Individual Differences and Development in Organisations

Individual Differences and Development in Organisations

Edited by

Michael Pearn

Chartered Occupational Psychologist, Dublin, Ireland

JOHN WILEY & SONS, LTD

Other Wiley Editorial Offices

John Wiley & Sons, Inc., 111 River Street, Hoboken, NJ 07030, USA

Jossey-Bass, 989 Market Street, San Francisco, CA 94103-1741, USA

Wiley-VCH Verlag GmbH, Boschstr. 12, D-69469 Weinheim, Germany

John Wiley & Sons Australia Ltd, 33 Park Road, Milton, Queensland 4064, Australia

John Wiley & Sons (Asia) Pte Ltd, 2 Clementi Loop #02-01, Jin Xing Distripark, Singapore 129809

John Wiley & Sons Canada Ltd, 22 Worcester Road, Etobicoke, Ontario, Canada M9W 1L1

Wiley also publishes its books in a variety of electronic formats. Some content that appears in print may not
be available in electronic books.

Library of Congress Cataloging-in-Publication Data

Individual differences and development in organisations / edited by Michael Pearn.
        p.   cm.—(Wiley handbooks in the psychology of management in organisations)
    Includes bibliographical references and index.
    ISBN 0-471-48540-3 (alk. paper)
    1. Psychology, Industrial.   2. Organizational behavior.   3. Employees—Training of.
  4. Diversity in the workplace.   5. Individual differences.   I. Pearn, Michael.   II. Series.

    HF5548.8 .I516   2002
    158.7—dc21   2002029633

British Library Cataloguing in Publication Data

A catalogue record for this book is available from the British Library

ISBN 0-471-48540-3

Typeset in 10/12pt Times by TechBooks Electronic Services Pvt Ltd, New Delhi, India
Printed and bound in Great Britain by TJ International Ltd, Padstow, Cornwall
This book is printed on acid-free paper responsibly manufactured from sustainable forestry,
in which at least two trees are planted for each one used for paper production.

*This Handbook is dedicated to my parents Barbara and Harry
who, in 2002, the Handbook's year of publication,
celebrated their 60th wedding anniversary*

Contents

PART IV   DEVELOPMENT METHODS AND PROCESSES

PART V   ORGANISATIONAL CONTEXT

About the Editor

Michael Pearn is a Chartered Occupational Psychologist based in Dublin. He is a Fellow of The British Psychological Society, the Chartered Institute for Personnel and Development, and the RSA. He is a graduate in Psychology and Philosophy, Dublin University and holds a PhD in Psychology from London University. He was a founding partner of Pearn Kandola in 1984 until retiring from the practice in 1999. Recent books authored include Learning Organisations in Practice (1995); Ending the Blame Culture (1998); Empowering Team Learning (1998) and The Manager's Book of Numbers (2002). He is currently a Director of the Centre for Leadership Learning in Dublin, a Director of Learn2improve Ltd, a Visiting Research Fellow at Lancaster University, and a Member of the Associated Faculty, Swedish Institute of Management, Stockholm.

About the Contributors

Professor John G. Burgoyne, *Department of Management Learning, University of Lancaster, Lancaster, LA1 4YW, UK*

John Burgoyne is a founding member of the Department of Management Learning in the Management School, University of Lancaster. He is a psychologist by background and has worked on the evaluation of management development, the learning process, managerial competencies and self-development, corporate management development policy, career formation, organisational learning, knowledge managing and virtual organisation. Recent books include the fourth edition of *A Manager's Guide to Self-Development*, 2001 (with M. Pedler and T. Boydell); *The Learning Company Toolkit*, 2000 (with M. Pedler, T. Boydell, K. Aspinwall, & T. Wakeman, T.); *Develop Yourself, Your Career and Your Organisation*, 1999; *Management Learning: Integrating Perspectives in Theory and Practice*, 1997, Editor with M. Reynolds.

Dr Ian Cunninghan, *Centre for Self Managed Learning, 13 Harrington Road, Brighton, BN1 6RF, UK*

Ian Cunninghan chairs Strategic Developments International Ltd. and the Centre for Self Managed Learning. He is Visiting Professor in Organisational Capability at Middlesex University. He works with organizations at various levels including assisting with organization-wide change, with Boards on strategy development, with teams (on their development) and through the mentoring and coaching of senior managers and CEO's. Past posts include CEO of Roffey Park Management Institute; Senior Research Fellow at Ashridge Management College; manager; trainer and research chemist. He has also been an Adjunct Faculty Member of the Fielding Institute, California and a visiting professor in India and at the University of Utah. He has published over 100 articles, papers and books.

Professor Victor Dulewicz, *Head of HRM & Organisational Behaviour Faculty, Henley Management College, Henley, Berkshire, UK*

Professor Victor Dulewicz is a Chartered Occupational Psychologist, a Fellow of both the British Psychological Society and the Chartered Institute of Personnel & Development, and a member of the Institute of Directors. He is Head of the Human Resource Management & Organisational Behaviour Faculty and Director of Assessment Services at Henley Management College. He led a major government funded project investigating Competences for Boards of Directors and is currently Research Director of Henley's Centre for Board Effectiveness. He is also a co-author of *Psychological Testing* (3rd edition, 1997), and of *Making Sense of Emotional Intelligence* (1999) with M. Higgs.

Professor Adrian Furnham, *University College London, Department of Psychology, 26 Bedford Way, London, WC1H 0AP, UK*

Adrian Furnham is Professor of Psychology at University College London, where he has taught for twenty years. A graduate of LSE and Oxford he has written 35 books and over 400 peer reviewed scientific papers. His books include *The Psychology of Behaviour at Work* (1997); *The Myths of Management* (1996); *The Psychology of Incompetence* (1998) and the *Psychology of Money*, 1998 (with M. Argyle); *Body Language at Work* (1999); *The Helpless, Hapless, and Hopeless Manager* (2000); and *The Psychology of Culture Shock* (2001). He is currently President Elect of the International Society for the Study of Individual Differences.

Dr Jane Henry, *Open University, 86 Mt Pleasant, Aspley Guise, Bucks, MK17 8JU, UK*

Dr Jane Henry is a Senior Lecturer at the Open University where she developed and chairs the Creativity, Innovation and Change Masters course. It is the OU's most popular MBA elective and is taken by around 1400 managers each year. Jane chairs the BPS Consciousness and Experiential

Psychology Section and is editor of *Consciousness and Experiential Psychology*. Her recent books include *Creativity and Perception in Management* (2001); *Creative Management*, (2nd edition, 2001); and *Managing Innovation and Change* (with P. Mayle), 2002. She is an active researcher working on personal development, change processes, intuition and creativity.

Dr Malcolm Higgs, *Faculty of HRM & Organisational Behaviour, Henley Management College, Henley, Berkshire, UK*

Malcolm Higgs is Dean of Henley Management College and a member of the Human Resource Management and Organisational Behaviour Faculty. He moved to Henley from a role as Principal Partner in Towers Perrin's London Human Resource Management practice. In addition he was responsible for the firm's European leadership development practice. Prior to joining Towers Perrin, Malcolm had eight years consulting experience with the Hay Group and Arthur Young. In 1997 he completed his Doctorate at Henley Management College based on research into factors impacting on senior managerial team performance. Malcolm is a member of the British Psychological Society and a chartered occupational psychologist.

Dr Jörg Iten, *ITEN & MÜLLER Executive Assessment & Management Development, Alte Land-strasse 136, CH-8802 Kilchberg, Switzerland*

Jörg Iten is the managing partner of ITEN & MÜLLER Executive Assessment & Management Development, a consulting firm located in Kilchberg/Zurich, Switzerland. He majored in work and organizational psychology at university and at the Federal Institute of Technology in Zurich. This was followed by eight years of practical management development experience in a corporate environment and at an internationally active major bank. In 1987, he founded the consulting firm ITEN & MÜLLER with his partner; together they advise companies in the areas of assessment and management development.

Dr Rajvinder Kandola, *Pearn Kandola, 76 Banbury Road, Oxford, OX2 6JT, UK*

Dr Rajvinder Kandola is a Chartered Occupational Psychologist specialising in assessment and development of people in organisations, and also the implementation of effective diversity strategies in organisations. He co-founded Pearn Kandola in 1984 and has carried out research and consultancy assignments all over the world. His books include *Job Analysis for Managers*, and the award-winning *Managing the Mosaic*. He is Currently Chairman of the British Psychological Society's Division of Occupational Psychology.

Satya Kartara, *Pearn Kandola, 76 Banbury Road, Oxford, OX2 6JT, UK*

Satya Kartara is a Chartered Occupational Psychologist with Pearn Kandola in Oxford.

Dr Nigel King, *University of Huddersfield, Department of Behavioural Sciences, Queensgate, Huddersfield, HD1 3DH, UK*

Nigel King has a Ph.D. in psychology from the University of Sheffield, and is currently Reader in Psychology at the University of Huddersfield. He has published widely in the area of creativity, innovation and change in organisations, including the recent book *Managing Innovation and Change: A Critical Guide for Organisations* (with Neil Anderson). His research has mostly been in health care settings, and he is Director of the Primary Care Research Group at Huddersfield. He has a strong interest in the use of qualitative methods in work and organisational psychology, especially those from a phenomenological perspective.

Dr Monica Lee, *Hare Appletree House, Quernmore, Lancaster, LA2 0QP, UK*

Monica Lee is Editor in Chief of the journal *Human Resource Development International* and Editor of the Routledge Research Monograph Series *Studies in Human Resource Development*. She can be found in the Department of Behaviour in Organisations at Lancaster University, UK. She has worked extensively in Europe and the CIS coordinating and collaborating in research and teaching initiatives, each of which have "confused her attempts to make sense out of life". Recent book contributions include "Management Education in the New Europe: Boundaries and Complexity" (1996) in R. Goodman, (ed.) *Modern Organisations and Emerging Conundrums* (1999); and in J. Burgoyne & M. Reynolds, *Management Learning* (1997).

Professor Victoria J. Marsick, *Adult Education Graduate Programs, Teachers College, Columbia University, TC Box 112, NY, NY 10027, USA*

Victoria J. Marsick is a Professor of Adult & Organizational Learning, Department of Organization and Leadership, Columbia University, Teachers College. She co-directs the J.M.Huber Institute for Learning in Organization at Teachers College with Martha Gephart. Recent books include: *Informal Learning on the Job* (1999, co-edited with Marie Volpe); *Action Learning* (1999, co-edited with Lyle Yorks and Judy O'Neil); and (all co-authored with Karen Watkins) *Facilitating the Learning Organization: Making Learning Count* (1999), *In Action: Creating the Learning Organization* (1996), *Sculpting the Learning Organization* (1993), and *Informal and Incidental Learning in the Workplace* (1990).

Dr Cynthia D. McCauley, *Centre For Creative Leadership, One Leadership Place, PO Box 26300, Greensborough, NC 27438-6300, USA*

Cynthia D. McCauley is Vice President of Leadership Development at the Center for Creative Leadership (CCL). She received her Ph.D. in 1984 in industrial and organizational psychology from the University of Georgia. Her research and publications have focused on strategies for enhancing leadership development through job assignments, feedback, developmental relationships, and formal programs. Dr McCauley is co-editor of CCL's *Handbook of Leadership Development* (with R. Moxley and E. Van Velsor). She is also the co-developer of Benchmarks, a 360-degree feedback tool (with M. Lombardo), and the Job Challenge Profile (with M. Ruderman and P. Ohlott).

Roger Mottram, *Chartered Occupational Psychologist, 8 Hesketh Avenue, Didsbury, Manchester, UK*

Roger Mottram is a Chartered Occupational Psychologist. He was Assistant Director of the Industrial Training Research Unit, University College London, where he worked with Meredith Belbin on the research and development of the Team Role concept. He joined Woolworths, Australia as Personnel Director where his main task was to help reorganise the Company's structure. Roger now lectures at Manchester University on Human Resource Management, and consults on management assessment and development. He is working on a multimedia approach to assessing individual and team effectiveness. His publications include co-authorship of the Equal Opportunities report on "Selection Tests and Sex Bias" (1986), and "Building Effective Teams" (1988).

Dr Alan Mumford, *2 Victoria Mews, Magdalen Road, London, SW18 3PY, UK*

Alan Mumford is a specialist in Director and management development. He is Visiting Professor of Management Development at International Management Centres, and a Visiting Fellow at the Department of Management Learning at the University of Lancaster. His main work is on improving management performance, especially through effective learning processes with senior managers and directors both in the UK and internationally. His books include *The Manual of Learning Styles* (3rd edition, 1992); *Management Development: Strategies for Action* (3rd edition, 1997); *Learning at the Top* (1995); *How to Choose the Right Development Method* (1997); and *How to Produce Personal Development Plans* (2001).

Professor Kevin R. Murphy, *Dept of Psychology, Pennsylvania State University, University Park, PA 16802-4104, USA*

Kevin Murphy is a Professor of Psychology at the Pennsylvania State University. He has served on the faculty of Rice University, New York University, and Colorado State University. He has served as President of the Society for Industrial and Organizational Psychology and is the editor of the *Journal of Applied Psychology*, and serves as a member of the editorial boards of *Human Performance*, *Human Resource Management Review*, *Journal of Industrial Psychology*, *International Journal of Management Reviews* and *International Journal of Selection and Assessment*. He is the author of over eighty articles and book chapters, and author or editor of eight books.

Dr Rob F. Poell, *University of Nijmegen, Department of Educational Science, PO Box 9104, 6500 HE Nijmegen, The Netherlands*

Rob F. Poell is a Lecturer in Human Resource Development in the Education Department of Nijmegen University. His Ph.D. thesis, entitled "Organizing work-related learning projects: A network approach", was granted the Malcolm S. Knowles Dissertation of the Year 1998 Award by the Academy of Human Resource Development. He was awarded a Marie Curie Fellowship by the

European Union to carry out a research project at the University of Sheffield, United Kingdom, in 1998. He teaches and conducts research in the areas of human resource development, vocational education, and learning in organisational contexts.

Dr Gilly Salmon, *Open University Business School, Walton Hall, Milton Keynes, MK7 6AA, UK*
   Gilly Salmon is at the Centre for Innovation, Knowledge and Enterprise at the Open University Business School and is Visiting Professor at Glasgow Caledonian Business School. In 2000–2001 she was inaugural MBA Program Director in the new online United States Open University. She has extensive experience of working with students, tutors and trainers through online learning and has been teaching online since 1989. She is the author of the widely used book "E-moderating: the key to teaching and learning online". She researches and speaks internationally about online teaching.

Professor Paul Sparrow, *Manchester Business School, Booth Street West, Manchester, M15 6PB, UK*
   Paul Sparrow is Professor in International Human Resource Management at the Manchester Business School. Before that he was Professor of Organisational Behaviour at Sheffield University. His principal research interests are in the field of international and comparative human resource management and in work and organisational psychology. He has written a number of books including *Designing and Achieving Competency, European Human Resource Management in Transition, Human Resource Management: The New Agenda* and *The Competent Organisation: A Psychological Analysis of the Strategic Management Process*. He is editor of the *Journal of Occupational and Organisational Psychology* and is on the Review Board of the *British Journal of Management*.

Professor Bruce Torff, *307 Mason Hall, Hofstra University, Hempstead, New York 11549-1130, USA*
   Bruce Torff is Assistant Professor of Education at Hofstra University in Hempstead, New York. He has published numerous books and articles on topics including intuitive conceptions, implicit learning, intelligence, and musical cognition. A recent volume entitled *Understanding and Teaching the Intuitive Mind* (edited in collaboration with Robert J. Sternberg) explores the educational implications of non-conscious cognitive processes. Torff is active as a leader of professional-development workshops for educators. Torff earned a doctorate at Harvard University, where he worked with Howard Gardner, and held a post-doctoral appointment at Yale University with Sternberg. He also moonlights as a jazz pianist and songwriter.

Dr Karen van Dam, *Dept of Work and Organisational Psychology, Tilburg University, PO Box 90153, 5000 LE Tilburg, The Netherlands*
   Karen van Dam is Associate Professor at the Department of Work and Organizational Psychology at Tilburg University in the Netherlands. Her research focuses on employee development, functional flexibility and job mobility on the one hand, and on recruitment, selection and assessment on the other hand. In 1997 she received the NITPB award for her dissertation "Dancing bears: judgment processes in personnel selection". Dr van Dam has also worked as human resource consultant management and has been on the editorial board of both Dutch and international journals.

Professor Ferd Van der Krogt, *University of Nijmegen, Department of Educational Sciences, PO Box 9104, 6500 HE Nijmegen, The Netherlands*
   Ferd Van der Krogt is a senior lecturer of Human Resource Development in the Education Department of Nijmegen University. He teaches and conducts research into the organisation of human resource development, in relation to developments in work and organisations. His publications in this domain focus on learning-network theory.

Edward C. Warburton, *3 Peter Cooper Road, Apt 10H, New York, NY, USA*
   Edward Warburton holds a Doctor of Education degree on Human Development and Psychology from the Graduate School of Education, Harvard University. He is currently Assistant Professor at The Steinhardt School of Education, New York University. Before that he was a Research Associate with MPR Associates, Berkley, CA.

Professor Karen E. Watkins, *School of Leadership and Lifelong Learning, University of Georgia, Athens, Georgia 30602, USA*

Karen E. Watkins is Professor of Human Resource and Organizational Development and the Director of the School of Leadership and Lifelong Learning at the University of Georgia. She is the author or co-author of over 70 articles and chapters, and 6 books. She has consulted with numerous businesses and industries. In 1999, Dr Watkins was voted Scholar of the Year by the Academy of Human Resource Development. She served as President of the Academy of Human Resource Development from 1994–1996. She was named a distinguished graduate by The University of Texas at Austin's Community College Leadership Program in 2001.

Jacqueline A. Wilson, *University of Georgia, Athens, Georgia 303602, USA*

Jacqueline Wilson received her Ph.D. in Adult Education from the University of Georgia in 2001. She is the Assistant Director of the Technical Career Academy of Northeast Georgia and has been a hotel manager, a human resources director, and an adjunct faculty member in hotel restaurant administration at the University of Georgia.

Dr Jac N. Zaal, *GITP International Research and Development, Box 12457, 1100 AL Amsterdam, The Netherlands*

Jac Zaal is Head of R&D with GITP International in Amsterdam. Before that he was head and founder of the Centre of Management Assessment at the Department of Psychological Services of the Dutch government. He studied industrial and organisational psychology at the Free University in Amsterdam, and obtained his doctorate at the same university in 1978. His consultancy work involved individual assessment for selection and top level promotion, career counselling and reviewing practices and structure of mainly professional organisations. He was President of the International Test Commission from 1986 to 1990.

Series Preface

Peter Herriot
The Empower Group

The dictionary definition (Random House, 1987) of 'handbook' runs as follows:

- A book of instruction or guidance, as for an occupation; a manual.
- A guidebook for travellers.
- A reference book in a particular field.
- A scholarly book on a particular subject, often consisting of separate essays or articles.

These definitions are placed in the historical order of their appearance in the language. So the earliest use of a handbook was as a set of instructions which members of particular occupations kept to hand, in order to be able to refer to them when they were at a loss as to how to tackle a problem at work. The most recent definition, by way of contrast, refers to a scholarly book consisting of separate essays or articles.

It is the modest ambition of the Wiley Handbooks in the Psychology of Management in Organizations series to reverse the course of (linguistic) history! We want to get back to the idea of handbooks as resources to which members of occupations can refer in order to get help in addressing the problems that they face. The occupational members primarily involved here are work and organisational psychologists, human resource managers and professionals, and organisational managers in general. And the problems they face are those that force themselves with ever greater urgency upon public and private sector organisations alike: issues such as how to manage employees' performance effectively; how to facilitate learning in organisations; how to benefit from a diversity of employees; and how to manage organisational change so that staff are engaged and supported.

Now the claim to provide something useful for professionals, rather than a set of scholarly articles, is a bold one. What is required if such a claim is to be justified? First, practising professionals need a clear theoretical basis from which to analyse the issues they face and upon which to base their solutions. Practice without underpinning theory is merely applying what has worked in some situations to other situations without knowing why, and hoping that they will work there too. This is blind empiricism.

Theory without practice, on the other hand, is mere indulgence. It is indulgent because theories in applied science can never be properly tested except by application, i.e. their attempted use in solving problems in the real world. A handbook in the original sense of the word will therefore contain elements of practice as well as statements of theory. The Wiley Handbooks in the Psychology of Management in Organizations seek to demonstrate, by descriptions of case studies, methods of intervention and instruments of assessment, how theory may be applied in practice to address real organisational issues.

It is clear that Work and Organisational Psychology is a core discipline for addressing such issues as those listed above, for they are all issues that depend for their solution upon an understanding of individuals' behaviour at work, and of the likely effects of various organisational interventions upon the stakeholders involved. These latter include employees, customers, shareholders, suppliers, and the wider community (Hodgkinson & Herriot, 2001).

The success criterion for these handbooks, then, is a simple one: will professionals find them useful in their practice? If they also help in the development of apprentice professionals, e.g. by being used on training courses, then so much the better. The field of Work and Organisational Psychology is currently at risk from a failure to integrate theory and practice (Anderson, Herriot & Hodgkinson, 2001). Theory and research often seem to practitioners to address issues of interest only to academics; practice appears to academics to lack careful empirical, let alone theoretical, underpinning. These handbooks will help to bridge this divide, and thereby justify the title of 'handbook'.

What is clear is that if we psychologists fail to impact upon the urgent issues that currently crowd in upon organisations, then those who claim to address them better or faster than us will gain power and influence. This will happen even if the solutions they provide offer little longer-term benefit to clients. The Wiley Handbooks in the Psychology of Management in Organizations provide a resource to help professionals serve their clients more effectively.

This second handbook in the series is edited by Michael Pearn, and addresses a highly important current issue. The increasing rate of organisational and technological change requires employees to develop new skills and knowledge and new ways of relating to colleagues, customers and clients. How do people differ in terms of their capacity to develop in these ways? To what extent do we have to accept that certain capabilities and characteristics are simply not amenable to development? And how do we best facilitate the development of those that are? Some would argue that the answers to these questions are close to being provided by scientific research. The different perspectives on development taken by the distinguished contributors suggest, on the contrary, that a wide variety of assumptions, values and practices currently populate this area. Perhaps this is just as well, since a similar variety characterises the organisational clients we seek to serve.

REFERENCES

The Random House Dictionary of the English Language, 2nd edn (1987) New York: Random House.

Hodgkinson, G.P. & Herriot, P. (2001) The role of psychologists in enhancing organisational effectiveness. In I. Robertson, D. Bartram & M. Callinan (eds), *The Role of Individual Performance in Organisational Effectiveness*. Chichester: Willey.

Anderson, N., Herriot, P. & Hodgkinson, G.P. (2001) The practitioner–researcher divide in Industrial, Work and Organisational (IWO) Psychology: where are we now, and where do we go from here? *Journal of Occupational and Organisational Psychology*, **74**, 391–411.

Preface

INDIVIDUAL DEVELOPMENT IN AN INCREASINGLY CONNECTED WORLD

The world as a whole is becoming increasingly connected, which creates both opportunities, and challenges, for individual development in organisations. Ever since the exploratory voyages of discovery from Portugal in the fifteenth century, instigated by Henry the Navigator, the world has become increasingly connected and at an ever faster rate. Before the voyages of discovery the recorded and the unrecorded journeys and migrations of people from one part of the world to another made connections, but it is over the last 500 years the world has increasingly become more interconnected. Now the speed, multiplicity, interactivity and diversity of connections are growing at an accelerating rate, especially in the last two decades with the advent of the internet, e-commerce and e-learning.

Opportunities for access to information of all kinds, the ease of interactions across traditional boundaries, the sheer speed of developments, and ease of communications for individuals and for organisations, all combine to create a different and more complex world in which organisations, made up of individual and diverse human beings, seek to go about their business and achieve their goals.

Paradoxically, the very connectedness of the world as we know it today with its potential for becoming a global village and for universal understanding and cooperation, brings with it a heightened sense of differences between groups, cultures and traditions. Exposure to and awareness of individual and group differences are enhanced with the rapidly evolving technologies of information and communication. The increased capacity, speed, and ease of access to communication across diverse groups brings with it an increased potential for mutual understanding and tolerance. Yet the same technologies make it easier for diverse groups (some feeling marginalised and alienated from others) to assert their identities and strike at the heart of more powerful and dominant groups. Never has it been more important for us to seek to understand, accommodate, and harness individual differences (often used as the basis for group attributions and stereotypes) we find in the people who comprise the political, public, commercial and voluntary organisations in society.

Yet in that 500-year period of accelerating world connectedness, and for that matter the tens of thousands of years that preceded it, we have shared the same physical apparatus that makes us distinctively human. In particular, we possessed the same brains and bodies that are recognisably similar across tens of millennia. The physical attributes include the ability to walk upright, and to put finger and thumb together, but above all it is the, still little understood, human brain that makes us distinctive as human beings. The physical human brain has been described by Greenfield (2000) "as weighing only some three pounds and with the consistency of a soft boiled egg" and yet has the capacity to give each and every human a unique sense of themselves as individuals, separate from the outer world, distinct from all other human beings, and at the same time with a sense of belonging to groups of one kind or another. Ultimately it is the brain that gives our sense of ourselves as individuals and our identities as members of groups of one kind or another, and enables a sense of humour and also spirituality. We still know very little about how the brain achieves these things.

In my view, the increasingly integrated discipline of the new neurosciences (see for example, Gazzaniga, Ivy and Mangan, 1998; Rose, 1999) which seek to combine the concerns and contributions of biology with psychology, and also philosophy, anthropology and sociology without the myopia and restraints that result from disciplines when they see themselves in competition with each other, will ultimately lead to significant breakthroughs in our understanding of how we develop our sense of ourselves as individuals, how we learn, create meaning, and a sense of belonging, and well-being. Psychology has an important role to play in devising frameworks and theories to aid the understanding that leads on to the creation of tools and processes that are empirically tested and proven and which result in genuine individual development.

As the world becomes increasingly connected and individuals are better and/or more educated the balance of power between the individual and the employing organisation has changed. Formerly, confident and domineering large organisations could not only offer jobs or careers for life, they could also dictate how their employees behaved. In essence, it was largely a relationship of dependency and compliance on the part of the individual employee, resisted in places only by collective action but not always with satisfactory outcomes. In general, the large employers, or any employer in periods of excess labour supply, maintained the upper hand. But with the decline and fall of once seemingly invincible organisations (Kanter, 1989), and the advances of the new technologies the change in the power relationship between individual and organisation has accelerated with the advent of e-business (Schwarttz, 1999; Kelly, 1999; Kanter, 2000) and even virtual organisations (Hedberg et al., 2000). Bridges (1998) has described the de-jobbed organisation, Cooper (1999) the short-term contracting culture, and Hakim (1994), in an aptly entitled book *We Are All Self-employed Now*, argues that we must all take full responsibility for our career mobility and job productivity and that without a "self-employed" mentality many people will not be able to cope with the rapid changes in the world of work.

One symptom of the changes in the world of work in the last few decades has been manifested in changing concepts of careers, and the nature of the psychological contract between employer and employed (Herriot and Pemberton, 1995), and Hirschorn (1998) has examined the implications of leadership and followership in the post-modern organisations with new concepts of authority relying less and less on command-and-control and more and more on cooperation, shared interests and psychological identity as individuals.

But what are the implications for individual development in organisations? There is a sense in which individual development is always occurring, in that to varying degrees learning and developing is continuous, even when we are asleep, (the possible exception being when someone is in a coma). By individual development, *from an organisational perspective*, I mean the planned and unplanned activities, which can be the conscious and unconscious basis for changes in individuals that result in them being better equipped to perform current and future roles within the organisation, and more prepared and ready for effective execution of future roles. By contrast, individual development *from the person's point of view* could be anything that leads to an increased sense of well-being, satisfaction and fulfilment, which may or may not overlap with the organisation's needs.

Individual development in an organisation at its worst is ad hoc, inconsistent, reactive to short-term needs, and bears little or no relation to the core purposes of the organisation, or where it does, is mechanistic and authoritarian. At its best, individual development in organisations is comprehensive, closely allied to the prime purposes of the organisation, is strategic, and recognises the dignity and as well the diversity and complexity of human beings, including the capacity for self-management and self direction.

Both the individual and the organisation have a stake in the outcomes of individual development activities and processes in organisations. The individual wants improved, or sufficient, performance capability, and the associated sense of well-being (from whatever source, be it spiritual or material or psychological or any combination). The organisation wants motivated and committed employees (or members) whose contribution to the goals of the organisation is improved as a result of activities associated with individual development, whether or not the individual or the organisation is the prime instigator.

Recruitment, selection, induction, training, performance management, organisational culture, values and the daily experience of people all play a part, but the organisation that seeks to harness and develop the potential of its members, and thereby increase their capability of contributing successfully to the achievement of organisational goals, is likely to increase its organisational effectiveness and, where appropriate, its organisational competitiveness.

THE MORAL DIMENSION

Ideally, there should be congruence between the individual's needs and the needs of the organisation. The relationship between individual and organisation raises many issues at a moral, philosophical, and practical level. To what extent should organisations seek to change the attitudes and behaviour of their employees? How much conformity with organisationally defined norms is it reasonable to expect? How much freedom to differ is the individual allowed or expected to have? Who decides what is best for the individual? What are the rights of the individual vis à vis the organisation? The answers are not straightforward and are dependant on contextual factors.

Some organisations require or condition their members into thinking and behaving alike, and to refrain from thinking for themselves beyond tightly defined limits, at least in their role as employees. Call centre operatives have little choice in the way they behave and speak to customers. The individual chooses or declines to be a member of such an organisation and to accept its rules. Other organisations encourage individualism, as do some cultures, as opposed to those who favour collectivism (Handy, 1991; Trompenaars and Hampden-Turner, 1997). The latter organisations could be said to be suppressing the individual in the interest of the greater good of the organisation and what it stands for. This was the prevailing attitude adopted by many organisations, especially in the nineteenth and the first half of the twentieth century. The power of the organisation to dictate to the individual how he or she should behave (and even think) is declining rapidly, but probably more slowly in more traditional, hierarchical and bureaucratic organisations.

THE SOCIAL DIMENSION TO INDIVIDUAL DEVELOPMENT

It is all too easy to disregard the social dimension when thinking about individual development in organisations. Ultimately all learning and development occurs in the brains of individuals but almost all learning takes place in a social context. It is by sharing with, interacting, and confronting others that we learn. There is always a social context defined by reference to others, though some go so far as to say that being individual is illusory and that we have evolved a "social brain" (Ratey, 2001) that is dependent on interaction with other brains, a view that is not inconsistent with the idea of the selfish gene (Dawkin, 1978) or the argument that the traditional focus on the individual self is misleading (Pinker, 1998; Blackmore, 1999).

It is misleading to regard individual development in organisations as though it is either totally individualistic or for that matter context free. Many of the chapters in this handbook make the point that context and interactivity of factors are crucial considerations. This applies to leadership development, innovation, emotional intelligence, competencies, and indeed to almost all topics in this handbook. It is not difficult to build specific skills and abilities in individuals, but if this is not done in a way that is integrated with the context and the core purpose of organisation the investment it is likely to be limited in value. It is relatively easy to watch videos and read books as isolated individuals, but unless there is dialogue with others and joint attempts to apply the learning then the scope for individual development is restricted.

Does this mean that it is meaningless to talk about individual development in organisations? Would we be better off focusing solely on social, group, team and collective development? The answer is probably not, because at the end of the day we all feel we are individuals, and we know that common experiences can be differently interpreted by individuals simply because individuals differ. It is difficult to escape from our sense of individuality. It would seem that, as individuals, we need to function and learn collectively, while at the same time retaining our sense of being unique individuals.

RATIONALE FOR THE HANDBOOK

This handbook is about the psychology of individual differences and development in organisations. It does not seek to provide simple answers to complex issues. It is not the kind of handbook that offers prescriptive solutions. It does, however, seek to provide insight and greater clarity on issues and on areas of research, thus enabling more informed choices to be made. The handbook is not primarily aimed at either academics or at practitioners, or both in parallel, for I believe the distinction is artificial and unhelpful in organisational and work psychology, as an applied branch of psychology. The distinction between academic and practitioner can only be clearly differentiated at the extremes and tends to result in caricatures. This handbook is aimed equally at what I like to call academically-minded practitioners and at practice-orientated academics.

The handbook contains only twenty chapters and therefore represents a trade-off between depth and breadth. Accordingly some topics are not expressly covered in this book. A guiding principle has been: what is likely to be of interest and/or practical benefit to readers over the next three to five years. The whole area of personal growth and personal effectiveness has not been included on the grounds that there is a huge "be a better or more successful person" literature (c.f. Covey, 1989; McCormack, 1990; Smith, 1994) which has little to do with the complex relationships between individuals and organisations. Training and formal education are not specifically included because the emphasis in this handbook is on developmental processes that lead to change within the individual rather than on the management of formal organisatioal processes.

I also decided to exclude any topic that is evolving so rapidly that what is written in 2001 (up to a year before publication date) would be obsolete by the time of publication or shortly afterwards. On balance, topics have been included where practical implications from conceptual analysis of an issue, or where summary and analysis of empirical research, point to practical implications; and where the case for or against a particular approach, or even partisan exposition of a particular approach, would help practitioners and academic researchers make more informed choices and decisions.

SUMMARY OF THE CHAPTERS

The handbook is divided into five parts. **Part One** is titled Approaches, Concepts and Theory. There are differing views about the nature and possibility of development and learning. In chapter one, **John Burgoyne** in a cerebral analysis, raises some fundamental questions about the differing concepts of self that are implicit, and sometimes explicit, in the varying approaches that have developed over the last 100 years. As he puts it: "Whatever else these do in terms of aiming at specific or general learning outcomes for the learner they make a 'pitch' at the learner as a certain kind of self. In some cases this may help to create the learner as the kind of self assumed by the learning approach—for example as an employable commodity to fit an organisational machine, or as an autonomous self asserting the right to self creation." He goes on to argue that the asserted "self" may be in conflict with some pre-established learner identity and self and that this conflict or clash may explain some of the "difficulties" that can occur in events to facilitate learning.

The main practical consequence of Burgoyne's analysis is that "acceptable constructions of the self" should be negotiated between learning facilitators and learners as part of the relationship. He argues that both theorists and practitioners can be more aware of the variety and alternatives, including those that may be different from their current beliefs and practices. He goes on to say that this is pivotal to the reproduction and revision of our social, economic and political lives. Burgoyne asserts that there is a clear sense of progression in the approaches that he summarises and distils into brief summaries and metaphors, which range from individual passive and active learning, through the social to a more fully integrated concept of learning. The message here is that inappropriate or undifferentiated concepts of the individual result in development initiatives that at best are not effective and at worst alienating.

Monica Lee in chapter 2 presents a more impassioned and experiential argument. Just as John Burgoyne showed that different concepts of the self are implicit (consciously or otherwise) in different theoretical and methodological approaches to developing the individual, Monica Lee reminds us that developing the self involves the whole person as a sentient, sense-making, enquiring individual. There is a need to understand oneself, and to understand that the other is different from oneself, and the nature of those differences, but this is a dynamic, co-regulated and often sub-conscious process. Other people might catalyse it, and in the longer term it is about relationships with others but other people cannot specify it, control it or manage it. It is not a quantifiable thing to be specified, controlled, or managed in any way—it cannot be prescribed for, mapped out, or planned. However, organisations can foster self development.

She describes a range of tools and processes that help foster self development, which tend to be those that help understanding, reflection and behaviour change but there is no clear relationship between different tools and different aspects of development. A culture is needed that supports self development which requires challenge and thus, risk. The culture of the organisation also needs to foster courage and support. By establishing a true open environment of co-regulation, resisting conceptual closure and capacity for "negative capability" the organisation is likely to foster self development in those who engage with it.

In chapter 3, **Jane Henry** describes how cognitive science now pictures how mind, brain, body and environment interact. In particular, she draws attention to the centrality of intuitive know-how and the limitations of rational thought and the part played by tacit processes and the development of the system within which individuals practice. Cognitive processes such as perception, thought, and memory and cognitive behaviour such as problem solving, learning, decision marking and creativity all have implications for individual development in organisations. Cognitive science has revealed how much information is processed tacitly and how little of this reaches the surface. This means most information processing, learning and decision making appears to happen below conscious awareness. She describes approaches or tools for individual development that are congruent with the findings of cognitive science. Perhaps the most important implication of recent developments in cognitive sciences is recognition of the limited capacities and fallibility of the conscious mind, and the importance of implicit learning and tacit knowledge, as opposed to the pre-occupation with rationality and logic. The author argues that development strategies should take greater account of intuitive ways of knowing and that we need to shift the balance of individual development away from reflection, analysis and competency towards more focus on well-being with greater attention to social support, physical involvement and "quietening".

She also concludes that the evidence for the part played by genetics in certain aspects of cognitive style is strengthening, reinforcing the need to allow for diversity in development. In addition there has also been a shift to a greater recognition of the part played by social systems in the way we think and an appreciation of the need to address the systems in which individuals develop in addition to their individual needs.

In chapter 4, **Kevin Murphy** provides a synoptic survey of one of the traditional fields of enquiry in psychology, viz. individual differences in the areas of cognitive ability, interests, and personality. His conclusion is that individual characteristics, particularly cognitive ability, will have a substantial influence on whether individuals will in fact benefit from training and development. For the author, the clear implication of the research is the dilemma: should training and development activities be offered to those individuals who are most clearly positioned to succeed or those who need it the most? He concludes by arguing that we cannot and should not ignore the findings from research on individual differences, but that there is no clear consensus at this point about how to use information about individual differences in making decisions about who gets access to which sorts of developmental opportunities. The answers do not lie within the realms of psychology, but in recognition of differing contexts and the application of policy, values and moral principles.

Part Two of the handbook, Individual Differences, contains more detailed summaries of what we currently know about individual differences in key areas of human functioning and the implications for individual development in organisations. There is a sense in which development is synonymous with learning. Part two focuses on individual learning within a team context, the critical role of informal or incidental learning, and the power of self-directed learning as embodied in Self Managed Learning.

Bruce Torff and **Edward Warburton** (chapter 5) examine old and new models of cognitive abilities. Akin to the argument presented by Burgoyne on the relativity of concepts of self, Torff and Warburton argue that there is no such thing as theory-neutral assessment of human abilities. As they put it, most old and new theories are packaged part-and-parcel with an assessment scheme, and each of these schemes assumes the existence of some sort of cognitive ability. They describe "intelligence-fair" assessments that encompass all of the individual's cognitive abilities, rather than solely linguistic or logical-mathematical intelligence. According to Torff and Warburton, a true assessment can be made only by evaluating the individual over time in context, using multiple measures. Torff and Warburton describe what they refer to as an assessment conundrum: it is impossible to evaluate candidates on what they have not learned, yet it is inadvisable to place too much confidence in de-contextualised measures. The theory of multiple intelligences (MI) has provided psychologists and educators with a way to think about human abilities, but the corresponding assessment revolution, according to Torff and Warburton, never materialised, and MI's popularity with educators and other professionals has been waning. Since no ability theory is dominant and all raise measurement problems, he argues that it is best to forsake the goal of assessing human cognitive abilities directly and focus instead on the evaluation of performance of authentic activities in particular domains and that the unit of analysis will be the context, not the person, at least initially. As they put it, for assessment, to tell the whole story, it must get beyond the one-shot-deal administration of a test. Needed are *ongoing* assessments that allow repeated measures over time, so that the development of the person's knowledge and skill can be charted. Assessment in context not only provides real-world tasks, materials, and settings; it also requires repeated measures. Torff and Warburton's position is opposite to that offered by Murphy and by Furnham in other chapters.

Adrian Furnham provides a major overview of research on personality and style preferences in chapter 6. He concludes that it is "certainly obvious that personality traits, cognitive and learning styles are fundamentally implicated in the whole business of development in organisations". He goes on to assert that there are systematic individual differences which in part predict every aspect of behaviour at work whether it be choice of occupation; productivity and satisfaction; absenteeism and accidents; turnover and training; decision making and development. He draws attention to the differences of emphasis of style researchers and trait researchers. He argues that style researchers are more interested in, committed to, and optimistic about change and development than trait researchers, but the renowned interest of organisational psychologists in trait measurement may mean all this is changing fast. He concludes that it is an exacting time for those interested in the topic of individual development in organisations. He also raises the question whether it is morally justifiable, sensible, even possible for an organisation to attempt to change an employee's personality or work style and examines both sides of the argument. As he puts, it the two schools of thought have different ideas, read different literatures and can, over time, be dismissive of one another. Thus just as the trait and style academic research grew apart so practitioners for-and-against individual development tend more to ignore each other than argue or research the case for their different positions.

In chapter 7, **Paul Sparrow** provides a series of frameworks that may be used to help position the approach taken to management competency both within organisational practice and academic research. He summarises three main approaches that have been taken in the study of management effectiveness: analysis of classical management functions, observation of behaviour and the study of intelligent functioning. He describes three different models of competency. The best known model, the behavioural competency approach, is then analysed and positioned within these frameworks. He argues that the HR process in organisations benefits from the application of competencies to external resourcing, individual development and internal career systems, generally outweighing any dysfunctions that might exist. He asks of competencies: Are they valid ? How are they made more organisationally relevant? Does this make it easy to identify which competencies are best selected for and which may be developed? Are they fair? He examines the decisions that are invoked when competencies are applied in the realm of pay and rewards, ard asks are some more important than others? Finally, he argues that we should only view individual behavioural competency in the context of the much larger quest for strategic competency of organisations.

Chapter 8 by **Victor Dulewicz** and **Malcolm Higgs** begins with elucidation of the Emotional Intelligence construct, in terms of what it is and why it has become significant for individuals and organisations. The authors assert that Emotional Intelligence can be measured and they describe the development of their own questionnaire, the EIQ. Measurement issues relating to assessment or development and the importance of a broad profile measure, as opposed to a unitary and definitive measure, are also discussed. They then describe the development of a model to explain how Emotional Intelligence adds to our understanding of the drivers of individual success and performance. They conclude that some of the elements of EI are readily developable while others are more enduring characteristics and should be exploited. They describe the relationship between EI and leadership, and with organisation culture, the extent to which EI can be developed, the nature of effective development methodologies, and the relationship to team performance.

Part Three contains three chapters under the heading Assessment Tools and Processes. Just as different approaches to development imply different concepts of self, different frameworks and different types of frameworks for human abilities have direct implications for approaches to individual development.

Chapter 9 by **Karen van Dam** focuses on methods and tools for assessment of employee development needs. The chapter outlines different objectives and effects of individual needs assessment. Needs assessment is considered an important tool for specifying the directions for future development activities. Critical features of needs assessment methods are described followed by an evaluation of those methods that are most commonly used in needs assessment. In the chapter she discusses several issues an organisation should consider in deciding whether and how to conduct an individual needs assessment. Finally, she reminds us that needs assessment indicates more than only the identification of weaknesses and development needs; it also provides the organisation and the employee with information about strengths and valuable future contributions.

In chapter 10, **Jörg Iten**, using a concrete case shows that the individual assessment method can be effective not only as a selection tool but also as a component of the individual professional development process. The example described illustrates the importance individual assessment can assume in achieving a balance between the individual's needs and organisational goals. He argues that effective development is rarely possible without a serious and individualized assessment of the person. He stresses that the goal of the individual assessment is to assess aspirational, intellectual, and social-communicative capacities on the one hand, and on the other, to give the participants the opportunity to gain clarity into their own motives and predispositions. The primary focus is not superficial behavior but the person as a whole. He describes the practical aspects of individual assessments that must be taken into account if organisations intend to conduct management development projects based on individual assessments. The function reserved for the individual assessment in many management development processes is frequently taken over by the assessment or development center but, Iten argues that in most development centers there is too much focus on behaviour and not enough on personality and the fit between the individual and the organisation's needs.

Jac Zaal in chapter 11 refers to Development Centers as a specific application of Assessment Center Methods (ACM) aimed at diagnosing, mostly managerial, skills that need to be developed to meet requirements of a target job. ACM is defined in part by the inclusion of different methods among which are exercises representing job samples. Although it has established its credentials as a valid predictor of management potential and career advancement, serious doubts have been raised about the skills it claims to measure. In this chapter basic characteristics of ACM are examined followed by the specific features of DCs. Generally it takes more effort to customise the design of ACM for developmental purposes and once the Development Center (DC) is ready for operation it takes more time to execute it. Are the extra efforts and cost in fine-tuning DCs paying of? What precisely are the strong and weak points to be considered in evaluating the benefits of DCs? In a critical review of available research the author challenges the construct validity of ACM and recommends ways to improve its validity. He argues that effective diagnosis of development needs can only be achieved when taking into account the situational determinants of managerial competencies. A primary goal of this chapter is to stimulate practitioners to take validity research more seriously in deciding on the use of ACM in different contexts. Depending on the type of use made, the design of assessment methods will have to meet different requirements to sustain its suitability for the purpose at stake.

Part Four, Development Methods and Processes, contains six chapters with a broad focus on tools and processes for development covering the choice of development methods, learning in teams, learning through experience, Self-Managed Learning, and learning through social networks and through electronic networks.

Alan Mumford in chapter 12 outlines four frameworks to help professional developers and advisers in organisations, and also individual learners, to choose development methods that are likely to be reasonably effective for them in a given context, by comparison with alternative development methods. He argues that it is not only the characteristics of the methods that should form the basis of the choice, nor just the characteristics of the learners or the context, but rather the interaction between them, as well as other factors. The four frameworks he outlines are (a) suitability for developing knowledge, skills and insight; (b) relationship to learning theories; (c) learning to learn potential; and (d) congruence with personal learning style preferences. The four frameworks are then used to assess the potential effectiveness of sixteen distinct development methods divided into three broad categories, viz. at work methods, of the job methods, and other methods.

Roger Mottram in chapter 13 considers the importance of balancing the needs of the team with the needs of the individuals in the team. He describes the increased frequency and relevance of team working in today's organisations, and the potential of team working to provide individual development opportunities. His main theme is that what is good for the team is not necessarily good for the individual, and that unless best practice is followed, the individual faces significant problems. He concludes that a well-managed, properly composed, relevant and effective team will, by its nature and set-up, encourage and facilitate individual development but that many team working situations do not meet these criteria and pose dangers for individual development and career progression.

In the following chapter, **Victoria Marsick**, **Karen Watkins** and **Jacqueline Wilson** present their model of informal and incidental learning, and the ways that this model can account for more effective use of what we already know, as well as creative, anticipatory learning. They analyse the dilemmas that occur when the demand for speed conflicts with the demand for accuracy and learning, especially in today's more pressurised world. They identify and illustrate ten strategies that individuals and organisations can use to come closer to meeting conflicting demands, or at the least, to better recognise the trade-offs they are making. Managers play a critical role in this process. They are often the facilitator of debriefing sessions, the questioner challenging assumptions in a planning or problem-solving session, and the coach and teacher when individuals come with a problem for which they do not now have the knowledge or skill to resolve.

Ian Cunningham in chapter 15 makes the case for Self Managed Learning (SML) as a basis for individual development in organisations. He reminds us that, despite attempts to force learning on people, adults in organisations will actually choose what they learn and that learners will interpret any "teaching" in terms of their own mental frameworks and existing patterns of thinking. He explores both research and theoretical support for the use of Self Managed Learning and concludes with speculation as to why SML is not more widely accepted, given what he calls the impressive theoretical and research basis for its practice. He goes on to argue that by locating SML in the social context people have to dialogue with their colleagues in order to plan and implement their own learning activities. In this sense learners decide *for themselves* what and how they want to learn but they do not decide *by themselves* and in this way contribute to the development of human *and* social capital of the organisation.

The next two chapters focus on the role of networks in individual development. Chapter 16 by **Rob Poell** and **Ferd Van der Krogt**, addresses the question how social networks in various organisational contexts create learning programmes for individual employee development. The authors use an actor-network approach to describe four models for learning programme creation in social networks, viz. contractual, regulated, organic and collegiate. They then relate the different types of learning programme to the prevailing work and learning contexts in which they take place. They conclude that these contexts have a powerful impact, but that learning networks have their own dynamics as well. They conclude by arguing that employees as learners, with their specific context interpretations and action strategies, should therefore be considered key to learning-programme creation.

In chapter 16, **Gilly Salmon**, explores the potential benefits that online networking can bring to individual development. She offers four approaches for using networked technologies for development in the future and reviews what is known to date of the significance of working online. She shows how working together online, suitably and carefully supported, offers special benefits as well as hazards. The chapter offers a 5-step model of development through online networking, together with examples of its application. She argues that the future of e-learning is open for shaping. She predicts that the most successful development experiences will derive from online networking rather than through delivery of static online "content". She sees online networking as a way forward for effective, individual development that can shape rather than become the victim of the future.

Part Five, Organisational Context, contains chapters on the development of leadership, innovation, and diversity in organisations, all subjects on which there is an abundance of, often simplistic, advice and exhortation. **Cynthia McCauley** in chapter 18 examines processes and strategies for developing the capabilities that enable individuals to be effective in leadership roles. She clarifies the tasks of leaders and the broad human capabilities applicable across many leadership roles. She then examines three main avenues for leader development: job experiences, relationships and formal learning experiences. The chapter summarises the conclusions of best-practice studies of leadership development and points to factors beyond individual development that affects an organisation's leadership capacity. She concludes with a look at the future of leader development, in terms of emerging capabilities needed in leadership roles, new methods or processes for developing the capabilities of leaders, and evolving frameworks for understanding leadership development in organisations. She argues for a systemic perspective that does not ignore the role of individual development in leadership development, but equally recognises the role of relationships, culture and systems in sustaining leadership capacity in organisations.

The next two chapters focus on two key areas of development that can have direct implications for organisational effectiveness, viz. innovation and diversity. In chapter 19, **Nigel King** provides an overview of the literature in work and organisational psychology on innovation in organisations. He examines definitions of the construct, and the ways in which the relationship between creativity and innovation may be understood. He then examines individual, group and organisational-level research, distinguishing between that which conceives of innovation as a product, as a process and as a characteristic of organisations. He also argues that greater attention should be paid to the ways in which innovativeness relates to organisational, group and personal identities. He criticises the general prescriptions for enhancing innovation, and suggests the qualities required of those facing the task of managing a process, which by its very nature is uncertain and hard to control. He sees organisational innovation as a social process that is heavily dependent on context. The implications for practice are less about specific structures to set up or procedures to follow, and more about the way managers interact with other people and the relationships they develop and use in the process of steering an innovation attempt.

Chapter 20 reinforces the increased connectedness of the world in the acknowledged heterogeneity of workforces, communities and markets. **Rajvinder Kandola** and **Satya Kartara** review models and strategies for managing diversity and present a vision of a diversity-orientated organisation. They examine the practice of managing diversity and how it applies to key fields of activity such as recruitment, selection, promotion, individual development and appraisal. Diversity competencies for diversity-orientated organisations are described together with a model for the effective implementation of an integrated diversity strategy. They argue against group-specific development initiatives as unnecessary and leading to marginalisation of groups who need to be "mainstreamed". The key argument for them is that culturally sensitive, and diversity aware development of all individuals in an organisation can only take place within the context of an integrated diversity strategy of the kind they describe in the chapter.

CONCLUSION

It has been a privilege for me to create this handbook in conjunction with 24 distinguished authors. I have learned a great deal. It has also given me an opportunity to stand back and reflect on the totality of what is contained within the twenty chapters representing as they do many years of research, thought and experience.

If there is a theme running through these chapters it is that is misleading to examine issues as though they occur in a vacuum. At one level this makes conceptual analysis, model building, and the construction of practical tools and processes for measurement or for development somewhat simpler, but the price to be paid is high in terms of wasted effort, undeveloped and frustrated people. There are no easy solutions to complex problems, and the contextual variations that abound in the world of work, together with the complexity and chaotic nature of the environment, all combine to suggest unitary concepts and hard-edged approaches have little practical sustainable value.

Context-sensitive, relativist, pluralistic and multi-dimensional approaches to the development of people in organisations are most likely to be most effective. That is perhaps why it is so difficult to find systematic empirical evaluations of development initiatives within organisations (Cascio, 1998). At best the results would be correlational and not conclusive. There is still the danger of vulnerability to fads and fashions taken up too readily, ranging from programmed instruction in the seventies, through CBT in the eighties and e-learning in the nineties. It is unlikely that fashions of this kind can be stopped, any more than fashions in art or science, which with hindsight we call schools of thought.

Individual development in organisations is not a simple process that can be managed and controlled, though it can be deliberately fostered. It is easier to pressurise and coerce people into degrees of acquiescence and compliance but that does not mean change and development has been achieved. The human capacity for resistance, and subversion is phenomenal when there is no genuine belief and acceptance. It is much harder, more complicated and more unpredictable to bring about genuine people- and context-specific development.

The findings of researchers into the long-term effectiveness of organisations, whether focused on HR practices (Fitz-Enz, 1997) or general characteristics (Collins and Porras, 1997; Collins, 2001) point not to specific techniques or processes but to collective attitudes and culture which though different across organisations add up to similar combined effects. If by reading the chapters in this handbook, or as many as you see fit, you move towards an more interactive, context sensitive and humanistic approach to the development of people then the handbook will have served a useful purpose. If, on the other hand, you are unconvinced but more informed of key developmental processes and tools, then it has also served its purpose well.

Michael Pearn
Dublin, December 2001

REFERENCES

Bridges, W. (1998) *Creating you & co*. London: HarperCollins.

Cascio, W.F. (1998) Applied Psychology in Human Resource Management, 5th edition. New Jersey: Simon & Schuster.

Cooper, C. (1999) *The changing nature of work*. In RSA On work and leadership. Aldershot: Gower.

Dawkins, S. (1978) *The selfish gene*. Oxford: Oxford University Press.

Collins, J.C. & Porras, J.I. (1996) *Built to last: Successful habits of visionary companies*. London: Century Press.

Collins, J.C. (2001) *Good to great*. New York: Random House.

Covey, S. (1989) *The seven habits of highly effective people: Powerful lessons in personal change*. New York: Simon & Schuster.

Fitz-Enz, J. (1997) *The eight practices of exceptional companies*. New York: AMACOM.

Hakim, C. (1994) *We are all self-employed: The new social contract for working in a changed world*. San Francisco: Berrett Koehler.

Handy, C. (1991). *Gods of management*. London: Business Books.

Hedberg, B., Dahlgreen, G., Hansson, J. & Olve, N. (2000) *Virtual organisations and beyond*. Chichester: Wiley.

Herriot, P. & Pemberton, C. (1995) *New deals: The revolution in managerial careers*. Chichester: Wiley.

Hirschhorn, L. (1997) *Reworking authority: Leading and following in the post-modern organization*. Cambridge, Ma: MIT Press.

Gazzaniga, M.G., Ivy, R. & Mangan, G. (1998) *Cognitive neuroscience*. New York: Norton.

Greenfield, S. (2000) *The private life of the brain*. Harmondsworth: Allen Lane The Penguin Press.

Kanter, R.M. (1989) *When giants learn to dance*. London: Simon & Schuster.

Kanter, R.M. (2001) *e-Volve!: Succeeding in the digital culture of tomorrow*. Boston: Harvard Business School Press.

Kelly, K. (1999) New rules for the new economy—10 ways the network economy is changing everything. London: Fourth Estate.

McCormack, M.H. (1990) *The 110% solution*. London: Chapmans.

Pinker, S. (1998) *How the mind works*. New York: Penguin.

Ratey, J. (2001) *A user's guide to the brain*. New York: Little, Brown.

Schwartz, E.J. (1999) *Digital Darwinism: Seven breakthrough strategies for surviving in the cut-throat web economy*. Harmondsworth: Penguin.

Smith, H.W. (1994) *The ten natural laws of successful time and life management*. New York: Warner Books.

Trompenaars, F. & Hampden-Turner, C. (1997, 2nd edition) *Riding the waves of culture: Understanding cultural diversity in business*. London: Nicholas Brealey.

PART I

Approaches, Concepts and Theory

Learning Theory and the Construction of Self: What Kinds of People Do We Create through the Theories of Learning that We Apply to Their Development?

John G. Burgoyne
Lancaster University Management School, Lancaster, UK

SUMMARY

It is argued that the great variety of theories of learning each imply very different conceptions of the self or person. Some of this variety is summarised and some of the different forms of self are explored. It is argued that in teaching and learning we may create the learners as certain kinds of 'selves', or run into resistance from pre-established selves different from the ones we assume. Finally, some sense of progression over time in the kinds of selves we envision through our theories of learning is explored, and our choices in supporting this progression is explored.

INTRODUCTION

Learning has been understood and theorised in a number of dramatically different ways over the last several decades. The variety of teaching, training and learning facilitation

Individual Differences and Development in Organisations. Edited by Michael Pearn.
© 2002 John Wiley & Sons, Ltd.

methods is also, and perhaps not surprisingly given this, vast and varied (Huczynski, 2001). The organisation-based practices of education, training and development, 'human resource development', organisational development and learning organisation initiatives look very different from the different theoretical perspectives. Furthermore, the different schools of thought are suggestive of very different lines of action that might be taken to facilitate learning and development.

The aim of this chapter is partly to offer an initial mapping of some of this variety so that both theorists and practitioners can be more aware of the variety and alternatives, including those that may be different from their current beliefs and practices. Another aim is also to argue that each different theoretical perspective on learning carries with it a 'concept of self' or concept of the 'learning entity', which is also extremely varied.

It is argued that whatever any effort to teach, educate, learn or develop tries to do, successfully or otherwise in the specifics of what is learned—understanding, ability, values, etc.—the notion that 'the medium is the message' (McLuhan, 1964) also applies. An attempt to facilitate learning asserts a form of self for the target of the learning. In some circumstances learning facilitation therefore has a second-order effect; it creates a self-concept or identity in the learner. However, this is not always the case; in other circumstances the subject of learning facilitation may have an identity or form of self concept already established which is at odds with, or at least different from, that assumed or asserted by the facilitation process. In this circumstance, the process and outcome of the interaction is likely to be varied and unpredictable, containing hidden or overt conflict, contestation and misunderstanding. It is a common finding on research on the learner's experience of being taught that the reactions and experiences generated by what appears outwardly to be the 'same' stimulus to learning is extremely varied between people (see Marton et al., 1984). This suggests that this pattern may be the norm rather than the exception.

It is also argued here that the differences in the concept of self embedded in learning theories, the practices applying them and people themselves subjected to attempts to facilitate their learning are not mere technical differences. The differences are about fundamental values, ethical stances about the human condition and philosophical stances on the nature of life and existence. The conclusion, whether we like it or not, is that both theorising about learning and working with the methods, styles and practices of facilitating learning is, in that sense, a philosophical and ideological endeavour.

Different theories of learning construct greatly contrasting views of the person or self that works in, on or for organisations. It follows from this that the differing forms of self asserted in learning facilitation in an organisational context, and how this interacts with existing employee identities, are likely to have a profound effect on the nature and form of the organisation in which this take place.

A final strand of the argument in this chapter is to do with change over time. Although it is certainly not the case that theories of learning, and the practices associated with them, have succeeded one another in a neat chronology that can be located in easily defined eras in recent history, there is without doubt a historicity to them. The theories and practices, and the people who developed and championed them, do belong to different time periods and their work reflects broader theoretical and practical trends crossing their eras. Something can perhaps be made of the complex evolutionary flow involving ideas and practices related to learning, linked to broader social, economic and organisational patterns.

SCHOOLS OF THOUGHT ON LEARNING AND THEIR EMBEDDED CONCEPTS OF SELF AND THE LEARNING ENTITY

This part of the chapter presents a summary of 14 perspectives on learning, and attempts to crystallise the essence of each of them. It then interprets the concept of self or the learning entity embedded in each As will be seen, this distinction is important. At the beginning of the broad progressions through the theories of learning are those that see the individual as a stand-alone learning entity. Next come those that see individuals learning, but very much in a social context. Then there are those that see learning as very much shaped by, and dependent on, features of the social and material context; and finally there are those that locate learning in some wider process in which the individual or 'person' is but one part, and by no means a special or privileged one.

A number of prefatory remarks are in order: first, a common format has been adopted, to assist comprehension [this is a reflexive issue in this chapter—how do I help you understand what I am arguing? Ausubel (1968), belonging to one of my earlier schools of thought, suggests that giving people an initial structure for cognitive material helps— and pragmatically I have always found this helpful in this kind of situation!]. Each school of thought is given a name and a brief description. Following that, an attempt is made to capture the essence of each school in the form of an indicative statement that tries to capture the general principle that might follow from it as a guide to an approach to facilitation of learning. Finally, the construct of the self or learning entity is labelled and described.

Second, as may be obvious, this enterprise involves summarising in a few sentences and paragraphs vast areas of thought and practice that can and do fill volumes, and constitute the work of whole careers and the programmes of whole research groups over long periods. Live members of these can be guaranteed to deplore the simplistic nature of my enterprise, dead ones to be spinning in their graves. I do aspire to be able to identify something of the essence of each approach to learning, but would be the first to admit to not capturing the full richness and variety or, perhaps more importantly, not being able to portray some of the differences and alternative formulations within each approach. I still hope it is worthwhile for the intended purpose.

Third, the split into 14 areas is somewhat arbitrary. It is a bit like a cake that can be cut into more or fewer pieces, and the dividing cuts make in different places. This is to some extent a personal choice.

Fourth, the ordering is somewhat personal, being roughly the order in which I have encountered them since hearing my first formal definition of learning in a first-year undergraduate psychology course in 1963. This may have some idiosyncratic properties, but it must also reflect some broad changes in interest and development in the theory and practice of learning.

Finally, some of the schools of thought are primarily about learning and quite recognisable as schools of thought on learning. Others, which tend to be the later ones like post-modernism, activity theory, actor network theory and critical realism, are broader meta-theories or philosophical orientations with foci well outside any specific boundaries of learning as a phenomenon. I include them because I believe they have special implications for learning not covered elsewhere. This is why I include them and why I concentrate on the aspects of them that I believe have implications for learning.

TABLE 1.1 Learning theories and implied concepts of self

Learning theory	Self
1 Conditioning and the connectionist approach	A mechanical view of the self
2 The trait modification view	A specification view of self
3 The information transfer approach	A recorder view of self
4 The cognitive school	A knowing view of self
5 The systems theory approach	The discovery view of self
6 The humanistic and existential approach	An essential view of self
7 Social learning theory	An identity view of self
8 Psychodynamics and related approaches	A mystical view of self
9 Post-modernism	The decentred and fragmented self
10 Situated learning theory	The communal self
11 Post-structuralism	The 'vacant' self
12 Activity theory	The contextualised self
13 Actor network theory	The co-evolving self
14 Critical realism	The hermeneutic self

Table 1.1 summarises the schools of thought on learning and the concept of self that I suggest is associated with them.

SCHOOL ONE: CONDITIONING AND THE CONNECTIONIST APPROACH

- *Summary*. The *conditioning* school of thought is the behaviourist psychological approach that represents learning as the establishment of a linkage between a stimulus and response in perception and behaviour, respectively. The classic sub-theories are those of classical conditioning (Pavlov, 1972) where a 'new' stimulus, through association with an existing stimulus attached to a response, becomes attached to that response also; and reinforcement theories, where a response that happens to follow a stimulus which is then rewarded becomes 'attached' to that stimulus, or the reverse if punished (Thorndike, 1913; Thomas, 1974). This approach to learning is the basis for a large amount of empirical experimental research and theorising, which accounts for complex behaviour like language through the chaining together of simple stimulus–response connections. In both cases the product can be thought of as habit, and the process as one of establishing association through the two different processes outlined. Although this way of thinking about learning has been criticised for its mechanistic nature, or interpreted as only applying to very basic forms of learning, and not 'higher' forms of intelligent and moral and conscious human behaviour, Skinner has argued that it can be the basis for a more general social theory of learning (1971).
- *Essence of orientation for facilitating learning*. One should be clear about what behaviours one wants people to be capable of, and arrange to elicit and reinforce them.
- *View of self and the learning entity*. A mechanical view of the self.

SCHOOL TWO: THE TRAIT MODIFICATION VIEW

- *Summary*. *Trait modification theory* is based on the concept of the learning person or entity being describable as a set of characteristics, and learning as a change in this profile of characteristics. As a theory it is more specific on learning as product than it is on learning as process. There are a whole variety of specific theories within this category, often associated with the psychometric tradition of research (Guilford, 1954), which proposes specific categorisations of traits and often associated measures and measuring instruments (e.g. 16PF, Myers Briggs type indicator—although the underlying constructs of this latter come from Jungian theory mentioned under the later school of psychodynamics). In the more applied world of training it is common for 'knowledge', 'skills' and 'attitudes' to be taken as three broad categories of traits, which define learning goals and outcomes. In the training and development world the whole approach of profiling people and jobs on trait profiles, and the great majority of 'competency' approaches to managing learning, are implicitly or explicitly based on an underlying trait modification perspective (Schroder, 1989; Short, 1984; Boyatzis, 1982). Within this perspective one of the main enduring debates is between 'nature', i.e. those characteristics which are fixed on the basis of genetics or some other assumed structure, and 'nurture', those characteristics which are changeable as a result of learning. Thus, this perspective emphasises the question of what can and cannot be changed, or change through a learning process. This perspective also raises the question of characteristics that affect the learning process itself, either directly through the idea of learning styles (Kolb, 1974, 1984; Honey & Mumford, 1992), or indirectly through the proposition that personality characteristics may influence how learning takes place. The complication that this perspective raises for both the theory and practice of learning is that not all learning entities may learn in the same way, which would imply that an adequate theory of learning would be a contingency theory, viz. different processes for different people.

- *Essence of orientation for facilitating learning.* It is essential that one should 'profile' the knowledge, skills, competencies, personality attributes, values, competencies and abilities that people do have and should have, understand which of these are capable of being influenced by training and development, and run programmes accordingly, with attention to their fits to learning styles.
- *View of self and the learning entity.* A specification view of self.

SCHOOL THREE: THE INFORMATION TRANSFER APPROACH

- *Summary.* The *information transfer* approach regards the product of learning as a stored product in the form of an informational commodity. The theoretical issues of the learning process are ones of transmission, communication, organisation, storage and retrieval in the learning entity. This way of thinking implies that the product of learning is knowledge as an objective commodity, publicly owned and acknowledged, and, at least in its simpler forms, having straightforward truth value. The primary orientation to learning as a process is learning as memory, and the theoretical and practical problems that are seen or acknowledged by this perspective are to do with how the learner takes in information, how it can be presented to be internalised, how the learner organises their knowledge—like a filing system or library so that it is stored and can be accessed (remembered) when it is called for. This perspective leads, in terms of the practice of helping learning, to a concern with imparting knowledge in an organised way and helping the learner achieve organisation as well as storage of knowledge. This way of thinking about learning (Ausubel, 1968) can be seen as embedded in practice as well as theory. For example, the design and rationale of higher education institutions can be interpreted as having activities of research that generate knowledge, libraries and the like that store it, and teaching that disseminates the knowledge to students. When this way of thinking is dominant, teaching staff are primarily seen and valued as subject experts, teaching methods are primarily one-way knowledge transfer ones, examination and assessment is primarily based on test of information recall. Arguably, many applications of information technology to learning are and will be, because of its information storage and transmission capability, primarily based on this perspective.

- *Essence of orientation for facilitating learning.* The primary task is to communicate information on ideas and procedures effectively and assist the learners to organize this information so that they can access it in their memories, and utilize it in appropriate circumstances.
- *View of self and the learning entity.* A recorder view of self.

School Four: the Cognitive School

- *Summary.* The *cognitive* school of thought sees the learning process as one in which the learning entity develops its own mental model or cognitive map of itself in its context, and uses this to plan and regulate its behaviour. Here knowledge is essentially personal and subjective, in contrast to the objective and public form envisaged in 'information transfer'. Learners develop their idiosyncratic cognitive maps, modifying them to help them make increasing sense of their experience and take actions that help them achieve their outcomes. Kelly's theory of personal constructs, and its associated repertory grid methodology, represents one formulation of this approach (see Bannister & Mair, 1968). Historically, the gestalt orientation to psychology (Kohler, 1929), in seeking to acknowledge a holistic mind behind behaviour, fits with this view. Miller et al. (1960) develop the metaphor of the cognitive map to account for behaviour and skill as the equivalent of 'itineraries' that are drawn from maps to suggest how skills and behaviour might derive from knowledge.
- *Essence of orientation for facilitating learning.* The important thing is to help students/learners develop, test and improve their own mental models of the organisational situations they do or will deal with.
- *View of self and the learning entity.* A knowing view of self.

School Five: the Systems Theory Approach

- *Summary.* The *cybernetic/autopoietic perspective* is essentially the application of systems theory to the issue of learning. The learning entity is seen as a system within a context, normally adapting to that situation by developing an understanding of it and using this understanding to guide its behaviour in its environment to allow it to survive and attain its purposes. The concept of autopoiesis modifies the standard systems view of an entity surviving as a system by adapting to its context, towards a view in which the system acts to modify its context in a way that is to the advantage of the system. Pask (1975) gives an academic treatment of this perspective; it is treated in a much more applied way by Romiszowski (1970). Maturana & Valera (1980, 1992) develop the concept of autopoiesis in the context of biology; Morgan (1989) applies it to the human development and organisation world. Much of business gaming and simulation in general as a teaching/learning process can be seen as based on this idea of learning, based around the notion of simulating a learning environment (Armitage, 1993; Gibb, 1974; Taylor & Walford, 1978). Systems thinking as also a major perspective in conceptualisations of organisational learning (Senge, 1990; Beer, 1972).

- *Essence of orientation for facilitating learning.* It is useful to put students/learners into situations that simulate the management and leadership work situations that they do or will face, where they analyse, decide and act, and get a simulated response to their actions.
- *View of self and the learning entity.* The discovery view of self.

SCHOOL SIX: THE HUMANISTIC AND EXISTENTIAL APPROACH

- *Summary. Humanistic/developmental approaches* to learning typically attempt to acknowledge an emotional, affective aspect of learning as well as an intellectual/cognitive one, and often encompass an idea of a natural trajectory of learning towards a 'fully developed' state. They tend, in their simplest forms, to assume a 'good and true' human nature for the learner that will lead to fulfilment and a good life and, indeed, society, if authentically acknowledged and expressed (see Rogers, 1969, for the classic treatment). Theories in this category are implicitly or explicitly normative, tending to the view that the natural trajectory of development is also the 'right' one. Some theories, notably Kohlberg (1981), address this directly, presenting the theory of one of moral development. The closely related existential point of view is essentially a philosophical one, but one with important implications for learning. The essential point for learning is that existentialism challenges the traditional assumption implicit in much thinking about learning, that ideas, beliefs, thought and decision making precede and determine action. Existentialism, at least as articulated by Sartre (1970), proposes that action precedes and generates meaning. In this perspective, learning and creativity are closely allied; wilful action, in a domain not prestructured by existing meaning and habits, is the generator of new meanings.
- *Essence of orientation for facilitating learning.* In helping people learn it is important to see them as complex, full human beings like ourselves, and not to use some model that simplifies them as learning entities. This involves respecting individuals' own processes for development and growth.
- *View of self and the learning entity.* An essential view of self.

SCHOOL SEVEN: SOCIAL LEARNING THEORY

- *Summary. Social influence* theories of learning take a more sociological or social psychological view of learning, in contrast to the more individualised psychologistic orientation of the schools of thought summarised so far. Here the learning entity is taken to be primarily a social construction, and what is at stake is identity or identity formation—how the learning entity is perceived and self-perceives, and including the question of whether the 'learner' has a unitary and individualised identity, which is not to be taken for granted in the more fully developed forms of this school of thought (see e.g. Gowler, 1972, for an articulation of the primarily social view of the person). Socialisation (see Van Mannen, 1976), both as a process and an outcome, are a prime focus in this perspective, and more psychological and empirical work in this tradition focuses on the processes by which identity and self-concept are formed and the conditions that influence this. However, this perspective does not only cover identity; it would interpret even technical skills as only being learnt to implement some kind of occupational or role identity, technical skill being as much or entirely about having reputation for a certain kind of performance, rather than some objective technical ability to achieve a material performance.

- *Essence of orientation for facilitating learning.* Central to educating managers and leaders is the creation of processes by which they achieve 'identities' as managers and leaders—in their own eyes and in the eyes of others.
- *View of self and the learning entity.* An identity view of self.

School Eight: Psychodynamics and Related Approaches

- *Summary.* The *psychoanalytic school* of thought is intended here in the broadest sense to label that body of approaches, following Freud (1938) and Jung (1923), that use the concept of the unconscious and various forces and sources of energy as a framework within which to propose interpretations of experience and behaviour as created by dynamic interactions between conscious and unconscious. As well as providing the theoretical basis of a whole class of therapeutic programmes, this approach has been embodied in popular methodologies such as transactional analysis (Barker, 1980) and, through the work of Bion (1961) to various group learning methods, and organisational change (DeBoard, 1978). Central to this view is the idea of the unconscious, which has content that interacts dynamically with the content of consciousness in the shaping of experience and behaviour. Different sub-schools within this general one differ on how they see this dynamic working, and how fixed this is, or itself open to change through learning. This school of thought also underlies and relates to various therapeutic practices and offers interpretations of the therapist—'patient' relationship. These ideas can be and are also applied to the teacher–learner relationship. Ideas like 'projection', in which either party sees in and attributes to the other features which are in fact their own, and 'dependency' in which one relies on the other for the validity of their beliefs and justifications for their actions, are examples.
- *Essence of orientation for facilitating learning.* It is important to recognize that any learning process that is going to affect a person's ability to perform a management and leadership role is going to involve the realignment of the dynamic balance between conscious and unconscious forces and processes in his/her psyche.
- *View of self and the learning entity.* A mystical view of self—in the sense that, via the notion of the unconscious, the person is a mystery to him/herself and others.

School Nine: Post-modernism

- *Summary.* Post-modernism is a broad intellectual movement asserting the end of modernism, the start of which is usually located anywhere between the beginning of the Enlightenment and the commencement of the industrial revolution. The end of modernism is located in recent decades, although the case for the continuation of modernism can be made. Post-modernism has, perhaps fittingly, multiple definitions and descriptions. These include the end of a sense of progress (the growth of science and technology and the sense that it will solve all problems), the end of an overarching purpose for knowledge—knowledge to cope better with the world, knowledge for human enlightenment, and knowledge for its own sake. In fashion and art it leads to a pastiche of former styles in new combinations. The notion of the 'end of progress' has profound implications for learning, since much of our implicit and explicit thinking about learning is that it is progressive—getting better, more skilled, more able to cope, more mature and so on. Post-modern learning is just a new temporary combination, a temporary alignment to a new temporary set of circumstances. The post-modern view also questions the notion of an integrated self that is the author, or agent, or point of origin of action. Post-modernism talks of the 'decentred and fragmented' self. Post-modernism is a sense takes the view that an integrated self-originating purposive action is a modernist idea. From a post-modern point of view, the idea of an individual self is something strange to the modernist era and perhaps to Western culture. From this point of view, the individual self is not something real or natural, but rather a cultural idea belonging to a particular era. The idea of self is a cultural idea that we absorb and the rolling, evolving culture in which we live 'prints' certain cultural identities on us, and we are the carriers rather than the creators of these. Decentering takes the person away from the position of being the origin of meaning and action. Many ways of thinking about learning support the idea of helping the person have a consistent self and identity that is stable and without inner contradictions. Post-modernism takes the other view—it is inevitable and necessary that we are multiple, inconsistent and changing selves all the time. Post-modernism comes in an optimistic and pessimistic forms—and typically the message is that both apply. The optimistic view is that we can be whoever we want to be, and create whatever realities we want to, in the carnival of life. The pessimistic view is nihilistic—life has no purpose or meaning, nothing is any more or less true than anything else. Gergen (1991) provides a good treatment of some of the issues that this perspective raises for us in contemporary life.

- *Essence of orientation for facilitating learning.* In today's world, managers and leaders have to be helped to feel comfortable with having confused and multiple identities, live with unclear or multiple senses of direction, and with being just a part of complex and chaotic flows that they cannot understand.
- *View of self and the learning entity.* The decentred and fragmented self.

SCHOOL TEN: SITUATED LEARNING THEORY

- *Summary.* The notion of *situated learning* (Lave & Wenger, 1991) emphasises the collective, local and informal nature of much learning. In this view, learning in the outcome, product or noun sense exists in 'communities of practice' that share a way of doing things. Individuals come to share this collective learning through a process of 'legitimate peripheral participation', from which they are slowly incorporated into collective practice and community membership. This view of learning casts it essentially as a natural and informal process in which individuals become absorbed into the beliefs and practices of a group as part and parcel of becoming a member of it.

However, there have been attempts to apply this idea to the deliberate facilitation of learning by setting up groups of people with shared areas of practices in a way which is intended to help them share their experiences and develop their practices.

- *Essence of orientation for facilitating learning.* Management and leadership is best, and perhaps can only, be learnt by a kind of informal apprenticeship involving being a beginner-participant in the situation where the management and leadership is going to be practised.
- *View of self and the learning entity.* The communal self.

School Eleven: Post-structuralism

- *Summary.* The *post-structural perspective* constitutes a broad conceptual movement in the social sciences (Sturrock, 1979), which may not be a learning theory as such but has important implications for it. Broadly speaking, this approach argues that there is very little, or in the extreme nothing, that is fixed that generates psychological, social, linguistic or cultural phenomena. Rather, behaviour, experience and phenomena of all kinds are generated by temporary learnt operating beliefs that determine both the generation and perception of behaviour. In a metaphor, these things are generated by 'software' rather than 'hardware'. This perspective reframes many existing theories of learning. For example, humanistic phase models of human development were mainly proposed by their originators as structural truths about human personality, but can be reformulated in a post-structural perspective as 'learnt' assumptions shared by certain cultural groupings in certain eras. In the psychoanalytic domain, a post-structural reformulation has been proposed by Lacan (1977), who has suggested that Freud was right to propose the unconscious, but that the way the unconscious is structured is not fixed. A reaction to this point of view, reasserting the significance of structure as an inherited characteristic only modified in the very long term by Darwinian processes, has emerged under the banner of evolutionary psychology (Barkow et al., 1992).
- *Essence of orientation for facilitating learning.* It is a mistake to think that there is anything fixed or 'hard-wired' about people in terms of what they are like and how they learn. People can be constructed, and construct themselves, in all kinds of ways, in terms of both how they learn and what they learn to be.
- *View of self and the learning entity.* The 'vacant' self.

School Twelve: Activity Theory

- *Summary.* Activity theory continues the theme that it is not possible to understand and locate learning as a phenomenon that is entirely within an individual. It does not deny or question the notion of the person or the individual, but argues that what they are and do, including how they learn, can only be understood in the context of some important features of their situations. These include the activity or task in which they are involved, the tools (in very broad sense of the word) and resources they have access to, and the other people, social systems and structures that are part of their context (see Blackler, 1993, for an introduction to activity theory applied to organisation and management. In this view the individual still learns, but in a way that is fundamentally shaped by his/her context in terms of the tasks and purposes he/she pursues alone and with others, the social and cultural context in which he/she operates, and the material and non-material tools that are available to him/her.

- *Essence of orientation for facilitating learning.* People only learn in a way that is deeply entwined and integrated with the tasks and purposes they are learning to achieve and perform, the tools they do and could have to do this, and the other people and social context in which they do this.
- *View of self and the learning entity.* The contextualised self.

SCHOOL THIRTEEN: ACTOR NETWORK THEORY

- *Summary.* Actor network theory, like activity theory, emphasises the notion that the 'individual' or 'person' is deeply embedded in, and just part of, a context. This includes tools and technologies, social processes and structures, and institutions. This whole context, including the person, is an interactive system. As far as learning goes, actor network theory argues that learning is a property of this whole system. Within this view it makes just as much sense to attribute learning to the tools and technologies in a situation as it does to attribute it to the individual or person. However, it cannot really be attributed to any single part of the system because it is a system-wide phenomenon (see Law & Hassard, 1999; Hassard, Law & Lee, 1999). Actor network theory thus casts learning as a long-term characteristic of human, social or material systems by which the individual is carried along, and sees very distinct limits on the extent to which the individual can unilaterally reshape him/herself and his/her contexts.
- *Essence of orientation for facilitating learning.* What actually learns is systemic networks, including people, tools, resources, purposes and tasks, the material, social and the cultural legacy associated with domains of practice. To the extent that we can address individuals as learners, we have to recognise that they are just one element in such complex systems, and no more important or significant than any of the other parts.
- *View of self and the learning entity.* The co-evolving self.

SCHOOL FOURTEEN: CRITICAL REALISM

- *Summary.* Critical realism is another broad philosophical view of the world with profound implications for what learning might be. In relation to learning, critical realism points us to the question, 'What is there that exists in the world that might be learnt about, and what are the implications for its form and nature for learning?'. Critical realism asserts that there are 'real' things in the world with properties—effects that occur regularly, but are contingent on surrounding circumstances. But included in the 'real' are the ideas and concepts that we have about things, and the second-order ideas that we have about our ideas. However, critical realism neither accepts that there is a predictable machine-like world out there that can be discovered as a predictable system, nor that (as implied by post-modernism) there is nothing but an evolving sea of ideas, concepts and cultural meanings. Rather, the world is a complex open system with emergent properties—new things happen all the time due to events and entities coming together in combinations never previously occurring. Critical realism focuses our attention on the question of what there is to learn about, what its properties are and what the implications of this are for how we learn about it. The outcome is that learning is a kind of active detective work to understand how events and entities are playing out in particular circumstances.

- *Essence of orientation for facilitating learning.* Helping people to learn to manage and lead is best done by developing them as practical action researchers, continuously working out the dynamics of the situations that they deal with, which have properties of varying degrees of stability that are always recombining in new forms, but none the less have some features capable of anticipation.
- *View of self and the learning entity.* The hermeneutic self—i.e. a self that reflects on itself as it tries to make sense of itself and the world of which it is part.

CONSTRUCTIONS OF THE SELF IN PERSPECTIVES ON LEARNING

This extremely, and probably dangerously, brief sketch of some of the main perspectives on learning suggests a range of constructions of the 'self' implicitly and explicitly formulated by them, as summarised in Table 1.1.

Whether the summaries are fair, and whether the specific concepts of self that I have associated with them are formulated as well as they could be, must be open to questioning and debate. However, the argument is hopefully sufficient to demonstrate that there is a great variety of conceptions of self at work in our theories of learning. Returning to some of the questions and arguments in the opening paragraphs of this chapter, this hopefully provides a basis for considering a number of points and the implications of these for any practice that is to do with attempts to facilitate learning.

Any attempt to facilitate learning is going to involve methods and approaches, and these are going to be based, implicitly or explicitly, on ideas like the above. Whatever else these do in terms of aiming at specific or general learning outcomes for the learner, they make a 'pitch' at the learner as a certain kind of self. In some cases this may help to create the learner as the kind of self assumed by the learning approach, e.g. as an employable commodity to fit an organisational machine, or as an autonomous self asserting the right to self-creation.

In other situations, the asserted 'self' may be in conflict with some pre-established learner identity and self, and this conflict or clash may explain some of the 'difficulties' that can occur in events to facilitate learning. It would be hard to argue that there are any decisive rights and wrongs in this field of learning theory and practice. To find a practical approach in the light of all this complexity, the best line to take is probably that acceptable constructions of the self needs to be negotiated between learning facilitators and learners as part of the relationship. This idea has probably been best developed in terms of the value of 'learning conversations' by Harri-Augstein & Thomas (1991), who advocate this kind of discussion as part of learning events.

The sources of variety and differences between the different ways of thinking about learning, and the constructions of self that they carry, are certainly more than factual and technical differences. They reach right back to major alternative philosophical views of the world and fundamental ideological and moral perspectives associated with them. It follows from this that 'learning conversations' need to be a dialogue to establish some working consensus (or way of working with a dissensus) on these philosophical and moral issues. Given the pivotal role of education, training and development in our

TABLE 1.2 Suggested clusters of learning theories and concepts of self

1–4	An individualised, passive and machine-like view of learning and the self
4–6 (and 8?)	An individualised but agentic, purposive view of the self as learner
7 and 10	A social view of self—individuals as existing in relation to other people
9, 11–14	Learning as a system- or context-located phenomenon with the person/self as a node in this process, with variations of status in relation to learning. In this category learning is in a system-wide context, in which the individual is deeply embedded in the totality of this, which is not only social, but technical and ecological as well

society and economy, it can be argued that the way we negotiate the forms of ourselves in learning events is pivotal to the reproduction and revision of our social, economic and political lives.

Mention was made of the historicity of our ideas about learning. The schools of thought discussed here do not fall into a neat chronology, but there is some rough ordering of them in relation to ideas that have been at the forefront over the last 80 years. These can be very roughly grouped. Using the numbering in Table 1.1, the clusters shown in Table 1.2 can be suggested, which give some sense of how our conceptions of learning and the self have themselves developed over recent history.

There is a clear sense of progression here from individual passive and active learning, through the social to a more fully integrated concept of learning. In choosing and negotiating approaches to learning and the views of self that go with them, we have the opportunity to choose towards which of these stages of development we wish to move the contexts in which we work. Post-modernism notwithstanding, if we move to the later concepts of learning we may have the opportunity to move humanity, and organisations through which it expresses may of its aspirations, to a more sustainable relationship with the world.

REFERENCES

Ausubel, D.P. (1968) Cognitive structures and transfer. In *Educational Psychology: a Cognitive View*. New York: Holt, Rinehart and Winston.

Bannister, D. & Mair, J.M.M. (1968) *The Evaluation of Personal Constructs*. London: Academic Press.

Barker, D. (1980) *TA and Training: the Theory and Use of Transactional Analysis in Organisations*. Aldershot: Gower.

Bion, W. (1961) *Experiences in Groups*. London: Tavistock.

Blackler, F. (1993) Knowledge and the theory of organisations: organisations as activity systems and the reframing of management. *Journal of Management Studies*, **30**, 863–4.

Boyatzis, R.E. (1982) *The Competent Manager: a Model for Effective Performance*. New York: Wiley.

Freud, S. (1938) *The Basic Writings of Sigmund Freud* (A.A. Bril, trans. and ed.). London: Random House.

Gergen, K.J. (1991) *The Saturated Self: Dilemmas of Identity in Contemporary Life*. New York: Basic Books/Harper Collins.

Gibb, G.I. (1974) *Handbook of Games and Simulation Exercises*. London: E. & F.N. Spon.

Gowler, D. (1972) On the concept of the person: a biosocial view. In Ruddock (ed.), *Six Approaches to the Person*. London: Routledge & Kegan Paul.

Guilford, J.P. (1954) *Psychometric Methods*. Maidenhead: McGraw-Hill.

Harri-Augstein, S. & Thomas, L. (1991) *Learning Conversations: the Self-organised Way to Personal and Organisational Growth*. London: Routledge.

Hassard, J., Law, J. & Lee, N. (eds)(1999) Themed section: actor-network theory and managerialism. *Organization*, **6**, 3.

Huczynski, A.A. (2001) *Encyclopaedia of Development Methods*. Aldershot: Gower.

Kohlberg, L. (1981) *Essays on Moral Development, Vol. 1: the Philosophy of Moral Development*. New York: Harper & Row.

Kohler, W. (1929) *Gestalt Psychology*. New York: Liveright.

Kolb, D.A. (1984) *Experiential Learning*. Englewood Cliffs, NJ: Prentice Hall.

Kolb, D.A. (1974) On management and the learning process. In D.A. Kolb, I.M. Rubin & J.M. McIntyre (eds), *Organizational Psychology*, 2nd edn. Englewood Cliffs, NJ: Prentice Hall. 27–42.

Lave, J. & Wenger, E. (1991) *Situated Learning: Legitimate Peripheral Participation*. Cambridge: University Press.

Law, J. & Hassard, J. (eds)(1999) *Actor Network Theory and After*. Blackwell Sociological Review: Oxford.

Marton, F., Entwistle, N. & Hounsell, D. (eds) (1984) *The Experience of Learning*. Edinburgh: Scottish Academic Press.

McLuhan, M. (1964) *Understanding Media*. London and New York.

Miller, G.A., Galanter, E. & Pribram, K.H. (1960) *Plans and the Structure of Behaviour*. New York: Holt, Rinehart & Winston.

Pask, G. (1975) *The Cybernetics of Human Learning and Performance*. London: Hutchinson.

Pavlov, I.P. (1972) *Conditional Reflexes*. Oxford: Oxford University Press.

Rogers, C. (1969) *Freedom to Learn*. Indianapolis, IN: Bobbs-Merrill.

Romiszowski, A.J. (1970) *A Systems Approach to Education and Training*. London: Kogan Page.

Sartre, J.-P. (1970) *Existentialism and Humanism*. London: Methuen.

Schroder, H.M. (1989) *Management Competence: the Key to Excellence*. Iowa: Kendall/Hunt.

Short, E.C. (ed.)(1984) *Competence: Inquiries into Its Meaning and Acquisition in Educational Settings*. Lanham: University of America Press.

Skinner, B.F. (1971) *Beyond Freedom and Dignity*. New York: Knopff.

Sturrock, J. (ed.)(1979) *Structuralism and Since: from Levi-Strauss to Derrida*. Oxford: Oxford University Press.

Taylor, J. & Walford, R. (1978) *Learning and the Simulation Game*. Milton Keynes: Open University Press.

Van Mannen (1976) Breaking in: socialisation to work. In Dubin, R. (ed.) *Handbook of Work, Organisation and Society*. Chicago, IL: Rand McNally.

CHAPTER 2

Who Am I? Self-development in Organisations

Monica Lee

University of Lancaster, Lancaster, UK

SUMMARY

This chapter suggests that self-development is always on-going. We can look back and see where we have developed from. We learn more about ourselves from others, and our interaction with others fosters our emergent self. However, not all 'good' experiences are developmental, and vice versa. Self-development (at least of the transformative kind) is often painful, and this needs to be managed. A range of tools and techniques are discussed in this chapter, but neither we nor the organisation can control self-development. However, by establishing a true open environment of co-regulation and negative capability, organisations are likely to foster self-development.

INTRODUCTION

The concept of self-development within an organisation appears quite simple: 'I want to develop myself so that I am better at my job and am more likely to get promoted or find a more challenging job elsewhere'. Unfortunately, the area is more contested and complicated than might initially appear. Therefore, in this chapter I shall explore what might be encompassed by the 'development' of one's 'self'. I shall then look at how self-development might occur within organisations, and how organisations might facilitate the self-development of their employees.

Individual Differences and Development in Organisations. Edited by Michael Pearn.
© 2002 John Wiley & Sons, Ltd.

The mechanical approach to self-development (see '*shaping*' below) within organisations, which is partially enshrined in the competency debate, would suggest the logic of establishing where I am or what I am like now. I should then look to where I want to be in the future, what sort of person I want to be and what sort of skills (etc.) I wish to possess, and then break down the distance between the two into small achievable steps. Finally, I need to decide how I will know when I have got where I want to be. What milestones will I have reached? What goals will I have attained? Then I take the first step on the route I have planned.

This approach might work well for clearly defined pre-set goals, similar to that recommended for self-managed learning. For most people, however, development is more than learning. I have described elsewhere (Lee, 1997b, 2001a) how 'development' is seen by the literature in four ways.

EXPLORING DEVELOPMENT OF THE SELF

FOUR TYPES OF DEVELOPMENT

In the first approach, *development as maturation* was used as if to refer to a pre-determined stage-like and inevitable progression of people and organisations. Development is seen as an inevitable unfolding, and thus the developmental force is the process itself, which, in turn, defines the end-point. The system, be it an individual, a group or an organisation, is seen as being a coherent entity with clearly defined boundaries existing within a predictable external environment. The organisation is discussed as if it were a single living element, whose structures, existence and change are capable of being completely understood through sufficient expert analysis. Concepts such as empowerment and change-agency are irrelevant in an approach that is essentially founded upon social determinism, with no place for unpredictable events or freedom of individual choice.

In the second, *development as shaping*, people are seen as tools who can be shaped to fit the organisation. Here, development is still seen to have known end-points, but these are defined by someone or something external to the process of development. The organisation is stratified and senior management define the end point for junior management—the wishes of the corporate hierarchy create the developmental force. This approach assumes that there is something lacking, some weakness or gap, that can be added to or filled by the use of the appropriate tools or blueprint, and that such intervention is necessary. Individuals, including their aspirations and their values as well as their skills, are malleable units that can be moulded to suit the wider system. Empowerment and individual agency can be part of the developmental agenda, but not in their own right. They are acceptable developmental endpoints only if ratified by senior management: empowerment becomes a tool to enhance performance and decision making.

The third approach, *development as voyage*, is as a life-long journey upon uncharted internal paths in which individuals construe their own frames of reference and place their view of self within this, such that each of us construct our own version of reality in which our identity is part of that construct. This is described as an active process in which the individual is continually re-analysing their role in the emergence of the processes of which they are part. In so doing they are also confronting their own ideas, unsurfaced assumptions, biases and fears, whilst maintaining a core of ethicality and strong self-concept (Adler, 1974; Argyris, 1990). Development involves a transformative shift in approach that enables critical observation and evaluation of the experience, such that the learner is able to distance themself from it rather than replay it. Experiencing becomes a way of restoring meaning to life (Vasilyuk, 1984). The external world (including organisation and management) might mirror or catalyse development, but it is the individual who is the sole owner and clear driving force behind the process. Empowerment would be within the individual's own terms, and might have little regard for organisational objectives.

The fourth approach I identified is *development as emergent*. Here development is seen to arise out of the messy ways by which societal aspiration becomes transformed into societal reality. This includes the 'individuals' unique perceptions of themselves within a social reality which is continuously socially (re)constructed' (Checkland, 1994); in which 'individuals dynamically alter their actions with respect to the ongoing and anticipated actions of their partners' (Fogel, 1993: 34), and in which they negotiate a form of communication and meaning specific and new to the group and relatively inaccessible or indescribable to those who were not part of the process (Lee, 1994). Selfhood is a dynamic function of the wider social system, be it a family grouping, a small or medium-sized enterprise, a large bureaucracy or a Nation, or parts of each, and as that system transforms, so do all the participants. Emergent development of the group-as-organisation is seen to be no different from the development of any social system, and is not consistently driven by any single subsystem, be it senior management or the shop-floor. Discussion about planned top-down or bottom-up change is irrelevant, as the words themselves imply some sort of structure to the change. This approach is, of course, in direct conflict with traditional ideas that organisational change is driven by senior management, although Romanelli & Tushman (1994) offer empirical support for rapid, discontinuous transformation in organisations being driven by major environmental changes.

These are four fundamentally different working definitions of development. When talking of our own development we normally address it as if it is a *voyage*. When senior managers talk of organisational development they normally talk of it as if it were *shaping*. When social theorists talk of development they normally adopt a *maturational* or *emergent* perspective, depending upon their theoretical bent. Development is clearly not a unitary concept. For the purposes of this chapter I shall assume that we are mainly talking about development as either a voyage or emergent—as the notion of 'self' development seems at odd with the idea that 'nature' or the organisational hierarchy establish the end-points of development, as occurs in *maturation* or *shaping*, respectively.

Examining Self

One of the exercises I sometimes use in workshops is to ask people to write down 10 words that describe themselves. Even at this first stage of the exercise people differ greatly—some initially focus on their appearance, their gender, or their possessions, whilst others focus on their emotions, attitudes, values or relationships. Depending upon my purpose for the exercise at the time, I might then ask them to go through their lists and underline those that they think really are them rather than qualities that have been given to them by others. An example of the latter can be seen in one person I worked with who suddenly realised that all her life she had been called brave, and had tried to act as bravely as she could—but that in trying to meet others' expectations in this way (and despite the fact that bravery is normally seen as a good quality) she had denied herself the opportunity to ever really trust or rely on anyone else, and what she really wanted was the chance to *not* be brave. In doing this exercise most people generally come to the conclusion that almost everything they think is part of 'them' has nearly always, at some stage in their life, been placed upon them by someone else, and that there are some aspects of themselves that they might wish to accept and own, and other aspects they wish to reject. The way in which we view ourselves is, to a large extent, a social construct, and thus ties in well with the notion of development as emergent.

SELF AS A SOCIAL CONSTRUCT

This does not imply that other people go out of their way to tell us what we are, and that we have to accept their views, although, as an aside, I do believe that part of the developmental process involves becoming more aware of what others have laid upon us—and why we have accepted that burden. Our view of ourselves, of others and the social situation is not laid down by some external force, but is constructed and co-regulated by the people involved. Fogel (1993) builds a strong case for the development of ourselves through a process of creative interaction, a process that starts at birth and by which we become acculturated. In this view, 'culture' is co-regulated by the participants, and the underlying processes of this are the same whether we are talking of family and friendship groupings, temporary 'micro-cultures', organisational or national culture. Culture and relationships are seen to exist within mutually constructed conventions or frames of reference, which can be mutually dissolved by participants through ratification (Duncan, 1991; Moreland & Levine, 1989). This is not, however, to imply that these processes are conscious, or easily accessible to conscious control. As Fogel (1933) argues, 'communication, self and culture are just different ways of talking about relationships, different points of view on the same phenomenon'.

This means that for each of us, when we feel part of a group, our notion of 'self' is influenced by that group—we identify ourselves with it in some way (and part of our 'selves'is identified with all the other groups we associate with). It is as if we seek to establish an equilibrium in which all of our relationships are consonant with each other and mutually supportive. However, we cannot easily describe what part of us is being influenced and how—it is hard to access that information or to interpret it—because to be able to do so, even if we were able to introspect sufficiently for an audit of our 'self', it would mean that we would have a well-laid-out and static sense of 'self'.

From the view of self as social construct, as we change we elaborate, dissolve, compare and consolidate our dialogical self-frames, seeking balance—there is, as it were, a drive for harmony within our relationships and multiple views of self. It is important to note here that to seek control of oneself or another would be seen to be breaking from the search for balance and to be counter-developmental. The need for control of self or another leads to relationships that are 'marked by rigidity and sameness, by a motivation to avoid creativity around particular themes, by a sense of obligation without pleasure' (Fogel, 1993). This split between consensual and rigid relationships is similar to Marshall's (1984) two states of union-seeking communion and independence-seeking agency, and Rogers' (1959) concepts of unconditional and conditional regard.

For both Marshall and Rogers, in the first case, others are prized for their intrinsic value as human beings, whilst in the second, the acceptance of others is conditional upon meeting evaluative criteria. The 'self' judges others from its own terms, rather than accepting that others are legitimately different:

> 'A self in which one voice and one relationship dominates all others is not cohesive: it is rigidified and exclusionary, it is one that experiences disjunction between each of its real and imagined relationships' (Fogel, 1993).

Within these terms, development of the self as a social construct occurs as we move towards equilibrium, reaching a balanced state between ourselves and others, whilst non-developmental change is a process marked by rigidity and control. So, development is partly about accepting this self-in-flux and about valuing the freedom which the process of choosing to be, do and think in particular ways allows us, as opposed to assuming that development leads to an essentially fulfilled (and static) way of being-in-the-world.

The idea of co-regulation is more in tune with Eastern concepts of interdependence (Cushman, 1991) in that the individual's experience of selfhood is seen to be a reflection of continual social interactions in the course of life (Scheibe, 1986). Although Eastern views of self are more diffuse, 'the multiple dialogical self does not preclude a sense of self-cohesion or a sense of harmony between different aspects of one's social or private life' (Fogel, 1993). This is different from the Western notion of mastery (Pascale, 1978), in which our sense of identity is a chimera—we cannot define or capture what it means to be our 'self' and we cannot easily say what or how we are 'developing' at any one particular time. When questioned, most of us would agree that we have different knowledge, skills and attitudes to those we had as children, and possibly even to those we held a couple of years ago, yet we still foster our sense of self and we still talk about ourselves as if we do have a well-bounded and static identity.

Perhaps our sense of a permanent self is a localised feeling, by which I mean that chronologically recent patterns, habits and memories are combined to form a feeling of predictability about one's daily routine and role in society. From day to day we continue as before—odd incidents occur, by which we might judge ourselves to be different from others (more on this shortly) but it is rare that we have an experience that shatters that sense of stability.

SELF AS A SEARCH FOR MEANING

Development of the self as a social construct is towards balance with others, but does not necessarily require understanding of self or others (although I will suggest later on in this chapter that it is very hard to move forwards without such understanding). For many people, however, self-development is about a search for meaning—trying to understand one's role in life. Within this view the self has a clear identity and individuality, and the developmental search is associated with better understanding the uniqueness of one's self and of one's transformation. In much of the literature development is seen as a reasonably slow move towards making sense of our lives, whilst transformation is seen as a fundamental shift in being. Transformative experiences are those self-shattering moments when nothing is the same again afterwards. We might not know what we will be like afterwards, but we do know that we have experienced something fundamental to our psyche, and that we are changing. Someone once wrote to me along the following lines: 'Encountering a starving woman in India trying to feed her child had more of a transformative effect upon me than all the exhortations of my senior manager'.

Transformation is therefore an active process and hard to describe. Notions of shift can be seen in double/triple loop learning (Garratt, 1987; Hawkins, 1991) and the Rogerian approach, in which a facilitator helps others to help themselves (Rogers, 1951, 1959). Similarly, Bartunek & Moch (1987) describe second-order change attempts as designed to phase in particular frameworks in which events are understood (schemata) and phase out others, and third-order change attempts as aiming to help people develop the capacity to identify and change their own schemata as they see fit. Each of these descriptions involves a shift in approach through some process, either internal or externally facilitated, that enables critical observation and evaluation of the experience, such that the person is able to distance themself from it rather than 'replay' it. Acting in this manner involves the 'knowledge and acceptance of a wider repertoire of ways of being' (Kinsman, 1990). This shift is described by Magala (1993) as 'a step from tolerance of other paradigms to solidarity with the carriers; acknowledgement of difference to safeguarding communication and interaction', and is similar to Lane & DiStefano's (1992) commitment in relativism 'in which a person understands the relativistic nature of the world, but makes a commitment to a set of values, beliefs, and a way of behaving within this expanded world view'. It requires individuals and organisations to create their own models and derive their own views of the dynamics of change, rather than rely on uncritically utilising off-the-shelf accounts of the future (Slaughter, 1993).

Developmental change (particularly transformative change) is often very painful. Schemata are disbanded, the individual's feelings of self-worth are challenged, inconsistencies are exposed, and a contented life stance overturned [cf. Marshall & Stewart's (1981a, b) contented middle managers]. To step outside the 'contented' box is hard (Lee, 2000). It involves stepping outside the 'known' and therefore cannot be planned for. How can one 'know' what the result of the 'unknown' will be? It is often a process forced upon the person by changing circumstance by which the person's frame of reference is found to be no longer adequate to represent existence, entailing a need for deconstruction and recomposition. Transformation, rather than change, is therefore discontinuous and is driven by conflict and the need for crisis resolution (Emery & Trist, 1965).

There are some contradictory threads in the discussion above—if it is about the search for meaning and maintaining an ethical core and strong self-concept, and thus the maintenance of a strong, meaningful, unique and essential self, how can we move to solidarity with others? How can we ever do more than tolerate them and their different ways of being, because we will interpret these ways of being from our own core self-standpoint instead of accepting them on their merits?

THE DIALECTIC DEVELOPMENT OF SELF

I have suggested elsewhere (Lee, 1995) that the development of one's own reality or view of life is a process of managing the tension between selfhood and individuality, and the subconscious pressure to conform to group reality. It seems to me that the development of self happens in a dialectic manner, shifting backwards and forwards between individual and other-related foci, such that the self develops in opposition.

The mechanism for development of the self in opposition can be explored through the idea of shifting frames of reference. Each of us creates our own version of 'reality' based upon the way in which we structure (or map) our individual perceptions and memories of our unique suite of experiences and anticipations of the future [see e.g. Construct Theory—Kelly (1955)—and more recent discussions of cultural differences in mapped concepts, such as Jankowicz (1994)]. Both the individual and the group prefer to maintain their existing frames of reference, and expend effort in order to do so. The individual is torn—it is important for the individual's sense of selfhood to maintain life as he/she 'knows' it, yet co-regulated socialisation necessitates elements of reframing. The easier, dialectic non-transformative, route would be for the individual to only seek acceptance from those who are 'known' to be similar—to see life as they do. Similarly, the easy, dialectic non-transformative, route for the group is to only accept implicit membership (regardless of explicit membership-on-paper) from those that are trusted not to unduly influence the group frame.

This assumes that we 'know' the frames of reference of ourselves and the group and can make clear cut decisions based upon that knowledge. Frames of reference, however, are not known in the absolute cognitive sense—much of the 'knowing' occurs through pivotal encounters with the frames of others, encounters that emphasise previously 'unknown' dissimilarity and disjunction. Whether intended or not, encounter with others holds the potential for transformation—potential for challenge to existing frames of reference through tension between self and socialisation, or between group identity and the dissenting individual. The pain and conflict of transformation is therefore closely associated with negotiating group membership and influence, with feelings of inclusion and exclusion. In other words, the development of one's own 'reality' is a process of managing the tension between individuality, and the underlying co-regulatory processes, or subconscious pressure to conform to group 'reality'.

Thus the co-regulated reification of implicit group norms (as with organisational personnel policy documents that sound grand but are not enforced, or as with 'contracting' exercises at the beginning of a workshop, when everyone says they will trust each other but rarely do) can lead to alienation, re-statements of individuality and the challenging of the group norms. Obviously, not all group influence is threatening to the self, and, in fact, development of the rounded person might best occur as the individual's 'selfhood' moves back and forward between that of the individual in opposition to that of the individual within consensual group development. The first leads primarily to individuation, creativity and innovation, whilst the second leads primarily to the consolidation of group vision and identity. This presents a view of the self as developing in different areas at different times, and thus focusing alternately on internal and external stimuli as the catalyst for development. In addition, as can be seen in Figure 2.1, development can be visualised as occurring in a cyclical manner, within which the balance between internal and external foci is important for the evolution of that development.

The dotted line in Figure 2.1 is to mark an area of focal shift—a preference, not an absolute division or categorisation (cf. Lee, 2001b). I am not arguing that self-development has to swing from the internal to the external and so on, but that I normally find that it does. In broader terms, neither development with the group nor individual development can occur in isolation from the other (Lee, 1994), although the point of equilibrium in

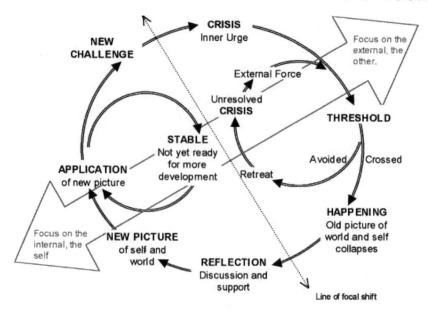

FIGURE 2.1   The developmental cycle. Adapted from Boydell (1998)

the see-saw, balanced between a focus on the individual at one end and a focus on the other (or the group) at the other end, is clearly sensitive to the wider culture. A strong individualist would seem as out of place and 'undeveloped' in the East, as would an ardent conformist in the West.

UNDERLYING PROCESSES

This tension between the individual and the other is inherent in a Jungian view of the world, and I shall make use of some of Jung's views to take this further. Carl Jung (1964, 1971) suggested that whilst everyone seeks to make sense of the world around them, we do not all focus on the same things—instead, our notion of self is also influenced by the underlying processes associated with gathering information and making decisions about what we have gathered. These are termed the processes of perception and judgement (Jung, 1961; McWhinney, 1992; Myers, 1962). Perception is the process by which individuals make sense (consciously or subconsciously) of their surroundings, and is thus mediated by previous understandings, expectation and anticipations, memory and unconscious influences, from the 'promissory notes' of metaphor, myth and rhetoric (Soyland, 1994) to primal drives. Judgement is the process of deciding which of the many alternative perceptual interpretations available at any one instant to adopt as 'reality'. Judgement is also, therefore, influenced by previous understandings, etc., and is more likely to be based upon *post hoc* rationalisation than the traditionally accepted view of 'scientifically' weighing up the alternatives and rationally choosing the best option in advance of the final decision.

Fishbein & Ajzen (1975) identified similar processes, termed 'perceived control' and 'self-efficacy', in their work on reasoned action. These were found to be empirically distinguishable (Terry & O'Leary, 1995) and to co-vary to provide a 'personal norm' (Parker, Manstead & Stradling, 1995). They were also found to be applicable to organisations (Elliott, Jobber & Sharp, 1995). Jung suggested that the two processes that he called perception and judgement are independent of each other, and that both are bi-polar, in that when gathering information people *prefer* to focus either on the 'here-and-now' information from their senses, or on the 'what-if' information they 'intuit' from the possibilities and patterns they see developing. Similarly, when deciding about the information they have gathered, people *prefer* to make decisions based on objective thinking, by analysing and weighing the alternatives from a wide perspective, or to make decisions based on their feelings for each particular situation in an individualised manner.

I have placed particular emphasis on the word 'prefer' in my description of Jung's dimensions, as he was concerned to emphasise that any one person was able to adopt either way of gathering information (sensing or intuition) and deciding upon it (thinking or feeling), but that he/she could only adopt one approach at any one time, and thus built up and normally demonstrated a preference over time. Jung's theory is about preference, rather than about type-casting people or about classifying someone according to his/her 'personality'. This means that, if we accept Jung's dimensions, we can say that different people might have different preferred ways of making sense of the world and their role within it, and that particular events or experiences might entail, or be better viewed, by one style of making sense, rather than another. The notions of *preference* and *style* carry with them the idea that people can choose to change their approach, and can adopt different approaches under different circumstances.

Within the organisational world the most common application of Jung's theory is the Myers Briggs Type Indicator (MBTI). I shall return to this shortly; however, it is worth noting that other people have applied Jung's theory to aspects of our existence. For example, Mitroff & Kilmann (1978) take these ideas and suggest that there are four psychological types which represent 'basic styles of thinking about and doing science'. The four basic styles they identify fit well with Jungian quartiles and the Myers–Briggs typology, as can be seen in Figure 2.2. But, as I have argued elsewhere (Lee, 2001b)

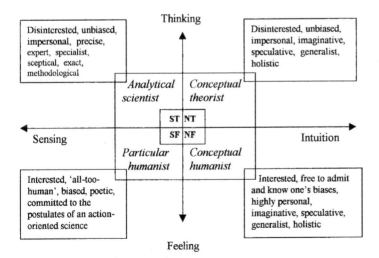

FIGURE 2.2 Combining Jungian dimensions with MBTI and Mittroff & Kilmanns typology

we live in a world that looks for certainties, and as illustrated by Mitroff & Kilmann, a system based on preference easily gets translated into one of fixed typology.

The danger from the point of view of development is that fixed typologies imply fixed personalities and thus the labelling of people with a permanence that denies the possibility of development. As I have described above, there is a need to understand oneself, and to understand that the other is different from oneself and the nature of those differences, but this is a dynamic, co-regulated and often subconscious process. We need to bear in mind that our own and other people's preferences are linked to context and situation; they are *situated* preferences rather than exclusive *personality* differences. (As an aside here, I do find that it easy it is for people to acknowledge that others are different, and yet they are surprised as they begin to understand that people *really are* different; they think in different ways, pay attention to different things, value and want different lives, and understand things differently.)

I find the notion of a personal norm useful. It extends the idea of frames of reference to allow for individual style or preference alongside that which is socially created. It thus accommodates possible genetically and physiologically related difference in the way people perceive and judge the world. It recognises the idea of 'self' as dynamic yet perceptually identifiable, thereby limiting any form of measurement to comparison, either with self or perceptions of others, and denying the possibility of statements of the absolute. It also allows for individual difference in the way in which 'learners as researchers' make sense of their experience holistically, such that their approach to meaning and their perception of their history and anticipation of the future will influence their current learning (Lee, 1994b). As Dewey (1938) pointed out:

> It is not enough to insist upon the necessity of experience, nor even of activity in experience. Everything depends upon the quality of experience which is had . . . every experience lives in further experiences.'

MATTERS ARISING

This leads me to a couple of points. Firstly, the outcome of developmental change, whether it is seen as positive or negative, is not necessarily the same as the quality of the experience itself. The transformative time recalled by two people was, in both cases, catalysed by the intense bullying of their domineering managers. One person, a senior PA, became withdrawn, timid and almost totally lacking in confidence. When I started working with her, she no longer felt able to take more responsibility than that required of a junior secretary. The other person had a similar experience but it sparked resistance and the negative experience became seen as a highly positive transformative event. A negative experience can lead to positive change (in the eyes of the individual), and a lovely warm experience could lead to negative change.

The second thing that I would like to emphasise is that self-development is, indeed, about the one self. Other people might catalyse it and in the longer term it is about relationships with others, but other people cannot specify it, control it or manage it. It is not a quantifiable thing to be specified, controlled or managed in any way—it cannot be prescribed for, mapped out or planned.

There are, however, aspects of self-development that can be fostered by oneself and by others and from which development of the self *might* emerge. In the next section of this chapter I shall move away from this more theoretical exploration of the notion and nature of self-development in order to look at practical aspects of how self-development might be fostered within the context of the organisation.

CONTEXTUALISING DEVELOPMENT OF THE SELF

As Malcolm Knowles (1975) pointed out, both the advantages and disadvantages of self-development stem largely from the fact that most of us know only how to be taught; we have not learned how to learn. It is clear that the development of ourselves entails greater understanding of ourselves, so that we are more able to make sense of why we act as we do in particular situations and circumstances and how and why we operate in particular relationships. It also entails more than understanding. For example, it is not really much use knowing that I always get cross with someone because he tries to control me as my father did, unless I use that information to try and respond differently, to widen my repertoire of behaviours and my ways of construing others.

Tools and techniques that help foster self-development therefore tend to be those that help understanding, reflection and behaviour change—and they tend to focus either on the individual or else on the individual's relationship with others as part of a group. As I have already stressed, whatever the intention, and however well-structured the experience, development of the self (as experienced by the self) is fragile and fickle and can not be controlled, planned or ordered. There is no clear relationship between different tools and different aspects of development. I cannot go to a group and say, 'Well, today we will do this and you will develop in this way'. I can, however, say, 'This is what I plan to do and this is what I hope it might bring out'. Therefore, the tools, techniques and practices described below help by fostering particular developmental aspects; they work in a situated experiential way and nothing is guaranteed or foolproof.

OUTLINING ONESELF: PSYCHOLOGICAL TYPE OR PREFERENCE

As described above, we all see life through our own, particular, eyes and have no real way of knowing whether others see it in the same way, or how we seem to them. The first set of tools I find useful are those that let us know (or give us the vocabulary to think about) how we compare with the rest of humanity, viz. personality tests or psychological profiles. They help us compare ourselves against others because, although they are often applied (wrongly, in my opinion) as if they can capture the essence of an individual and so type-cast that individual for life, they are generally based on small, culturally-specific and relatively biased samples. A person's profile, therefore, is only specified in relation to that sample.

Some personality tests, such as the Cattell 16PF, are derived from rigorous experimentation and solid statistical procedures, yet despite this the 16PF also has its problems. It provides a view of the person as compared with urban white western society of the 1960s. It is important to check that the normative data are representative and recent for profiling purposes. Along with other tools that look at preference rather than type, the MBTI offers the opportunity to look at one's own preferences and also to examine them in relation to those of other people (the sample population was rather out of date but has been recently updated, and can be standardised to several different cultural norms). It is beyond the remit of this chapter to go into the MBTI-based literature in any depth, Briggs Myers & McCaulley (1987) and Krebs Hirsh & Kummerow (1987) offer more detail.

Most people, however, do not have easy access to such instruments unless the organisation is providing them for specific purposes. Also, a lot of the development impact of the instrument resides not in the instrument itself, but more in the circumstances under which it is used, and the benefit (or otherwise) of these is related to the skill of the facilitator or test administrator, because the illuminative aspects of the session for the person are those that give the person accurate and non-judgemental feedback and help the person work through what the results might mean for him/her.

These fundamentals can be obtained in many other ways, ranging from attending structured developmental workshops and sessions, to unstructured encounter and T groups, through to asking friends for their honest feedback (and then not taking it out on the friends when they are being honest!). Management, and particularly senior management, can find it hard to take the risk of exposing themselves within the work team (although those that have done so have, in my experience, found it to be beneficial to the team as well as themselves). One alternative that is becoming increasingly popular is that of mentoring. Some organisations run formal mentoring programmes, which I shall discuss later on, but the sort of mentoring I am referring to here is that of a personal mentor external to the organisation to act as a sounding board and developer. The developmental benefit of this, though, as with formal instruments and workshops, depends to a certain extent upon the quality or skill of the mentor, but it also depends upon the quality of the relationship. In my experience it helps if the mentor and mentee are able to think about, discuss and justify their preferred style and approach.

REFLECTING UPON ONE'S SELF

The tools and techniques suggested above all hold the opportunity to foster reflection about oneself and one's relationships; however, there are several ways of doing this by oneself. The most obvious, perhaps, is that of the reflective journal or learning log used as a diary about key incidents, events and thoughts. Those who use such a log as a developmental tool find that it rapidly shifts from a 'what I did today' sort of account to one in which they are able to record their views and feelings in an open and honest manner. This has the benefit of helping reflection on the immediate issue, checking that reflection and planning action, and also of highlighting 'development'. As discussed earlier, development is normally only seen or understood for what it was in retrospect. The log book can help shift one's perception of the painful transformative event into something that had a major positive developmental effect, to let the author know that he/she has come through the pain and is 'really' a different person now.

The log book also helps the author shift around the Kolb cycle of experience, reflection, theorising and planning, and so back to further experience (Kolb, 1974, 1976, 1984; Honey & Mumford, 1979). As I mentioned earlier, we could question whether 'development' occurs if it is limited to increasing knowledge of oneself and of one's relationships with others without making use of this information to alter one's behaviour. We need to explore and implement our new 'selves' as they develop, and so we need to seek action as well as reflection.

This leads nicely to a brief discussion of action learning sets within organisations. As with organisationally-driven mentoring systems or psychological profiling, action learning sets might well be established for the benefit of the organisation rather than the individual, whatever the rhetoric. Indeed, they might be so structured that they are more like project teams than sets focused on action learning, but even so, they do offer developmental opportunity. Ideally, action learning sets are entirely participant-defined—a group of people get together and agree to support each other in either individual or joint (developmental) projects. They agree the 'rules' of their participation; how they will each help facilitate the other's reflection and movement into action, what support they want from each other and how and what they can give. I have facilitated a wide range of action learning sets and I am still amazed how an hour or so of positive regard and support from the rest of the group can be a fundamentally developmental experience for many. Perhaps it is just an indication of the lack of time we normally have for each other in our (organisational) lives.

Aspects of the Organisation

Although the development of self is not directly linked to organisational initiatives, there are certain aspects of organisational policy and practice that can help or hinder self-development. As with the tools and techniques mentioned above, the degree to which the organisation is seen as 'developmental' is a matter of perception, which, as discussed previously, is a matter of individual style, it is also a matter of opportunity and culture.

Opportunity might be about what courses are available at the person's particular job level. Are they entirely functional or do they encourage or inspire reflection and self-development? Is there a system of mentoring? Are there assessment and feedback policies? Are these systems and policies entirely to 'fit the person in the job' or are they sufficiently flexible to enable the individual to set his/her own agenda and goal posts? The more flexible the organisation in these respects, the more it is moving towards a system of open learning. Ideally, open learning systems are entirely at the behest of the individual. Employees are given time and money to further their education as they see best, and the culture of the organisation is such that studying Ancient Greek is seen to be as important as learning a new management technique. It is clearly much easier to seek self-development within an organisation that offers such freedom to the individual.

Culture of the Organisation

As many parents and trainers know, it is possible to help the child or learner too much, to take away the necessary exploration that they have to go through in order to 'save time' or save them from the pain that is often associated with such exploration. Life is much more simple if we stay as we are in our contented ruts. It could be that a contended and 'helpful' organisation is as discouraging to self-development as is the classic machine-like interpretation of organisation. A culture that supports self-development needs to create challenge, and thus risk. It also needs to foster courage and support. To change we need to have the courage to wonder and to look outside our self-imposed boundaries. As shown in Figure 2.1, we need the courage to reach the threshold of the known and to accept the challenge of stepping outside that.

People can develop their selves under all sorts of different conditions, but some organisational and individual qualities do foster the courage to develop more than others,

namely: openness, lack of blame, honesty in feedback, minimisation of needless hierarchy and negative capability (even hanging loose). This quality is one of resisting
conceptual closure, and thereby creating the necessary 'space' for the formulation of personal insights, and was described by the early nineteenth century English poet John Keats:

> And at once it struck me, what quality went to form a man of Achievement . . . meaning
> Negative Capability, that is when a man is capable of being in uncertainties, mys-
> teries, doubts, without any irritable reaching after facts and reason (Keats, letters of
> 21 December 1817).

I have argued elsewhere (Lee et al., 1996, 2001b) that the push for early closure and
compartmentalisation that appears to be an inherent part of organisational life and the
desired quality in a 'good' manager is counter-productive to the development of the self
and of the organisation.

In looking to the future, and to the qualities that managers and organisations will need,
the vast majority of writers talk of the need for increasing flexibility and willingness to
handle and work with uncertainty. Thus, as management becomes more complex and
more generalist (Dobson & Stewart, 1990), managers need to be able to adapt and change
in response to the changing environment, such that learning becomes a new form of labour
and knowledge is a resource (Drucker, 1993). This entails the erosion of distinctions
between managers and managed, with organisations structured around human beings and
the relationships between them (Zuboff, 1989). The manager is seen as a manipulator
of organisational symbols (Johnson, 1990), who can inspire and influence others by
managing the communicative climate through process skills, whilst maintaining a core
of ethicality and strong self-concept.

What is so interesting about this is that the qualities that foster and support self-
development in organisations also seem to be those that are promoted alongside notions
of the learning organisation or of the development of the managerial role. In other words,
'good' managers know themselves and others, and are able to balance self and other and
to manage the search for meaning in their lives. In other words, a 'good' manager is a
self-developing manager (Freedman, 1992; Handy, 1985; Kanter, 1982).

PROBLEMATISING DEVELOPMENT OF THE SELF

FROM THE ORGANISATIONAL PERSPECTIVE

One of the problems with this view of a fulfilling organisational life in which:

> . . . one or more persons engage with others in such a way that leaders and followers
> raise one another to higher levels of motivation and morality . . . a process of mutual
> exchange where the function of leaders and followers is fused (Burns, 1978).

is that it seems to be more of a vision than an achievable reality. Pascale (1990) talks
of a business environment in which people can flourish spiritually and emotionally by
nourishing creative tension generated by a balance between a focus on human resources
and personal well-being on one hand and a clear, hard, management on the other, yet
who is nourished in this way? All employees or the chosen few? When we are talking
about fostering a culture for self-development, do we really mean for everybody? The
temporary and part-time workers? The menial workers? Or those that have a direct and
obvious impact on the organisation—senior and rising management?

The literature talks of fostering particular aspects of organisational culture as if a magic wand can be waved and all falls into place but, for example, how can we create negative capability whilst all the strictures of organisational economics are demanding that life be measured, organised and closed? What do we do about those who do not want to take the challenge and engage on this voyage of self-discovery—those who are happy as they are and cannot be tempted into 'self-development'? 'You will develop or else...'isn't easy to enforce, and is just a little hypocritical!

What about the different layers of the organisation? Do we really expect senior staff to have the time to attend developmental courses, and if they did, do we expect them to feel able to talk openly and honestly about things deep within them to subordinates whom they have to 'manage' the next day? Or the subordinates to talk truthfully in front of senior management? Some senior management can, and do, do it, but in fact not many. Do we really expect peers, who are in direct competition with each other for promotion, to easily trust each other?

Finally, from the organisational perspective, there is the issue of 'the bottom line'. The rhetoric holds up vague promise that a developed and motivated workforce will save money by working more creatively and with absence, and the organisation is more likely to survive (nebulous) threats in the future. The reality suggests that if Joe and Jane say they want to develop, it is in their own interests, and if they are keen enough they will pay for it themselves in their free time, and if not that interested, they shouldn't be doing it anyway.

In fact, many organisations take a middle role. They might build internal mentoring systems alongside assessment systems that promote reflection and feedback for all staff, and provide team/group-based development opportunities for key middle-level staff. Senior staff are more likely to be offered one to one mentoring with external specialists. This is increasingly being seen as part of the senior management package.

FROM THE INDIVIDUAL PERSPECTIVE

There are also problems to be faced by the individual. Whether or not the organisation offers opportunity for development, how do we know if it is what we want? How can we judge for ourselves or others what might help self-development at any one time? How can we know where we are going if we don't ever really know who or where we are? How do we develop the confidence to 'go with the flow'? How do we find the courage to take a risk? It is almost an endlessly repeating circle, because until we take the risk we don't know whether we have the courage to do so. We can develop mechanisms for helping our self-confidence, negative capability and courage, which is, of course, self-development in its own right. We can look to others for example and to urge us on and talk it through, but they may well be part of the self-developmental equation. We can look to ourselves, start noting down key incidents or aspects of our learning, and make some conclusions that mean we have to move a step forward.

We have taken the plunge, and it might hurt. How do we stop ourselves retreating back to our safe shell and deciding *never* to come out again? How do we find the emotional energy or the time to reflect upon it and make sense of it? Can we school ourselves to be patient in the knowledge that it will make sense eventually—learning that looking back (sometimes after many years) is often pivotal in sense making? How do we know that it is not just us—that other people have similar experiences? How can we describe it to others when we can barely describe it to ourselves? How can we find the words so they can help us make sense of it?

Although self-development 'happens' in the same way experiences happen, we also need to be quite organised if we are going to make the most of it—we need to organise ourselves so that we can reflect upon it and learn from it, and we need to organise others. We rely on other people to give us feedback and support, and we need to choose these other people carefully. We also need to manage the perceptions of those close to us; as we change, their view of us will lag behind our 'new' self. If we want their help and support we need to prepare them for that change and involve them with it. In changing our self we are changing our relationship with them, and we are also changing them, and so on. It is very, very hard to try and develop when all around are trying to prevent it, because one person's looked-for and fostered development can be another person's painful, externally-imposed forced change.

This raises a series of ethical questions about who has the right to force someone to change, that are beyond the scope of this chapter but which are central to any discussion about change and can be applied to organisations as well as individual actors.

CONCLUSION

In this chapter I have suggested that self-development is always on-going—we never really know who we are, where we are or where we are going. We can look back and see where we have developed from. We learn more about ourselves from others, and our interaction with others fosters our emergent self. We can try and build the qualities that help us develop, and we can learn from ourselves and others, however, not all 'good' experiences are developmental, and vice versa.

There are a range of tools and techniques that we can employ to help our self-development and organisations can also attempt to foster a developmental environment, but neither we nor the organisation can control self-development. Not everyone develops at the same pace, in the same direction, and not everyone wants to develop. But, establishing a true open environment of co-regulation and "negative capability" is likely to foster self-development in those who engage with it. Building systems of trust and support, with colleagues and those close to us, is also important, not only to help us in our development but also because changing ourselves changes them.

Were such an environment to be established, it might feel like an organisational utopia, but self-development (at least of the transformative kind) is often painful, and it could be argued that there is no true development without pain. One bonus is that as we look back over the years and start to make sense of the pain we can feel a spark of achievement in the fact that we have survived and grown stronger.

ACKNOWLEDGEMENT

I would like to thank Jo Brewis for her comments on an earlier draft.

REFERENCES

Adler, P.S. (1974) Beyond cultural identity: reflections on cultural and multicultural man. *Topics in Culture Learning*, Vol. 2. Honolulu: East–West Culture Learning Institute.

Argyris, C. (1990) *Overcoming Organisational Defences*. Boston, MA: Allyn and Bacon.

Bartunek, J.M. & Moch, M.K. (1987) First-order, second-order, and third-order change and organization development interventions: a cognitive approach. *Journal of Applied Behavioural Science*, **23**: 483–500.

Boydell, T. (1998) Self-development methods. In J. Prokopenko (ed.), *Management Development: a Guide for the Profession*. Geneva: ILO Publications.

Briggs Myers, I. & McCaulley, M.H. (1985) *A Guide to the Development and Use of the Myers–Briggs Type Indicator*. Palo Alto, CA: Consulting Psychologists Press.

Burns, J.M. (1978). *Leadership*. New York: Harper and Row.

Checkland, P. (1981). *Systems Thinking, Systems Practice*. London: Wiley.

Cushman, P. (1991) Ideology obscured: political uses of self in Daniel Stern's infant. *American Psychologist*, **46**, 206–19.

Dewey, J. (1938) *Experience and Education*, New York: Kappa Delta (then Collier)

Dobson, S. & Stewart, R. (1990) What is happening to middle management? *British Journal of Management*, **1**, 3–16.

Drucker, P. (1993) *Post-capitalist Society*. New York: Harper Business.

Duncan, S. (1991) Convention and conflict in the child's interraction with others. *Developmental Review*, **11**, 337–67.

Elliott, R., Jobber, D. & Sharp, J. (1995) Using the theory of reasoned action to understand organisational behaviour: the role of belief salience. *British Journal of Social Psychology*, **43**, 161–72.

Emery, F.E. & Trist, E.L. (1965) The causal texture of organisational environments. *Human Relations*, **18**, 21–32.

Fishbein, M.J. & Ajzen, I. (1995) *Belief, Attitude, Intention and Behaviour: an Introduction to Theory and Research*. Reading, MA: Addison-Wesley.

Fogel, A. (1993) *Developing through Relationships: Origins of Communication, Self and Culture*. Hemel Hempstead: Harvester Wheatsheaf.

Freedman, D. (1992) Is management still a science? *Harvard Business Review*, **November**, 26–38.

Garratt, B. (1987) *The Learning Organisation* London: Fontana.

Handy, C. (1985) *Understanding Organisations*. Harmondsworth: Penguin.

Hawkins, P. (1991) The spiritual dimension of the learning organisation. *Management Education and Development*, **22**, 172–87.

Honey, P. & Mumford, A. (1989) *The Manual of Learning Opportunities*. Maidenhead: Peter Honey.

Jankowicz, A.D. (1994) Parcels from abroad: the transfer of meaning to Eastern Europe. *Journal of European Business Education*, **3**(2), 1–19.

Johnson, G. (1990) Managing strategic change: the role of symbolic action. *British Journal of Management*, **1**, 183–200.

Jung, C.G. (1938) Psychology and religion: West and East. In *Collected Works*, Vol. II: 167; cited in Jung, C.G. (1961) *Memories, Dreams and Reflections*. London: Flamingo; 416.

Jung, C.G. (1961) *Memories, Dreams and Reflections*. London: Flamingo.

Jung, C.G. (1964) *Man and His Symbols*. London: W.H. Allen.

Jung, C.G. (1971) *Collected Works* (R.F.C. Hull, revised translation), Vol. 6, *Psychological Types*. Princeton, NJ: Princeton University Press.

Kanter, R. (1982) The middle manager as innovator. *Harvard Business Review*, 95–105.

Kelly, G. (1955) *A Theory of Personality: the Psychology of Personal Constructs*. New York: Norton.

Kinsman, J. (1990) *Millenium: Towards Tomorrow's Society*. London: Allen and Co.

Knowles, M. (1975) *Self-directed Learning*. New York: Associated Press.

Kolb, D. (1974) On management and the learning process. In D.A. Kolb, I.M. Rubin & J.M. McIntyre (eds), *Organisational Psychology*, 2nd edn. New Jersey: Prentice Hall.

Kolb, D. (1976) *Learning Style Inventory: Technical Manual*. Boston, MA: Mcber.

Kolb, D. (1984) *Experiential Learning*. Eaglewood Cliffs, NJ: Prentice Hall.

Krebs Hirsh, S. & Kummerow, J. (1987) *Introduction to Types in Organisational Settings*, Palo Alto, CA: Consulting Psychologists Press.

Lane, H. & DiStefano, J. (1992) *International Management Behaviour*, 2nd edn. Boston, MA: PWS-Kent.

Lee, M.M. (1994) The isolated manager: walking the boundaries of the micro-culture. *Proceedings of the British Academy of Management Conference*, Lancaster: 111–128.

Lee M.M. (1995) The opposing self: the truth is that there is no truth. In Gustafsson, C. (ed.), *Standing Conference on Organisational Symbolism, Self and Identity in Organisations*, Turku; 1–13.

Lee, M.M. (1997a) Strategic Human Resource Development: a conceptual exploration. In R. Torraco (ed.), *Academy of Human Resource Development Conference Proceedings*, Baton Rouge, LA: Academy of HRD; 92–9.

Lee, M.M. (1997b) The developmental approach: a critical reconsideration. In J. Burgoyne & M. Reynolds (eds), *Management Learning*. London: Sage; 199–214.

Lee, M.M. (1999) Text, gender and future realities. In R. Goodman (ed.), *Modern Organisation and Emerging Conundrums*. Lanham, MA: Lexington Books; 109–126.

Lee, M.M. (2000) HRDI: the catalyst. *Human Resource Development International*, **3**(1), 1–8.

Lee, M.M. (2001a) On seizing the moment as the research question emerges. In J. McGoldrick, S. Watson & J. Stewart (eds), *Understanding Research in HRD*. Studies in HRD Research Monograph Series. London: Routledge (in press).

Lee, M.M. (2001b) A refusal to define HRD. *Human Resource Development International*, **4**(3) (in press).

Lee, M.M., Letiche, H., Crawshaw, R. & Thomas, M. (eds)(1996) *Management Education in the New Europe*. London: International Thompson Publishing.

Magala, S. (1993) Postmodernism as management of ambiguity. Paper presented at TEMPUS: Central European Management Teacher Development Programme, Vienna.

Marshall, J. (1984) *Women Managers: Travellers in a Male World*. Chichester: Wiley.

Marshall, J. & Stewart, R. (1981a) Managers' job perceptions: part 1—their overall frameworks and working strategies. *Journal of Management Studies*, **18**, 177–89.

Marshall, J. & Stewart, R. (1981b) Managers' job perceptions: part 2—opportunities for and attitudes to choice. *Journal of Management Studies*, **18**, 263–75.

McWhinney, W. (1992) *Paths of Change*. London: Sage.

Mitroff I.I. & Killman R. H. (1978) *Methodological Approaches to Social Science: Integrating Divergent Concepts and Theories*. San Francisco, CA: Jossey Bass.

Moreland, R.L. & Levine, J.M. (1989) Newcomers and oldtimers in small groups. In Paulus, P. (ed.), *Psychology of Group Influence*, 2nd edn. Hillsdale, NJ: Erlbaum; 143–86.

Myers, I. (1962) *The Myers Briggs Type Indicator*. Palo Alto, CA: Consulting Psychologists Press.

Parker, D., Manstead, A.S.R. & Stradling, S.G. (1995) Extending the theory of planned behaviour: the role of the personal norm. *British Journal of Social Psychology*, **34**, 127–38.

Pascale R.T. (1978) Zen and the art of management. *Harvard Business Review*, **March–April**.

Pascale, R. (1990) *Managing on the Edge*. London: Penguin.

Rogers, C.R. (1951) *Client-centred Therapy*. Boston, MA: Houghton Mifflin.

Rogers, C.R. (1959) A theory of therapy, personality, and interpersonal relationships as developed in the client-centred framework. In Koch, S. (ed.), *Psychology: a Study of a Science*, Vol. 3. New York: McGraw-Hill.

Romanelli, E. & Tushman, M.L. (1994) Organisational transformation as punctuated equilibrium: an empirical test. *Academy of Management Journal*, **37**: 1141–66.

Scheibe, K.E. (1986) Self narratives and adventure. In T.R. Sarbin (ed.), *Narrative Psychology: the Storied Nature of Human Conduct*. New York: Praeger; 129–51.

Slaughter, R. (1993) Looking for the real 'megatrends'. *Futures*, **25**(8): 351–64.

Snell, R. (1993) *Developing Skills for Ethical Management*. London: Chapman and Hall.

Soyland, A.J. (1994) *Psychology as Metaphor*. London: Sage.

Terry, D.J. & O'Leary, J.E. (1995) The theory of planned behaviour: the effects of perceived behavioural control and self-efficacy. *British Journal of Social Psychology*, **34**, 199–220.

Vasilyuk, F. (1984) *The Psychology of Experiencing: the Resolution of Life's Critical Situations* (English translation, 1991). Hemel Hempstead: Harvester Wheatsheaf.

Zuboff, S. (1989) *In the Age of the Smart Machine*. Oxford: Heinemann.

CHAPTER 3

Cognitive Science and Individual Development

Jane Henry
Open University

SUMMARY

This chapter introduces work on cognitive processes such as perception, thought, and memory and cognitive behaviour such as problem solving, learning, decision marking and creativity with implications for individual development in organisations. This includes discussion of mind-sets, cognitive style, implicit learning, situated knowledge, expert recognition, group-think and complexity. The chapter makes reference to approaches or tools for individual development that are congruent with the work presented such as reframing, metaphor, mapping, visualisation, cognitive therapy, problem-finding, acceptance finding, and culture-change.

It goes on to examine certain issues that affect the frame within which cognitive science and individual development are practised. These include a deficiency orientation, a Western cultural bias, and the possible limitations of reflection as a development tool. The chapter acknowledges a shift away from focusing on purely rational cognitive processes in individuals to take greater account of the part played by tacit processes and the development of the system within which individuals practice.

INTRODUCTION

Cognitive science refers to the study of processes that underpin mental life such as attention, perception, thought and memory and the interplay of such processes in learning, problem solving, decision making, and creativity. Cognitive psychology burgeoned in the 1970s and 1980s when investigations into the brain's information processing

Individual Differences and Development in Organisations. Edited by Michael Pearn.
© 2002 John Wiley & Sons, Ltd.

capacities began to develop; (French and Colman, 1995 and Gellaty, 1986 offer introductions to the field). From the 1990s interest focused on the cognitive sciences in which an alliance of cognitive psychologists, cognitive neuroscientists and artificial intelligence specialists combined their expertise in an attempt to establish how the brain and mind work.

A cognitive perspective in management science has a long history dating from work by Simon (1947) but it is only much more recently, (in the late 1990s), that interest in managerial cognition has begun to develop, perhaps partly as a natural response to the increasing role that knowledge, imagination and creativity now play in organisational life (Walsh, 1995). Over the last thirty years cognitive science's understanding of how the brain works has changed considerably. Cognitive investigations have shown the mind operates in a very different manner from that which common sense suggests in a number of respects. For example, the brain is actively involved in construing perceptions and re-construing memories, and it is characterised by distributed activity, plasticity and parallel processing.

Many development tools assume we process information consciously and rationally and that there is a single self that makes decisions, essentially advocating that we should set our goals, plan action and evaluate better. Cognitive science highlights the limited capacities and fallibility of the conscious mind and the importance of implicit learning and tacit knowledge. It also shows how individualised our ways of thinking and learning are. As such it calls into question both the information processing and humanistically derived frames within which much individual development in organisations operates.

The first part of this chapter looks at various cognitive processes and their implications for individual development, the second looks at issues affecting the practice of cognitive science and individual development in organisations. For an accessible cognitively-oriented approach to individual development see Butler and Hope (1995).

COGNITIVE PROCESSES

PERCEPTION

The popular conception is that our perceptions match reality. The brain is assumed to record whole images passively somewhat like a video. In fact different cells in our brains specialise and pick up different aspects of a scene, some react only to movement, others to shape, size, colour and so on. How the brain reassembles these bits of information into a coherent whole that approximates to reality is not clear. Our perceptions are also influenced by what we expect to see, so our expectations actively co-determine what we see. If we are not expecting something, it may be cut out of our image, hence a magician can perform close up magic and hide a scarf in a plastic thumb that is edited out by the brain if the thumb is roughly the right shape and colour that it expects. Work on visual illusions illustrates just how easy it is to trick the brain into seeing something that is not there (Hubel, 1979; Marr, 1982).

We are also programmed to look for meaning, hence we see recognisable images in Rorschach ink blots and equally, faced with an ambiguous picture or degraded image see a meaningful image after a period (e.g. Henry, 2001a, p. 60). Once such an image has been seen it is almost impossible for the brain to go back to seeing the jumble of dots and lines they first saw.

Mental set

The phenomena of seeing what we expect to see and getting set in our ways applies to cognitive processes as much as sensory perception. The mind is faced with more information that it can deal with thoroughly every second of the day and the way it copes with this is to rely on heuristics, short cuts that have worked in the past and so our thinking is heavily conditioned by how we have tackled problems to date (McCaskey, 1982). The danger is that our thinking becomes set in certain patterns which restricts the options we consider.

The classic demonstration of the ease with which the mind is conditioned was provided by Luchins (1942). He provided subjects with three jars of different sizes and asked them to obtain a set amount of water. After only six trials where the formula 'jar B minus jar A minus two jar C' produced the correct quantity, four-fifths of subjects used the same formula for two subsequent problems in which the far simpler 'jar A minus jar C' or 'jar A plus jar C' achieved the desired result. In one case jar A held 28 litres, jar B 76 litres and jar C held 3 litres, yet 60% of subjects were so conditioned to using the earlier formula they were unable to solve the problem of obtaining 25 litres (jar A – jar C).

Cyert and March (1963) claim managers have a similar tendency to search in areas close to those where previous solutions have been found to work. We see many examples of getting set in particular ways of working or in particular ways of viewing a problem in everyday life. For example, IBM famously took a long time to see the potential of PCs and for years people exerted enormous amounts of energy trying to drag sunken ships up to the surface until Kroyer reversed the problem, and realised the answer was to make the ships lighter than water so they would float up on their own. This he achieved by pumping polystyrene balls into sunken ships (Brown, 1988).

In the development literature this phenomena is known as the problem of mind-set. There are many approaches that endeavour to help individuals break out of their set ways of thinking (de Bono, 1984; Adams, 1974). Procedures such as brainstorming and nominal group technique rely on building on other people's naturally different mind-sets. De Bono advocates various forms of lateral thinking to help break out of mental tramlines and bring forth new alternatives. Lateral thinking employs provocations such as a random input, problem reversal, or analogy to introduce an artificial prompt and then going on a mental excursion away from the problem and subsequently force-fitting the new associations back into useful solutions.

Self-fulfilling prophecy

One particular form of mind-set that has received attention in the development literature is the case of self-fulfilling prophecies. Rosenthal (1969) conducted a series of experiments which show the extent to which negative expectations can affect our judgement of others and ourselves. When groups of schoolchildren were matched for ability and teachers were told one group were less able than the other, that group did indeed perform worse. People, it seems, perform close to their labels. Brown (1971, 1988) has reported similar phenomena in work settings, in that foreman's opinions of their staff and the output of those staff was closer to the view of the staff member passed to the foreman initially, than their actual ability.

Reframing

One tool that attempts to overcome unwarranted perceptions is the use of reframing. In the case of individuals suffering from low self-esteem and those with a negative self-image, reframing may entail rephrasing a statement more positively, e.g. saying I am determined rather than stubborn, or I am sensitive rather than weak. Some people use positive affirmations more systematically, writing down their good qualities, reframing any negative belief about themselves into something positive. One can equally well reframe consistently negative beliefs for colleagues, carefully listening to what they say and rephrasing it in a more positive light. Reframing can become a tool for helping people develop a more positive attitude to life generally. For example, reframing the need to visit staff on the other side of the building as an opportunity for exercise or a temporary work move as a chance to experience a new town, or the stress management course's favourite example—of seeing being stuck in a traffic jam an opportunity to listen to the music you are normally too busy to listen to. Creativity courses sometimes refer to this as the 'yes and' rather than the 'yes but' phenomena. Negotiators similarly advocate adopting a win-win perspective. The use of positive thinking as a tool for individual development has a long history including the well-known proponent Dale Carnegie (1953).

Metaphor

Metaphor is another tool that can be used to encourage the mind to see things differently (Lakoff and Johnson, 1983). Morgan (1993) has suggested metaphors can consciously be used to help us 'imaginize' the world differently. His own work encompassing most of management science under eight metaphors can be used to help develop management thinking about different approaches to management (Morgan, 1986): 'In recognizing the close links between thought and action in organizational life, we recognize that the way we "read" organizations influences how we produce them. Images and metaphors are not just interpretive constructs used in task analysis. They are central to the process of imaginization through which people enact or write the character of organizational life' (Morgan, 1986, pp. 333–4).

Deconstruction

This phenomena or set constrained thinking applies to domains of thought as well as individuals or organisations. Foucault (1977, 1980) has shown how professionals develop a discourse, e.g. management, or individual development, within which they frame and discuss the problems facing their field. This discourse structures the way issues are seen, and inevitably certain aspects are given privileged attention at the expense of others. Thus creativity and innovation training may privilege discourse around new products and services and neglect lessons to be learnt from organisations that have been great survivors. One way of getting round this is to deconstruct the underlying assumptions, acknowledge the privileged aspects and consciously pay attention to the reverse.

MEMORY

People commonly assume that their memory holds an accurate record of events, and that they remember things as they happened. Cognitive science presents an entirely different picture. Though specific parts of the brain are involved in auditory and visual memory, much memory seems to be distributed across the brain (Lashley, 1929). Far from locating and reviewing the video of a particular event in your mind, the brain appears to reconstruct memory anew each time you attempt to recall the same event. Cognitive science has also revealed the fallibility of human memory. Work on eyewitness testimony shows people regularly believe things were other than they were and work on the false memory syndrome shows it is quite easy to get people to believe they have experienced something and recall memories of this event when it has not happened at all (Loftus and Loftus, 1975; Loftus, 1994). The fallibility of memory calls into question development strategies based round re-experiencing and perhaps discharging negative emotions associated with past experiences.

Short-term verbal memory is very limited. People are hard pushed to remember more than five to seven digits in short term memory (Miller, 1956; Simon, 1976) unless they are repeatedly reviewed or some visual mnemonic is used to aid recall. Memory can be improved by chunking information into larger units as in recalling chunked telephone numbers—44 1904 653 728 (Anderson, 1985).

Visual memory on the other hand is superior to verbal memory in many ways. People can discriminate whether or not they have seen a photograph they were exposed briefly even when it is placed among 1000 others seen only momentarily. As the saying goes a picture is worth a thousand words.

Mapping techniques are powerful in large part because visual memory is vastly superior to verbal memory, admittedly also because they force us to organise our thoughts. Numerous mapping and diagrammatic tools are available to help individuals in organisations. These include mind maps (Buzan, 1974), cognitive maps (Eden et al.,1992), rich pictures (Checkland and Scoles, 1990), etc. Martin (1991) offers many other examples. The position of keywords on a mindmap aids recall, as can colour and size cues, e.g. using different colours for different branches and larger letters for the main branches of ideas.

Mnemonics procedures to improve memory employ visual, narrative and dramatic techniques as memory aids. For example, imagining the names of people you meet on the forehead, or linking a number of different items into a story with memorable symbols. They work because it is easier to recall visual, unusual and dramatic images than semantic information.

Recently there has been considerable interest in narrative approaches to development for example the use of stories, myths and metaphors (Shaw et al., 1998). Gabriel (1995) argues that stories are episodic in character and offer a form of sense-making that is easier to remember and identify with. Short-term memory worsens from the mid-forties, thus in the later half of their career people find information they previously held in their head has to noted and planned. Time planners, Filo-faxes and personal organisers can be a great help. Baddeley (1983) offers an authoritative but accessible review of work on memory and ways of improving it.

THINKING

Work on cognition has highlighted the limited information processing capacity of the brain. Basically there is too much information coming into the brain for it to process it all with equal attention so its resorts to short cuts, such as mind sets and heuristics, that have worked in the past to speed up its processing. These normally serve us well but can on occasion mislead. Thus asked how much space there would be between the earth and a rope, if a rope placed round the earth had two metres added to it's length, most people reply negligible, actually it's 32cm (Claxton, 1997). We are misled by applying an inappropriate heuristic that where large size is concerned a smaller change can be expected. (This heuristic would work in the apparently analogous situation of adding two litres of water to the ocean which would raise the level of the ocean infinitesimally.) In certain circumstances conscious thought can interfere with a good performance. For example, Masters (1992) found people who had learnt to play golf intuitively through practice performed better under stress than those who had learnt from explicit instructions.

Thinking style differs across individuals. For example some people have a cognitive preference for considering the big picture, considering many options and being prepared to questions basics. Others are more likely to search a narrower area, develop ideas in more detail, and work within existing frames (e.g. Kirton, 1989). These cognitive preferences have implications for the way people communicate, take decisions, their leadership style, and approach to problem solving. There are numerous inventories designed to measure different aspects of cognitive style commonly used to aid individual development in organisations. See Bartram (1995) for a review of the reliability and validity of inventories commonly used in occupational settings and Furnham's chapter later in the Handbook.

Over the years people have attempted to determine what the common factors are underlying the different inventories. There has been increasing consensus that there maybe be five factors, known as the Big Five—extraversion, openness, agreeableness, conscientiousness and neuroticism (e.g. Goldberg, 1993). Over time we learn to behave in ways that are not natural to our style but a number of commentators (e.g. Kirton, 1989) argue that we revert to our natural style under pressure.

Development courses often use one or more inventories to alert participants to their and their colleague's cognitive style and its consequences. Some advocate participants aim to build up their natural deficiencies. Others that participants should seek to work with those with alternative styles (Belbin, 1981) and strengths. If cognitive style is genetically underpinned, as seems likely, there will be a limit to the extent to which people can change comfortably. Participants may be better off aware of this rather than feeling bad for failing to master something that is not natural to their style. For example, those with a high MBTI Perception preference tend to find it harder to do things on time than those with a high Judging preference.

Another line of development seeks to improve people's capacity to argue their case more effectively. Part of this entails an understanding of logic, but skills in the art of rhetoric and persuasion as just as important (Thoulness, 1953). Cognitive therapy is centred round improving thinking skills (for example, by analysing what works personally and what does not, and challenging one's own unwarranted generalisations). Individual development texts are increasingly drawing on this type of approach rather than the more traditional psychodynamic or humanistic approaches (e.g. Nelson-Jones, 1989).

LEARNING

At birth our brains are not fully formed and continue growing. Evidence suggests that the way they operate is determined by our experience. Neuro-imaging studies have made it clear that different areas of the brain are used by different people performing the same task, so brains exhibit plasticity, i.e. they develop differently in different people. That brains are organised differently in different people, gives further weight to the argument for individualising development programmes so that individuals can learn in ways that suits their particular cognitive style, schema and habits of mind. It also means learning is an active process, new ideas are not absorbed passively but have to be actively accommodated in our existing schemas. Active learning is encouraged where students have to formulate, organise, analyse and synthesise material and relate new ideas to their existing schema. This is considerably more effective that passive learning, such as learning by rote.

Cognitive science has revealed how much information is processed tacitly and how little of this reaches the surface. This means most information processing, learning and decision making appears to happen below conscious awareness. For experimental evidence to support this see Berry and Broadbent (1984), Lewicki et al. (1992), Schooler (1997), and Marcel (1993) and Reber (1993) for a review. It takes half a second of brain activity before any image is registered consciously (Libert, 1993) so the conscious mind is registering events after they have happened. Fortunately, in accidents and many other situations our unconscious bypasses conscious thought and slams the foot on the brake long before the conscious mind has realised it is about to crash into the car in front. This work has highlighted the importance of tacit knowledge in many situations.

We know explicit knowledge often lags behind tacit knowledge and that knowledge can be known tacitly but at the same time be too complex for the conscious mind to comprehend. Berry and Broadbent (1984) describe studies of a sugar factory simulation. Here participants learnt to manipulate the required output long before they were able to state explicitly how they were doing this. The superiority of implicit over explicit processing in complex tasks has been replicated in a variety of settings (Claxton, 1997).

Mintzberg (1975) has shown how in practice managers tend to rely much more on intuitive thinking than the management rhetoric of planning would lead one to expect. Our conscious mind is often only brought into play after the event, once we have already implicitly decided what to do. This suggests that individual development in organisations would do well to utilise development strategies that take greater account of intuitive ways of knowing. We need to shift the balance of development away from reflection, analysis and competency development to take more cognisence of apprehension.

Until recently most of the procedures for developing individuals in organisations addressed explicit ways of knowing, especially reflection and analysis. Nonaka and

Takeuchi (1995) have drawn attention to the extent to which Japanese companies consciously endeavour to tap tacit knowledge through tools like metaphor and analogy.

Recently there has been more interest in development procedures that are better placed to elicit subconscious hunches and half-formed ideas (Agor, 1986). One approach long used by certain psychotherapists and sports psychologists, and now applied to management development, is the use of visioning and guided imagery (Vaughan, 1979; Gawain, 1982). Visualisations often have two parts, first a relaxation to alter the participants' state of mind so that they can more easily access ideas and feelings that are normally just below conscious awareness; for example suggesting people relax each part of their body in turn. Then a guided visualisation where a facilitator (or tape) talks the participant through a sequence designed to address the issue in question either directly or indirectly. This may involve visualising a positive outcome, as in mental rehearsal, and sometimes includes a sense of how you got there but procedures are also available to help find direction, decide between alternatives, develop a plan of action or resolve conflict (Gloubermain, 1991).

Cognitive science has shown that knowledge is situated, i.e. known only in the area in which it was learnt, so things known in one context do not necessarily apply to similar problems in different contexts (Berry and Dienes, 1992). Thus Brazilian street children can perform arithmetic wonders in connection with gambling odd calculations and be quite unable to answer essentially the same questions in a classroom. Similarly, Berry and Broadbent's managers learnt how to get the best out of a particular sugar factory simulation after a period of practice but did not transfer that knowledge to related problems (Berry and Dienes, 1992). The implication is stark; knowledge does not transfer from one field to another, the good private sector manager is not necessarily the good public sector manager. Skills are bound up with our knowledge about particular fields. This presents a picture of learning that is diametrically opposite to the standard image of transferable skills inherent in management science, development education and the competency movement. Recently we have seen a shift to more learning on the job, which perhaps this is more likely to capitalise on situated know-how than off-site development.

Notions of individual development in organisations are often heavily influenced by rationalistic notions of information processing which underpin theories about learning being largely a matter of skill acquisition. The central image of learning appears to be one where skills need to be input into the brain. This is based on an idea of learning as information processing and development as making good skill deficiencies. This thinking lies behind the competency movement, an approach that has been wholeheartedly championed by the government, and taken up by the educational establishment, management and organisations, despite educational critiques. Development is seen as a process of inputting missing skills and in organisations these skills are assumed to be transferable.

There are many other approaches to learning, some operating from a very different perspective. Notably, psychodynamics which seeks to get the participant to relax defences so they can be more honest. Argyris (1994) has shown how most managers tend to avoid personally threatening situations and decisions and opt to play it safe or by the book, thereby forgoing opportunity to deal with important underlying issues and learn from differences of opinion. Psychodynamics highlights the part played by unlearning, where individual development is not so much a matter of acquiring skills as relinquishing schemas and assumptions that have been blocking perception (e.g. Gabriel, 1995).

PROBLEM SOLVING

Studies of problem solving suggest it is can be split into stages and that three may be fundamental. These have been variously described as preparation, production and judgement (Johnson, 1955); intelligence, design, selection (Simon, 1976a) identification, development, selection (Mintzberg, 1975); exploration, development, implementation (Henry, 1991). Many organisations have a particular problem-solving procedure they favour and organisational development procedures such as quality or re-engineering approaches also often advocate particular problem-solving procedures. Management problems are often messy or ill-structured (Simon, 1976). Such novel, uncertain and complex problems may require non-standard approaches, partly addressed by creative problem solving procedures (Kaufmann, 1991). Creative problem solving introduces a divergent phase prior to a convergent phase at each stage. The divergent phase precludes criticism so any idea goes, in the hope of widening the range of approaches considered. For a variety of problem solving procedures for managers see Stevens (1988) or Hicks (1991).

Cognitive science has shown that experts tackle problems very differently from novices (Kahney, 1986). Part of the reason for this is that experts chunk information differently. Experts' high level organised knowledge gives access to superior problem finding and problem solving abilities (Getzels, 1987). Superior *problem finding* ability is hard to develop other than through long experience in the field.

Changes in problem representation have been shown to cause a large difference in performance (Hayes & Simon, 1977). Imagine a chessboard of alternating black and white squares where a rectangular domino covers two squares. If two diagonal corner squares are cut from the board, would 31 dominoes cover the remaining squares? Most people think about this for quite a time before arriving at a conclusion, and do not immediately attend to the colour of the squares. Had they done so they would realise each domino has to cover two adjacent squares, i.e. a black and a white one and the two corners squares are the same colour so this is not possible. Asked if all 32 women in a village can marry when two of the 32 single men in the adjoining village die, people immediately say no.

There are a class of problems, known as insight problems that are very hard to deduce logically, they are more usually grasped as a holistic insight. A classic illustration of this is the nine-dot problem (Scheerer, 1963).

The task is to join the nine dots with four straight lines without taking your pen off the paper. Adults can struggle for a long time to work out this task, though quite young children can sometimes find the solution more readily. The difficulty lies in the fact that people assume (unnecessarily) that the pen must stay within a square bounded by the outer dots. Incubation, i.e. a period away from the problem, can aid insight into this kind of problem. Attempts to articulate what you are doing has been shown to hinder attempts to find the solution (Claxton, 1997). Here silence is more effective than verbal reflection.

DECISION MAKING

Decision making procedures often emphasise a rational approach, however several lines of work serve to counter the idea that decision making is broadly rational. Mintzberg (1975) and Isenberg (1984) have shown how managers appear to rely heavily on intuition rather than rational procedures when making decisions. In the 1950s, Simon popularised the idea of 'satisficing' and bounded rationality (Simon 1947, 1976) as a counter against the search for optimal decisions. Satisficing involves recognizing limitations of time and lack of information to advocate making a decision that is good enough. Cohen, March and Olsen (1972) have elaborated the garbage can model where decisions are as poor as the information they are based on. In another line of work, Janis (1982) has showed how the influence of social factors like group-think biases decision making. The danger of group-think is well-appreciated in the development literature, though hard to guard against unless conscious attempts are made to bring in those with different viewpoints.

Cognitive science has shown how decision makers often attend to only a subset of data and just how fallible decisions are. Under time pressure negative informative gets more weight and fewer variables are taken into account (Wright, 1974). Decision makers in organisations seem to commit early to a decision and take insufficient consideration of alternatives (Schwenck, 1984.) Under pressure the quality of decisions seems to suffer (Arnold et al., 1991).

In addition, the mind is prone to certain *judgement biases* which affect our capacity to judge events accurately. Tversky and Kahnemann (1974) document a number of these including the following. The *availability* bias refers to our tendency to assume events are more frequent if they come to mind readily. Recent, familiar and vivid events are easier to remember. Thus we overestimate the frequency of dramatic plane crashes and underestimate the likelihood of undramatic accidents in the home. We exhibit a *confirmation* bias in that we incline to stick with our initial judgements, noticing confirming evidence and dismissing evidence that does not fit our beliefs. We also show a *hindsight* bias believing ourselves to be more certain about our judgements than we initially were. We tend to be *overconfident* in our decisions believing lung cancer is more likely to affect others than ourselves. Haley and Stumpf (1987) present preliminary evidence suggesting managers with certain cognitive preferences may be more prone to some judgement biases than others. There is also evidence of cultural differences in decision making style, notably the Western tendency to rush to closure and the Japanese tendency to take longer before reaching a decision (Abramson et al., 1993).

Tools for improving decision making often advocate a *rational approach* in which, for example, one is encouraged to list and weigh costs and benefits of favoured options (e.g. Philip, 1985; Heirs, 1989). Recently some fascinating studies by Schooler (1997) suggest that verbalisation can interfere with decision satisfaction. In his studies, more of the participants who had been asked to decide intuitively proved happier with their decisions than those who were asked to think through the logic of their decision at the time of making it. Perhaps basing a decision on only those aspects of a case that can be verbalised misses some critical information intuition can take into account. Claxton (1997) reviews other experiments where verbalisation is shown to interfere with learning in complex, unfamiliar and unexpected situations. If this work on verbalisation interfering adversely with learning and decision making is replicated in other settings it could have considerable implications for individual development practice, as these frequently ask people to develop and articulate their reasons for decisions at a point that may be premature.

Work on social cognition has emphasised the importance of *gaining acceptance* for the proposed plan, an idea well accepted in organisations and embodied in tools like stakeholder analysis. In group settings, the idea of meeting both parties' needs is emphasised in *win-win* procedures, that seek to meet needs for both parties. Negotiation procedures similarly advocate listing where parties agree before tackling their disagreements.

A more fundamental critique argued by some cognitive psychologists is that there is no central self that makes decisions, rather that what we do is largely determined by whichever group of neurons happen to have the highest level of activity and come to the fore at any particular point in time (Blackmore, 1999). This line of thinking derives from connectionist studies of parallel processing, showing that different bits of the brain work on different problems simultaneously. One implication is that different parts of the brain might be trying to pursue different agendas that may not be consistent with one another. The conscious mind can be aware of only one of these at a time and which part comes to the fore appears to be determined pre-consciously. The Buddhist approach to this problem is to quieten the mind, become mindful and gain access to the brain's decision process a bit further upstream. Development practitioners have long recognised the existence subpersonalities which perhaps goes some way to acknowledging competing neuronal nets in the brain (e.g. Rowan, 1990). Intrapersonal development practice typically encourages the different subpersonalities to acknowledge each other's needs and wants and negotiate a way forward that takes account of these.

CREATIVITY

The approach taken to individual development in organisations is determined in large part by the theories practitioners hold as to its genesis. The development of creativity in organisations is a good example of how theories about development have affected the development tools advocated. It is an area that has been studied by cognitive scientists (e.g. Guildford, 1959; Simon,1976, 1988; Csikszentmihalyi, 1996; Amabile, 1990) and one of interest to many organisations at this time.

For many years efforts focused on the individual as the source of creativity but more recently attention has shifted to looking at creativity as an emergent property of a social system. This raises the question as to whether creative development is best aimed at individuals or groups.

Table 3.1 summarises how approaches to developing creativity differ in line with theories about its genesis. Those viewing creativity as an ability of the chosen few are likely to buy into the idea of creativity testing to identify staff for their R and D labs. (A weakness here is whether creativity tests do measure creative ability.) Those believing we are all creative in different ways may wish to ensure teams include staff with a variety of different cognitive styles who will naturally gravitate to different roles (Belbin, 1981).

Those believing creativity to be a skill will send staff to creative thinking and creative problem solving courses designed to enhance participants' creative thinking abilities. Those appreciating the time and experience it takes to be in a position to be truly creative may think twice before downsizing and losing the potentially valuable tacit knowledge locked in employee's heads.

TABLE 3.1 Implications of creativity theory for approaches to developing creativity

Perceived causes of creativity	Implications for the nature of creativity	Implications for developing creativity
Ability	Some are creative	Test for creative ability
Style	All are creative	Build differing cognitive styles in teams
Skill	It can be taught	Attend creative problem solving course
Experience	Non-transferable	Retain staff with tacit knowledge
Motivation	Non-transferable	Allow staff time free-time to pursue own projects
Systems	Needs nurturing	Open climate, attend to recognition, encourage networking
Complexity	Cannot be taught	Facilitate relationships, relax controls

Those realising that creativity is much more likely in areas staff care about will allow staff some time to pursue projects that motivate them even if the potential application is not yet obvious. Many organisations such as 3M allow scientists up to 15% of their time for such projects and award genesis grants to support them. Post-it notes came from such a project (Nayak and Ketteringham, 1988). Those appreciating the importance of the social context in allowing creative endeavour to emerge will make a point of opening the organisational climate to encourage challenge (Ekvall, 1991), forgive mistakes (Handy, 1999) and encourage staff to network with colleagues within and outside the firm.

Those who believe creativity emerges naturally in complex adaptive systems will relax their efforts to predict and plan for the future and monitor and control staff, and give greater attention to facilitating relationships and connections in the expectation that creativity will emerge naturally in due course (Wheatley, 1994; Stacy, 1996). See Henry (2001a) for amplification of the link between theory and practice in creative development.

ISSUES

Development practices are necessarily influenced by culture and history. In the West this seems to have led us to emphasise individual development at the expense of social influence, focus on growth rather than acceptance, stress processes aimed at solving problems rather than realising visions, value explicit reflection and insight over intuitive feelings and structure programmes round inputting skills to develop competency rather than releasing assumptions that block perception. In addition, cognitive science and complexity theory now present more fundamental challenges to our notions of how to develop the individual. An introduction to several of these issues follows.

DEFICIENCY ORIENTATION

Many development practices are derived from psychotherapeutic approaches and the underlying clinical orientation there is about fixing deficiencies and aiming to cure emotional hurt. Since the second World War psychology has also concentrated on study-ing pathology, deficiency and failure and approaches to individual development have tended to reflect this orientation (Seligman and Csikszentmihalyi, 2000). Organisations too tend to concentrate on inputting missing competencies and solving problems (rather than unblocking perceptions or chasing visions). Fritz (1989) argues that aiming for where you want to be and trying to get there ends up in a very different place than starting by trying to solve the problem.

Recently approaches to development in organisations have given greater attention to the alternative strategy of modelling the best, e.g. benchmarking best practice and seeking to emulate or learn from that. A few individual development strategies adopt a similar strategy: Covey (1989) tells us of the seven habits of highly effective people and NLP (neuro-linguistic programming) based their communication strategies on studies of the way masterly therapists, such as Satir, Erikson and Perls, and subsequently managers and teachers set about their work (Bandler, 1984; Dilts, 1990). Strategies derived from studying 'what works well' have tended to end up placing more emphasis on process—the way people communicate rather than the content.

PERSONAL GROWTH OR ACCEPTANCE

Humanistic notions of the blocked but basically loving and creative human, tends to support the idea that humans can get beyond their current woes and flourish into self-actualised and largely untroubled beings. The westerner seeks individual growth and often assumes they can metamorphise into a better and changed person. Managers' faith in the latest fad suggests they also seek the quick fix. Some empirical work presents a less optimistic picture. Studies of recovery from major trauma, such as loss of a child, find that people are just as pained by the loss two years after the event. So the capacity for personal change may be more limited than the consultants rhetoric would sometimes suggest. Elsewhere in the world greater stress seems to be given to the idea of self-acceptance, forbearance and balance. The Chinese emphasise on balance leads to development practices aimed at relaxing and balancing the body, such as Tai chi and Shiatsu, for example.

ROLE OF SOCIAL GROUP AND INVOLVEMENT

Psychotherapy and individual development have been critiqued as being overly con-cerned with the individual and failing to appreciate the extent to which people's state of consciousness arise out their social situation (Hillman and Ventura, 1993). Organi-sations on the other hand, aware that much of the work within them is done by teams, generally offer considerable group-based development, in the form of interpersonal skill development, team building, role preference awareness training, focus groups, creative problem solving and outdoor education for example.

Studies of well-being show consistently that people who are socially well supported rate themselves as happier than more isolated individuals (Argyle, 1987). They also show that people more often rate themselves as satisfied when actively engaged in a task, rather than passively watching TV (Csikszentmihayli, 1988). Self-report studies of long-term development also find social support and active physical involvement are effective strategies for long-term personal development. They also highlight the effectiveness of contemplation and other strategies for quietening the mind for self-development (Henry 2000). This work suggests a wider range of individual development strategies would be advisable, notably intuitive, social and physical approaches (rather than relying so heavily on reflection and skill development).

Value of Reflection and Insight

Much management rhetoric takes place in a rationalistic frame that emphasises planning, monitoring and control. This privileging of explicit analysis over intuitive apprehension has also applied to individual development in organisations, where insight and reflection are arguably the dominant routes to personal improvement. There can hardly be a manager alive who has not been asked to reflect on and articulate the learning point(s) they felt they have gained from a management development course. Counselling and allied approaches also tend emphasise insight through reflection. In cognitive terms development processes can be seen as a process of goal clarification through verbal analysis which develops self-awareness through a discussion of problematic feelings and a rational analysis of present and possible actions. There are however a number of problems with this dependence on reflection and insight as the main routes to development.

At face value stressing insight through reflection seems plausible, if managers are better placed to understand their situation they will be placed to deal with it. However this is not always the case, understanding that you have a habit does not necessarily supply the will-power to break it, often some other mediating variable such as confidence or support from a trusted other is necessary.

It is also questionable whether people are reliable guides to their own motivation. Nisbett and Wilson (1977) have shown how the driving human need to account for their actions leads to people presenting stories, they may believe, that are inaccurate. More fundamentally a series of experiments by Taylor and Brown (1994) show that depressives tend to have a more realistic self-image and estimate of their future prospects than happier people. This work shows the adaptive potential of positive illusions, and brings into question whether accurate insight into oneself is a desirable development strategy!

The general thrust of recent work in cognitive science is to acknowledge that much perception, thought, learning and decision making may be unavailable to the conscious mind. Individual development practice has tended to try to bring into consciousness aspects of experience that were previously unacknowledged. Cognitive science suggests there are inherent limits to this process.

TRENDS

Table 3.2 summarises some of the major shifts in cognitive science and parallel trends in individual development. They accord with a wider shift to a more participatory discourse that places greater emphasis on perceiving relationship than analysing elements. See Henry (1998) for discussion of privileged and neglected practices in personal and professional development.

Both cognitive science and development have historically focused largely on the individual level. Both fields are having to take greater cognisance of the social system within

TABLE 3.2 Trends in cognitive sciences and individual development

Cognitive science	Individual development
Individual representation > Social embeddedness	Individual reflection > Team based learning e.g. team-building, focus groups, developing organisational climate
Explicit > Implicit processing	Rational > Intuitive processes e.g. visioning, analogical, narrative approaches
Disembodied > Embodied self	Purely cognitive > Physical approaches e.g. relaxation, stress, health, outdoor education
Linear > Connectionist models	Individual development > Networking e.g. peer community support, cross organisational meetings

which cognition and development occur. In organisations we now have networking, partnership and community-based approaches to development for example.

We have seen earlier how a reliance on explicit reflection is being supplemented with development tools that take account of intuitive and less tangible ways of knowing. This trend in individual development practice parallels developments in cognitive science. Cognitive science now appreciates the greater role of implicit learning and unconscious processing, and development practice seems to feature a greater role for procedures that aim to tap intuitive understanding whether through the use of visualisation, metaphor, or narrative approaches.

Cognitive science has been criticised for operating in a frame that emphasises representation at the expense of embodiment and is now beginning to grapple with this problem (Varela et al., 1993). In individual development strategies that aim to reach the mind through the body seem to be gaining prominence. These include stress and health-related tools, exercise, Yoga, massage, Alexander Technique and the like. In professional development we are also beginning to see increasing interest in physical approaches to individual development.

Other trends in individual development include a shift away from developing individual qualities to a greater concern with developing relationships and attention to the community seen in attempts to develop teams and organisational climate and encourage networking rather than focusing solely on individuals themselves. We have also seen a move to more learning on the job and a shift away from expert-led to self-managed development processes such as mentoring and focus groups.

CONCLUSION

There has been a major shift in the way cognitive science now pictures how mind, brain, body and environment interact. Notably a new appreciation of the centrality of intuitive know-how and the limitations of rational thought. The evidence for the part probably played by genetics in certain aspects of cognitive style is firming, reinforcing the need to allow for diversity in development.

There has also been a shift to a greater recognition of the part played by social systems in the way we think and an appreciation of the need to address the systems in which individuals develop in addition to their individual needs. Nevertheless currently much work in individual development in organisations is dominated by two main approaches—competency and counselling. Studies of well-being suggest greater attention to social support, physical involvement and quietening the mind would be beneficial.

REFERENCES

Abramson, N. Lane, H. Nagai, H. and Tagagi, H. (1993) 'A comparison of Canadian and Japanese cognitive styles: implications for management interaction', *Journal of International Business Studies*, 24, 3, 575–87.

Adams, J.L. (1974) *Conceptual block-busting*. San Francisco: W.H. Freeman.

Agor, W. (1986) The logic of intuition: how top executives make important decisions, *Organisational Dynamics*, 14, Winter, 5–18.

Amabile, T. (1983, 1990) *The social psychology of creativity*. New York: Springer Verlag; also 2nd edn, *Creativity in Context*, 1990.

Anderson, J.R. (1983) *The architecture of cognition*. Cambridge, MA: Harvard University Press.

Arnold, J., Robertson, I.T. and Cooper, C.L. (1991) *Work psychology: understanding human behaviour in the workplace*. London: Pitman.

Argyle, M. (1987) *The Psychology of Happiness*, London: Methuen.

Argyris, C. (1994) 'Communication that blocks learning', *Harvard Business Review*, July/August, pp. 77–85.

Baddeley, A. (1986) *Your memory: A user's guide*. London: Pelican.

Bandler, R. (1984) *Using your brain for a change*. Moab, UT: Real People Press.

Bartram, D. (1995) *Review of personality assessment instruments (level B) for use in occupational settings*. Leicester: British Psychological Society.

Belbin, M. (1981,1993) *Management teams: why they succeed or fail*. Oxford: Butterworth Heinnemann.

Berry, D. and Broadbent, D. (1984) 'On the relationship between task performance and associated verbalized knowledge.' *Quarterly Journal of Experimental Psychology*, 36A, 209–31.

Berry, D.C. and Dienes, Z. (1992) *Implicit learning*. London: Lawrence Erlbaum.

Blackmore, S. (1999) 'Me, myself and I', *New Scientist*, Mar 13th, 40–44.

de Bono, E. (1984) *Lateral thinking for management*. Harmondsworth, Middx: Penguin.

Brown, M. (1988) *The dinosaur strain*. London: Element.

Butler, G. and Hope, T. (1995) *Manage your mind: a guide to mental fitness*. Oxford: OUP.

Buzan, T. (1974) *Use your head*. London: British Broadcasting Corporation.

Carnegie, D. (1953) *How to win friends and influence people*. London: Cedar.

Checkland, P.B. and Scoles, J. (1990) *Soft systems methodology in action*. Chichester: Wiley.

Claxton, G. (1997) *Hare brain, tortoise mind: Why intelligence increases when you think less*. London: Fourth Estate.

Cohen, M.D., March, J.G. & Olsen, J.P. (1972) 'A garbage can model of organizational choice'. *Administrative Science Quarterly*, 17, 1–25.

Covey, S. (1989) *The 7 habits of highly effective people*. New York: Simon and Shuster.

Csikszentimihalyi, M. and Csikszentmihalyi, I.S. (1988) *Optimal experience: Studies in the flow of consciousness*. New York: CUP.

Csikszentmihalyi, M. (1996) *Creativity: flow and the psychology of discovery and invention*. New York: Harper Collins.

Csikszentmihlyi, M. (1997) 'A systems view of creativity', in Henry (2001) op.cit.

Cyert, R. and March, J. (1963) *A behavioural theory of the firm*. Englewood Cliffs, NJ: Prentice Hall.

Dilts, R. (1990) *Changing belief systems with NLP*. Cupertino, CA: Meta Publications.

Eden, C. (1992) 'On the nature of cognitive maps'. *Journal of Management Studies*, 29, 261–265.

Ekvall, G. (1991) 'The organizational culture of idea management', Chapter 7 in Henry and Walker, op.cit.

Eysenck, H. (1947) *Dimensions of personality*. London: Routledge.

Eysenck, H.J., Barret, P. and Eysenck, S.B. (1985) 'Indices of factor comparison for homologous and non-homologous personality scales in 24 different countries', *Personality and Individual Differences*, 6, 503–4

Eysenck, H.J. (1967) *The biological basis of personality.* Springfield: Thomas.

Foucault, M. (1977) *Discipline and punish: The birth of the prison.* London: Penguin.

Foucault, M. (1980) *Power/Knowledge.* Brighton: Harvester.

French, C.C. and Colman, A.M. (eds) (1995) *Cognitive psychology.* New York: Longman.

Fritz, R. (1989) *The path of least resistance.* New York: Ballantine.

Gabriel, Y. (1995) 'The unmanaged organization: stories, fantasies, subjectivity'. *Organization Studies*,16, 3, 477–501.

Gawain, S. (1982) *Creative visualization.* New York: Bantam.

Gellatly, A. (1986) *The skilful mind: An introduction to cognitive psychology.* Milton Keynes: Open University Press.

Getzels, J.W. (1987) 'Creativity, intelligence and problem finding: Retrospect and prospect', in S. G. Isakson, *Frontiers of creativity research.* Buffalo, NY: Brearly, 88–102.

Glouberman, D. (1989) *Experiences with imagery.* London: Unwin Hyman.

Goldberg, L.R. (1993) 'The structure of phenotypic personality traits'. *American Psychologist*, 48, 26–34.

Haley, U. and Stumpf, S. (1987) 'Cognitive trails in strategic decision-making: linking personalities and cognitions'. *Journal of Management Studies*, 26, 5, 477–97.

Handy, C. (1999) *Beyond certainty.* London: Arrow.

Hayes, J.R, and Simon, H.A. (1977) 'Psychological differences among problem isomorphs', in N.J. Castelan, D.B. Pisoni and G.R. Potts (eds) *Cognitive Theory Vol. 2.* Hillsdale NJ: Erlbaum.

Henry, J. (1991) *Creative management.* London: Sage.

Henry, J. (1998) 'Privileged practice in personal development'. *Life-long Learning in Europe*, 3, 3, 161–5.

Henry, J. (2000) 'Effective change strategies'. *Consciousness and Experiential* Psychology, 5, 13–18.

Henry, J. (2001) *Creative management*, 2nd edn. London: Sage.

Henry, J. (2001a) *Creativity and perception in management.* London: Sage.

Hicks, M.J. (1991) *Problem-solving in Business and Management.* London: Chapman and Hall.

Hiers, B. (1989) *The professional decision thinker.* London: Grafton.

Hillman, J. and Ventura, M. (1993) *We've had a hundred years of psychotherapy and the world is getting worse.* San Francisco: Harper.

Hubel, D.R. (1979) 'The brain'. *Scientific American*, 214, 3, 44–53.

Isenberg, J. (1984) 'How senior managers think'. *Harvard Business Review*, 62, 81–90.

Janis, I.L. (1982) '*Groupthink*'. 2nd edn. Boston: Houghton Mifflin.

Johnson, D.M. (1955) *The psychology of thought.* New York: Harper and Row.

Kahney, H. (1986) *Problem solving: A cognitive approach.* Milton Keynes: Open University Press.

Kaufmann (1991) 'Creativity and problem solving' in J. Henry, *Creative management*, 1st edn. London: Sage.

Kirton, M.J. (1989) *Adaptors and innovators: Styles of creativity and problem solving*, London: Routledge (1st edn) and 1994 (2nd edn).

Lakoff, G. and Johnson, M. (1980) *Metaphors we live by.* Chicago: University of Chicago Press.

Lashley, K.S. (1929) *Brain mechanisms and intelligence.* Chicago: University of Chicago Press.

Lewicki, P., Hill, T. and Crysweka, M. (1992) 'Non-conscious acquisition of information'. *American Psychologist*, 47, 796–801.

Libet, B. (1993) 'The neural time factor in conscious and unconscious events'. *Consciousness.* Chichester: Wiley.

Loftus, G.R. and Loftus, E.F. (1975) *Human memory: The processing of information.* New York: Halstead Press.

Loftus, E.F. (1994) 'The repressed memory controversy'. *American Psychologist*, 49, 5, 443–45.

Luchins, A.S (1942) 'Mechanization in problem solving'. *Psychological Monographs*, 54, 6, 248.

Marcel, T. (1993) 'Slippage in the unity of consciousness', in *CIBA Symposium*, 174, op. cit.

Marr, D. (1982) *Vision: A computational investigation into human representation and processing of visual information.* San Francisco: W.H Freeman.

Martin, J.N.T. (1991) *Creative Management Techniques.* Milton Keynes: Open University.

Masters, R.S.W. (1992) 'Knowledge, nerves and know-how: the role of the explicit versus implicit knowledge in the breakdown of complex skill under pressure'. *British Journal of Psychology*, 83, 343–58.

McCaskey, M. (1982) 'Mapping: creating, maintaining and relinquishing conceptual frameworks', in *The Executive Challenge: Managing Change and Ambiguity*, Pitman 14–33, reprinted in J. Henry (1991) *Creative management*. London: Sage.

Miller, G.A. (1956) 'The magical number even plus or minus two: Some limits on our capacity for processing information'. *Psychological Review*, 63: 81–97.

Mintzberg, H. (1973) *The nature of managerial work*. New York: Harper and Row.

Mintzberg, H. (1975) 'The manager's job: folklore or fact'. *Harvard Business Review*, July–August, 49–61.

Morgan, G. (1986, 2nd edn 1997) *Images of organization*. London: Sage.

Morgan, G. (1993) *Imaginization*. London: Sage.

Nayak, P.R. and Ketteringham, J.M. (1988) '3M's little yellow note pads', Chapter 27 in Henry and Walker (1991) op.cit.

Nelson-Jones, R. (1989) *Effective thinking skills*. London: Cassell.

Nisbett, R. and Wilson, T. (1977) 'Telling more than we know, verbal reports on mental processes?' *Psychological Review*, 84, 231–59.

Nonaka, I, and Takeuchi, H. (1995) *The knowledge-creating company*. Oxford: Oxford University Press.

Philp, T. (1985) *Improve your Decision Making Skills*. London: McGraw-Hill.

Reber, A. (1993) *Implicit learning and tacit knowledge*. Oxford: OUP.

Rosenthal, R. (1969) *Artefact in Behavioural Research*. New York: Academic Press.

Rowan, J. (1990) *Subpersonalities*. London: Routledge.

Schooler, quoted in Claxton 1997, op.cit.

Scheerer, M. (1963) Problem solving, *Scientific American*, 208, 118–28.

Schwenk, C.R. (1984) 'Cognitive Simplification Processes in Strategic Decision Making'. *Strategic Management Journal*, 29, 51–71.

Seligman, M. and Csikszentmihalyi, M. (1990) 'Positive psychology'. *American Psychologist*, Special Issue, Jan.

Shaw, G., Brown, R. and Bromiley, P. (1998) 'Strategic stories: How 3M is writing business planning'. *Harvard Business Review*, May–June.

Simon, H. (1947, 1976) *Administrative Behavior*. New York: Free Press. 3rd edn 1976.

Simon, H. (1976a) Identifying basic abilities underlying intelligent performance of complex tasks. In L.B. Resnick (ed.) *The nature of intelligence*, 65–98, Hillsdale, NJ: Erlbaum.

Simon, H. (1988) 'Understanding creativity and creative management', in Kuhn, R., *Handbook for creative and innovative managers*. New York: McGraw-Hill.

Stacy, R.D. (1996) *Complexity and creativity in organizations*. San Francisco: Berrett-Kohler.

Stevens, M. (1988) *Practical problem-solving for managers*. London: Kogan Page/BIM

Taylor, S.E. and Brown, J.D. (1994) 'Positive illusions and mental well-being revisited: Separating fact from fiction'. *Psychological Bulletin*, 116, 1, 21–27.

Thoulness, R.H. (1953) *Straight and crooked thinking*. London: Pan.

Tversky, A. and Kahnemann, D. (1974) 'Judgement under uncertainty'. *Science*, 185, 1124–31.

Varela, F.J., Thompson, E. and Rosch, E. (1991) *The embodied mind*. Cambridge, Mass: MIT Press.

Vaughan, F. (1979) *Awakening intuition*. New York: Doubleday.

Walsh, J.P. (1995) 'Managerial and organizational cognition: notes from a trip down memory lane'. *Organizational Science*, 6, 280–321.

Wheatley, M. (1994) *Leadership and the new science*. San Francisco, CA: Brett-Koehler.

Wright, P. (1974) 'The harassed decision maker: Time pressures, distractions and the use of evidence'. *Journal of Applied Psychology*, 59, 555–561.

CHAPTER 4

Individual Differences can both Facilitate and Limit Individual Development

Kevin R. Murphy
Pennsylvania State University

SUMMARY

Individual differences in cognitive abilities, interests, and personality provide both opportunities and challenges for individual development. Cognitive ability is directly related to the ease, speed and efficiency of learning. Interests and personality traits are likely to be related to individuals' motivation to develop and change. These individual differences can enhance development, but they can also be a significant barrier to development. Unfortunately, individuals who are most in need of development (e.g. individuals who have low levels of cognitive ability, flat interests, dysfunctional personality traits) may be least likely to profit from developmental activities. Similarly, individuals who start out with strong abilities, healthy personalities, and well-developed interests are most likely to develop new abilities, skills, and talents, particularly if the developmental activities they have access to are consistent with their interests and personalities. A clear understanding of the characteristics of the abilities, interests and personalities of individuals is the first step towards understanding the success or failure of developmental efforts.

INTRODUCTION

There are a number of characteristics of individuals, of the situations they find themselves in, and of the methods that are used to induce or foster change that might influence the

Individual Differences and Development in Organisations. Edited by Michael Pearn.
© 2002 John Wiley & Sons, Ltd.

process and the success or failure of individual development. The purpose of this chapter is to consider the role of individual differences as factors that might facilitate or limit development. It is well known that broad and stable differences between individuals that influence a wide range of behaviors and outcomes, including those that are related to individual development. As a result of these individual differences, some individuals are more likely to develop and change than others, and the success of specific methods of development is likely to vary across individuals as a function of specific differences in their cognitive abilities and skills, their personalities, their values and interests, etc.

In this chapter, I will focus on three broad individual difference domains that are likely to be especially relevant to understanding opportunities for, and limits on, individual development. First, the implications of individual differences in cognitive abilities are considered. There is a substantial body of research, in settings ranging from the classroom to the workplace, showing that learning, success in training, acquisition of new skills, etc. is profoundly affected by general (and perhaps also by specific) cognitive abilities. Second, I will review the potential influence of interests on individual development. Interests are likely to influence both the individual's motivation to develop and his or her acceptance of specific developmental plans, methods, and assignments. Finally, I will consider the domain of personality. Several aspects of normal personality are likely to be relevant for understanding the process of and the likely success of individual development efforts.

The sections that follow lay out some of the principal models, theories and findings in the areas of cognitive ability, interests, and personality. Following these general descriptions, I will take up the question of how individual differences in cognitive ability, interests and personality are likely to affect development.

COGNITIVE ABILITY

Abilities are stable individual differences that are related to performance on some set of tasks, problems, or other goal-oriented activities. Cognitive abilities are involved when performing tasks that require the active manipulation of information. Tasks that require coordination between perception and physical action typically involve psychomotor abilities. It is possible to define more specific abilities that are restricted to a relatively narrow range of goal-directed activities (e.g., music); the focus here will be on the broad domain of cognitive ability, which is likely to subsume a number of specific abilities.

The key to understanding the structure of human cognitive abilities is the fact that scores on almost any reliable measure that calls for mental processing, retrieval, or manipulation of information will be positively correlated with any other reliable measure that also involves cognitive activity (Allinger, 1988; Carroll, 1993; Guttman & Levy, 1991; Jensen, 1980). Thus, scores on paragraph comprehension measures will be correlated with scores on numerical problem solving, which will be correlated with scores on spatial relations tests, and so on. One key issue in the history of research on cognitive ability has been the development of models of cognition that account for this phenomenon.

Spearman (1927) suggested that the correlations between various cognitive tests might be explained *solely* in terms of a general factor labeled "g". Although he later abandoned this theory, one of its key predictions has held up well. Measures of general cognitive ability ("g") do in fact predict performance across a wide array of contexts and tasks, and there is sometimes little to be gained by adding measures of more specific facets of ability to prediction equations.

MULTIPLE-ABILITY MODELS

While admitting the importance of a general intellectual factor, many psychologists object to the notion that the correlations between psychological tests could be completely explained in terms of their relationship to "g". Thurstone (1938) noted that there are factors common to groups of tests, labeled group factors, which are related to "g" but clearly not identical to "g". For example, tests of reading comprehension, verbal analogies, simple addition, and subtraction involving fractions all will be positively correlated as a consequence of their relationship to "g". Yet we would expect higher correlations between the two verbal tests and between the two numerical tests than we would between a verbal test and a numerical test. In Thurstone's terms, we would say that the first two tests share a group factor, labeled verbal comprehension, whereas the third and fourth tests share a different group factor, labeled numerical ability. These group factors are somewhat independent of one another, but both are related to "g".

Thurstone (1938) suggested that intelligence could best be understood in terms of a number of group factors, or primary mental abilities including verbal comprehension, word fluency, spatial visualization ability, associative memory, perceptual speed and reasoning. Since these mental abilities are thought to be as at least somewhat independent, it might be possible for two people who are identical in their level of "g" to differ dramatically in terms of their strengths and weaknesses in primary mental abilities. Thus, the most practical implication of Thurstone's theory is that intelligence should be measured at the level of primary mental abilities; the measurement of a single general factor would obscure much of the information conveyed by these group factors. While Spearman might argue that our attention should be focused on measuring "g", Thurstone and his followers suggest that intelligence tests should be developed to tap each of a number of factors.

Guilford's (1967, 1988) model represents a strong departure from the theories discussed so far in that Guilford does not accept the existence of a general intellectual factor. Rather, Guilford proposes that intelligence is organized according to three dimensions: (1) operations—what a person does, (2) contents—the material on which operations are performed, and (3) products—the form in which information is stored and processed. There are six types of operations, five types of content, and six types of products. Guilford proposes that each combination of a specific operation, a specific type of content, and a specific type of product defines a unique type of intelligence. In other words, there are 180 different types of intelligence, defined by all possible combinations of six operations, five types of content, and six types of product. Later versions of the theory proposed even more types of intelligence.

Although Guilford and Hoepfner (1971) claim to have identified 98 of the 180 factors suggested by the model (see also Guilford, 1988), the theoretical and practical implications of Guilford's model are somewhat in doubt (Allinger, 1988; Ulosevich, Michael, & Bachelor, 1991). To date, Guilford's model has not greatly affected the practice of intelligence testing.

Pursuing a similar line, Gardner (1983, 1993) suggested that there are several distinct types of intelligence, including logical-mathematical, linguistic, spatial, bodily-kinesthetic, interpersonal and intrapersonal. This theory focuses on assessing broad competencies, and many of the proposed applications of this theory have included naturalistic assessment (e.g., assessing intelligences by observing peoples' day-to-day activities). This theory suggests that the concept of general intelligence is not a very useful one, in part because people can be "intelligent" in many different ways.

This type of theory has potential implications for education and development. If Guilford's or Gardner's theory was correct, it might be better to tailor development to each individual's patterns of strengths and weaknesses than to focus on global evaluations of candidates. These theories suggest that global comparisons between people or groups (e.g., describing individuals in terms of IQ) are misleading, because they tend to emphasize only a small portion of the domain of intelligence. For example, if Joe is strong in spatial intelligence and interpersonal intelligence, and Sarah is strong in linguistic and logical-mathematical intelligence, it might be impossible to say which one is "smarter".

Hierarchical Models of Cognitive Ability

Vernon (1960) suggests that in a sense both Spearman and Thurstone were right. Vernon's model suggests a general factor, "g", that pervades all tests of intelligence and that can be broken down into two broad categories, called major group factors. There are two major group factors, verbal–educational and spatial–motor, which can be further divided into minor group factors, such as verbal or spatial factors; in some respects, these minor group factors resemble primary mental abilities. Minor group factors, in turn, summarize patterns of association among individual tests.

Carroll's (1993) three-stratum model of cognitive ability (based on the results of a large number of factor-analytic studies) nicely illustrates the nature of modern hierarchical models. At the most general level, there is a "g" factor, which implies stable differences in performance on a wide range of cognitively demanding tasks. At the next level (the broad stratum), there are a number of areas of ability, which imply that the rank-ordering of individuals' task performance will not be exactly the same across all cognitive tasks, but rather will show some clustering. The broad abilities in Carroll's (1993) model include: (1) fluid intelligence, (2) crystallized intelligence, (3) general memory ability, (4) broad visual perception, (5) broad auditory perception, (6) broad retrieval ability, and (7) broad cognitive speediness. The implication of distinguishing these broad abilities from "g" is that some people will do well on a broad range of memory tasks, and these will not be *exactly* the same set of people who do well on a broad range of tasks tapping cognitive speed, visual perception, etc. Finally, each of these broad ability areas can be characterized in terms of a number of more specific abilities (the narrow stratum) that are more homogeneous still than those at the next highest level. Examples corresponding to each of the broad spectrum abilities labeled above include: (1) induction, (2) language development, (3) memory span, (4) spatial relations, (5) sound discrimination, (6) word fluency, and (7) perceptual speed. Once again, the implication of distinguishing specific narrow abilities from their broad parent abilities is that the individuals who do well on inductive reasoning tasks might not be exactly the same as those who do well on other fluid intelligence tasks (although the groups will once again overlap substantially, and also overlap with those classified as high on "g").

Hierarchical models suggest that general vs. specific ability constructs will be used for different purposes. If your purpose is parsimonious prediction, "g" may be all that is needed. If your goal is to communicate or understand the meaning of human performance, lower levels in the hierarchy are likely be more useful. Saying that a person is high on "g" is the same as saying that he or she is likely to perform above average on some wide range of tasks. Saying that a person shows a high level of inductive reasoning ability (which implies relatively high "g") helps to describe the content and nature of the tasks he or she performs well.

THE DEBATE OVER "G"

One of the most hotly contested topics in research on cognitive ability is the importance of the general factor "g" that is central to the theories of Spearman, Vernon, Carroll, and the like. On the one hand, there is abundant evidence that there are broad and general differences in people's performance on a wide range of cognitively demanding tasks and that a general factor emerges from analyses of virtually any set of cognitive tests. People's standing on this general factor is probably the best single predictor of their performance in school, on the job, and in other settings where cognitively demanding tasks must be performed. Finally, once you have taken "g" into account, considering additional, more specific abilities does not seem to help much in predicting performance in these settings (for extensive recent analyses of these points, Ree & Earles, 1992; Ree, Earles, & Teachout, 1994; see also Hunter & Hunter, 1984; Murphy, 1996). From a pragmatic point of view, it is hard to doubt the utility of the "g" factor.

On the other hand critics of "g-ocentric" theories of intelligence (e.g., McClelland, 1993; Sternberg, 1985; Sternberg & Wagner, 1993) rightly note that, if you concentrate too much on the g factor, you are likely to lose sight of key questions such as why a person is intelligent, or what intelligent people do, or how they do it. It is clearly not enough to simply say that people differ on "g" and leave it at that. Murphy (1996) suggests that models of intelligence that focus on "g" are most useful for pragmatic purposes (e.g., predicting future performance), whereas models that focus on facets of intelligence other than "g" may be more useful for structuring research on the nature and origins of intelligent behavior.

Theories of cognitive ability that posit many different types of intelligence are appealing for a number of reasons, not the least of which is the sense that if you don't do well in one type of "intelligence" test, perhaps there is another type that would show just how smart you really are! Unfortunately, theories that strive to identify multiple and distinct types of intelligence have not fared well in terms of their empirical support (Cronbach, 1986; Lubinski & Benbow, 1995; Messick, 1992). These theories, all of which downplay the importance of "g", fail to explain a wide range of phenomena, especially the tendency for measures of performance on most cognitively demanding tasks to be positively correlated. If "g" is not an important facet of cognitive ability, it is very hard to explain why people who do well on vocabulary tests tend do well on math tests, or why people whose spatial abilities are generally good also tend to do well in remembering long strings of numbers.

One of the most potent criticisms of research on cognitive ability is that it implies a very narrow vision of what it means to be "smart." Cognitive ability is clearly relevant to success in school or in performing a wide array of cognitively demanding tasks (everything from completing a crossword puzzle to completing your doctoral dissertation), but there is more to life than cognitively demanding tasks. In recent years, social and interpersonal facets of "intelligence" have received considerable attention. Empirical research on emotional and social skills has a long history (Salovey & Mayer, 1990; Sternberg, 1985), but it was not until 1995, with Goleman's best-selling book, that the topic received widespread public attention. In the last few years, emotional intelligence has been the cover story for magazines like Time and Newsweek and the focus of numerous articles and television reports.

Although some proponents of emotional intelligence or EQ suggest that this concept "redefines what it means to be smart" and that it "can matter more than IQ" (both claims are made on the cover of Goleman, 1995), it would be a mistake to throw out cognitive ability tests with the hope of replacing them with measures of social or emotional intelligence. First, we are still far from consensus in defining emotional intelligence. Research in this area suggests that attributes such as impulse control, self-monitoring, and empathy are all part of emotional intelligence, but it is not yet clear how these diverse elements go together or whether social intelligence is a monolithic general ability (e.g. perhaps there is a social or emotional counterpart to the "g" factor in cognitive ability research) or a set of diverse abilities. Second, and more important, there is no good measure of emotional intelligence that could be used in the ways that cognitive ability tests are currently used.

Consider, for example, the most widely discussed measure of social or emotional intelligence, the marshmallow test. Suppose that you place a marshmallow on a table in front of a 4-year old and tell him that he can either have this marshmallow now, or if he waits a few minutes until you return from an errand, he can have two marshmallows. If you leave the room, you will find that some children grab the marshmallow right away and eat it, while others are able to delay gratification long enough for you to return so that they receive the two-marshmallow reward. Remarkably, children who exhibit the ability to delay gratification in this test turn out to be better students, more well-adjusted, more resilient, confident, and dependable, and these differences are still apparent when they are assessed years later (Shoda, Mischel, & Peake, 1990). In other words, this simple measure of the ability to delay gratification at age 4 predicts a wide range of behaviors and outcomes throughout childhood and adolescence (and perhaps beyond).

The marshmallow test may very well be a good measure of emotional intelligence (although it is still far from clear exactly what this test really measures), but it is still not a good substitute for cognitive ability tests. Similarly, emotional intelligence seems to be a very important attribute, and in some settings it might be more important than IQ, as it is traditionally assessed. Nevertheless, it is unlikely that EQ will someday be a substitute for IQ. Rather, as the concept of emotional intelligence continues to develop and as good measures of this concept start to emerge, it is likely that a combination of IQ and EQ measures will become increasingly common. Rather than being viewed as competitors, it is probably best to view these as complementary aspects of "what it means to be smart" and to look for ways to use information about EQ and IQ in tandem.

THE ORIGINS AND CONSEQUENCES OF INDIVIDUAL DIFFERENCES IN COGNITIVE ABILITY

The only thing that can be said with any certainty about the origin of individual differences in cognitive ability is that there is a great deal of uncertainty. It is clear that genetic factors are important; like most broad constructs in psychology, and cognitive ability shows strong evidence of heritability (Plomin & Rende, 1991; Vandenberg & Vogler, 1985). On the other hand, there is substantial evidence of environmental effects (Dickens & Flynn, 2001). For decades, controversy has raged over the relative contributions of nature and nurture to the development of cognitive abilities, but it is now clear that the nature-nurture dichotomy is oversimplification (Ceci & Williams, 1999; Young & Pursell, 2000). Current models of the development of cognitive ability focus on the interaction between nature and nurture.

Dickens and Flynn (2001) present a comprehensive model that helps to explain the interaction of genetic and environmental factors in the development of cognitive abilities. They note that people tend to choose environments in which they experience success and rewards. Children with stronger cognitive abilities and skills tend to be more comfortable in and more frequently rewarded by cognitively-demanding environments, and these environments, in turn contribute substantially to their further development. Children with weaker cognitive skills tend to prefer less demanding environments, and as a result, develop their abilities more slowly and less fully.

There is much less controversy about the implications of individual differences in cognitive ability. It is abundantly clear that differences in general cognitive ability contribute strongly to success in school, in job training, in the workplace, and in life in general (Gottfredson, 1997; Jensen, 1980: Neisser et al, 1996). Cognitive abilities, especially general abilities, are relatively stable over the adult lifespan, and their effects can be long-lasting. Cognitive ability is most clearly important in academic settings, where the acquisition and mastery of new knowledge and skills is such a major focus, but there is unmistakable evidence that measures of general cognitive ability predict a wide array of criteria (Jensen, 1980, Herrnstein & Murray, 1994). As I will note in a later section, individual differences in cognitive ability may have a profound effect on individual development.

INTERESTS

Strong (1943) defined an interest as "a response of liking" (p. 6). It is a learned affective response to an object or activity; things in which we are interested elicit positive feelings, things in which we have little interest elicit little affect, and things in which we are totally disinterested elicit apathy or even feelings of aversion. For example, some people enjoy (are interested in) opera, other people can take it or leave it, and still others hate it.

Interests are different from abilities. The fact that you like opera does not make you an opera singer. However, interests and abilities tend to show some similar patterns. People often learn to like things that they do well and learn to dislike things that they do not do well (Strong, 1943). One practical distinction between abilities and interests is in terms of the variables that they tend to predict. Measures of ability tend to predict measures of performance or efficiency. Interests are typically related to persistence and satisfaction, rather than to performance. Thus, although the fact that a person is extraordinarily interested in opera does not necessarily indicate that he or she will succeed as an opera singer, it does indicate that the person would be happy as an opera singer (the audience, however, might not be so happy).

Interests can be used to predict choices, especially when there are few external constraints. For example, when a person goes to a bookstore, his or her interests (together with the price of the book) have a substantial impact on the choices of which book to buy. Even in decisions that have substantial consequences, such as choosing a career, interests have a substantial effect. A person who hates to work with figures is not likely to choose a career in accounting, even if very lucrative jobs are available.

Interests differ in terms of their specificity. The typical conception of interests is that they are tied to specific objects or activities, such as interest in baseball, interest in ships, or interest in dentistry. However, very broad domains of interest have been identified; examples include scientific interests, masculine interests, and humanitarian interests. Within the occupational domain, interests in specific occupations (e.g., air traffic controller), in broad occupational fields (e.g., medical jobs), and in general types of fields (e.g., business) have been assessed. To date, measures of specific interests have been more useful than measures of general interests in predicting future choices and future satisfaction (Super, 1973).

A distinction is typically made between interests and values; values are regarded as more general and more resistant to change than interests. Super (1973) has suggested that interests and values are best defined in a sort of a means—end relationship. Thus, values are objectives one seeks to satisfy a need, while interests are linked to specific activities through which values can be obtained. Examples of the work values proposed by Super are quality of life, material outcomes, self-expression, and behavior control.

Holland's (1973) model of occupational interests has been one of the most influential models in applied psychology (e.g., it forms the basis for most measures used in vocational counseling; for comparisons to other models of vocational interests, see Tracey & Rounds, 1993). Holland identified six major interest areas that could be used to describe both work environments and types of people: (1) Realistic—interest in practical things, dealing with machines and physical skills, (2) Investigative—interest in scientific activities, solving abstract problems, (3) Artistic—interest in creativity and self-expression, (4) Social—interest in the welfare of others, social interactions and relationships, (5) Enterprising—interest in selling, leading, persuading others, and in power, wealth and domination, and (6) Conventional—interest in well-ordered activities, predictability, and stability. His theory suggests that, the optimal vocation choice involves matching people with their appropriate environmental type. Holland further postulated that the hexagonal model illustrated in Figure 4.1 best represented the relationship that exists among these six interest areas; as the distance along the hexagon increases, the similarity or correlation among interests diminishes. Consequently, the least similar areas are those that lie diagonally across from one another. For example, people with conventional interests do not share much in common with artistic individuals, nor do scientists have many interests in common with people in business.

It is likely that interests develop through a process similar to that suggested by Dickens and Flynn's (2001) model of cognitive development. That is, people differ in the activities,

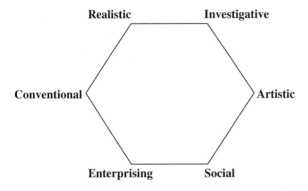

Realistic   Investigative

Conventional   Artistic

Enterprising   Social

FIGURE 4.1   Holland's Vocational Interest Taxonomy

environments, etc., that they find rewarding, and they are increasingly likely to seek out environments that provide satisfaction and positive rewards, and avoid those that lead to failure, boredom or negative consequences. Although interests in specific jobs may wax and wane, broad occupational interests crystallize by the late teens, and remain remarkably stable throughout adulthood. Interest measures have been widely used to predict occupational choice and occupational satisfaction and success (Campbell & Borgen, 1999; Campbell & Hansen, 1981).

PERSONALITY

Frank (1939) noted that "an initial difficulty in the study of personality is the lack of any clear-cut conception of what is to be studied" (p. 389). More modern reviewers suggest that the situation has not fundamentally changed in the intervening years (Carson, 1989; Pervin, 1985). There still is some uncertainty over what personality is, over the usefulness of the term personality, and over the contribution of personal factors, as opposed to environmental factors, to the understanding of behavior.

A definition of personality must take into account several facts. First, individuals are unique in the sense that no two people are exactly alike in terms of temperament, behavior, or preferences. Second, individuals do not behave in identical ways in all situations. A person behaves differently at a football game than he or she would in a religious setting. Third, although individuals are unique and are not completely consistent across situations, there is considerable commonality in human behavior. That is, although there are great differences in detail, many people show similar patterns of behavior. The description of broad personality types may allow us to group individuals meaningfully in a way that accurately describes some important behavior patterns.

In theory, two extreme positions could be put forth to explain behavior, the purely trait oriented position and the purely situational position. The former concentrates solely on the person and ignores the situation in which behavior occurs, whereas the latter ignores the person and concentrates solely on the situation. Neither position represents a fruitful or even adequate description of personality (Carson, 1989; Pervin, 1985). A more comprehensive definition that considers both the person and the situation has been suggested by Pervin (1980). Personality is defined as the set of characteristics of a person or of people that account for consistent patterns of response to situations.

During the 1970s and 1980s, the dominant issue in research on personality was the debate over the consistency of behavior across situations (Epstein, 1980; Mischel & Peake, 1982). This controversy can be traced back to the 1930s and probably has roots as old as those of psychology (Maddi, 1984; Pervin, 1985). The core issue in this debate was whether persons do in fact behave in relatively consistent fashions across a wide range of situations.

If you accept (in its most extreme form) the argument that behavior is not at all stable across situations, it would make no sense to measure personality, interests, ability, or any other individual difference variable (Rorer & Widigor, 1983). The data do not support this extreme interpretation, but neither do they support the opposite extreme, that behavior is completely stable across situations. The heart of the person–situation debate is not which factor is completely dominant but, rather, how much emphasis should be placed on consistency versus inconsistency.

Personality psychologists appear to have reached a consensus that individual behaviors are unstable, but that broad patterns of behavior show some consistency (Epstein, 1980) and that persons show more relative than absolute stability in their behavior (Maddi, 1984; Pervin, 1985). This suggests that personality measures may provide a useful means of predicting individual differences in general patterns of behavior, but that to accomplish this, both the personality dimension(s) measured and the behavior being predicted must not be too narrow or specific.

PERSONALITY TAXONOMIES

Although many personality psychologists believe that it is useful to measure traits, there has been a long history of disagreement about what traits to measure. A quick look through the textbook used in any personality course shows that different theories have emphasized very different sets of traits. Until the 1980s there was no broad agreement about what traits best summarized the domain of personality.

There is now some consensus that the domain of human personality can be character-ized in terms of the five factors listed in Table 4.1; these factors are often referred to as the "big five" (Digman, 1990; McCrae & Costa, 1985, 1987, 1989; Saucier & Goldberg, 1996).

TABLE 4.1 The five-factor model of personality

Extroversion	People high on this dimension are sociable, gregarious, assertive, talkative, and active.
Emotional stability	People low on this dimension are anxious, depressed, angry, emotional, embarrassed, and insecure.
Agreeableness	People high on this dimension are courteous, flexible, trusting, good-natured, cooperative, and tolerant.
Conscientiousness	People high on this dimension are dependable, careful, thorough, responsible, hard-working, and persevering.
Openness to experience	People high on this dimension are imaginative, cultured, curious, original, and artistically sensitive.

These five factors are highly robust and have been replicated in a number of studies using different methods of measurement (e.g., paper-and-pencil inventories, interviews, peer ratings) and in different linguistic and cultural groups. There are personality inventories specifically designed to measure these five factors (e.g., the NEO Personality Inventory; Costa & McCrae, 1992); but perhaps more important, several of these five factors seem to be present in many, if not most, well-designed personality inventories (Barrick & Mount, 1991). Thus, this taxonomy provides a basis for organizing and comparing studies involving a wide range of personality inventories.

As you might expect, given the long history of disagreement over the basic structure of personality, this taxonomy is not universally accepted. There are still controversies over the meanings and the names of several of the factors, particularly the factor "openness to experience." There are also several studies showing that factors not in this taxonomy are important predictors of a variety of criteria (e.g., performance on the job; Barrick & Mount, 1991; Hough, Eaton, Dunnette, Kamp, & McCloy, 1990; Salgado, 1997; Tett, Jackson, & Rothstein, 1991). Nevertheless, this taxonomy appears to provide a good starting point for describing what personality inventories should measure, and it helps to organize the previously fragmented body of research on personality and its correlates.

The origins of individual differences in personality are still uncertain. Like cognitive abilities, broad personality dimensions show strong evidence of heritability (e.g., Tellegen, Lykken, Bouchard et al., 1988). Environmental effects may be harder to pin down, in part because of probable differences in the way genetic and environmental determinants of personality vs. ability and interests are linked. In the cases of abilities and interests, there does seem to be evidence that people choose environments that fit them, and that these environments foster the stronger development of particular patterns of ability and interest. It is not yet clear whether a similar matching model will account for the development of personality. Regardless of how they develop, individual differences in personality are likely to play a strong role in individual development.

IMPLICATIONS FOR INDIVIDUAL DEVELOPMENT

Individuals differ in a number of ways, and the three domains described here (i.e., abilities, interests, personality) represent just the tip of the iceberg. Furthermore, all three of these domains overlap in part with demographic variables, socioeconomic status, etc. As a result, it is often impossible to take individual differences in ability, interest and the like into account without also indirectly taking into account variables such as race, gender, education, etc. Nevertheless, these three variables do provide a good starting point for discussing the potential role of individual differences in facilitating or inhibiting individual development.

First, individual differences in these three domains are thought to be relatively stable, at least throughout the adult lifespan. As a result, it is unlikely that general abilities, broad interests or broad aspects of personality are likely to change much, regardless of what else develops or fails to develop during "individual development". More to the point, these three domains subsume a wide range of activities and behaviors. Cognitive ability is relevant to virtually anything that involves active information processing, ranging from learning in school to solving problems at work to making and using a grocery list. Interests, such as those that define the Holland Taxonomy, represent responses of liking and disliking to broad patterns of behavior and activity (e.g., working with people vs. working with things). Personality dimensions represent consistent patterns of behavior that span situations. Thus, a person who is high on conscientiousness can be expected to be diligent, responsible, achievement-oriented, etc. is a fairly wide array of settings. Finally, psychometrically sound measures of all three domains are widely available. Therefore, it should be possible to obtain credible information about abilities, interests, and personality in many situations where individual development is thought to occur, and use these to understand the potential opportunities for or limits to development.

COGNITIVE ABILITY

Individual differences in cognitive ability have both obvious and profound implications for individual development. The acquisition of new knowledge, the integration of new knowledge with existing knowledge and skills, the ability to translate what one has learned into action, and even one's willingness to embark on efforts to develop are likely to be correlated with cognitive ability. Unfortunately, this is a domain in which the rich are likely to get richer. That is, individuals who receive high scores on measures of general cognitive ability are more likely to learn, to succeed in training, in integrate knowledge, etc., whereas individuals who score lower on such measures find it more difficult to learn or to profit from experience (especially in information-rich environments). Different patterns of strength and weakness in specific abilities and cognitive skills may have implications for specific types of development (e.g. success in programs designed to increase skills in analyzing and understanding data may depend more on analytic and mathematical abilities than on other abilities), but given the strong positive correlations among most cognitive abilities, it is reasonable to focus on general cognitive factors and to conclude that learning and development is most likely for those who are highest in ability (and who might need development the least) and least likely for those lower in ability (who might have more pronounced developmental needs).

Several studies have examined the concept of "trainability" (Casey, 1984; Robertson & Downs, 1989; Wexley, 1984), i.e., the likelihood that particular skills, abilities, knowledge can be developed through structured training. On the whole, this literature suggests that low cognitive ability is not necessarily an absolute barrier to learning and development. Rather, it represents a serious impediment, which can often be overcome only with substantial time and effort. Thus, high ability does not guarantee success in learning or development, and low ability does not guarantee failure. However, ability does tell you quite a bit about the likelihood that particular developmental efforts will succeed, and about the effort and motivation that may be needed for a particular individual to succeed. On the whole, high-ability individuals are drawn to situations that involve learning, mastery, and development, in part because they often find it relatively easy to learn. Low-ability individuals might, given sufficient time and effort, learn and master the same material, but they will often find the process more difficult, less rewarding, more frustrating, etc.

The relationship between cognitive ability and development will depend in part on exactly what you mean by "development". Individual development might refer to an array of activities, ranging from those that focus on acquiring knowledge to those that focus on developing interpersonal skills. The influence of cognitive ability on development will be strongest for developmental activities that focus on acquiring, manipulating and using information, and weakest for programs that focus on skills outside of the domain of active information processing. However, because "information processing" underlies such a wide range of developmental activities, it is fair to say that the first question you might ask in predicting whether an individual will succeed or fair in a particular developmental activity or program is "where does this person stand in terms of general cognitive ability". The answer to this question will not always allow you to predict success or failure in individual development, but the empirical research on the ubiquitous role of cognitive ability does suggest that this ability is a critically important determinant of success. People with relatively low levels of cognitive ability will find it relatively difficult to develop new skills, abilities, and patterns of behavior, and this effect will be progressively stronger the more heavily the activities in question draw upon information processing and retrieval. People with relatively high levels of cognitive ability will often find it easier to learn, change, and develop, particularly in areas that involve active information processing.

INTERESTS

Whereas cognitive ability appears to affect the ease of learning and development, interests appear to influence individuals' motivation to change and develop. Motivation is often defined as a construct that relates to the direction and to the persistence of behavior, and interests are likely to exert both types of effects. First, because interests represent responses of liking, it is reasonable to infer that people will be drawn toward developmental opportunities that are consistent with their interests (i.e., opportunities that provoke consistent positive reactions) and will be repelled from developmental opportunities that are associated with activities or domains that they dislike. Second, individuals are likely to persist in developmental activities that produce positive experiences (responses of liking) and remove themselves from activities that do not.

Consider, for example, an individual with strong Conventional interests. That person will tend to respond positively to activities, situations, etc. that involve order, predictability and stability, and will tend to respond less positively to activities that involve creativity and self-expression (Artistic interests). Developmental opportunities that focus on dealing with things (Realistic) or on persuading and dominating others (Enterprising) are likely to be more motivating that opportunities that involve research (Investigative) or group interactions (Social).

Traditionally, vocational counselors have focused on the *relative* strength of the interests in the Holland typology rather than the absolute strength, but this is not always the best strategy. Consider, for example, two individuals, one of whom has a very flat profile of interests, not really showing a high level of interest in any single domain, with only a slight elevation in one or more interest domains (e.g., Enterprising). The other has very sharp likes and dislikes, showing strong Social interests, elevated interests in Enterprising activities, and strong aversion to Realistic of Investigative activities. If the developmental activity in question focused on Enterprising activities (e.g., persuading others), the second individual (whose Social interest is higher than Enterprising) might be a better candidate than the first (who is not interested in anything, but less bored with Enterprising activities than with others).

Interests might prove useful for predicting both the choice of developmental activities (e.g., the more options and the fewer constraints the individual has in choosing developmental activities, the higher the likelihood that choices will be consistent with interests) and persistence in those activities. Also, because interest taxonomies (e.g., Holland's theory of vocational interests) often include specifications of the correlations among interests, it should be possible to predict individual preferences for and persistence in a fairly wide range of developmental activities. As noted earlier, strong interests in one domain (e.g., Conventional) tend to be linked with relatively weak interests in other domains (Artistic). As we will note below, the same cannot be said for broad facets of normal personality.

PERSONALITY

Despite decades of research and theory, it is still not completely clear what "personality" really means. For the purposes of this chapter, I will treat "personality" as a description of broad consistencies in behavior, that can be reasonably captured by the "big five" dimensions. That is, if I know your standing on the dimensions Conscientiousness, Extroversion, Agreeableness, Emotional Stability, and Openness to Experience, I can make some useful statements about your behavior. A person who is high on Conscientiousness will tend to be more reliable, dependable, rule-abiding, achievement-oriented, etc. than people who are lower on this dimension, and these comparisons will hold up across a range of situations. A conscientious person will not always focus on reliability, dependability, etc. (e.g., at a concert, he or she will probably think more about the music and the performers than about being dependable), but compared to other people in the same situation, his or her behavior will tend to show more of these characteristics (e.g., if your group need someone to go back to the car and get umbrellas, it is a good bet that the person who ends up doing this is high on Conscientiousness).

One notable difference between the domains of cognitive ability, interests, and personality is that personality is made up of several essentially uncorrelated dimensions. Cognitive abilities are almost all inter-correlated, and it is often possible to describe a person's ability at a fairly general level and do a good job capturing most of the variance in ability. Interests tend to be correlated; Holland's (1977) hexagonal model summarizes the pattern of inter-correlations (e.g., Realistic and Social Interests are less highly correlated than Realistic and Investigative interests). Personality dimensions, on the other hand, tend to be independent, and finding that a person is high on Conscientiousness does not tell you much about his or her levels of Agreeableness, Extroversion, etc.

There is a common thread running through the "big five" personality dimensions—i.e. social desirability. On the whole, most people would prefer to spend time with someone who is dependable, outgoing, agreeable, stable, and curious than with someone who is unreliable, withdrawn, disagreeable, neurotic, and close-minded. However, beyond this broad generalization, there may be no "general factor" underlying personality. As a result, any speculation about the role of personality factors in individual development must be recognized as such, and categorical statements about the implications of personality for development must be made with caution. For example, it seems obvious that people who score at the low end of the "Openness to Experience" dimension might be less likely to engage in and profit from developmental efforts that those who are more open-minded and curious, this may not always be true. Individuals who are low on Openness to Experience might have a variety of other attributes that contribute to their development (e.g., a combination of high Conscientiousness and Extroversion might lead to a strong motivation to develop skills in teamwork).

Whereas a great deal of information about cognitive abilities can be summarized by a broad general factor, and the structure of interests understood in terms of a small number of dominant facets, personalities must usually be thought of in terms of profiles. That is, there are many combinations of personality dimensions that are likely to be encountered, and each of these might have different implications for development. For example, suppose that you know that an individual is highly Conscientious. That person is equally likely to be high or low on Extroversion, on Agreeableness, on Openness to Experience, or on Emotional Stability (because these dimensions are essentially uncorrelated), and it is not hard to imagine that some combinations of personality traits might make a person more conducive to development than others (e.g., high Conscientiousness coupled with high Extroversion and Agreeableness may more strongly incline a person toward developing social skills and knowledge than high Conscientiousness coupled with low Extroversion and Agreeableness).

INDIVIDUAL DIFFERENCES AND THE WHO AND HOW OF INDIVIDUAL DEVELOPMENT

Suppose you were the Director of Training and Development in a large organization. You want to offer a wide range of developmental opportunities to your employees. You have a finite budget, and you need to decide who will get what types of opportunities for training and development. The research reviewed in this chapter suggests that individual characteristics, particularly cognitive ability, will have a substantial influence on whether individuals will in fact benefit from training and development. Interests and personality characteristics might also be quite important, particularly as they bear on the individual's motivation to pursue and stick with training and development programs. From one perspective, this research paints a discouraging picture, because it is reasonably clear that the people who are most likely to benefit from a particular developmental activity are quite often those who need it the least. That is, people who are motivated, conscientious, emotionally stable, bright, etc. tend to do well in a wide range of training and development programs, while people who have less ability, less stable and functional personalities, less interest, etc. tend to fail. If your goal is to maximize the benefit to the organization, you will rarely go too far wrong by following a "rich get richer" strategy—i.e., offering training and development activities to those individuals who are most clearly positioned to succeed. On the other hand, if you start from the individual perspective rather than from the perspective of the organization, you should probably offer training and development to those who need it the most (e.g., people who are not as bright, capable, etc.). Even if many of these individuals turn out to do poorly in training, the ones who do get something out of it will benefit immensely.

The most critical issue in thinking about the influence of individual differences on individual development is what to do with information about individuals' abilities, interests, personalities, etc. It is clear that we cannot and should not ignore this information, but in my view there is no clear consensus at this point about how to use information about individual differences (described in more detail in chapters five and six) in making decisions about who gets access to which sorts of developmental opportunities.

REFERENCES

Allinger, G.M. (1988). Do zero correlations really exist among measures of different cognitive abilities? *Educational and Psychological Measurement, 48*, 275–280.

Bachelor, P.A. (1989). Maximum likelihood confirmatory factor-analytic investigation of factors within Guilford's structure of intellect model. *Journal of Applied Psychology, 74*, 797–804.

Barrick, M.R. & Mount, M.K. (1991). The big five personality dimensions and job performance: A meta-analysis. *Personnel Psychology, 44*, 1–26.

Block, J. (1995). A contrarian view of the five-factor approach to personality description. *Psychological Bulletin, 117*, 187–215.

Campbell, D.P. & Borgen F.H. (1999). Holland's theory and the development of interest inventories. *Journal of Vocational Behavior, 55*, 86–101.

Campbell, D.P. & Hansen, J.C. (1981). *Manual for the SVIB-SCII* (3rd edn). Stanford, CA: Stanford University Press.

Carroll, J.B. (1993) *Human cognitive abilities: A survey of factor-analytic studies*. Cambridge, UK: Cambridge University Press.

Carson, R.C. (1989). Personality. *Annual Review of Psychology, 40*, 227–248.

Casey, J.J. (1984). Trainability diagnosis: A humanistic approach to selection. *Training and Development Journal, 38*, 89–91.

Ceci, S.J. & Williams, W.M. (1999). *The nature–nurture debate: The essential readings. Essential readings in developmental psychology*. Malden, MA: Blackwell.

Costa, P.T. & McCrae, R.R. (1992). Normal personality assessment in clinical practice: The NEO Personality Inventory. *Psychological Assessment, 4*, 5–13.

Cronbach, L.J. (1986). Signs of optimism for intelligence testing. *Educational Measurement:Issues and Practice, 5*, 23–24

Dickens, W.T. & Flynn, J.R. (2001). Heritability estimates versus large environmental effects: The paradox resolved. *Psychological Review, 108*, 346–369.

Digman, J.M. (1990). Personality structure: Emergence of the five-factor model. *Annual Review of Psychology, 41*, 417–440.

Epstein, S. (1980). The stability of behavior II. Implications for psychological research. *American Psychologist, 35*, 790–806.

Gardner, H. (1983). *Frames of mind: The theory of multiple intelligences*. New York: Basic Books.

Gardner, H. (1993). *Multiple intelligences: The theory in practice*. New York: Basic Books.

Goleman, D. (1995). *Emotional intelligence: Why it can matter more than IQ*. New York: Bantam.

Gottfredson, L. (1997). Why "g" matters: The complexity of everyday life. *Intelligence, 24*, 79–132.

Guilford, J.P. (1967). *The nature of human intelligence*. New York: McGraw-Hill.

Guilford, J.P. (1988). Some changes in the Structure-of Intellect Model. *Educational and Psychological Measurement, 48*, 1–4.

Guilford, J.P. & Hoepfner, R. (1971). *The analysis of intelligence*. New York: McGraw-Hill.

Guttman, L. & Levy, S. (1991). Two structural laws for intelligence tests. *Intelligence, 15*, 79–103.

Herrnstein, R.J. & Murray, C. (1994). *The bell curve: Intelligence and class structure in American life*. New York: Free Press.

Holland J.L. (1973). *Making vocational choices: A theory of vocational personalities and work environments*. Englewood-Cliffs, NJ: Prentice Hall.

Hough, L.M., Eaton, N.K., Dunnette, M.D., Kamp, J.D. & McCloy, R.A. (1991). Criterion-related validities of personality constructs and the effects of response distortion on those validities. *Journal of Applied Psychology, 75*, 581–595.

Hunter, J.E. & Hunter, R.F. (1984). Validity and utility of alternate predictors of job performance. *Psychological Bulletin, 96*, 72–98.

Jensen, A.R. (1980). *Bias in mental testing*. New York: Free Press.

Lubinski, D. & Benbow, C.P. (1995). An opportunity for empiricism. *Contemporary Psychology, 40*, 935–940.

Maddi, J. (1984). Personology for the 1980s. In R. Zucker, J. Aranoff & A. Rabin (Eds), *Personality and the prediction of behavior*. New York: Academic Press.

McCrae, R.R. & Costa, P.T., Jr. (1985). Updating Norman's "adequate taxonomy": Intelligence and personality dimensions in natural language and questionnaires. *Journal of Personality and Social Psychology, 49*, 710–721.

McCrae, R.R. & Costa, P.T., Jr. (1986). Clinical assessment can benefit from recent advances in personality psychology. *American Psychologist, 51*, 1001–1002.

McCrae, R.R. & Costa, P.T., Jr. (1987). Validation of the five-factor model of personality across instruments and observers. *Journal of Personality and Social Psychology, 52*, 81–90.

McCrae, R.R. & Costa, P.T., Jr. (1989). The structure of interpersonal traits: Wiggin's circumplex and the five-factor model. *Journal of Personality and Social Psychology, 56*, 586–595.

McClelland, D.C. (1993). Intelligence is not the best predictor of job performance. *Current Directions in Psychological Science, 2*, 5–6.

Messick, S. (1992). Multiple intelligences or multi-level intelligence? Selective emphasis on distinctive properties of hierarchy: On Gardner's Frames of Mind and Sternberg's Beyond IQ in the context of theory and research on the structure of human abilities. *Psychological Inquiry, 3*, 365–384.

Mischel, W. & Peake, P.K. (1982). Beyond déjà vu in the search for cross-situational consistency. *Psychological Review, 89*, 730–755.

Murphy, K.R. (1996). Individual differences and behavior in organizations: Much more than g. In Murphy, K.R. (Ed.), *Individual differences and behavior in organizations* (pp. 3–30). San Francisco: Jossey-Bass.

Neisser, U. et al. (1996). Intelligence: Knowns and unknowns. *American Psychologist, 51*, 77–101.

Pervin, L.A. (1980). *Personality theory and assessment*. New York: Wiley.

Pervin, L.A. (1985). Personality: Current controversies, issues and directions. *Annual Review of Psychology, 36*, 83–114.

Plomin, R. & Rende, R. (1991). Human behavioral genetics. *Annual Review of Psychology, 84*, 782–799.

Ree, M.J. & Earles, J.A. (1992). Intelligence is the best predictor of job performance. *Current Directions in Psychological Science, 1*, 86–89.

Ree, M.J., Earles, J.A. & Teachout, M.S. (1994). Predicting job performance: Not much more than "g". *Journal of Applied Psychology, 79*, 518–524.

Robertson, I.T. & Downs, S. (1989). Work-sample tests of trainability: A meta-analysis. *Journal of Applied Psychology, 74*, 402–410.

Rorer, L.G. & Widigor, T.A. (1983). Personality structure and assessment. *Annual Review of Psychology, 34*, 431–463.

Salgado, J.F. (1997). The five factor model of personality and job performance in the European Community. *Journal of Applied Psychology, 82*, 30–43.

Salovey, P. & Mayer, J. D. (1990). Emotional intelligence. *Imagination, Cognition and Personality, 9*, 185–211.

Saucier, G. & Goldberg, L.R. (1996). The language of personality: Lexical perspectives on the five-factor model. In J.S. Wiggins (Ed.), *The five-factor model of personality: Theoretical perspectives* (pp. 21–50). New York: Guilford.

Shoda, Y., Mischel, W., & Peake, P. (1990). Predicting adolescent cognitive and self-regulatory competencies from preschool delay of gratification. *Developmental Psychology, 26*, 978–986.

Spearman, C. (1927). *The abilities of man*. New York: MacMillan.

Sternberg, R.J. (1977). *Intelligence, information processing, and analogical reasoning: Thecomponential analysis of human abilities*. Hillsdale, NJ: Erlbaum.

Sternberg, R.J. (1985). *Beyond IQ: A triarchic theory of human intelligence*. New York: Cambridge University Press.

Sternberg, R.J. & Wagner, R.K. (1993). The g-ocentric view of intelligence and performance is wrong. *Current Directions in Psychological Science, 2*, 1–5.

Strong, E.K. (1943). *Vocational interests of men and women*. Stanford, CA: Stanford University Press.

Super, D.E. (1973). The Work Values Inventory. In D. Zytowski (Ed.), *Contemporary approaches to interest measurement*. Minneapolis: University of Minnesota Press.

Tellegen, A., Lykken, D.T., Bouchard, T.J., Wilcox, K.J. et al. (1988). Personality similarity in twins reared apart and together. *Journal of Personality & Social Psychology, 54*, 1031–1039.

Tett, R.P., Jackson, D.N. & Rothstein, M. (1991). Personality measures as predictors of job performance: A meta-analytic review. *Personnel Psychology, 44*, 703–742.

Thurstone, L.L. (1938). *Primary mental abilities*. Psychometric Monographs No. 1. Chicago: University of Chicago Press.

Tracey, T.J. & Rounds, J.B. (1993). Evaluating Holland's and Gati's vocational-interest models: A structural meta-analysis. *Psychological Bulletin, 113*, 229–246.

Ulosevich, S.N., Michael, W.B., & Bachelor, P. (1991). Higher-order factors in structure-of-intellect (SOI) aptitude tests hypothesized to portray constructs of military leadership: A re-analysis of an SOI data base. *Educational and Psychological Measurement, 51*, 15–37.

Vandenberg, S.G. & Vogler, G.P. (1985). Genetic determinants of intelligence. In B. Wolman (Ed.) *Handbook of intelligence* (pp. 3–57). New York: Wiley.

Vernon, P.E. (1960). *The structure of human abilities* (rev. edn). London: Methuen.

Wexley, K.N. (1984). Personnel training. *Annual Review of Psychology, 35*, 1984, 519–551.

Young, J &. Persell, R. (2000). On the evolution of misunderstandings about evolutionary psychology. In D. LeCroy and P. Moller, Peter (Eds). *Evolutionary perspectives on human reproductive behavior*. Annals of the New York Academy of Sciences, *907*, 218–223.

PART II

Individual Differences

CHAPTER 5

Old and New Models of Cognitive Abilities: the Assessment Conundrum

Bruce Torff
Hofstra University, and
Edward C. Warburton
New York University

SUMMARY

In this chapter we review old and new cognitive ability theories and suggest that the quest for valid assessment methods has been somewhat problematic. Our argument in brief is as follows. Traditional models of cognitive abilities, favoring a single over-arching "general" factor of intelligence and the tests that measure it, have waned in direct influence in recent decades. Many psychologists and educators have criticized "g" for overemphasizing a small subset of the full range of human abilities and also for relying on questionable "decontextualized" assessment instruments (pencil-and-paper tests) that deny individuals a true opportunity to demonstrate all they know.

More recently, a number of influential "pluralistic" models favoring multiple cognitive abilities have been posited, including Guilford's multifactorial theory, Sternberg's tri-archic theory, and Gardner's theory of multiple intelligences. These pluralistic theories have considerable promise to facilitate, among other things, richly detailed matching of the individual's profile of abilities with the demands of specific scholastic and occu-pational contexts. Such matching would have considerable benefits in school and on the job.

Despite the promise of pluralistic models, they remain difficult to bring to fruition, largely because of the difficulties inherent in assessing complex performances in an authentic, contextualized manner. As a result of these assessment problems, reliance on traditional psychometric models and instruments is likely to persist despite widespread dissatisfaction among psychologists and educators. That does not mean efficacious

Individual Differences and Development in Organisations. Edited by Michael Pearn.
© 2002 John Wiley & Sons, Ltd.

assessment is precluded, however. The chapter concludes with a section describing some fundamental tenets of contextualized multiple-ability assessment.

INTRODUCTION

In schools and occupational settings, a persistent need exists to determine which individual has the right stuff for a particular task (e.g. graduate studies or a more challenging job). Who, for example, to accept to law school or promote to vice president? What sorts of skills are lawyers and vice-presidents required to demonstrate successfully? Inherent in these questions is the need to conduct a valid and reliable evaluation of the individual's intellectual mettle and to analyze what sorts of abilities are needed in a particular domain. Ultimately the goal of cognitive-ability assessment is to match individuals with specific scholastic or occupational contexts so as to allow them to maximize their competencies and work where their skills are best utilized.

Such assessments have been attempted for over a century by a diverse group of psychologists and educators, among others. But it is important to note that any attempt to measure human cognitive abilities perforce grows out of a particular theory of how the mind works and how its workings should be assessed. There is no such thing as theory-neutral assessment. Most contemporary theories are packaged part-and-parcel with an assessment scheme, and each of these schemes assumes the existence of some sort of cognitive ability. Hence, if one wishes to address the assessment needs of schools and organizations, one must dive into the murky realm of cognitive ability theory.

GENERAL INTELLIGENCE AND THE PSYCHOMETRIC TRADITION

Most psychometricians agree that the source of modern intelligence testing stems from Alfred Binet's work on predicting school performance (Jensen, 1998). In 1905, together with his colleague Theodore Simon, Binet developed a test of intelligence that measured things such as vocabulary, comprehension, and verbal relations. Binet's mission was to distinguish children who are genuinely mentally retarded from those who have behavior problems but are otherwise intellectually competent. The result was that tests of intelligence were designed, and continue to be designed, in ways that predict school performance.

The industry of intelligence testing grew substantially during the war years of the early to mid-1900s. In America psychologists were increasingly called upon to screen soldiers for varying levels of responsibility. The research and development of those early intelligence tests form the basis of a series of tests that today are used to measure various kinds of achievements and abilities (Perkins, 1995). Foremost among these standardized assessments are intelligent quotient (IQ) tests. IQ tests use multiple-choice and short-answer questions to measure specific domains of cognition including verbal fluency, mathematical deduction and computation, spatial visualization and memory. All tests of mental ability rank individuals in about the same way, or so the argument goes, and this overlap or intercorrelation suggests that all such tests measure some global element of intellectual ability or "general intelligence" (abbreviated as "g") (Thorndike, 1932; Thurstone, 1938).

Proponents of "g" contend that several decades of military and civilian research have converged to draw a convincing portrait of career potential, training style, and life success along the IQ continuum (Gottfredson, 1997). Individuals in the top 5 percent of the adult IQ distribution (above IQ 125) can essentially train themselves, and few occupations are beyond their reach intellectually. Persons of average IQ (between 90 and 110) are not competitive for most professional and executive-level work but are easily trained for the bulk of jobs in the global economy. This middle group must work hard to keep up with their neighbors. In contrast, adults in the bottom 5 percent of the IQ distribution (below 75) have an uphill battle in school and work; they are very difficult to train and cannot compete for many occupations on the basis of ability.

Criticism of the notion of general intelligence comes from diverse quarters, but especially from contemporary psychologists and educators. A pair of common threads runs through this diverse work. First, there is the argument that tests for general intelligence focus on a narrow slice of the full range of human cognitive abilities. Intelligence tests are limited largely to logical abilities, and yet much of what defines the human species is not logical in any formal sense. For instance, how does one account for the combination of interpersonal skills, intrapersonal (self) knowledge, and creativity that is required to manage a project or "close a deal" in business?

A second critique of general intelligence is a methodological one concerning the traditional psychometric instruments with which "g" is measured. Critics of IQ and Scholastic Aptitude Tests (SAT) argue that these assessments are imperiled by problems of ecological validity—the extent to which individuals' responses in artificial "test" settings correspond to their behavior in the real world (Cole, 1971). Researchers have found that once populations, situations or tasks change so do the results. For example, while IQ positively predicts leadership success under conditions of low stress, in high stress situations the tests negatively predict success (Sternberg, 1998). According to this viewpoint, what little predictive capacity "g" research provides is tainted by questions of ecological validity. Still, even while "g" and the assessment models that accompany it suffer from such critiques, they continue to exert an enormous influence in schools and occupational settings.

Those contemporary psychologists and educators who want to see "g"—and the psychometric instruments spawned by this construct—lose influence point to new models of human cognitive abilities that began to appear in the mid-1900s. Often described as pluralistic, each puts forth a theory of human mental life consisting of a number of separate cognitive abilities (c.f. Anderson, 1992; Gardner, 1983, 1993; Guilford, 1967; Karmiloff-Smith, 1992; Sternberg, 1988; see also Hirshfeld and Gelman, 1994). Three of the most prominent of the pluralistic theories are the focus of the following sections.

GUILFORD'S STRUCTURE OF INTELLECT THEORY

While some have argued against "g" on theoretical and methodological grounds, others like the psychologist J.P. Guilford looked beyond "g" to statistical approaches that suggest a multiplicity of factors involved in intelligence. In the early 1960s Guilford proposed a theory of intelligence that involves over one hundred different components (Guilford, 1967). A psychometrician, Guilford was one of the first to challenge the mathematical technique behind the idea that intelligence is a unitary, one-of-a-kind ability.

The statistical extraction of "g" involves a statistical technique called factor analysis. Factor analysis determines the minimum number of underlying dimensions necessary to explain a pattern of correlation among measurements. Psychometricians interested in intelligence have long recognized that explanations of intelligence shift somewhat in response to particular uses of factor analysis. The technique also allows for dividing people's performance into a number of subfactors. It depends upon how the analysis is set up, and that, according to Guilford, depends upon whether one views intelligence as unitary or as a composite of different contributing abilities.

In the course of developing her *structure of intellect* theory, Guilford ultimately arrived at 150 components through considering five cognitive *operations* that could be applied to any of five kinds of *content* to yield any of six kinds of *products* ($5 \times 5 \times 6 = 150$).

- *Operations:* Cognition, Memory, Evaluation, Convergent Production, and Divergent Production
- *Content:* Behavioral, Visual Figural, Auditory Figural, Symbolic, Semantic
- *Products:* Units, Classes, Relations, Systems, Transformations, Implications

Putting forth a variation on traditional psychometrics, Guilford suggested that each combination had a distinct statistical presence and a psychological reality. So when you try to remember a friend's new telephone number, you have to use a *memory* operation on a *symbolic* representation (i.e., the numeric notation) to produce a single *unit*, your friend's phone number.

The work of Guilford and those who followed her has been criticized from several perspectives. The model proves difficult to implement in educational and occupational settings, and some argue that the sheer volume of cognitive abilities posited is so large that the theory has few practical uses. Others reject the assumption that intelligence is a measurable entity, that the right set of tests will demonstrate that the mind consists of a number of relatively independent *stable* factors. For many, to present intelligence in this reified way—as a concrete, stable, measurable quantity—is something of a scientific anachronism (Feuerstein & Kozulin, 1995). In the end, Guilford's theory has had little impact on assessment practices, despite a period of considerable popularity among psychologists.

STERNBERG'S TRIARCHIC THEORY

Sternberg's "triarchic" theory holds that human abilities are comprised of three separate but related cognitive processes. This first is *analytical* ability, the capacity to render critical judgments. Analytical ability is in evidence when one weighs the factors inherent in choosing the sporty car or the practical one. The second is *creative* ability, the capacity to generate novel responses, which is evinced when coming up with a story to tell the police after being pulled over for speeding in the sporty car. Finally there is *practical* ability, the capacity to adapt to the situation at hand. Practical ability can be seen when one uses one's understanding of the real-world system of justice to pay the fine and be done with it.

Sternberg suggests that individuals pull together these three sets of abilities as needed to accomplish objectives in real-world disciplines and domains. Hence, successful performances result from using these three abilities in a coordinated and domain-specific way. At the same time, Sternberg argues, there is a tendency in many settings to overemphasize analytical ability and underplay creative and practical abilities. Educational benefits follow from a pedagogical regimen that restores balance to the three sets of abilities (Sternberg, Torff & Grigorenko, 1998).

Sternberg's ideas have found a receptive audience in both education and business, but assessment vehicles based on the three types of intelligence have been somewhat more problematic. Like Guilford, Sternberg has relied on the traditional psychometric model. Sternberg devised a set of assessments for each of the three types of intelligence. Sternberg's research ostensibly substantiates the construct validity of the three types (Sternberg, Wagner, Williams, & Horvath, 1995), but the efficacy of the individual assessments has been disputatious. While there has been little argument about Sternberg's subtest for analytical ability, the tests of creative and practical abilities have proven harder to defend. Both tests suffer from complaints of low ecological validity. Moreover, quantitative assessments of creative ability lack reliability in general and thus garner little confidence from psychologists and educators (Gardner, 1993). Sternberg's practical-intelligence assessments have also been criticized as conflated by analytical ability. Sternberg's theory, like Guilford's, has been of limited help to psychologists and educators faced with assessment challenges.

The pluralistic models of human cognitive abilities put forward by Guilford and Sternberg grow out of a strong belief in psychometrics, but an alternative theoretical perspective on human abilities has gained influence in the last two decades—one that relies less on statistical concepts and more on alternative sources of evidence.

GARDNER'S THEORY OF MULTIPLE INTELLIGENCES

All of the theories of cognitive abilities we have discussed heretofore share the conviction that the nature of intelligence can be determined by psychometric testing. More a reaction to than a variation of psychometric theories, Gardner (1983, 1998, 1999) began examining research with groups that evinced distinctive profiles of abilities. These groups included children who displayed precocious performance in a particular area, such as a prodigious ability in visual art, and adults who suffered from strokes that compromised specific capacities while sparing others. These early forays into the nature of intelligence convinced Gardner that human beings are better thought of as possessing a number of relatively independent faculties rather than as having a certain amount of intellectual brainpower.

Gardner defines an intelligence as "a biopsychological potential to process information that can be activated in a cultural setting to solve problems or create products that are of value in a culture" (1999, p. 34). To proceed from a definition of intelligence to a set of human intelligences, Gardner developed criteria for analyzing candidate intelligences. These criteria were drawn from several sources, including psychology, anthropology, and biological sciences.

- **Potential isolation by brain damage**. For example, linguistic abilities can be compromised or spared by strokes.
- **The existence of prodigies and savants**. Case studies of extraordinary individuals permit intelligence to be observed in relative isolation.
- **An identifiable core operation or set of operations**. Musical intelligence, for instance, consists of a person's sensitivity to melody, harmony, rhythm, timbre and musical structure.

- **A distinctive developmental history within an individual, along with a definable nature of expert performance**. The examination of skills of an expert in dance for example, as well as the steps to attaining such expertise.
- **Support from experimental psychology and psychometric findings**. The existence of correlations (or lack of) between certain capacities.
- **Susceptibility to encoding in a symbol system.** The existence of symbol systems that encode certain kinds of meanings, such as language, arithmetic, and maps, capture important components of intelligences.

Based on these criteria and others (see Gardner, 1983), seven abilities were initially included in the theory of "multiple intelligences" (MI). Later, Gardner (1999) added an eighth intelligence. These eight intelligences encompass abilities not previously categorized as "cognitive" abilities:

1. **Linguistic intelligence** describes the ability to perceive or generate spoken or written language. Linguistic intelligence is exemplified by poets, lawyers, and journalists.
2. **Logical/mathematical** intelligence involves using and appreciating numerical, causal, abstract, or logical relations. It figures heavily in mathematics, science, and engineering.
3. **Spatial intelligence** describes the ability to perceive visual or spatial information, to transform and modify this information, and to recreate visual images. Spatial intelligence is used in sculpture, architecture, and navigation.
4. **Musical intelligence** refers to the ability to create, communicate, and understand meanings made out of sound. It can be seen in musicians but also can be discerned outside the musical sphere (e.g. auto mechanics and cardiologists make diagnoses based on careful listening to patterns of sound).
5. **Bodily/kinesthetic intelligence** involves controlling all or part of one's body to solve problems, communicate, or fashion products. It is used, for example, in athletics, dance, surgery, and dramatic performances.
6. **Interpersonal intelligence** involves the capacity to recognize and make distinctions among the feelings, beliefs, and intentions of other people. Interpersonal intelligence enables individuals such as Winston Churchill or Mohatma Gandhi to successfully communicate and work with others.
7. **Intrapersonal intelligence** enables individuals to form a mental model of themselves and to draw on that model to make decisions about viable courses of action. The core operations of intrapersonal intelligence include the capacity to distinguish one's feelings and to anticipate reactions to future courses of action.
8. **Naturalist intelligence** involves the ability to understand and work effectively in the natural world. Naturalist intelligence is exemplified by biologists, zoologists, and naturalists.

Multiple Intelligences (MI) Theory makes several key claims that distinguish it from other pluralistic theories. To begin with, the theory holds that each intelligence is characterized by a set of core information-processing mechanisms dedicated to specific kinds of input. Our biological inheritance ensures that all normal humans possess the potential for successful use of all eight intelligences. At the same time, people are born with differing degrees of promise in these eight areas. We all have different profiles of intelligences. Gardner also suggests that the intelligences are potentials that may or may not be activated, depending upon the opportunities available and values inherent in a specific cultural setting. In this way the intelligences *develop*: they change over time as individuals gain culturally-specific experiences and education. So, not only do we have unique profiles of intelligences but these profiles are also changing constantly.

Gardner also suggests that real world activities are supported by *combinations* of intelligences. A concert pianist activates a number of different intelligences in addition to the musical one, including—at a minimum—linguistic, logical-mathematical, spatial, and bodily/kinesthetic intelligences. As such, Gardner makes the claim the intelligences are integrated, unlike the "encapsulated" abilities posited in other theories.

INTELLIGENCE-FAIR ASSESSMENTS

The theory of multiple intelligences also makes some noteworthy claims concerning the methods used in cognitive-ability assessment. MI calls for "intelligence-fair" assessments that encompass all the individual's cognitive abilities, explicitly avoiding the measurement of an individual's mettle through the "window" of linguistic or logical-mathematical intelligence.

Intelligence-fair assessment has two requirements. First, assessment procedures should be contextualized or "authentic." Individuals must be assessed in situations that closely parallel conditions typical of the domain. For example, the best assessment of a lawyer's ability would focus on the activities that practitioners in this domain actually do (e.g., briefing a case, interacting with clients). Secondly, intelligence-fair assessments are by definition *ongoing*, that is, structured with repeated data collection events as opposed to one-shot-deal psychometric tests. Even if tests could be devised to capture the lawyer's work, Gardner argues, a single test-administration could not capture long-term aspects of the target performance (e.g. degree of motivation, ability to bring difficult projects to fruition). A true assessment can be made only by evaluating the individual over time, using multiple measures.

While Gardner's theory has been profoundly influential among educators around the world, it has also been criticized in a number of ways. One common critique holds that MI is not really a theory because it cannot be proved (or disproved) empirically. This criticism misses the mark. The configuration of intelligences can change (and likely will do so) as new research influences the way in which MI's criteria are interpreted. The number of intelligences, which intelligences are posited, and how the intelligences work are all subject to revision in the light of new findings.

A somewhat more robust criticism of MI concerns the assessment of the intelligences. Gardner's belief in assessing how people carry out valued performances under realistic conditions and his insistence on "intelligence-fair," multi-dimensional measurement has been somewhat problematic for assessment specialists. As noted, Gardner opposes the development of a set of eight MI tests, because the intelligences are thought to operate in combinations and thus cannot be independently assessed in a valid way.

So, if the intelligences can be assessed only in context, then assessment practices must focus on real-world (often termed "authentic") tasks in a domain, which by definition the beginner has yet to learn much less master. How can one assess candidates' worthiness for medical school when they have not yet been taught to be a doctor? Medical-school admissions personnel are left only with assessments of isolated skills that may or may not be predictive of success in medicine. It is an assessment conundrum: it is impossible to evaluate candidates on what they have not learned, yet it is inadvisable to place too much confidence in decontextualized measures. In some cases, there may be no valid way to assess the abilities needed in a particular educational or occupational context.

This conundrum has resulted in a situation wherein MI theory has become well known as a taxonomy of human abilities, but its assessment implications—its potentially most profound statement—are all but ignored. The theory has provided psychologists and educators with a way to think about human abilities, but the corresponding assessment revolution never materialized.

Taking stock, pluralistic theories have opened new vistas on the nature of human cognition. It is worth noting that the movement toward pluralistic theories of intelligence is consistent with trends in related sciences. Neuroscience recognizes the modular nature of the brain; evolutionary psychology is based on the notion that different capacities have evolved in specific environments for specific purposes; and artificial intelligence increasingly embraces expert systems rather than general problem-solving mechanisms. Psychologists who believe in a single IQ or general intelligence are increasingly isolated.

On the other hand, pluralistic models have also caused methodological problems not easily solved. Guilford's and Sternberg's theories revert to traditional psychometric methods with sharply limited results and negligible impact on schools and other organizations. Gardner alone insists that MI is inconsistent with what he calls "psychometrics as usual" (Gardner, personal communication). But his insistence on authentic assessment ultimately makes MI theory every bit as problematic as other pluralistic models.

GENERAL INTELLIGENCE: HIDDEN BUT NOT GONE

Among psychologists and educators, dissatisfaction with the concept of general intelligence is at an all-time high. Few commentators find general intelligence to capture what is important about human cognitive performances. In contrast, pluralistic theories have attracted widespread interest in psychological circles and plenty of support from educators and other practitioners. But none of these theories is dominant and all pose daunting assessment challenges. Pluralistic theories have simply not developed a compelling assessment alternative.

Under these conditions one might not expect pluralistic theories to topple the deeply entrenched traditional psychometric model of assessment. Indeed, the psychometric-testing establishment continues to expand as this chapter is written. These tests have the benefits of being quick, easy, and inexpensive to administer, and at present there is only sporadic debate about their efficacy. Traditional assessment practices will likely persist despite widespread acknowledgement of their limitations. Indeed, psychologists and educators facing assessment decisions have few new tools to work with, despite a marked increase in focus on the multiplicity of cognitive abilities and the need for ecologically valid assessment. General intelligence may then be said to be hidden, but not gone; the theory has few vocal adherents, but its assessment instruments remain in active use and implicit belief in "g" has not waned.

TOWARD CONTEXTUALIZED MULTIPLE-ABILITY ASSESSMENT

In this chapter we have argued that theories of general intelligence look too narrowly at human cognitive abilities. We have presented alternative "pluralistic" views of intelligence, but have found serious difficulties in constructing valid and reliable assessment vehicles based on these theories. However, our purpose here is not to suggest that assessment of intellectual functioning is impossible or inadvisable. On the contrary, cognitive-ability assessment remains a pressing need in schools and other organizations. In this final section, we conclude with a four-point analysis of the fundamental tenets of contextualized multiple-ability assessment.

THE PROBLEM WITH THEORY-DRIVEN ASSESSMENTS

In modern science, many fields benefit from the existence of a paradigm—a widely-held theoretical framework that structures discourse in the domain, at least for a time before a new paradigm displaces it (Kuhn, 1991). Contemporary physics, for example, rests heavily on the standard paradigms growing out of Newton and Einstein.

But such a dominant paradigm in physics has no equal in human ability theory. Various models of human abilities and, more generally, models in human cognition and perception, have waxed and waned in influence at least since Plato's *Meno* over two millennia ago. (Plato was a pluralist, dividing the mind into four parts.) Clearly, single-ability and multiple-ability models have a long and contentious history. And while there have been theories with considerable influence, no theory of human abilities can rightfully be called a paradigm at the present time.

But various assessment schemes have come into widespread use nonetheless, chiefly because they answer pressing evaluative needs and are easy, quick and inexpensive to administer. There exists at present a bewildering array of tests for intelligence, such as the Otis Lennon Scales, and for personality characteristics, such as the Myers-Briggs Type Indicator. But these assessment schemes have been endowed with a confidence that often exceeds those of the test developers. Most tests are accompanied by a warning, often unheeded, that the results of the test should be aggregated with other assessments in the making of evaluative decisions.

In fact, the track record of psychometric assessments leaves much to be desired. In predicting school performance, conventional intelligence tests correlate about 0.4 to 0.6 with school grades, which is a respectable if modest level of correlation. A test that predicts performance with a correlation of 0.5, however, accounts for only about 25 percent of the variation in individual performances, leaving about 75 percent of the variation unexplained. Thus, there has to be much more to school performance than that which tests show.

Moreover, the predictive validity of cognitive-ability tests declines when they are used to forecast outcomes in later life, such as job performance, salary, or even obtaining a job in the first place (Sternberg, 1997). On average, the validity coefficient between cognitive ability tests and measures of job performance is about 0.2 (Wigdor & Garner, 1982). This means that only four percent of the variance in job performance is accounted for by scores on ability tests.

Even after validity coefficients are corrected for a) unreliability in test scores and criterion measures, and b) restriction of range caused by the fact that only high scorers were hired, the average validity coefficient rises only to 0.5 (Hunter & Hunter, 1984; Schmidt & Hunter, 1981). Thus, even with the corrections, only 25 percent of the variance in job performance is accounted for by ability test scores. Put the other way, even the corrected estimates leave unexplained a full three-quarters of the variance in job performance. Sternberg et al. (1995) conclude that "even the most charitable view of the relations between intelligence test scores and real-world performance leads to the conclusion that the majority of the variance in real-world performance is not accounted for by intelligence test scores" (p. 913). Clearly, there is more influencing adult success than the academic skills captured on ability tests.

The dismal performance of cognitive ability in predicting outcomes in school and on the job has prompted educators and occupational professionals to look for alternatives. Gardner's MI theory has been remarkably popular with educators, who have warmed to the optimistic and hopeful outlook on the child that MI fosters. MI seems to endow everyone with something that can be called a strength. The theory has also garnered interest in the business community, where human-resources professionals have looked to MI as a way to conceptualize the abilities needed in occupational contexts.

Recently, however, MI's popularity with educators and other professionals has been waning. MI was embraced by educators but never by psychologists, who questioned the theoretical status of the intelligences, criticized the lack of experimental support for the theory, and generally bristled at MI's bold reconfiguration of human intellect. This lack of respect for the theory, coupled with too few concrete assessment strategies based on MI, has begun to trickle down to professionals in the field. Now even educators and occupational professionals are looking elsewhere for answers to the assessment conundrum. In the science of human abilities, both theory and assessment methodologies remain chaotically pre-paradigmatic.

That does not mean that psychological work has no value, however, as we describe below. Instead, professionals with important assessment decisions to make ought not cast their lot with a particular theory and go with it to the exclusion of all else. Unfortunately, that is exactly what has been done in the past, as part of the influence of MI theory that Gardner did not intend. Some psychometricians have reasoned that if there are eight intelligences, then there ought to be a set of eight tests, one for each intelligence. In this way, a chart quantifying the individual's intelligences could be procured, allowing the evaluation of his/her readiness for various educational programs and occupational challenges.

This flawed approach indicates a lack of understanding of MI theory's fundamental tenets. It fails to consider MI's call for contextualized assessment. An example may help to illustrate the point. Let's say for the sake of argument that chess (a hoary example domain in cognitive science) calls upon four kinds of intelligence: logical, spatial, intrapersonal, and interpersonal. How well would separate tests of these intelligences predict who might be at promise to develop a high level of skill in chess? A battery of subtests will neither capture these intelligences in isolation nor capture important real-world skills in a valid manner. Few chess experts would accept such test results as meaningful, and ultimately they would prove poor predictors of prowess in chess. More likely, the chess experts would call for contextualized assessment, such as having candidates play a few chess matches so that their potential might be predicted.

The point is that it is inadvisable to employ MI or any other model of intelligence as a guide to assessment practice. A single dominant theory does not exist, and even if it did, the direct assessment of cognitive abilities remains a questionable undertaking. Perhaps what's needed is to switch the focus of assessment from the individual to the domain.

A DOMAIN-SPECIFIC APPROACH TO HUMAN ABILITIES

In this chapter we have described several theories that respond to one of the basic questions in the human sciences: what abilities do people have? But these theories fail to provide a sound basis for assessment, leaving educators and occupational professionals without reliable and valid tools for the job.

Perhaps a different question might be helpful: what abilities are required by specific contexts of knowledge use? What does it take to be a good teacher, lawyer, or CEO? Since no ability theory is dominant and all raise measurement problems, it is best to forsake the goal of assessing human cognitive abilities directly and focus instead on the evaluation of performance of authentic activities in a domain. Turning the issue on its head as such means that the unit of analysis will be the context, not the person, at least initially. The goal of this "situated" approach is to develop assessments that fit a particular domain or discipline (Seely Brown, Collins & DuGuid, 1989).

In the next section we describe what such an assessment scheme looks like; here we focus on the implications of the domain-specific view. To begin with, the domain-specific approach begins with a detailed analysis of the domain for the types of cognitive skills it requires. To develop assessments well situated to a particular context, experts in the field must create taxonomies of abilities evinced by successful participants. Consider teacher preparation, for example. It may be difficult to measure all the skills that make a teacher an expert, but there is no shortage of candidate abilities. The expert teacher must, among a great many other things be able to plan instructional units and lessons linked to discipline-based curriculum objectives; foster productive relationships with students, colleagues, and parents; and think reflectively about teaching practice and to generate strategies for improvement.

Teacher educators focus on such things in their classes, because these are the abilities they believe that teachers need. And they are also the abilities one would need to assess if one wanted to be sure that the teachers given professional certificates were qualified to do the job. It is hard to imagine an intelligence test or personality inventory handling such a task, and in practice few teacher educators expect such tests to tell them much. One can easily imagine a wonderful teacher with low scores and an abysmal teacher with high ones, as might be expected given the low predictiveness of cognitive-ability tests. Consequently, many teacher educators proceed not by examining the prospective teachers who sign up, but by strengthening the needed skills and then assessing the results—the same strategy employed by the chess experts discussed above.

A domain-specific approach means the performances assessed will be very complex. It is an easy matter to develop a multiple-choice test to examine, say, mathematical reasoning. It is immensely more difficult to assess something as complex as a teacher's ability to establish and maintain productive relationships with students. It seems clear that no pencil-and-paper, tabletop assessment will suffice for so complex a task. Only interaction in the real world of the classroom can yield useful information. And such an approach is considerably more costly. Assessment done well is both difficult and expensive. Theory-driven, tabletop assessment schemes are inexpensive to administer and score. Sending observers to classrooms to rate teachers' performance requires a nontrivial investment

Finally, and unsurprisingly, it can be difficult to gain consensus in a domain concerning what sorts of abilities to assess. Here again teacher education provides an apt example. Some teacher educators stress the prospective teachers' knowledge base in the domain; others are most concerned with methods of instruction; other put a premium on relationships with students and classroom atmosphere; others make activism for social justice the central issue. It is no easy matter to encourage the advocates for these diverse opinions to agree on a comprehensive assessment scheme. How, then, to evaluate student teachers?

Switching from the individual to the domain as the unit of analysis has the advantage of bringing assessment more closely in line with the domain at hand. On the other hand, the domain-specific approach requires assessment of complex performances—an onerous task—and challenges assessment professionals to agree on what are the precise competencies needed for a specific task.

ASSESSMENT IN CONTEXT

Once the valued skills in a domain are identified, the next step is to devise assessment procedures that capture these skills in the way they will be needed in the real world. If certain skills needed by teachers, for example, are deemed essential, then the next consideration is how to develop procedures for assessment of these real-world skills. The issue is one of *assessment in context*: that is, the extent to which assessment procedures employ the tasks, materials, and settings used in professional practice or pedagogy in a domain or discipline. If teaching requires certain skills, assessment instruments and procedures are needed that capture these skills in a valid and reliable manner.

In professional literatures in a variety of fields, the notion of *assessment in context* has a variety of monikers, including performance assessment, genuine assessment, and authentic assessment, alongside related notions like portfolio assessment. Terms such as "authentic" and "genuine" are often used to describe assessment in context, but these terms are in part problematic. These words imply a fealty to the final products of a domain, often to the exclusion of skills needed along the way and which may not appear in public products. In music, for example, scales are not played on concert stages, and are thus technically inauthentic, but the deliberate practice of scales is an indispensable component of music learning. Our purpose here is to avoid the confusion attendant to words such as "authentic" and instead focus on the common sense underpinning here: assessment must resemble the products and proven pedagogical activities in a domain or discipline. Scales, as part of the musician's training, may not be especially authentic, but they are a valuable part of assessment in context in music. That's why piano "juries"— panels of expert pianists who act as gatekeepers in music schools—typically require pianists to play scales, especially for novice performers. In our view, assessment in context includes both final products (e.g., a Chopin nocturne) and traditional pedagogical activities (e.g., scales, sight singing).

Assessment in context means that assessment *schedules* must change as well. A photograph hints at the action going on; a series of photographs tell more of the story of the scene's action; a movie provides even more information. For assessment to tell the whole story, it must get beyond the one-shot-deal administration of a test. Needed are *ongoing* assessments that allow repeated measures over time, so that the development of the person's knowledge and skill can be charted. Assessment in context not only provides real-world tasks, materials, and settings; it also requires repeated measures (Hatch and Gardner, 1990).

Assessment in context means that the fodder for assessment will be exceptionally rich. But such complex performances are notoriously hard to evaluate. Returning to the piano example, how can reliable and valid evaluation be conducted when the target performance is as complex (and seemingly "subjective") as piano performance?

We have two suggestions to make. First, consider using narrative assessment where possible. Many private schools use narrative evaluation procedures instead of grades, with considerable benefit to students and parents. Similarly, occupational professionals also have a long history of narrative assessment. These assessments may not have always been based on a rigorous domain-specific taxonomy of abilities, as we suggest here, but there is much to recommend qualitative analysis of contextualized data.

Second, it is possible to develop "rubrics" for scoring of complex performances. A rubric is scoring system that allows complex performances to be evaluated quantitatively. A rubric is in essence a 2 X 2 table that includes "dimensions" (the valued skills to be scored) and "indicators" (descriptions of excellent, good, fair and poor performance of each dimension). With four points assigned to maximum performance, three to good, and so on, it is possible to generate a total score. The total score is a quantity that represents the person's overall skill competency with respect to the requirements of the task. Hence, assessment can be contextualized without loss of quantitative analysis of task performance.

The rich information that rubrics yield allows teachers and supervisors to design future learning experiences for maximum benefit to these individuals. Rubrics thus aid in *formative* assessment. And they also support summative assessments every bit as mathematically rigorous as an exit test.

Assessment in context means that individuals have to prove they are more than book smart. It may be difficult and costly, but it delivers a great deal of value to the organization that undertakes it. A detailed assessment of a person's work processes and products provides a far more valid and reliable evaluation of the person's mettle than any theory-driven test.

INTERPRETING THE RESULTS OF DE-CONTEXTUALIZED ASSESSMENTS

There are many cases in which assessment decisions depend on determining who is eligible for a new job or academic program that by definition the applicants can not have previously participated in or know much about. As noted, how can we assess people's readiness for medical school when we have not yet taught them to be doctors? In this case, and in other cases, some form of de-contextualized assessment is needed.

In settings where contextualized assessment is precluded, strategies can be used to improve assessment practices. To begin with, just because a test is de-contextualized does not mean it cannot be designed to capture valued skills particular to the domain. There is much to be said for developing test items that assess individuals in as contextualized a way as possible, across as much of the full range of skills in the domain as possible. A good example of this is the LSAT, the Scholastic Assessment Test for prospective law students. Recent versions of this exam require test takers to evaluate the strength of a particular piece of evidence in relation to given legal action—a reasoning task that closely parallels the kind of thinking needed in law school and in the legal profession. The LSAT may not test all the skills that lawyers need, but it captures some of them, by focusing on real-world requirements in the domain.

De-contextualized assessments can be continuously validated and checked against more fully contextualized measures that are administrated later. Once the prospective lawyers have finished school, their performance as barristers can be assessed in context, and these results can be used to examine the predictiveness of the decontextualized admissions test.

In our view, it is best to interpret the findings of de-contextualized assessments carefully, to avoid placing more confidence in them than is warranted. Being a lawyer is more than the admissions test reveals, and it would be a mistake to admit people to law school or the legal profession strictly on the de-contextualized instrument. Unfortunately, that is exactly what many law schools in the USA do. But we still think it best to heed the warning found on most commercial test packages: test results should be aggregated with other sources of information in the making of assessment decisions.

CONCLUSION

In this chapter we have criticized modern theories of human abilities and their assessment instruments, calling for assessments that are domain specific and contextualized, whenever possible. And when fully contextualized assessment is not possible, a great deal of caution is warranted in the interpretation of test results. Assessment in context, if brought to fruition through intensive research in a domain, has the potential to facilitate more detailed evaluation practices in schools and organizations. At present this promise remains largely unrealized. But for individuals interested in creating pioneering new assessment devices in the discipline in which they work, there is much to recommend assessment in context.

REFERENCES

Anderson. M. (1992) *Intelligence and development. A cognitive theory.* Oxford: Blackwell.

Cole, M. (1971). *The cultural context of learning and thinking.* New York: Basic Books.

Feurerstein, R. and Kozulin, A. (1995). The bell curve: getting the facts straight. *Educational Leadership*, April, 71–74.

Gardner, H. (1983). *Frames of mind: The theory of multiple intelligences.* New York: Basic Books.

Gardner, H. (1993). *Creating minds: An anatomy of creativity as seen through the lives of Freud, Einstein, Picasso, Stravinsky, Eliot, Graham, and Gandhi.* New York: Basic Books.

Gardner, H. (1998). Are there additional intelligences? The case for naturalist, spiritual, and existential intelligences. In J. Cain (Ed.) *Education: Information and transformation.* Englewood Cliffs, NJ: Prentice Hall.

Gardner, H. (1999). *Intelligence reframed.* New York: Basic Books.

Gottfredson, L. (Ed.) (1997). Intelligence and social policy. Special issue of *Intelligence*, January/February, 24, 1.

Guilford, J. (1967). *The nature of human intelligence.* New York: McGraw-Hill.

Hatch, T. and Gardner, H. (1990). If Binet had looked beyond the classroom: The assessment of multiple intelligences. *International Journal of Educational Research*, 415–429.

Hirschfeld, L. & Gelman, S. (1994*). Mapping the mind: Domain-specificity in cognition and culture.* Cambridge: Cambridge University Press.

Hunter, J. & Hunter, R. (1984). Validity and utility of alternative predictors of job performance. *Psychological Bulletin*, 96, 72–98.

Jensen, A.R. (1998). *The G factor: The science of mental ability*. New York: Praeger.

Karmiloff-Smith, A. (1992). *Beyond modularity*. Cambridge: Cambridge University Press.

Kuhn, D. (1991). *The skills of argument*. Cambridge: Cambridge University Press.

Perkins, D. (1995). *Outsmarting IQ*. New York: The Free Press.

Schmidt, F. & Hunter, J. (1981). Employment testing: Old theories and new research findings. *American Psychologist*, 36, 1128–1137.

Seely Brown, J., Collins, A., & Duguid, P. (1989). Situated Cognition and the culture of learning. *Educational Researcher*, 18(1), 32–42.

Spearman, C. (1927). *The abilities of man*. New York: Macmillian.

Sternberg (1988). *Beyond IQ: The triarchic theory of human intelligence*.Cambridge: Cambridge University Press.

Sternberg, R. (1998). Abilities are forms of developing expertise. *Educational Researcher*, 27, 11–20.

Sternberg, R., Torff, B., & Grigorenko, E. (1998). Teaching triarchically improves school achievement. *Journal of Educational Psychology*, 90(3), 374–384.

Sternberg, R., Wagner, R., Williams, W., & Horvath, J. (1995). Testing common sense. *American Psychologist*, 50, 11, 912–927.

Thorndike, E. (1932). *The fundamentals of learning*. Englewood Cliffs, NJ: Merrill/Prentice Hall.

Thurstone, L.L. (1938). *Primary mental abilities*. Chicago: University of Chicago Press.

Wigdor, A. & Garner, W. (Eds) (1982). *Ability testing: Uses, consequences, and controversies*. Washington, D.C.: National Academy Press.

CHAPTER 6

Personality, Style Preference and Individual Development

Adrian Furnham
University College London, London, UK

SUMMARY

This chapter looks at the interface between the concepts and measurement of personality traits and styles (cognitive, learning) and more importantly whether they have
predictive validity in the work place. It is argued that recent thorough meta-analyses
have demonstrated conclusively that traits do predict job performance and two examples (sales and absenteeism) are considered in detail. It is also suggested that the
concept of style is less clear though very popular. Finally the issue of how, when and
why personality traits influence development in organisations is discussed.

INTRODUCTION

Researchers and managers have long noticed and been intrigued by individual differences
at work. Employers differ in their accident and absenteeism rate; their motivation and
productivity; their needs for status and for security (Furnham, 1994). Cook (1998) has
argued that there is abundant evidence that, in terms of measurable productivity, the
best employee is twice as good as the worst. He notes that the ratio between salary and
difference in value between good and average workers is between 40% and 70%. "If
the salary for the job is £30,000 then the difference in value to the organisation between
a good manager and an average manager is somewhere between £12,000 and £21,000,
while the difference between a good manager and a poor manager is twice as great,
£24,000 to £42,000". (p. 2).

It is no wonder then that recruitment, selection and training have been seen to be so
important in business. Curiously however, organisations do not always attempt to assess

Individual Differences and Development in Organisations. Edited by Michael Pearn.
© 2002 John Wiley & Sons, Ltd.

abilities and aptitudes of potential employees (Cook, 1998). Indeed, it is more likely that job interviewees are given personality tests than ability tests. There may be many reasons for this: employers may be worried about litigation following test results, or they may believe personality and other individual differences (i.e. values) are better predictors of productivity and overall motivation than ability.

Thus over the past 30 years there has been a significant growth in the testing industry as HR managers attempt to assess individual differences such as personality, learning style etc. Despite this, the relationship between personality research and organisational psychology has never been close (Hogan, Hogan & Roberts, 1996). Whilst some personality psychologists have allied themselves most often with clinical and social psychologists, applied and organisational psychologists have tended to focus on situational explanations of work-related behaviour. Although both personality and organisational psychologists tended to favour correlational, rather than experimental methodologies, it was the case for most of this century that organisational psychologists stressed external or interpersonal, rather than intrapersonal determinants of the work-related behaviours most often studied like motivation, productivity and satisfaction.

Still many organisational psychologists are ignorant of latest thinking and developments in personality research; while few personality researchers have taken much interest in testing their theories in the work-place. However the interest of organisational psychologists and practitioners in personality and individual difference is to some extent a function of fashion and the number of test publishers currently aggressively marketing their tests. Inevitably laws of supply and demand dictate the number of organisations selling and using individual difference test data used in recruitment, selection, development and training. Fashions in the use of personality questionnaires can however abruptly change as a function of academic reports on their shortcomings (Blinkhorn & Johnson, 1990).

This chapter will consider the literature on the theories behind, uses of, and research into, personality and style preference measures in the workplace. The literature on these two areas has however remained largely distinct. Personality theory has been closely linked to biological and clinical psychology while the literature on cognitive learning and thinking styles has been much more closely associated with educational psychology. Neither has greatly influenced organisational psychology as any inspection of the major journals in the area show. However this situation is changing.

This chapter will deal initially with personality and style preference separately but consider how they are related. Finally the chapter will consider possible implications for individual development in organisations.

PERSONALITY AT WORK

Personality measurement has a long history in psychology. However, during the 1960's personality psychology was attacked repeatedly and very effectively by social psychologists and behaviourists (Mischel, 1968). In his book, Mischel (1968) argued that traits are an illusion and that behaviour is explained more by differences in social situations than differences in stable, internal traits. There was also no consensus regarding what to measure, even if there was some agreement regarding why it should be measured (Roberts & Hogan, 2001). Concurrent with this view, many psychologists thought that personality variables were poor predictors of social and work behaviours. Guion and

Gottier (1965), in what later turned out to be a very influential review, considered the criterion-related validity of personality variables. They concluded that the empirical evidence suggested that personality variables have little or no systematic relationship to the various important criterion variables relevant to organisational psychologists. Similarly Ghiselli and Barthol (1953) concluded that there was very little evidence to support the use of personality measures in personnel selection context. This conclusion was based on the fact that validity coefficients for personality measures were so low (most below 0.30). These factors, in combination, conspired against using personality variables or any other individual difference variables in research or applied settings resulting in their virtual demise in organisational psychology.

In the last ten years, personality measures have been reborn in industrial and organisational psychology and much research has focused on the exploration of personality performance relationship (Barrick & Mount, 1991; Hough, 1992, 1996, 2001). In particular, organisational psychology rediscovered the utility of personality measures in selection contexts. There were three main reasons for this. Firstly, other than an interview (and application form and references) the selection method of choice for organisational psychology was a cognitive test. However, cognitive ability tests almost always result in adverse impact for certain "protected classes" of employees. Meta-analytic evidence suggests that most personality variables have significantly less adverse impact on the protected classes than those of cognitive ability variables do (Hough, 1996). Secondly, research has provided a general agreement on the taxonomy of personality variables, enabling psychologists to organise the literature on personality and job performance (Furnham, 1999). Exploration of personality performance relationships within, rather than across, personality constructs revealed statistically and practically significant relationships where they had not been revealed before (Hough & Schneider, 1996). Thirdly, meta-analytic reviews by Barrick & Mount (1991) and by Tett, Jackson and Rothstein (1991) provided further evidence that personality measures were more valid predictors of work outcomes than generally believed.

The multidimensional conceptualisations of job performance have also been critically important in highlighting the relevance of personality and measurement variables for predicting job performance (Campbell, 1990). It is now evident that personality variables correlate differently with different job performance constructs (Day & Silverman, 1989, Hough, 1992). Another factor that has prompted the rebirth of personality variables in organisational psychology is the fact that more than half of the developed economies are considered service economies. This growth in both the service and sales sector has affected how organisational psychologists define and measure job performance (Hough & Schneider, 1996) and has highlighted the importance of investigating the link between personality and job performance.

It has now been recognised that part of the reason for the decline of personality variables in psychology, particularly organisational psychology, was due to the fact that no well-accepted taxonomy existed for classifying personality traits (Barrick & Mount, 1991). Taxonomies are critically important to the advancement of science as they facilitate the organisation and accumulation of knowledge, hypothesis generation, efficient communication among scientists, and retrieval of information (Digman, 1990). Thus it is recent personality taxonomies that have provided the organising principles that have enabled researchers to establish relationships between personality constructs and job-related criteria (Hough & Schneider, 1996) and has highlighted the importance of investigating the link between personality and job performance.

In general, the taxonomies used are based upon measures of normal and adult personality. The initial purpose in the construction of these was the accurate description of individual differences in personality, therefore providing a broad description of personality that could be used in a whole range of settings (Ones & Viswesvaran, 2000). Examples of inventories relevant to this study are the Five-Factor Model (FFM). However, it has been argued that the taxonomy the organisational psychologists use makes a difference to the outcome of the analysis. Conclusions about the usefulness of personality and the nature of personality-performance relationship depend upon the taxonomy used. Many respected personality psychologists believe that the Five-Factor Model (FFM) is an adequate taxonomy for organisational psychology (Costa & McCrae, 1995; Digman, 1990; Goldberg, 1990). Indeed, the FFM has been shown to be useful as an organising taxonomy for organisational research (Barrick & Mount, 1991). However, some scepticism regarding the adequacy of the FFM has been raised (Block, 1995; Hough, 1992).

DOES PERSONALITY PREDICT JOB PERFORMANCE?

Research clearly suggests that personality variables correlate differently with different job performance constructs (Day & Silverman, 1989; Hough, 2001). Current research on the relation between personality and job performance has involved the integration of personality measures with the FFM. This method was used in various reviews of criterion validity (Barrick & Mount, 1991; Tett et al., 1991).

Barrick & Mount (1991) was a large scale meta-analysis using 117 validity studies and a total sample that ranged from 14,236 people for Openness to Experience to 19,721 for Conscientiousness. Performance measures within these groups were classified into three broad criteria that included: job proficiency, training proficiency and personnel data. They reported that Conscientiousness was consistently found to be a valid predictor for all five occupational groups and for all performance criteria. However, the other four personality factors only generalise their validity for some occupations and some criteria. Extraversion was observed to be a valid predictor (across the criterion types) for two occupations: managers and sales. Emotional Stability was a valid predictor for police; Agreeableness was a valid predictor for the Police and managers while Openness to Experience was found to predict the training proficiency criterion relatively well, as did Emotional Stability and Agreeableness. Similarly, Openness to Experience was found to be a valid predictor of training proficiency, but not for the other two criterion categories, job proficiency or personnel data. In a follow up study Mount & Barrick (1995) found that overall validity of Conscientiousness has been underestimated and that the overall score and both of its dimensions (dependability and achievement), predicted specific performance criteria, better than global criteria (e.g. overall rating of job performance).

Tett et al. (1991) used only confirmatory studies, that is studies based on hypothesis testing or on personality-orientated job analysis. Mean validities derived from confirmatory studies were considerably greater than those derived from exploratory studies. These results generally supported those reported by Barrick & Mount (1991), but are distinctly more positive for the predictive validity of traits. In essence, Tett et al. (1991) found that all personality dimensions were valid predictors of job performance. However, Extraversion and Conscientiousness had lower validity coefficients, whereas Neuroticism, Openness to Experience and Agreeableness had higher validities than had been previously shown.

A third review of the relationship between personality measures and performance criteria was reported by Hough, Eaton, Dunnette, Kamp and McCloy (1990) who investigated the relationship of nine personality dimensions and a range of performance criteria, specific to military settings. Results indicate that Adjustment (Emotional Stability) and Dependability (Conscientiousness) were valid predictors for the two most used performance criteria: training and job proficiency; and that the Big Five are predictors of training criteria. Thus, the findings of Hough et al. (1990) were partly convergent with those of Barrick & Mount (1991) but also provided evidence of some divergence. Further research by Hough (1992) suggest that each of the nine personality constructs correlates with important job and life criteria and that each of the nine constructs has a different pattern of relationships with that criteria. On the basis of Hough's data it has been suggested that Barrick & Mount overemphasised the broad dimensions of Conscientiousness at the expense of other useful personality traits (Furnham, 2001). The fact that other personality variables are not correlated with all occupational categories or criterion types does not necessarily mean that they are unimportant. Different jobs make different demands on employees and may contribute to a pattern of job dependent validity coefficients (Furnham, 2001a).

In a further European contribution to the debate, Salgado (1997) undertook a meta-analytic review differed from previous studies in that it only included studies conducted in the European Community. Salgado (1997) found that the overall validity of personality constructs is small, excepting Emotional Stability (Neuroticism) and Conscientiousness even when effects of measurement error in predictors and criteria and range restrictions have been corrected. In this respect the results show a great similarity to Barrick & Mount (1991) and Hough et al. (1990). Again, concurrent with Barrick & Mount (1991) and Hough et al. (1990), but partially divergent from Tett et al. (1991), Conscientiousness showed the highest estimated true validity which could be generalised for all occupations and criteria. A third finding of Salgado (1997) was that the estimated true validity for Emotional Stability was comparable to that for Conscientiousness. Moreover, as with Conscientiousness, Emotional Stability could be generalised across jobs and criteria. This finding is contrary to Barrick & Mount (1991) but is consistent with Hough et al. (1990). Openness to Experience was found to be a valid predictor for training proficiency, thus consistent with Barrick & Mount (1991) and Hough et al. (1990). Other results support the suggestion that individuals with high scores in Openness to Experience may be those who are most likely to benefit from training programs (Dollinger & Orf, 1991). A positive correlation as found between Extraversion and two occupations in which interpersonal characteristics were likely to be important, confirming Barrick & Mount (1991) and Hough et al. (1990). However, contrary to Barrick & Mount (1991), Extraversion did not seem to be a valid predictor for training proficiency (Salgado, 1997). Finally, the results for Agreeableness suggest that this factor may be relevant to predicting training performance. This is consistent with Barrick & Mount (1991) and Hough et al. (1990).

PERSONALITY, SALES AND ABSENTEEISM

This section will look at two quite different examples of how personality traits have been shown to predict positive (sales) and negative (absenteeism) work-related behaviours. In the past classic studies investigating personality as a predictor of sales performance have generally found inconsistent and inconclusive results and it was suggested that no significant relationship existed (Mattesson, Ivancevich & Smith, 1984). Schmidt, Gooding, Noe & Kirsch (1984) analysed sales validity coefficients and found an uncorrected r of 0.17 for all types of predictors and criteria for sales jobs. They found personality factors to have the lowest validity coefficient of any predictor group. Furnham (2001a) suggested that this under-estimation of the predictive validity of personality in sales performance was due to lack of understanding of the nature of the sales job itself. Another possible reason why research into personality as a predictor of sales performance has failed to find predictive validity, is that investigations have tried to predict performance across different types of sale people, in different types of sales jobs and in different industries, using the same performance criteria and the same set of predictor variables (Furnham, 2001a). Research suggest that personality may be a more useful predictor when performance is broken down into components and specific work-related personality dimensions are targeted (Robertson & Kinder, 1993).

A recent meta-analytic review of predictors of job performance of sales by Vinchur, Schippmann, Switzer and Roth (1998) found more positive results than those noted above. They reported that Extraversion and Conscientiousness predicted sales success in terms of both objective sales volume and managerial ratings. This study confirms previous findings by Barrick & Mount (1991). The sub-dimensions suggested by Hough and co-workers were particularly strong predictors of sales success. It was found that Potency (which includes Assertiveness) appeared to be the key part of Extraversion that predicted sales performance and it was suggested that Achievement was the key part of Conscientiousness that predicted objective sales success (Vinchur et al., 1998). The results from this study indicate that specific personality sub-dimensions are able to more accurately predict specific sales performance criteria than broad personality dimensions (Furnham, 2001a).

In earlier studies Churchill, Ford, Hartley and Walker (1985) examined, by meta-analyses, a range of predictors of different types of sales-person's performance. Their results indicated that aptitude and personal characteristics (i.e. personality) account for only 2% of the work outcome measures, based on self-report, manager and peer-ratings and objective company data. Churchill et al. (1985) postulated that the strength of the relationship between the major determinants and sales performance is affected by the type of products sold, the specific tasks to be performance and the type of customer to be targeted. Furthermore, it has been argued that there are aspects of the sales job that make unique demands on an employee and may contribute to a pattern of validity coefficients different from other jobs (Vinchur et al., 1998). Churchill et al. (1985) suggested that the most prominent of these demands are the degree of autonomy and the degree of rejection experiences by many salespersons. Vinchur et al. (1998) further reasoned that given this level of autonomy, persons in sales must be self-starters, relying on their own initiative and powers of persuasion to see tasks through to completion.

The literature cited has suggested that personality dimensions or patterns of dimensions are predictive of sales success and job performance in general (Vinchur et al., 1998; Barrick & Mount, 1991). It could be suggested that bio-data variables such as gender and age, known to play a role in personality (Costa & McCrae, 1988), can also be used to predict occupational success and failure (Gunter & Furnham, 2001). However, research has found age to be a poor predictor of both productivity and ratings across a wide cross-section of jobs (McEvoy & Cascio, 1989). Hunter & Hunter (1984) reviewed over 500 validity coefficients and found age alone has zero validity as a predictor, whether the criterion is supervisor rating or training grade. Similarly, Vinchur et al. (1998) found evidence to partially support this view. They found age to be a valid predictor of the rating criterion but not actual sales.

The research into gender differences have mainly focused on issues such as occupational values, preferred rewards, occupational interest. The results however, are equivocal. There has been little investigation into the gender differences and sales performance. In terms of personality, it has been suggested that women score more highly than men on Neuroticism and Conscientiousness (Costa & McCrae, 1988). However, from the findings discussed, high scores on Neuroticism (low score HPI Adjustment) do not predict high sales performance (Vinchur et al., 1988) but high scores on conscientiousness do (Barrick & Mount, 1991; Salgado, 1997). Therefore there is conflicting evidence to suggest whether females will, show a higher or lower sales performance compared to men and the debate continues to whether gender differences exist in the workplace.

Personality can also predict absenteeism. A study by Judge, Martocchio & Thoresen (1997) considered the degree to which dimensions of the FFM and personality are related to absence. Their results supported the proposition that absenteeism can successfully be predicted by employee's personalities as described by the FFM. Specifically, Judge et al. (1997) reported Extraversion and Conscientiousness as moderately strong predictors of absence. The carefree, excitement-seeking nature of extraverts and the dutiful, reliable nature of conscientious employees lead the former to be absent more and the latter to be absent less. Previous research by Bernardin (1977) reported the effects of extreme anxiety levels on absence. However, Judge et al. (1997) reported no evidence of such an association. Alloy & Abramson (1979) suggested that neurotic individuals, although impulsive, are more realistic in evaluating contingencies and consequences of their actions. Thus neurotic individuals may be more attuned to the potentially negative consequences of absence. Results by Judge et al. (1997) also suggest the absence history (measured by the previous year's level of absence) partly mediated the relationship between the personality variables and absence.

At the turn of millennium there is a new sense of optimism among personality theorists. There is broad agreement on the fundamental, higher-order, orthogonal superfactors and impressive developments in the construction of measures. Moreover there has been a rapprochement between personality theorists and consistent evidence that personality tests do indeed predict behaviour at work. Organisational psychologists openly recognise that personality factors are important in predicting all facets of behaviours at work including productivity and satisfaction. Personality traits, along with ability factors, no doubt also in part predict individual development . . . or indeed lack of development.

Researchers and recruiters are increasingly aware of the usefulness of measuring personality traits both as select in and select out decisions. But a knowledge of an individuals learning style may also be important to help understand preferences, predilections as well as capacity for development.

THE CONCEPT OF STYLE AND PREFERENCE

The concept of style in psychology can be traced back seventy years (Wulf, 1922). It is probably true that the concept of cognitive style preceded others like learning style. The concept of style is particularly attractive, more so than trait; at least in popular and applied rather than academic circles. Applied psychologists in educational, clinical and work settings have embraced the concept and this has led in turn to a profusion of concepts and measures.

Learning, teaching and personality style, as well as the later styles (attribution, coping) were more broadly based, linking cognition and affect, but tending to be focused on specific areas of social behaviour. Thus we have: Attribution style; Brain style; Cognitive style; Coping style; Learning style; Personality style; Teaching style (Furnham, 2001b).

Messick (1976) listed nineteen cognitive style variables alone. Messick (1994) has argued that human activity displays both substance (content/level or performance) and style (manner/form or performance), though as we shall see is more a distinction between ability and style, than traits and style.

The idea of style is for many people intuitively appealing. Style seems to imply choice, preference and therefore change. One can choose a learning style, adopt a cognitive style and moderate an attributional style. It seems much easier and more natural to change style than personality, let alone ability. Hence style is much more likely to imply development than does traits. It may therefore particularly appeal to optimists or those in the training and development business to use this sort of language. The traditional view of styles is that they are stable (but learnt as opposed to biologically based) dispositions to behave in a certain way (Baron, 1985). According to Baron, this does not mean that individuals always behave in the same way. "Styles, like other traits may be somewhat situation specific" (p. 380). Baron uses the example that although each person has a modal style of walking, people will walk faster when in a hurry or swing their arms more when in a carefree mood. This property of styles is shared by learning styles and cognitive styles. Inherent in the notion of style, whenever it is learning style, cognitive style or walking style is that, despite some variability, individuals tend to exhibit consistent patterns of behaviour across situations and over time. However they can choose to change those styles and learn other forms of behaviour. It is relatively easy to develop another style.

Yet many personality and cognitive theorists and psychometricians have given up on stylistic concepts and measures. The field is therefore fragmented, idiosyncratic and egocentric. There remains confusion about the two major style concepts: cognitive style and learning style. Cognitive styles determine the amount and organisation of information available to the individual at the moment. It mediates the influence of personality tests and motivation and intellectual functioning. However different 'style' researchers have used very different concepts. Thus we have cognitive controls; cognitive attitudes; cognitive system principles; cognitive strategies; intellectual executive functions; and preferences in information processing (Furnham, 2001b).

Cognitive styles have three distinct research origins: Perceptual factors—speed and strength of closure; Ego adaptation—maintaining harmony and equilibrium of feelings/impulses; and Developing cognitive systems—gestaltism. Compared to cognitive styles however, learning styles are both broader and more focused; include cognitive, affective, sociological, and physiological preferences specifically in relation to the learning situation; are stable but innate or learned; and tend to confound ability with style.

Messick (1976) explains that cognitive styles "have their roots in the study of perception and thus have had close ties since their inception with the laboratory and the clinical psychologists . . . have tended to utilise measures derived from laboratory apparatus or clinical tools" (p. 10). It is not surprising, therefore, that cognitive style instruments are generally projective and are assessed in terms of accuracy and correctness of performance. In contrast, most learning style instruments have been designed for easy administration in a classroom context by teachers. They are generally self-report inventories that measure typical or usual ways of behaviour and preferences. The concept of preference is an important one in learning style measurement. While style refers to the processes a learner is likely to use, preference refers to the choices a learner makes. The notion that people choose one learning situation or condition over another is termed learning preference. Thus, learning styles instruments are not measuring the accuracy of correctness of responses but merely gathering information on how a student 'likes', 'tends' or 'prefers' to learn. Learning styles instruments do, in fact, measure preferences.

Learning style is the composite of characteristic cognitive, affective, and physiological factors that serve as relatively stable indicators of how a learner perceived, interacts with, and responds to the learning environment. It is demonstrated by the pattern of behaviour and performance by which an individual approaches educational experiences. Messick (1984) defines cognitive styles as "characteristic self-consistencies" in information processing that develop in congenial ways around the underlying personality trends" (p. 61). According to Messick:

> "They are conceptualised as stable attitudes, preferences, or habitual strategies determining a person's typical modes of perceiving, remembering, thinking, and problem solving. As such, their influence extends to almost all human activities that implicate cognition, including social and interpersonal functioning" (Messick, 1976, p. 5).

It has always been easier to distinguish ability from style, compared to personality and style (Messick, 1976, 1984, 1994; Tiedemann, 1989). Ability questions refer to how much and what; style questions to how. Ability refers to what kind of information is being processed, by what operation, in what form, and how efficiently. Style refers to the manner or mode of cognition. Ability implies maximal performance; style implies typical propensities. Ability is measured in terms of accuracy, correctness, and speed of response, whereas style emphasises the predominant or customary processing model.

Abilities are unipolar; style is bipolar. Ability levels range from none to a great deal, whereas styles usually have two different poles with quite different implications for cognitive functioning. Abilities are value directional; styles are value differentiated. Usually, having more of an ability is considered better than having less, whereas supposed stylistic extreme poles have adaptive value but in different circumstances. Abilities are often domain specific; styles cut across domains. Abilities are often specific to various domains (e.g. verbal, numerical, or spatial areas), whereas styles often serve as high-level heuristics. Abilities are enabling variables because they facilitate task performance; styles are organising and controlling variables. Abilities dictate level of performance, whereas styles contribute to the selection, combination and sequencing of both topic and process.

The difference between traits and styles is, however, much less clear. Studies in the area suggest correlations between established traits (i.e. Extraversion/Neuroticism) and well measured styles (i.e. learning styles) to be in the $r = .20$ to $r = .40$ range (Furnham, 1996). Indeed, most styles are measured and thought about in trait-like terms (Furnham & Steele, 1993). Several researchers have attempted to integrate personality traits and style theory. However, as Messick (1994) notes, these efforts do not fulfil the aspiration of style theorists, who believe styles embrace personality and cognition. It is, of course, a moot point to argue that trait theorists themselves do not take cognisance of cognitive variables.

Furnham (1995) has pointed out a number of unsatisfactory answered problems for the issue of style:

- Aetiology of a cognitive/teaching style. The question arises as to their origin: are they biologically based, the result of early learning, neither, or both? This is a fundamental question that must be answered to avoid tautology. Aetiology determines both how much a style may be changed and therefore developed.
- Variance accounted for. Even if styles exist and determine in part the learning that takes place in social behaviour, few would argue that they are the only—or even the most important—factor that determines learning. The question then needs to be asked whether the amount of variance accounted for by this factor is so small as to be trivial, or, indeed, a major and central feature. Do styles have incremental validity over ability, personality or value measures?
- The nature of style as a variable. If cognitive/learning style is a moderator variable between intelligence, personality and performance the precise nature of this relationship needs to be spelt out. Indeed, it is necessary to list all relevant variables that relate to learning and specify how they interact.
- The process's underlying mechanism. So far, a great deal of the research in this field has been descriptive and taxonomic, aimed at identifying various styles and their consequences. Less work has gone into describing the mechanism or process whereby the style operates.

He concludes:

> "A pessimist might argue that despite fifty years of research into cognitive/learning style, we still know precious little if the above questions have not been answered or even attempted. An optimist, though, might be impressed by the research effort that has gone into this topic, by the proliferation of ideas, and by the evidence already accumulated. Nevertheless, pessimists sound more profound that optimists, and hence most recent reviewers in the field tend to be highly critical of developments in this area"(p. 411).

Messick (1994) likewise notes:

> "The literature of cognitive and learning styles is peppered with unstable and inconsistent findings, whereas style theory seems either value in glossing over inconsistencies or confused in stressing differentiated features selectively" (p. 131).

Sternberg & Grigorenko (1997) remain strong, articulate defenders of the style concept. They argue that thinking style is a subset of cognitive style, which itself is a subset of style (a distinctive/characteristic method/manner of acting/performing). They provide three explanations for why psychologists should be interested in cognitive styles, none of which have anything to do with predictive validity or parsimonious explanations. The first is that style bridges the concept of cognition and personality, though they overlook the extensive work on relationship between cognitive processing and personality traits (especially Neuroticism) (Furnham & Cheng, 1996). Next, cognitive style added to measures of ability improve the predictability of school behaviour, yet very little evidence is brought to bear supporting this assertion. Third, cognitive styles help explain occupational choice and performance. Yet again, any reviewer of this literature may be equally impressed by the poor predictive power of cognitive styles in the work place (Furnham, 2001b).

They then set out the five criteria for the evaluation of theories of style:

1. Theoretical specification: the positing of a reasonably complete, well-specified, and internally consistent theory of styles that make connection with extant psychological theory.
2. Internal validity: a demonstration by factor analysis or some other method of internal-analysis that the underlying structure of the item or subset day is as predicted by the theory.
3. Convergent external validity: a demonstration that the measures of styles correlate with other measures with which, in theory, they should correlate.
4. Discriminant external validity: a demonstration that the measures of styles do not correlate with other measures with which, in theory, they should not correlate.
5. Heuristic generativity: the extent to which the theory has spawned, and continues to spawn, psychological research and ideally, practical application" (p. 703).

They argue:

> "We believe that styles have a great deal of promise for the future. First, they have provided and continue to provide a much-needed interface between research on cognition and personality. Second, unlike some psychological constructs, they have lent themselves to operationalisation and direct empirical tests. Third, they show promise for helping psychologists understand some of the variation in school and job performance that cannot be accounted for by individual differences in abilities. For example they predict school performance significantly and add to the prediction provided by ability tests. Finally, they can truly tell something about environments as well as individuals' interactions with these environments, as shown by the fact that correlations of styles with performance that are significantly positive in one environment ate significantly negative in another environment" (p. 710).

Suffice it to say that the concept of style in psychological theory and measurement remains problematic. Indeed, it could be argued that because style affects many forms of social behaviour—particularly in applied settings like work and leisure—certain behaviours in the testing situation may themselves be indices of style. That is, how people complete tests, be they behavioural or self-report, may be a good individual difference measure, be it trait or style.

PERSONALITY, STYLE AND LEARNING

To illustrate this literature the educational psychology literature on teaching/learning style will be briefly reviewed. There is a small experimental literature on the relationship between personality and teaching style. Over 25 years ago Shadbolt (1970) measured pupils' personality and exposed them to a structured-deductive or unstructured-inductive teaching method. Based on post-test assessments, there was an interactive effect of extraversion and teaching style/strategy in the first study and an interaction between Neuroticism and strategy in the second study. In the first study introverts performed better with a structured approach, and in the second neurotics performed better with a structured approach. Rowell and Renner (1975) found scores on the Eysenck Personality Inventory were unrelated to a preference for written essay work vs. formal examinations and also unrelated to performance. Extraverts outperformed introverts in only one course, educational sociology, and the authors surmised that this may have been the result of a lower degree of class structure in that course.

There also is an extensive experimental literature on the relationship between learning, memory and personality that would suggest a coherent and consistent relationship between personality and preferred learning style (Campbell & Hawley, 1982). Eysenck (1978) noted that except in primary school, Neuroticism works against scholastic achievement while extraverts compared to introverts seemed "handicapped" as far as secondary school and university education are concerned. "This seems obvious on common-sense grounds; the high N scorer worries about his work, suffers from examination anxiety, and lets his 'nerves' interfere with his studies. The extravert socialises, instead of concentrating on his work, seeks non-academic outlets (sport, sex) for his energies, and has difficulty in concentrating (extraverts score poorly on tests of vigilance in the laboratory)" (pp. 141–143).

Eysenck (1981) summarised the findings thus:

> "In spite of the relatively small volume of research on the effects on introversion-extraversion on learning and memory, there appear to be a number of fairly robust findings. Some of the more important of these have been discussed earlier and will now be listed:

- Reward enhances the performance of extraverts more than introverts, whereas punishment impairs the performance of introverts more than extraverts.
- Introverts are more susceptible than extraverts to distraction.
- Introverts are more affected than extraverts by response competition.
- Introverts take longer than extraverts to retrieve information from long-term or permanent storage, especially non-dominant information.
- Introverts have higher response criteria than extraverts.
- Extraverts show better retention-test performance than introverts at short intervals, but the opposite happens at long retention intervals.

While it is probably premature to attempt any theoretical integration of these various findings, it is nevertheless tempting to argue that introverts are characteristically better motivated on performance tasks the extraverts, with the consequences that their normal expenditure of effort and utilisation of working memory capacity is closer to the maximum. Since introverts, as it were, start from a high motivational baseline, it follows that they are less able than extraverts to utilise extra processing resources to handle increasing processing demands (e.g. from distracting stimulation, from response competition or from difficult retrieval tasks)" (pp. 203–204).

There is also a small but interesting an important literature on the interaction between personality and teaching method. For instance Leith (1974) demonstrated that extraverts learn much better than introverts with the discovery method of learning, while introverts learn much better than extraverts with the direct (reception) method. Earlier Leith (1972) found personality interacts with test conditions to predict learning. Other studies on task conditions and pair learning confirm the importance of personality variables (Trown & Leith, 1975).

Eysenck (1978) has listed six practical applications for personality variables to learning situation: selection (advice based on personality traits as to fit); streaming and setting (streaming pupils/students by personality or setting the different tasks); re-education (intervention in learning difficulties based on the understanding of traits); ascertainment (monitoring of personality development over time to anticipate problems); training (the education of teachers in differential psychology); and research which takes seriously the role of individual differences.

PERSONALITY, STYLE AND DEVELOPMENT IN ORGANISATIONS

Both individuals and organisations change over time; possibly the latter more often and radically than the former. However, most organisations have to manage change, to grow and to develop. This means that any "fit" between an individual and the job he/she is in, is able to change. Furnham (2001a) has argued that four dynamic forces come into play.

People choose their job and working environments. Personal occupational choice is a matter of a number of things like pay, location, job security, training, etc. It is also a function of personality traits, attitudes and values. This choice is always a matter of balancing various factors that may be implicit or explicit. The organisation also makes a choice in the selection process and may well have a number of quite specific criteria like size (minimum height) fitness (not wearing spectacles) skills (literacy, numeracy) or demography (sex, age, education). These criteria might change radically so that one selection cohort may differ radically from another. Further employees' values, and needs may change making them agree eager for different things and very responsive to develop- ment opportunities. Equally they may deeply resent an organisation breaking its implicit contract and try to change them, which is a protracted and painful experience.

People adapt to the job they are in. They adapt aspects of their working style to the requisites of the job often quite soon after they start a job. Most organisations attempt through primary socialisation (induction, mentoring, training) to mould individual be- haviour into the then currently acceptable pattern of work behaviour. They try to adapt workers to the job they are in by specifying the time of day they are required to work, the pace of work, responsiveness to colleagues and customers. Some adaptations are relatively easy; others very difficult because they represent a style of work that maybe fairly incompatible with traits. Thus if extraverts trade off accuracy for speed to increase arousal and introverts the precise opposite it may be very difficult to an extrovert to adapt to say the requirements of a proof-reader while introverts may have great difficulty being an auctioneer. People change various aspects of the job. They change their physical social environment and personalise many aspects of their working lives.

People arrange their personal working space given identical offices or equipment. These changes may be to facilitate better or different working styles or maybe little more than an impression management exercise. The less technical, team-based or computerised the work the more scope people have to change the job to suit their needs, traits and values. Workers can negotiate or earn or unilaterally change the way in which they do the job that may or may not affect their outputs and that of their colleagues. Jobs themselves evolve with new technology, markets and global requirements. Many aspects of a job may change while a person is still in it. Increased automation, the different needs of clients, a change in the market may mean the job have to change.

People have to learn new skills; new ways of behaving and unlearn some deeply ingrained habits. Organisations may choose very different ways to develop their staff. They may use in-home trainers or hire them from outside the organisation. They may opt for experimental learning, or classroom learning. They may prefer short, distributed courses (every Monday for two months) or massed courses of longer periods (a week long course). They may "sheep-dip" all staff on similar programmes or offer very different programmes for those on different levels or in different specialities. They may really "believe in " training and development which is reflected in their budgets or else hope for miracles on a shoe-string budget.

Both trainers and trainees report wide variations in attitudes towards, behaviour at, and learning from organisational development and learning programmes. Some people are antagonistic towards training and development trying best to avoid it; others seem almost addicted. Some learn quickly; others do not. For some the teaching style fits perfectly with their preference; for others the opposite is true.

CONCLUSION

It is certainly obvious that personality traits, cognitive and learning styles are fundamentally implicated in the whole business of development in organisations. There are systematic individual differences which in part predict every aspect of behaviour at work: Choice of occupation; productivity and satisfaction; absenteeism and accidents; turnover and training; decision making and development. The style vs. trait researchers tend to agree on some things more than others. The former are more clinical, educational and counselling oriented and unlike the latter tend to be more aligned to biological and clinical psychology. Whilst there are differences within each camp it is probably true to say they share an interest in, and commitment to individual differences. But they differ most on the origin and causes of those differences that inevitably impact on how to change them. Development is about change, whether it is an attempt to encourage a natural process or alter it in some way. It is perhaps fair to say that style researchers are more interested in, committed to, and optimistic about change and development than trait researchers. But the renowned interest of organisational psychologists in trait measurement may mean all this is changing fast. It is indeed an exacting time for those interested in the topic of individual development in organisations.

Organisations tend to both select and train to achieve a particular end. They may have in mind a very clear profile of the ideal employee that they attempt to 'clone'. If they are correct in the sense that the abilities, traits and styles do predict the desired work related behaviours *and* the world remains stable this may be a good strategy. The problem with work-force homogeneity is that it trades off internal climate for adaptability. That is people in groups with similar abilities, personalities and values "get along" easily. But because they see things in the same way they may all equally have difficulty in adapting to new conditions.

Another very fundamental question concerns whether it is morally justifiable, sensible, even possible for an organisation to attempt to change an employee's personality or work style. Some organisations take a sceptical, even cynical, approach to change and development arguing that change is too difficult and expensive even to contemplate. They cite the extensive therapy industry (from alternative medicine to psychoanalysis) that attempts to change people many (or at least some) of whom really do want to change but who fail. Sceptics argue that through contingencies of reward and punishment one can change employees' behaviours in the work place and even their beliefs and values over time but that is all. The dim can never be made intelligent, the extraverted can never become introverted.

Sceptics also argue that it is morally wrong to change people. Today we are horrified to read how Victorians tied the arm of left-handers behind them when they were learning to write to force/encourage them to become right-handed: that is dextrous not sinister. Is this any different going on in workshops, training courses and other events to encourage people to change their natural style of work? Presumably organisations would not dream of physiological or pharmacological methods to change behaviour: why then do they accept or even encourage educational methods to do so. Sceptics argue for selection rather than training and development.

Developmental enthusiasts on the other hand believe it beneficial for both the employee and the organisation that attempts are made to increase the 'fit' in values, goals and approaches between the two. They believe this is time and money well-spent as it increases both satisfaction and ultimately profits. They see development as more proactive than therapy and more wide ranging than training. They see it as a necessity.

It is probably the case that developmental sceptics would side with those trait theorists who see personality as pretty fixed while the developmental enthusiasts side with the style theorists who feel styles are relatively easy to adopt and adapt. They have different ideas, read different literatures and can, over time, be dismissive of one another. Thus just as the trait and style academic research grew apart so practitioners for-and-against development tend more to ignore each other than argue or research the case for their different positions.

REFERENCES

Alloy, L.B., & Abramson, L.Y. (1979). Judgement of contingency in depressed and non-depressed students: Sadder but wiser? *Journal of Experimental Psychology: General*, **108**, 441–485.

Baron, J. (1985). What kinds of intelligence components are fundamental? In J.W. Segal, S.F. Chipman, & R. Glaser (Eds.), *Thinking and Learning Skills*, Vol. 2: Research and open questions (Chapter 16). London: Lawrence Erlbaum Associates.

Barrick, M.R., & Mount, M.K. (1991). The Big-five personality dimensions and job performance: A meta-analysis. *Personnel Psychology*, **44**, 1–26.

Bernardin, H.J. (1977). The relationship of personality variables to organisational withdrawal. *Personnel Psychology*, **30**, 17–27.

Blinkhorn, S., & Johnson, C. (1990). The insignificance of personality testing. *Nature*, **348**, 671–672.

Block, J. (1995). A contrarian view of the five-factor approach to personality description, *Psychological Bulletin*, **61**, 159–179.

Campbell, J.B., & Hawley, C.W. (1982). Study habits and Eysenck's theory of extraversion-introversion. *Journal of Research in Personality*, **16**, 139–146.

Campbell, J.P. (1990). Modelling the performance prediction problem in industrial and organisational psychology. In M.D. Dunnette & L.M. Hough (Eds.), *Handbook of industrial and organisational psychology* (2nd edn, Vol. 1, pp. 687–732. Palo Alto, CA: Consulting Psychologists Press.

Churchill, G.A., Ford, N.M., Hartley, S.W., & Walter, O.C. (1985). The determinants of sales person performance: A meta-analysis. *Journal of Marketing Research*, **22**, 103–118.

Cook, M. (1998). *Personnel Selection*. Chichester: John Wiley.

Cooper, R., & Payne, R. (1967). Extraversion and some aspects of work behaviours. *Personnel Psychology*, **20**, 45–47.

Costa, P.T. Jr., & McCrae, R.R. (1988). From catalogue to classification: Murray's needs and the five-factor model. *Journal of Personality & Social Psychology*, **55**, 258–265.

Costa, P.T., & McCrae, P.R. (1995). Solid ground in the wetlands of personality: A reply to Block. *Psychological Bulletin*, **117**, 216–220.

Day, D.V., & Silverman, S.B. (1989). Personality and job performance: Evidence of incremental validity. *Personnel Psychology*, **42**, 25–36.

Digman, J. (1990). Personality structure: Emergence of the five-factor model. *Annual Review of Psychology*, **41**, 417–440.

Dollinger, S.J., & Orf, L.A. (1991). Personality and performance in 'personality': Conscientiousness and openness. *Journal of Research in Personality*, **25**, 276–284.

Eysenck, H. (1978). The development of personality and it's relation to learning. In S. Murray-Smith (Ed.). *Melbourne studies in education*. Melbourne: Melbourne University Press, pp. 134–181.

Eysenck, M. (1981). Learning, memory and personality. In H. Eysenck (Ed.). *A model of personality*. Berlin: Springer-Verlag.

Furnham, A. (1995). The relationship of personality and intelligence to cognitive learning styles and achievement. In O. Saklofske & M. Zeidner (Eds.). *International handbook of personality and intelligence*. New York: Plenum, pp. 397–413.

Furnham, A. (1996). The FIRO-B, the learning Style questionnaire, and the five-factor model. *Journal of Social Behaviour and Personality*, **11**, 285–299.

Furnham, A. (1992). Personality and learning style: A study of three instruments. *Personality and Individual Differences*, **13**, 429–430.

Furnham, A. (1994). *Personality at work*. London: Routledge.

Furnham, A. (1999). *The psychology of behaviour at work*. Hove: Psychology Press.

Furnham, A. (2001a). Personality and Individual Differences in the Workplace. In B. Roberts and R. Hogan (Eds.). *Personality psychology in the workplace*. New York: APA, pp. 223–252.

Furnham, A. (2001b). Test taking style, personality traits and psychometric validity. In J. Collis & S. Messick (Eds.). *Intelligence and Personality*. NJ: LEA.

Furnham, A., & Steele, H. (1993). Measuring locus of control. *British Journal of Psychology*, **84**, 443–479.

Furnham, A., & Cheng, H. (1996). Psychiatric symptomology on the recall of positive and negative personality information. *Behaviour Research and Therapy*, **34**, 731–733.

Ghiselli, E.E., & Barthol, R.P. (1953). The validity of personality inventories in the selection of employees. *Journal of Applied Psychology*, **37**, 18–20.

Goldberg, L.R. (1990). An alternative "description of personality": The Big-Five factor structure. *Journal of Personality and Social Psychology*, **59**, 1216–1229.

Goldberg, L.R. (1993). The structure of phenotypic personality traits. *American Psychologist*, **48**, 26–34.

Guion, R.M., & Gottier, R.F. (1965). Validity of personality measures in personnel selection. *Personnel Psychology*, **18**, 135–164.

Guildford, J. (1980). Cognitive styles: what are they? *Educational and Psychological Measurement*, **40**, 715–730.

Gunter, B., & Furnham, A. (2001). *Assessing Business Potential: A Biodata Approach*. London: Whurr.

Hogan, R., Hogan, J., & Roberst, B. (1996). Personality measurement and employment decisions. *American Psychologist*, **51**, 469–477.

Hogan, J., Rybicki, S., Motowildo, S., & Berman, W. (1998). Relations between contextual performance, personality, and occupational advancement. *Human Performance*, **11**, 189–207.

Hough, L.M. (1992). The 'Big-Five' personality variable construct confusion: Description versus prediction. *Human Performance*, **5**, 139–155.

Hough, L.M. (1996). Personality at work: Issues and evidence. In M.D. Hakel (Ed.), *Beyond multiple choice: Evaluating alternatives to traditional testing for selection*. Hillsadle, NJ: Erlbaum.

Hough, L.M. (2001). I.Owes Its Advances to Personality. To appear in B.W. Roberts & R. Hogan (Eds.), *Applied Personality Psychology: The Intersection of Personality and I/O Psychology.* Washington, D.C.: American Psychological Association, pp. 19–44.

Hough, L.M., Eaton, N.L., Dunnette, M.D., Kamp, J.D., & McCloy, R.A. (1990). Criterion-related validities of personality constructs and the effect of response distortion on those validites (Monograph). *Journal of Applied Psychology*, **75**, 581–595.

Hough, L.M., & Schneider, R.J. (1996). Personality Trait, taxonomies, and applications in organisations. In K.R. Murphy (Ed.), *Individual Differences and Behaviour in Organisations* (pp. 31–88). San Francisco: Jossey-Bass.

Hunter, J.E., & Hunter, R.F. (1984). Validity and utility of alternative predictors of job performance. *Psychological Bulletin*, **96**, 72–98.

Leith, G. (1972). The relationship between intelligence personality and creativity under two conditions of stress. *British Journal of Educational Psychology*, **42**, 240–247.

Leith, G. (1974). Individual differences in learning: interactions of personality and teaching methods. In Personality and Academic Progress: Conference Proceedings (pp. 14–15). London: Association of Educational Psychologists.

Mattesson, M.T., Ivancevich, J.M., & Smith, S.V. (1984). Relation to Type A behaviour to performance and satisfaction among sales personnel. *Journal of Vocational Behaviour*, **25**, 201–214.

McEvoy, G.M., & Cascio, W.F. (1989). Cumulative evidence of the relationship between employee age and job performance. *Journal of Applied Psychology*, **74**, 11–17.

Messick, S. (Ed.) (1976). *Individuality and learning.* San Francisco: Jossey-Bass.

Messick, S. (1984). The nature of cognitive styles: Problems and promise in educational practice. *Educational Psychologist*, **19**, 59–74.

Messick, S. (1994). The matter of style: Manifestations of personality in cognition, learning and teaching. *Educational Psychologist*, **29**, 121–136.

Mischel, W. (1968). *Personality and assessment.* New York: Wiley.

Mount, M., & Barrick, M. (1995). The big five personality dimensions. *Research in Personnel and Human Resources Management*, **13**, 153–200.

Ones, D.S., & Viswesvaran, C. (2000). Personality at work: Criterion-focused occupational personality scales (COPS) used in personnel selection. In B.W. Roberts & R. Hogan (Eds.), *Applied Personality Psychology: The intersection of Personality and I/O Psychology.* Washington, D.C.: American Psychological Association.

Ones, D.S., Viswesvaran, C., & Schmidt, F.L. (1993). Comprehensive meta-analysis of integrity test validities. *Journal of Applied Psychology Monograph*, **78**, 679–703.

Judge, T.A., Martocchio, J.J., & Thoresen, C.J. (1997). Fve-factor model of personality and employee absence. *Journal of Applied Psychology*, **82**, 745–755.

Petrides, K., & Furnham, A. (2000). *On the dimensional structure of emotional intelligence. personality and individual differences.* In Press.

Roberts, B., & Hogan, R. (Eds.) (2001). *Personality psychology in the workplace.* Washington: APA.

Robertson, I., & A. Kinder (1993). Personality and job competency. *Journal of Occupational and Organisational Psychology*, **66**, 225–44.

Rowell, J., & Renner, V. (1975). Personality, mode of assessment and student achievement. *British Journal of Educational Psychology*, **45**, 323–338.

Salgado, J. (1998). Big five personality dimensions and job performance in army and civil occupations: A European Perspective. *Human Performance*, **11**, 271–288.

Schmidt, N., Gooding, R.Z., Noe, R.A., & Kirsch, M. (1984). Meta-analysis of validity studies published between 1964 and 1982 and the investigation of study characteristics. *Personnel Psychology*, **37**, 407–422.

Shadbolt, D. (1970). Interactive relationships between measured personality and teaching strategy variables. *British Journal of Educational Psychology*, **48**, 227–231.

Sternberg, R., & Grigorenko, E. (1997). Are cognitive styles still in style? *American Psychologist*, **52**, 700–712.

Tett, R.P., Jackson, D.N., & Rothstein, M. (1991). Personality Measures as predictors of job performance: A meta-analytic review. *Personnel Psychology*, **44**, 703–742.

Tiedemann, J. (1989). Measures of cognitive styles: A critical review. *Educational Psychologists*, **24**, 261–275.

Trown, E., & Leith, G. (1975). Decision rules for teaching strategies in primary schools. *British Journal of Educational Psychology*, **45**, 130–140.

Vinchur, A.J., Schippmann, J.S., Switzer, F.S., & Roth, P.L. (1998). A meta-analytic review of predictors of job performance for sales people. *Journal of Applied Psychology*, **83**, 586–597.

Wulf, F. (1992). Transformation of images-memory and Gestalt. *Psychologische Forschung*, **1**, 33–37.

CHAPTER 7

To Use Competencies or Not to Use Competencies? That Is the Question

Paul Sparrow
Manchester Business School, UK

SUMMARY

In this chapter I begin by providing a series of frameworks that may be used to help position the approach taken to management competency both within organisational practice and academic research. A range of dispositional characteristics that can be considered at the individual level are outlined. I also summarise three main approaches that have been taken in the study of management effectiveness: analysis of classical management functions, observation of behaviour and the study of intelligent functioning. Finally, three different models of competency are introduced, namely the technical/functional specification of management competence, the analysis of behavioural competencies that may be input to the organisation, and the consideration of strategic skills necessary to achieve outcomes associated with longer term sources of competitive advantage.

The best known model—the behavioural competency approach—is then analysed and positioned within these frameworks. I then outline the reasons why this approach became attractive in the wider context of human resource management. The perceived benefits of using competencies and subsequent areas of criticism are discussed by reviewing recent benchmarking survey data and assessment of practice. It is argued that the HR process benefits of the application of competencies to external resourcing and individual development and internal career systems generally outweigh any dysfunctions that might exist. The pressures that led to competencies being used more extensively within organisations and pushed in particular into rewards systems are outlined.

Individual Differences and Development in Organisations. Edited by Michael Pearn.
© 2002 John Wiley & Sons, Ltd.

Some attention is given to the more difficult questions that have arisen from the wide application of competency-based HR strategies. Are they valid? How are they made more organisationally relevant? Does this make it easy to identify which competencies are best selected for and which may be developed? Are they fair? Having noted some of the issues that arise from this questioning, I examine the decisions that are invoked when competencies are applied in the realm of pay and rewards. Some of the questions that this move invokes, such as which competencies are more important than others, are actually very important issues to consider from a developmental perspective. Finally, I form some linkage with the previous chapters by noting some of the more telling individual differences to which attention has been turned recently, and argue that we should only view individual behavioural competency in the context of the much larger quest for strategic competency organisations.

INTRODUCTION: THE EARLY ARGUMENTS FOR THE USE OF COMPETENCIES

In order to develop the arguments that have been used in support of a competency-based approach to management, I shall briefly recap in historical sequence the main debates within the field. The first reason why the competency approach began to take centre stage was that it was a technology whose time had come. It provided an apparently ready set of answers to the questions being asked in the academic and practitioner management literature of the time (Sparrow and Boam, 1992). The centrality of some definition of competency to human resource management—whatever the construct of competency was to become—can be traced back to the beginnings of the US human resource management (HRM) movement.

It is useful to remind ourselves of the different perspectives that have been taken on the issue of dispositions which are important for the successful execution of management tasks. Psychologists tend to focus on three dispositional characteristics (Campbell, Dunnette, Lawler and Weick, 1970):

- Abilities (viewed as potentialities inherent and developed in a person)
- Values, interests and motivation (stable individual preferences which influence choice and perseverance at a task)
- Personality traits (stable attributes which distinguish individual character)

Within the abilities domain, a distinction was made between skills (which tended to be derived in the context of specific-routine tasks, in task-driven environments, and were often therefore seen as non-generalisable) and a softer set of skills which with hindsight became seen as competencies (which were considered to be generalisable indicators of resourcefulness that could be derived from non-routine discretionary tasks in people-driven environments) (Kanungo and Misra, 1992). By the late 1970s there was general disappointment with the poor predictive validity for managerial performance that was found through the use of demographic indicators, experience, skills, aptitude and personality tests, interviews and assessment centres. Three different research strategies into the problem of better capturing the nature of managerial effectiveness can be discerned (Kanungo and Misra, 1992):

Classical management function approach: Driven by the theoretical argument by people such as Fayol (1949) and Urwick (1952) the view was taken that classicial management functions such as planning, organizing, co-ordinating, directing and con-trolling required generic technical, problem solving, decision-making and people-handling skills. An article by Shenhar (1990) reminds us that even early models of executive management skills made the distinction between technical, human (interpersonal) and conceptual skills (see for example Katz, 1955, later re-articulated in Katz, 1974) that was later supported by empirical studies (Boyatzis, 1982; Carroll and Gillen, 1987).

Observation of what managers actually do: Studies identified clusters of overt activity and roles and then established lists of the skills required to do this work. A common denominator was the view that critical management behaviours relate to the need to plan and co-ordinate resources. In order to achieve the classical management functions outlined above, managers engage in covert mental activity and overt behaviours (Carroll and Gilenn, 1987). The work of Stewart (1967) demonstrated the importance of time spent interacting. Mintzberg (1973) grouped ten roles under interpersonal, informational, negotiating and decision-making domains. Landmark studies from the US such as Boyatzis's (1982) study on the nature of managerial competence and Kotter's (1982) longitudinal analysis of general managers tended to concentrate on the overt behavioural agenda (using overt behaviours as a proxy for covert mental functioning). They demonstrated that a great deal of effective managerial behaviour was situation-specific and had to be developed over time. It directed attention towards people skills such as networking ability, but recognised that problem solving in the context of complex and constantly changing environments was an invisible process that underpinned the people skills.

The role of intelligence and intelligent functioning in managerial jobs: Boyatzis (1982) drew attention to the cognitive and intellectual processes involved in executing managerial work agendas, but it was people such as McClelland (McClelland, 1973; Klemp and McClelland, 1986) who drew attention to the nature of intelligent functioning in coping with external and internal demands, with particular emphasis being given to planning and causal thinking, diagnostic information seeking and conceptualisation/synthetic thinking. These competencies, as revealed through behavioural event investigation techniques, were felt to lie at the root of both the directive influence styles of supervisors and the more symbolic influence/leadership strategies of senior managers. The investigation of multiple intelligences and emotional intelligence falls into this category.

Closely associated with the intelligent functioning perspective has been work on competence as revealed through expert judgement and decision making and cognitive skills (Shanteau, 1992). He argued that work on competence within experts demonstrated that competence depended on five components: a sufficient knowledge of the domain, psychological traits associated with the designation of 'expert' status, the cognitive skills necessary to make tough decisions, the ability to use appropriate decision strategies, and a task with suitable characteristics on which to apply competence.

However, work on the intelligent functioning of experts presented a conflicting picture from a competency perspective. Judgement and decision research generally showed that even experts made flawed decisions, largely through the biasing effect of reliance on judgemental heuristics and susceptibility to cognitive illusions (Kahneman, 1991). Their decisions lack validity, reliability and coherence, reflect surprisingly low information use, and lack complexity (Shanteau, 1989). In contrast, cognitive science studies have tended to view experts as competent and different to novices on nearly every aspect of cognitive functioning. Expertise is

- domain specific (Anderson, 1990);
- acquired through stages of mental development that progress through cognitive memorisation, associative connection and strengthening, and autonomous rapid practice of skill (Fitts and Polson, 1967);
- based on different thinking strategies (accessed usually through verbal protocols) that lead to more efficient approaches to thinking, problem solving and decision making (Slater, 1987); and
- based on automated processes that operate in the same way as visual perception and pattern recognition (Shiffrin and Schneider, 1977).

Cognitive scientists then view experts as being skilled within their domains, competent, and capable of thinking in qualitatively different ways than novices (Chi, Glaser and Farr, 1988). They operate using quasi-rational thought, which cognitive continuum theory proposes (Brunswick, 1956; Hammond, Hamm, Grassia and Pearson, 1987) sits at the mid point between analytical (explicit, sequential and recoverable transformation of information according to certain rules) and intuitive (implicit, non-sequential and non-recoverable) thinking. In an analysis of work on organisational learning, knowledge management, top team cognition, and a range of individual differences variables, including locus of control, need for achievement, flexibility, cognitive style, insight and intuition, creativity and intelligence, Hodgkinson and Sparrow (2002) have summarised the evidence behind a dual processing competence in which both modes of processing are fruitfully combined.

In reality '. . . experts are neither as deficient as suggested by the decision making literature nor as unique as implied by the cognitive science perspective' (Shanteau, 1992, p. 256). Nor, of course, should it be assumed that managers have to be experts (although there are cross-cultural differences in the required intellectualisation of the managerial task, see for example, Whitley 1989).

WHAT IS A BEHAVIOURAL COMPETENCY?

So then, what is a behavioural competency and how does the approach claim to access and synthesise the above perspectives on managerial effectiveness? It seems somewhat strange to write a chapter having to define the nature of management competency from a behavioural perspective at a juncture in time when the movement has probably reached the end of its centrality to the management discourse. (See the comments of Sparrow and Marchington (1998) on the dominating impact of contract over competence, and Hodgkinson and Sparrow (2002) on the changing nature of strategic competence within organisations). However, at this juncture, we must revisit the original debate that developed throughout the 1990s. Sparrow (1997) delineated three contexts or models of competence that emerged throughout this decade:

1. management competence (often called the technical/functional approach),
2. behavioural competency (sometimes also called the soft skills approach), and
3. organisational competency (or strategic core competence).

The first model used a task-centred approach via functional analyses of job roles and responsibilities (cf. the classical management function approach noted in the Introduction) to analyse expectations of workplace performance. This is usually in the form of entry or threshold standards that could act as common denominators of management competence. Management educationalists and trainers influenced this perspective and used it to specify occupational standards of performance or expectations of workplace performance. In the UK this formed the initial core of developments in the Management Charter Initiative (MCI) and National Vocational Qualifications (NVQs).

Boyatzis (1982) is credited with the advancement of the second model—the behavioural competency approach. This was a more person-centred approach intended to identify excellent behaviours. He studied 2,000 managers holding 41 different jobs in 12 (mainly Anglo-Saxon) organisations. He distinguished between 'threshold' management competencies which usually means the minimally acceptable level of work and 'superior' management competencies, defined as the level achieved by one person out of ten. Central to the competency approach is the proposition that a skill can only be identified when there is reference to a specific behavioural component (the behavioural component may be either covert or overt). Identification of these behavioural competencies—whether against such an explicit performance criterion or a less well defined one—relies on one or more of a range of job analysis techniques. These include such techniques as repertory grids, critical incidents, structured skills questionnaires, observations, diaries, and behavioural event interviews. They are used to gather data from a neutral or blind stance by tapping into the employee's constructs of 'effective' performance without specifying what sort of criteria the organisation believes are most appropriate. Alternatively, they are used with a values-driven stance (specifying performance criteria that the organisational culture or strategy suggest are most appropriate).

It is the relevance (causal link to performance) of the behaviours identified and the quality and consistency of the rules applied to govern the way in which they are expressed that makes the competency approach so potentially powerful. A characteristic is not a competency unless it predicts something meaningful in the real world, i.e. predicts behaviour and performance. It must be '... causally related to criterion-referenced effective and/or superior performance in a job or situation' (Spencer and Spencer, 1993, p. 9). Boyatzis (1982) therefore views competencies as an underlying characteristic of a person that results in effective and/or superior performance in a job. By using a post-hoc labelling process, competencies draw upon a variety of individual dispositions and fields of knowledge:

- **Fields or bodies of knowledge:** i.e. what the employee needs to know in order to achieve the goals that the job specifies—insights into information in specific content areas.
- **Skills:** i.e. what the employee has to possess in order to do the job—the ability to perform a physical or mental task and demonstrate a sequence of behaviour that is functionally related to a performance goal and can be applied to a range of situations.
- **Attitudes and values:** i.e. what the employee needs to display in connection with achieving tasks—attitudes and values that predict behaviour in the short or long term.
- **Traits:** i.e. characteristic or quality of a person that is associated with effectiveness—physical characteristics and consistent responses to situations or information.
- **Motives:** i.e. drive or thought that is related to a particular goal—the things a person consistently thinks about or wants that cause a desired action or goal.

- **Self-image:** i.e. the understanding an individual has of themselves in the context of values held by others.
- **Social roles:** i.e. the perception of social norms and behaviours that are acceptable and the behaviours that a person needs to adopt in order to fit in.

This breadth of 'source evidence' does appear to capture many of the views on management effectiveness noted in the previous section. I would argue that it is immediately clear that competencies are an *inferred construct* rather than an *actual dispositional characteristic*, despite the official definitions. They use the elicitation of a series of effective overt individual behaviours—behaviours that cross several levels of the psychological structure of human beings—to capture all three levels of individual disposition specified by Campbell et al. (1970).

Behavioural competencies are a context-specific specification of effective individual behaviours (the context specificity is set by the performance criteria built into the behavioural event investigation techniques). This specification of behaviours is then operationalised in terms of what people actually do—as opposed to what they say they do (Sparrow, 1997). Competencies are viewed as behavioural repertoires (sets of behaviour patterns) that some people can display more effectively than others, and that enable them to develop (subsequently or in parallel) particular fields of knowledge (i.e. the aspects of the job that a person must perform effectively). A behavioural competency therefore includes all those behaviours that individuals input into a broad organisational context (ranging from success in an individual job, a role or career stream, or within the organisation as a whole given its structure and strategic purpose) in order to perform well. They involve an implicit performance criterion (excellence) and are expressed in terms of performance outputs—i.e. what is achieved and produced from a situation by managing it effectively.

The third context that drew upon the language of competency delineated by Sparrow (1997) and began to emerge more towards the latter half of the 1990s was the organisational or strategic core competency model. Here practitioners were interested in the resource and capabilities of the organisation that were linked to business performance. As the attention of strategists turned to longer-term sources of competitive advantage, the importance of the intangible assets of the organisation and the strategic management skills that engendered this began to grow. Management competency was viewed through the lens of the organisational and business processes that led to superior records of innovation and organisational learning. This approach focused on the outcomes required of the managerial role (such as thought leadership, vision, customer focus, and innovation), with the assumption that there was some reflection of these outcomes in the behaviours that managers should input into their role.

COMPETENCY LINKED TO HUMAN RESOURCE MANAGEMENT SYSTEMS

Organisational practice has of course muddied the distinction between the three perspectives, with competency-based systems operating using different elements of managerial competence, behavioural competency and organisational competency thinking at different levels of the hierarchy and at different points of time. This chapter is concerned primarily with an evaluation of the second approach—the behavioural competency approach—as it became adapted and applied through competency-based approaches to human resource management (HRM).

A few years after the early 1980s re-conceptualisation of management effectiveness that resulted from the work of people such as Boyatzis and Kotter, HRM academics articulated what became known as the Harvard model of HRM (Beer, Spector, Lawrence, Mills and Walton, 1985). This called for two processes of integration within HR policies and practices. The first involves vertical integration in which the policies were *aligned with the business strategy*. The second involves horizontal integration in which a sense of *coherence* (a planned logic or a purposeful stream of HR activities and programmes) and *consistency* (mutual behavioural reinforcement across policies) was created across the various HR systems. The latter typically include resource acquisition and development, rewards and performance management, works design and systems, and employee relations.

Strategic HRM was later to be defined as comprising all those activities affecting the behaviour of individuals in their efforts to formulate and implement the strategic needs of the business (Schuler, 1992). Competency-based HRM as first articulated was never seen as a panacea for all HR ills within the organisation. Sparrow and Boam (1992) pointed out that it was just one—albeit an important one—of six typical responses (the others being concerned with issues such as structural change, cultural change, and human resource planning).

Nonetheless, the focus on the need to foster behavioural change in many organisations had by this time become self-evident. Research within organisations had shown that many of the change programmes that they had pursued had been helpful in creating *representational learning*—the use of new words, language and mental schema—but had been much less successful in creating *behavioural learning*—actual changes in skilled performance (Beer, Eisenstat and Spector, 1990). There was increasing consensus in the UK too that effective management behaviour comprised of growth in interpersonal and intellectual skills, in business and corporate knowledge, and the creation of relevant networks and relationships (Sisson and Storey, 1988; Storey, 1990). Development needs within organisations were seen as being diverse, highly dependent on the context, and in need of being located within organisational policies and procedures. The relative success of a more strategic approach to human resource management was also being demonstrated. Competencies—through their articulation of a model of individual and organisational effectiveness and their focus on behaviours—were easily associated with the sorts of outcomes desired by organisations at the time. Moreover, the behavioural focus enabled the design and development of a plethora of tools, techniques and frameworks that could be mobilised to bring about the desired coherence and consistency, ranging from application forms, situational interviews, assessment centre exercises, appraisal behavioural checklists, to career development workshops.

A second reason why competencies became so important was that they suited the *'realpolitik'* that was taking place within HRM practice. Jobs-based HR systems—in which the focus of attention was the need to fit the person to the job, which in turn required a clear system of sizing jobs, comparing their skills difficulty and worth in the pay market—were falling into disrepute. Technological and structural pressures had essentially reduced the 'half life' of many technical and functional skills (the period in which the skill still had some potency before its influence began to wane) and with this, the relevance of the relative job worth enshrined in the job evaluation systems. The evolving set of tasks and activities that were being built into people's roles could no longer be compared accurately—or priced—in the labour market. Roles were becoming a much more individualised affair, and the competencies that people developed within them more highly dependent on the HR policies and practices of the employing organisation.

The experience of working for some organisations truly provided the employee with a sense of added-value, stretch in competency-development, and employability in the labour market. In other organisations, people with the same job title were developed to far less demanding levels. Moreover, a decade of process re-engineering had altered the 'pecking order' of many surviving jobs (for they were still called that) and organisations were finding themselves surprisingly dependent on the competency of the job holder in certain areas, even though the value of these jobs was not formally recognised in the job evaluation system (Sparrow, 1998). Therefore, the argument went, jobs no longer had easily assessable value, but perhaps the people did. To the extent that organisations could assess potential, and the 'external transfer value' of the individual in terms of their skill, qualification, experience and productivity, and then factor in an assessment of the internal value that they added (in terms of their contribution to the business strategy), then people-based HR systems made more sense. In the mid-1990s the American Compensation Association argued that organisations pay for what they value, and to the extent that they were becoming more committed to using competencies as the basis for managing performance, then they would need to reflect those competencies in the way that they paid employees.

I use the challenge of linking or basing pay on the demonstration of competency later in this chapter to tease out some of the principles that should be used to decide whether to use competencies or not. However, first I summarise the position based on evidence of application of the competency approach and critical analysis of some of the weaknesses with the technology.

PERCEIVED BENEFITS AND CRITICISMS OF COMPETENCIES: EVIDENCE FROM RESEARCH AND PRACTICE

APPLICATION OF COMPETENCIES: BENCHMARKING EVIDENCE

Sparrow and Boam (1992) noted that there was an evolution in the way in which competencies were applied to organisations as part of a human resource strategy. The early applications were in the field of individual career development and recruitment and selection. Here the benefits that could be achieved seemed to outweigh any dysfunctions that the use of competencies might create, and usage was relatively 'safe'. Changing the profiles against which you recruit or promote can be threatening, but core staff do not feel immediately challenged. Having achieved relative success in these two areas, the potential of competencies to articulate business and cultural change initiatives also became evident. Again, their usage was generally seen as being constructive in that they helped articulate complex change processes and were generally adopted in conjunction with other changes in HRM systems (Sparrow and Bognanno, 1993). It was argued at that time that the next step—and the most significant challenges—would come from

TABLE 7.1 Employers use of competencies and associated effectiveness

HRM application	% of firms using competencies in this area	% of firms feeling most effective use of competencies
Training and development	87	21
Appraisal/performance management	82	25
Personal development/career planning	82	17
Recruitment and selection	77	22
Job/role design	51	3
Change management/culture change	39	5
Grading/job evaluation	33	2
Team building/working	31	2
Succession planning	26	1
Pay/bonuses	24	3
Other	2	0

Source: After Rankin, N. (2001) Benchmarking survey of the 8th Competency Survey: Raising Performance Through People. *Competency and Emotional Intelligence 2000/2001 Benchmarking Report.* London: IRS Eclipse Group Ltd.

moving the use of competencies into performance management and reward. I return to this challenge in the next section.

The picture painted at the beginning of the 1990s is still reflected in recent evidence from practice based on a survey of 156 employers in the UK in October 2000, ten in-depth examples of practice and 64 named competency sets (Rankin, 2001). The bench-marking exercise estimated that 3.2 million employees in the UK alone are covered by competency frameworks. Of those using competencies, 89% used the behavioural or soft skill approach and 35% used the technical/functional approach with externally specified competencies. 48% of employers used more than one type of competency for different employee groups. Table 7.1 summarises the main application areas for competencies in terms of the percentage of organisations using them for each application (left hand column) and the percentage of organisations that feel that each application area benefits from the application of competencies to it (a measure of impact). The right hand column is based on a total sum of 100%, with organisations electing which one of all the applications is the most effective. Therefore the rank order of perceived effectiveness is more telling than the actual percentage figure.

Based on a review of practice, Sparrow (1997) summarised the perceived potential benefits of using a behavioural competency approach for external recruitment and selection, internal resourcing, performance management, and business/culture change applications (see Table 7.2). The rest of this chapter of course concentrates on the more problematic issues associated with the use of competencies, but it is important to note that for many organisations the benefits noted in Table 7.2 are sufficient to justify using competencies. It is also important to note that many of the criticisms levelled at the use of competencies could equally well be levelled at any alternative approach—if not more so. Moreover, it does not appear as if there is any obvious alternative. Rankin (2001, p. 2) notes that 'no other fresh approach to the management of people has emerged in the past decade that has succeeded in embedding itself so firmly in mainstream personnel management practice ... other innovative contemporaries of competencies, such as business-process re-engineering, have failed to consolidate their initial presence'.

TABLE 7.2   The HRM content and process benefits associated with well-designed competency approaches

---

HRM content benefits

Recruitment and selection
- Visible and agreed set of standards to systematic assessment
- More rigorous job analysis process to defend against equal opportunities legislation
- Reduces variable practice by individual selectors and assessment on irrelevant person characteristics
- More sophisticated and flexible targeting of applicants e.g. women returners, untried labour pools, freedom from previous norms
- Conveying of relevant information to assist self-selection in adverts or assessment centre exercise design
- Enhancement of application form design to focus on more important aspects of previous experience
- More informed initial screening and sifting decisions based on targeted questionnaires
- Informed choices about the types of assessment tools best used in the selection procedure to ensure adequate coverage of competencies
- Provision of information for situational interviews to assess potential

Career development
- Promotes career restructuring by identifying real 'career bridges' or 'break-points' as opposed to the status quo ie. results in more cross-functional movement and technical to professional moves
- Informs decisions about the underlying number of vertical hierarchies in the structure
- Standards set for progression based on behavioural sets and not the individual
- Career decisions made on the basis of future potential not just current competency
- Facilitates succession planning
- Strengths and weaknesses provide a referent for planned development

Performance management
- Provides a guideline for decisions about grading in job evaluation
- Provides a framework under which objectives for the appraisal system may be developed and set
- Broadens appraisal systems to consider 'how well it is done' measures as well as the more traditional 'what is achieved' measures
- Facilitates the development of behaviourally-anchored rating scales or language ladders for more accurate performance management assessment
- Concentrates the appraisal interview discussion on performance and effectiveness
- Provides a language for feedback on sensitive and emotive issues

HRM Process benefits
- Involvement of line managers in the identification process and design of assessment tools results in higher ownership of the results
- Forces a link between the strategic direction and recruitment criteria
- Identification process creates a shared understanding of the types of people needed in the organisation
- More informed decisions about the most appropriate resourcing decision ie. buy, make or design out the competencies
- Provides a language for self-development and self-assessment and a basis for coaching and training
- Generates useful information to help build successful teams
- Represents a tool for developing the business culture, forcing clearer articulation of the strategy, or consideration of how new structures or business processes may actually work

---

Source: Sparrow, P.R. (1997) Organisational competencies: creating a strategic behavioural framework for selection and assessment. In N. Anderson and P. Herriot (Eds.) *International handbook of selection and assessment.* Chichester: John Wiley. Reproduced with permission from John Wiley.

Problems, Issues and Critical Evaluation

There are clear HR process benefits that can result from the use of competencies and there is also as yet little consensus on any valid alternative. Yet, we should not ignore the more difficult questions that traditionally have to be considered in pursuing a competency-based HRM strategy. A major problem—and a rather critical one for HR managers—is what to do about an assessment of an individual against a competency framework. What if they score poorly? Is any given competency more selectable (a deep stable and enduring source of individual difference) or developable (individuals are capable of learning and enriching their competence)?

Closely linked with this question is the 'time to competence' issue. Competencies have been used as part of a human resource strategy. Clearly, pragmatic decisions about whether the best solution is to select against competencies or develop towards competencies will be based on soft judgements about the time it takes to build a specific competency within others. I have always had a problem with the language of competency with regard to this question. The spirit behind the movement has been a positive one that stresses human development. Yet, even the initial language sounded as if competencies are fairly well set: '. . . a fairly *deep* and *enduring* part of a persons' *personality* [that] can predict behaviour in a fairly wide variety of situations and tasks (Spencer and Spencer, 1993, p. 9). This was never intended to be the case.

Original competency theory viewed competencies as being of different 'types'. The same authors used an iceberg and onion model (see Figure 7.1) to address the select or develop question, with there being a core of enduring and hard to develop competencies bases on traits and motives, with successive layers of competencies based on self-concept and attitudes and values (more difficult to develop, but possible over lengths of time) and finally competencies based on skills or knowledge that were more 'visible', lying

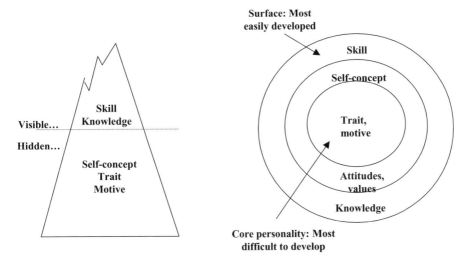

Figure 7.1 Central and surface competencies
Source: Spencer, L.M. and Spencer, S.M. (1993) *Competence at work: Models for superior performance*. London: Wiley Reproduced with permission from John Wiley.

at the surface of the onion. This is neat thinking from a psychological perspective, but sadly bears little or no relationship to the competency labels, or actual collection of behavioural indicators, that have been used by most organisations.

As has been made clear throughout this chapter, there is poor conceptual clarity in the field. There are at least three ways in which the language of competency is used and organisations tend to use combinations of these (really quite different) constructs. The question of validity then for competency profiles has always been a very difficult one to address. There have been a handful of evaluations of the competency-sets used by organisations (see for example the work of Cockerill and Schroder). This then leads us onto the validity issue. The validity of the competency approach lies in its use of 'criterion samples' i.e. people who have clearly had success in their jobs. It also lies in the use of BEI (Behavioural Event Investigation) techniques that are presumed to identify only those behaviours that are causally related to a successful outcome (as we have seen, competencies have to include a 'causal intent' that generates action towards the desired outcome). However, the ways in which competencies were put into practice soon saw them being operationalised in ways that makes validation nigh impossible.

From an HR process perspective, the labels used to make the long lists of behavioural indicators identified through a competency identification process more palatable are actually of less importance than the indicators themselves (Sparrow and Bognanno, 1993). The labels served to cluster indicators into organisationally meaningful constructs, rather than into traditionally assessable psychological constructs (although in the early years the conceptual, and interpersonal clusters were evident in competency specification, usually in conjunction with a set of competencies associated with getting things done or specific leadership styles). The labelling process was a post hoc activity, merely a tool for reducing potentially hundreds of effective behaviours into simpler labels and a short hand to convey the essence of effective behaviour. It was based traditionally on three options:

1. mathematical clustering in which behaviours rated on a series of dimensions are grouped on the basis of a factor analysis or similar technique and competency labels attributed to describe and make sense of the grouped behaviours
2. interpretation by trained psychologists, grouping behaviours along traditional grounds (frequently distinguishing between analytical, interpersonal and results achievement attributes)
3. allocation of behaviours to labels that have some other purpose or meaning within the organisation (for example, to support statements of culture or mission).

The latter perspective began to dominate the competency specifications as the approach was applied in more strategic areas of HRM. Herein lies both the strength of the process, and its Achilles Heel. Culturally-derived or organisation strategy-relevant clusters of behaviour are clearly not easily assessable by psychologists. Any one competency contains behavioural indicators that may be sourced from surface level or much deeper dispositions.

Another oft-cited danger of using competencies based on behavioural event investigation of an existing set of effective job holders is that it runs the risk of building a picture of past effectiveness, which can be problematic in settings where the consensus is that the rules of the past may no longer apply (Sparrow and Boam, 1992). From a pragmatic perspective, organisations often introduce competencies because they perceive that they have a gap in capability. The need to introduce a competency therefore often comes at a time when an organisation has limited internal understanding of what the competency looks like (or there are very few—and somewhat atypical in other ways–job holders who currently evidence the competency).

Identifying an appropriate set of competencies is often a values-driven and educational process in itself. Organisations tend to handle this issue in one of three ways. First, they attempt to build in competencies that are assumed to lead to a learning orientation—recognising attributes such as conceptual flexibility, creativity and balanced learning habits—in the profile whether they were evidenced through BEI identification or not. The assumption is 'if we cannot specify what future roles will look like (and we cannot) then let's resource people who are generally flexible and open to learning and trust that they will be the best equipped to handle an uncertain future'.

The second approach is to drill down a more targeted and socio-cultural view of intelligent functioning within organisations. This is where the organisation will shape certain competencies to pick up very specialised styles of thinking—talking about attributes such as future forecasting, fluid intelligence, or the ability to spot major fracture lines or discontinuities.

The third approach is to manage the total portfolio of competencies within the HR system in a more planned way. Sparrow and Boam (1992) argued that competencies could be plotted on two axes (centrality to the business strategy, and time from today through to five years forward) thereby distinguishing competencies that could be classified as emerging, maturing, played a transitional role, or remaining of stable/core relevance over time. This requires continual adaptation of competency sets, and differential management across the various HR systems. You might wish to recruit for competencies that are deemed to be emerging in importance in the future, but it would be unfair to pay people purely on the evidence of these when current systems dictate the display of other competencies.

ARE COMPETENCIES FAIR?

Finally, the question can be asked, are competencies fair? Competencies, like any other management technique, have the potential for unfair discrimination, especially in terms of equal opportunities. On the one hand, it is argued that they can reduce discrimination through transparency, consistency and objectivity in areas such as recruitment, training and promotion (Rankin, 2001). On the other hand, they can have an in-built tendency to reinforce discrimination (Kandola, 1995; Strebler, Thompson and Heron, 1997). Rankin (2001) draws attention to two dangers. Where the only means of identifying competencies relies on research among existing employees then the competency sets identified will reflect the current composition of the workforce, and thereby over-emphasise the attitudes, culture and behaviours of white males. Although without the use of competencies covert biases will still exist, and the competencies can make such bias more visible, charges of *gender cloning* can still apply. Gender roles can be built into the competency set at identification stage. Leadership competencies in particular can be influenced by a macho-rhetoric that over emphasises transactional and transformational styles. The second danger is through the use of *poorly trained assessors* whose unskilled judgements can bring even the best competency framework into disrepute.

I would draw attention to a third potential source of bias, which forces us to consider the ways in which judgements are made on the basis of competencies. This is based on the possibility first that competencies have a different currency—some competencies help people feel that you are doing a good job whilst others serve to get you promoted. Second, men and women show different leniencies when assessing themselves and the other gender through 360 degree. The evidence here tends to be sparse and tentative, based on practitioner report and study (Sparrow, 1998). However, the data-set analysed in a study by Robertson et al. (2000) examined assessments of competencies made by supervisors with separate assessments that they made about their subordinates' current level of performance and promotability. Different competencies correlated with the two outcomes. High ratings on the competencies of being flexible, articulate, co-ordinating, innovative, persuasive and decisive were significantly correlated with assessments of promotability. Being expert, strategic, analytical, organised and quality-driven did not make supervisors view you as being more promotable, but they thought that you were a better performer!

Consider this in relation to a study by the Peachell Group (People Management, 1997) that looked at how men and women rated themselves and the other gender differently on 360 degree feedback schemes. Men gave women higher ratings on planning, organising (performance), listening skills, interpersonal sensitivity and quality (performance) competencies. Women gave men higher scores on analytical problem-solving, creative (promotion) and constructive thought, customer service, decision-making (promotion) and judgement competencies. There were no areas where women rated women higher than men. There were fewer differences in self-rating, but women were more severe on themselves. Men saw themselves better in terms of: being more resilient to stress, better at goal orientation, influencing people and assertiveness, whilst women scored themselves better on people development, quality, self-development and team-working competencies. The danger is clear. Men over-rate women's possession of the competencies that will get you judged to be doing a good job currently. Women may over-rate men's possession of the competencies that will get you promoted.

THE END GAME: COMPETENCY-LINKED PAY, COMPETENCY-BASED PAY AND HUMAN RESOURCE STRATEGY

The previous section has discussed some of the more critical charges levelled against competencies—even if the original concept has some integrity—the nature of operationalisation within organisations has been loose. The more the approach has been successful the more pressure there has been for systems to be implemented in ways that make the language of competency more organisationally-relevant, but at the same time psychologically unassessable. The more important it has become to ensure that competency-based HR systems use constructs and labels that are organisationally-relevant, the more future-orientated and selective becomes the range of competencies built into the system. The more selective the choice of competencies, the more they focus on desired outcomes, rather than requisite inputs, as envisaged by the original writers in the area. This criticism is not meant to imply that organisations are wrong to have gone down this path. Far from it, but it does mean that we should be a little more honest in our claims.

So, let us finally consider the issue that has come to dominate competency-based HRM on the last few years. Should we pay for competencies and what is the impact of doing so on development thinking? The question of reward has to be considered even in a Handbook on individual development simply because the possession of, or capability to demonstrate a competency, is only the first part of the equation. Individuals also have to be motivated to *display* their potential (see the distinction between in the discussion of individual predispositions). As they do not always do so, competency capabilities have to be reinforced. Linking, or even totally basing, the display of competency to rewards is an obvious reinforcement tool. The political difficulties—and complex underlying human resource management questions and philosophies—that are triggered once what began as a developmental behavioural technology is applied to the thorny problem of reward and compensation become evident once we examine the multitude of approaches that have been adopted in the quest of this goal. It has also split opinion amongst commentators on the competency movement. Notable cautioners, i.e. people who argue that whilst technically possible the risks may often outweigh the potential benefits, have included Lawler (1996), Sparrow (1996) and Boyatzis (1998). Proponents of forging greater linkage include Brown and Armstrong (1997).

Sparrow (1996) argued that it is possible to match situations when using competencies makes sense or not across the different HR applications. In terms of rewards there are indeed some situations when paying for competency can make sense. These include situations when:

- departmental or individual performance is seen to require the acquisition of new skills or training
- a department's reputation is very dependent on the level of professional and competent behaviour by staff (being the right sort of person),
- the overall performance of a department can be made or destroyed by one or two extremely competent or incompetent staff.
- it is relatively easy to determine the skills (which may be converted into competency language) needed to deliver each key result area,
- a small set of focused core skills are clearly involved in job,
- a direct link between higher skill use and actual job performance clearly exists in the minds of managers and employees (and all managers attribute the same elements of performance to the same demonstration of competencies),
- similar job titles do not require similar task specifications across departments and so the measurement of individual competency raises fewer pay equity issues.

Under such conditions, the argument at least can be made that reward systems should reflect the demonstration of individual competency (even though as we shall see the actual implementation might create too many dysfunctional side effects). There are of course contra-indicators—situations when even the thought of linking reward and individual competency would be hard to justify. This is in situations when:

- It is important not to produce an overly structured picture of the job
- The nature of the work means that it is easy to achieve a set output (objective) by using very different skills or strategies
- Conscientiousness (doing whatever goes) is more important than skill level
- It is difficult to create a clear skills progression path across jobs (i.e. most jobs have a similar skills content), or the job families are so distinct that progression across them is technically too risky.
- Much work is carried out off-site or out of view, and so only very complex multi-stakeholder assessment systems might capture observed performance, and even here

different stakeholders are likely to only glimpse and capture different sets of competencies. Centralising data or weighting of competencies is unjust.
- The possession or display of skills is arguably not a black or white affair, but open to very subtle judgement (for example, roles in which the job holder themselves is primarily using judgement or complex cognitive skills, the outcome of which cannot truly be judged for several years), and any assessment becomes subjective
- Where the appraisal system has been designed to encourage strongly two-way problem solving, but the current sophistication of managers will likely mean that any discussion of a single set of competencies will resort to counter-productive 'telling' about the right way to demonstrate performance.
- A department has a series of very different jobs, each with its own particular skill needs. Some employees can claim that their ability to display certain specialised competencies has been 'designed out' of the real roles
- Job holders start from very different skills levels, so rewards have to be focused on having made some progress towards up-skilling, rather than reaching an absolute level of competency
- The competency framework cannot be defended against possible discrimination charges, such as implicit sex discrimination caused by competency-sets identified on male-biased samples.

Clearly, this is a political process that requires subtle judgements to be made about the readiness of the existing HR systems and managerial attitudes and skill-sets within the organisation to handle a complex technology. We saw some important distinctions emerging in the rewards field, between for example skills-based pay (where organisations directly paid for and rewarded the acquisition of a formal set of vocational skills) and competency-based pay (where the reward was not driven simply by the acquisition of skill but by the ability of employees to actually put their personal attributes into successful practice) (Lawler, 1996). The distinction is an important one.

When this thinking is fed into the use of competencies in relation to rewards, it can be used politically within human resource management systems. Does the organisation wish to reward the acquisitions of competencies (the motivation to create a linkage is to jump-start a transition towards a different competency set) or does it assume that the selection and development system has created an even spread of competencies and instead it needs to reward the successful and continual application of existing competencies?

The first and as yet more common approach is to forge a link between competencies and pay through the job evaluation process. Organisations pursue more flexible and broader grade bands and create more generic job evaluations based on broad sets of competencies. To the extent that job evaluations are linked to salary bandings, then new sets of competencies influence pay levels by regulating the proportion of people moving through pay bands. In this sense, the organisation has introduced competency-linked pay. This is also often called the job-focused approach (Brown and Armstrong, 1997). Competency headings are used to evaluate jobs or roles, and jobs are allocated to pay bands or job families using competency definitions. Even within this approach, two different methods have been detected. The non-analytical approach uses broad bands based on generic competency profiles. This has been seen at Glaxo Wellcome and at Guinness. The analytical approach replaces traditional job evaluation factors by competence-related factors. ICL and Volkswagen have been cited as firms adopting this method.

A more adventurous and complicated form of linkage is to link pay and competencies through the appraisal system and performance-related systems. Organisations feed competency definitions into their traditional 'what you achieve' (output, targets, standards, objectives) and 'how you achieve it' (competencies, values, behaviours) appraisal measures. 'Link' is the key word here, for in most schemes the competencies are but one factor, and the linkage is based on an implicit calculation in the appraiser's mind which presumably will weight the performance based on the 'what you do' type measures as well as the 'how you do it' type measures. Complex maths or simple managerial judgement is then used to roll the 'how you achieve it' element (described in terms of competency) into an overall performance rating, which in turn may be linked to an element of individual pay. The systems are the same as before, but the labels to rate performance contain competency language.

A very small number of organisations base all their performance-related pay solely on an assessment of competencies. This has variously been called a competency-based pay approach or people (not jobs) based approach (Brown and Armstrong, 1997). Competency levels are defined and job profiles are developed. Pay increases are linked to the levels of competency attained by individuals against these pre-defined profiles. This approach has been seen in firms such as Abbey Life, Derby City General Hospital, and Scottish Equitable. Staff are assessed against each competency area and growth in each competency area is rewarded. People, not jobs are placed in a four-banded pay structure and paid for growth in competencies irrespective of job needs. This may be combined with other pay elements such as a team-based performance pay scheme.

For example, Guinness adopted this approach in May 1996. The pay budget was aimed at the recruitment and retention of the most talented staff. In order to reward talent, it replaced a 24-grade structure and lengthy job descriptions with broad role profiles and three pay bands. Role profiles had three elements: need to do; need to know; and need to be (which was the competency element). Seven competencies were specified (such as commitment to results, and interpersonal effectiveness). An individuals' actual competency was compared against the role profile in the performance management process. Pay movement within the band was based on three factors: company affordability, level of market movement, and the individual's demonstrated competency.

If we consider the ways in which competencies are being operationalised in relation to rewards, two models can be discerned: The first is what may be termed a Super Person Model. Under this approach a handful of bottom-line competencies associated with generic effectiveness are built into rewards systems. The logic associated with the de-selection of competencies from the performance management or reward system tells you much about the nature of HRM within the organisation.

The second approach is what may be termed a Graded Mastery Model. The roots to this thinking were noted by Mosley and Bryan (1992) when they outlined the use of language ladders at BSS Ltd. in order to define 14 levels at which a single competency could be evidenced. Taking the competency of 'Motivating others' as an example, the language ladder *deconstructed* the competency such that at minimal levels individuals tended to be uninvolved, distant and aloof when dealing with others. Then, when they might demonstrate some attention to others, but still lack knowledge of others' aspirations. Then they might appreciate others' aspirations but set unrealistic targets and impose their own standards. After learning how to set more realistic targets they might not provide much positive feedback and still tend to criticise others. Then they provide constructive feedback and also demonstrate sensitivity to development needs. By this level of display, they show that they enjoy listening to others and building a team spirit, getting involved with others and finding interesting things for them to do, at which point it becomes a small step to demonstrating a wide range of motivational skills and naturally gaining the commitment of others. A clear developmental logic is *implied* (if not supported by actual mastery attainment) by such scaling!

Graded mastery approaches then tend to outline a series of progressive capability levels, which are defined for each competency. The gap-between *expected levels of competency display* for the role and *actual display* are then assessed, and reward is progressively linked to levels of display of competency. Typically systems seem to differentiate three or four levels of mastery (using language such as: baseline, developing, experienced and mastery; or point of recruitment, developing within the role, expected operating level, advancing and advanced). This type of model forces a series of difficult design decisions to be made. Some of the questions that have to be resolved are quite testing and indicative of the thinking that underlies managerial competency.

For example, can a simple linear progression in terms of mastery be built into the behavioural indicators used to evidence a competency, and built in such a way that someone will evidence a clear majority of behaviours within one level of mastery such that they cannot make a case for display at a much higher level of mastery? Are the different levels of competency mastery best treated as being *generic* across a wide range of jobs (such that a single set of competencies may be used across the whole organisation, or such that jobs of different levels of complexity may be 'scaled' against a single competency mastery scale as expressed in a single language ladder)?

This means that competencies have to be scaled using indicators that cannot be interpreted in ways in which a secretary might be able to argue that, for example, leadership has been displayed in the same way as indicated in a language ladder that was intended to delineate mastery behaviours at the level of Chief Executive! Or, should different levels of mastery be created for *each* major job role, allowing assessors to make their own implicit assumptions of what baseline or mastery behaviours might look like for a Chief Executive as opposed to a secretary? Once these language ladders have been articulated, at what point do the behavioural indicators across progressive levels of apparent mastery of the competency really evidence a higher level of attainment, or actually a different capability within the individual? I know of no scientific approach to making such judgements. Nor do rewards consultants.

In order to ensure that the use of competencies for rewards as opposed to developmental purposes is appropriate, organisations need to consider the motivation to form the linkage between the two more deeply. From a psychological perspective, the two important questions seem to be: Are the competencies in question of a more selectable or developable nature? and Is the problem one of competency capability or competency display? In theory, organisations pay for the more 'selectable' competencies (i.e. those that are very strongly rooted in individual personality and cognitive traits and therefore a source of stable individual difference) through their recruitment and selection systems, and then the career development workshops that serve as promotion filters across management layers. It could legitimately be asked, why should other parts of the HR system then have to bear the cost of paying for all competencies when the organization should have already assessed whether people have the competencies and should have deselected the incompetent?

The counter to this question is to draw attention to the distinction that I made above between the *capability or potentiality* to evidence competency, and the incentive to actually *display* the competency. By pushing competencies into the reward field, we see a return to the opening distinction in this chapter between different dispositional characteristics. The second category—values, interests and motivational disposition—have suddenly become separated once more from the other elements of competency (abilities and personality traits) as an important predictor of the likelihood that an individual will display a competency.

This distinction between potentiality and motivational disposition to display is muddied by a further distinction between the inherent stability or development that is assumed to be associated with a particular competency. This leads us to a distinction between *pull-based* or *push-based* competency-based rewards strategies. Whilst it would make sense for the majority of payment for competencies to focus mainly on the 'developable' competencies (i.e. to create a 'pull effect' that ensures that the new behaviours gravitate towards the competency specification through the motivational and reward aspects of the pay system.), there is one situation in which an organisation might argue that it should pay for competencies that are of a more selectable nature.

A 'push-effect' might still be justified in a situation when having selected people who are clearly all capable of demonstrating the competence (potential is assured) they need to be nudged more towards the continual display of the competency. If the lack of display cannot be attributed to more serious problems of job design, for example (whereby individuals can legitimately argue that their competency cannot be displayed by design), but instead is seen as a matter of lack of individual commitment to display, then differential reward can be justified. Although a rather obvious distinction, few HR departments will admit to having a pull or a push motivation to reward competencies, or more importantly, think through the design of the system to consistently and coherently reflect this strategy.

There is also the deeper question of why, if the situation is a display problem rooted more in a lack of commitment rather than design, does the organisation consider that paying for competencies is the best route? We cannot engage this question in any depth here, but it is important to note that elsewhere I have argued that by the late 1990s the most pressing problem facing organisations was not one of Competency but one of Contract (Sparrow and Marchington, 1998). The pressures of globalisation, deterioration of the psychological contract and changing focus of commitment (away from the organisation towards commitment to profession, to project and to team) are just as likely to explain a reluctance to display competency as is their being a lack of 'push' towards the display.

WHAT ARE THE LATEST 'HOT' COMPETENCIES?
IS THE COMPETENCY-MOVEMENT FAD OR EVIDENCE-BASED?

One of the indirect consequences of the shift of attention towards paying for competencies was that it forced organisations to consider the *relative value* of competencies. Many original competency-protagonists felt uncomfortable about this, arguing that the whole point of the competency approach was the fact that you had to accept that the total spectrum of competencies influenced performance—attention could not just be given to one small part of the picture. However, HR practitioners had to take a more pragmatic stance, asking 'If I am going to pay for it, surely the competency must have some real bottom-line value?' Once their minds became concentrated on such questions, they turned their attention once more to the search for the most telling individual differences.

Again, it should be made clear that there is nothing new in the argument that I am about to forward—which is that there are a series of particular competencies moving to centre stage in the hunt by organisations for this series of telling individual differences. I shall draw attention to intuitive decision-making and creative reasoning, innovation, information load management competencies, and the debate associated with discussion of emotional intelligence.

The challenge in this chapter is to set the attention to such competencies in the context of competency-based HR systems. First, I would note that these individual differences have become the focus of attention in part because of more recent change in the nature of the management task and a questioning of the nature of managerial effectiveness in a highly uncertain world: '. . . we must question what intelligence in modern organisations really looks like. The discussion of levels of information load, richness of a managers' required cognitive maps, and increased reliance on the intelligent unconscious suggests that cognitive skills should take the center-stage in future competency profiles' (Sparrow, 1999). However, in drawing attention to some of these telling individual differences, the point should not be lost that much of the rhetoric in this area is simply a product of academic and practitioner followership. Again we can see that many people have been there before, though in the slightly different context of their times.

For example, Katz's (1955) analysis of conceptual skills pointed to the need for executives to see the organisation as a whole, and to understand the impact of its various components on the entire business. Similarly, by the early 1990s, when the first significant critiques of the competency movement began to emerge, the argument was put forward that the linkage of competencies to the topic of human resource strategy ran the danger of giving too much importance to human resource management, as opposed to resourceful human management! Consequently, '. . . the skills needed to handle the emergent, non-routine, and dynamic components that characterise a large chunk of managerial work tend to get neglected' (Kanungo and Misra, 1992, p. 1312).

There has understandably also been a debate about the construct of emotional intelligence. Sparrow (1999) noted that much of the discussion on it clearly described previously understood emotion-handling competencies such as self-awareness, emotional management, empathy, relationships, communications and personal style. Indeed, if there were one lasting contribution of the behavioural competency movement it surely must be the way in which it re-articulated the nature of 'intelligent behaviour' within organisations and moved us beyond our fascination with general intelligence. Of course this contribution was made long before the emergence of talk about emotional intelligence, and so we would be right to maintain a sense of scepticism and to feel uncomfortable about the commoditisation of the construct (Fineman, 2000). Nonetheless, it would be churlish to reject *all* the messages that have emerged from the more recent debate as simple fadism. Chapman (2001) argues that it serves some purpose as a metaphor signalling a paradigm shift within organisations.

I would argue that some of the discourse that it has created is even more solid than this. For example, when treated as a *meta-ability* or *meta-cognition*—i.e. an aptitude that provides the individual with awareness of one's own cognitions that determines how well people use the other skills they have, including their intellect—then there appears to be some value in the construct (the emotion-handling competencies aside). If a novel contribution were to be sought, it is in the attention that it draws to the role of the intelligent unconscious, and the operation at a pre-conscious level of neurological processes that have also been given attention by recent research into intuition and creativity.

Another contribution is through the legitimacy that it gave to talk about the down-side of management in modern organisations, and the help that it gave to other (totally independent) researchers investigating:

1. the heightened levels of emotionality that exist within the workforce through: emotions being built into the labour process in many occupations (emotional labour), breach of the 'implicit' or 'psychological contract' and the HRM consequences of this (Morrison and Robinson, 1997; Rousseau, 1995);
2. an endemic lack of trust, and change in the nature of trust within organisations (Kramer and Tyler, 1996; Herriot, 1998);
3. increased attention into perceptions of fairness and the role of organisational jus-tice in managing accountability for events that have negative impact on material or psychological well-being (Folger and Cropanzano, 1998);
4. the need for better retrospective sense-making (and hence emotionally-tinged cogni-tion) and an ongoing creation of reality in what is a complex and ambiguous organi-sational world (Weick, 1995); and
5. the growing need for organisations and their managers to make the knowledge and experience of individuals and groups more explicit and understandable in an environ-ment that is tinged with the conflicts and emotions (Briner, 1999; Herriot, 2001) that I cited above.

CONCLUSION

If we consider the debates around the competency movement since the early 1980s until today, we can see that although on the surface there has been little alternative but for organisations to use competencies, and apparently little shift in the issues faced over the last ten years or so, we have in fact come a very long way. As some of the more difficult questions have been asked, the manoeuvres by organisations to either avoid the need to answer such questions, or to prove the irrelevance of such academic grumblings, has in itself sent powerful signals about what seems to be important in terms of managerial effectiveness. Competency is clearly a multi-level phenomenon that is best viewed in the context of the psychological contributions that individuals make to the strategic effectiveness of the organisation. Hodgkinson and Sparrow (2002) define this strategic competence as the ability of organisations (or more precisely their members) to acquire, store, recall, interpret and act upon information of relevance to the longer-term survival and well being of the organisation.

In part, this competence resides within individuals—comprising the cognitions and behaviours that are required in order to be best equipped to deal with what is becoming an increasingly complex and highly turbulent business world. At the individual level, dual-processing strategies act as a means of enabling managers to skilfully alternate the ways in which they process information, switching back and forth between automatic and controlled modes, as and when required. Other aspects of this competence, however, reside among intra- and inter-organisational collectives.

Managers are engaged in processes of dialogue and interaction within distributed teams and across communities of practice. The creation of collective memory and learning across such collectives is central, as is the design of appropriate systems and structures, i.e. systems and structures of a form that enable both a matching and stretching of individuals, and organisational collectives, in terms of their ability to procure and utilise strategic information. They argue that the strategically competent organisation and the learning organisation are one and the same entity. This combination of the messages that have emerged from the analysis of behavioural competency and the more recent cognitive insights into the nature of intelligent functioning within *organisations (not just individuals)* is likely to provide us with more powerful insights into the development of people within organisations. How we chose to operationalise such constructs will inevitably need to be tinged more by pragmatism than by science.

REFERENCES

Anderson, J.R. (1990) *Cognitive psychology and its implications*. 3rd edition. New York: Freeman.

Beer, M., Eisenstat, R. and Spector, B. (1990) *The critical path to corporate renewal*. Boston: Harvard Business School Press.

Beer, M., Spector, B., Lawrence, P., Mills, D.Q. and Walton, R. (1985) *Human resource management: A general manager's perspective*. Glencoe, Ill.: Free Press.

Boyatzis, R. (1982) *The competent manager: A model for effective performance*. New York: Wiley.

Boyatzis, R. (1998) Interview with Richard Boyatzis. *Competency*, 1998/99 Annual Survey.

Briner, R.B. (1999) The neglect and importance of emotion at work. *European Journal of Work and Organizational Psychology*, 8: 323–346.

Brown, D. and Armstrong, M. (1997) Terms of enrichment. *People Management*, 3, 11th September.

Brunswik, E. (1956) *Perception and the representative design of psychological experiments*, 2nd edition. Berkeley: University of California Press.

Campbell, J.P., Dunnette, M.D., Lawler, E.E. and Weick, K.E. (1970) *Managerial behavior, performance and effectiveness*. New York: McGraw-Hill.

Carroll, S.J. and Gillen, D.J. (1987) Are the classical management functions useful in describing managerial work? *Academy of Management Review*, 14: 333–349.

Chapman, M. (2001) Emotional intelligence—critical competency or passing fad? Beyond the rhetoric. *The Occupational Psychologist*, No. 43, August, 3–7.

Chi, M.T., Glaser, R. and Farr, M.J. (1988) *The nature of expertise*. Hillsdale, NJ: Erlbaum.

Fineman, S. (2000) Commodifying the emotionally intelligent. In S. Fineman (ed.) *Emotion in Organisations*. 2nd edition. London: Sage Publications.

Fitts, P.M. and Polson, M.J. (1967) *Human performance*. Belmont, CA: Brooks Cole.

Folger, R. and Cropanzano, R. (1998) *Organisational justice and human resource management*. London: Sage.

Hammond, K.R., Hamm, R.M., Grassia, J. and Pearson, T. (1987) Direct comparison of the efficiency of intuitive and analytic cognition in expert judgement. *IEEE Transactions On Systems, Man and Cybernetics*, SMC 17, 5, 753–770.

Herriot, P. (2001) Future work and its emotional implications. In R. Payne and C. Cooper (eds) *Emotions at work*. London: John Wiley and Sons.

Hodgkinson, G. and Sparrow, P.R (2002) *The competent organization: A psychological analysis of the strategic management process*. Milton Keynes: Open University Press.

Kahneman, D. (1991) Judgement and decision-making: a personal view. *Psychological Science*, 2, 3, 42–145.

Kandola, B. (1995) Competencies: An in-built bias against diversity. *British Psychological Society Occupational Psychology Conference, Brighton.* 3rd–5th January.

Kanungo, R.N. and Misra, S. (1992) Managerial resourcefulness: A re-conceptualisation of management skills. *Human Relations,* 45 (12), 1311–1332.

Katz, R. (1955) The skills of an effective executive. *Harvard Business Review,* 33 (1): 33–42.

Katz, R. (1974) Skills of an effective administrator. *Harvard Business Review,* 52 (5): 90–102.

Klemp, G.O. and McClelland, D.C. (1986) What characterises intelligent functioning among senior managers? In R.J. Sternberg and R.K. Wagner (eds) *Practical intelligence: Nature and origin of competence in the every day world.* Cambridge: Cambridge University Press.

Kotter, J. (1982) *The general manager.* New York: Free Press.

Kramer, R.M. and Tyler, T.R. (eds) (1996) *Trust in organizations: Frontiers of theory and research.* London: Sage.

Lawler, E. (1996) Competencies: a poor foundation for the new pay, *Compensation and Benefits Review,* November/December.

McClelland, D.C. (1973) Testing for competence rather than for intelligence. *American Psychologist,* 28, 1–14.

Mintzberg, H. (1973) *The nature of managerial work.* New York: Harper and Row.

Morrison, E.W. and Robinson, S.L. (1997) When employees feel betrayed: a model of how psychological contract violation develops. *Academy of Management Review,* 22, 1, 226–256.

Mosley, C. and Bryan, J. (1992) A competency approach to performance management. In R. Boam and P. Sparrow (eds) *Designing and achieving competency: A competency based approach to developing people and organisations.* London: McGraw-Hill.

People Management (1997) Sex differences in 360 degree competency ratings. *People Management,* 4th December 1997.

Rankin, N. (2001) Benchmarking survey of the 8th Competency Survey: Raising Performance Through People. *Competency and Emotional Intelligence 2000/2001 Benchmarking Report.* London: IRS Eclipse Group Ltd.

Robertson, I., Baron, H., Gibbons, P., MacIver, R. and Nyfield, G. (2000) Conscientiousness and managerial performance. *Journal of Occupational and Organizational Psychology,* 73, 2, 171–180.

Rousseau, D.M. (1995). *Psychological contracts in organizations: understanding written and unwritten agreements.* Thousand Oaks, CA: Sage

Schuler, R.S. (1992) Linking people with the strategic needs of the business. Organization Dynamics, 20: 18–32.

Shanteau, J. (1989) Psychological characteristics and strategies of expert decision-makers. In B. Rohrman, L.R. Beach, C. Vlek and S.R. Watson (eds) *Advances in decision research.* Amsterdam: North Holland.

Shanteau, J. (1992) Competence in experts: the role of task characteristics. *Organizational Behavior and Human Decision Processes,* 53, 252–266.

Shenhar, A. (1990) What is a manager? A new look. *European Management Journal,* 8 (2): 198–202.

Shiffrin, R.M. and Schneider, W. (1977) Controlled and automatic human information processing: II. Perceptual learning, automatic attending, and a general theory. *Psychological Review,* 84, 127–190.

Sisson, K. and Storey, J. (1988) Developing effective managers: a review of the issues and an agenda for research. *Personnel Review,* 17 (4): 3–8.

Slatter, P.E. (1987) *Building expert systems: Cognitive emulation.* Chichester: Ellis Horwood.

Sparrow, P.R. (1996) Linking competencies to pay: too good to be true? *People Management,* 2 (23), 1–6.

Sparrow, P.R. (1997) Organisational competencies: creating a strategic behavioural framework for selection and assessment. In N. Anderson and P. Herriot (eds) *International handbook of selection and assessment.* Chichester: John Wiley.

Sparrow, P.R. (1998) Why integrate skills and competencies into HR strategy? *Gender, Competencies and Skills Conference.* London: Institute of Employment Studies/Equal Opportunities Commission.

Sparrow, P.R. (1999) Strategic management in a world turned upside down: The role of cognition, intuition and emotional intelligence. In P. Flood, T. Dromgoole, S. Carroll and L. Gorman, (eds) *Managing Strategy Implementation*. Oxford: Blackwell.

Sparrow, P.R. and Boam R. (1992) An assessment of the strengths and weaknesses of competency-based approaches: where do we go from here? In R. Boam and P. Sparrow (eds) *Designing and achieving competency: A competency based approach to developing people and organisations*. London: McGraw-Hill.

Sparrow, P.R. and Bognanno, M. (1993) Competency requirement forecasting: issues for international selection and assessment. *International Journal of Selection and Assessment*, 1 (1), 50–58.

Sparrow, P.R. and Marchington, M. (1998) Re-engaging the human resource management function: re-building work, trust, and voice. In P. Sparrow and M. Marchington (eds) *Human resource management: The new agenda*. London: Financial Times Pitman Publications.

Spencer, L.M. and Spencer, S.M. (1993) *Competence at work: Models for superior performance*. London: Wiley.

Stewart, R. (1967) *Managers and their jobs: A study of the similarities and differences in the way that managers spend their time*. London: Macmillan.

Storey, J. (1990) Management development: a literature review and implications for future research—Part 2: Profiles and Contexts. *Personnel Review*, 19 (1): 3–11.

Strebler, M., Thompson, M. and Heron, P. (1997) *Skills, competencies and gender: Issues for pay and training*. IES report 333. London: Institute of Employment Studies.

Weick, K.E. (1995) *Sensemaking in organisations*. Thousand Oaks, CA: Sage.

Whitley, R. (1989) On the nature of managerial tasks and skills: Their distinguishing characteristics and organization. *Journal of Management Studies*, 26(3): 206–235.

CHAPTER 8

Emotional Intelligence and the Development of Managers and Leaders

Victor Dulewicz and Malcolm Higgs
Henley Management College, UK

SUMMARY

The chapter begins with clarification of the Emotional Intelligence construct, in terms of what it is and why it has become significant for individuals and organisations. Its significance stemmed from an early interest in non-cognitive capabilities and more recently from evidence of relationships with success and superior performance found by the authors and others from their research. Physiological and educational studies, and recent research within organisations, are covered in the chapter.

Measurement issues are also addressed. The authors demonstrate that Emotional Intelligence can be measured and they describe the development of their own questionnaire, the EIQ. Measurement issues relating to assessment or development and the importance of a broad profile measure, as opposed to a unitary and definitive measure, are also discussed. The authors then describe the development of a model to explain how Emotional Intelligence adds to our understanding of the drivers of individual success and performance.

Individual Differences and Development in Organisations. Edited by Michael Pearn.
© 2002 John Wiley & Sons, Ltd.

Another major issue concerns whether or not Emotional Intelligence is developable. The authors conclude that some of the elements of EI are readily developable while others are more enduring characteristics and should be exploited. Some approaches to development of EI are described.

The relationship between EI and Leadership is discussed within the context of current thinking about leadership, with research evidence to support the claims. The authors also cover some contextual issues such as the potential impact of corporate culture on EI and exploratory research on cultural influences; trends in understanding sustainable competitive advantage; and the limitations of our current understanding of EI and the related need for further research. Finally, they outline current applications of EI and of their instrument.

INTRODUCTION

Judging by the extensive media coverage given to Emotional Intelligence (EI) over the last two years or so, and the great interest shown in the topic by people in all walks of life, there is no doubt that EI is a very hot topic in Human Resource Management. It has tremendous potential value not only for managers and HR professionals but also for teachers, educationalists and counsellors. However, it is a topic that is surrounded by controversy. In the UK, Charles Woodruffe (2001) challenged the growth in the popularity of the concept on the basis that it was both unproven and indeed nothing new. In our view the critical questions are not whether it is new, but whether it is a valid concept and has real value for developing people.

In this chapter we explore the nature and development of thinking in relation to Emotional Intelligence, the evidence for its validity as a concept and its practical applications. In the case of applications we will examine important implications in relation to leadership thinking and approaches to the development of EI. Finally we will consider the extent to which an organisation's culture can impact on the development of an individual's EI. In the chapter we will draw on both our own work and that of others working in this field.

From our own research and consultancy we have found relatively strong evidence to show that EI:

1. Explains a high proportion of individual success in an organisational context and much more than cognitive competencies alone.
2. Is clearly related to the performance of managers, team leaders and sales staff.
3. Becomes even more significant at higher leadership levels, right up to board level, and
4. Is clearly related to leadership competencies.

THE SIGNIFICANCE OF EMOTIONAL INTELLIGENCE

THE CASE FOR EI AND THE HISTORIC CONTEXT

In their quest to explain what determines success, psychologists have been investigating qualities other than intelligence for many years. As long ago as the 1920s, Thorndike reviewed the predictive power of IQ. He developed the concept of "Social Intelligences" to explain aspects of success that could not be accounted for by IQ. The behavioural and cognitive psychologists stifled this early venture into the field in the 1930s and it was not until the early 1980s that Harold Gardner, a Harvard psychologist, resurrected interest in these "social intelligences" in his book *Frames of Mind* by developing and exploring the concept of Multiple Intelligences. These included interpersonal, self-awareness and emotional traits. Subsequently, Peter Salovey, a Yale Psychologist, mapped the way in which we can bring intelligence to our emotions, and was the first to coin the term Emotional Intelligence in 1990 and then, in 1996, Farnham used the term Emotional Literacy to refer to the process involved in developing Emotional Intelligence. But the concept of Emotional Intelligence was brought to the world's attention in the same year by Dr Daniel Goleman, a psychologist and journalist, in his best selling book *Emotional Intelligence—Why it can Matter More than IQ* (Goleman, 1996). Over 4.5 million copies have been sold around the world so far.

We reviewed over 60 books and articles on the subject and found that much of the "evidence" produced by Goleman and others working in the field is anecdotal or based on case-studies. Very few of these studies produced hard evidence (Dulewicz & Higgs, 2000a). However, a small number of interesting examples of those that did show some fairly hard evidence, from different fields of psychology, are summarised below.

Damasio studied brain-damaged patients who had received damage to the pre-frontal, amygdala circuit of the brain. Their decision-making capabilities had deteriorated, even though no deterioration was found in their IQ scores. He concluded that these patients had lost access to the emotional learning necessary for effective decision-making. Herrnstein & Murray (1994) advocates of the *primary importance* of IQ, studied the relationship between IQ and "broad measures of life success". They concluded that "the link between tests scores and achievements is dwarfed by the totality of other characteristics which are *relevant*". The implication is that many of these are EI factors. Kelley and Caplan (1993) studied research teams in Bell Laboratories. Although all members had very high IQ, some were rated as "Stars" by their peers. Neither IQ nor academic talent differentiated between the Stars and the others, but "interpersonal strategies" did. These strategies were similar to many of the elements of Emotional Intelligence. Both Gordon and Martinez (1997) describe studies of salesmen in financial services. Groups who had undergone training to develop their Emotional Intelligence achieved higher rates of performance and productivity than control groups which had not received this training.

The physiological basis of Emotional Intelligence is used by Goleman (1996) to support his case. As can be seen in Figure 8.1, the brain stem, at the bottom, controls our body and also our basic instincts, including survival. This part we share with our ancestors, the primates. Above that, we find the hippocampus which controls our feelings and emotional responses, and in particular the amygdala region—the brain's emotional memory bank. At the top of the brain we find the neo-cortex, the part unique to man, which covers thinking, memory and reasoning functions. According to Goleman, when we are calm the cortex functions at its optimal level. However, when we become emotional, especially when under pressure, the brain shifts into self-protective mode, stealing resources from memory and reasoning, and transferring them to other sites, in order to keep the senses hyper-alert—the survival responses. Whilst the circuitry for emergencies evolved millions of years ago, we still experience it today in the form of troubling emotions: worries, surges of panic, anxiety, frustration and irritation, anger and rage. So "intelligence" and "emotion" are found in different parts of the brain.

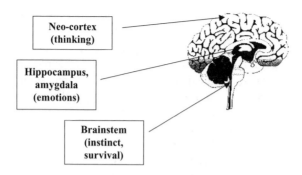

Neo-cortex
(thinking)

Hippocampus,
amygdala
(emotions)

Brainstem
(instinct,
survival)

FIGURE 8.1 Physiological basis of emotional intelligence

The core proposition put forward by Goleman and others is that success cannot be explained by IQ alone. It is the combination of IQ and Emotional Intelligence that together explain those personal qualities that contribute to a person's success in different fields. Now this is common sense, not rocket-science, especially to occupational psychologists who for the last 80 years or more have been researching and assessing traits other than IQ. Personality questionnaires, assessment centres, competency frameworks and appraisal schemes have been designed to measure emotional responses, motivation and other personality characteristics, in the search for explaining high performance. Since the evidence for the validity of EI produced by Goleman and others was rather weak, the authors began to conduct their own organisational research.

RESEARCH STUDY OF GENERAL MANAGERS AND THEIR EMOTIONAL INTELLIGENCE

Goleman (1997) presented a paper at a conference on Competencies in which he defined Emotional Intelligence in competency terms. This enabled the authors to relate Emotional Intelligence to research already in progress. In 1988, 100 members of Henley's General Management Course had been invited to take part in a longitudinal research study (Dulewicz & Herbert, 1999). They had undertaken a personality assessment and had assessed their own performance using a Personal Competencies questionnaire, the JCS. Their bosses had also rated their performance. In addition, they had provided information about their job level and responsibilities, and in particular the number of levels between them and the CEO; their salary; their budget; and the number of staff for whom they were ultimately responsible. Seven years later they were followed up, and asked for an update of their data on level and responsibility. Almost three-quarters of the original sample responded. The main aim of the study was to identify the personality characteristics and personal competencies that predicted long-term managerial advancement.

Based on a review of all the relevant literature, the authors redefined Emotional Intelligence in competency-terms, and the data from the follow-up study was used to test whether Emotional Intelligence was able to predict long-term managerial advancement. Of the 40 Competencies assessed, 16 appeared to be relevant to different aspects of Emotional Intelligence. Examples of these competencies are Listening and Sensitivity; Motivation & Energy; Emotional Resilience; Influence & Adaptability, Decisiveness; and Integrity. Aggregating performance on all these competencies into one measure predicted, statistically, their advancement up their respective organisations over the seven-year period.

Recalling the basic proposition that EQ and IQ were both important for success, those Competencies in our questionnaire that were concerned with intellectual performance were identified. Examples of IQ competence include: Analysis, Judgement, Planning, Organising, Strategic Perspective, Creativity and Risk-Taking. An aggregate of these ratings also predicted organisational advancement. After analysing the remaining 12 Competencies in the competencies questionnaire, it became clear that they were all essentially concerned with important aspects of Management. To complete the picture, these were referred to as "MQ" Competencies, which included: Supervising; Communication, Business Sense, Initiative and Tenacity. An aggregate measure of MQ also predicted managerial advancement.

In order to try to put some figures on the proportion of the total Advancement figure explained by each of the three scales, a multiple regression analysis was conducted on each. It was found that the IQ competencies accounted for 27%, quite close to Goleman's own estimate of 20%. EQ accounted for over one third of the variance, 36%; and finally, MQ explained 16% of Advancement. It was concluded that, whilst EQ factors appear to be particularly important for explaining managerial success, the core proposition, IQ + EQ = success, was supported although one must not overlook other competencies which are more specifically related to the task, in the case of management, MQ.

Therefore, the result of the authors' initial study of General Managers made them less sceptical and indeed convinced them that there might be something in the value of EI for organisations. However, before more evidence is provided, let us first address the important issue of whether EI can be measured at all.

MEASUREMENT OF EI

Throughout the literature on Emotional Intelligence there is considerable debate around the *reliability* of the construct (e.g. Goleman, 1996; Steiner, 1997; Stuller, 1998; Mathews, 1996). In broad terms Goleman suggests that a competence-based measure is more likely to yield an effective measure of Emotional Intelligence than a "pencil-and-paper" test. This point is reinforced in his more recent work that focuses on the relationship between Emotional Intelligence and the McBer Competence model (Goleman, 1998). The problems of measuring Emotional Intelligence are highlighted by other authors (e.g. Steiner, 1997; Martinez, 1997; Fisher, 1998). In particular, Fisher (1998) points to the difficulty of measuring Self-awareness:

> "It's very tough to measure your own Emotional Intelligence, because most of us don't have a very clear sense of how we come across to other people . . ." pp. 297.

The original study just described by the authors had one major limitation—it used an existing competence-based measure rather than a tailored EI instrument. However, having established the validity of a competence-based measure, it appeared feasible to develop a questionnaire-based measure to capture the competence on a self-report basis and, furthermore, to capture the missing elements which related to self-awareness.

In spite of the acknowledged difficulties in validly measuring Emotional Intelligence, the appetite for such tests and abundance of unvalidated attempts to provide a single measure are evidenced by the number of self-score questionnaires available in popular journals and the Internet (Fisher, 1998). Building on the earlier study of general managers, the authors started to develop a questionnaire designed to assess an individual's level of Emotional Intelligence on a self-report basis (Dulewicz and Higgs, 1999).

Emotional Intelligence Questionnaire (EIQ) Design

The questionnaire was designed from the literature survey of Emotional Intelligence and relevant personal competencies mentioned above. Items were drafted to capture the meaning of the behaviours related to the personal competencies shown to be good predictors of success and other elements of emotional intelligence identified as being of potential relevance to the new scale, derived from the authors' literature review. In addition, items were designed to sample the under-represented element, Self-awareness. In the original prototype version of the questionnaire, 72 items appeared. A conceptual, deductive approach to design, was adopted based upon the framework and model derived from the review of the literature. This method of test construction produces what Saville et al. (1993) refer to as Homogeneous Item Clusters (HICs). Item analysis was conducted using part-whole correlations, and involved five iterations. Three items were dropped because of low Part-Whole correlations, so the original 72 items were reduced to 69 (Dulewicz & Higgs, 1999; 2000c). On the basis of these analyses, seven separate elements of Emotional Intelligence were identified. These are defined briefly below:

- *Self-awareness:* Being aware of one's feelings and being able to manage them;
- *Emotional Resilience:* Being able to control ones emotions and to maintain one's performance when under pressure;
- *Motivation:* Having the drive and energy to attain challenging goals or targets;
- *Interpersonal Sensitivity:* Showing Sensitivity and Empathy towards others;
- *Influence:* The ability to influence and persuade others to accept your views or proposals;
- *Intuitiveness:* The ability to make decisions, using reason and intuition when appropriate; and finally
- *Conscientiousness:* Being consistent in one's words and actions, and behaving according to prevailing ethical standards.

In view of the nature of the EI construct, and in particular the importance of Self—awareness, the authors soon saw the need for a version of the EIQ which could be completed by colleagues. The 69 items in the original version of the questionnaire were modified so that they could be rated by a third party (Dulewicz & Higgs, 2000b).

EVIDENCE FOR THE VALIDITY OF THE EIQ

The authors and others have recently shown that EI does seem to be related to work performance. This has been demonstrated by taking the EI scores of staff in managerial and sales positions and relating them to job performance measures taken at the same point in time in a number of companies. A study of Team Leaders in a pharmaceutical company (Dulewicz & Higgs, 2000b) provided an opportunity to investigate the validity of the EIQ since measures of current performance were available. The results provided clear evidence for the concurrent validity of the original (Self) EIQ. The total EIQ score was highly significantly related to the performance measures. Furthermore, all Elements, apart from Sensitivity, were significantly related to three performance measures. In particular, Motivation and Influence were highly related to successful performance.

Turning to the 360° "Colleague" version of EIQ, the results provide further support. Once again, total score on EIQ-360° was significantly correlated with the performance measures. Focussing on the Elements, Resilience and Motivation were significantly related to the performance measure, whilst Sensitivity (unlike the self-reports) Influence and Decisive were related to some aspects of the performance. In contrast to the self-assessments, Self-awareness and Conscientiousness were not significantly related to performance. Finally when the results for the combined Self & Boss scores were combined, the results demonstrated the importance and value of aggregating the scores from the two. First, the total EQ score is highly significantly related to all the performance measures whilst on the specific Elements, six of the seven were significantly related to performance.

Further evidence to support the value of EI has been produced by Mark Slaski, a doctoral student at UMIST who was studying stress and job satisfaction within a large UK retail company. One part of his research involved the investigation of Emotional Intelligence using two measures, the Bar-on EQ-i and the EIQ. Scores from the various questionnaires were correlated with job performance ratings on a sample of 59 middle to senior managers. The results showed a significant relationship between EIQ Total score, Self-awareness, Emotional Resilience, Motivation and job performance. As noted, the researchers also administered the Bar-on EQ-i test, a widely used and validated US measure of EQ, to the same sample and correlated total score results with the total EIQ scores. A highly statistically significant correlation was found, confirming that both tests were measuring broadly the same construct (Dulewicz, Higgs & Slaski, 2001).

In view of the two studies reported by Goleman (above) on sales staff, another concurrent validity study was conducted by the authors in an Electrical Distribution company on a sample of 32 salespeople (Dulewicz & Higgs, 2000b). They all took the EIQ and their bosses completed the EIQ-360. The overall performance of the salespeople was assessed by their Regional Managers (their bosses' superiors) in order to avoid "contamination", and the results were inter-correlated. The correlations between the seven Elements (and total) and the Self, Boss and combined scores were calculated. Two elements, Emotional Resilience and Motivation, were significantly related to performance on the Self form. In contrast, when one combines the two sets of EIQ scores, four Elements—Self-awareness, Resilience, Motivation and Influence—and the overall score were significantly related to sales performance. These results provide further evidence of validity, and from a non-managerial sample.

CROSS-VALIDITY

It has already been noted above that the authors' original study had shown that an "EQ Competencies" scale, derived from 16 of the personal competencies from the Job Competencies Survey, had predicted organisational level advancement for a large group of General Managers. This finding was cross-validated on the 201 managers involved in the development phase of EIQ. Their EIQ scores were found to be highly significantly correlated with their Emotional Intelligence competencies scores from the JCS (see section 2 above).

Further evidence of cross-validity was found in the pharmaceutical company study. The participants and their bosses had rated their performance on the same JCS, and so it was possible to cross-validate not only the Self EIQ, but also the Colleague EIQ (using the Boss ratings) and the combined EIQ against the "EQ Competencies" scale. The correlation co-efficients showed that the total score on EIQ from all three sources (Self, Boss & Combined) were all highly significantly correlated with the EI total score derived from the 16 EQ competencies. The results from these two studies provide the critical link with the original study of General Managers that had produced evidence of predictive validity over seven years.

Taking all of these results together, we believe that quite extensive evidence now exists to support the validity of the EIQ-360°, as well as evidence for the "Self" EIQ. But an even more powerful case is made for combining the two inputs to provide a very effective indicator of job performance.

MAKING SENSE OF EMOTIONAL INTELLIGENCE

A major concern of the authors has been the disparate nature of the seven different elements. There is much evidence, above, to suggest that each one contributes to managerial performance. But how do they relate to each other, so that the whole is greater than the sum of the parts? The relevant literature, covering competency and personality theory, and Freud's work, with his model of the Id, the Ego and the Super-ego, was reviewed. In particular, the conflict between the Ego (our Consciousness) and the Super-Ego (our Conscience) and the need for Balance in order to achieve maturity seemed relevant. A new model, devised by the authors (Higgs and Dulewicz, 1999), has three main components:

1. **The Drivers**—Motivation and Intuitiveness (Decisiveness). These traits energise people and drive them towards achieving their goals, which are usually set very high.
2. **The Constrainers**—Conscientiousness, & Emotional Resilience—on the other hand, act as controls, and curb the excesses of the Drivers, especially if they are very high and undirected, or mis-directed.
3. **The Enablers**—those traits that facilitate performance and help the individual to succeed—Self awareness, Interpersonal Sensitivity and Influence.

The components of the Model and the Elements of Emotional Intelligence are summarised in Figure 8.2. High Performance should result, firstly, if the individual has high scores on all seven elements. They are all contributing, and in balance; or secondly, if all scores are average or above, and there are no large disparities between Drivers and Constrainers. On the other hand, Low Performance should result firstly, if scores are below-average on all seven elements; or secondly if overall EQ, and the Enablers scores are average, but the Drivers are high and the Constrainers are low, or vice-versa. In these cases, there would be imbalance.

The model shown in Figure 8.2 also brings in two more dimensions of particular importance. First, the importance of IQ, and MQ (the management competencies) has already been noted. High scores on these two scales would also clearly be Enablers

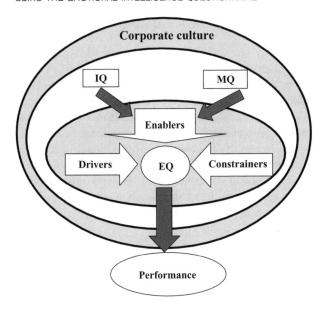

FIGURE 8.2 The model of emotional intelligence

of high performance. Secondly, the culture of the organisation will have a significant influence on whether managers with high Emotional Intelligence are selected in the first place, and then, whether or not they can prosper and survive. Managers with high Emotional Intelligence cannot thrive or exist in cultures which value short-term financial performance above all else. And they cannot thrive if consideration for other people, emotional expression and ethical standards are not valued or encouraged. Such organisations may be successful now, but are they really healthy enough to continue to be highly successful in the long-term? We will explore the issue of culture later in the chapter.

USING THE EMOTIONAL INTELLIGENCE QUESTIONNAIRE

SELECTION OR DEVELOPMENT

The EIQ was designed primarily for *development*, and test-takers should be reminded that it is in their interests to be as honest and frank with themselves as possible. There is no point in presenting a false description—that is tantamount to cheating at Patience or Solitaire—and will most probably produce misleading development advice. The report given to test-takers afterwards is designed to produce a number of ideas to facilitate self- development. Nevertheless, the EIQ is used for *personnel selection* and can provide valuable data, especially on those elements that are more enduring and less easy to develop, i.e. the Drivers and Constrainers. If used for selection, the results should not be used in isolation of other data available on the candidate. Cross-references should also made in subsequent interviews or assessment centres. It is very difficult to spot what many of the items are really measuring. Candidates should be warned about these two points when the form is administered.

THE IMPORTANCE OF A BROAD PROFILE, RATHER THAN A UNITARY MEASURE

The EIQ report provides information on the overall test score, together with information on the seven element scales which taken together comprise the overall test score to obtain a overview of the results. Thus, in interpreting the EI profile it can be useful to begin with the overall test score, which is derived from the average of the Sten scores on the seven Elements, and which thus determines the overall "EI" level. However, the overall shape of the profile is much more important and informative. It is essential to examine the individual scale scores in order to identify the elements of Emotional Intelligence which need to be both reinforced and developed in order to enhance the individual's abilities in relation to this significant area of competence. The EI report also provides data on these seven scales, derived again from the norms, which together comprise the overall measure of Emotional Intelligence.

THE RELATIONSHIP TO LEADERSHIP

Over the last few years there has been a significant and sustained growth in interest in the area of leadership in an organisational context (e.g. Chaudry, 2000; Bagshaw & Bagshaw,1999; Goffee & Jones, 2000). Indeed the rate and range of publications in the academic and practitioner journals attest to this growth. For example, in 1999 alone it was estimated that over 2000 new books on the topic of leadership were published (e.g. Goffee and Jones, 2000). In terms of research publications, the growth has been equally stunning in the last decade (Alimo-Metcalfe, 1995).

THE NATURE OF LEADERSHIP

Whilst the interest in leadership is growing in its perceived importance to business, the interest in exploring its nature, and attempting to identify what makes for effective leadership, is by no means new. Indeed the topic, as an area of both academic and business interest, has a recent history which dates back to at least the 1930s. In spite of this sustained interest, and associated research, there appears to be little emerging which enables us to define the nature of effective leadership and related requirements of effective leaders in a meaningful way (Kets De Vries, 1994). Furthermore, the linkages between academic research and practical experience appear to cause difficulty (e.g. Kets De Vries, 1995; Kouznes & Posner, 1999). Researchers, who also work as consultants in the business world, highlight the problem of building generic models to describe the nature of characteristics of effective leadership by pointing to the difficulty of finding a consistent way of exploring the realities of accounting for a huge variety of leadership styles, which lead to effective business performance (e.g. Kets de Vries, 1994; Goffee and Jones, 2000; Collins, 2001; Cacioppe, 1997).

AN HISTORICAL PERSPECTIVE

The difficulty of defining the nature of leadership, and i) the relationship of this research to the needs and concerns of organisations; and ii) the challenge of identifying what leads to effective leadership; may be elucidated by considering the development of the topic from an historic perspective. There is little doubt that mankind has been intrigued by the nature of leaders and leadership since the times of Plato. However, as Goffee and Jones (2000) point out, the belief in rationality, which dominated our thinking since the Enlightenment, was challenged by the work of Max Weber and Sigmund Freud. This led to the start of a reappraisal of our thinking about leadership and attempts to define and understand the phenomenon. This development in thinking may be grouped into five categories. These categories, and their historical development, are summarised in Table 8.1.

TABLE 8.1 Historical development of thinking on leadership

Period	Predominant "School"	Predominant constructs	Key references
1920s	Trait Theory	Leadership can be understood by identifying the distinguishing characteristics of great leaders	• Weber (1947)
1950s	Style Theory	Leadership effectiveness may be explained and developed by identifying appropriate styles and behaviours	• Tannenbaum & Schmidt (1958)
1960s	Contingency Theory	Leadership occurs in a context. Leadership style must be exercised depending on each situation	• Fiedler (1967) • Hersey & Blanchard (1969)
1970s	Charismatic Theory	Leadership is concerned with the charismatic behaviours of leaders and their ability to transform organisations	• House (1976) • Burns (1978) • Conger & Kanungo (1988) • Bryman (1992)
1980s	New Leadership/Neo-Charismatic School	Leadership and management are different. Leaders require a transformational focus which encompasses a range of characteristics and behaviours in addition to charisma	• Bass (1985) • Avolio & Bass (1995; 1997) • Conger & Kanungo (1988) • Shamir (1992) • Bennis (1985) • Alimo-Mecalfe (1995)
Late 1990s	Emerging Approaches a) Strategic Leadership b) Change Leadership	a) Leadership may be understood by examination of strategic decision-making by executives b) Leadership is inexorably linked to the management of change. Leader behaviours may be understood in the context of the work of delivering change	a) • Finhelstein & Hambrick (1996) • Hambrick & Brandon (1998) b) • Kotter (1994) • Higgs & Rowland (2000) • Conner (1999)

LEADERSHIP AND CHANGE

In practice (as outlined above) one of the main focuses of the current interest in leadership relates to the linkage between leadership and the ability of an organisation to manage and deliver significant organisational change (Kotter, 1998; Carnall, 1999, Higgs & Rowland, 2000). Many argue that up to 70% of change initiatives fail to deliver expected benefits (e.g. Kotter, 1996, 1998, Hammer & Champy, 1993; Higgs & Rowland, 2000). The explanations for this failure, and the nature of leadership behaviour required to deliver success, are often positioned in relation to successful transformational behaviours (e.g. Kotter, 1996; 1994). However, in spite of identifying generic delivery failures, the above authors tend to avoid specifics in terms of alternative leadership behaviour patterns. Perhaps the issue in addressing proposed routes forward lies with a belief in the role of individual leaders, as an enduring and pervasive set of behaviours, rather than linking leadership behaviours to specific activities in the work involved in making change happen (Higgs & Rowland, 2000). Whilst the research on leadership and change is still an emerging area (Conner, 1999; Chaudry, 2000), there is some evidence that a competence-based framework, combined with planned development, can impact on both business results and the building of leadership capability (Higgs & Rowland, 2001).

In reviewing the Emotional Intelligence research Higgs & Dulewicz (1999) indicated that there was a developing view that Emotional Intelligence may be strongly related to leadership. A number of assertions to this effect have been made by both researchers in the field of Emotional Intelligence and leading authors on the topic of leadership (e.g. Goleman, 1998; 2000; Bennis, 1985). Indeed Goleman (1998) claims that the evidence from competency research shows that, whilst for all jobs Emotional Intelligence is twice as important for high performance as IQ and technical competencies, for leadership roles it accounts for 85% of the variance in high performing individuals. Specifically he states that:

> "Emotional competence made the crucial difference between mediocre leaders and the best. The stars showed significantly greater strengths in a range of emotional competencies, among them influence, team leadership, political awareness, self-confidence, and achievement drive. On average close to 90 per cent of their success in leadership was attributable to Emotional Intelligence". (Daniel Goleman, 1998, p. 33)

In exploring this claim in our own research we have found that there is indeed a relationship between organisational level and EI. In particular, in a study of 100 directors we found that CEOs and Chairmen had higher EI than other directors. In further exploring this by revisiting our original 7-year follow-up data we found that directors had higher levels of EI than other managers. However, understanding the relationships between EI and leadership is about more than looking at its relationship to hierarchical progression.

In looking more broadly at leadership and, in particular, the future nature of leadership, a number of authors and researchers have identified the growing significance of Emotional Intelligence (e.g. Cacioppe, 1997; Sosik & Magerian, 1999; Chaudry, 2000). In part, this shift in focus from the rational to emotional aspects of leadership represents the continuation of a trend encountered more broadly in thinking on organisational behaviour and leadership (e.g. Fineman, 1997; Goffee & Jones, 2000). Indeed, although not explicitly surfaced, much of the literature on transformational leadership implies that leaders require Emotional Intelligence (Higgs & Rowland, 2001). In reviewing the leadership literature from the "Transformational" period onwards there appears, on the basis of a content analysis of the constructs, to be a strong indication that there is a linkage between leadership and Emotional Intelligence. Table 8.2 provides a "map" of some of the key leadership models and their potential relationship to the elements of Emotional Intelligence as defined by Higgs and Dulewicz (1999). Turning to the core role of leaders in making change happen (as described above) it is likely that the linkage between behaviours in this context is likely to require a combination of cognitive competencies and those associated with Emotional Intelligence. Such a linkage was proposed by Channer and Hope (2001). They identified three important dimensions of change management. These were: i) rational, ii) political; and iii) emotional. They further assert that guiding an organisation along a transformational journey demands the ability to recognise where, on all three dimensions, the business is, and then to be able to design interventions, and manage communications and behaviours accordingly. They suggested that the need to handle all the multifarious requirements of change places a unique strain on the leadership of the business.

Similar themes emerge from other authors exploring leadership and change (e.g. Conner, 1999; Goffee & Jones, 2000; Collins, 2001). Transformational leadership is described by Selzer and Bass (1990) as: "The process of fast dramatic changes in an organisation by building commitment to the organisation and its mission". Ashford and Humphrey (1995) comment that:

> "... this process is largely dependant upon the evocation, framing, and mobilisation of emotions which the leader does by articulating a compelling, higher-order, utopian vision, and emphasising the contribution that the individual makes to the whole", (Ashford & Humphrey, 1995; p. 36).

Channer and Hope (2001) describe the role of leaders during transformation as entailing: i) planning; ii) mobilising and organisation; iii) building the vision; iv) personal risk; v) sending the right signals; vi) holding course; vii) making the tough calls; viii) asserting themselves; ix) handling anxiety; x) coping with overload. Once again the linkages between this description of the leader's role in change and Emotional Intelligence elements, identified by Higgs and Dulewicz (1999), become evident. However, a means of exploring this needed to be found. Such an opportunity arose from the work on Change Leadership competencies conducted by Higgs and Rowland (2000, 2001). In a study of change leaders in a large multi-national, Higgs and Rowland (2000, 2001) identified a distinct set of leadership competencies which were associated with the work involved in implementing change successfully. These were:

i) **Creating the case for change**. Effectively engaging others in recognising the business need for change;

ii) **Creating structural change**. Ensuring that the change is based on depth of understanding of the issues and supported with a consistent set of tools and processes;

iii) **Engaging others** in the whole change process and building commitment;

iv) **Implementing and sustaining changes.** Developing effective plans and ensuring good monitoring and review practices are developed; and

v) **Facilitating and developing capability.** Ensuring that people are challenged to find their own answers and that they are supported in doing this.

This clearly indicates a number of behaviours or traits which appear to be related to Emotional Intelligence. In reviewing the leadership literature from the "Transformational" period onwards, there appears, on the basis of a content analysis of the constructs,

TABLE 8.2 Relationships between leadership "models" and Emotional Intelligence

Elements of Emotional Intelligence (from Higgs & Dulewicz, 1999)	Leadership models and frameworks					
	Bass (1985) Transitional/ Transformational	Alimo-Metcalfe (1995) leadership constructs	Goffee & Jones (2000) four factors	Kouznes & Posner (1998)	Kotter (1990) - what leaders do	Bennis (1985)
Self awareness		• Self-awareness	• Reveal differences • Selectively show weaknesses			• Develop Self-knowledge • Develop feedback sources
Emotional resilience			• Tough empathy	• Challenges processes • Enable others		• Balance change & transition • Learn from adversity
Motivation	• Charismatic leadership	• Achieving, determined	• Tough empathy	• Challenge processes • Model the way	• Motivating and inspiring • Setting directions	• Role model
Interpersonal sensitivity	• Individual consideration • Charismatic leadership • Intellectual stimulation	• Consideration for the individual • Sensitive change management	• Tough empathy • Selectively show weaknesses • Enable others	• Challenge processes • Inspire shared vision • Model the way • Encourage the heart	• Aligning people	• Open style
Influence	• Charismatic leadership • Individual consideration	• Networking	• Reveal differences • Tough empathy	• Inspire shared vision • Enable others	• Aligning people • Motivating and inspiring • Setting direction	• Open style
Intuitiveness	• Intellectual Stimulation	• Decisive, achieving	• Intuition	• Inspire shared vision		• Capacity to concentrate • Curious about innovation
Conscientiousness & integrity	• Individual consideration	• Integrity and openness	• Tough empathy • Reveal differences	• Model the way • Encourage the heart	• Aligning people	• Role model

to be a strong indication that there is a linkage between leadership and Emotional Intelligence. Table 8.2 provides a "map" of some of the key leadership models and their potential relationship to the elements of Emotional Intelligence as defined by Higgs and Dulewicz (1999).

Moving to demonstrate these linkages became possible through a study conducted by Higgs and Rowland (2001). Using a combination of their Change Leadership competency assessment questionnaire and the EIQ in a study of 74 "change leaders" (i.e. individuals responsible for leading significant change projects) they were able to demonstrate strong correlations between EI and Change Leadership competencies. The results of their study are shown in Table 8.3.

From Table 8.3 it is evident that clear relationships exist between EI and Change Leadership Competencies (as measured by the CLCQ). Of the seven EI elements, there are positive and significant relationships with all except Intuitiveness. At the overall level there are significant relationships between EI and Change Leadership (as measured by the total CLCQ). Clearly, research evidence to demonstrate the relationship between EI and Leadership has some way to go. However the early explorations are encouraging and have considerable implications for future development and selection of leaders.

DEVELOPING EMOTIONAL INTELLIGENCE

In the literature on Emotional Intelligence there is considerable debate around the extent to which such a concept is developable (e.g. Goleman, 1996; Steiner, 1997; Dulewicz and Higgs, 1998a, 1998b). In supporting the concept of Emotional Intelligence, the earlier arguments of Gardner (1983) in terms of his broader Multiple Intelligences construct should be borne in mind. Gardner observes that cognitive abilities (in the sense of multiple intelligences, which encompass inter- and intra-personal intelligences are not static, but can, indeed, be developed. With this viewpoint in mind and given the theoretical underpinnings of the current test, the authors propose that the results of an individual assessment should be used to aid personal development. The ways in which the results might be employed for this purpose are discussed below.

The nature of Emotional Intelligence as discussed above is such that it is possible to enhance the overall level by planned and sustained personal development. Much of this development will result from reflecting on the individual's behaviours which tend to be exhibited in different situations, consciously practising different behaviours and actively seeking feedback on the way in which others interpret and respond to these new behaviours. In broad terms it is important to reflect on how the feedback might apply in a range of situations which the individual has faced and to capture and reflect on the following (in these different situations):

- What did they feel?
- How did they feel about the outcomes of their decisions?
- How did they feel about the outcomes of their actions?
- How could the outcomes have been improved in terms of the solution of the problem/ situation?
- How could the outcomes have been improved in terms of their feelings?
- What have they learned from this situation which could help them in dealing with future issues?

TABLE 8.3 Results of analysis of EIQ versus change leadership competencies (CLCQ) emotional intelligence

Change leadership competencies		EI total	Self-aware	Emotional resilience	Motivation	Interpersonal sensitivity	Influence	Intuitiveness	Conscientiousness
Creating the case	r	**0.333**	**0.388**	0.249	**0.340**	**0.298**	**0.332**	−0.113	**0.306**
	sig	**0.025**	**0.008**	0.100	**0.022**	**0.047**	**0.026**	0.461	**0.041**
Structural change	r	0.269	**0.461**	0.189	**0.290**	**0.362**	0.225	−0.131	0.208
	sig	0.074	**0.001**	0.214	**0.054**	**0.015**	0.138	0.391	0.170
Engagement	r	0.287	**0.326**	0.176	0.268	**0.346**	**0.368**	−0.144	**0.317**
	sig	0.056	**0.029**	0.246	0.075	**0.020**	**0.013**	0.344	**0.034**
Implementation	r	**0.418**	**0.445**	**0.311**	**0.391**	**0.381**	**0.371**	−0.043	0.279
	sig	**0.004**	**0.002**	**0.038**	**0.008**	**0.010**	**0.012**	0.780	0.063
Facilitation	r	**0.333**	**0.483**	**0.325**	**0.308**	**0.384**	0.241	−0.162	0.286
	sig	**0.025**	**0.001**	**0.029**	**0.040**	**0.009**	0.111	0.287	0.056
Overall change Competency	r	**0.377**	**0.486**	0.284	**0.367**	**0.411**	**0.354**	−0.134	**0.317**
	sig	**0.011**	**0.001**	0.059	**0.013**	**0.005**	**0.017**	0.381	**0.034**

Bold = statistically significant

The appropriate way in which to use the overall feedback is to examine each of the Emotional Intelligence scales and identify:

i. Those where individuals have strengths which may be developed and generalised.
ii. Those where there are specific opportunities for improvement.

Detailed guidance on feedback and development relating to each of the scales are presented by Dulewicz & Higgs (1999) in the Emotional Intelligence Questionnaire User Guide.

CONTEXTUAL ISSUES AND FURTHER RESEARCH

Given the competence-base underpinning the measurement of Emotional Intelligence, its potential value for personal development is reinforced. Once again, the conclusions from the current research are supported by those of Goleman (1998). However, in an organisational context practitioners will observe that, in some organisations, the general construct will either be rejected and/or neglected in the selection and promotion of the individual for important leadership roles. Indeed, in some organisations the exhibition of a number of elements of Emotional Intelligence may be "punished" (Lazear, 1991). Gardner (1983), in presenting the concept of multiple intelligences, which include elements of Emotional Intelligence, observed that central to the "abilities" (i.e., multiple intelligences) argument is the experience of the individual and the environmental factors which allow these "abilities" to develop. Thus, in an organisational context, these "abilities" can be ignored or "punished". This can result in either voluntary or involuntary loss of employees, or the achievement of conformity at the cost of underperformance, under-utilised potential and/or low morale.

Once again, whilst the case for a relationship between organizational culture and Emotional Intelligence is intuitively clear there has been no research to test the assertion. In part, this may be due to the relative recency of interest in the EI construct. However, there is also the challenge of operationalising 'culture' for research purposes. There is wide agreement that organizational culture is a difficult and complex area (e.g. Deal & Kennedy, 1999; Goffee & Jones, 1996; 1998). In order to explore culture, a number of authors have accepted that the most productive way to operationalise the construct is to examine the manifestations of an organisation's culture in terms of policies, practices, structures, etc. (e.g. Schein, 1985; Goffee & Jones, 1996, 1998). This approach is in line with the view that ". . . culture is simply the way we do things around here . . . " (Goffee & Jones, 1998, p. 32).

Using this framework, the authors developed an instrument for assessing an organisation's culture in terms of practices and behaviours which relate to the reinforcement and recognition of elements of EI. For example, Self-Awareness may be supported by the use of 360 degree feedback in appraisal and development programmes; Interpersonal Sensitivity may be developed and reinforced by training activities which include behavioural as well as technical components. The questionnaire is completed by a sample of people within an organization and an overall profile developed which provides an indication of the degree to which the perceptions of the organisation's practices and policies are supportive of the development and exhibition of EI by those working there. An initial pilot of the questionnaire showed that it had good levels of reliability (Higgs & McGuire, 2001). In order to explore the relationship between organization culture and individual

EI, Higgs and McGuire conducted an exploratory study in 9 companies. In total, 160 individuals took part in the study with an average of 17 from each organization. The participants completed an EIQ to provide data on their individual EI, and the "EI Culture Inventory" to provide perceptions of the organizations level of cultural support for EI. Using t-tests, significant relationships were found between the level of cultural support for EI and the mean levels of individual EI (Higgs & McGuire, 2001). Clearly the study has many limitations. However, it does provide some support for the view that culture plays a part in supporting the development of EI.

PRACTICAL APPLICATIONS OF EMOTIONAL INTELLIGENCE

Although we see a clear need for further research which will enhance our understanding of Emotional Intelligence, we are aware that the concept has developed well beyond being a "new age", theoretical idea. The practical application, based on the evidence to date, would seem to be in the broad areas of Development and Selection.

INDIVIDUAL PERSONAL DEVELOPMENT

The work we have carried out (both in terms of research and consultancy) suggests that EI has a significant role to play in personal development. The primary value of EI is for identifying individual's development needs, as a starting point and initial input to a systematic and on-going personal development programme, ideally facilitated by a coach. Our EIQ report provides data on where the individual stands, compared to a reference group, e.g. managers, general staff, and provides guidance on what can be done to develop areas which are below average. It also highlights strengths which can be exploited.

GROUP DEVELOPMENT

EI can be helpful in looking at how groups of people can be developed in line with behaviours needed to build a new organisational culture and means of behaving. The links between EI and corporate culture do indicate that interventions can help in supporting the growth of individual EI which will support a significant change in the style of working in an organisation which will develop in infrastructure, to support a building of capability for coping with increasing organisational change, complexity and competition in the business environment.

Turning to *personnel selection*, in our model of EI we propose that three of the elements are clearly capable of development, i.e. the Enablers, Self-awareness and the two inter-personal elements, Sensitivity and Influence. For years, courses have been available to develop these competencies. However, the other four elements, the Drivers, Motivation and Intuitiveness, and the Constrainers, Resilience and Conscientiousness, are more enduring characteristics which we believe should be "exploited". Therefore, it seems appropriate to use the EIQ for selection, to assess these elements. Many companies are now using the EIQ for general personnel selection and for graduate recruitment in particular. Some specific potential applications of Emotional Intelligence are summarised below.

IDENTIFICATION OF LEADERSHIP POTENTIAL AMONGST EXISTING STAFF

The importance of leadership and relationships between EI and leadership suggest that EI has a practical role to play in the context of identifying and developing future leaders (preferably as a part of an overall assessment/development centre).

IDENTIFICATION OF POTENTIAL AT SELECTION

Building on the above comment, there is clear potential for EI to play a part in graduate and high level new entrant assessment. Graduate Assessment Centres that include an assessment of EI elements will clearly add to the predictive power of assessment of future potential when making such hiring decisions. It is particularly appropriate to use EIQ as part of an Assessment Centre to assess the EI competencies since many of these are difficult to assess by Observers in Assessment Centre exercises. Results provide an objective input to the assessors conference and many companies are currently using EIQ on their Assessment Centres.

GENERAL SELECTION

Our EIQ is primarily concerned with the building of individuals, rather than their selection. However, if we explore the respective ability of the elements to be developed rather than exploited we do need to recognise that the EIQ, especially the versions for general staff below management, may have a significant role to play in initial selection.

CULTURE CHANGE

If the core premises of EI and the link between organisation culture and performance are accepted, then an assessment of current EI levels is worthwhile. It helps to identify significant changes in organisational practice that are necessary to implement in order to build a future culture designed to be aligned with the organisational strategic content.

CONCLUSION

In this chapter we have explored a range of aspects of Emotional Intelligence. Whilst it is a "Hot Topic" which is attracting widespread interest, it is evident that the practical interest and desire to exploit the concept has been running ahead of the research evidence. However, we believe that the evidence that we have presented demonstrates that the core constructs and assertions relating to EI have a degree of grounding in reality. Although we have described a number of exploratory studies, it is clear that more research is needed. Our research and review of the literature have indicated that EI is a potentially valid construct and one which has linkages to, and implications for, leadership behaviour and development. Furthermore, there is some evidence that organisational culture is related to the level of EI within a company. The research to date is generally supportive of many assertions. However, areas which do need to be examined further are:

- The relationship with leadership.
- The relationship to organisation culture.
- The extent to which EI can be developed and the nature of effective development methodologies.

In addition to these areas, there is also scope for conducting research into the relationship between EI and team performance.

REFERENCES

Alimo-Metcalfe, B. (1995). An investigation of female and male constructs of leadership. *Women in Management Review*, 10, 2, pp. 3–8.

Ashforth, B.E. & Humphrey, R.H. (1995). Emotion in the workplace: A reappraisal. *Human Relations*, 48(2): pp. 97–99.

Bagshaw, M. and Bagshaw, C. (1999). Leadership in the twenty-first century. *Industrial and Commercial Training*, 31 (6) pp. 236–240.

Bass, B.M. (1985). *Leadership and performance beyond expectations*. New York: Free Press.

Bass, B.M. (1997). Does the transactional-transformational leadership paradigm transcend organisational and national boundaries? *American Psychologist* 52, 130–139.

Bass, M.B. (1990). *Bass and Stodghill Handbook of Leadership: Theory, Research and Applications*. New York: Free Press.

Beer, M. (1980). *Organisational change and development: A systems view*. Santa Monica, CA: Goodyear.

Bennis, W. (1989). *On Becoming a Leader*. London, Hutchinson.

Bryman, A. (1992) *Charisma and leadership in organisations*. Santa Monica CA: Sage.

Buchanan, D. & Boddy D. (1992). *The expertise of the change agent*. Hemel Hempstead: Prentice Hall.

Burns, J.M. (1978). *Leaders' work*. New York: Harper & Row.

Cacioppe, R. (1997). Leadership moment by moment! *Leadership and Organisation Development Journal*, 18 (7), pp. 335–346.

Carnall, C. (1999). *Managing change in organisations*. London: Prentice Hall.

Channer, P. & Hope, T. (2001) *Emotional impact: passionate leaders and corporate transformation*. Basingstoke: Palgrave.

Chaudry, S. (2000). *Management 21C*. London: Pearson Education.

Collins, J. (2001). Level 5 leadership: The triumph of humility and fierce resolve. *Harvard Business Review*, Jan–Feb, pp. 67–76.

Conger, J.A. & Kanungo, R.N. (1988). The empowerment process: Integrating theory and practice. *Academy of Management Review*, 13, 471–482.

Conger, J.A. & Kanungo, R.N. (Eds.). (1988). *Charismatic leadership: The elusive factor in organisational effectiveness*. San Francisco, CA: Jossey-Bass.

Conner, D. (1999). Leading at the edge of chaos. New York: John Wiley.

Damasio, A. (1994). Descartes' error: emotion, reason and the human brain. New York, NY: Gosset, Putnam.

Deal, T. & Kennedy, A. (1999). *The new corporate cultures*. New York: Perseus.

Dulewicz, S.V. & Herbert, P.J. (1999). Predicting advancement to senior management from competencies and personality data: A 7-Year follow-up study. *British Journal of Management*, 10, 13–22.

Dulewicz, S.V. & Higgs, M.J. (2000a). Emotional intelligence: Managerial fad or valid construct? *Journal of Managerial Psychology*, 15, 4, pp. 341–368.

Dulewicz, S.V. & Higgs, M.J. (2000b). 360 degree assessment of Emotional Intelligence: A study. *Selection & Development Review*, 16, 3.

Dulewicz, S.V. & Higgs, M.J. (2000c). *EIQ-Managerial user guide*. Windsor: NFER-Nelson.

Dulewicz, S.V. & Higgs, M.J. (1999). Can Emotional Intelligence be measured and developed? *Leadership and Organisation Development*; 20 (5), pp. 242–252.

Dulewicz, V., Higgs, M.J. & Slaski, M. (2001). Emotional Intelligence: construct and concurrent validity. *Henley Working Paper Series, HWP 2001/021*.

Easterby-Smith, M., Thorpe, R. & Lowe, A. (1991). *Management research: An introduction*. London: Sage.

Farnham, A. (1996). Are you smart enough to keep your job? *Fortune*, 133, 1, 34–6.

Fiedler. F. (1967). Theory of leadership effectiveness. New York: McGraw-Hill.

Fineman, S. (1997). Emotion and management learning. *Management Learning*, 28 (1), pp. 13–25.

Finkelstein, S. & Hambrick D. (1996). *Strategic leadership—top executives and their influence on organisations*. St. Paul, Min: West Publishing Company.

Fisher, A. (1998). Success secret: A high emotional IQ. *Fortune*, October 26, pp. 293–298.

Fletcher, C. (1997). Self-awareness—a neglected attribute in selection and assessment? *International Journal of Selection and Assessment*, 5 (3), pp. 183–187.

Gardner, H. (1983). *Frames of mind: The theory of multiple intelligences*. New York: Basic Books.

Goffee, R. & Jones, G. (2000). Why should anyone be led by you? *Harvard Business Review*, Sept–Oct, pp. 63–70.

Goffee, R. & Jones, G. (1998). *The character of a corporation*. New York: HarperCollins.

Goleman, D. (1996). *Emotional intelligence: why it can matter more than IQ*. London: Bloomsbury Publishing.

Goleman, D. (1997). Beyond IQ: Developing the leadership competencies of Emotional Intelligence. *Paper presented at the 2nd International Competency Conference*: London, Oct. 1997.

Goleman, D. (1998). *Working with Emotional Intelligence*. London: Bloomsbury Publishing.

Goleman, D. (2000). Leadership that gets results. *Harvard Business Review*, March–April, pp. 78–91.

Hair, J., Anderson, R.E., Tathum, R.T. & Black, W.C. (1995). *Multivariate Data Analysis* (4th Edition). Englewood Cliffs, NJ: Prentice Hall.

Hambrick, D.C. & Brandon, G.L. (1988). *Executive Values*, in Hambrick D.C. (Ed.) *Executive effectiveness—Concepts and methods for studying top managers*. Greenwich, Connecticut: JAI Press, pp. 74–106.

Hammer, M. & Champy, J. (1993). *Re-engineering the corporation: A Manifesto for Business Revolution*. New York: HarperCollins.

Herrnstein, R. & Murray, C. (1994). *The Bell Curve: Intelligence and Class Structure in American Life*. New York: Free Press.

Heifetz, R.A. & Laurie, D.L. (1997). The work of leadership. *Harvard Business Review*, Jan–Feb, 1997, pp. 71–97.

Hersey, P. & Blanchard, K.H. (1969). Life cycle theory of leadership. *Training and Development Journal*, 23 (5), pp. 26–34.

Higgs, M.J. & Dulewicz, S.V. (1999). *Making sense of Emotional Intelligence*. Windsor: NFER-Nelson.

Higgs, M.J. & McGuire, M. (2001). Emotional Intelligence and culture: an exploration of the relationship between individual EI and organisational culture. *Henley Working Paper Series HWP 2001/006*.

Higgs, M.J. & Rowland, D. (2001). Developing change leadership capability: The impact of a development intervention. *Henley Working Paper Series, HWP 2001/004*.

Higgs, M.J. & Rowland, D. (2000). Building change leadership capability: The quest for change competence. *Journal of change Management*, 1, 2, 116–131.

House, J. (1995). Leadership in the twenty-first century: A speculative inquiry. In A. Howard (Ed.), *The changing nature of work* (pp. 411–450). San Francisco: Jossey-Bass.

House, R.J. (1976) A theory of charismatic leadership. In J.G. Hunt & L.L. Larsons (Eds.) Leadership: The cutting edge, pp. 189–207. Carbondale, IL: Southern Illinois University Press.

Kelley, R. & Caplan, J. (1993). How Bell Labs creates star performers. *Harvard Business Review*, July–Aug, pp. 100–103.

Kets de Vries, M. (1995). *Life and death in the executive fast lane*. San Francisco: Jossey-Bass.

Kets de Vries, M. (1994). The leadership mystique. *Academy of Management Executive*, 8(3), 73–5.

Kets De Vries, M. (1993). *Leaders, fools, imposters*. San Francisco, CA: Jossey-Bass.

Kotter, J.P. (1990). What leaders really do. *Harvard Business Review*, May–June 1990, 37–60.

Kotter, J.P. (1994). Leading Change: Why Transformation Efforts Fail. *Harvard Business Review*, May–June, pp. 11–16.

Kouznes & Posner (1998). *Encouraging the heart*. San Francisco: Jossey-Bass.

Levinson, H. (1996). The leader as analyser. *Harvard Business Review*. January/February. pp. 63–70.

Martinez, M.N. (1997). The smarts that count. *HR Magazine*, 42, 11, pp. 72–78.

Mathews, L. (1996). The EQ factor. *Management*, 43, 3, 29–31.

Mintzberg, H. (1975). The manager's job: Folklore and fact. *Harvard Business Review*, July–August, 1–36.

Norusis, M.J. (1994). *SPSS Advanced Statistics, 6.1*. Chicago: SPSS Inc.

Salovey, P. & Mayer, J.D. (1990). Emotional intelligence. *Imagination, Cognition and Personality*, 9, 185–211.

Saville, P., Holdsworth, R., Nyfield, G., Cramp, L. & Mabey, W. (1993). *Occupational Personality Questionnaire Manual*. Esher: SHL.

Schein, E.H. (1985). *Organisation culture and leadership*. San Francisco: Jossey-Bass.

Seltzer, J. & Bass, B.M. (1990). Transformational leadership: Beyond initiation and consideration. *Journal of Management*, l6, pp. 693–703.

Senge, P. (1990). *The fifth discipline*. New York: Doubleday.

Senge, R., Kleiner, A., Roberts, C., Ross, R., Roth, G. & Smith, B. (1999). *The dance of change*. New York: Nicholas Brealey.

Shamir, B. (1992). Attribution of influence and charisma to the leader. *Journal of Applied Social Psychology*, 22(5), 386–407.

Sosik, J.J. & Magerian, L.E. (1999). Understanding leader Emotional Intelligence and performance. *Group and Organisation Management*, 24 (3), pp. 367–391.

Steiner, C. (1997). *Achieving emotional literacy*. London: Bloomsbury Publishing.

Stuller, J. (1998). Unconventional smarts. *Across the Board*, 35, 1, 22–23.

Tannenbaum, R. & Schmidt, W.H. (1958) How to choose a leadership pattern. *Harvard Business Review*, 36, 2, March–April, 95–l01.

Tichy, N.M. & Devanna, M.A. (1986). *The transformational leader*. New York: Wiley.

Ulrich, D. (1997). HR of the future: Conclusions and observations. *HR Management*, 36 (1), 175–179.

Williams, M. (2000). *The war for talent*. London: IPD.

Wright, G. & Fowler, C. (1986). *Investigative and design statistics*. Middlesex: Penguin Books.

Zaleanik, A. (1992). Managers and leaders: Are they different? *Harvard Business Review*, March–April, 126–35.

PART III

Assessment Tools and Processes

CHAPTER 9

Assessing Individual Development Needs

Karen van Dam
Tilburg University, Tilburg, The Netherlands

SUMMARY

This chapter focuses on the assessment of employee development needs. Needs assessment is considered an important tool for specifying the directions for future development activities. The chapter starts with discussing several objectives and effects of individual needs assessment. Following, several critical features of needs assessment methods are introduced. Next, an evaluation is given of those methods that are most commonly used in needs assessment. Finally, the chapter discusses several issues an organization should consider in deciding whether and how to conduct an individual needs assessment.

INTRODUCTION

Over the last two decades many companies have come to view employee development as a key to organizational survival and success. Rapid technological developments and changes in market conditions are some of the factors that have implied changes in the types of work that people perform and, consequently, changes in skills, knowledge, and abilities required. Although learning and development may occur informally in the daily work situation, unstructured learning generally does not suffice to reach the organization's or the individual's goals. Employee development is concerned with the way the learning process is structured towards these goals.

Individual Differences and Development in Organisations. Edited by Michael Pearn.
© 2002 John Wiley & Sons, Ltd.

A careful assessment of employees' development needs is a crucial first step to effective employee development. Needs assessment helps specifying the directions for development efforts. At the same time, the assessment's outcomes can serve as a base line for evaluating training efforts. Companies that implement development programs without conducting a needs assessment may be making errors or spending money unnecessarily.

There exist different definitions of needs assessment. Bernardin and Russell (1998, p. 176) emphasize the importance of adequate measurement when describing needs assessment as "a systematic, objective determination of development needs". Thomas and Mellon (1996, p. 21) point to the assessment's objectives when defining needs assessment as "a process of gathering and interpreting relevant information in order to determine the most effective and efficient ways of enhancing learning, potential and performance". Finally, Rossett (1987, p. 3) refers to possible causes when defining needs assessment as "the systematic study of a problem or innovation [...] in order to make effective decisions or recommendations about what should happen next". All three aspects, measurement, objectives, and causes, are important when conducting a needs analysis.

Needs assessment may involve three types of analyses (Goldstein, 1991): organizational analysis, task analysis, and person analysis. The focus of organizational analysis is on organizational goals, on where in the organization a development emphasis is required, and on organizational constraints that may hinder the transfer of learning to the work setting. Task (or job) analysis provides information on important work activities and on the individual competencies that are required to perform those activities. Task analysis should be in line with organizational analysis. For instance, if an organizational analysis reveals that the organization should become more customer-oriented, customer-orientation should be incorporated into the analysis of future jobs. Person analysis is aimed at assessing individual competencies, such as skills and abilities. To be most effective, the person analysis should be directed at those competencies that have resulted from the task analysis. In that case the assessment will provide information that is relevant to the needs assessment's objectives, namely which employee needs development, and which kind of development is required.

Individual needs assessment thus involves a comparison between the outcomes of the person analysis and some standard. Ideally, this standard is derived from the outcomes of the organizational and task analyses. Development need is indicated when the comparison reveals a discrepancy between what is desired and what exists. Since the required standards usually are incorporated into the personal assessment, this comparison is rather implicit. Employees that perform well on the assessment dimensions seem to have little development needs. When performance on the assessment dimensions is lacking, this may indicate needing attention. Performance discrepancies should not be automatically interpreted as a need for development, however. Sometimes the problem is motivational and requires some other type of organizational intervention.

This chapter focuses on individual needs assessment, i.e. the assessment of the competencies of individual employees. In organizations, a variety of techniques are being used for conducting individual needs assessment. These assessment techniques differ with respect to the quality and acceptation of the method and it's outcomes. In this chapter, we will examine some critical features of assessment methods in general. Next, an overview of individual needs assessment techniques and their features is presented. Finally, several issues are discussed that are important for implementing assessment programs. The chapter starts with outlying different objectives and effects of individual needs assessment. For information on organizational or task analysis, the reader is referred to other texts (e.g., Harrison & Shirom, 1999; Harvey, 1991).

OBJECTIVES AND EFFECTS OF NEEDS ASSESSMENT

Assessment of individual development needs can serve different goals. Most of these goals are tightly related to the objectives of employee development. The first and main objective of needs asssesment is a strategic one, aimed at keeping the work force optimally shaped for reaching the organization's goals. From this point of view, both needs assessment and employee development can be seen as keys to effective implementing business strategy. The strategic value of these tools is critical to improving the organization's competetiveness, enhancing productivity, and organizational change. Ideally, needs assessment should be conducted in the context of a human resource policy that is linked to organizational strategy.

Despite the strategic value of needs assessment, only a few organizations conduct such an analysis in the context of their strategic plans (Bernardin & Russell, 1998; Cox & Blake, 1991). More often needs assessment occurs on instigation from the operational level of the organization. Most organizations become interested in identifying development needs only after receiving signals from the shop-floor, such as declined performance, when implementing new technologies, or on specific supervisor or employee request (Fisher, Schoenfeldt & Shaw, 1996). On this operational level, needs analysis can help improve person-task fit. Person-task fit exists when the skills and abilities of the employee match the skills and abilities required by the job. A good fit has advantages for both the organization and the employee, since it may result in improved job performance as well as enhanced work-related attitudes (Anderson & Ostroff, 1997).

While organizations recognize the value of needs assessment and employee development to help them reach their goals, so too do employees. Employees too have aspirations, and they understand that development opportunities may enable them to grow and advance in their career. Therefore it seems important that the organization's efforts should be in line with their employees' needs. Employees that perceive a discrepancy between personal and organizational objectives may react with resistance to the needs assessment. Resistance may also arise when employees fear the outcome of the assessment. Resistances and fears may affect the motivation and performance of employees, and undermine the validity of assessment outcomes. Employees that react positively towards the needs assessment procedure are likely to be more satisfied with the development program content (Noe & Schmitt, 1986). Therefore, it is important that organizations try to overcome these resistances, for instance by offering vocational guidance and emphasizing the value of the assessment for individual career development.

Besides contributing to the organization's or the employee's goals, needs assessment can have an important spin-off by communicating the organization's anticipated directions and desired performance to the work force. Both task analysis and person analysis contain activities by which important skills, abilities and achievements are communicated throughout the organization (cf. Altink, Visser & Castelyns, 1997). Providing employees with the opportunity to participate in task analysis and assist in developing criteria for future behavior and performance, may lead to a better understanding and incorporation of the organization's goals. Similarly, by experiencing a needs assessment, employees may better realize which competencies are necessary for achieving desired work outcomes.

CRITICAL FEATURES OF NEEDS ASSESSMENT METHODS

If managers are to take development decisions based upon a needs assessment, they have to be sure that the outcomes of the assessment are accurate and acceptable. In this section we will discuss some critical features of assessment methods; features that are important for the application of assessment techniques and for the interpretation of assessment outcomes. Two categories of features may be distinquished: psychometric features, such as reliability and validity, and utilization criteria, such as relevance, fairness and acceptability.

RELIABILITY

Reliability can be defined as the extent to which a set of measurements is free from measurement error (Guion, 1998). When a measure contains error, repeated measurements of the same aspect will yield different outcomes. The observed measurement outcome thus can be perceived as the algebraic sum of a true measure (true score) and a measurement error (error score). Measurement error, by definition, is purely random, i.e. error scores are neither related to true scores nor interrelated.

There are several methods for estimating reliability. Generally, such an estimation involves computing a correlation between two sets of measures that are presumed to measure the same thing in the same sample in the same way. For instance, *test-retest* reliability is evaluated by giving the same test at two different points in time, and computing the correlation between these scores. Using the same test twice involves some practical problems however. Candidates or employees might not be available a second time, and practice or memory effects may affect performance at the second assessment. Parallel forms reliability and split halves reliability are ways to avoid these problems. In case of *parallel test* reliability, two forms of the same test are developed, and the correlations of the scores on these two alternate forms are used to estimate reliability. In case of *split halve* reliability, a test is split randomly into two halves and the scores of these two halves are then correlated. Another indication for reliability results if one splits a test in all possible ways, and averages the estimated split halves reliabilities. The resulting coefficient alpha is considered an *internal consistency* estimate of reliability, and indicates the effect of random error as well as the degree to which the test measures more than one construct.

Some of the measures used in needs assessment involve the use of raters. Different observers seeing the same behavior or the same product may make different evaluations, however. Thus, when raters are used as source of information, differences between raters are an important source of error. Like test reliability, *interrater* reliability is often expressed as a correlation, or—if there are more than two raters—an average correlation. High interrater reliability does not necessarily imply that raters make the same ratings, but only that they put raters in roughly the same relative order. The reliability of ratings can be increased by pooling raters.

VALIDITY

A measure is valid to the extent that it measures what it is purported to measure (Cronbach, 1984). Like reliability, validity has different forms, with predictive validity and construct validity being most important (Drenth, 1998). The *predictive* validity of an assessment method is the degree to which it is capable of predicting future performance or behavior. The predictive validity of measures is important for job selection or for a programme of instruction where the measure is intended to predict eventual success in these areas. Evidence on predictive validity can be obtained by calculating a correlation between the obtained scores and indices that represent the degree of success in the selected field, for instance supervisor ratings of work behavior. Since a needs assessment is directed at diagnosing strengths and weaknesses more than predicting future work behavior, predictive validity is not the most relevant feature of an assessment technique. Instead, predictive validity can serve as an indication for an instrument's quality, although its ability to predict work behavior and training proficiency remains important of course.

More important for needs assessment is *construct* validity. Construct validity refers to the extent to which a measure correctly provides information on the underlying construct it is supposed to measure. If the forgoing organizational and task analyses have indicated that customer orientation is an important future employee characteristic, then the measure used in the person analysis should tap customer orientation and not some other characteristic. Invalid measures may lead to wrong decisions concerning the necessity and content of development programs. Also, providing employees with invalid feedback on their skills or behavior may affect their self-image or self-confidence unjustly.

Unlike reliability and predictive validity, construct validity can not be expressed in a single correlation coefficient, but has to be derived from a pattern of correlations. Construct validity is higher as the correlation between the measure and other indices of the same characteristic or behavior is higher (*convergence* validity), and if there exist low correlations with indices of different characteristics or behaviors that are obtained by a similar method (*discriminant* validity). In order to obtain high validity, it is important that the measures used are highly reliable, since unreliability will lower correlations between measures. As such, reliability is imposing a ceiling for validity.

Two more forms of validity warrant attention: content validity and face validity. An assessment method has *content* validity if it adequately represents all job or construct domains. *Face* validity refers to the subjective evaluation of the validity of an assessment method. Content validity and face validity are important for needs assessment since they are thought to affect the acceptability of assessment methods. Candidates appear to react more favorably towards assessment methods that show a clear relationship with important job dimensions (e.g. Gilliland, 1994). Similarly, organizations prefer measures that resemble the job or in which important job criteria can be easiliy identified.

RELEVANCE

Needs assessment should be directed at those competencies that follow from the organizational and task analyses. An assessment is said to be relevant when it provides an adequate representation of those competencies. Two issues are important here (Drenth, 1998): *deficiency*, i.e. whether all important parts of the competency domain are adequately

considered; and *excessivess*, i.e. whether the assessment contains elements that are irrelevant. If deficiency and excessiveness are avoided, the assessment will provide valid
information on which organizations subsequently can base decisions about employee development. Relevance thus can be considered a feature of an assessment program more
than an intrinsic feature of a specific assessment technique. For example, we cannot
assert that supervisor ratings in general have more relevance than development center
outcomes. Being a program feature, relevance will receive no attention in the overview
of assessment methods given below.

FAIRNESS

An assessment is said to be fair if it reflects real differences in competencies without
treating groups differently. The major issues of unfairness involve race, ethnic minorities,
and gender; but other categorizations may be important as well, such as social class, age,
height, sexual orientation, and physical attractiveness (Rust & Golombok, 1999). In
many countries it is now illegal to select or promote individuals on the basis of group
characteristics. The 1976 Race Relations Act, the 1986 Sex Discrimination Act, and the
1995 Disabilities Discrimination Act, are examples of anti-discrimination legislation in
the UK.

There are different ways in which unfairness can occur (Cook, 1998). *Intrinsic* unfairness for instance exists when a measurement device shows differences in the mean
score of two groups that are due to test characteristics and not to any differences between the groups in the characteristic that is being measured. *Extrinsic* unfairness exists
when decisions leading to inequality are made following an assessment procedure that
by itself contains no bias. These decisions are perceived as unfair since they tend to
maintain—and even strengthen—existing inequalities between groups. For instance, if
a measure for leadership qualities shows that female employees have significantly lower
scores than male employees, and the organization uses leadership qualities as a criterion
for promotion, this combination of assessment method and decision making will uphold
the under-representation of women in the management of this company. This situation
generally is known as *adverse impact*. Some methods, for instance cognitive ability tests,
display a greater adverse impact than others, such as work samples.

In needs assessment, we also should be aware of *pre-assessment* unfairness; where
the decision which employees will participate in a needs assessment, and consequently
in a development program, may exclude specific groups. Like relevance, this aspect of
unfairness concerns a whole program and not specific assessment methods, and therefore
will receive no further attention.

ACCEPTABILITY

For obtaining optimal results and avoiding resistance, it is crucial that the individual
needs assessment program is acceptable for participants. Besides reacting to the objectives of an assessment program or being fearful of the assessment outcome, as previously
discussed, employees may react to features of the assessment program itself. Assessment
experiences can have several psychological and behavioral consequences. For instance,
Noe and Schmitt (1986) observed direct links between candidates' reactions to their

assessment, such as finding the assessment credible and agreeing with the assessment outcome, and later training program satisfaction. Other studies (e.g. Ployhart & Ryan, 1998) have shown important side-effects of assessments on a range of withdrawal behaviors, such as lowered job involvement and organizational commitment, increased withdrawal cognitions and career search behavior.

Candidates may react to both assessment procedure and assessment outcome. When evaluating the assessment *procedure*, candidates focus on features such as job relatedness of the assessment methods used (Gilliland, 1994); opportunity to demonstrate one's ability (Lind & Tyler, 1988); information provided about the assessment (Bauer, Maerta, Dolen, & Campion, 1998); invasion of privacy (Steiner & Gilliland, 1996); and interpersonal treatment (the degree to which assessment methods are perceived as warm and personal as opposed to being cold and insensitive, Bies & Moag, 1986). Some features have been found to relate to test motivation and test performance (Arvey, Strickland, Drauden & Martin, 1990).

Evaluations of assessment *outcomes* appear to relate to organizational attractiveness, job acceptance intentions, turnover intentions, and testing attitudes (Bauer et al., 1998). Process and outcome evaluations may affect each other. Candidates that have received a negative outcome tend to be less positive about the assessment process than candidates with a positive outcome, especially when they had high expectations about the assessment outcome (Gilliland, 1994). On the other hand, candidates can accept a negative outcome better when they consider the process to be fair (Van Yperen & Baar, 2000). Together, these findings emphasize that organizations should be careful when designing and administering individual needs assessment.

METHODS FOR INDIVIDUAL NEEDS ASSESSMENT

A great number of methods are available for conducting an individual needs assessment. Whereas some of these methods concentrate on the employee's performance on the job, others focus on evoked job behavior in standardized job simulations.

RATINGS OF JOB PERFORMANCE

Ratings of job performance are usually made by the employee's supervisor. Performance ratings are used for different purposes, such as promotion, salary, training, and research (validation). Ratings are typically based on observation; more specifically they are based on remembered observations since ratings seldom occur during the actual work performance. In some cases the time from observation to evaluation may amount to a year, which puts a heavy demand on the way observations are stored and remembered. During the rating process, these remembered observations are quantitatively evaluated by means of scales or checklists. Besides numerical anchors (1 = low, 5 = high) and verbal anchors (agree—disagree), BARS (behaviorally anchored rating scales) (Smith & Kendall, 1963) have been used. BARS describe which behavior is expected at each performance level, which makes the ratings obtained useful for performance feedback.

Ratings are often criticized for their weak psychometric properties and rater bias. Several rating errors have been observed. Some raters for instance are reluctant to give poor ratings (leniency error) or use the extremes of the scale (central tendency). In the same vein, some people tend to rate more highly those targets they perceive to be like themselves (similar-to-me effect). Also, the evaluation of one important performance dimension has been found to affect the evaluations of other dimensions (halo error). The quality of performance ratings can be improved with appropriate training, and carefully designed rating scales, such as BARS.

The quality of ratings is usually evaluated through inter-rater reliability. Supervisor reliability appears to be modest. Rothstein (1990) found a ceiling of .60, which only could be reached after 20 years of acquaintance. Reliability is higher if the same supervisor makes both ratings (Viswesvaran, Ones & Schmidt, 1996); when raters are from different levels of the organization, inter-rater reliability is typically lower. The reliability of ratings can be improved by pooling the judgments of several raters. As follows from the Spearman-Brown equation, a single reliability estimate of .50 can improve up to .80 or even higher, when four or more parallel ratings are used (Houston, Raymond & Svec, 1991). If the ratings are not parallel, i.e. when each rater evaluates a slightly different construct, pooling is not an appropriate solution.

It is difficult to evaluate the validity of supervisor ratings at this point. Often supervisor ratings are used as criteria themselves, and accepted uncritically as measuring whatever the scale label says (Guion, 1998). Thus, after checks on inter-rater reliability, no further psychometric evaluation of construct validity is sought. Validity estimation by itself is difficult since no obvious criterion for supervisor ratings exists, although convergence over organizational levels of raters is sometimes proposed. Supervisor ratings have demonstrated a low correlation with objective criteria (Heneman, 1986), suggesting that ratings and objective criteria measure different aspects of work behavior.

With respect to fairness, some studies (e.g. Kraiger & Ford, 1985; Mount, Sytsma, Hazucha & Holt, 1997) have found a small but consistent own-race bias where Whites were rated higher by Whites and Blacks were rated higher by Blacks (for a different interpretation, see Sackett & DuBois, 1991). In another study (Pulakos, White, Oppler & Borman, 1989), the occurrence and direction of race bias in performance ratings varied with job dimension. Note that the observed differences are always small.

Job performance ratings can also be provided by others than supervisors, for instance by peers. Peers are considered a uniquely valuable information source for several reasons (Ladner & Greguras, 2001). First, peers often work closely with ratees and have more opportunities to observe certain behaviors than supervisors. Second, peers may be more aware of the behaviors that are critical for job performance. Finally, peers most likely do not experience the same restraints that other sources may experience when rating. Indeed, peers have been found quite honest in expressing what they think of each other (Cook, 1998). Thus, peer ratings have been noted as being potentially the most accurate judgments of employee behavior assuming that the raters are well acquainted with the ratee. Peer assessments are of acceptable inter-rater reliability and temporal reliability, and have shown predictive validity (Pollack & Pollack, 1996). However, peer ratings are not always favored by assessees.

Yet another information source for performance ratings consists of the rated employees themselves. Self-assessments have become increasingly popular, especially for development purposes. More than other methods self-assessments are considered an effective way of developing self-awareness (Kidd, 1997), and enhancing acceptance of others' feedback (Riggio & Cole, 1992). However, self-assessments have shown only moderate validity and reliability (e.g. Mabe & West, 1982), correlating rather low with other ratings (Atwater, Ostroff, Yammarino & Fleenor, 1998). Correlations between self and other (supervisor, peer) ratings are consistently lower than correlations between peer and supervisor ratings (Harris & Schaubroeck, 1988). Self-ratings tend to be more lenient than the ratings made by colleagues, which seems due more to over-estimation of abilities, than to faking (Nilsen & Campbell, 1993). Although this self-enhancing bias reflects a positive self-view, it may lead employees to ignore criticism and discount failure, which in turn may result in poorer future performance (Atwater et al., 1998). Indeed, congruence in self-others' ratings has been found to relate to performance and promotion recommendations (Atwater & Yammarino, 1992). The extent to which self-ratings are congruent with others' assessments is typically taken as indicating employees' self-awareness, i.e. the degree to which individuals understand their own strengths and weaknesses (Fletcher & Baldry, 2000). Increased self-awareness has been shown to lead to changes in behaviors and improved performance (Johnston & Ferstl, 1999).

In *multi-source feedback* systems, or *360 degree feedback* systems, ratings from various raters are combined. Besides supervisors, peers, and ratees, ratings may be obtained from subordinates, customers, and other external experts. Obtaining feedback from multiple sources is considered advantageous since it provides information from a broad spectrum of people on various aspects of the employee's performance. At the same time, a greater objectivity may be achieved; having multiple raters may result in a fairer and possibly less biased view than simply relying on a supervisor's ratings (Fletcher, Baldry & Cunningham-Snell, 1998). Multi-source feedback is rapidly growing in popularity as development tool; besides it has been used for performance appraisal, succession planning, and organizational change initiatives.

Despite their popularity, there has been serious criticism levied against multi-source feedback systems. According to Waldman, Atwater, and Antonioni (1998), 360 degree feedback has "gone amok" with many organizations implementing these systems solely ~~political~~ to keep up with competition, and without understanding how these systems fit into their culture and how they may, in turn, impact culture. Others have criticized organizations' lack of attention for the psychometric properties of these systems. As Fletcher et al. (1998) argue, systems of these kinds are just as likely to display deficiencies in psychometric properties, and show rater bias, as do ordinary ratings.

A great deal of research has explored the relationships among various types of raters, trying to reveal why ratings from different sources vary. Inconsistencies have been attributed to different frames of reference being applied in judging job performance, different opportunities to observe the ratee, or the ratee's actually behaving differently in the presence of different raters (Schmitt & Chan, 1998). Due to their varying perspectives, ratings from different sources are likely to be somewhat inconsistent (London and Smither, 1995). According to Borman (1974) high agreement might be an erroneous requirement, since raters at different levels probably observe different facets of the employee's performance, and that, accordingly, their ratings should reflect these differences. To what degree discrepancies between raters follow from divergent rater perspectives rather than from inadequate measures, or invalid and unreliable ratings, is of course difficult to establish.

However, the fact that ratings—both within and between sources—do correlate, can be taken to indicate that they do measure something in common. According to Campbell et al. (1990) ratings are more likely to be explained by ratee performance than by contaminants. Improving rating formats, training raters, and guarding the rating process are recommended ways to increase the quality of performance ratings. In conclusion, when constructed and used competently, rating systems, like the multi-source feedback system, can be considered reliable and relevant measures of job performance.

 ## PERFORMANCE TESTING

The main objective of performance tests is to elicit relevant work behavior. Performance tests consist of a task central to the job in question, which is presented, performed and rated under standardized conditions. There exists a large range of performance tests. Whereas some of these simulations may imitate a task almost exactly, as in work samples, others may present only the general flavor of reality, as in assessment center exercises. But there are many more performance tests, ranging from work knowledge tests to situational video-based tests, that all use standardized, work related stimuli. Below, we will focus on work samples and development centers.

A *work sample* test is a standard sample of a job content domain, presented in such a way that specific aspects of the work process, the outcome, or both, can be observed and scored. The most literal example of a work sample test is the hands-on performance test (such as a typing test) in which an employee is required to actually perform a job-related task under the same conditions as those required on the job. Scores are usually ratings, although in some cases more objective measures are obtained. Work sample tests are often used as predictor measures in personnel selection, but they have also served as indices of trainability and as criterion measures to validate training outcomes.

Work samples possess several positive features. Work samples have demonstrated high predictive validity; some types have even shown higher predictive validity than cognitive ability tests (Schmidt & Hunter, 1998). Besides, they know little adverse impact against minority groups (Schmitt, Clause & Pulakos, 1996), and—due to their job-relatedness and opportunity for demonstrating ability—evoke positive candidate reactions (Steiner & Gilliland, 1996). Test-retest reliability is usually adequate but can be lower depending on the number of sub-tasks performed (Shavelson, 1991). Finally, work samples tend to measure maximum performance shown under conditions of high motivation; they indicate what people can do but not what they typically will do. Maximum performance is useful information since it indicates the presence of training needs without a motivational aspect.

Work samples also have a number of limitations. A first limitation concerns their costs; work samples are expensive to develop and administer. Each job, or group of jobs, requires an individually tailored and validated work sample. Often expensive equipment is required, and the testing situation may involve one examiner for each candidate. And because work samples are job-specific, they have limited usability, which hinders writing down development costs. Second, work samples usually do not entail the full range of actual working tasks or elicit the full range of relevant work behaviors. Thus, sampling issues may arise and content validity may be questionable. Third, work samples can only be applied when candidates have already some job experience and are able to perform the tasks without prior training. Fourth, there is the issue of construct validity. Most work samples are multi-faceted (Schmitt et al., 1996); the observed work behavior is the result of several underlying factors. Indeed, work samples have been found to correlate with general mental ability, work experience, job knowledge, while at the same time they are also thought to tap performance-related factors unrelated to intelligence, "tacit knowledge", and practical work habits (Callinan & Robertson, 2000). The scoring process rarely allows the isolation of these multiple dimensions. Thus, in case of a needs assessment, it will be difficult to entangle, and feed back, the reason for a less-than-adequate test score. Finally, work samples are most appropriate for assessing skilled work performance. They are less useable when the job requires social interactions, complex information processing, or decision making. Due to these limitations, work samples have not been used too often for development purposes.

Increasingly popular for needs assessment are *development centers*, which have their origins in assessment center practice. Assessment centers (and thus development centers) work on the principle of multi-trait, multi-method assessment; a specific assessment center includes at least two different methods of assessing each competency. For example, decision making can be assessed through an in-tray exercise and a role-play. According to the logic of multiple methods of assessment, the resulting measure should be better generalizable across methods (exercises) and to actual job performance. Although assessment centers may include standardized tests, their core feature is the situational exercise meant to elicit relevant work behavior by simulating central work settings. Exercises most often used are the leaderless group discussion, in-tray exercises, and role-plays.

As assessment centers came to be more widely used, there was an increasing recognition of their possible benefits for employee development. Following, development centers have been developed along traditional assessment center lines, aimed at identifying individual strengths and weaknesses, and diagnosing development needs. Moreover, development centers have been perceived as interventions that by itself may act to change the behavior of assessors (usually managers) and candidates. Thus, some development centers have been designed not just to be diagnostic but also for developmental events in their own right.

To what degree has research supported these positive expectations about development centers? Since most studies have concentrated on assessment centers, this question will be answered more generally. Assessment centers have several positive features. Besides adequate parallel test and interrater reliabilities, assessment centers have demonstrated substantial predictive validities. Assessment center scores predict both work performance criteria and career advancement rather well. In addition, assessment centers do not seem to create adverse impact; neither gender nor race bias has been found. Finally, they are popular with candidates and organizations. Candidates commonly perceive the assessment outcomes to be accurate and fair, and as furthering their understanding of their strengths and weaknesses (Iles & Robertson, 1997). Organizations value the range of insights about candidates resulting from the assessment center.

But there are some drawbacks as well. Like work samples, assessment centers are costly to develop and administer; the average assessment center includes seven exercises, lasts two days and uses managers as assessors. And despite positive candidate reactions, assessment centers can have a de-motivating impact, particularly on those who "failed". But the biggest problem of the assessment center concerns construct validity. Research findings indicate that assessment centers have low construct validity; evaluations of different dimensions in the same exercise show higher inter-correlations than evaluations of the same dimension in different exercises (e.g. Robertson, Gratton & Sharpley, 1987).

This *"exercise problem"* has led some researchers (e.g. Robertson et al., 1987; Russell & Domm, 1995) to propose that assessments should be based on exercises, developed as work samples, rather than on dimensions. In Russell and Domm's (1995) study indeed a greater construct validity was observed for task-based ratings than for dimension-based ratings. For needs assessment, however, the exercise solution seems less appropriate since dimensional feedback is necessary in order to improve practice. Telling participants that they did not perform well on some exercises will not suffice; in order to develop they need to know why and how they were ineffective (Carrick & Williams, 1999). Also, the exercise approach directly undermines the AC's logic of multiple assessments, and might stripp off the component by which predictive validity and generalizability are delivered (Callinan & Robertson, 1999).

Other solutions to the exercise problem have focused on improving construct validity. Research has revealed several factors that moderate construct validity (see Lievens, 1998), such as dimension factors (number, conceptual distinctiveness, and transparency), assessor factors (type of assessor, type of training), and exercise factors (exercise form, use of role-players). Paying careful attention to these factors may help organizations to reach adequate construct validity of the development center in use.

 ## INTERVIEW ASSESSMENT

Interviews are recommended widely in the needs assessment literature (e.g. Goldstein, 1991). Interacting with top management, line management and employees is an important way to convey needs and objectives, collect information on current problems and anticipated developments, and reach general acceptance of the needs assessment program. Thus, the interview can serve as an important tool for communication.

However, can the interview also serve as a tool for assessing individual development needs? The answer to this question is: It depends. Meta-analytic reviews (e.g. Huffcutt & Arthur, 1994) have demonstrated that the value of the interview is greatly affected by its structure; the less structured the interview, the lower its reliability and (predictive) validity. Structure results from a thorough preparation of interview content, followed by a systematically conducted interview and rating process.

Distinguishing four levels of structure, Huffcutt and Arthur (1994) showed that adding only a little structure to the interview, i.e. deciding on the topics to be discussed (level 2) already resulted in improved validity compared to the situation in which no constraints existed (level 1). Validity improved even more when questions were specified in advance, while varying probes were allowed (level 3). The most structured level (level 4) in which no deviations or probing questions were allowed, did not show improved validity compared to level 3, suggesting that the effect of structure had reached its ceiling. In conclusion, when properly structured, interviews can show satisfactory reliabilities and predictive validities. In predicting work performance and training proficiency, structured interviews appear competitive with other assessment methods (Schmidt & Hunter, 1998).

Recently, the construct validity of interviews has become a serious research issue, with researchers focusing on the constructs that might be assessed in the interview (Lievens, van Dam & Anderson, 2001). Correlations have been observed between interviews and other constructs, such as personality (Caldwell & Burger, 1998; van Dam, 2001a), social skills (Schuler & Funke, 1989), and job knowledge (Maurer, Solamon & Troxtel, 1998). For some types of interviews, correlations with mental ability tests have been observed, suggesting that some interviews actually may tap cognitive abilities. Behavior-oriented structured interviews however show little correlation with mental ability (Motowidlo et al., 1992; Salgado & Moscoso, 2001). Salgado and Moscoso (2001) found that behavioral structured interviews were most strongly related to job experience, job knowledge and social skills.

With respect to fairness, interviews appear to create only little adverse impact. Whether adverse impact occurs depends on interview content and structure. Deviding interviews according to interview content, Huffcut, Roth and Conway (1999) found that mainly background credentials showed high racial and gender group differences. In addition, highly structured interviews show lower adverse impact then less structured interviews (Huffcutt & Roth, 1998), whereas bias is lowest for behavioral structured interviews compared to conventional structured interviews (Lin, Dobbins, & Fahr, 1992). Thus, the small adverse effect of interviews might be even reduced if behavioral structured interviews are used.

The message to be drawn from these studies appears that structured interviews, especially when they are behavior oriented, can be applied in individual needs assessment. However, structured interviews in general are not very popular with organizations nor with candidates, at least in a job selection context (Dipboye, 1997). Although interviews that are more structured are perceived to be more complete, thorough and fairer than unstructured interviews, they are also rated as more difficult and stressful (Janz & Mooney, 1993). Besides, the tight format of the structured interview is thought to threaten the needs of both interviewer and candidate, leaving no room for individual contributions (Van der Zee, Bakker & Bakker, 2001). Since the unfavorability of structured interviews is established mainly in a job selection context, one could argue that the situation might be different in a development context. Assuming that employees experience a needs assessment as a means towards personal growth, they can be expected to react more positively to a structured interview format.

For a summary of the key issues raised see Table 9.1.

ISSUES IN IMPLEMENTING NEEDS ASSESSMENT PROGRAMS

There are several issues an organization should consider in deciding whether and how to conduct an individual needs assessment. Some of these issues have been the topic of this chapter and concern the features of the assessment methods used. As noted before, it is important the individual needs assessment is geared towards those competencies that result from the organizational and task analyses. In addition, the methods used should provide reliable and valid information about these competencies. Only when a method is reliable and construct validity is satisfactory, one can use the information it provides for feedback and curriculum development. Construct validity however is difficult to establish, and in many cases it will be impractical to engage in this endeavour, for instance when assessment instruments are tailor made and infrequently used. In these cases, it is crucial to pay careful attention to validity issues when designing and administering assessment methods (e.g., Lievens, 1998).

Albeit important, psychometric features tell only one side of the tale; there is another side that is relevant as well, viz. the social impact of assessment programs. Needs assessment takes place within a social framework. Usually assessees are employees that—during their employment—have established an exchange relationship with the organization (van Dam, 2001b). A needs assessment may endanger this relationship in several ways. As this chapter has shown, some assessment methods have lower acceptability

TABLE 9.1   Summary of methods for individual needs assessment

Methods	Favourable	Not favourable
Ratings of Job Performance		
1. Supervisor ratings	• convenience • low cost • readily improved with rater training, formats and scoring processes	• rater bias • reliance on memory • poor psychometric properties
2. Self-assessment	• increases self-awareness	• poor psychometric properties • low correlation to ratings by others
3. Multi-source feedback (360 degree)	• integrates information	• psychometric properties can be weak
Performance tests Work samples	• high predictive validity • little adverse impact • reasonable reliability • measures 'maximum' performance	• costly • restricted sampling of tasks • needs experienced people • best for assessing skilled work performance
Development centres	• good predictive validity • little adverse impact • popular with participants • valued by organisations	• costly to develop and administer • can be de-motivating to participants • the 'exercise problem' (construct validity
The interview	• poor psychometric properties when not structured • useful as communication tool • little adverse impact	• when highly structured perceived as stressful • not popular with organisations or individuals • high structure inhibits flexibility

than others. Acceptability is related to adverse impact, but also to job-relatedness; those methods that are clearly related to the job are better received by assessees.

Besides assessment program features, there are other factors that may affect the acceptablity of an assessment program and put the employee-organization relationship under strain. Employees might object to a needs assessment because they dread its consequences. Even though the assessment is geared towards development, there exists some point where the observed discrepancy between what is and what should be, is too large to be remedied. In that case, the assessment may have consequences for the employee that where not foreseen initially, such as job transfer, voluntary or involuntary turnover, and loss of self-esteem. Resistance may also arise when a needs assessment mainly emphasizes the organization's goals and ignores the objectives of the individual employee. Employees vary in career objectives and development needs (van Dam, 1998). Whereas some employees are clearly development and career-oriented, others may experience little need for development and change. By paying attention to their employees' career orientations, the organization may improve the commitment of employees to the employee-organization relationship.

A related issue concerns the choice of assessees: who are going to participate in a needs assessment? It is sometimes proposed that top-managers should be the first ones to take part in a needs assessment. Management participation as such can be considered a gesture; by showing their personal vulnerability, managers serve as a role-model, and thus may enhance the acceptability of the assessment program. At the same time, the outcomes of the assessment might produce some useful information that can be used to prepare these managers better for the organization's future. Participation of top-management is more evident when a needs assessment serves a strategic objective. In needs assessments that are instigated by the operational (shop-floor) or personal (employee) level, management participation is not required.

Although participant selection by the organization is more common than self-nomination, it is clear that some employees will be more eager to participate in needs assessment and development activities than others. The decision to participate in these activities is likely to be influenced by the expectancy that it will result in positive outcomes (van Dam, 2001b). Here a paradox seems to exist (Carrick & Williams, 1999), since those with greater potential for advancement may expect to gain more, may be motivated more, and may be offered more developmental opportunities. In contrast, those that perform less well, and in fact have greater development needs, may be less motivated to develop themselves since they expect to gain only little. Thus, a needs assessment in the end might have an opposite effect, increasing instead of diminishing the differences between those that already perform well and those that do not.

Resistance and low acceptability can have severe consequences. Within the assessment and development context, the acceptability of an assessment program may affect test motivation and test performance (Arvey et al., 1990), as well as training attitudes and satisfaction with the training content (Noe & Schmitt, 1986). Assessment participation has been found to affect certain psychological states, such as self-esteem or well-being (Iles & Robertson, 1997). In addition, assessment procedures and decisions can have an impact on candidates' job performance (Gilliland, 1994), as well on their post-assessment attitudes to the organization, and the intention to leave their jobs and careers (Francis-Smythe & Smith, 1997). This effect appears to be stronger for participants that dread the consequences the assessment will have for their careers. Some employees may eventually decide to leave the organization.

What can organizations do to prevent these negative effects to occur? In the first place, it should be emphasized that a trustful, well-balanced employee-organization relationship is a prerequisite for successful change efforts. This relationship presupposes that organizations pay attention to employees career objectives and development needs besides their own objectives. Participation in task analysis and the definition of critical work behaviors, consultation in program design, as well as supplying information on the program and methods used, will further increase employees' commitment to the needs assessment. Acceptability of assessment methods and their outcomes may also be enhanced by providing employees with the opportunity to supply additional information; for instance through self-assessments or interviews.

In addition to raising motivation, it is important that the organization acts on the outcomes of the assessment. Employees will have expectations with respect to development activities, career guidance, job changes, or other activities that are to follow a needs assessment. However, there are many organizational constraints that may prevent subsequent activities to take place, or hinder the transfer of learning to the work setting, such as organizational climate, lack of managerial support, and fixed production standards. For development to happen, it is important that it takes place in a supportive environment where all parties see it as a valuable process. This again illuminates the necessity to place needs assessment within a broader framework of career development policy and even human resources management. Only within a broad organizational framework, employee development will be assured for all employees.

CONCLUSION

In this chapter we have focused on methods to be used for assessing individual development needs. In the introduction, a development need was said to exist if the assessment shows a discrepancy between what is desired and what exists. Thus, the emphasis in needs assessment, and in this chapter, is on assessing the employee's shortcomings. However, a needs assessment also provides information about employees' strengths. Both from an organizational and from a personal perspective, it would be unwise to emphasize only weaknesses and ignore these strengths. The strengths of the work force are an important factor for the organization's competitiveness. Besides, even the most motivated and development oriented employee will be disappointed if only weaknesses are noticed. Obviously, a needs assessment indicates more than only discrepancies and development needs; it also provides the organization and the employee with information about positive characteristics and valuable future contributions.

REFERENCES

Altink, W.M.M., Visser, C.T. & Castelijns, M. (1997). Criterion development: The unknown power of criteria as communication tools. In N. Anderson & P. Herriot (eds), *International handbook of selection and assessment*. Chichester: Wiley.

Anderson, N. & Ostroff, C. (1997). Selection as socialization. In N. Anderson & P. Herriot (eds), *International handbook of selection and assessment* (pp. 413–440). Chichester: Wiley.

Arvey, R.D., Strickland, W., Drauden, G. & Martin, C. (1990). Motivational components of test taking. *Personnel Psychology, 43*, 695–716.

Atwater, L.E. & Yammarino, F.J. (1992). Does self-other agreement on leadership perceptions moderate the validity of leadership and performance predictions? *Personnel Psychology, 45*, 141–164.

Atwater, L.E., Ostroff, C., Yammarino, F.J. & Fleenor, J.W. (1998). Self-other agreement: Does it really matter? *Personnel Psychology, 51*, 577–598.

Bauer, T.N., Maertz, C.P., Jr., Dolen, M.R. & Campion, M.A. (1998). Longitudinal assessment of applicant reactions to employment testing and test outcome feedback. *Journal of Applied Psychology, 83*, 892–903.

Bernardin, H.J. & Russell, J.E.A. (1998). *Human resource management*. Boston: Irwin McGraw-Hill.

Bies, R.J. & Moag, J.S. (1986). International justice: Communication criteria of fairness. *Research on Negotiation in Organizations, 1*, 43–55.

Borman, W. (1974). The rating of individuals in organizations. An alternative approach. *Organizational Behavior and Human Performance, 12*, 105–124.

Caldwell, D.F. & Burger, J.M. (1998). Personality characteristics of job applicants and success in screening interviews. *Personnel Psychology, 51*, 119–136.

Callinan, M. & Robertson, I.T. (2000). Work sampling testing. *International Journal of Selection and Assessment, 8*, 248–260.

Campbell, C.H., Ford, P., Rumsey, M.G., Pulakos, E.D., Borman, W.C., Felker, D.B., de Vera, M.V. & Riegelhaupt, B.J. (1990). Development of multiple job performance measures in a representative sample of jobs. *Personnel Psychology, 43*, 277–300.

Carrick, P. & Williams, R. (1999). Development centres—a review of assumptions. *Human Resource Management Journal, 9*, 77–91.

Cook, M. (1998). *Personnel selection* (3rd edn). Chichester: Wiley.

Cox, T. & Blake, S. (1991). Managing cultural diversity: Implications for organizational competetiveness. *Academy of Management Executive, 5*, 45–56.

Cronbach, L.J. (1984). *The essentials of psychological testing* (4th edn). Cambridge: Harper & Row.

Dipboye, R.l. (1997). Structured selection interviews: Why do they work? Why are they underutilized? In N. Anderson & P. Herriot (eds) *International handbook of selection and assessment* (pp. 455–473). Chichester: Wiley.

Drenth, P.J.D. (1998). Personnel appraisal. In P.J.D. Drenth, H. Thierry & C.J. de Wolff (eds). *Handbook of work and organizational psychology* (Vol. 2, pp. 59–87). Hove: Psychology Press.

Englebrecht, A.S. & Fischer, A.H. (1995). The managerial performance implications of a development center. *Human Relations, 50*, 149–167.

Fisher, C.D., Schoenfeldt, L.F. & Shaw, J.B. (1996). *Human Resource Management* (3rd edn). Boston: Houghton Mifflin.

Fletcher, C. & Baldry, C. (2000). A study of individual differences and self-awareness in the context of multi-source feedback. *Journal of Occupational and Organizational Psychology, 73*, 303–319.

Fletcher, C. Baldry, C. & Cunningham-Snell, N. (1998). The psychometric properties of 360 degree feedback: An empirical study and a cautionary tale. *International Journal of Selection and Assessment, 6*, 19–34.

Francis-Smythe, J. & Smith, P.M. (1997). The psychological impact of assessment in a development center. *Human Relations, 50*, 149–167.

Gilliland, S.W. (1994). Effects of procedural and distributive justice on reactons to a selection system. *Journal of Applied Psychology, 79*, 691–701.

Goldstein, I.L. (1991). Training in work organizations. In M.D. Dunnette & L.M. Hough (eds), *Handbook of industrial and organizational psychology* (Vol. 2, pp. 507–619). Palo Alting: Consulting Psychology Press.

Guion, R.M. (1998). *Assessment, measurement, and prediction for personnel decisions*. Mahwah, NJ: Erlbaum.

Harris, M.M. & Schaubroeck, J. (1988). A meta-analysis of self-supervisor, self-peer, and peer-supervisor ratings. *Personnel Psychology, 41*, 43–62.

Harrison, M.I. & Shirom, A. (1999). *Organizational diagnosis and assessment; Bridging theory and research*. Thousand Oaks: Sage.

Harvey, R.J. (1991). Job analysis. In M.D. Dunnette & L.M. Hough (eds), *Handbook of industrial and organizational psychology*, (Vol. 2, pp. 71–163). Palo Alting: Consulting Psychology Press.

Heneman, R.L. (1986). The relationship between supervisory ratings and results oriented measures of performance: a meta-analysis. *Personnel Psychology, 39*, 811–826.

Houston, W.M., Raymond, M.R. & Svec, J.C. (1991). Adjustments for rater effects in performance assessment. *Applied Psychological Measurement, 15*, 409–421.

Huffcutt, A.I. & Arthur, W., Jr. (1994). Hunter and Hunter (1984) Revisited: Interview validity for entry-level jobs. *Journal of Applied Psychology, 79*, 184–190.

Huffcutt, A.I. & Roth, P.L. (1998). Racial group differences in employment interview evaluations. *Journal of Applied Psychology, 83*, 179–189.

Huffcutt, A.I., Roth, P.L. & McDaniel, M.A. (1996). A meta-analytic investigation of cognitive ability in employment interview evaluations: moderating characteristics and implications for incremental validity. *Journal of Applied Psychology, 81*, 459–473.

Huffcutt, A.I., Roth, P.L. & Conway, J.M. (1999). Assessment of employment interview constructs: A content approach. In R. Dipboye (chair), From both sides of the desk: applicant and interviewer perspectives. Symposium presented at the 14th Annual Conference of the Society of Industrial and Organizational Psychology, Atlanta, Georgia.

Iles, P.A. & Robertson, I.T. (1997). The impact of personnel selection procedures on candidate. In N. Anderson & P. Herriot (eds), *International handbook of selection and assessment* (pp. 543–566). Chichester: Wiley.

Janz, T. & Mooney, G. (1993). Interviewer and candidate reactions to patterned behavior description interviews. *International Journal of Selection and Assessment, 1*, 165–169.

Johnson, J.W. & Ferstl, K.L. (1999). The effects of interrater and self-other agreement on performance improvement following upward feedback. *Personnel Psychology, 52*, 271–303.

Kidd, J.M. (1997). Assessment for self-managed career development. In N. Anderson & P. Herriot (eds), *International handbook of selection and assessment* (pp. 599–618). Chichester: Wiley.

Kraiger, K. & Ford, J.K. (1985). A meta-analysis of ratee race effects in performance ratings. *Journal of Applied Psychology, 70*, 56–65.

Ladner, H.S. & Greguras, G.J. (2001). Effects of mean rating level, interrater agreement, and self-other agreement on ratee reactions to peer feedback. In J. Williams (Chair), Has 360-degree feedback really gone amok? New empirical data. Symposium conducted at the 16th annual conference of the Society for Industrial and Organizational Psychology, San Diego, April.

Lievens, F. (1998). Factors which improve the construct validity of assessment centers: A review. *International Journal of Selection and Assessment, 6*, 141–152.

Lievens, F., Van Dam, K. & Anderson, N. (2001). Recent trends and challenges in personnel selection. Submitted for publication.

Lin, T-R., Dobbins, G.H. & Fahr, J.L. (1992). A field study of race and age similarity effects of interview ratings in conventional and situational interviews. *Journal of Applied Psychology, 77*, 363–371.

Lind, E.A. & Tyler, T. (1988). *The social psychology of procedureal justice*. New York: Plenum Press.

London, M. & Smither, J.W. (1995). Can multi-source feedback change perceptions of goal accomplishment, self-evaluations, and performance-related outcomes? Theory-based applications and directions for research. *Personnel Psychology, 48*, 803–839.

Mabe, P.A. & West, S.G. (1982). Validity of self-evaluation of ability: a review and meta-analysis. *Journal of Applied Psychology, 67*, 280–296.

Maurer, T., Solamon, J. & Troxtel, D. (1998). Relationship of coaching with performance in situational employment interviews. *Journal of Applied Psychology, 83*, 239–260.

Motowidlo, S.J., Carter, G.W., Dunnette, M.D., Tippins, N., Werner, S., Burnett, J.R. & Vaughan, M.J. (1992). Studies of the structured behavioral interview. *Journal of Applied Psychology, 77*, 571–587.

Mount, M.K., Sytsma, M.R., Hazucha, J.F. & Holt, K.E. (1997). Rater-ratee race effects in developmental performance ratings of managers. *Personnel Psychology, 50*, 51–69.

Nilsen, D. & Campbell, D.P. (1993). Self-observer rating discrepancies—once an overrater, always an overrater? *Human Resource Management, 32*, 265–281.

Noe, R.A. & Schmitt, N. (1986). The influence of trainee attitudes on training effectiveness: Test of a model. *Personnel Psychology, 39*, 497–523.

Ployhart, R.E. & Ryan, A.M. (1998). Applicants' reactions to the fairness of selection procedures: The effects of positive rule violations and time of measurement. *Journal of Applied Psychology, 83*, 3–16.

Pollack, D.M. & Pollack, L.J. (1996). Using 360-degree feedback in performance appraisal. *Public Personnel Management, 26*, 245–256.

Pulakos, E.D., White, L.D., Oppler, S.H. & Borman, W.C. (1989). Examination of race and sex effects on performance ratings. *Journal of Applied Psychology, 74*, 770–780.

Riggio, R.E. & Cole, E.J. (1992). Agreement between subordinate ratings of supervisor performance and effects on self and subordinate satisfaction. *Journal of Occupational and Organizational Psychology, 65*, 151–158.

Robertson, I.T., Gratton, L. & Sharpley, D. (1987). The psychometric properties and design of managerial assessment centres: dimensions into exercises won't go. *Journal of Occupational Psychology, 60*, 187–195.

Rossett, A. (1987). *Training needs assessment*. New Jersey: Englewood Cliffs.

Rothstein, H.R. (1990). Interrater reliability of job performance ratings: growth to asymptote level with increasing opportunity to observe. *Journal of Applied Psychology, 75*, 322–327.

Russell, C.J. & Domm, D.R. (1995). Two field tests of an explanation of assessment validity: *Journal of Occupational and Organizational Psychology, 68*, 25–47.

Rust, J. & Golombok, S. (1999). *Modern psychometrics*, (2nd edn). London: Routledge.

Sackett, P.R. & DuBois, C.L.Z. (1991). Rater-ratee race effects on performance evaluation: Challenging meta-analytic conclusions. *Journal of Applied Psychology, 76*, 873–877.

Salgado, J.F. & Moscoso, S. (2001). Construct validity of employment interview: A meta-analysis. Submitted for publication.

Schmidt, F.L. & Hunter, J.E. (1998). The validity and utility of selection methods in personnel psychology: Practical and theoretical implications of 85 years of research findings. *Psychological Bulletin, 124*, 262–274.

Schmitt, N. & Chan, D. (1998). *Personnel selection; A theoretical approach*. Thousand Oaks: Sage.

Schmitt, N., Clause, C.S. & Pulakos, E.D. (1996). Subgroup differences associated with different measures of some common job-relevant constructs. In C.L. Cooper & I.T. Robertson (eds), *International Review of Industrial and Organizational Psychology*, Vol. 11. Chichester: Wiley.

Schuler, H. & Funke, U. (1989). The interview as a multimodal procedure. In E.W. Eder & G.R. Ferris (eds), *The employment interview: Theory, research and practice* (pp. 183–192). Newbury Park: Sage.

Shavelson, R.J. (1991). Generalizability of military performance measurements: Individual performance. In A.K. Wigdor & B.F. Green, Jr. (eds), *Performance assessment for the workplace* (Vol. 2, pp. 207–257). Washington, DC: National Academy Press.

Smith, P.C. & Kendall, L.M. (1963). Retranslation of expectations: An approach to the construction of unambiguous anchors for rating scales. *Journal of Applied Psychology, 47*, 149–155.

Steiner, D.D. & Gilliland, S.W. (1996). Fairness reactions to personnel selection techniques in France and the United States. *Journal of Applied Psychology, 81*, 134–141.

Thomas, K. & Mellon, T. (1996). *Planning for training and development: A guide to analysing needs*. London: Save the Children.

van Dam, K. (1998). Employee flexibility: A model of individual differences and organizational characteristics. Paper for the 24th International Congress of Applied Psychology, San Francisco, August.

van Dam, K. (2001). Understanding job mobility intentions: A test of the extended investment model. Paper presented at the 16th Annual Conference of Industrial and Organizational Psychology, San Diego, April.

van Dam, K. (2003). Trait perception in the employment interview: a five factor model perspective. *International Journal of Selection and Assessment* (in press).

Van der Zee, K.I., Bakker, A.B. & Bakker, P. (2001). Why are structured interviews so seldomly used in personnel selection? *Journal of Applied Psychology* (in press).

Van Yperen, N.W. & Baar, A.P. (2000). Betrouwbaarheid en rechtvaardigheid van de 360°graden feedback beoordelingsmethode (Reliability and procedural justice of the 360° feedback method). *M & O, 4*, 39–52.

Viswesvaran, C., Ones, D.S. & Schmidt, F.L. (1996). Comparative analysis of the reliability of job performance ratings. *Journal of Applied Psychology, 81*, 557–574.

Waldman, D.A., Atwater, L.E. & Antonioni, D. (1998). Has 360 degree feedback gone amok? *Academy of Management Executive, 12*, 86–94.

CHAPTER 10

Individual Assessment as an Integrated Tool in a Systematic Management Development Process

Jörg Iten
Executive Assessment & Management Development, Kilchberg/Zürich, Switzerland

SUMMARY

Using a concrete case, this chapter is intended to show that the individual assessment method can yield excellent results not only as a selection tool but also as a component of the individual professional development process. The example described illustrates the importance individual assessment assumes as the link between the requirements and goals of the organization and those of the employee. It makes it clear that focused—and thus profitable—development is rarely possible without a serious and individualized assessment of the person to be developed. Practical indications are given that show which (high) demands should be placed on the application of individual assessments and what must be heeded if organizations intend to conduct similar management development projects based on individual assessments.

INTRODUCTION

In our work with prospective management candidates or those already in positions of responsibility, we are continuously confronted with two questions: What essential qualities must a person have in order to be successful in management functions, and what must be done to further existing potential so that it can be applied to the optimum degree possible? Optimum here means efficiency from the company's point of view as well as from the employee's point of view, where his or her own personal qualities can be used and professional goals realized.

There are a great number of instruments, which to a greater or lesser degree provide information, which can be used to answer these questions. The electronic processes on the open market, which impress more often through the economy of use than through the validity of the results, have made their contribution in the creation of a confused market. Our long-term experience in the conduct of individual and group assessments (assessment and development centers) and the procedures for conceiving systematic management development processes have taught us that the selection of valid instruments and procedures is a necessary but not an adequate prerequisite to answering the key questions posed. In the end, much depends upon the qualitative demands with which these are applied and their effective association.

This chapter emerged from a consulting practice, and it thus addresses those in organizations, who are responsible for employee development and especially for new recruits and managers. Using a concrete example, it is intended to show how an individual assessment—linked with 360° feedback—can be applied successfully as the foundation for the systematic development of management staff. In this, I will focus on those points that make the difference if one wants to bring about change.

Although this chapter refers to a specific company in an effort to provide application-related, practical information, the observations and remarks still are intended to address fundamental issues and enable them to be transferred to other organizations.

The individual assessment and the assessment center method are probably the methods, which in the last two decades have been used most often to achieve valid evaluations of the personal and leadership-related qualities of people. Generally speaking, the most common areas of application were for selection as well as for personnel and management development. Whereas the assessment center has found broad application for both selection and development (often the term development center is used for the latter), the individual assessment has clearly been used more frequently as a selection tool. The individual assessment provides valuable, requirement-specific information about the essential personal qualities that the applicant possesses, which can be especially important when filling important management positions through internal or external candidates. Compared to the assessment center as a selection tool, the individual assessment offers the group addressed the advantages of greater privacy in the area of personality, flexibility in terms of time and facilities, and lower financial expense.

The 360° feedback method has become more important in recent years. In some companies, it is used in addition to previously established performance assessments; in others, it has replaced the usual internal annual assessments. Most of the employed 360° feedback systems use questionnaires as the basis for the assessment; in these, participants can compare self-assessments with the ratings of other selected groups of people (for the most part supervisors, colleagues, employees, and clients). As interesting as the application of the 360° feedback appears initially, it is equally limited when it comes to assessing fundamental personal capacities. In some instances, the 360° feedback can provide the basis for a change of attitude, as, for example, when the participants in a 360° feedback round are not just "hit by the lightning" of a comprehensive computer printout, but rather when the user sees that a serious personal assessment and interpretation takes place. The 360° feedback takes place, however, on a behavioral plane; the person himself or herself, his or her essential qualities, capacities, and motives remain outside the realm of consideration. Whoever sets his or her sights on real employee development will come up short if he or she disregards these psychological and fundamental levels.

Whoever is serious about promoting the development of people in an organization must accept that not all abilities can be improved; in fact, there is often less range for improvement than one would care to admit. Furthering one's development within an organization does not mean merely signing up for further training courses, attending seminars, and improving strengths and combating weaknesses, but rather it means above all learning to size up oneself realistically, recognize one's own motives, and, on this basis, formulate realistic development targets. Educational and further training measures are then most efficient if they are planned and undertaken on the basis of such goals. A company can support this process—as discussed below—to its own and to the advantage of its employees.

In order to create conditions under which it is possible to define realistic targets and formulate purposeful development measures from both the employee's and the company's points of view, an assessment basis is necessary that encompasses not only motives, predispositions, and values but also reveals potential in the sense of fundamental, individual capacities. And this, in turn, has implications for the quality of the instruments, which come to bear for the assessments of these aspects. Clearly insufficient are methods that merely scratch the behavioral surface. The individual assessment, however, is one method available that can fulfill these requirements. Both the conception and the quality of implementation, however, must meet a higher standard.

Using a concrete example, we will show how the individual assessment, combined with a 360° feedback, can assume a pivotal role within a management development process. Initial results will be discussed and conclusions drawn.

THE INDIVIDUAL ASSESSMENT AS A CENTRAL ELEMENT IN THE MANAGEMENT DEVELOPMENT PROCESS: AN EXAMPLE OF BEST PRACTICE

The company we have selected for this report is a middle-sized, established Swiss private bank. It was taken over by a major bank some years ago but retained its name and concentrated its activities on private banking. Management development activities were discontinued after the takeover, and the parent company's program was used. Around two years ago, they came to the conclusion that this offering did not sufficiently address their own needs, and the management board decided to establish their own management development program tailored to the bank's needs.

One target group, which was to be the focus with the management development program, was made up of members of junior management. The bank's management recognized that in a competitive environment and a difficult labor market, members of management play a much more important role. Leadership in this bank was traditionally rather discreet; seniority and professional skills were the key criteria, which were to a large extent decisive when filling a management position in the past. Through the takeover by the major bank, the situation may have changed radically, but there was a feeling that leadership was not proactive enough within management. For this reason and because they were convinced that an above-average management team is an important factor in attracting good quality employees and that real value-added could be gained by highlighting the prospects for young people in a very competitive labor market. Consequently, a project was set up with the objectives of recognizing management potential as early as possible, registering it, and developing it in a meaningful way.

VARIATIONS IN INDIVIDUAL ASSESSMENTS

A wide variety of products are offered under the guise of an individual assessment. They differ in length, structure, content, and professionalism. It is not my intention to outline the breadth and assess the various forms of these, but I will illustrate briefly which standards an individual assessment must meet in order to achieve the aim of describing the capacities, values, and motives of personalities of individual employees.

An assessment must be conceived in such a way as to take into consideration both the social, communicative, and intellectual complexity and the required dynamics and ability to learn required in today's work environment. And it must be directed towards presenting an image of the individuality of each assessed person. These requirements make clear that the assessment program must offer the candidate the greatest possible creative freedom and must also be laid out in such a way as to capture both the essence and entirety of the candidate's personality. Whoever has not taken the time to understand the personality of the candidate will have a hard time forecasting whether that person will be successful in the target position. The key task of management diagnostic activity is highlighting the available skills and capacities against the background of the personality. Making a purely technical determination of potential performance on the basis of simulated situations or the non-dynamic interpretation of test results (from written tests or by using electronic methods, which can spit out multi-page reports at the click of a mouse) leads to a one-dimensional, short-sighted view of the requirements needed.
Table 10.1 provides an overview of the process.

OBJECTIVES AND SELECTION CRITERIA FOR THE MANAGEMENT DEVELOPMENT PROGRAM

With the goal of recognizing potential management candidates early on, young employees with several years' experience, above-average performance, and showing aspirations of taking on additional responsibilities over the medium-term are given the opportunity to participate in this management development program. The direct supervisor submits the application after consulting with human resources specialists; the final nomination is then made by the second-level management supervisor (the line manager responsible for management development tasks in his or her own area). A cycle with twelve to fifteen participants is planned every half year.

THE INDIVIDUAL ASSESSMENT PROCESS

Phase 1: Assessment

The foundation of the program is an individual assessment combined with a 360° feedback. The latter, which an external provider also conducts, allows the program participants the opportunity to examine their conduct in everyday professional life. The individual assessment, on the other hand, goes into greater depth. The goal of the individual

TABLE 10.1 Overview of the individual assessment process

Phase 1 *Assessment*	Individual assessment with external consultant lasting nine hours, report written
Phase 2 *Evaluating the assessment results*	
First feedback session	With external consultant, development implications
Second feedback session	With line manager and 360 degree data available
Phase 3 *Development Planning*	Preparation of the development plan Implementation of the development plan
Phase 4 *Monitoring*	

assessment is to uncover willingness-related, intellectual, and social-communicative capacities on the one hand, and, on the other, offer the participants the opportunity to gain clarity into their own motives and predispositions.

The individual assessment is conducted externally. It usually lasts nine hours. Around one-third of the time is spent discussing in-depth the candidate's life experience and personal record as well as the individual assignments from the assessment; six hours are devoted to the written portion. In the latter, analytical and conceptual problems and case studies are worked through on the one hand, and, on the other, assignments are worked on which serve as the basis for an examination and evaluation of the essential personality-related qualities. In addition, the participants are asked to reflect on their careers until now and to put their imagined future careers in concrete terms. The interview consists of a biographic and a semi-structured behavior-related portion. The primary focus is not superficial behavior but the person as a whole.

Phase 2: Evaluating the assessment results

First feedback session

The responsible consultant prepares a comprehensive report on the basis of the assessment results; this refers in detail to the motivational, intellectual, and social-communicative capacities and draws on the personality and abilities profile, the imagined future career as defined by the participant, and questions relevant to the company about the extent and quality of the participant's available leadership potential.

The assessment results and report are discussed in detail during the feedback session between the consultant and the participant. In accordance with the demand for a deeper and personality-oriented discussion, the assessment report must provide more than a mere superficial description of the participant's behavior and characteristics, as is often observed with such. Admittedly, the effect on the behavioral level should also be addressed as an important theme and supplemented through the evaluation of a 360° feedback, but to create the foundation for controlling a professional career, statements about fundamental potential are necessary. The combination of an individual assessment and 360° feedback is appealing, because the personal essential qualities of the candidate can be explained through external behaviors, and primarily because the candidate can see which non-superficial behavioral changes are necessary in order to further himself or herself as a person.

This session is highly sensitive, since it is ultimately a discussion about fundamental questions concerning the possibilities for professional development. This often means being willing to admit weakness and accept corrective plans, and this is something that is not always possible without a degree of anguish.

The participants receive a copy of the assessment report; the original is kept in a special management development file with the head of human resources. Access is limited to the participant's supervisors and those responsible for management development.

Second feedback session

In the second session, the direct supervisor is included and the evaluation from the assessment is supplemented by input on everyday professional life. The inclusion of the direct supervisor is especially important, because he or she will play a central role in the planning and implementation of the development measures.

360° feedback

This feedback session was separated from the individual assessment up until now, and it was based, first and foremost, on a comprehensive computer print out. This was unsatisfactory and therefore was changed. In the next cycle, the 360° evaluation will be discussed with the external provider initially, the important results filtered out, and then integrated into the first feedback session.

After the end of the feedback rounds, the participant should be capable of positioning himself or herself more precisely and formulating the professional career goals for the next three to five years.

Phase 3: Development planning

Preparation of the development plan

The responsibility for the conception and implementation of the development plan is borne jointly by the participants and the person responsible for management development. The latter steers the processes, arranges discussions with the direct and second-level supervisors, and counsels the participants and the line manager involved about the internal and external possibilities for further education and training.

Before individual development measures are contemplated, common short- and medium-term goals must be formulated: Should the journey be one involving the taking on of leadership and management responsibilities or does the compass point more toward a professional career? Should one strive for sales-oriented or advisory duties? Should the assignment provide more of a conceptual challenge? Are the medium-term professional goals and the company's expectations compatible with the personal and familial requirements of the candidate? These are just some of the central questions, which must be discussed openly.

On the basis of these goals, measures are spelled out and a schedule drawn up. Emphasis is placed on taking advantage of all particularly promising on-the-job opportunities (job rotation, job enrichment, and project work). Instead of comprehensive leadership training courses, workshops are offered on a variety of subjects (communication within the management team; increasing one's powers of persuasion and forcefulness; project management; solving complex problems; etc.), which are attended selectively as needed. Group workshops take place within a cycle; these focus on general topics that concern the bank as a whole (organization, strategy, market development, and current projects). Members of the management team are involved in these workshops. An intensive exchange of ideas is consciously sought that offers both sides the opportunity of getting to know each other better. Project work is linked to these workshops; group participants carry this out at the behest of a member of the management team.

Implementation of the development plan

The individual development plan, besides the goals, contains all of the discussed measures, including deadlines and responsibilities. In it, the individual implementation steps are spelled out. Wherever the matter requires it, the person responsible for management development influences the plan.

Phase 4: Monitoring

The person responsible for management development within human resources monitors the implementation of the development plans and provides support wherever necessary. When plans stretch out over a greater length of time, periodic discussions take place with the participants to provide encouragement in the form of interim results controlling. The person responsible for management development is also in charge of the continual effectiveness control of the program; he or she periodically schedules discussions with the participants (internal and external) and optimizes the system.

What has yet to be done is the setting up of an management development file, which can systematically process all of the relevant participant's personal electronic data (curriculum vitae, potential assessment, career plans) and thus enable quick access to suitable internal candidates when job vacancies arise or new positions are created.

WHAT HAVE WE LEARNED FROM THE INITIAL CYCLE?

The response we have received up until now has been overwhelmingly positive. Since only nine months have passed since the beginning of the program, a serious examination of the results is not yet possible. The reactions from the participants have shown that our efforts to orient the assessment and the resultant development plans to the individual and to take into consideration the participant's personality are especially valued.

It was clear that the transformation of assessment results into a realistic development and career planning program requires a significant amount of time and intensive discussions. More feedback discussion time must be set aside especially for those employees whose own future career plans do not or only partially match their own essential qualities and for whom a certain rethinking process is necessary before they can move on to participating in the conception of the development plan. The consultant responsible for the individual assessment, who has the greatest insight into the employee's personality, can take on an additional role similar to a coach during this phase in the future.

Room for improvement was found in the assessment results from the 360° feedback. Many of those involved found the evaluation as too standardized to permit the drawing of personal conclusions. One missed an individual assessment discussion with the responsible provider of the assessment system.

Since internal communication about the management development program did not always function optimally, this led to some uncertainty during the selection of the participants by the supervisors as well as to a lack of clarity about the intensity and standing among the participants themselves. In the future, the selection criteria will be interpreted more strictly to avoid turning the program into a mass event. Only those employees who distinguish themselves as key players and have expressed a certain willingness to take on leadership responsibility should complete the program. The supervisor nominating an employee should sense a clear potential for development in the employee based on the latter's past performance.

CRITICAL FACTORS

When setting up a comparable program, attention must be paid to four critical factors on which the basic success of the endeavor depends: transparency, involvement of management, the person responsible for management development, and the selection of the external consultant.

TRANSPARENCY

If one starts a management development program, which—as in the example illustrated—begins with the premise of an in-depth potential analysis, open and absolutely transparent information is the highest principle. Just as such a process can be useful for the individual and the company, it can also bring about detrimental results if the participant has false expectations or is not in the clear as to what he or she will go through. Being judged, assessed, or evaluated is a highly sensitive process for most people, especially when the assessment does not remain on a superficial behavioral level but plumbs the depths of fundamental personal qualities. This must be taken into consideration.

In concrete terms, this means the following: The potential participants must be informed about the program and the individual steps before their definite nomination. It should be underscored that participation is appealing because it is instructive. But it should also be mentioned that the process is not without its risks and requires the willingness to thoroughly examine one's self and one's career. The nominating supervisor should also provide his or her reasoning for the nomination of the employee to the program. Everyone should be informed of the detailed program and therefore be free to decide about active participation. A healthful measure of maturity, open-mindedness, and inner resolve are prerequisites for a successful process.

The content and the sequence of events when carrying out each of the individual program elements must be conveyed openly. The participants must be able to perceive why he or she is doing whatever and who plays which part, especially during the individual assessment and the 360° feedback. It must also be clear to those involved what information is passed on to whom and in which form, or rather, who has access to the assessment report. An uncontrolled handling of confidential data can cause lasting damage to the process and inflict damage on the image of the entire program.

INVOLVEMENT OF MANAGEMENT

Not only must management approve the budget for the implementation of a rather comprehensive management development program, but also lend the material a necessary weight through a recognizable commitment during the realization phase. The involvement of the participant's direct or second-level supervisor is especially important as in the feedback sessions, or in the planning and implementation of the development program. Ideal supervisors are those who can take the time for the active promotion and development of young colleagues despite the demands of everyday business matters. This includes a willingness to recognize promising management talent and pass that information along to other units within the organization, even if this is often related to more work and effort in the first instance. Narrow-minded thinking does not pay off for anyone in the long run.

THE PERSON RESPONSIBLE FOR INTERNAL MANAGEMENT DEVELOPMENT

The person responsible for management development can be the same as the head of human resources depending on the size of the company. It is important, however, that this function is so positioned within the organization, that no hierarchical barriers hinder a purposeful and efficient exercising of this role. It goes without saying that the person responsible for management development must be established somewhere in the higher echelons, since he or she is responsible for the furthering and development of upper management as well as for that of the new management recruit target group. The demands on the personality of the person responsible for management development are greater if this role is not just administrative but active, as shown in the example discussed above. In order to earn broad acceptance and trust as a partner in discussions and feedback sessions, he or she must be a mature and sensitive person with good communication skills, who has assembled organizational and leadership experience. A strong network of contacts to relevant persons within the organization is an advantage that should not be underestimated. This person must be regarded as someone in a position of trust by representatives from different levels within the hierarchy, and he or she must be someone who can make things happen.

THE SELECTION OF AN EXTERNAL CONSULTANT

Although it is conceivable that a large corporation would put together its own team of assessment specialists, most decide to collaborate with external partners. The reasons for this are basically twofold: the greater independence of the external partners and their broader overview of the benchmarks within the industry. In addition, it has been demonstrated that internal specialists, if they are really good and experienced, eventually seek their independence, which is counter-productive for the project in terms of continuity.

The market for personnel consultants and assessment providers is large and confusing. Who is the right partner for the conduct of individual assessments? Some pointers should help to separate the wheat from the chaff. In terms of professional qualifications, a recognized and sound education background in psychology is just as necessary as a wealth of experience in management diagnostics. In addition, organization and management experience are desirable. Partners should also have a persuasive personality and still be able to gain the confidence of both the participants and management. A careful evaluation is indicated in any case. An assessment of concrete results is more informative than reading color brochures conceived for marketing-related purposes. If one is looking at large international consulting firms, one should look into who precisely carries out individual assessments. The character of the consultant is essential to a successful collaboration. It is also worthwhile checking to what extent other services (e.g. headhunting) are offered by the consulting firm that could lead to a conflict of interests and, ultimately, objectives. The continuity of the collaboration directly benefits the quality of the consulting performance for both the company as well as for the external consultants.

When selecting providers of other products such as the 360° feedback or computer-aided personality tests, one should not be distracted by the simplicity of operation, colorful diagrams, or the number of assessments churned out. Whereas control criteria (reliability and validity) must be checked for tests, quality and the individuality of the evaluation are important in the case of the 360° feedback. It is literally child's play to spit out a fifty-page printout with the click of a mouse; carefully interpreting the results, discussing them with the candidate, and deducing measures confront the provider with a greater challenge.

INDIVIDUAL ASSESSMENT VERSUS ASSESSMENT CENTER

The function reserved for the individual assessment in such a management development process is variously taken over by the assessment or development center. If this is the case, this must be set up in such a way that sufficient attention is devoted to the capturing of the candidate's personality—and not just the behavioral data—and that the evaluation and follow-up is individualized—similar to the example depicted above. An examination of existing practice shows that assessment centers are operated with too much focus on technology and remain stuck on the superficial behavioral level, and that companies often lack the energy and perseverance to perform functional and individual development work. It is basically possible to carry out individualized and in-depth potential analyses in an assessment center, but this places great demands on those responsible for implementation (similar demands to those described under "The selection of external consultants" above). Since the evaluation in an assessment center must be standardized, however, an individual assessment will always be superior to an assessment center in terms of individualization. The more heterogeneous the employee group under observation is, the more an individual assessment recommends itself. The individual assessment will be the method of choice as well when the focus is on the evaluation and ongoing development of seasoned managers and a high level of confidentiality and anonymity must be guaranteed.

ETHICAL PRINCIPLES

The application of the individual assessment is only then responsible if the following principles are maintained. The responsibility for compliance with them lies both with the consultant in charge and the contracting corporation.

THE CONSULTANT'S RESPONSIBILITIES

In 1992, the American Psychological Association defined six ethical principles addressing the professional competence and fundamental approach to be demanded of consultants, who conduct individual assessments. In his article on "Ethical, Legal, and Professional Issues for Individual Assessment in Individual Psychological Assessment" (Jeanneret & Silzer, 1998), Richard Jeanneret summarized these succinctly as follows:

1. *Competence*: Psychologists have appropriate education, training and experience to conduct assessments; they update their knowledge in assessment practices and properly use assessment techniques and information for their intended purposes.
2. *Integrity*: Psychologists provide truthful information and deal fairly with others; they clarify their roles and relationships; and they avoid conflicts of interest related to assessment practices.
3. *Professional and scientific responsibility*: Psychologists accept responsibility for the influences of assessment results; they confer, refer, or cooperate with other psychologists when appropriate; they do not promote the practice of assessment by unqualified individuals; and they do not use instruments that scientific research has found not to meet professionally accepted standards.
4. *Respect for people's rights and dignity*: Psychologists recognize the rights to privacy, confidentiality, self-determination, and autonomy of those undergoing an assessment; they are respectful of individual differences and the diversity of others; they realize that an individual's participation in an assessment is voluntary; and they understand that assessees have a right to receive feedback about their assessment results.
5. *Concern for other's welfare*: Psychologists are sensitive to the welfare and needs of assessees; they attempt to avoid or minimize any harm that might result through the assessment process; and they are cognizant of the individual's well-being when interpreting assessment results.
6. *Social responsibility*: Psychologists comply with the law and maintain an awareness of social conditions that might influence how they conduct assessments.

THE CORPORATION'S RESPONSIBILITIES

The three most important aspects that a corporation should take to heart are:

1. *Selection of the consultant*: It is part of a corporation's responsibility to find a partner for the conduct of an individual assessment, who meets the above requirements without question.
2. *Nominations for an individual assessment*: Persons, with whom a corporation intends to conduct an individual assessment, must be informed of the plans and purpose in advance. A voluntary decision to participate must be guaranteed.
3. *Treatment of data*: Prior to the assessment, the corporation communicates how the gathered data (which is generally presented in the form of a report) will be used, who will have access to it, as well as how and over what period it will be kept. Those responsible must ensure compliance with these agreements.

CONCLUSION

The early recognition of leadership potential and the systematic development of junior staff are part of the central tasks of a professionally run management development program as are the continual and ongoing development of existing management personnel. Purposeful and efficient development work can only then be carried out if it is individualized, or, in other words, if the potential, motives, and goals of the person in the development program are recognized and brought into line with the profile of the career goals as formulated by the employee and the company. Development programs tailored to individual persons promise greater success than broad standardized educational and further training pursuits.

Through the individual assessment a valuable instrument is available that is highly suited as the foundation for such a development process. However, it is important that it is not just blindly arranged but rather integrated into the management development process as defined by the client company, and that its form and conduct meet high diagnostic standards. Promising development work demands the professional involvement of all participants and requires an open corporate culture based on trust.

REFERENCES

Chivers, W. and Darling P. (1999). *360-Degree feedback and organisational culture.* London: Institute of Personnel and Development.

Jeanneret, R. (1998). Ethical, legal, and professional issues for individual assessment in individual psychological assessment. In Jeanneret and Silzer (1998).

Jeanneret, R. and Silzer, R. (1998). *Individual psychological assessment: Predicting behavior in organizational settings.* San Francisco: Jossey-Bass, 1998.

Kaplan, R. E. (1994). *Enhancing 360-degree feedback for senior executives: how to maximize the benefits and minimize the risks.* Greensboro, NC: Center for Creative Leadership.

CHAPTER 11

Development Centers: A Neglected Perspective[1]

Jac N. Zaal

GITP International B.V., Amsterdam

SUMMARY

Development Centers (DCs) represent a specific application of Assessment Center Method (ACM) aimed at diagnosing skills, mostly managerial, that need to be developed to meet requirements of a target position. Like any other assessment procedure ACM can be used for different purposes. To qualify for those purposes procedures have to meet different sets of measurement qualities. ACM is known by the inclusion of different methods among which are exercises representing job samples. Although it has established its reputation as a valid predictor of management potential and career advancement, serious doubts have been raised about the skills it claims to measure. In this chapter basic characteristics of ACM are examined followed by specific features that qualify DCs for its specific purposes.

In a critical review of available research the construct validity of ACM is challenged. Recommendations to improve its construct validity are presented. It will be argued that effective diagnosis of development needs can only be achieved when taking into account the situational determinants of managerial competencies. Finally additional conditions are discussed that need to be considered in order to realize the full potential of the developmental impact of DCs.

INTRODUCTION

Assessment Center Methods (ACM) like any other kind of psychological or educational testing procedure can be used for different purposes. The most well known purpose

---

[1] The author would like to thank Dr. Martin Ippel for his helpful comments on an earlier version.
Individual Differences and Development in Organisations. Edited by Michael Pearn.

for the use of ACM is assessing management talents or management potential in order to help organizations in making job entry or job advancement decisions. More recently these methods have been used for licensing or certification (Joyce, Thayer & Pond, 1994; Hambleton, 1996; Norske Veritas, Personal communication). Apart from applications to support pass/fail decisions, ACM is also used to assess strength and weaknesses of skills of an individual to use these outcomes to promote the development of some of these skills. When ACM is primarily used for developmental purposes the centers are frequently referred to as development centers (Feltham, 1989).

A primary goal of this chapter is to stimulate practitioners to take validity research more seriously in deciding on the use of ACM in different contexts. Depending on the type of use made, the design of assessment methods will have to meet different requirements to sustain its suitability for the purpose at stake.

Generally it takes more effort to customize the design of ACM for developmental purposes and once the Development Center (DC) is ready for operation it takes more time to execute it. Are the extra efforts and cost in fine-tuning DCs paying of? What precisely are the strong and weak points to be considered in evaluating the benefits of DCs? As we will see, ACM has many features that make it very attractive for use for feedback on developmental needs. It is perhaps due to this face value that more often than not developmental consequences were used as by-products of a procedure designed for decision-making on selection or promotion (Goodge, 1991).

There is at least one reason to reconsider the design and execution of DCs. That reason has to do with crucial measurement qualities that would justify its suitability for that use, which are seriously questioned by research findings over and over again. Despite efforts to carefully define transparent and coherent performance dimensions to be evaluated in clearly job relevant exercises, empirical results fail to demonstrate the expected coherence and generality of these performance constructs. If assessment center dimensions are not valid constructs, this would imply we do not really understand what the meaning is of the feedback we are providing. Implications of these findings for practice will need attendance to this neglected perspective.

In the next paragraph we will first describe basic and shared characteristics of both ACM and Development Centers. We then focus on the features that discriminates DCs from other AC applications. The main research findings that challenge its construct validity will be presented and discussed. In the concluding part of this chapter we will attend to factors effecting developmental impact e.g. the use of alternative concepts in communicating feedback, in-depth analysis of behavior including personality, values and motives and post-assessment activities that might even have a greater impact on the ultimate purpose of development centers: making development happen.

BASIC FEATURES OF ASSESSMENT AND DEVELOPMENT CENTERS

Assessment centers manifest themselves in many different forms. This is according to Finkle (1976) inherent to the very nature of the method. Not surprisingly, the definition has been the subject of international conferences on this method (Moses, 1977). According to the latest document endorsed by the 2000 International Congress on Assessment Center Methods in San Francisco, three successive task forces have been working on as many editions of Guidelines and Ethical considerations. By definition, ACM consists of a standardized evaluation of behavior based on:

- **Multiple inputs** that can include techniques such as interviews, questionnaires, sociometric devices, besides a number of job related simulations (exercises).
- Several, specially **trained assessors**.
- Evaluations (ratings) in terms of **observed behavior** (behavioral dimensions).
- **Definition of dimensions** in advance on the basis of a task (job) analysis. This holds of course for the exercises as well.
- Overall evaluation of the performance of the assessees on the dimensions/competencies (or other variables it is designed to measure) reached in a **joint assessor meeting** in which comprehensive accounts (and often ratings) of behavior are discussed and integrated.

A warning is added to the definition that procedures in which some but not all of these features are used, do not fall within the definition of ACs, such as when a person acting as an assessor, works alone (so called individual assessments) even if the procedure consists of the various techniques just described. Another example of a procedure not considered as an ACM is one in which assessors report only on the separate exercises instead of making an integrated final report as well.

In short, assessment centers and development centers constitute an integrated assessment procedure, reporting results in a conceptual framework of performances measurements (behavioral dimensions) observed in (at least some) work sample type of exercises, based on the evaluations of more than one specially instructed observer (called assessor).

However restrictive this definition may sound it is more liberal than the description of methods referred to in the APA guidelines for educational and psychological measurement (APA, 1966; American Educational Research Association, American Psychological Association & National Council on Measurement in Education, 1999; Evers, Caminada, Koning et al., 1988; International Test Committee, 2000).

ACs may differ in many ways from one another, viz the number and type of exercises, the conceptual framework of behavioral dimensions, the number and type of dimensions, the number and type of assessors, to the procedures of collecting and integrating observations. As we will see later on in this chapter several of these variations can have a serious impact on the validity of ACs. These findings underline the fact that the term ACs stands for a class of methods just like other labels for generic measurement methods like intelligence tests and personality questionnaires. That is why guidelines for ACs should require documentation of the specifications of a specific AC as well as of the research that should underpin its validity, just as it is done for psychological tests and test research. See, for example, several editions of Buros Mental Measurement Yearbooks, or the Dutch editions of Documentation of Tests and Testresearch (Evers, Van Vliet-Mulder & Groot, 2000). Up till now this kind of systematic documentation of specific ACs has been needed but not available.

Development Centers (DCs) by this view do not differ from other ACs other than by the purpose for which it is used. In the same sense one might equally speak of SACs (selection), PACs (promotion or potency), CACs (career or certification) (Joyce et al.,1994). DCs, however, should be distinguished from other applications in more ways than purpose alone. Before turning to more specific design features of DCs let us first look in more detail to the three basic design features of any AC: (1) conceptual framework of performance dimensions; (2) exercises; and (3) ownership: internal versus external development and execution.

THE CONCEPTUAL FRAMEWORK OF PERFORMANCE DIMENSIONS

Performance dimensions basically are derived from inferences made by management, specialists and professionals about skills required for successful performance of activities and tasks. They are based on perceptions and judgments and represent at best implicit performance theories held both by managers, subordinates and others involved in analyzing the target jobs such as psychologists and HRM specialists. These insights are nevertheless indispensable starting points in developing useful concepts and descriptive clarity in the complex and diversified domain of managerial activities and responsibilities.

Gathering accurate and up-to-date information on target jobs is the first and necessary step in designing a DC. Job analysis serves two purposes. It provides the set of skills/behavioral dimensions agreed upon by major stakeholders as essential for effective performance and it provides the situations and tasks to build exercises that are proven representations of the domain of work situations and task settings of target positions. It is important to note that it is not of prime interest to give a complete description as long as it does not overlook settings, situations and behaviors that are crucial for effective performance.

Many job analysis methods are available. See, for example Algera and Greuter (1998) for a recent and comprehensive overview. Given the prime focus of ACs on describing and evaluation of observable behaviors, methods aimed at describing work activities or behavior requirements are most suitable such as the Critical Incidents Technique (Flanagan, 1954) or questionnaires such as the PAQ (McCormick, Mecham & Jeannerete, 1989) or the WPS (Saville and Holworth, 1989). Latter methods do not focus on a limited number of critical incidents, but sample from a large number of basic activities. Alternatively, AC practitioners may use different types of information in designing job relevant procedures as well. They can put together performance models from published research, the collective inheritance of previous ac applications, written information and folklore available in the client organization using abbreviated standard procedures for verification and fine-tuning. However in doing so one should take to heart the warning of Jeswald (1977) against the danger of too readily following badly defined and invalidated performance criteria, which traditionally take root in practice in organizations.

Within the realm of assessment center practice, a list of some forty behavioral skills (dimensions) published by Thornton and Byham (1982) often serves as a basis for local adaptations. It is also in use as a shortcut questionnaire for drawing up a job profile of the 10 to 15 most important skills for effective functioning. The number of skills as well as the groupings may change over time and different users, but on the whole such lists will include skills of communication, planning & organizing, interpersonal effectiveness including leadership, decision making, including judgement and analyses, professional & technical knowledge and personal & motivational skills.

To apply these behavioral concepts in DCs they need to be worked out in more readily observable details, both for reasons of clarifying the meaning and for instructional purposes for assessors who have to observe and evaluate these skills in exercises. This can be done in different ways. For example one might provide a sample of statements expressing required behaviors as is done in checklists. Statements can be worked out in bipolar scales including the description of unwanted (negative) behaviors. Finally behaviors at different levels of mastery can described so as to construct a behaviorally anchored rating scale (e.g. Zaal, 1998).

Specific behavior indicators, though more elaborated are still of a general nature. That is they are not specified according to situational demands. They should be to help assessors identify skillful behavior in each exercise. This implies that dimension ratings cannot be accurately interpreted without referring to specific exercises.

For the correct understanding of dimensions it is important to realize that we deal with skill concepts and that these concepts like any other can vary in level of abstraction. Which level is appropriate depends on the purpose for which they are used. If they are to be used for developmental feedback a low level of abstraction, giving details of observed behaviors in situ is helpful in understanding and accepting feedback. For communication to decision makers a higher level of abstraction serves better.

Although Thornton and Byham (1982) discuss leadership research at some length especially those based on use of questionnaires, the number of dimensions (33) exceeds by a couple of times the number of factors in even the most extended model (e.g. Tornow & Pinto, 1976). So skill dimensions as such are on the whole more specific concepts then factors in leadership models. Some dimensions can be traced back more easily than others.

Throughout AC applications reported in literature, taxonomies of dimensions are inconsistent. This is not helpful in getting a better understanding of management effectiveness ratings in AC applications. Moreover it opens the door for conceptual confusion by entering behavioral management dimensions of different abstraction levels in one and the same list, e.g. entrepreneurship as one dimension together with vision, risk-taking and creativity. Yukl (1987) presents a more explicitly argued integration of earlier findings by a taxonomy of 14 specific leadership behaviors each defined by several behavioral components. He thus arrives at categories that maintain continuity with major lines of research and are generic enough to be widely applicable to different kind of management positions and yet specific enough to relate to unique situational demands and constraints of the individual manager (Yukl, 1998). The higher order grouping of Yukl in Task, Person and Change oriented behaviors compare rather well to three of the four management rolesin the leadership models of Adizes (1979) and Quinn (1984, 1988), namely that of the Producer, Integrator and Entrepreneur. Their fourth role, the Administrator is part of Yukl's Task oriented factor.

The relationship between dimensions and traits on the one hand and management roles on the other does not fit in a simple hierarchical structure model in which dimensions reflect just a lower of level of abstraction. The same dimension as more specific skill concept such as decision making or communication and influencing skills may relate to different management roles.

In conclusion, the AC dimensions that have been derived in a bottom-up process by elaborating on implicit theories of skills held by managers and others involved do not have a strong relation with theoretical models based on academic leadership research. Furthermore, there is little empirical evidence for hierarchical ordering of behavior dimensions at various levels of abstraction or for a neat "simple structure" relationship with leadership models. A conceptual framework of a limited number of higher order clusters such as those of Yukl and Quinn however may provide descriptive clarity and can serve as a conceptual anchor point (Hunt, 1991) in communicating the meaning of managerial skills.

ASSESSMENT CENTER EXERCISES

Multiple methods are used in ACs. The use of work samples (exercises) however differentiates AC most typically from the content of other assessment procedures. The simulation of specific management situations (the exercises) is as important for defining the content of the assessment center program as are management behavior dimensions. The exercises typically represent the job level and the situational constraints in which the participant has to operate. They should provide candidates ample opportunities to demonstrate the relevant behavioral skills in situations and circumstances, which are characteristic for the target positions in the organization. The repertoire that has developed over the years shows a large variety of oral and written exercises. They need to be considered as global scripts for prototypical situations that can easily incorporate specific job level demands and situational constraints and are not intended as examples of job replica.

Traditionally these exercises are semi structured assignments leaving the subject room for his personal interpretation of the problem situation and the goals and objectives that should be reached. These characteristics are in general representative for situations one encounters in daily work situations, but hinder standardization. It is though specifically required when certain skills have to be assessed like vision and goal setting. Oral exercises in which role playing is involved are provided with specific instructions to gear the exercise in measuring skills like adaptation, resilience, flexibility, decisiveness, etc.

Settings of ACs differ widely depending on the type of organization to be served. Some take place in a simulated business setting and those for government in a simulated government setting. Exercises differ depending on the level of the target position. Exercises do not represent assignments in the sense of achievement testing. The participant is not so much judged by what is achieved as well by the demonstrated level of required skills.

There is no system or prescription that guides us in deciding on the representativeness of the characteristic task settings (situations). Aiming at job replica certainly serves both the content and face validity for that specific job. However it is easily understood most applications even within one organization are aimed at a broader range of positions. So design efforts are focused on constructing proto typical tasks rather than job replica. It therefore would mean a major improvement for efficient design and use of ACM if there were a better understanding of precisely which situational determinants counts for content validity. One of the questions is how far one should go in customizing exercises to organizational settings. Could exercises still be considered as valid prototypical task elements if specifications of a different branch setting were used. And what about differences in other settings? In this respect one also has to consider different instructional variants of the same exercise including scoring instructions (Sackett, 1987).

These questions have not attracted much attention either from the designers or from researchers. A possible explanation can be that exercises were initially merely thought of as a vehicle to create opportunities for demonstrating and assessing behavioral skills (dimensions) which are conceptualized as highly general across settings and exercises. Researchers also have to face practical limitations due to the limited number of exercises presented to the same participants.

Apart from aspects such as face value and acceptance, (the organization wants it and the candidate expects it), answers to the above question will also have to be traded off against the requirement that the setting should be equally familiar and accessible to each candidate to give every one a fair chance to demonstrate their ability. A matrix combining methods (including exercises) used and dimensions to be assessed is often used to illustrate the full extent of an AC as an assessment and measurement device (see Thornton and Byham, (1982) and Zaal, (1998) for examples). Different exercises provide ample opportunities to observe dimensions. Preferably they can be observed in more than one method.

OWNERSHIP: INTERNAL VERSUS EXTERNAL DEVELOPMENT AND EXECUTION

At first glance it might be surprising to consider ownership as a design feature of AC. However several qualities of the method are associated with what we call ownership. "Whether used for selection or for diagnosis of development needs, whether used for external or intern candidates, an assessment center... in its most effective form... is usually part of a selection-promotion system" (Thornton & Byham, 1982, p. 127). Taking all relevant information into account, including documented performance appraisals and other relevant information in the personnel file enhances effectiveness of a decision-making procedure. What Thornton & Byham have in mind is that the optimal integration of information from different sources can be greatly enhanced by the use of a common conceptual framework. This is more than a semantic accommodation. It takes a serious investment on the part of the organization to develop and implement ACM and related HRM practices. One of these investments is participation of managers as assessors. Assessor training is in itself an effective medium to transfer and implement the conceptual framework. Apart from that, getting involved in the assessment of (future) employees raises their commitment in taking part in developmental activities for those particular persons. This could be done in several ways such as offering projects, training on the job, or acting as a mentor (Yukl, 1998; Seegers, 1989).

Assessment centers have additional qualities such as acceptability (Moses, 1977; Thornton & Byham, 1982; Zaal, 1998), and can offer preview of and exposure to organizational values (Iles & Robertson, 1989). Although comparative data are lacking it seems logical that ownership, especially taking part as assessor make a contribution to these qualities. When applied as DC an assessor might well be as decisive for the acceptance of feedback and participation in developmental activities as it is for performance appraisal (Lee & Akhtar, 1996).

SPECIAL FEATURES OF DEVELOPMENT CENTERS

Thus far I have discussed three basic characteristics of ACM. The conceptual framework of skill dimensions, the exercises as representative work samples of target jobs, and ownership. Some elements of ACM are considered more basic then others. So we left out elements such as assessor training, how and to whom results are reported, the target population, the introduction and preparation of candidates and the operation of ACM.

Different shades of ACM can be distinguished that are relevant for DCs (Jeswald, 1977; Thorton & Byham, 1982; Zaal, 1998). Differences not only concern the basic elements viz. behavioral dimensions, methods and ownership, but also the target groups, the extensiveness of the written report, the oral feedback and activities and precautions prior to and after assessment. In contrast to assessments for selection, admission and or potential (advanced career track programs) no definitive decisions about future position are involved in DCs. This characterizes DC as low stake assessments. In discussing contributions of ACM to management development, Thornton & Byham, (1982) take a broader perspective, which includes "Early identification AC" and participation as an assessor. In this chapter I restrict the term Development Centers to designs aimed at diagnosing development needs. In any case purpose, career implications, administrative conditions and procedures should be made clear to participants beforehand.

In addition the following features make the difference between DCs and plain decision-oriented ACs as summarized below:

- **Methods** DC methods should include personality and aptitude tests as well as exercises. Trait information should be used to better understand development needs and how to tackle them.
- **Ownership** Preferably in-house and managers acting as assessor to enhance impact and credibility. Joint ventures with outside consultancy firms should ensure ample visibility and commitment of client organizations.
- **Assessor training** This should include special attention to behavior dynamics and situational demands in exercises; assessors will have to work together with psychologist in preparing the final report and participate in oral feedback sessions.
- **Assessments** These will be made using multiple sources, which may include peer ratings, self-ratings and ratings by role players.
- **Written reports** They should be extensive and detailed; going into behavior dynamics, handling situational demands, goal setting. Interpretations integrating basic skills at an aggregate level have to be entered. Reports may need to be re-edited to enhance better understanding by the participant and to comply with development needs.
- **Oral feedback sessions** They will have to be scheduled of a highly interactive nature, focusing on acceptance, problem solving and raising commitment to personal development planning and activities. It might have to be repeated after some days of reflection. The feedback provider should be trained in signaling subtle distress and defense reactions and be skilled in handling defensive, aggressive and indifferent attitude/responses of the participant. (See, for example, the protocol of the Canadian Federal Government reproduced by Slivinsky & Bourgois, 1977).

Finally, DCs will profit from special attention to:

a.   Drafting tailor made documents containing standards and guidelines for all participants, covering topics like responsibilities, regulations and rules, privacy of information, handling of complaints and re-assessments, opportunities and references to other relevant policy documents and

b.   Arrangements made for video taping exercises so participants and/or coaches can review performances at later times.

DCs are the most extensive and most costly of ACM applications. However when their contribution to reach developmental objects are realized their costs compare favorably to other training and development efforts. Care should be taken that tight budgeting does not lead to cutting down on reporting and post-assessment activities such as feedback sessions.

VALIDITY ISSUES OF DCs

WHAT QUALITIES ARE AT STAKE?

In the introduction, I mentioned psychometric qualities associated with different uses of measurement methods. I referred to other attractive features as well. Psychometric qualities refer to the dependability, accuracy and validity of measurements. In general, standardization of the assessment situation is seen as a precondition to achieve these qualities. For subjective measurements like assessing exercises, agreement among different assessors rating the same individual is an appropriate estimate of its reliability. Validity in a broad sense deals with the extent to which a measure serves the purpose for which it is mend to be used. Depending on its purpose, validity can take different forms such as predictive, content and construct validity. For DCs the construct validity is of prime importance.

Construct validity refers to the theoretical concepts intended to be measured. These concepts serve to understand and explain the psychological meaning of measurement. To be theoretical is not to say it is without practical meaning (see Klimosky & Brickner, 1987). It is not sufficient for predictive validity to have a demonstrated relation between assessment and criterion performance. It is essential that alternative explanations that have nothing to do with individual performances can be excluded. In that sense, demonstration of test fairness (cf. lack of cultural, race, or sex bias) is also part of the construct validity of an assessment or test method. Equally important to know is what kinds of skills are being measured when giving feedback on skills that need improvement is the main focus.

Setting standards is a subject lightly touched upon in assessment center literature. It is treated as part of the content validity issue in that exercises should both represent the content and the level of jobs. It is indirectly covered in the discussion of dimensional profiles as related to job level. However this treatment falls short of what is needed to make dependable judgments to underscore decision making as is done in certification and job classification. These latter methods can be applied when standard setting really matters. In most applications it does not, not even in DCs for which reference to existing job levels in the organization will normally suffice. When off-the-shelf DCs are used from external providers, and applied to applicants from different organizations they do. Special measures have to be taken to demonstrate the adequacy of represented job levels (Hambleton, 1996). Besides measurement qualities, methods have to meet other requirements to prove value to users. Quality of manuals and test materials for one thing, cost effectiveness (utility) and ease of execution for another. Opinions of those taking tests become more and more important to users (Iles & Robertson, 1997; Francis-Smithe & Smith, 1997). Qualities relevant in this respect are acceptability, transparency, and credibility or face validity.

Finally we may point to additional benefits. By this, I refer to benefits that lie beyond the prime purpose for which the method is intended. This is not to say these qualities are not being sought. Examples are the similarity of the conceptual framework (the vocabulary) of methods and other existing practices in the organization, applicability of learning experiences outside the test situation both of assessees and assessors, tuning of measurement approach to existing training approaches, expressing desired organizational values, sustaining or setting off processes of organizational change and development, etc.

Measurement qualities of ACM in its different forms and applications have been extensively researched. The study that added most to its fame is the well-known follow-up study by Bray and colleagues (Bray, 1964; Bray, 1982; Bray, Campbell & Grant, 1974) based on assessment center data that ATT kept in its files without using it for decision making. It demonstrated impressive predictive validity for management advancement over periods of four, eight and more years. Many studies on predictive validity of overall assessment ratings (OAR) followed this famous one. Meta-analysis summarizing these studies supported the findings (Gaugler, Rosenthal, Thornton & Bentson, 1987; Schmitt, 1990) adding new insights on the generality of the predictive power of ACs.

Other qualities of ACM have also been documented by research findings. Many surveys among participants (managers, assessors, participants) confirm the credibility, acceptance, transparency and content validity of ACs (Dodd, 1977; Thornton & Byham; 1982; Zaal, 1990). Such perceived qualities like these, affect the participants' willingness to accept feedback from DCs and to commit themselves to follow-up developmental activities (Thornton, & Byham, 1982; Lee & Akhtar, 1996; Francis-Smythe & Smith, 1997).

EVIDENCE FROM RESEARCH DATA FOR CONSTRUCT VALIDITY OF DIMENSIONS

Empirical evidence on the construct validity of dimensions can be based on four different type of data such as ratings of job requirements, overall dimension ratings (ODRs), respective exercise ratings in ACs, and 360° feedback ratings. Most relevant for DCs are data derived from ACs. First, data on ODRs will be presented followed by exercise ratings.

Overall dimension ratings in ACs

An overview of results from different studies using dimension ratings in assessment centers—without making references to purpose—is presented in Thornton and Byham (1982). These studies have in common that assessors integrate observations from different exercises into overall dimension ratings in a council or "wash-up" meeting. Not all factors are replicated in all studies due to differences in exercise but three common broad factors are reported:

1. Administrative skills like Planning and Organizing, Decision-Making and Writing skills.
2. Interpersonal skills like Human relations skills, Flexibility, First impression, Leadership (group and individual), Forcefulness and Oral communication.
3. Amount of activity with personal skills like Persuasiveness, Forcefulness, Aggressiveness, Energy and Self confidence.

Other factors only surfaced in two different studies such as Intellectual ability, Work-oriented behavior, Sensitivity, Oral communication and Written communication.

In a more recent study on the construct validity of final dimension ratings two factors are reported that proved to be related to personality and aptitude factors (Shore,

Thornton & McFarlane-Shore, 1990). Subscales of "Interpersonal Style" including Amount of participation, Impact and (to a lesser extend) Personal acceptability correlated substantially (mean r ± .30) with Cattell 16PF scales like shy-bold, submissive-dominant and sober-enthusiastic. "Performance Style" (Originality, Oral Communication, Recognizing priorities, Thoroughness, Work Quality and Drive) only correlated moderately though consistently with the 16PF scale Concrete-Abstract Thinking. Performance Style correlated stronger with aptitude (average r. 25) than did Interpersonal Style.

In summary final dimension ratings reveal at least two common factors that mirror task (administration) oriented and person oriented skills that are well known from management literature. These factors have found to be related in a predictive way to personality and aptitude traits.

Dimensions rated in exercises

Data of the third type are the only ones that represents observational data on exercises in a direct way. A variety of analysis techniques have been used such as MTMM analysis (Campbell and Fiske, 1959), confirmative factor analysis (Jøreskog & Sørbom, 1986) and structural covariance analysis (Jöreskog, 1974). All studies report consistent results meaning that exercise dimension ratings fail to generalize over exercises (lack of convergent validity) and within exercises dimension ratings fail to discriminate from one another (lack of discriminant validity). Factor structures reveal only independent exercise factors (Sacket and Dreher, 1982; Turnage, 1982; Van de Velde, Born & Hofkes, 1984; Zaal en Pieters, 1985; Herriot, 1986; Silverman, Dalessio, Woods & Johnson, 1986; Bycio, 1987; Robertson, 1987; Joyce, Thayer & Pond, 1994; Schneider & Schmitt, 1992; Fleenor, 1996).

So exercise ratings do represent overall proficiency. Even within exercises skill ratings can hardly be differentiated. Also alarming for construct validity is the fact that exercise factors do not cluster. So it is not surprising that construct validity achieved a high priority ranking on the ACM research agenda for the next decade (Howard, 1997). Zaal (1990, 1998) highlighting nuances in data of Zaal & Pieters (1985), showed evidence of cross situational validity of some dimensions like Motivation, Sensitivity measured in Group Discussion Assigned Roles and Oral communication measured in Leaderless Group Discussions. Comparable observations with regard to Oral and Written Communication can be found in results reported, for example, in Harris, Becker & Smith (1993) and Fleenor (1996). In a recent study by Zaal & VanLeeuwen (in preparation) these results were partly replicated using behavioral checklists following the promising results in Reilly, Henry, & Smither (1990). Performances in both an interview exercise and a fact-finding could be explained by two specific exercise factors and four trait or skill factors: Sensitivity, Stress tolerance, Oral communication and Listening. Skill factors were related to personality and aptitude as were the exercise factors. Most revealing is the finding that Decision-making and Analyses/judgment in the fact finding exercise correlated with aptitude, but comparable exercise factors in the Interview did not, thus illustrating that skills seemingly alike at a behavioral level could well represent different skill constructs depending on the situational setting of the exercise.

These results may point to a promising approach to enhance construct validity of skill dimensions rated in exercises, especially when taking account of the short checklist with which dimensions are rated (two items for each dimension).

In summary, preventing situational determinants of behavior to operate (as is the case in ODRs) the picture of common factors seems to have some foundation. However the key data as far as the construct validity of DCs is concerned reveal a dominance of situational determents of management effectiveness. Before discussing the implications of these findings for applying DCs let us first turn to measures that might improve construct validity of these ratings.

MEASURES TO IMPROVE CONSTRUCT VALIDITY

The use of checklists can enhance controlled and balanced construction of dimensions at various levels of abstraction (e.g. generality) by carefully selecting relevant behavioral items but what more can be done? Lievens (1998) reviews studies in which features of AC design were varied to evaluate their effect on construct validity of ratings. Several measures prove to be effective thus providing useful prescriptions of adapting the design and procedures of DCs. Of special interest in this respect are findings indicating that using a limited number of conceptually distinct dimensions enhances discriminant validity (Gaugler, 1989) as does giving assessees information on dimensions to be assessed and the relevant behaviors defining them (Kleinmann, Kuptsch & Köller, 1996). Other recommendations relate to exercise design and execution. Exercises should be designed to provide abundant opportunities to elicit behaviors on relevant dimensions. Non-relevant behaviors should not be encouraged (Schneider, 1992). Role players should be instructed to play an active part in their play (Tan, 1996).

Also the quality and not so much the amount of assessor training is important. Training should be focused on familiarizing assessors with the definition and operationalization of performance dimensions (Woehr, 1992) and on establishing a common frame of reference in using evaluative standards (Woehr & Huffcutt, 1994). In other words, assessors should be provided with examples of efficient and non-efficient behaviors in each dimension and each exercise.

It does not follow from research on construct validity that a different conceptualization of dimensions e.g. more closely related to managerial tasks like Staffing, Structuring jobs, Establishing work group relations, Performance management, etc. is making much difference on discriminant and convergent validity (Joyce, Thrayer & Pond, 1994).

In short, both in the design of exercises and the definition of dimensions as well in the quality of assessor training and the execution of DCs, much can be done to improve the construct validity of ratings of dimensions:

1. Use of a limited number of salient dimensions in each exercise.
2. Exercises geared at exhibiting the most salient behaviors; endorsed by active role playing and prior tuning of assesses.
3. Focusing assessor training on use of behavior dimensions and applying common evaluation standards.
4. Use of carefully constructed behavior related checklists in making dimensions ratings.

Having said this we should not close our eyes to the situational specificity that is inherent in certain performance dimensions (Reilly et al., 1990; Zaal, 1998). These effects are also found in performance measurement in other settings such as using standard patients in assessing skills in medical diagnosis (Vleuten, 1990; Swanson, 1995). Skills are believed to be important concepts to guide exercise construction and understanding of exercise performance. Skills do not take the same form in all contexts (Messick, 1994). If it is conceivable that behaviors related to decision-making in different exercises may be content-specific representatives of different aspects of the same construct (Reilly et al. 1990), then we should adopt the concept of management effectives as best described by the matrix of exercises times dimensions instead of the one (dimensions) or the other (exercises). Consequences for practice are discussed in the next section.

IMPLICATIONS FOR DC PRACTICE

The situational specificity of AC ratings expressed in different but alarming titles such as "Dimensions or Job samples" (Herriot, 1986) or "Dimensions into exercises won't go" (Robertson, Gratton & Sharpley, 1987) seems to be a neglected perspective as far as practitioners are concerned. It did not change dimension oriented AC-practices very much. At best references are made to situational departures from the overall dimensional rating. Reporting on work sample performances instead of dimensions, such as advocated in the Netherlands by Jansen (1993), violate the concepts, assumptions, expectations and needs of most parties involved. For one thing, HRM policies and related developmental programs are centered on dimensional concepts like competencies. It would mean a significant step forward in improving accuracy of feedback on development needs if one could bring DC practices more in line with empirical findings by complying to some of the following recommendations:

1. Feedback on dimensions should always be related to each of the situations considered to be relevant. These situations can be best thought of in terms of exercises. Exercises also provide the natural setting in which training sessions will be framed that are based on behavior modeling approaches. We should abandon giving feedback on developmental needs solely based on personality traits as advocated by Goodstein & Lanyon (1998), no matter how transparent the concepts seem to be. The use of personality questionnaires for these purposes always should be accompanied by post hoc analysis in which the situational relevance is verified and specified. This recommendation holds equally for 360° applications (Kaplan, 1993).
2. To provide accurate feedback on development needs, it is better to rely on performance samples displayed in exercises rather than on personality data. In making accurate predictions of future management success on the other hand it is better to rely on both data sets. Giving more weight though to personality data would be in line with the recommended use of employee appraisal data (Drenth, 1998, page 62). This is not to say that one can do without personality data in giving feedback on development needs. As is illustrated in research by Zaal et al. (in preparation), personality questionnaire data are necessary to in-depth understanding of the meaning of behavioral dimensions in specific settings. These kinds of relationships should be addressed in post hoc analysis and will be decisive in answering questions about the ease and the prospects of the development of specific dimensions.
3. Performance models of exercises in terms of skill dimensions should be formulated. In contrast with present practice one should not aim at describing all the possible behavior dimensions that can be observed, but instead only determine the most salient and crucial skills needed to perform well in that particular exercise. This approach

to exercise analysis is comparable to job analysis. Performance models should reveal patterns of skills rather than isolated skill dimensions.

4. In the absence of sound empirical models of leadership behavior based on assessment data, dimensions or management skills can best be modeled on taxonomies of well-researched leadership behavior models based on survey data. The better these models relate to managerial roles or tasks, the better they will be understood by assesses (Joyce et al., 1994).

5. The number of exercises is at least as critical but probably more so for representing the desired domain of job relevant behaviors than are dimensions. This is in line with the findings of Gaugler et al. (1987) who report the predictive validity to be moderated by the number of exercises and not by time spent observing assessees.

Finally, in line with what has been concluded above regarding the enhancement of construct validity, reducing the number of behavior dimensions to be rated is becoming a critical factor. Reduction can be achieved by using more general behavior constructs discussed earlier. This need not and should not be at the expense of behavior-specificity of ratings and feedback. Use of checklists can ensure a well-balanced representation of relevant behaviors.

ADDITIONAL FACTORS AFFECTING DEVELOPMENT IMPACT OF DEVELOPMENT CENTERS

Without special attention to the following factors the impact of DC will stay below its potential and expectations. Factors to be considered are setting realistic expectations, providing accurate and specific feedback, raising understanding of what lies behind behavior, commitment of key figures in the organization, integration of planned activities in HRM policy and activity plans of the organization and post assessment activity planning and monitoring.

Accuracy of feedback is a necessary but certainly not a sufficient condition for DCs to be effective in making a developmental change. Giving feedback will moderate opinions of candidates about themselves, about their well being (Robertson et al., 1991; Francis-Smythe & Smith, 1997), the assessment procedure (Dodd, 1977), and it can make a difference to effectiveness of post-assessment training (Thornton & Byham, 1982, page 328), but more often than not effects of DCs are absent (Boehm, 1985; Goodge, 1993).

DCs are well known for their reliability and behavioral feedback. However it is certainly not sufficient for the understanding of someone's development needs to be told on what dimensions scores are below average. Thus a weak score on leadership, problem-solving or sensitivity should be illustrated with key behaviors exhibited in relevant exercises. To relieve assessors from this extra burden, Goodge (1993) makes the interesting suggestion to involve participants in report writing, thus making the feedback process more of a collaborative action. It also fits equally well with integrating information from different sources such as self and peer ratings.

A strict behavioral perspective in providing feedback is too narrow to ensure full understanding of development needs. It disregards the complexity of determinants of managerial competencies (Kaplan, 1993; Hoekstra & Vander Sluis, 1999). Behaviors do result from a mixture of interwoven skills, personality dispositions and drives, interacting with environmental constraints. Kaplan (1993) gives an overview of what he calls

"Boosters for 360°s feedback" that serve equally well to articulate the requirements for DC feedback processes. These include, besides follow-through verbal descriptions in own words in addition to standard scores, data on motivation, data from early history and data from personal life.

Commitment of the participant to developmental activities is dependent on complex relations which include the quality of feedback, the involvement of the individual's manager and the perceived availability of developmental opportunities. This is nicely reflected in a causal model based on a study to identify determinants of employee willingness to use feedback from performance appraisals (Lee & Akhtar, 1996). Supervisor's "Knowledge of the job" strongly predicted Perceived Fairness and Accuracy of feedback (.37) together with Trust in Supervisor (.04) and Agreed Performance Plan (.11), the latter directly determined Willingness to Use Feedback (.18) jointly with Perceived Fairness and Accuracy of Feedback (.04).

Developmental activity planning obviously tries to relate developmental needs to appropriate actions. These actions can take different forms such as special outdoor training programs, training on the job, special assignments, formal and informal mentoring, etc. (see e.g. Baldwin & Padgett, 1993; Yukl, 1997).

Finally, the decision on which of the competencies diagnosed as in need of development should be worth the effort needs special consideration. This question not only involves return on investment, it also relates to ethical standards in as far one runs the risk of raising false hopes on improvement (Thornton & Byham, 1982). Although this problem has to do with different notions (who is willing to pay, who is making the effort, which pre-conditions in the working place have to be met, etc) the one that is of special relevance here has to do with stability and change of behavior. Some behaviors are more resistant to change than others especially those related to personality such as Cognitive style or Flexibility; Motivation to work, Need for achievement and probably Leadership and Decision Making (Boehm and Hoyle, cited in: Thornton & Byham, 1982, page 402). However, evidence is scarce and far from conclusive. In a more recent study by Engelbrecht (1995) significant improvement is reported for all clusters of dimensions used (Action, Human Resources, Information Management and Problem solving). In part, this way of thinking can be traced back to the trait-like concepts included in assessment center lists of dimensions. One runs the risk of talking about dimensions without separating trait like connotations from skills. Trait-like dispositions such as Need for achievement, Assertiveness, Intelligence, Creativity are by definition more or less stable characteristics of a person. However at a behavioral level, many more determinants come into play besides a person's disposition. Some may be inclined to work harder than others, but may be equally well responsive to measures to raise morale and effort. Many training courses are known to be effective in raising innovation in the work place (Guilford, 1967). Although dispositions play a dominant role in selection, be it for educational streaming or for fast track assignments, once these decisions have been made, training and educational efforts are geared on those other factors that promise maximum development of skills.

REFERENCES

Adizes, I. (1979). *How to solve the Mismanagement Crises: Diagnosis and Treatment of Management Problems*. California: Adizes Institute.

Algera, J.A. & Greuter, M.A.M. (1998). Job Analyses. In P.J.D. Drenth, H. Thierry & C.J. de Wolff (Eds), *Handbook of work and organizational psychology*, 2 edn, Vol. 3. Hove: Psychology Press.

Anderson, N. & Herriot, P. (1997). *International Handbook of Selection and Assessment.* New York: John Wiley & Sons.

American Educational Research Association, American Psychological Association & National Council on Measurement in Education (1999). *Standards for educational and psychological testing.* Washington, D.C.: AERA.

American Psychological Association (1966). *Standards for educational and psychological tests and manuals.* Washington, D.C.: APA.

Baldwin, T.T. & Padgett, M.Y. (1993). Management development: A review and commentary. *International Review of Industrial Organisational Psychology, 8*, 35–85.

Boehm, V.R. (1985). Using assessment centers for management development-Five applications. *Journal of Management Development, 4*, 40–51.

Boehm, V.R. & Hoyle, D.F. (1977). Assessment and management development. In J.L. Moses & W.C. Byham (1977). *Applying the assessment center method.* New York: Pergamon Press.

Bray, D.W. (1964). The management process study. *American Psychologist, 19*, 419–429.

Bray, D.W. (1982). The assessment centers and the study of lives. *American Psychologist, 37(2)*, 180–189.

Bray, D.W. & Grant, D.L. (1966). The assessment center in the measurement of potential for business management. *Psychological Monographs, 80 (17, Whole No 625).*

Bray, D.W., Campbell, R.J. & Grant, D.L. (1974). *Formative years in business: A long-term AT&T study of managerial lives.* New York: John Wiley.

Bycio, P., Alvares, K.M. & Hahn, J. (1987). Situational specifity in assessment center ratings: a confirmatory factor analysis. *Journal of Applied Psychology, 72(3)*, 463–474.

Cascio, W.F. (1998). *Applied psychology in human resource management (5th edition).* London: Prentice-Hall International Ltd.

Dodd, W.E. (1977). Attitudes Towards Assessment Center Programmes In J.L. Moses & W.C. Byham (1977). *Applying the assessment center method.* New York: Pergamon Press.

Drenth, P.J.D. (1998). Personnel Appraisal. In P.J.D. Drenth, H. Thierry & C.J. de Wolff (Eds), *Handbook of work and organizational psychology*, 2nd edn, Vol. 3. Hove: Psychology Press.

Engelbrecht, A.S.F., A.H. (1995). The managerial performance implications of a development assessment center process. *Human Relations, 48*, 1–18.

Evers, A. Caminada, H., Koning, R. Laak, J. ter, Measen de Sombreff, P.van der & Starren J. (1988) *Richtlijnen voor ontwikkeling en gebruik van psychologische tests en studietoetsen.* Amsterdam: Nederlands Instituut voor Psychologen.

Evers, A. Van Vliet-Mulder, J.C. van & Groot, C. (2000). *Documentatie van tests en testresearch in Nederland, dl 1 en dl 2.* Assen: Van Gorcum.

Feltham, R.T. (1989) Assessment Centers. In P. Herriot (Ed.), *Assessment and selection in organizations.* Chichester: John Wiley & Sons.

Feltman, R. (1988). Validity of a police assessment center: A 1–19 year follow up. *Journal of Occupational Psychology, 61*, 129–144.

Finkle, R.B. (1976). Managerial assessment centers. In M.D. Dunnette (Ed.) *Handbook of industrial and organizational psychology.* Chicago, IL: Rand McNally, 891–888.

Flanagan, J.C. (1954). The critical incident technique. *Psychological Bulletin, 51*, 327–349.

Fletcher, C. (1990). Candidates' reactions to assessment centres and their outcomes: A longitude study. *Journal of Occupational Psychology, 63*, 117–127.

Francis-Smythe, J. & Smith, P.M. (1997) The psychological impact of assessment in a development center. *Human Relations, Vol 50, 2*, 149–167.

Gaugler, B.B., Rosenthal, D.B., Thornton, G.C. & Bentson, C. (1987). Meta-Analysis of assessment center validity. *Journal of Applied Psychology, 72*, 493–511.

Gaugler, B.B.T., G.C. (1989). Number of assessment center dimensions as a determinant of assessor accuracy. *Journal of Applied Psychology, 74*, 611–618.

Goodge, P. (1991). Development centres: Guidelines for decision makers. *Journal for Management Development, 10 (3)*, 4–12.

Goodstein, L.D. & Lanyon, R.I. (1999). Applications of personality assessment to the workplace. *Journal of Business and Psychology,13*, 3, 291–322.

Hambleton, R.K. (1996). Advances in Assessment Models, Methods and Practices. In D.C. Berliner & R.C. Calfee (Eds), *The Handbook of Educational Psychology*. New York: Macmillan.

Harris, M.M., Becker, A.S. & Smith, D.E. (1993) Does the assessment scoring method affect cross-situational consistency of ratings? *Journal of Applied Psychology, 78*, 675–678.

Herriot, P. (1986). *Assessment centers: Dimensions or job samples*. European Conference on the Benefits of Psychology, Lausanne.

Hoekstra, H. & Sluis, E. Vander (1999). *Management van competenties: het realiseren van HRM*. Assen: Van Gorcum.

Howard, A. (1997). A reassessment of Assessment Centers, challenges for the 21th century. *Journal of Social Behavior and Personality, 12*, 12–52.

Hunt, J.G. (1991). *Leadership: A new synthesis*. Newbury Park, CA: Sage.

International Test Commission (2000). *International Guidelines for Test Use, Version 2000*. ITC.

Iles, P.A. & Robertson, I.T. (1989) The impact of personnel selection procedures on candidates. In P. Herriot (Ed.), *Assessment and selection in organizations*. Chichester: John Wiley & Sons.

Jansen, P.G.W. (1993). De werking van het assessment center. Zurück zu den Sachen (Husserl). *Gedrag en Organisatie, 6: 10.*

Jeswald, T.A. (1977). Issues in establishing an assessment center. *Applying the assessment center method*. New York: Pergamont Press.

Jøreskog, K.G. (1974). Analysing psychological data by structural analysis of covariance matrices. *Contemporary development in mathematical psychology*. D.H. Krantz, Luce, R.D., Atkinson, R.C., Uppes, P. San Francisco: Freeman. 2.

Jøreskog, K.G. & Sørbom, D. (1986) *LISREL: Analysis of linear structural relationships by the method of maximum likelihood* (4th edn) Chicago: National Educational Resources.

Joyce, L.W., Thayer, P.W. & Pond, S.B. (1994). Managerial functions: an alternative to traditional assessment center dimensions. *Personnel Psychology, 47*, 109–121.

Kaplan, R.E. (1993). 360-degree feedback Plus: Boosting the powers of co-worker ratings for executives. *Human Resource Management, 32*, 299–314.

Kleinmann, M. (1993) Are rating dimensions in assessment centers transparent for participants? Consequencies for criterion and construct validity. *Journal of Applied Psychology, 78*, 988–993.

Kleinmann, M., Kuptsch, C. & Köller, O. (1996) Transparency: a necessary requirement for the construct validity of assessment centres. *Applied Psychology: An international Review, 45*, 67–84.

Klimosky, R.J. & Brickner, M. (1987) Why do assessment centers work? The puzzle of assessment center validity. *Personnel Psychology, 40*, 243–260.

Lee, J.S.Y. & Akhtar, S. (1996). Determinants of employee willingness to use feedback for performance improvement: cultural and organizational interpretations. *The International Journal of Human Resource Management (7:4)*, 878–890.

Messick, M. (1994). The interplay of evidence and consequences in the validation of performance assessments. *Educational Researcher, 23*, 13–23.

Moses, J.L. & Byham, W.C. (1977). *Applying the assessment center method*. New York: Pergamon Press.

Quinn, R.E. (1984). Applying the competing values approach to leadership: towards an integrative framework. In J.G. Hunt, Hosking, D., Schriesheim, C., Steward, R. Elmsford (Eds), *Leaders and managers: international perspectives on managerial behavior and leadership*. New York: Pergamon Press.

Quinn, R.E. (1988). *Beyond rational management: Mastering the paradoxes and competing demands of high performance*. San Francisco: Jossey-Bass.

Reilly, R.R., Henry, Sarah, Smither, James W. (1990). An examination of the effects of using behavior checklists on the construct validity of assessement center dimensions. *Personnel Psychology, 43*, 71–84.

Robertson, I.T., Gratton, L. & Sharpley, D. (1987). The psychometric properties and design of managerial assessment centers: Dimensions into excercises won't go. *Journal of Applied Psychology, 60*, 187–195.

Sackett, P.R. (1987). Assessment centers and content validity: some neglected issues. *Personnel Psychology, 40*, 13–25.

Sackett, P.R. & Dreher, G.F. (1982). Constructs and assessment center dimensions: Some troubling empirical findings. *Journal of Applied Psychology, 69*, 187–190.

Saville, & Holdsworth Ltd. (1989). *Work Profiling System* (WPS). London: Saville, & Holdsworth Ltd.

Schmitt, N., Schneider, J., Cohen, R. & Scott, A. (1990). Factors affecting validity of a regionally administered assessment center. *Personnel Psychology, 43*, 1–12.

Schneider, J.R. & Schmitt, N. (1992). An exercise design approach to understanding assessment center dimensions and exercise constructs. *Journal of Applied Psychology, 77*, 32–41.

Seegers, J.L. (1989). Assessment centers for identifying long-term potential and for self-development. In *Assessment and selection in Organization.* Chichester: Wiley

Silvermann, W.H., Dalessio, A., Woods. S.B. & Johnson, R.L. (1986) Influence of assessment center methods on assessor ratings. *Personnel Psychology, 30*, 565.

Slivinsky, L.W. & Bourgois, R.P. (1977). Feedback of assessment centers results. In *Applying the assessment center method.* New York: Pergamont Press.

Swanson, D.B., Norman, G.R. & Linn, R.L. (1995). Performance-based assessment: Lessons from the health professions. *Educational Researcher, 24*, 5–11, 35.

Tan, M. (1996). *Het effect van rolstandaardisatie op de begripsvaliditeit van de gedragscriteria in assessmentoefeningen.* Amsterdam: Universiteit van Amsterdam/GITP.

Thornton, G.C. & Byham, W.C. (1982). *Assessment centers and managerial performance.* New York: Academic Press.

Tornow, W.W. & Pinto, P.R. (1976). The development of a managerial job taxonomy: A system for describing, classifying and evaluating executive positions. *Journal of Applied Psychology, 61*, 410–418.

Velde, E.G. van der, Born, M.Ph. & Hofkes, K. (1994). Begripsvalidering van een assessment center met behulp van confirmatieve factoranalyse. *Gedrag & Organisatie, 1*, 18–25.

Vleuten, C.P.M. v. d. & Swanson, D.B. (1990). Assessment of clinical skills with standardized patients: State of the art. *Teaching and Learning in Medicine, 2*, 58–76.

Woehr, D.J. (1992). Performance Dimensions accessibility: Implications for rating accuracy. *Journal of Organizational Behavior, 13*, 357–367.

Woehr, D.J. & Huffcutt, A.I. (1994). Rater training for performance appraisal: A quantitative review. *Journal of Occupational and Organizational Psychology, 67*, 189–205.

Yukl, G.A. (1987) *A new taxonomy for integrating diverse perspectives on managerial behavior.* Paper presented at annual meeting of the American Psychological Association, New York.

Yukl, G.A. (1998, 4th edn) *Leadership in organizations.* New Jersey: Prentice-Hall International.

Zaal, J.N. (1990). Assessment Centers at the Dutch Central Goverment. In R.K. Hambleton & Jac N. Zaal (Eds), *Advances in Educational and Psychological testing.* Boston: Kluwer Academic publishers.

Zaal, J.N. (1998). Assessment Centre Methods. In P.J.D. Drenth, H. Thierry & C.J. de Wolff (Eds), *Handbook of Work and Organizational Psychology*, 2nd edn, Vol. 3. Hove: Psychology Press.

Zaal, J.N. & Pieters, J.P.M. (1985). Assessment Centers at the Rijks Psychologische Dienst. Paper Presented at the West European Conference on the Psychology of Work and Organization, Aachen.

Zaal, J.N. & VanLeeuwen, R. (in preparation). Applying 360° feedback methods in individual assessment program. Amsterdam: GITP Research & Development.

PART IV

Development Methods and Processes

CHAPTER 12

Choosing a Development Method

Alan Mumford
London, UK

SUMMARY

In this chapter, I outline four frameworks to help professional developers and advisers in organizations, and also individual learners, to choose development methods that are likely to be reasonably effective for them in a given context, by comparison with alternatives development methods. This argument is based on the view that it is not only the characteristics of the methods that should form the basis of the choice, nor the characteristics of the learners or the context, but rather the interaction between them as well as other factors. The four frameworks are:

1. Suitability for developing knowledge, skills and insight
2. Relationship to learning theories
3. Learning to learn potential
4. Congruence with personal learning style preferences

The key point is that the effectiveness of any development method is influenced by a number of factors not inherent in the method itself. The four frameworks are used to assess the potential effectiveness of sixteen distinct development methods divided into three broad categories, viz., at work methods, of the job methods, and other methods.

Individual Differences and Development in Organisations. Edited by Michael Pearn.
© 2002 John Wiley & Sons, Ltd.

INTRODUCTION

There is a bewildering array of methods, techniques, processes that can be brought
to bear on helping people to learn in order that they can improve their performance.
Huczynski's (2001) encyclopaedia of development methods, helpfully recognizing the
overlap between individual development and organizational development methods, contains 700 entries, half of which have a prime focus on the individual.

There is a degree of confusion as to what exactly is meant by a method as distinct
from technique, tool, process or approach. Also there is no commonly agreed framework for classifying and describing different development methods. Having reviewed
attempts to classify development methods from different perspectives (viz. learning objectives, number of learners, level of learner autonomy, learning theories), Huczynski
(2001) comes to the view that it is unlikely that there will "ever be one best way of
classifying development methods let alone a way of selecting the most appropriate ones
for a task" (p. 21). He argues that the personal philosophy of the teacher or developer is
a prime determinant, and that the sheer complexity of the skills and competencies being
developed mitigate against such an approach.

I broadly agree with this argument that there is unlikely to ever be one best way
of classifying development methods where the aim is to create a taxonomy allowing
identification of critical similarities and differences such as that used in biology for
classification of plants. I would argue that such an enterprise is unhelpful and unnecessary.
Instead utilitarian frameworks are desirable that enable practitioners faced with an array
of possible methods to make more informed choices about the appropriate use, and
combination, of development methods in different contexts.

There is a lack of rigorous research on the comparability and effectiveness of development methods. Many development methods have been taken up because they became
available for the first time and their proponents extolled their virtues (e.g. outdoor training), or the technology became available (as with programmed instruction in the Sixties
and Seventies, and with computer-based training or CBT in the Eighties). There is a risk
that e-learning has now become current fashion and is being adopted without critical
evaluation or evidence. In addition, the variables of gender and culture have not been
researched.

From the individual perspective there is still a need for guidance on what is likely
to work best in a given context, and organisations still need to make informed rather
than blind decisions, even though there is no all-purpose prescriptive method of known
predictive validity. The effectiveness of a development method can only be judged within
an overall context. Mumford (1997a) has argued that there are eight key elements:

1. Needs—established by a process generating commitment from an individual or a
   group.
2. Goals—for learning, agreed with, if not created by, the learner.
3. Facilitation—at the appropriate level of skill and ethical responsibility by a line manager or adviser.
4. Resources—at the required level of financial and other priorities, e.g. time and
   attention.
5. Support—by the organisation and especially the learner's direct manager.
6. Relationship between the method and the desired learning output.

7. Congruency with motivation and learning preferences of the individual.
8. Evaluation—assessing what results have occurred, in relation to what objectives or needs.

This chapter is concerned with items 6 and 7 above. The model is presented to reinforce the point that the effectiveness of any method is influenced by a number of other factors not inherent within the method itself. An individual who has not been helped to recognize the need to develop a particular knowledge or skill may respond unfavorably to any method intended to develop that knowledge or skill. (It may be, however, that some methods are better than others at helping individuals to recognize such needs.)

Mumford (1997) defined management development as "an attempt to improve managerial effectiveness through a learning process" and this applies to all members of an organization, not just those in professional roles. Not all individual development is planned and/or conscious; much learning still occurs in an unplanned way, sometimes unconsciously. For the purposes of this chapter, a development method is the specific means by which learning is acquired by individuals. Specific in this context implies stipulated, prescribed or broadly recommended, i.e. a consciously chosen method.

FOUR FRAMEWORKS FOR SELECTING DEVELOPMENT METHODS

1. SUITABILITY FOR DEVELOPING KNOWLEDGE, SKILLS AND INSIGHT

The tri-partite distinction of Knowledge, Skills and Insights is sufficient to make critical distinctions when choosing development methods. The term "Insight" is preferred to the more usual "Attitude" which itself is very hard to define precisely. Insight is closer to perceptions, conclusions, or generalizations from experiences. I am using Skills, Knowledge and Insights here in the sense that they can be broadly differentiated from each other without getting tangled in different definitions or types of knowledge. Development methods can be assessed for suitability and effectiveness in helping acquire these three outcomes.

2. RELATIONSHIP TO LEARNING THEORIES

Learning and the development of learning theory has been a perennial and active part of psychology and educational research for over a hundred years. There are literally hundreds of theories, conceptual models and formulations but I have confined my focus to a few theories that have a practical focus and application to the kinds of learning engaged in by adults in the world of work.

The major theories described and used inn this chapter recognize the way adults learn; encourage questioning action; encourage double-loop learning; allow the full learning cycle; and develop appropriate types of learning (cognitive, affective, interpersonal learning and self-insight.

Knowles' work (1985) focused on adult learning and has influenced many in the field of management development and management education. He argues, in particular, that adults differ from children in the way they learn:

• The learner is self-directed but has been conditioned into expecting to be dependent and to be taught.

- Adult learners bring substantial experience to bear on new learning, and therefore themselves provide the richest resource for other learners, especially in a group
- Adults are ready to learn where there is a need to perform more effectively in some aspect of their lives
- For the most part adults do not learn for the sake of learning; they learn in order to perform a task, solve a problem, or to live in a more satisfying way
- Although adults will respond to some external motivators (salary increase, a better job) the more potent motivators are internal (self-esteem, recognition, self-confidence, self-actualisation).

Reg Revans (1982), the pioneer of action learning formulated the Learning Equation $(L = P + Q)$ where Learning = Programmed Knowledge + Questioning Insight. The point here is that pure knowledge acquisition is unlikely on its own to lead to improved performance. Any development method can be assessed in terms of the balance, or lack of balance, between the two. Pedler (1991) defines action learning as "an approach to the development of people in organizations which takes the task as the vehicle for learning. It is based on the premise that there is no learning without action and no sober and deliberate action without learning. ... It proceeds particularly by questioning taken for granted knowledge." Action learning is essentially social and interactive and focuses on the resolution of real-world problems in context, resulting in the potential to change the context itself.

David Kolb's (1984) formulation of the learning cycle has also been very influential. Ideally a development method should allow optimum opportunities for the four phases of the cycle, though in practice the sequence may not always be followed. Kolb was the originator of the idea that, within the cycle individuals have different preferences about how to learn.

Single-loop learning (Argyris 1982) occurs where solutions to problems are discovered leading to the removal of the problem, but without addressing the underlying issues or the wider context in which the problem occurs. This may lead to the problems occuring elsewhere in the system, or cause or exacerbate other problems outside the framework of the learner. By contrast, double-loop learning addresses the underlying causes and the interdependencies of different parts of the system. It addresses and challenges fundamental assumptions, including the goals of the organization, as well as indirect causes. Single-loop learning is incremental and can result in improved performance of what

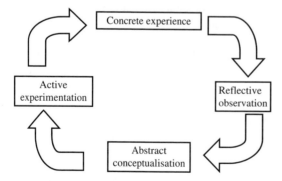

FIGURE 12.1   The learning cycle

is already being done. By contrast, double-loop learning is generative and can lead to step-changes in performance.

Organisational defence routines, according to Argyris (1990), are self-deluding (often unconscious) rationalizations that can make problems appear to go away or belong to someone else. They are powerful, and often deeply rooted in the culture and belief systems of organisations. They have the comforting benefit (at least in the short term) of explaining away problems. *Espoused theories* are expressions of what people say they believe and what they say they do. By contrast, *theories-in-use* are the inferred or observed expressions of what really happens and the actual theories/beliefs causing the actions. Unless the *theories-in-use* are actually surfaced and the discrepancies acknowledged they cannot be addressed and may block effective learning and the implementation of change processes. Double-loop learning helps overcome defence routines.

Aygyris influenced the more recent work of Peter Senge (1990, 1994) who has placed considerable emphasis on helping individuals learn new ways of becoming a learning organisation by continually refining a shared vision; bringing to the surface and challenging prevailing mental models; and fostering systems thinking, resulting in new action.

There have been many classification of learning types. A convenient classification of types of learning helpful to practitioners is that offered by Pedler (1978):

- Psychomotor (physical and manual skills)
- Cognitive (acquisition of theory and knowledge)
- Affective (attitudes and feelings)
- Interpersonal (person to person skills such as persuasion, influencing)
- Self-knowledge (personal growth)

3. Learning to Learn Potential

Learning to learn is a process through which individuals (or groups) understand the principles of effective learning and acquire and continuously improve the skills and discipline for future learning (Mumford, 2001).

This is a poorly understood and neglected aspect of the potential of any development method. Learning to learn is the most fundamentally important kind of learning because all other learning depends on it. For example, if at the same time as learning financial planning the individuals learn to improve their reflection skills, their questioning, and their ability to formulate and test their own assumptions then they have learned the morst important skill of all, i.e. their ability to learn and improve their learning skills.

Development methods can be assessed for the potential to help learners understand the learning process, the variety of learning experiences involved, and also on the suitability for the different kinds of learning that may be involved (cognitive, affective, interpersonal, and self-knowledge).

4. Congruence with Learning Style Preferences

A method may be inherently well suited to a particular purpose but individual learners may react well or badly to it. The Learning Styles Questionnaire (LSQ) developed by Honey and Mumford (1992) provides a closer examination of learner preferences than Kolb's Learning Style Inventory.

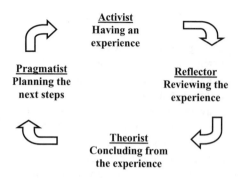

Figure 12.2   Learning styles and the learning cycle

The four learning styles are summarized here:

Activists learn best from relatively short here and now tasks. These may be managerial activities on the job or on courses: such things as business games and competitive team-work exercises. They learn less well from situations involving a passive role such as listening to lectures or reading.

Reflectors learn best from activities where they are able to stand back, listen, and observe. They like collecting information and being the opportunity to think about it. They learn less well when they are rushed into things without the opportunity to plan.

Theorists learn best when they can review things in terms of a system, a concept, a model, or theory. They are interested in and absorb ideas even when they are distant from current reality. They learn less well from activities presented without this kind of implicit or explicit design.

Pragmatists learn best where there is an obvious link between the subject matter and the problem or opportunity on the job. They like being exposed to techniques or processes that can be applied inn their immediate circumstances. They learn less well from learning events that seem distant from their own reality: "Does it apply to my own situation?"

Over 15 years' use of the LSQ indicates that many people have a strong or very strong preference for one of the 4 learning styles as the table below indicates:

Strong or Very Strong preference	
One strong preference	35%
Two strong preferences	24%
Three strong preferences	20%
Four strong preferences	2%
No strong preferences	19%

The fact that one in three have a strongly preferred method indicates that if there is a mis-match between their preference and the mode embodied in the development method then their learning could suffer. One answer is to provide a range of methods so that no individual is turned off throughout an experience. It may be preferable for an individual to avoid a method altogether. Of course, the best answer is to help individuals develop additional learning strengths. At the very least advisors should know which methods suit which learning styles.

SIXTEEN DEVELOPMENT METHODS

The following summary charts are indicative not prescriptive (Mumford, 1997a). The judgments offered are partly based on experience but also on the potential of the methods rather than on actual achieved performance. In practice development methods are rarely pure. For example, there may be considerable overlaps. Lectures can be used with participative group discussion. However, the methods are assessed here in their singular role because this clarifies what is actually happening rather than concealing it behind other methods when used in combination.

The 16 development methods are divided into three broad categories:

On the job methods

1. Manager as developer
2. Through the job
3. Coaching
4. Mentoring

Off the job methods

5. Action learning
6. Case study
7. Distance learning
8. Lecture
9. Outdoor
10. Reading
11. Role play
12. Simulations
13. Technology-based training
14. Video (talking head and case/drama)

Other methods

15. Group learning (Process and Content)
16. Learning review/logs

AT WORK METHODS

MANAGER AS DEVELOPER

This is the manager who has direct line responsibility for the development of others. Within a formal system of development this can include performance appraisal, analysis of development needs and goals, and recognizing and facilitating opportunities for development. Within the direct managerial context it includes establishing learning goals, acting as a model of learning behaviour, accepting risks in behaviour, and direct coaching (Mumford, 1993). The opportunities for on the job learning are extensive and in many organizations the importance of developing subordinates in this way is fully recognized.

The real challenge lies in the readiness and ability of the line manager to identify the learning needs of individuals and provide the means of meeting those needs (Mumford, 1995).

The method is most suitable for developing the skills, knowledge and insights particular to the job currently being done, and can also provide insights to the line manager's own job. The method provides an opportunity for the line manager to pass on his/her own learning, by modeling and provision of immediate and relevant feedback. The method is less suitable for generalizing to other contexts, and widening knowledge outside the immediate environment, or developing skills and knowledge not possessed by the line manager. It is of course dependent on skilful feedback and coaching skills, and there is also the risk of inappropriate skills being modeled. McCall, Lombardo, and Morrison (1988) describe how line managers may help others learn from experience at work, and Hill (1992) describes the development of new first line managers.

LEARNING THROUGH THE JOB

This method centers on real work performed in real work conditions. While most learning from experience is left to chance, this method focuses on planned, deliberate and conscious learning from experience. The opportunities for learning in this context may be existing tasks, identified and used additionally as learning opportunities or additional tasks deliberately proposed and taken up as learning opportunities. This can include project work, presentations, working with consultants, negotiating, networking, especially if these are not normally done by the individual. Grundy (1994) provides a good illustration of learning through a major work issue by developing strategy, though some of it is based on special workshops.

The main purpose underlying this method is to take advantage of work situations that either are already present or can easily be created. This approach can create learning opportunities which may not exist at all in off-the-job learning or which may have lower credibility if simulated in some way.

The method is most suitable for learning from current situations, problems and relationships. It is most suitable for relatively slower learning and development over time with repeated situations. It may be attractive to people who are suspicious of formal training and education. The method is less suitable for developing skills or knowledge not currently within the organization or at least not accessible. It is not likely to encourage double-loop learning or challenges to the status quo.

COACHING

Megginson and Boydell (1979) describe coaching as "a process in which a manager, through direct discussion and guided activity, helps a colleague to solve a problem, or to do a task than would otherwise have been the case". A useful practical guide to coaching is provided by Parsloe (1992), and Megginson (1988) provides a helpful basis for distinguishing coaching from mentoring. The sports coaching analogy has been developed by Whitmore (1992).

Coaching can be directive or non-directive in style. Non-directive coaching involves:

- An open style between participants in which the nature of the problem is discussed and becomes part of the coaching process

- Both leaner and coach engage in dialogue and not one-way communication.
- The coach primarily asking questions, enabling the learners to identify for themselves what the issues are and possible solutions
- Some confronting behaviours by the coach
- Using the coaching process to build up confidence and self-esteem

By contrast, directive coaching involves explicit guidance, how-to instruction, and data provision. As a coach, a manager is providing a role model and a provider of learning. Coaching is most suitable for feedback on performance issues, discussions about those issues and the knowledge and skills involved. It often involves demonstration of some of the skills, especially where there is work on a particular issue or problem or opportunity. The coach can provide new or alternative views on an issue, can test and possibly correct data held by the learner, and can model effective styles and skills possessed by the coach.

Coaching in work situations may be less appropriate where there are delicate interpersonal problems that may require counseling, or situations where the needs of the learner are not matched by the skill or experience of the coach. It is not appropriate where individuals do not recognize or accept the need for coaching on a particular issue or the credibility of the coach is questioned. It is less effective if there are time pressures or no support for development activities outside the coaching relationship. Coaching can also be carried out by course tutors, and co-coaching by participants can also be very powerful.

MENTORING

Mentoring has been defined by Mumford (1993) as "a protected relationship in which experimentation, exchange and learning can occur and skills, knowledge and insight can be developed". Although a line manager may use skills appropriate to mentoring with a subordinate it is unlikely that a mentoring relationship could develop in this context. The kind of developmental issues and discussions that can take place between a mentor and someone for whom he or she has no direct managerial responsibility is often different from that which can occur between a line manager and the same person.

The potential benefits of mentoring to the organization are to improve individual performance, and assist personal development for the individual. It can also form part of succession management and it also demonstrates a commitment to personal development. Another use of mentoring in organizations is to help under-represented groups "catch up".

For mentors the benefits include personal satisfaction in helping someone grow, developing their own skills and insights as a results of the discussions, and demonstrating that they can improve performance of others. For the learner the potential benefits of mentoring includes advice on particular problems, advice on career issues, having doors opened, acquiring knowledge about the politics and culture of the organisation, introduction to networks inside and outside the organization, knowledge and insights from an outsider, and feedback on one's own behaviour and attitudes.

Mentoring is most suitable for escaping from sole dependence on the boss as developer, providing alternative views about managerial problems, structure, objectives and strategy. Also the learners gains feedback on reported or observed behavior, and a role model of effectiveness. Mentoring is especially good for development grounded in managerial reality.

Mentoring is less suitable for issues not grounded in current personal or organizational reality and situations where either the learner or the mentor is not in practice willing to find time to develop and act on the relationship, or where there are clashing expectations between mentor and learner. Mentoring requires organisational support. It is easily undermined if it is perceived as management flavour of the month, or a quick fix is being sought. Mentors are usually provided from within the organization but consideration needs to be given to the provision of external mentors especially for senior executives (Mumford, 1988).

TABLE 12.1   On the job methods summary

Framework 1 Development methods and their suitability for learning outcomes
Ratings *** = most suitable ** = moderately suitable * = least suitable

At work methods	Suitability for knowledge	Suitability for skills	Suitability for insights
Manager as developer	***	***	**
Through the job	***	***	**
Coaching	***	***	**
Mentoring	***	**	***

Framework 2 Development methods and their relation ship to learning theories
Ratings *** = strong link ** = moderate link * = weak link
Knowles = refers to at least one major element in Knowles' theory, Argyris = refers to double-loop learning, Kolb 1 = learning cycle fully available, Kolb 2 = influence of learning styles on acceptability of method

At work Methods	Knowles	Revans	Argyris	Kolb 1&2	Cognitive learning	Affective learning	Inter-personal	Self-knowledge
Manager as developer	***	***	*	1*** 2***	*	**	**	***
Through the job	***	***	**	1*** 2***	**	**	**	**
Coaching	***	*	*	1*** 2***	*	**	**	***
Mentoring	***	*	*	1*** 2***	*	**	**	***

Framework 3 Development methods and impact on learning to learn
Ratings *** = Strong likelihood ** = Moderate likelihood * = Low Likelihood
Each method is assessed on whether it potentially helps individuals understand the learning process, provides a variety of learning processes, and assists particular types of learning

At work Methods	Potential	Variety	Cognitive learning	Affective learning	Interpersonal learning	Self-knowledge
Manager as developer	***	***	*	**	**	***
Through the job	***	***	*	**	**	***
Coaching	***	***	*	**	**	***
Mentoring	***	***	*	**	**	***

TABLE 12.1 *(continued)*

Framework 4 Development methods' congruence with strong learning styles
Ratings *** = Strong congruence ** = Moderate congruence * = Low
congruence

At work Methods	Activist	Reflector	Theorist	Pragmatist
Manager as developer	*	***	**	***
Through the job	***	***	***	***
Coaching	*	***	**	***
Mentoring	*	***	**	***

OFF THE JOB METHODS

ACTION LEARNING

Action learning has a strong theoretical, as well as defined philosophical basis which has already been referred to above (Revans, 1982; Pedler, 1997). Action learning has great power to enhance learning to learn, and provides ample scope for preferred learning styles. In particular, it offers the opportunity to learn from the task as a desirable end in itself and in a transferable manner. It provides experience in and knowledge about effective resolution of problems, and provides conscious experience of how people learn in groups and team dynamics, and it also provides a strongly bottom-line orientated development method as part of an overall development strategy.

Action learning is most suitable where real organizational issues are used as the basis for learning and there is a preference for learning from experience and not being taught, and by tapping into the experiences of a wide variety of people. Action learning challenges the status quo and encourages generative learning. It allows people to cross over boundaries and share common organizational issues. It encourages people to take action in a controlled way to see what happens, allows for a variety of approaches, and is thus well adapted to learning about change. Action learning regards evaluation as integral to the process and seeks double value, to the learner and to the organization.

Action learning is less well suited where it is possible to follow an appropriate programmed learning course where the focus is primarily on data and information. Action learning is less suitable where a result is needed quickly, or where people cannot escape their dependency on being taught. It can be expensive and even disruptive, leading to unwanted challenge, and sometimes unacceptable action. Action learning requires sympathetic understanding by senior management and trust across the organization.

CASE STUDY

A case can be defined as a depiction (in words or video) of a situation, specially written for development purposes, which exists or existed in an organization. Learners study the case and analyse what has happened, which may or may not be jointly discussed. The size of the discussion group will vary considerably and the facilitation skills of the presenter are critical. Cases vary in the degree to which they are convergent on implicitly correct interpretations or are divergent, allowing a variety of interpretations leading to a range of insights as a result of the debate. Helpful books on the case study method are Barnes, Christensen and Hansen (1994), and the earlier Easton (1982). The skills and learning potential of writing your own cases are covered by Saint Germain (1995).

Cases provide experience in solving a problem and a process through which general principles of good practice can be perceived. Cases are useful for helping to prove or illustrate theory or techniques or for deepening understanding of theory, for applying skills learned elsewhere in a programme. Much of the learning through cases comes from responding to challenges provided by the presenter and debate within the group. Cases also generate possibilities for self-analysis. In addition cases can help develop analytical reasoning, sifting and data evaluation skills, questioning, diagnosing and problem-solving skills, communication and influencing skills, as well as group generalizing, integrating, decision-making, and argument winning skills. Unfortunately, the potential of the case method for learning to learn is under-utilized (Burgoyne and Mumford, 2001). Cases are less suitable for knowledge giving and are not realistic simulations and may lack credibility with particular groups. The discussion and interaction is critical to the learning.

DISTANCE LEARNING

Distance learning can be defined as a programme involving one or more channels of delivery in which a tutor is not usually physically present and which is designed to meet the needs of learners who may be physically dispersed who are unable or unwilling to come together to attend a course. Most forms of distance learning now make provision for interaction between facilitators and learners, and between learners themselves, either through meetings or electronic means or satellite communication. Distance learning is particularly suitable for meeting the requirements of large numbers of learners who all need the same input and a consistent level of quality. Alternatively it can be used with small numbers or even solo, but physically remote, learners.

Distance learning is most suited to the delivery of data and information. It can give insight to the value of skills development but is less likely to be effective in development of those skills. Distance learning may be less appropriate in its pure version where there is little or no interaction with other learners for the development of understanding through dialogue or joint problem-solving and team skills. Useful books on open and distance learning include Harrison (1994), Rowntree (1992) and a good general review of key issues associated with open and distance learning is provided by Snell and Binsted (1985).

LECTURES, TALKS AND PRESENTATIONS

Lectures have been defined as "fifty to fifty-five minutes of largely uninterrupted discourse from a teacher with no discussions between between students and no student activity other than listening and note-taking" (Gibbs and Habeshaw, 1992). The pros and cons of the lecture method vis-a-vis the discussion method have been outlined by Griffin and Cashin (1989), and Hodgson (1984) provides an account of research on students' experience of lectures rather than that of the tutors.

Usually the learner is passive and solitary even though they are in a group. The lecture can effectively be used to pass on information and data though it can, in the hands of a highly skilled presenter, also be used to stimulate, enthuse, explain, or even stir things up. The skills of the lecturer are crucial. Although primarily geared towards cognitive learning, responses from learners are often emotional, responding more to the lecture's style and behaviour than to the content of the lecture. Lectures can be effective for providing brief introductions to a subject, or for launching a programme where there is a desire to get a message across. Many well known management gurus have built reputations on their lecturing skills and their ability to rouse or excite an audience. Lectures can describe skills and theories but may not be well suited to develop deeper understanding or the practice of those skills. It would seem that timing and context is crucial to the effectiveness of a lecture. Despite the known limitations of lectures the vast majority of universities, business schools and executive programmes still depend greatly on lectures, the Harvard Business School being a notable exception.

OUTDOOR TRAINING AND DEVELOPMENT

Outdoor activities are designed to provide task-centred experiences that are meant in some way to relate to experiences at work. The tasks are done in real time and the physical nature of the task is critical. The aim is to learn things relevant to the workplace. The tasks and the environment are unfamiliar, are always carried out by groups and the decisions made have direct consequences for the group. Timescales and contexts for the tasks vary enormously, but there is usually some psychological risk-taking involved and/or endurance involved.

The aim of outdoor training is usually to enable people to break out of familiar routines and shock the individuals into new ways of thinking and doing. A wide range of purposes can be served by outdoor training including personal development through self-insight, team building, development of leadership, practice at problem-solving, attitudinal change, interpersonal skills and acceptance of diversity. The tasks are not designed for people to become better at the them but to gain insights, etc. Bank (1994) and Tuson (1994) claim a wide range of skills that can be developed through outdoor activities. There is a strong element of learning with and from others and skilled facilitation of reviews and feedback is critical. Outdoor training is less applicable to the learning of cognitive elements of functional management and technical skills. Krouwel and Goodwill (1994) have attempted comparative evaluation of outdoor training against feasible alternatives.

READING

Reading is clearly an important part of other development methods, e.g. handouts to support lectures, but the focus here is on reading as a stand-alone or prime source of individual development. Reading can be paper-based or electronic (e-mail or internet when not in an interactive mode.) Reading when used as a stand-alone development method is solitary, self-paced and non-interactive. Reading can be used to absorb and comprehend information, analyse information, form views, consider practical applications, and plan next steps.

Reading, or at least the purchase of, books is a major potential resource for individual development whether as part of courses or for the independent reader. Crainer (1996a,

1996b) has summarized the 50 most influential books and also the most influential ideas in management theory.

Novels have also been written to illustrate management themes (see, for example Goldratt and Cox, 1993 on quality management) or existing novels, (e.g. Richard Adams's Watership Down) can be used for illustration and discussion of management themes. The writings and exploits of famous adventurers and explorers such as Ernest Shackleton are also used as aids to learning about leadership. Also, some management books are written in a semi-fictional style such as Blanchard's book on team-working (Blanchard & Bowles, 2001).

On the whole, reading is most suitable for provision of information, development of understanding and for practical guidance which may or may not result in changed behaviour and improved performance. Reading is less suitable for the development of skills and questioning insight. The style, level, and content is important as it easy to de-motivate or even alienate readers if the reading material is not appropriate to the audience or the purpose. Reading is often a compensatory device where the teaching is perceived to be ineffective. Reading is best used as a stimulus to group discussion and dialogue.

Curiously there is little if any evaluation research on the role and effectiveness of reading in personal development yet the success of books by Stephen Covey, Kenneth Blanchard, Warren Bennis, Tom Peters and Charles Handy to name but a few of recent gurus suggests that reading plays an important role in individual development.

ROLE PLAY

Role play is described by Van Ments (1999) as "asking someone to take on the role of imagined people, real people, and themselves" in a simulation that focuses on the interaction of people with one another. Individuals are asked to behave in a role, the nature of which is set for them. The amount of structure presented to the individual varies greatly from a few guiding principles to detailed scenarios. The roles are usually designed to allow individuals to enact behaviour that they then review in the light of their own experience and feedback from others. Role plays can also be designed to help individuals become more sensitive, or to question or challenge attitudes as expressed in behaviour. Role plays can be used to illustrate a situation or problem, take things from discussion to practice, or can be used to emphasise different skills at different levels of significance.

Role plays are most suitable for the improvement of affective and interpersonal skills such as counseling, interviewing, conflict management, and assertiveness. Standard texts on role plays are Maier, Solem and Maier (1975), Turner (1992) and Van Ments (1999).

SIMULATIONS AND GAMES

Simulations include business games, in-tray exercises, and practical tasks such as Lego Tower. Outdoor exercises, role-plays and cases are also simulations. Simulations can cover a wide range of activities but are probably most effective when used as a development method when choices are involved which lead to consequences arising directly from the decisions made. The consequences can then be reviewed by the individuals or the group.

Simulations are intended to be realistic, and representative of problems and issues encountered in the real world. They are usually compressed in time, are dynamic and unfold, allowing progressive feedback on outcomes. People can get very involved and excited about simulations and there is a risk that there is more focus on the simulation as a task than as a means to learning. As a development method simulations can serve a very wide range of purposes. Simulations are most suitable for the development of personal and interactive skills and for gaining personal insights. Simulations also offer the opportunity to learn and develop under realistic conditions in the absence of normal time and other pressures. Simulations also work well in conflicting or uncertain conditions where decisions result in feedback that aids learning but do not have disastrous consequences for the learner.

Scenario-planning (De Geus, 1997) is a simulation technique in which groups of people learn together within teams examining realistically created possible situations, make strategic decisions and experience the long term systemic consequences of the decisions. The technique also provides practice in surfacing and examining mental models in a low-risk setting.

Simulations are least suitable for the passing on of theory or knowledge and are often used after the presentation of knowledge or guiding principles. On the other hand, simulations can be powerful when used as a means for a group to generate their own theory or working models. Good general sources on the use of simulations can be found in Elgood (1996), Fripp (1993), and Saunders (1995). Micro-Worlds and learning laboratories have also been described by Senge (1994).

TECHNOLOGY-BASED METHODS

This broadly defined development method is delivered by means of a screen and the technology behind it. Interactive video, computer based training, interactive sites on the internet or intranets, e learning, and interactive CD-ROM, and DVD are all included in this category.

In many cases the material delivered is little different from the paper version, and the technology is little more than a delivery channel. In others, the full interactive capability and flexibility to meet the changing and evolving needs of individual learners is utilized. The learning design is still critical as with all development methods and the appropriateness to the context. The recent rapid growth in e-learning may have more to do with the appeal of the technology and potential cost savings than the quality of learning achieved.

Evaluation is needed. One of the great features of this cluster of development methods is that there is less reliance on the availability and personal skills of tutors. Computer-based development enables distance learning of a high quality, and is amenable to on-demand learner-led provision. It also allows individual record-keeping and tracking, and for some is appealing because of the high status aspects of using the latest technologies. One advantage is that material can easily be customised and updated, especially if delivered on intranets. The potential impact on individual learning and development is high, though this needs to be demonstrated.

Technology-based development methods can be used for the development of knowledge, skills and insights, and when used to create realistic simulations can be used for the development of physical as well as cognitive skills. It has great potential, yet to be achieved, to adapt to different learning styles and to help people improve their ability to learn. The potential for interactivity, flexible resourcing, multi-media and tailoring to the individual's on-demand needs, irrespective of time and location of the learner, suggest that the true potential of e-learning is only just being discovered. As with all breakthroughs the claims of it proponents must not be accepted uncritically and without evidence of effectiveness. Not all individual development needs are going to be met through e-learning. A judicious blend, as ever, is required.

VIDEO

Again the focus is on pure video (or film) on a stand-alone basis as a means of conveying rather than recording. Videos tend to divide into talking heads (virtually a filmed lecture) or enacted drama that is specially created or excerpted from other sources. Videos can be used in a variety of ways including elaborating material already delivered, illustrating things in practice, providing a basis for discussion, presenting role models, or presenting cases.

Talking heads allows vivid exposure to people that the individuals might not otherwise meet, such as famous experts or gurus. The video can be entertaining and can present more vividly material that is also presented in book form. Videos are suitable for presenting information, and data, and can be used for the development of skills, and insights. One of the potential disadvantages of videos is that they can distract attention from the real learning that is needed, but again this depends on how the video is used. They can also be somewhat general and can get out of date quickly. Ellet and Winig (1996) have produced a critical guide to management training videos and Binsted and Armitage (1994) provide a useful discussion of the kinds of learning achievable with interactive video.

TABLE 12.2   Off-the job methods summary

Framework 1 Development methods and their suitability for learning outcomes

Ratings *** = most suitable ** = moderately suitable * = least suitable

Off the job methods	Suitability for knowledge	Suitability for skills	Suitability for insights
Action learning	**	**	***
Case study	**	***	**
Distance learning	***	**	*
Lecture	***	*	**
Outdoor	*	**	**
Reading	***	*	**
Role play	*	***	***
Simulations	*	***	***
Technology-based training	***	*	*
Video (talking head)	***	*	**
Video (case/drama)	**	**	**

TABLE 12.2 (*continued*)

Framework 2 Development methods and their relation ship to learning theories
Ratings *** = strong link ** = moderate link * = weak link
Knowles = refers to at least one major element in Knowles' theory, Argyris = refers to double-loop learning, Kolb 1 = learning cycle fully available, Kolb 2 = influence of learning styles on acceptability of method

Off the job methods	Knowles	Revans	Argyris	Kolb 1&2	Cognitive	Affective	Inter-personal	Self-knowledge
Action learning	***	***	***	1*** 2***	**	***	***	***
Case study	***	*	**	1*** 2***	**	*	**	*
Distance learning	*	*	*	1* 2***	***	**	*	*
Lecture	*	*	*	1* 2***	***	**	*	*
Outdoor	**	*	*	1*** 2***	*	***	***	***
Reading	*	*	*	1* 2***	***	*	*	**
Role play	**	*	*	1*** 2***	*	***	***	**
Simulations	**	*	*	1*** 2***	*	***	***	***
Technology-based training	*	*	*	1*** 2***	***	*	*	*
Video (talking head)	*	*	*	1* 2***	***	*	*	*
Video (case/drama)	**	*	*	1* 2***	**	**	**	*

Framework 3 Development methods and impact on learning to learn
Each method is assessed on whether it potentially helps individuals understand the learning process, provides a variety of learning processes, and assists particular types of learning
Ratings *** = Strong likelihood ** = Moderate likelihood * = Low Likelihood

Off the job methods	Potential	Variety	Cognitive learning	Affective learning	Interpersonal learning	Self-knowledge
Action learning	***	**	**	**	**	**
Case study	**	*	**	*	**	*
Distance learning	*	*	***	**	*	*
Lecture	*	*	***	*	*	*
Outdoor	***	*	*	***	***	***
Reading	*	*	***	*	*	**
Role play	***	*	*	***	***	**
Simulations	***	*	*	***	***	***
Technology-based training	*	*	***	*	*	*
Video (talking head)	*	*	***	*	*	*
Video (case/drama)	*	*	**	**	**	*

continues overleaf

TABLE 12.2 *(continued)*

Framework 4 Development methods congruence with preferred learning styles
Ratings *** = Strong congruence ** = Moderate congruence * = Low congruence

Off the job methods	Activist	Reflector	Theorist	Pragmatist
Action learning	***	**	**	***
Case study	**	**	**	**
Distance learning	*	***	***	**
Lecture	*	***	***	**
Outdoor	***	**	*	**
Reading	*	***	***	***
Role play	***	***	**	**
Simulations	***	**	**	**
Technology-based training	*	***	**	**
Video (talking head)	*	**	***	**
Video (case/drama)	*	**	**	***

OTHER METHODS

GROUP LEARNING—PROCESS AND CONTENT

This group of development methods covers existing groups where there is also a learning objective, such as management teams, task groups, and project teams. It also covers groups specially created for learning purposes, usually off the job. This includes discussion groups, syndicates, project groups, brainstorming groups, action learning sets and observation groups (e.g. fishbowl, role plays). The prime focus of group learning is that it is explicitly social and features interpersonal exchange rather than an external source of delivery as the means of learning. The group could have a task focus, with a focus on shared problem analysis and problem-solving. Some groups are created to share knowledge and gain insights across conventional boundaries and disciplines. Process learning groups focus on the participants themselves in relation to each other and the interpersonal and group dynamics (e.g. T group training, laboratory training, gestalt).

Group learning is most suitable for facilitating people learning from each other, and learning about what happens in groups and teams. There is opportunity for exchange and interpretation of knowledge as well as emotional expression and examination of feelings. Group learning provides direct experience of how others behave and think, and opportunity to understand new and different perspectives. Group learning is less well-suited for transmitting detailed knowledge, or where the members of the group have no reason to trust each other or the members of the groups are unequal in status and power. As with other interactive methods the skill of the facilitator (if there is one) is crucial. Useful descriptions of behaviour in learning groups have been provided by Dixon (1994), Cunningham (1994), Mumford (1993), and Watkins and Marsick (1993) have provided descriptions of four types of learning in a group.

LEARNING REVIEWS AND LEARNING LOGS

A learning review is a process through which an individual or a group reviews what has been learned from experience. It is a process of reflection, "the process of stepping back from am experience to ponder carefully and *persistently* the meaning to the self, through the development of inferences" (Daudelin, 1996). Learning reviews as a development method are not haphazard but are conscious, planned and structured. Learning logs are written records with varying degrees of structure to enable reviews to take place.

The key thing is to capture and record experience in a way that allows reflection, the identification of key lessons or insights and the implications of applying the insights or lessons in action. The review can be general or highly focused and may be a solo or group activity or combinations of both. The learning review is both a method of learning and a method of reviewing what has been learned from other methods, which of

TABLE 12.3   Other methods summary

Framework 1 Development methods and their suitability for learning outcomes
Ratings *** = most suitable ** = moderately suitable * = least suitable

Other methods	Suitability for knowledge	Suitability for skills	Suitability for insights
Group learning—Process	***	***	***
Group learning—content	**	**	***
Learning review/logs	*	***	***

Framework 2 Development methods and their relation ship to learning theories
Ratings *** = strong link ** = moderate link * = weak link
Knowles = refers to at least one major element in Knowles' theory, Argyris = refers to double-loop learning, Kolb 1 = learning cycle fully available, Kolb 2 = influence of learning styles on acceptability of method

Other methods	Knowles	Revans	Argyris	Kolb 1&2	Cognitive	Affective	Inter-personal	Self-knowledge
Group learning—Process	***	***	***	1*** 2***	*	***	***	***
Group learning—content	***	***	***	1*** 2***	*	***	***	***
Learning review/logs	**	***	***	1*** 2***	**	*	*	***

Framework 3 Development methods and impact on learning to learn
Ratings *** = Strong likelihood ** = Moderate likelihood * = Low Likelihood
Each method is assessed on whether it potentially helps individuals understand the learning process, provides a variety of learning processes, and assists particular types of learning

Other methods	Potential	Variety	Cognitive learning	Affective learning	Interpersonal learning	Self-knowledge
Group learning—Process	***	***	**	***	***	***
Group learning—content	***	***	*	***	***	***
Learning review/logs	***	*	**	*	*	***

continues overleaf

TABLE 12.3   *(continued)*

Framework 4 Development methods congruence with preferred learning styles
Ratings *** = Strong congruence ** = Moderate congruence * = Low
congruence

Other methods	Activist	Reflector	Theorist	Pragmatist
Group learning— Process	**	***	***	***
Group learning— content	**	**	**	**
Learning review/logs	*	***	***	***

course is part of the learning process. The learning review enables the construction, or reconstruction, of meaning through reflection, recording, recall and reasoning leading to planned action. The practicalities of different forms of logs will vary with circumstances and the individuals' preferences. Boud, Keogh and Walker (1985) offer a useful model of reflection and learning, and Boud, Cohen and Walker (1993) focus on the practicalities.

CONCLUSION

In this chapter I did not set out to survey all available methods for effective individual development. Much learning is social and therefore the distinction between individual and group or interactive learning is hard to maintain. The individual develops mostly in a social context (groups, teams, organizations and communities) but at the same time growth of the individual leads to personal growth and also growth within those social contexts.

In this chapter I offered four broad sets of considerations to be taken into account when choosing development methods that are likely to be most effective within a given context. I have provided a general and practical aid to decision-making but it is not prescriptive. There is an almost total lack of research evidence on the effectiveness of development methods in general, and also when combined into development programs. Unfortunately considerable amounts of money, time and human effort and also frustration will be consumed without evident benefit, in the absence of such research. Meanwhile the individual can only make more informed choices with the aid of models such as the one presented here. Choice based on faith, partial experience, anecdote and the tutor's own preference are not acceptable in the 21st Century.

ACKNOWLEDGEMENTS

This chapter draws on material originally published (Mumford, 1997a) and is re-produced with permission of Honey Publications.

REFERENCES

Argyris, C. (1982) *Reasoning, learning and action.* San Francisco: Jossey Bass.
Argyris, C. (1990) *Overcoming organisational defences: Facilitating organisational learning.* Boston: Alyn and Bacon.

Bank, J. (1994) *Outdoor development for managers*. 2nd Edition. Aldershot: Gower.

Barnes, L.B, Christensen, C.R. & Hansen, A.J. (1994) *Teaching and the case method*. 3rd Edition. Cambridge, MA: Harvard Business School.

Binsted, D. & Armitage, S. (1994) Facilitating managerial learning with interactive learning. In Mumford, A. (Ed.) *Handbook of management development*. 4th Edition. Aldershot: Gower.

Blanchard, K. & Bowles, S. (2001) *High five! The magic of working together*. London: HarperCollins Business.

Boud, D., Keogh, R. & Walker, D. (1985) Reflection: *Turning experience into learning*. London: Kogan Page.

Boud, D., Cohen, R. & Walker, D. (1993) *Using experience for learning*. Milton Keynes: Open University Press.

Burgoyne, J. & Mumford, A. (2001) *Learning from the case method*. Cranfield: European Case Clearing House.

Clutterbuck, D. (1991) *Everyone needs a mentor*. London: IPD.

Crainer, S. (1996a) *The ultimate business library: 50 Books that made management*. Oxford: Capstone.

Crainer, S. (1996b) *Key management ideas: Thinking that changed the world*. London: FT Pitman.

Cunningham, I. (1994) *The wisdom of strategic learning*. Maidenhead: McGraw-Hill.

Daudelin, M. (1996) Learning from experience through reflection. *Organisational Dynamics*, Winter, 38–48.

de Geus, A. (1997) *The living company*. Cambridge: Harvard Business School Press.

Dixon, N. (1994) *Organisational learning cycle*. Maidenhead: McGraw-Hill.

Easton, G. (1992) *Learning from case studies*. Englewood Cliffs: Prentice Hall.

Elgood, C. (1996) *Using management games*. Aldershot: Gower.

Ellet, W. & Winig, L. (1996) *A critical guide to management training videos*. Cambridge, MA.: Harvard Business School Publishing.

Fripp, J. (1993) *Learning through simulations*. Maidenhead: McGraw-Hill.

Goldratt, E. & Cox, J. (1993) *The Goal*. 3rd Edition. Aldershot: Gower.

Harrison, I. (1994) *Practical instructional design for open learning material*. London: McGraw-Hill.

Hill, L.A. (1992) *Becoming a manager*. Boston: Harvard Business School Press.

Huczynski, A. (2001) *Encyclopaedia of Development Methods*. Aldershot: Gower.

Gibbs, G., Habeshaw, S. & Habeshaw, T. *53 interesting things to do in your lectures*. 4th Edition. London: Technical and Education Services Limited.

Griffin, R.W. & Cashin, W.E. (1989) The Lecture and discussion method: pros and cons. *Journal of Management Development*, 8, 2, 25–32.

Hodgson, V. (1992) *Learning from lectures*. In Marton, F., Hounsell, D. & Entwistle, H. (Eds) The Experience of Learning. Edinburgh: Scottish Academic Press.

Honey, P. & Mumford, A. (1992) *Manual of learning styles*. 3rd Edition. Maidenhead: Peter Honey Publications.

Kolb, D. (1984) *Experiential learning*. Englewood Cliffs: Prentice Hall.

Knowles, M. (1985) *Androgy in action*. San Francisco: Jossey-Bass.

Kram, K. (1988) *Mentoring at work*. Genville, Ill: Scott Foresman.

Krouwel, B. and Goodwill, S. *Management development outdoors*. London: Kogan Page.

Maier, N.R.F., Solem, A.R. & Maier, A.A. (1975) *The role play technique*. San Francisco: University Associates.

McCall, M., Lombardo, M. & Morrison, A. (1988) *Lessons of experience: How successful executives develop on the Job*. Lexington, Mass: Lexington.

Megginson, D. (1988) Instructor, coach, mentor: Three ways of helping for managers. *Management Education and Development*, 19, 1.

Megginson, D. & Clutterbuck, D. (1995) *Mentoring in action*. London: Kogan Page.

Mumford, A.(1993) *How managers can develop managers*. Aldershot: Gower.

Mumford, A. (1994) A review of action learning literature. In Pedler, M. (1997) *Action Learning in Practice*. Aldershot: Gower.

Mumford, A. (1995) Managers developing others through action learning. *Industrial and Commercial Training*, 27, 2.

Mumford, A. (1997a) *How to choose the right development method*. Maidenhead: Peter Honey Publications.

Mumford, A. (1997b) *Management development: Strategies for action*. 3rd Edition. London: IPD.

Mumford, A. (2001) *How to produce personal development plans*. Maidenhead: Honey Publications.

Parsloe, E. (1992) *Coaching, mentoring and assisting*. London: Kogan Page.

Pedler, M. (1978) Learning to negotiate. *Journal of European Industrial Training, 2, 7*.

Pedler, M. (1991) *Action learning in practice*. 2nd Edition. Aldershot: Gower.

Revans, R. (1982) *The origins and growth of action learning*. Bromley: Chartwell Bratt.

Rowntree, D. (1992) Exploring open and distance learning. London: Kogan Page.

Saint Germain (1995) *How to bring learners to write cases*. In Saunders (Ed.), *Simulation and gaming yearbook*. London: Kogan Page.

Saunders, D. (Ed.) (1995) *The simulation and gaming yearbook*. London: Kogan Page.

Senge, P. (1990) *The fifth discipline*. New York: Doubleday.

Senge, P., Kleiner, A., Roberts, C., Ross, R. & Smith, B. (1994) *The fifth discipline fieldbook*. London: Nicholas Brealey.

Snell, R. & Binsted, D. (1985) Issues in management development: Implications for open and distance learning. Lancaster: Centre for Managerial Learning.

Turner, D. (1992) *Role plays*. London: Kogan Page.

Tuson, M. (1994) *Outdoor training for employee effectiveness*. London: IPD.

Van Ments, M. (1999). *The effective use of role play*. 2nd Edition. London: Kogan Page.

Watkins, K. & Marsick, V. (1993) *Sculpting the learning organisation*. San Francisco: Jossey-Bass.

Whitmore, J. (1992) *Coaching for performance*. London: Nicholas Brealey.

CHAPTER 13

Teamworking and the Implications for Individual Development

Roger Mottram

Chartered Occupational Psychologist

SUMMARY

This chapter considers the importance of balancing the needs of the team with the needs of the individual in the team. It describes the increased frequency and relevance of team working in today's organisations, and the potential of teamworking to provide individual development opportunities. The main theme is that what is good for the team is not necessarily good for the individual, and that unless best practice is followed, the individual faces significant problems.

The nature of effective team work is looked at, together with the principles of effective team training and development. The implications of poorly composed and managed teams, and of poorly planned and managed development programmes, for individual development are outlined.

Particular attention is paid to the idea of Team Roles in individual development, and to the need to manage "cultural" expectations in both the team and the organisation. The cross-functional project team is described as, perhaps, the most typical teamworking challenge an individual will face; a challenge that can offer rewards but also dangers. The chapter concludes with a plea for properly composed and managed

Individual Differences and Development in Organisations. Edited by Michael Pearn.
© 2002 John Wiley & Sons, Ltd.

> teams, for well-designed development programmes, and for individuals to be equipped
> with effective and *portable* team skills to ensure their survival and the development of
> their full potential.

INTRODUCTION

Life at work today being the way it is, we are more and more likely to find ourselves in a
team of one sort or another. Team working can offer us great opportunities for learning,
but, if we are not careful, the personal development may compare with surviving a life-
threatening illness: you are sure you are a better person as a result but you do not want
to repeat the experience.

In this chapter we shall look at the potential development opportunities that team working can offer the individual, starting with best practice but moving on to the consequences
for individuals when best practice is not followed.

Different types of teamworking will be considered, together with different approaches
to development. Different perspectives will be taken in the chapter: the individual's
capacities and inclinations, the composition and management of the team, the climate
within the team and the culture of the organisation in which the team operates. All have
relevance to individual development as well as to the success of the team.

The main issues involved in team skills training and development will be discussed.
The underlying theme of the chapter is that what may be good for the team may not
necessarily be good for the individual team member; but that careful management of
team working and of team training/development programmes *can* achieve positive results
for all involved. While the chapter is written from the point of view of managing the
development of others, it is equally applicable to those of us who still hope to develop a
bit more; and who may need some guidance on how to get the best out of our experiences
in teams.

WHY TEAMWORKING?

CENTRAL ROLE PLAYED BY TEAMS IN WORKING LIFE

I shall start with a brief look at why teams have become so central to personal development
in the last few years, and why it is likely that they will continue to play an important role
in individual as well as organisational development. Teams have always been with us, but
never quite so ubiquitously. Diverse trends in organisational life have come together to
promote the "team" as the optimum vehicle for harnessing people's efforts, and as one of
the major environments for personal development. The team, we are urged, must produce
more than the sum of its parts. We all need to learn to be effective team players, but at
the same time we must seize the opportunity to develop as individuals. With properly
managed team building and development these two objectives are compatible; handled
poorly, they can become antagonists.

The importance of the team as a development opportunity for the individual has
grown in the last few years. In the move to emphasise self-development and to consider
the organisation as a learning entity, we can see a number of interlinked trends: line

managers are taking more responsibility for the development of people; organisations are restructuring with a consequent emphasis on cross-functional team working; and performance management systems are embracing both self-development and the development of others as specific performance criteria. If we add in such factors as the trend towards shorter employment contracts and the pressure to keep up to date in rapidly changing technologies, we have a challenging situation facing everyone who works with others.

SELF DEVELOPMENT AND HELPING OTHERS DEVELOP

DUAL RESPONSIBILITIES OF MANAGERS

The manager today finds her or himself responsible both for their own development and for the development of others. Like the organisation he or she works in, they face the demand both for delivery and for the need for renewal; for earning their keep as well as for continuous learning.

People generally find they need to re-evaluate where and how they direct their efforts. Not only is there the need for continuous learning but also the need for "portability": the readiness to transfer both the learning and the capacity to learn between very different situations and teams within the organization, and often to different organisations. "Today's organisations are rapidly breaking up boxes" (McCrimmon, 1990), with the result that the membership of a number of cross-functional teams together with active networking is becoming the normal way of working life for most people in management and professional roles.

The training and development world is changing at the same time as the organisational world, with fascinating interrelationships of initiating and responding between them. There are changes in *who* delivers, *where* delivery takes place, and *how* training and development are delivered. It is no longer a separate activity but is becoming inextricably intertwined with day-to-day work: "work-based learning through live projects" (O'Connell, 1997). The assumption is made that all work has development potential, and it is the responsibility of the employer to provide both opportunity and structure to ensure the learning can take place; to allow the individual to work in changing and challenging situations, and to encourage him or her to reflect on their experiences. Learning becomes integral to all jobs. There is also a pragmatic aim, of course: to reduce costs, simplify structures, and increase efficiency by harnessing people-power more effectively.

WHAT IS A TEAM, EXACTLY?

And so we see the rise and rise of the team, of individuals being grouped together in different permutations to achieve corporate objectives. Disruptive and stifling barriers between departments, functions and specialisms are to be pulled down. People find themselves working more and more in a number of different team situations. If learning on the job is what is expected, then learning in teams looks like the major opportunity on offer.

SUMMARY OF DEFINITIONS

So, what is this entity we call a team? Most definitions of what constitutes a *team* as opposed to a group of individuals include the following related concepts:

1. Reliance on group collaboration to achieve both individual and team goals. (Dyer, 1977).
2. Individuals working together to achieve more than they could achieve alone. (Woodcock, 1979).
3. The definition and acceptance of common goals. (Hunt, 1979).
4. Team members *considering* themselves to be a team. (Larson & Lafasto, 1989) and "seeing themselves as interdependent". (Lewis, 1993).
5. Team members actually meeting and working together as a team.
6. Katzenbach and Smith (1993) sum up the differences between a "Pseudo" team: where there is "no clear sense of purpose or direction, no joint goals or accountability" and a "Real" team: which is "committed to a common purpose, performance goals and approach, holding themselves mutually accountable".

Not all "teams" will meet all these criteria, but we may as well have the concept of the ideal team in mind as we continue. Similarly, not all the teams we find ourselves in are fully effective, but it will help us examine the idea of learning in teams if we set up a model of a truly effective team.

CRITERIA FOR EFFECTIVE TEAMS

There seems to be agreement between observers of team operations that to be fully effective a team must:

1. Generate the right climate, which includes care for one another, open and truthful communication, and a high level of trust. (Larson and Lefasto, 1989; West, 1994).
2. Have a strong commitment on the part of all team members to the successful achievement of the team's objectives; "a perception of unity even when uncertainty hangs over them". (Zander and Cartwright, 1996).
3. Practise effective team processes: including decision-making processes, conflict resolution and effective use of resources. (Bell, 1992).
4. Recognise the importance and extent of individual contributions. (Guzzo and Shea, 1992).
5. Be *appropriately* led.
6. Maintain effective relationships with the organisation and with other teams.
7. Have the capacity to manage external pressures.
8. Reflect continually on how to develop and improve its way of working and be ready to adapt to changed demands and circumstances. (West, 1994).
9. Accommodate individual needs as well as meet team objectives. (Herriot, 1995).
10. Include the right combination of experience, expertise and personal attributes for meeting the team objectives. (Belbin, 1991).
11. Be able to accommodate changes to team membership speedily and effectively.

One thing is clear from this list: true and effective teams are rare beasts. As Hackman (1994) says: "Calling a set of people a team or exhorting them to work together" doesn't make them a team. Teams are all too prone to fail to "use their resources effectively, create an atmosphere of fear, allow a leader to dominate and to avoid conflict".(Dyer, 1977).

IMPLICATIONS FOR INDIVIDUAL LEARNING

The implications for individual learning in a "team" are consequently quite complicated. One can imagine that, in a perfect team operation, effective personal development is a natural outcome. Individual strengths and weaknesses are acknowledged, and individuals are encouraged to expand the scope of their team contributions in line with their potential. Individual contributions are valued and positive feedback is given at the appropriate moment in the team's operations. All this flows naturally as a consequence of the team process, and individuals blossom.

I have seen this happen, but all too often the reality is somewhat different. We find ourselves, for example, in "teams" with little idea of why we are there or what the team is supposed to achieve; where the team leader is so dominant that we have to fight to achieve any sort of recognition, and where the pressure to deliver is combined with a lack of time and resources to the extent that everyone is stressed and demoralised, with interpersonal conflict disrupting any possible progress. I've been in one of these teams too; the scope for personal learning is certainly there, but it is all too often a matter of acquiring survival skills at the expense of personal growth.

Let me summarise the main points so far:

1. Managers and professionals are likely to have a good deal of responsibility for their own learning and development.
2. They are also likely to be responsible for creating learning opportunities for others.
3. They are going to be working more and more in teams of varying degrees of true "teamness" and effectiveness.

Given this prospect, let us look at the potential opportunities for individual learning and development. Whether or not they can all be realised will depend to a great extent on the nature and context of the team and how well the team and the learning are managed.

POTENTIAL LEARNING OPPORTUNITIES OF TEAMWORKING

The focus of the chapter is on the development of personal skills rather than of professional disciplines and technical expertise. Within the area of personal skills a rough distinction can be made between personal growth: a holistic development of our self-awareness and awareness of others; and the more specific skills of working effectively in a team. The particular learning opportunities for an individual in a team can be summarised as follows:

PERSONAL GROWTH

1. Receiving informed feedback on performance/behaviour from colleagues who have considerable direct experience of working with you in a relatively controlled environment.
2. Learning to *give* feedback to colleagues in a positive and acceptable fashion.

3. Experiencing the potential synergies of working collaboratively with individuals of different disciplines and styles of working.
4. Exploring and understanding the potential range of your own contributions to team working. Learning to accept help and support from others; and to seek it when appropriate.
5. Understanding what colleagues can contribute to the team, especially those who offer different contributions; appreciating the potential of diversity in team membership.
6. Acquiring skills of establishing relationships and working with people, skills that are transferable to working in other teams and to working life generally.

SPECIFIC SKILLS

These relate to understanding the dynamics and practicalities of team behaviour and how to manage them effectively:

1. Learning how to put together the right mix of individuals to achieve a team's objectives. (Belbin, 1983).
2. Employing effective team processes that make the best use of team resources.
3. Practising/observing leadership styles that are appropriate to the needs of the task, the circumstances and the people involved.
4. Identifying your own potential range of team roles and recognising its relevance to any team of which you may be a member. (Mottram, 1994).
5. Learning the skills of establishing and managing a productive team climate; of managing relationships with other teams and with the organisation within which the team operates. (West, 1994).

There could be more to be learned and gained from working in a team than is covered in this list; but it is clear that the potential for individual development is considerable. These opportunities apply to on-job experiences, action learning generally (Revans, 1982), but the "Team" situation can offer a relatively contained, structured environment that allows for experimentation and change, speedy and informed feedback, and continuous monitoring of progress. That is the good news, but what can go wrong?

POTENTIAL PITFALLS OF TEAMS FOR LEARNING AND DEVELOPMENT

The list above is impressive (and probably incomplete) but it must be balanced by considering the dangers or pitfalls that can be presented by the experience of working in a team. There are several main danger areas, and they are most likely to be a problem in an ineffective team.

THE CONSTRAINT OF INDIVIDUAL DIFFERENCES

The skills we acquire in one team may be less than usefully transferable because they are specific to the culture and circumstances of that team. Nevertheless, they can be powerful influences on our behaviour even when they are inappropriate to the changed situation and circumstances. Teams develop their own ways of operating and of dealing with the "outside" world. Extreme examples are those which have allowed a culture of "Group Think" (Janis, 1982) to grow, where the team erects barriers to the outside world, rationalises its own actions and decisions including its mistakes, and demonises any opposition, real or imagined, internal or external.

While few teams would operate the full "Bay of Pigs" culture, most teams do tend to build up a sense of identity that, while essential for team spirit, can encourage a degree of insularity of feeling and thinking. For the individual, the danger is that any divergence from the team line is seen as disloyal; individual challenge or diversity is discouraged or even penalised. The trick, as is so often the case, is to achieve an effective balance. The individual needs to feel able to challenge and to question the team's decisions and ways of behaving; to put forward a contrary point of view without feeling he or she is being awkward, holding up the action, or being disloyal to team spirit.

The team as a whole should develop a culture of reflection and of challenging its own assumptions; of actively exploring opportunities for developing relationships with other parties in the organisation to allow fresh views and perspectives to be introduced and to foster collaboration. If this is not the case, the problem for the individual, never mind the likely fate of the team, is that their learning is non-transferable and their personal growth prone to distortion. If they are strong and assert themselves as individuals they can be rejected and marginalised by the team. While they may emerge as stronger characters the experience can be painful and their attitude to team work can be prejudiced, especially if the team effort ends in failure.

POOR TEAMS, POOR MANAGEMENT

Membership of a team that is definitely neither organised nor harmonious poses its own problems for learning and development. It is even more important that the individual separates out the generalisable principles of their learning from the tactics they evolve to survive if they are not to develop a deep distaste for team working altogether.

Two typical problems are, unfortunately, all too common. The first concerns clarity of role: for the team and for the individual. Why are you in the team? What is the team designed to achieve? It is obviously extremely difficult to harness your resources effectively and play to your strengths when there is no clear brief, and a lot of unproductive energy is expended in feeling your way with equally confused colleagues to discover the meaning of life in this team. The second can be a consequence of the first: relationships between team members are poor, and conflicts between team members are frequent (West and Slater, 1995).

The individuals finding themselves in such a team have a real problem. They can get stuck in and try to resolve the ambiguities and to disentangle the conflicts, but the wisdom of such initiative will depend on their skill and experience in team working and their status in the team. All too often, their most practical option is to take what small steps they can to ease matters or at least not add to the problem. Frequently, the learning will be in terms of "this is what I would do if I had the opportunity"; and "this is where I would take positive steps to avoid such situations occurring".

These situations have been described as essential stages of team formation (Forming, Storming, Norming, and Performing: Tuckman, 1965) but too many teams continually fall back to the Storming stage because Forming was not properly managed and achieved. But even stable, effective teams present learning problems to the individual.

TEAM DEPENDENCY

All teams develop their own ways of operating. For example, membership of a harmonious and well-organised team can become very comfortable, and pose problems for individual learning. Team members know just what is expected of them and what to expect of their colleagues, there are efficient systems for achieving results, and individual styles and contribution becomes known, accepted and rewarded; in fact, less effective characteristics and ways of behaving may come to be regarded as tolerable weaknesses and benevolently indulged.

The push to maintain harmony can result in divergent views being suppressed and learning diluted (Souder, 1985) much as in the Group Think Team. If an individual is to develop, he or she needs not only to be open to change but to seek it actively. This involves both a readiness to trust others *and* a readiness to confront them; to challenge their views and their way of behaving.

Unless the individual makes an active effort to learn generalisable principles from their experience, any move outside the team or to another team can be traumatic. Team members need to look beyond the obvious and make sure they understand the mechanics and principles that underlie both what the team does well and what it does less well. They need to distinguish between behaviour that is successful because of the particular circumstances, composition and operating procedures of the team, and behaviour that will be effective in any group of people, or even when there are no other people involved. In short, the individual needs to learn the principles of effective behaviour and their relevance to their personal set of resources, and to apply these principles to whatever situation they meet.

Those responsible for managing the team and/or the development of the team members need to be aware of this potential problem, and encourage people to take a critical look at their behaviour and its relevance to *all* the situations they may work within, even when they are doing well in the present circumstances.

DIFFERENT TEAMS, DIFFERENT LEARNING, DIFFERENT PROBLEMS

We need to consider the potential development opportunities together with the potential dangers in all types of team situation, not only structured training programmes in formal or specifically composed teams, but also more opportunistic learning in less formal groupings. A useful way of distinguishing between different types of team is on the basis of "formality" and "time span" (Critcheley and Casey, 1984). Formal teams are those set up by the organisation and which are therefore officially recognised. Informal teams are initiated by groups of individuals; they may be acknowledged and even encouraged by the organisation but they do not figure on any organisation chart.

LONG-TERM FORMAL TEAMS

These teams are usually established work groups such as an Audit Unit or a Direct Mail Marketing group. Just about every organisational employee will be a member of one of these teams, though whether or not it qualifies as a true team is an interesting question. Often an enlightened manager will make the effort to weld the work group into a team, but, is this always a good idea? Often, the only relationship actually required for efficient working is that people's efforts are co-ordinated and necessary information is shared at the right time. If, in addition, a feeling of shared commitment and purpose can be built up, then people will feel more motivated and co-operative; but the process can be taken too far in the pursuit of that elusive ghost in the team machine: Team Spirit.

Individuals may be led to believe that all their endeavours should be *team* endeavours; that getting on with your work by yourself, even when this is the most effective way of getting things done, is not acceptable in a team culture. As well as causing operational inefficiencies, this misguided concept of team culture can result in a lack of individual initiative and a weariness with the whole idea of team working, and to the acquisition of behaviours which relate more to etiquette than to personal growth or learning (Higgs, 1992). The point is made by Katzenbach and Smith (1993) that a "working group" may be a better option than a real "Team"; i.e. a group that "combines individual efforts and specific inputs into an additive output, but which does not work on tasks jointly" may be more appropriate than a team "committed to a common purpose, performance, goals and approach" that "holds themselves mutually accountable", with all the emotional effort and dependence on team skills that this requires.

SHORT-TERM FORMAL TEAMS

These teams are usually those which are set up for a specific project of limited life span, and which are disbanded on the completion of the project. This form of team working is becoming more common, and usually involves *cross-functional* work groups. Such teams offer excellent learning opportunities, but they also pose most of the potential dangers referred to in a concentrated form.

INFORMAL TEAMS

These teams include alliances of individuals with similar interests or concerns, either for a specific purpose, in which case they may disband on achieving that purpose, or on a continuing basis for mutual support and sharing of information: a sort of structured long term networking. There may be little pressure to learn and develop in such teams, but for individuals who are ready to take the initiative to do so, they offer useful opportunities in a non-threatening environment.

STRUCTURED LEARNING

WHAT CAN BE ACHIEVED?

The other dimension we need to consider in looking at the learning potential of teams for the individual is the degree of structure and guidance in the learning. This can vary from a formal training course using teams as a major vehicle for learning, through coaching (Hackman, 1994), to self-initiated, undirected learning on the part of the individual in the course of their day-to-day work. Most of the research and implementation of learning in teams is based on teams taking part in a planned training programme, either established work teams or teams put together for the purpose.

Making Sure Objectives Are Achieved

A good example in this category is the structured Development Programme for an established work or project team. The objectives usually include both team building needs and individual learning needs:

a. understanding and practice of effective team processes,
b. understanding the principles of team composition and making best use of team resources,
c. encouragement of team spirit and morale,
d. building an effective and adaptable team unit,
e. development of personal teamworking skills,
f. personal growth and realising of potential;

all leading to improved team effectiveness and the enhanced performance of the individuals making up the team.

The structured team exercise enables participants both to learn about themselves and to develop their skills, and to understand their *need* to learn these things. It should offer a careful balance between complacency shock and alerting the team/individual to their need to learn and develop, while providing an experience and an environment that encourages and guides the learning. If this balance is not managed effectively, not only are opportunities lost but harm can occur. The exercise can vary from an hour's event in a hotel conference room involving eggs and balloons to a week on a yacht, all involving physical challenge, emotional resilience and mental flexibility to different degrees.

Safeguarding Individual Learning

Both these extremes of context and content require the same *elements of preparation, planning and management,* even though the degree of the potential consequences is not quite the same:

1. Participants must *want* to take part; they must understand what they can gain from the experience and why it is important that they do so. All too often people find themselves on a Team Event without knowing why they are there; or not accepting the reason they have been given. Apart from the lack of motivation that ensues, the potential learning and development is not only inhibited from the start but participants are also likely to erect defences to protect themselves from this unwanted experience and intrusion; defences which can neutralise any learning on offer.
2. The contract between the participant and the sponsoring organisation must be clear in terms of the responsibilities and outcomes of the event; especially the question of who has access to information on individual performance and how it is used. The natural concerns an individual has regarding their career prospects and how they may be affected need to be addressed if he or she is to approach the experience positively and to take the risks they need to take for optimum learning.
3. Participants must be prepared for the event: and in particular they should (a) understand where they are now and where they can hope to be in terms of skills/knowledge and personal growth; (b) be able to cope with the demands of the tasks they will be

expected to undertake; and (c) know how to take advantage of the learning opportu-nities and resources, (e.g. coaching) offered.

Learning to learn is probably one of the most neglected of skills (Pearn et al, 1995). Many individuals have hung on to their natural talent for learning, but too many have allowed it to atrophy, or have developed a fear of learning. Even where this is not the case, proper guidance and preparation are needed if people are not to find themselves spending valuable time and emotional energy orientating themselves as well as trying to survive on the training event.

4. The team(s) involved must have the resources, in terms of skills, knowledge and personal characteristics, to achieve something worthwhile in terms of the objectives of the exercise, but potential unwanted complications owing to differences in the status, expertise and experience of individual participants should be anticipated and avoided.

5. The training targets must be perceived to be achieveable if full learning is to be gained. It is all too easy for a team or individual to write off the experience, especially if it has identified gaps in ability or weaknesses in behaviour, and to blame lack of resources or the impossible nature of the task.

CRITICAL ISSUES FOR THE DESIGN OF LEARNING EVENTS

The exercises themselves should be designed to provide an adequate structure and context for the necessary learning to take place. The following considerations are particularly important for individual learning:

1. The degree of within/between team competition: a degree of competition can help encourage motivation and put some zest into the exercise, but too much will obscure the real learning objectives; and can also lead to loss of self-esteem for some individuals, unjustified complacency for others.

2. A possible role for *every* participant in achieving a result: an exercise which allows one or two individuals to dominate by virtue of their particular expertise and leaves others searching for a credible input to make will not achieve the learning objectives for any of its participants; unless it is conceived as a tutorial.

3. The balance of providing a stretching challenge with allowing for the satisfaction of the possibility of achieving a good result: those taking part will need to feel the exercise is a meaningful challenge to them both as individuals and as a team, but they should also be able to see it as an achievable challenge if they are to continue to take it seriously and stay motivated.

4. The dependence of outcomes on team performance rather than chance: again, this is an issue of motivation. If an exercise is to stimulate effort and commitment, and thus learning, then the outcome must be seen to depend on that effort and com-mitment, and each member of the team must feel that their personal contribution counts.

Both the exercise task and the observation of team performance need to be carefully and thoroughly managed. The learning in a poorly run exercise loses credibility, and the feedback on behaviour and performance to the team must provide valid evidence to carry conviction.

MAIN OPPORTUNITIES FOR INDIVIDUAL LEARNING IN A STRUCTURED PROGRAMME

There are two main interconnected areas of specific individual learning in teams: Team Processes and Team Roles. These encompass such skills as interpersonal influencing, team management, leadership and planning, and belong to the individual to take away with them.

DEVELOPING TEAM PROCESS SKILLS

Process skills in a team are all about making best use of team resources in the time available. They involve the obvious moves such as deciding whether or not to have a team leader/chair/facilitator, through to more complex issues such as agreeing a decision-making process. All too often, however, a team training programme will leap ahead to grander themes that involve missions, visions and team spirit before resolving the basic but essential questions of just how they are going to *operate* as a team. The result will often be that time is wasted, dissension grows, objectives remain unachieved, and individuals have any prejudices regarding teamwork reinforced because they are unclear on how to behave in order to contribute to the team's success. They may also feel guilty because they have not achieved that elusive team magic.

As is often the case, the answer is to have skilled facilitators to manage the process, whichever route is followed. They should observe team performance throughout whatever activity has been chosen and intervene at appropriate times to facilitate learning and preempt negative disruption and tension. Facilitators need to be perceptive in their handling of the debrief: making sure that both team and individuals recognise and face up to their learning needs while safeguarding individuals in particular from erosion of self-esteem.

The team members themselves should be encouraged to review their performance critically, and to give feedback to each other. Preferably, they should all have had some training, or at least guidance, in giving feedback (De Board, 1983). If all goes well, the team will be in a position to perform more effectively, and each of the team members will have received personal feedback on how they performed in the team: what they did that was valued, what they may need to do differently. This feedback needs to be translated into individual learning objectives, which can be done in conjunction with the other strand of team training: Team Roles.

TEAM ROLE DEVELOPMENT

Team Roles are distinguished from functional roles such as Accountant or Market Researcher. They describe the type of contribution an individual is likely to make to the team as a consequence of their personality and brainpower. The idea prompted research into team working, (Belbin 1976, 1991; Mottram 1982; Margerison, 1990) and the identification of "team roles" that an individual can act in; each with its particular contribution to make to the team's process and performance. These roles define different styles of managing and leading the team, contributions in terms of creative thinking and critical analysis, of managing personal relationships, and of the practical implementation of policies and plans. Most individuals have strengths in one, two or three of these roles; giving them a role-profile which identifies the potential pattern of strengths they can offer a team. The implications of the team role approach for training and development include:

1. Diagnosis of individual strengths and development needs in relation to teamworking. This is not a simple matter of identifying "missing" roles and working hard to develop them, but of considering carefully how to play to strengths and how to mitigate potential weaknesses. Often, the best strategy could be to encourage a team colleague to fill a role, or to support a particular team process rather than to try oneself to behave in a way which does not fit one's capabilities or disposition comfortably. Team Roles can, in fact, be used as a starting point for an individual's broader management development.

2. Team composition in terms of team roles. In practice, the consideration of individual team roles is usually linked to a diagnosis of the team's strengths and weaknesses in terms of its composition, and the team's composition is reviewed with respect to the aims and objectives of that team. A well planned and expertly managed training and development programme will enable a team to make the best use of its resources in terms of team roles; to harness and organise the individual differences towards achieving the team objectives. Most importantly, a team needs to perform in a manner appropriate to the task before it; and this means adapting its strengths and weaknesses to meet the particular challenges that are posed at each stage of the project. Effective teams will adapt and change their approach as the project progresses. While all the roles must have their input at all times, the balance will change as the challenges facing the team change. Within these dynamics, there is a danger that the individual may tend to be treated as a pawn on the team board, and individual differences regarded as team assets or team liabilities as the circumstances shift. In all team enterprises there will be a tension between recognising and promoting individual differences and encouraging such differences to be sacrificed for the good of the team. The team role approach can help maintain a reasonable balance, if applied with understanding.

3. The dangers of stereotyping. There is a real danger that our love of labelling individuals will lead to an over-prescriptive application of what should be a flexible concept. An exercise in assessing the team roles of individual team members can lead to their being stereotyped with all the strengths and weaknesses possibly associated with a role, and to their being seen, consequently, as an unchanging component of the team machine. This mechanistic approach can lead to the team's task being broken up into defined chunks which are then apportioned to the "appropriate" team members according to their individual team roles. An individual's attempts to involve themselves in matters outside their assigned chunk are discouraged: "It's not your role".

   The team and the individual must fight this stereotyping. The team must make flexible use of all its resources at all times, while recognising the relevance of particular attributes at particular stages or for particular challenges. The individual must fight to have an input at all stages and on all issues, while recognising the particular strengths one or more colleagues may bring to the party on an issue. The strengths of a team lie in achieving optimum synergy from its members, not in role discrimination;

and an individual has the right to push out the boundaries of their personal team role profile: they need, in fact, to develop "fluid, evolving skill sets" (McCrimmon, 1995).

4. The team of one. It is this concept of adaptation and flexibility that can be the most valuable learning for the individual as well as for the team as a whole (Mottram, 1994). When we tackle our own individual projects we move through similar stages: from scoping through strategic thinking to planning and innovation, and thence to implementation with periodic pauses for review and rethinking.

Our Team Role profile inevitably affects the way we operate, even in our individual ventures. Creative characters may try to move from idea to incarnation without an intervening period of planning and organisation. Critical evaluators may find it hard to get past the stage of analysing options and anticipating problems, while the practically inclined may get their heads down and achieve the obvious with accustomed diligence.

Awareness of our disposition and capacities in team role terms can help us avoid these exaggerations. We *know* we must submit our original concepts to rigorous scrutiny: if not our own, then that of an appropriate colleague. We *know* we must get down to the boring bits of planning and organising resources, and of checking progress against well-thought out milestones. Again, our approach will be a combination of developing and acting in different roles and of involving appropriate colleagues at appropriate times. We must be the Chair or Co-ordinator of our own team of one, and we must manage our relationships outside our unique team: with other individuals, with other teams, and with the organisation we work within.

5. Fitting into different teams. The self-awareness we can achieve from team role training will also allow us to move effectively between different teams in the organisation, formal or informal. There are the usual problems of "Forming, Storming and Norming" which can be greatly facilitated by a team role approach, and which can be managed by the individual on their own behalf to a considerable extent, whether or not the team has bought in to a team role approach. Obviously, an individual will have a functional role to perform in any team they join, whether it is a specialism such as Regulatory Affairs, a management responsibility such as Section Head, or a combination of both. This is not, usually, a problem in itself, though managing the inter-departmental dynamics can be an issue (which we shall discuss later in talking about cross-functional teams).

The problems and challenges are more likely to revolve around questions of "fit": the style and nature of the personal contribution an individual makes to the team processes. The smart newcomer will quickly:

a. Observe and weigh up the way the team works: how discussions are managed, how people make their views known, how decisions are made.
b. Identify the key players: those who appear to carry the most weight in the team, and work out why: is it expertise, personality, seniority or a combination of these? What team role profile describes their behaviour? Do any team roles dominate the team's way of operating?

c. Work out the strengths and weaknesses of the team's behaviour: does it tend to stay cautiously within safe, established parameters when its remit is to develop new approaches, for example?

d. Decide where she or he can best make an input to help the team progress and, perhaps, restore balance to the team processes by reinforcing a team role area: by encouraging creative thinking for example.

It will all be a delicate combination of winning acceptance by fitting the existing team climate while taking perceptive action to add value to the team processes. The perspicacious individual will develop these subtle skills from observation and practice when working with others in all situations, but also using such concepts as team roles flexibly and perceptively.

ORGANISATION CULTURE, TEAM CLIMATE AND THE INDIVIDUAL

Much recent research has focused on the concept of the social relationships within a team or the *team climate* (Slater & West, 1995). Earlier research has described the *organisation culture*: the environment within which a team operates, (Harrison & Stokes, 1986). These concepts, put together, can provide an invaluable perspective on how to make teams work effectively, and on how an individual can contribute to team performance and develop their personal skills.

The idea of organisation culture, while developed in the 1960s and 1970s, still provides a useful way of looking at the way things are done and the way decisions are made in an organisation. Team effectiveness has been found to depend to a considerable extent on how supportive the organisation is of the team. Obviously a team's strategy must fit the corporate strategy, but the organisation culture needs to support the dangerous notion of a relatively autonomous team operating within its bounds (Gladstone, 1984).

Formal work teams may or may not reflect the culture-profile of the host organisation. In practice, they may differ in their degree of hierarchy, the formality of their structure, the efficiency of their processes, the degree of participation in decision-making, the need for effective relationships, and in the premium they place on the individual within the team. However, they can run into problems if they do *not* reflect the organisation's culture mix in these terms. In spite of the fact that a team has been specifically set up to blaze new ground, for example, it can meet opposition, resource starvation and the epithet "Elite" unless it is adroit and perceptive, at least camouflaging its style to blend with the dominant culture, and managing its relations with other teams carefully with attention to Company etiquette.

The idea of team climate is more recent and refers to the style and effectiveness of co-operative working within the team. The model put forward by West and Anderson emphasises how people work together within the team, the team vision, support for innovation, task-orientation and "participative safety": the extent to which individuals both feel and actually are involved in decisions and the team processes. It reflects current beliefs in leadership backed by "management" and the importance of participation in decisions.

If an individual is to succeed as an effective team member he or she must learn to work within both the team climate and the organisation culture. Some individuals do this instinctively; others have to learn to do it. This takes us back to the need for the individual to work out how best they can contribute to any particular team in terms of their style and behaviour as well as their knowledge and expertise. She or he needs to weigh up the team climate, consider the degree of accommodation they may need to make in terms of their personal style of working, and decide what, if anything, they are going to do about it. What, in fact, is in it for them?

This last point is not often recognised, or is felt to be somehow unworthy of a loyal team member. But the degree of accommodation expected of the individual in terms of their way of working to meet the desired Team Climate can be significant. And what is more, it may not be completely relevant to the individual's working life in the organisation at large. The expectations of someone's behaviour may vary between their line or functional management and the project team to which they are seconded, for example. Ideally, someone with the readiness to learn and the capacity to adapt will benefit from expanding the range of their behaviours, and both their team working and their work outside the team will develop positively. In practice, however, a sort of role dissonance tends to be created that imposes a good deal of stress on individuals, especially when the differences in expected behaviour are pronounced.

THE PROJECT TEAM

The best practical example of both the opportunities and the dangers for individual learning is the Project Team. "One of the most dramatic trends in organisational design" is the emergence of the cross-functional team, assembled for a specific purpose and a finite time span (Griffin, 1997). The probability of finding oneself in one or more of these teams is significant. Team working skills need to be developed to play a full part in such a team while taking the opportunity to expand individual skills while working in the team. For the most part, the learning needs of the team and the individuals who make up the team are the same, and require the following conditions (Colton and Bailey, 1997):

1. The team needs to be given the authority and resources to achieve significant results without interference.
2. Team members must be committed to achieving the team goals.
3. In order to "qualify" for a "real" team approach the team goals should involve exploring new territory and dealing with uncertainty, giving it scope for taking risks and trying new ideas; and the goals should not be attainable by team members independently. (Critcheley and Casey, 1984).
4. The mix of disciplines and functions within the team should reflect the demands made of it; and the assignment of functional roles, responsibilities and authority should be clearly laid out. No one function should dominate, or managers outside the team pull the strings of power.
5. Any pressure should come from the nature of the team's task and the challenge it poses, not from a scarcity of time, resources and availability of team members.
6. The organisational climate should be supportive of the team goals and the team's existence. On the other hand, the way the team behaves should not be at odds with the behavioural norms of the organisation or of other teams it may need to deal with. (Schein, in Evans 1990).

Even though the conditions may be right for the establishment and success of the project team, specific training is needed: the team should be trained in process skills, including the need to encourage members to contribute to all aspects of the team's operations and not to confine their contribution to their specific area of expertise or function; and the team leader/manager should be trained in team building and facilitating skills.

There are delicate balances involved. The individual must be willing to change his or her approach to working and be ready to learn new ways of achieving results (Jussawalla and Sashiel, 1998), while the team must allow its members the freedom to express their views and, to a certain extent, the scope to behave as individuals. There will be an equally critical balancing act that must be managed between the individual team member's loyalty to his/her functional department and to the team. An essential part of the change in attitudes needed for a successful project team involves the demolition of inter-departmental barriers and the building of cross-functional collaboration.

If this culture shift is not achieved, then team members may interact but they will not truly collaborate. The effect of such a state of affairs will affect not only the achievement of team goals but also the individual's learning and motivation, (Kahn and McDonough, 1997). The main casualty from the team member's point of view, apart from the pain and frustration of the dysfunctional-team experience, can be her/his capability to work interdependently in the future: the inhibiting of their "portable team skills", not to mention their growth and personal well-being (Hackman, 1990).

It would seem that a project team must be effectively developed and managed if the defensive barriers carried with them by the team's members are to be broken down and an environment for change and learning created: barriers of personality, culture, jargon, expectations, priorities and measures of success. Even on the corporate level, organisations will only develop if their interfaces are not allowed to become barriers. The growth of cross-functional project teams can be very positive in this respect *but only if* they are properly put together, trained and managed, and supported. Otherwise they will confirm the prejudices and suspicions which cemented the barriers together in the first place.

Again, however, there is a balance to be struck and maintained. The individual team member should not be encouraged to develop a split personality: loyal to his/her home function when at home, loyal to the project team when at project team meetings. Nor should he or she try to disregard or smooth over important differences. Functional conflict is to be encouraged in so much as ideas, beliefs and assumptions held by both "sides" need to be challenged. Again, the onus falls squarely on the management and training of the project team, enabling it to achieve the positive interaction and sharing of ideas that can result in positive conflict. It must encourage the maintenance of individual identity, and avoid dysfunctional hostility with its symptoms of "information as power", unproductive competitiveness and points-scoring that we see all too often in a mixed function team. Jehn (1995) sees it as a matter of "Task" conflict being acceptable and productive, with conflict in "Relationships" being destructive. It will be important for the relationships to be right if the arguments and debates on the task are to lead anywhere.

The project team today is the most notable and prevalent example of teamworking and it has important implications for individual development. The opportunities for positive development are tremendous, but the dangers for disillusionment, confirmation of bad habits and negative attitudes, and stunted development are all too real. The answer to achieving the best in development, and to minimising the dangers, is to ensure best practice is followed. If you are not in a position to influence this directly, then this chapter will at least have given you the material to engage in productive guerilla action and to ask some pertinent questions.

CONCLUSION

This chapter has been written from the practitioner's perspective. Relevant research on teamworking has been referred to, but not much of it has been specifically targeted at the impact of the team on the individual. Many assertions will not be directly backed by research, therefore, but they are based on many years' practical experience of composing, diagnosing, training and managing teams, and encouraging the development of the individual's who sail in them. The main points that have emerged are:

1. Teamworking plays a major part in most working lives, and has the potential to offer significant learning and development opportunities for the individual.
2. Teamworking has tended to take on a life of its own, with the result that people may find themselves struggling to achieve results in a team when team working is not the best way to go.
3. A well-managed, properly composed, relevant and effective team will, by its nature and set-up, encourage and facilitate individual development.
4. Many team working situations do not meet these criteria and pose dangers for individual development and career progression.
5. Formal training in teamworking is essential, not only for effective team operations but for developing portable skills which will enable the individual to fit all the varieties of team he or she might encounter, effective and ineffective, and to deal more capably with people generally. Team working skills are often an essential prerequisite for demonstrating the individual's other skills and attainments to best effect.

The transferability of learning is critical. Much has been written on the need for organisations to develop a culture of learning, where individuals are encouraged and helped in learning to learn (Senge, 1990, 1995; Pearn, 1995). Any team activity within the organisation should reflect this culture and use the potential strength of the team environment to help the individual to:

1. Understand her/his own strengths and development needs in terms of achieving results with and through people.
2. Understand and appreciate the full range of the ways in which people operate: their individual styles and their different contributions.
3. Achieve effective working partnerships with all the people they work with, in all the different situations they work within.
4. Develop both their self-awareness and their empathy: "emotional intelligence" has now become a fashionable concept (Goleman, 1999) but it has always been the life blood and the product of good team work.
5. Understand and operate adaptively in a range of environments or cultures.

It should not be assumed that an individual will automatically benefit from finding themselves in a team. Whatever social anthropologists may claim, my experience supports the view that "being part of a team is not a natural human function; it has to be learned" (Crosby, 1979). Teamworking can offer the individual great opportunities for learning and development, but he and she need to be "team-fit" to take advantage of these opportunities even in the best of teams, and to avoid the potential demoralising and growth-limiting forces at work. Team-fitness is even more important given the need, these days, for "multi-teaming" ability: to move rapidly and seamlessly between teams of differing make-ups, styles and effectiveness.

The individual must be skilled-up beforehand. It is not enough to rely on an aptitude for learning on the job as you move through a succession of teamworking experiences. Some guidance, whether it be in the shape of formal training, coaching, or even written instruction on the basics of how to work in a team and make a team work, will help even those individuals who have a low emotional intelligence IQ survive, learn, and contribute to the team's operations. There are too many people who have "earned" the label of "non-team player" and consequently find their careers and job satisfaction limited to a level below their actual potential, when some induction into the noble art of teamworking would have allowed them to play to their fuller strengths.

REFERENCES

Adair, J. (1973). *Action-centered leadership*. Maidenhead: McGraw-Hill.

Adair, J. (1986). *Effective team building*. London: Gower.

Belbin, R.M. (1981). *Management teams: why they succeed or fail*. Oxford: Heinemann.

Belbin, R.M. (1993). *Team roles at work*. Oxford: Heinemann.

Belbin, R.M., Aston, B.R., & Mottram, R.D. (1976). Building effective management teams. *Journal of General Management*, 3, 3, 23–29.

Bell. L. (1992). *Managing teams in secondary schools*. London: Routledge.

Burgoyne, J. (1994). *Towards the learning company*. London: McGraw-Hill.

Critchely, B. & Casey, D. (1984). Second thoughts on team building. *Management Education and Development*, 15, 2, 163–175.

De Board, R. (1983). *Counselling people at work*. Aldershot: Gower.

Crosby, P.B. (1979). *Quality is free*. New York: McGraw-Hill.

Dyer, W.G. (1997). *Team building: Issues and alternatives*. AddisonWesley.

Evans, P. (ed.) (1990) *Human resource management in international firms*. London: Macmillan.

Gladstein, D. (1984). Groups in context: a model of task group effectiveness. *Administrative Science Quarterly*, 29, 499–517.

Goleman, D. (1998). *Working with emotional intelligence*. London: Bloomsbury.

Guzzo, R.A. & Shea, G. P., (1992). Group performance and intergroup relations in organisations. In Dunnette, M.D. & Hough, L.M. (eds). *Handbook of industrial and organisational psychology*, Vol. 3. Palo Alto, C.A.: Consulting Psychology Press.

Hackman, J.R. (ed.) (1989). *Groups that work (and those that don't): Creating conditions for effective teamwork*. San Francisco: Jossey Bass.

Hackman, J.R. (1994). Trip wires in designing and leading workgroups. *The Occupational Psychologist*, 23, Sept. 3–8.

Handy, C. (1993). *Understanding organisations*. London: Penguin Books.

Harrison, R. & Stokes, H. (1986). *Diagnosing organisational culture*. Harrison Associates Inc.

Herriot, P. (1992). *The career management challenge: Balancing individual and organisational needs*. London: Sage publications.

Herriot, P. (1992). The changing psychological contract: The human resource challenge of the 1990's. *European Management Journal*, 13, 3, 283–294.

Higgs, M. & Rowland, D. (1992). All pigs are equal? *Management Education and Development*, 23, 4, 349–362.

Janis, I.L. (1982). *Group think: A psychological study of foreign policy decisions*. Boston, M.A: Houghton Mifflin.

Jassawalla, A.R. & Sashiel, H.C. (1998). An examination of collaboration in high technology new product development processes. *Journal of Product Innovation Management*, 15, 237–254.

Jehn, K. (1995). A multi-method examination of the benefits and detriments of intra-group conflict. *Administative Science Quarterly*, 44(2), 245–282.

Kakabadse, A. Ludlow, R. & Vinnicombe, S. (1988). *Working in organisations.* London: Penguin Business.

Katzenbach, J.R. & Smith, D.K. (1993). *The wisdom of teams*: *Creating the high performance organisation.* Massachusetts: Harvard Business School Press.

Kline, T.J.B., Mcleod, M. & McGrath, J-L. (1996). Team effectiveness: Contributions and hindrances. *Human Systems Management*, 15, 183–181.

Larson, C.E. & Lafasto, M. (1989). *Teamwork: What must go right/what can go wrong.* London: Sage Publications,

Lewis, J. (1993). *How to build and manage a winning project team.* American Association.

Manning, A. (1997). Using team role theory in management development. *Organisations and People*, 4, 4, 6–10.

Makin, P., Cooper, C. & Cox, C. (1996). *Organisations and the psychological contract.* Leicester: BPS Books.

Margerison, P. & McCann, D. (1990). *Team management: Practical new approaches.* London: Mercury.

Margerison, C. & McCann, D. (1995). *Team management.* Oxford: Management Books.

Mottram, R.D. (1982). Team skills management. *Journal of Management Development*, 1, 1, 22–33.

Mottram, R.D. (1994, 2002) *Teamability: Measure your impact in teams.* Manchester: Robertson Cooper Ltd.

McCrimmon, M. (1995). Teams without roles: Empowering teams for greater creativity. *Journal of Management Development*, 14, 6, 35–40.

O'Connell, C. (1997). Current trends in management development and training. *M.Ed.paper, School of Education*, Manchester University.

Pearn. M., Roderick, C. & Mulrooney, C. (1995). Learning organisations in practice. Maidenhead: McGraw-Hill.

Schein, E. (1992). *Organisation culture and leadership.* New York: Jossey-Bass.

Senge, P. (1990). The leader's new work: Building learning organisations. *Sloan Management Review*, Fall, 7–22.

Slater, J.A. & West, M.A. (1995). Satisfaction or source of pressure: The paradox of teamwork. *The Occupational Psychologist, 24, 30–34.*

Tuckman, B.W. (1965) Development sequences in small groups. *Psychological Bulletin*, 63, 6, 384–99.

Tuckman, B.W. & Jensen, N. (1977). Stages of small group development revisited. *Group and Organisational Stress.* 2, 419–27.

West, M. (1994). *Effective teamwork.* Leicester: BPS Books.

West, M. & Slater, J. (1995). Teamwork: myths, realities and research. *The Occupational Psychologist*, 24, 24–29.

Woodcock, M. (1979). *Team development manual.* Farnborough: Gower press.

CHAPTER 14

Informal and Incidental Learning in the New Millennium: the Challenge of Being Rapid *and/or* Being Accurate!

Victoria J. Marsick
Columbia University, USA, and

Karen E. Watkins, and Jacqueline A. Wilson
University of Georgia USA

SUMMARY

This chapter examines how Marsick and Watkins' (1990) theory of informal and incidental learning can be operationalized in the climate of rapid change and knowledge
creation that defines the dawn of the twenty-first century. It distinguishes between
anticipatory learning and learning from experience and identifies strategies that individuals and organizations can use to stay ahead of the curve, create new knowledge, and
detect and correct—or even avoid—errors. An action science case is analyzed, using
the Potential Sources of Error in Informal and Incidental Learning model, to illustrate
what can happen in practical management situations when tacit knowledge leads to a
cycle of error. Ten strategies for enhancing individual learning are recommended and
discussed.

INTRODUCTION

Today, more than ever, companies and individuals turn to informal and incidental learning to meet their needs in keeping up with continually-changing knowledge demands.
Education has not gone out of style, although in many companies, traditional classroom
instruction, known as "seat time," has. Even so, the time it takes to craft excellent courses,

even if delivered online, often exceeds the timeliness and value of much of the knowledge embedded in the course. As a consequence, companies benefit when they support informal and incidental learning—learning that is integrated with work tasks, independently pursued, or gained almost unintentionally while doing something else. Moreover, it is impossible to accurately predict knowledge and learning needs given rapid market shifts and innovative product offerings. To stay ahead of the curve, companies seek to harness and direct employee learning—to effectively use both what people already know and to provide an environment for creating new knowledge. However, we ask whether, in the quest of learning fast, we may often sacrifice learning without errors.

In this chapter, we examine a theory of informal and incidental learning that we proposed in the early 1990s in light of these demands. We look particularly at several dilemmas faced when trying to learn informally and incidentally under these conditions of rapid change. First, informal and incidental learning is based on theories of learning from experience. Such theory inevitably starts with what we know, not what we don't know. Yet, the challenges of today's workplace often push people into uncharted territory. How can people simultaneously learn proactively from the past and in the present moment, as well as anticipate and form the future?

In addition, people and companies need to learn rapidly without giving up accuracy. Yet, there is a well-known learning curve when charting new territory—when an individual is a novice mastering known expertise and especially when people are creating new knowledge. Learning from experience often involves making mistakes. How can informal and incidental learners use what we know to quickly detect and correct errors made, or even better, to anticipate and avoid errors? This is very important since, when the error is not detected, it creates a cycle of escalating error that is often tacit or unnoticed until considerable damage is done.

We first turn to our model of informal and incidental learning, and to ways that this model can be re-interpreted to account for more effective use of what we already know as well as creative, anticipatory learning. We then analyze the dilemmas that occur when the demand for speed conflicts with the demand for accuracy and learning, especially in this era of rapid trial-and-error learning. We conclude by identifying and illustrating strategies that individuals and organizations can use to come closer to meeting conflicting demands, or at the least, to better recognize the trade-offs they are making.

THEORY UNDERLYING INFORMAL AND INCIDENTAL LEARNING

We begin with Marsick and Watkins' (1990) work on informal and incidental learning as the basis for our understanding of reflective learning:

> Formal learning is typically institutionally-sponsored, classroom-based, and highly structured. Informal learning, a category that includes incidental learning, may occur in institutions, but it is not typically classroom-based or highly structured, and control of learning rests primarily in the hands of the learner. Incidental learning . . . is defined by Watkins as a byproduct of some other activity, such as task accomplishment, interpersonal interaction, sensing the organizational culture, trial-and-error experimentation, or even formal learning. Informal learning can be deliberately encouraged by an organization or it can take place despite an environment not highly conducive to learning. Incidental learning, on the other hand, almost always takes place although people are not always conscious of it. (p. 12)

This definition is based on the action science perspective of Argyris and Schön (1974, 1978), which has roots in John Dewey's (1938) theories of learning from experience and in Kurt Lewin's (1935) understanding of the interaction of individuals and their environment. We also draw on work by Mezirow (1991, 2000) on transformative learning, that is, learning that is based on questioning of assumptions which leads to a fundamental re-conceptualization of experience.

Fundamental to our thinking is the action science theory of Chris Argyris and Donald Schön (1974, 1978). We have built on their idea of single-loop and double-loop learning, with an added emphasis on the role of context, which has emerged as particularly significant in many recent studies of informal and incidental learning (Cseh, 1998; Marsick and Watkins, 2001; Callahan, Watkins, and Marsick, 2001). Action science rests on the idea that individuals are guided by tacit assumptions, values and beliefs. Intentions (whether or not they are consciously or explicitly articulated) guide actions (strategies), but often, there is a gap between what people wish to do (espoused theories-of-action) and what they actually do (theories-in-use). Actions produce outcomes. A check on whether outcomes match intentions, or whether there is a mismatch, leads one to be satisfied or dissatisfied with the situation. When there is a mismatch, people may notice this error (a mismatch, which is not the same thing as a "mistake") and seek to learn new ways of correcting errors and achieving intentions. They might modify their tactics to better achieve a match with intentions (single-loop learning). If they revisit assumptions, values and beliefs, and therefore reframe the way in which they understand the situation and set intentions, they may engage in double-loop learning.

A MODEL FOR LEARNING FROM EXPERIENCE

Cseh (1998) found 143 dissertations between 1980 and 1998 that discussed aspects of informal learning, including over twenty that built on the Marsick and Watkins' informal and incidental learning model. Some of these studies were reviewed in Cseh, Watkins, and Marsick (1999), in which the authors re-conceptualized the informal learning model (Figure 14.1), based on Cseh's work. Summarizing themes from selected research, Marsick and Volpe (1999) suggested that informal learning is:

- Integrated with work and daily routines
- Triggered by an internal or external jolt
- Not highly conscious
- Often haphazard and influenced by chance
- An inductive process of reflection and action, and
- Linked to the learning of others.

The circle in the center represents a new life experience that offers a challenge, a problem to be resolved, or a vision of a future state. The context within which the experience occurs—the personal, social, and cultural context for learning—plays a key role in influencing the way in which people interpret the situation, their choices, the actions they take, and the learning they take away.

Learning begins with some kind of a trigger, that is, an internal or external stimulus that signals dissatisfaction with current ways of thinking or being. In our model, people use reflection to become aware of the problematic aspects of the situation, to probe

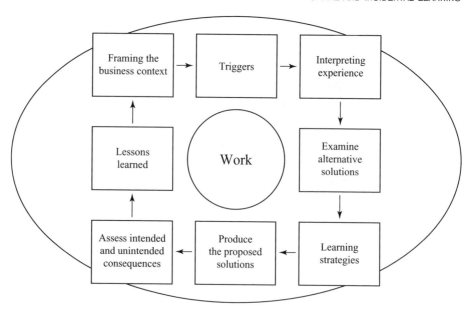

FIGURE 14.1 Marsick and Watkins' informal and incidental learning model as adapted with Cseh. Reprinted with permission from Marsick and Watkins, Informal and incidental learning, in S. Merriam (ed.) *The New Update on Adult Learning Theory*, San Francisco: Jossey-Bass, Figure 3.1, p. 29.

the characteristics of the problem or challenge, and to learn new ways to understand and address it. Our model shows that people diagnose or frame a new experience that they encounter. They assess what is problematic or challenging about it. They compare the new situation with prior experience, identify similarities or differences, and use their interpretation to make sense of the new challenge. People refine their diagnosis by deconstructing the context. They attend to the different factors in the context that influence their interpretation. The context might involve one other person, say a family member or co-worker, and a relatively routine interaction. Or it might be highly complex, with multiple actors and many political, social or cultural norms that have never before been addressed. Deconstructing the context is a greater challenge when social norms and expectations are in a state of flux, or when the person himself is learning something new. Also, people do not have the same level of skill or awareness around contextual factors that influence an interpretation, and they are subject to blind spots that can, at times, be strengthened due to emotional factors that come into play.

Interpretation of the context leads to choices around alternative actions. These choices are guided by recollections of past solutions and by a search for other potential models for action. Success in implementation depends on drawing on capabilities that are adequate to the task. If the solution calls for new skills, the person needs to acquire these. Many contextual factors influence the ability to learn well enough to successfully implement the desired solution. These include, but may not be limited to, the availability of appropriate resources (time, money, people from whom to learn), willingness and motivation to learn, and the emotional capability to take on new capabilities in the middle of what could be a stressful challenge.

Once an action is taken, a person can assess the outcomes and decide whether or not they match her goals. It is relatively easy to assess intended consequences if a person takes the time up front to make her goals clear and explicit. Perhaps because of the speed of everyday living, or the unanticipated nature of many new experiences, a person may not be highly aware of her intentions. Also, many consequences are not intended and hence, not easily observable without a systematic effort. This step of judging consequences then enables a person to draw lessons learned, and to use these lessons in planning future actions. These concluding thoughts are the new understandings that a person would bring when encountering a new situation, which brings us back full circle to the beginning of the cycle.

ANTICIPATORY LEARNING FROM EXPERIENCE FOR KNOWLEDGE CREATION

This model of learning from past experience needs modification to explain how people learn when they confront ambiguity and cannot draw on adequate kinds of prior experience on which to base their learning; or when learning requires creative leaps of imagination into the future. One way to stretch informal learning theory in such situations is to think of it as anticipatory learning from experience through the simulation of future states—through creative visualization strategies or through fact-based futures activities (for example, scenario planning, War Games, expert panels). Essentially, people use their understanding of history, other people's experience, and futures work to think through and learn from experience that has not yet occurred.

Single-loop or double-loop learning can mark this kind of learning as it marks learning from past experience. For example, Arie de Geus (1988) first introduced scenario planning into Shell Oil in order to help strategists anticipate their response to oil shortages, a prospect that was, at the time, unthinkable. The use of the computer allowed them to peer into a fact-based crystal ball. Because Shell strategists eventually did think outside their mental models, they were better prepared for the oil crisis that eventually occurred. A similar story can be told in many industries. But in the past, anticipatory learning often occurred among select groups in an industry, and may have been predicated on bodies of knowledge that changed more slowly than today. In many organizations today, people at many levels must learn in innovative ways that require creativity, visioning, and thinking outside of the box.

One of the differences between anticipatory learning and learning from prior experience is that people expect errors to occur and find ways to look for them. They know they are discovering new territory, and hence, expect to make mistakes. The smartest of these are companies that wish to "Fail Fast" in small ways as they move quickly through successive cycles of trial-and-error so that they can avert future, large errors at critical, visible junctures. They engage in iterative cycles of framing of the challenge, seeking and trying out a solution, collecting information about matches and mismatches, and using their assessment of success or failure to guide next steps. Leaders of innovative companies expect confusion and divergence, and invite frequent challenges to the prevailing view in order to tease out potential flaws that will avert larger and longer-term disasters. As one practitioner noted, many of the smartest people in the company often "feel stupid" because, even with the best minds on board, they are charting completely new territory.

People can go through this learning cycle in simpler or more complex ways depending on the depth with which they probe and question themselves and others; and on the breadth of their understanding of the context in which a new problem, situation, or challenge is situated. The model is not linear although it is presented as such. People move back and forth between steps and may skip steps. They may not move fully around the cycle each time they encounter a new experience. Most people do this almost automatically when confronted with a new problem or experience. The model is especially effective for reflecting on past experience prior to, or in the middle of, a new challenge. Some version of this kind of learning is at the heart of most post-mortems and of the After Action Review (Sullivan and Harper, 1996) developed by the US Army.

Nonetheless, people who learn informally may not be able to detect and correct their errors. They may not recognize contextual factors or adequately assess their influence on a particular situation. They may find it hard to confront and assess values, assumptions and beliefs. They may not understand or gain the skills and abilities they need to implement a solution, recognize errors, or see unintended consequences. When informal learning goes awry, it is often because such learning suffers from its very strength, that is, that it takes place rapidly and almost unconsciously as people meet demands that require the acquisition of new mental models, knowledge, and skills.

DILEMMAS OF LIVING IN THE FAST LANE

What happens when the demand for *speed* conflicts with needs for *accuracy* and *learning*? Everyone does not work in a company that values "failing fast," and even when they do, all of the company's managers may not tolerate learning from mistakes. What we have noted is that the informal learning process may become a process of escalating error if individuals move too quickly to a definition of the problem to a solution. In our work with managers in action learning teams, for example, we engage in a systematic process of defining and redefining the problem after challenging the underlying assumptions embedded in their definitions of the problem. Repeatedly, people find that the problem they were moving quickly to solve was not in fact the real problem. Implementing the proposed solution would not only solve the wrong problem; it would often also exacerbate the real problem.

Drawing on examples from our practice, and from work of our students, we illustrate what happens when individuals and organizations learn and perform under these conditions. Intuition and rapid response are often valued more than accuracy and learning from experience. We have developed a model of potential sources of error in incidental learning that illustrates this pattern of embedding mistaken or incomplete information that leads to escalating error. In this model, an individual faced with an experience or problem may frame or set the problem incorrectly or incompletely. For example, if a person goes to start a car, turns the key, and nothing happens, he or she may follow a chain of reasoning that suggests that the problem is electrical. From this understanding of the problem, we formulate solutions. The individual may assume that the battery is dead and begin to check the battery. If it is not dead, they may jiggle the key or examine wires. In this way, framing the problem too narrowly limits the range of solutions that we will try. On the other hand, we may also attempt to take action, to produce a solution that we do not have the expertise to implement. This too leads to less desirable outcomes

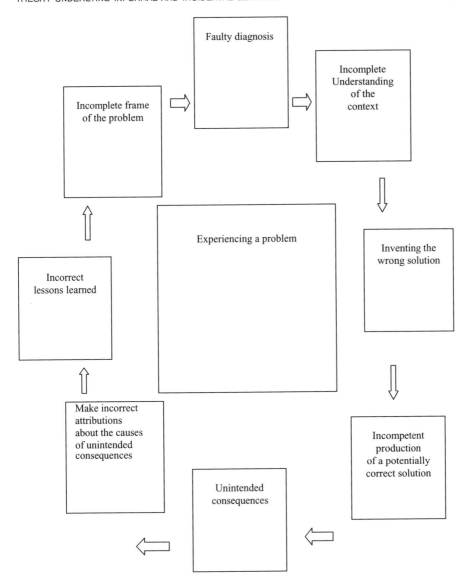

Figure 14.2   Potential sources of error in informal and incidental learning

yet we may be unaware that it is our inability to perform the task competently that led to the inappropriate outcome and may therefore "learn" that the solution does not work. Figure 14.2 depicts our model of escalating error in informal and incidental learning.

As can be seen in the model, we may enter a problem solving cycle with an inadequate or partial frame on a problem. The following example demonstrates what can happen in practical management situations when tacit incorrect knowledge shapes decisions. Wilson (2001) interviewed hotel managers for problematic encounters they had experienced at work. The encounters, transcribed in action science case format (Argyris, 1985, 1990), illustrate the speed at which managers frame and diagnose a problem and, relying upon their intuition, intervene and draw possibly flawed conclusions without testing their assumptions. The following case, analyzed using the Potential Sources of Error in Informal and Incidental Learning model, highlights how the cycle of error operates.

Anne, a twenty-eight year old resort hotel recreation manager for five years, recounted a problem she had faced with a newly hired subordinate, Sara, who on her fourth day at work expressed concern about her new job. This particular encounter was important to Anne because it was typical of other exchanges she had experienced with her staff. Table 14.1 depicts the conversation.

The action science case format gives us a window into Anne's thoughts as the conversation transpired. Anne's left column illustrates her familiarity with this type of conversation as she thinks "here we go again." Having "been there before," she frames her responses based on her intuition that Sara is not going to make it, and challenges her employee to show how she was misled about the job duties despite the fact that we have no indication that the employee felt misled. Furthermore, the encounter illustrates how automatic the framing process is. In a matter of seconds, Anne has diagnosed the situation and categorized it based on her prior experience. She never slows the process down enough to reflect on the accuracy of her conclusions about her employee.

The encounter also illustrates how lack of information (incomplete contextualisation) impedes the learning process. Even though Sara is able to answer Anne's question, repeating "verbatim" what she was told in the hiring interview, Anne makes no attempt either to probe the reasons for Sara's dissatisfaction or to help Sara understand the importance of her present job and how performing successfully can lead to future opportunities. By slowing down the conversation and asking questions to verify if her assumptions are correct, Anne might be able to learn some of the reasons why she is having similar encounters with other subordinates. Based on her knowledge of the context, she acts as if she knows what Sara is thinking.

Instead, the conversation quickly deteriorates as Anne moves rapidly from wanting to help to focusing on getting rid of a "bad apple." Anne's justification for her strategy of counseling her employee to leave is self-protection: "She's not going to help me in any way, shape or form and we get nailed a lot." Without testing her private reasoning and conclusions about Sara's motivation, Anne cannot be sure she is right. More importantly, she misses an opportunity to challenge her own preconceived beliefs about new employees and to help this particular subordinate learn how to build a career. By not reflecting on her own assumptions and not realizing she is contributing to the turnover she wants to avoid, Anne misses the opportunity to address a recurring problem.

By her own admission, Anne has had fifteen similar encounters in less than a year's time. Ironically, Anne is perpetuating the problem by counseling the employee to leave rather than examining how the organization or her own management style is producing repeated errors in hiring. She appears to be stuck in a self-sealing pattern of rapid response based on intuition rather than accuracy. A manager who does not know the full context of a problem cannot hope to resolve it. Anne has decided that her method of interviewing potential employees was producing this problem. She said, "Right after I came here I rethought the way I was doing my interviewing. And that's when I started doing more of the talking . . . We don't want to make any mistakes here." Once again, her framing and diagnosis of the problem are based on her belief that one-way (downward) communication is the best way to transmit what is expected. By dominating the interview and conversations with employees, she illustrates how the wrong strategy (poor invention)

TABLE 14.1 The "New Hire"

What Anne thought	What was said
	Sara:
OK, let me not say the first thing that comes to mind. Let me try to empathize. Let me really help.	I'd like to talk with you about a couple of issues.
	Anne:
Here we go again.	Certainly, what is it?
	Sara:
	Well, my job isn't what I thought it was going to be.
	Anne:
Honestly, I dare you to contradict what I originally told you, 'cause I've had this conversation with 15 employees so far this year.	Tell me what you expected it to be.
	[Sara described the job verbatim.]
	Anne:
Go ahead. Give me your best shot. Try to sway me on what you originally told me.	You were hired specifically for weekend work, and I told you what your job would be correct?
	Sara:
OK. Same old song. I heard this two months ago with so-and-so.	Correct, you're absolutely right. I made a lot of assumptions. I think I blocked that out.
	Anne:
OK. Bye-bye. She's under probation. I can send her out right now and not have any repercussions.	If you feel the need to leave, then I'll support you in your decision. And I will help you in any way that I can. If you need to find another job here, I'll help you do that. If you need to move on, then I'll be glad to help you do that, because if you don't want to be here, I don't want you here.
	Sara:
I can cover the schedule. I'll cover it myself if it gets rid of this bad apple.	Well, you've already made out the schedule for the next 3 weeks, so I'll work out the schedule.
	Anne:
If she continues whining—especially to other staff members—then she'll be headed out pretty soon.	If you don't want to be here, then I don't want you here. This doesn't make for a good situation for you or for our department. Whatever you decided is ok. I'll cover the schedule. Don't worry about that.
	Sara:
She needs to go. Even though she's trying a little bit, it's half-hearted and she's still gonna end up leaving.	No, I feel like I've made a commitment to working here, and the schedule is made out. So I'll think it over for the next 3 weeks. I'll work out the schedule, and then we'll talk then.
	Anne:
I'm just giving her fluffy stuff to help her out mentally. I empathize with her to some degree. I really understand how boring her job may be, how unchallenging it may be. And she's seeking more. But the flip side is I was up front with her and I think she needs to pay her dues before she gets that title and that big money and all of that stuff.	That's fine, but if you have any issues that arise between now and then, please come to me and know that the schedule is related to the original job that I had described. I'm not going to change your job description because you have an assumption.
	Sara:
	I understand.

leads to error, producing both unintended consequences (higher turnover and dissatisfied employees) and reinforcing her incorrect generalizations (that dissatisfied employees need to do what is expected or leave). This case well illustrates the problems that occur when error enters the informal and incidental learning cycle. In the section that follows, we outline organizational and individual strategies to enhance this learning that help interrupt the recurring cycles of escalating error seen in Anne's case.

ENHANCING INFORMAL AND INCIDENTAL LEARNING WHILE HONORING THE NEED FOR SPEED

In developing our original theory of informal and incidental learning, we noted that such learning is enhanced when people can become more proactive, critically reflective, and creative. We believe these characteristics pertain today as much as they did then.

We defined proactivity as "a readiness to take initiative. Its opposite, reactivity, suggests a victim-like, almost fatalistic stance toward events in which one lets circumstances dictate one's response" (Marsick and Watkins, 1990, p. 28). Proactivity involves a mental state of readiness to bring into awareness that which often remains tacit, or somewhat hidden and unconscious about informal and incidental learning. People have to pay attention to their intentions and outcomes. Often, it is difficult to "see" outcomes, though it is not always clear why that is so. Sometimes this is due to a deeper internal process, such as denial, and sometimes primarily to distracting external events and the pressure of time. Feedback loops are central to using what one notices as information for changing either tactics or fundamental, shaping values, assumptions, and beliefs. Argyris (2000) notes that management advice is often flawed because it implies a causal loop such that if you do X, you will get Y result, but does not specify either how to actually do X or how to know if you are doing it right. Managers need to know both how to implement advice such as "fail fast," and how to know if their interpretation is accurate and effective. Without testing the advice against their unique context and abilities, it is more likely to fail than to succeed. Moreover, few managers create systems to collect data on their own and others' behavior so that feedback will be data-based. Proactivity, then, can lead individuals to create habits, systems, and tools for obtaining data-based feedback on their practice, for challenging and testing advice, and for surfacing tacit knowledge.

Recognition and awareness, coupled with reflection that is often critical, enables people to continually scan an environment, become conscious of espoused and actual intentions, probing of values and assumptions that shape understanding, and alert to ways in which one crafts and implements learning or work strategies. Proactive, reflective learners are on the lookout for matches and mismatches that lead to error. They more easily engage in anticipatory learning because they are in tune with what might be needed in the future. Critical reflection involves learning a set of checks on one's tacit knowledge that prevent us from embedding erroneous information or acting on inappropriate generalizations from experiences.

Creativity involves imagination, the ability to engage in a process of "seeing-as" (Schön, 1983, p. 182), the willingness to nurture and examine one's intuitive judgments, and a comfort with divergence. Creativity allows for ambiguity and gives birth to the new patterns engendered at points far from equilibrium. Among other things, "imagination enables us to adopt other perspectives across boundaries and time, to visit "otherness" and let it speak its own language" (Wenger, 1998, p. 217). Through imagination, people become aware of the rich context within which their interaction occurs. Imagination helps people to understand and negotiate the meaning of context with one another through conversations and collaborative action. If people are aware of context and differences, then they can address these factors and use them to re-think intentions and action strategies. Mental rehearsal, for example, is a technique used often by leaders, athletes, and others to mentally walk through a process, a talk, or a difficult meeting. This and other similar strategies enable individuals to learn through their imagination.

ENHANCING INFORMAL AND INCIDENTAL LEARNING AT THE ORGANIZATIONAL LEVEL

While individuals can do much to enhance their informal learning, the organization plays perhaps an even more critical role because people need the company's support and encouragement to carry out many informal learning strategies in ways that benefit both themselves and the company as a whole. Organizations create conditions that nurture or suppress proactivity, critical reflectivity, and creativity through their reward systems, leadership and management practices, and cultures.

Rewards for learning demonstrate the value that the organization places on these investments by employees. For example, some companies such as Johnsonville Sausage give employees money for learning. Each employee is given an educational fund that they can spend to learn whatever they choose. At Skandia, the company has created a "competence benefits package" in which individuals can set aside part of their pay check each month into a fund that the company also invests in monthly. When there is sufficient money in that fund, an individual may take a sabbatical to go to any place that will enable them to acquire new skills. At other organizations, skills assessments are used to help employees determine what current or future skills they will need to acquire to remain productive, and desktop courses, tuition funds, and other means are then provided to learn the needed skills. While these strategies focus on providing resources, they assume that learning will be rewarded. Rewards for investing in learning may include retaining a job, future promotions, enhanced employability by other organizations or departments, and self-satisfaction. Some organizations such as banks have created career ladders for teller positions that tie time, skill development, and performance to movement to higher paying positions. Pay for knowledge schemes are examples of explicit financial rewards for learning.

Leadership and management strategies to support continuous informal and incidental learning include changing the role of the manager to become more of a coach or mentor who facilitates the learning of his or her employees and must model being a continuous learner themselves (Marsick and Watkins, 1999). Yet organizations must also create a learning infrastructure to support informal and incidental learning (Watkins and Marsick, 1993). They cannot focus only on formal training strategies when everyone in the organization must engage in continual renewal nor can they expect individuals to carry all of the responsibility for their own development. Some professions, such as accounting, have endorsed and documented learning from experience as a legitimate part of both the certification and re-certification process. A senior accountant is designated as a mentor for new accountants and that mentor is expected to assign increasingly challenging work, to give specific corrective feedback on all work performed, and to meet with the individual to discuss their development needs. Learning for mandatory continuing professional education for accountants can include things like watching a teaching videotape and discussing it with other accountants, reading professional journals, attending conferences, or other meetings of one's professional community. Organizations can build a supportive climate for employees to engage in these kinds informal learning opportunities and provide resources to support involvement. Benveniste (1987) wrote that the way to create a learning organization is to professionalise it: to encourage every individual to view themselves as professionals and to adopt a professional code of behavior that incorporates continuous improvement, self monitoring, and a long term vision of one's own development.

A high learning culture enables informal and incidental learning to flourish. This culture depends upon companies that hire and promote the best and the brightest people they can, and then essentially get out of these employees' way since talented, creative, intelligent people are attracted by a challenging job that provides them with opportunities for development through their work. The company's biggest challenge is to capture the wisdom of their employees, to extract lessons learned so that this knowledge is available to others as needed, and does not disappear when employees move on to new challenges. Informal and incidental learning are expected in these companies; and may be channeled and supported through clear statements of desired competencies, financial and other incentives for earned knowledge and developed capability, effective knowledge management systems, and infrastructure for knowledge networks and learning communities. Such companies, at least in theory, recognize that learning involves risk-taking, trial-and-error, and learning from experience.

The work of Nonaka and Takeuchi (1995) adds to our understanding of how to create a high learning culture and offers a framework for creating knowledge that builds on the distinction between tacit and explicit knowledge that is at the heart of informal and incidental learning. Explicit knowledge is articulated and codified; tacit knowledge is implicit, that is, knowledge that people have but may not know they have. Nonaka and Takeuchi propose a knowledge creation cycle that moves back and forth between tacit and explicit knowing.

Using Nonaka and Takeuchi's framework, it is possible to identify ways in which informal learning, which is largely tacit, can be supported and enhanced. It is critical to make time and space available so that people can learn while they work yet the press of meeting task demands often precludes the opportunity to learn while working. Some companies have tried to change this. For example, Arthur Andersen & Co. SC experimented with a strategy through which they incorporated learning into their work engagements. At the beginning of a work assignment, teams took time to plan for learning as well as work. Team members determined what knowledge and skills they might need that they did not already have, established learning objectives along with work objectives, developed and discussed a plan to acquire needed knowledge, and set out pre-work tasks. As the team worked, they found time for coaching, reflection and feedback. They built facilitated reflection into the process, and thought about evaluation and rewards for learning.

Corporations are using many strategies to more effectively draw out tacit knowledge in and among employees. Dixon (2000), for example, describes the way a manager at Ford Motor Company asked linesmen at different plants to visit other plants, "walk the line," and identify "pretty good practices" that they could bring home and use. He reasoned that these linesmen could socialize with other employees, and would ask very different kinds of questions about their work because they shared the same background. Dorothy Leonard-Barton (1995) has described the way in which strong marketing-oriented companies "live in the shoes of their customers" to find out how customers use products and to tap into tacit knowledge about what they do or do not like about these products. Many companies have adopted storytelling as a way to engage employees in sharing what they know because a story conveys a different kind of energy and experience than does an abstracted list of principles. And finally, companies have become captivated by the idea of multiple intelligences (Gardner, 1993) and the notion that some experiences are better explained and understood through non-cognitive, non-rational means such as music, art, poetry and metaphor.

People need opportunities to find out what others are doing that they might draw upon for improving their own work, and they need opportunities to experiment with possible solutions to problems. Benchmarking—within and outside one's company—is a way of meeting this need, but in addition, organizations need to encourage and reward experimentation.

STRATEGIES FOR ENHANCING INDIVIDUAL LEARNING

In 1990, we recommended six strategies that individuals could use for enhancing informal and incidental learning that we revisit in light of the above discussion (Marsick and Watkins, 1990, pp. 226–227):

1. Surface tacit theories.
2. Be aware of our own attributions about people or about situations and look for examples that prove and/or disprove them.
3. Problematize situations.
4. Engage in deliberately reflective, transformative learning.
5. Make private theories or assertions public so that they can be challenged.
6. Try to take a long-term view of the learning task.

We also add four new suggestions:

7. Use personal cycles of action research to "fail and recover fast."
8. Stretch one's tolerance and capability for divergent thinking and conflicting views.
9. Don't put off learning today that which one might not be able to do tomorrow.
10. Become active in knowledge networks and learning communities.

We begin with the value of surfacing tacit theories. People are often blind to what they know or don't know. Hence, tacit understanding is best surfaced when other people ask us questions, when they express surprise, or when others provide us with feedback that startles us into seeing something about ourselves and our work that we have come to take for granted. Once surfaced, it is also easy to ignore such outside input, especially if it takes us outside of our comfort zone or otherwise disrupts our self-image; and when the organization's culture does not encourage openness and trust. Yet, surfacing tacit theories—our own and those of others—provides us with insight into what goes wrong and right, into the logic of our reasoning, and the limits of our capabilities.

One way of surfacing one's tacit theories is to make opportunities to visit others that do similar and different work, and to create agreements with those people to put time aside to ask questions about what it is that you or they see during such visits. Goldberg (1998) attests to the value of using non-judgmental, inquiry-oriented questions to get in touch with one's thinking and explore new points of view.

The second suggestion is linked to identifying and testing attributions made by ourselves and others. While making attributions is not new, the speed at which people work and the frequency with which they interact with others who do not share their background and history, makes it highly likely that different parties to the same interaction will come away with completely different interpretations of the interaction. Moreover, it is very likely that they will not share and test their understanding of what just occurred, but instead, will selectively identify validating support for the conclusions they have drawn and the judgments they have made. These conclusions will then lead them to actions that may well be unfounded but also likely to create some of the same consequences that they are trying to avoid.

Argyris and Schön (1974, 1996) have built their scholarly reputations on the documentation of these kinds of attributions as a critical tool in their theory of action science. Their advice to people has been that slowing down in the early stages of interactions—in order to inquire about meanings and test understandings—often saves people a lot of time and error in the longer run. Slowing down is not easy in the Internet Age, yet its value is proven in many circles, including sports. A tool that has become commonly used in the last few years is the ladder of inference, a device adopted by Chris Argyris and Donald Schön (1996) to explain the way in which people can understand and test their attributions. The ladder shows how directly observable data in our experiences, the lowest rung on the ladder of inference, are run through successive rungs of interpretation (cultural, personal, and organizational meanings), each of which then leads to certain actions. Action Science provides a process of reflection that enables people to first increase their awareness of this rapid mental leap from fact to inference and then uses cases such as Anne's above to help people learn to test these successive interpretations and inferences against others' interpretations. Well-framed, open-ended, inquiry-oriented, nonjudgmental questions are a highly useful tool for opening thinking and learning about latent traps set by limitations in one's own understanding of the situation.

A third suggestion is problematizing situations. By taking familiar situations and looking at them as though they were problematic or unfamiliar, people can reframe situations and consider alternatives. One strategy that many organizations use is to ask "What if?" questions that question taken for granted assumptions about how things work. This can be applied both to situations and to people. What if your boss was not really wrong about the current strategic priorities? What might be some reasons why he or she was right? What would happen if we changed...? Many of the strategies used in creative problem solving are essentially ways to help people make the familiar strange and the strange more familiar. These approaches help clarify the underlying assumptions that determine our view of a problem or situation so that we can question whether or not these assumptions still hold.

A fourth recommendation is to engage in reflective learning that at times can become oriented to double-loop or transformative learning. In fact, we find that people often have little time for simple reflection in their fast-paced lives. "Reflection breaks" need to be built into regular work routines to allow people to learn from their own experience and that of others. They must become as habitual as the "to do" list, but for that to happen, they often have to first be "staged." Individuals might find it easier to build reflection breaks into their work at first when they are planning new activities because they are not routine and therefore need more conscious planning attention. The questions that guide the After Action Review (Sullivan and Harper, 1996) are good places to start: What were / are my goals? What actually happened? (Or, if before the fact: How can I track what actually happens?) Without ascribing blame, what went right and what went wrong? (Or, if before the fact, based on past experience: What can I anticipate going right or wrong?) And finally, what lessons does this hold for next steps? (Or, if before the fact, based on past experience, what lessons can I draw on from past experience to guide first steps?). One organization we know of created a practice of "one minute reflection" at the beginning of each meeting in which participants were asked to think about the purpose of the meeting and what they personally hoped to accomplish in this day's meeting. They found that their meetings were more productive, less tense, and that differences in understandings about the purpose of the meeting were more likely to be surfaced and resolved.

Our fifth recommendation involves making private theories public so that they can potentially be challenged, which is in some ways easier, and in other ways more difficult, in today's work environments than it was in the past. This recommendation requires individuals to develop ways to get feedback on how others see their practice, and ways to disclose to oneself and to others what one actually said or did, along with the underlying reasoning. Organizational cultures vary in the degree to which they make giving and receiving feedback available. In too many organizations, this is still high risk behavior. At the same time, there are more mechanisms available today for getting feedback when it is desired through personal and social networks, mentoring and coaching, 360 degree assessment instruments, or communities of practice and face to face or virtual knowledge networks. Success or failure is often evident in shorter and shorter timeframes, making performance feedback almost real time. Even if it is not culturally appropriate to do a post-mortem, a proactive learner can find ways to learn from mistakes with a circle of associates inside or outside of his or her workplace.

Our sixth recommendation—an effort to take a "big picture," long term view of the learning task is likewise easier and harder in today's environment. The value of this for informal learning is a richer learning environment and a richer source of expertise for the company. Organizations often have a short-term, quarterly results mentality driven by stockholder value. While it is not always possible to succeed individually within a quarter, it is possible for individuals to take a long term view of the development of their own capacities. In some cases, an individual's development plan may easily span several organizations over a five year planning cycle. One individual commented that employees often derided organizational initiatives as "the latest fad, here today and gone tomorrow." Yet, from a learning perspective, he added, new knowledge is left behind by every new initiative that can never be erased completely, only added to by the next new initiative. Organizations solve this problem by relying increasingly on teams that are multi-functional and multi-site in nature. Individuals solve this problem by viewing their work across organizations or jobs, rather than within, a particular organization.

Our seventh recommendation flows directly from the imperatives of speed. It is essential to try things out that move one beyond one's comfort zone. The organization, or interested individuals on their own, can create a learning laboratory within which it becomes acceptable to "be stupid" when venturing into unknown territory to solve challenges that are new to either the individual or the company. In order to maximize the benefit of such experiences, individuals can be helped to develop personal skills of action research that they can use in their own trial-and-error learning as well as in company initiatives. They can learn how to effectively frame the actions they undertake as problems and experiments; consciously think about success criteria and the information they need to collect in order to assess success; sharpen skills in data collection and analysis; solicit others to help them in their interpretation of the data they collect; and think through the way in which lessons learned should be incorporated into their next steps. They can also create successive cycles of action research that build on lessons learned to question their understanding of the situation and reassess goals and directions.

Our eighth recommendation involves stretching one's tolerance and capability for divergent thinking and conflicting views. Effective informal and incidental learning increasingly requires thinking outside of the box, and this necessarily requires people to put aside their favored perceptions of the world and participate imaginatively and openly in the alternative, often conflicting, views of a situation posed by people who are very different from themselves. Innovative informal and incidental learning occurs through clashes of personality, perspective, and culture. At the same time, without cultivating openness and conflict management skills, people might find that difference pushes them further within existing frameworks. This recommendation is well suited to the speed at which people function in today's organizations. Limited time often breaks down boundaries that were harder to negotiate because deadlines require collaboration across silos. However, without cultivating the capabilities needed to hear and argue within such cultures, individuals and the organization often do not benefit from rich divergent views that call into question the way in which a person or a company or a profession organizes its world-view.

Our ninth recommendation involves not putting off learning today that which one might not be able to do tomorrow. The speed with which knowledge grows and priorities shift argues that people learn for learning's sake. One cannot wait to learn only that which is proven essential today because new capabilities will easily be needed tomorrow. Speed again is a benefit as well as a liability in this environment. Individuals can make a sound argument for what used to be considered as non-essential learning. Moreover, as a number of organizations have found, getting employees engaged in learning anything often spills over into greater interest in job-related learning. Most people enjoy learning new things and the pace and stress of work may have repressed this natural inquisitiveness. Keeping one's mind actively engaged in learning keeps it open to learning more effectively from experiences and problems. Use it or lose it is the underlying theory here. Organizations can proactively provide for this kind of learning by building learning into the work process through strategies such as on-line help, desktop learning programs that tutor individuals through specific tasks, etc.

Our tenth and final recommendation is to become active in knowledge networks and learning communities. Many companies support web-based communities that are expected to share information and jointly problem solve challenges. Informal learning cannot easily occur in isolation, especially when it involves innovation and creativity. On-line communities make it possible to expand one's mental boundaries without physical travel. Informal learning is enhanced by deliberately and frequently crossing boundaries. Forays into alternative communities often hold up a mirror to one's own thinking and, at the same time, open doors to unanticipated points of view.

CONCLUSION

In this chapter, we have explored our model of informal and incidental learning and the implications for changing how we think about learning in the workplace. We have also looked at an illustration of how this learning may, without careful use of strategies to enhance this learning, lead to embedding mistaken information and ultimately to cycles of escalating error. Managers play a critical role in this process. They are often the facilitator of debriefing sessions, the questioner challenging assumptions in a planning or problem-solving session, and the coach and teacher when individuals come with a problem for which they do not now have the knowledge or skill to resolve. By consciously building a repertoire of skills to aid their own and others' informal and incidental learning, managers help to ensure that these potential debilitating errors are interrupted before they cause serious or long term harm.

REFERENCES

Argyris, C. (2000). *Flawed advice and the management trap*. New York: Oxford University Press.

Argyris, C. (1985). *Strategy, change and defensive routines*. Boston: Pitman.

Argyris, C. (1990). *Overcoming organizational defenses: Facilitating organizational learning*. Boston: Allyn and Bacon.

Argyris, C. & Schön, D. (1974). *Theory in practice: Increasing professional effectiveness*. S.F., CA: Jossey-Bass.

Argyris, C. & Schön, D. (1996). *Organizational learning II: A theory of action perspective*. Reading, MA: Addison Wesley.

Benveniste, G. (1987). *Professionalizing the organization: Reducing bureaucracy to enhance effectiveness*. San Francisco: Jossey-Bass.

Callahan, M.W., Watkins, K.E. & Marsick, V.J. (2001). Every-time, Every-place Learning: A 21st Century Imperative, unpublished manuscript under review.

Cseh, M., Watkins, K.E. & Marsick, V.J. (1998). Informal and Incidental Learning in the Workplace. *Proceedings of the Annual Conference of the Academy of Human Resource Development*. Baton Rouge, LA: Lousiana State University.

de Geus, A. (1988). Planning as learning. *Harvard Business Review, 66*(2), 70–74.

Dewey, J. (1938). *Experience and education*. New York: Macmillan.

Dixon, N.M. (2000). *Common knowledge: How companies thrive by sharing what they know*. Boston: Harvard Business School Press.

Gardner, H. (1993). *Multiple intelligences: The theory in practice*. New York: Basic Books.

Goldberg, M.C. (1998). *The art of the question: A guide to short-term question-centered therapy*. New York: Wiley.

Leonard-Barton, D. (1995). *Wellsprings of knowledge: Building and sustaining the sources of innovation*. Boston: Harvard Business School Press.

Leonard-Barton, D. (1999). *When sparks fly: Igniting creativity in groups*. Boston: Harvard Business School Press.

Lewin, K. (1935). *A dynamic theory of personality*. New York: McGraw-Hill.

Marsick, V.J. & Volpe, F.M. (1999). Informal learning on the job. *Advances in Developing Human Resources, No. 3*. San Francisco: Academy of Human Resources Development and Berrett-Koehler.

Marsick, V.J. & Watkins, K. (1990). *Informal and incidental learning in the workplace*. London: Routledge.

Marsick, V.J. & Watkins, K.E. (1999). *Facilitating the Learning Organization: Making Learning Count*. London: Gower.

Mezirow, J. (1991). *Transformative dimensions of adult learning*. San Francisco: Jossey-Bass.

Mezirow, J. & Associates. (2000) *Learning as transformation*. San Francisco: Jossey-Bass.

Nonaka, I. & Takeuchi, H. (1995). *The knowledge-creating company*. New York: Oxford University Press.

Schön, D. (1983). *The reflective practitioner*. New York: Basic Books.

Sullivan, G.R. & Harper, M. V. (1996). *Hope is not a method: What business leaders can learn from America's army*. New York: Broadway Books.

Watkins, K. & Marsick, V. (1993). *Sculpting the learning organization*. San Francisco: Jossey-Bass.

Wenger, E. (1998). *Communities of practice*. Cambridge, UK: Cambridge University Press.

Wilson, J.A. (2001). *Defensive routines and theories-in-use of hotel managers: An action science study*. Unpublished doctoral dissertation, The University of Georgia.

CHAPTER 15

Individual Development and Self Managed Learning

Ian Cunningham

Centre for Self Managed Learning, Brighton, UK

SUMMARY

This chapter makes the case for using Self Managed Learning (SML) in order to promote individual development in organisations. However the emphasis is on the social context of learning and development and not on purely individualistic processes.

The chapter explores both research and theoretical support for the use of Self Managed Learning. In the latter context the chapter draws on evidence from, inter alia, education, economics and sociology. The chapter concludes with speculation as to why SML is not more widely accepted, given the impressive theoretical and research basis for its practice.

INTRODUCTION

This chapter makes a case for the Self Managed Learning approach to individual development in organisations. I first need to clarify what I mean by some terms in this sentence. As regards the notion of 'development', I will equate it with 'learning'. As regards 'individual development' I do not take this to mean necessarily 'individualistic learning.' Learning in organisations occurs in a social context and I want to look at that context. Also learning by individuals may need to go beyond contributing to the human capital of the organisation and also add to its social capital. See, for example, Cohen and Prusak (2001) and Baker (2000.)

Individual Differences and Development in Organisations. Edited by Michael Pearn.
© 2002 John Wiley & Sons, Ltd.

The term 'Self Managed Learning' is used now more widely and has started to be equated with any approach that is outside the traditional course framework. This creates major conceptual confusion. In a previous text (Cunningham, 1999) I compared lower case 'self managed learning' with upper case 'Self Managed Learning'. It's the latter that I'll be writing about here. The former can be characterised as a re-naming of anything to do with self-development or self-directed learning or related terms.

In this chapter I will indicate first some ways of defining Self Managed Learning (SML) before moving into the theoretical and empirical bases of its practice. Some of this analysis may seem initially to be detached from the theme of development but I hope to show the connections. One of my aims is to address scepticism about learners taking charge of their own learning and the personal and social consequences of such a mode of working. This will require some detours into the wider issues of the nature of organisational life. I specifically want to challenge statements such as the following: 'The central challenge of management development is to control and manage the learning process of managers.' (Van der Sluis and Hoeksema, 2001, p.1). The learning process of managers cannot be 'controlled' in a simplistic way: Managers will make their own decisions about what they learn even if senior people try to control it. What is needed is assistance to people to help them to manage their own learning more effectively.

In making the case for Self Managed Learning (SML) I will mention some links to other approaches to development and comment on where they fit (or not) with Self Managed Learning. I will indicate also some aspects of the SML methodology, though I will need to refer readers to other texts if they want more information on practical applications and on the numerous evaluation studies carried out on SML in organisations (e.g. Cunningham et al., 2000).

SELF MANAGED LEARNING (SML)

An easy way to characterise SML is to say that it's about learners identifying for themselves what they want to learn, how they want to learn, when they want to learn—and where. It is distinct from most open learning, distance learning and e learning in not just allowing the person to learn when and where they want but also to drive the what and the how. Most open/distance/e learning dictates the 'what' and the 'how'. The learner has an imposed content (the what) and an imposed methodology (the how). (A minority of e learning practitioners are using the medium to free up learners on the 'what' dimension – and I'll refer to those later.)

So far the description of Self Managed Learning indicates some differences from supposedly similar approaches, but the distinctions become more fundamental when we move to the strategic dimension of SML. Figure 15.1. shows the notion that, in Self Managed Learning, the learner is able to choose methods of learning to suit themselves. Hence SML does not reject the use of any of the standard learning methods available. People on SML programmes may attend workshops, read books, get coaching assistance, and use the Internet. But the basis for them doing it is that they have thought through their learning goals and then looked for ways to meet them. It is here where the strategic dimension comes in. Learners are assisted to develop a coherent strategy for their learning within which various tactics may be appropriate.

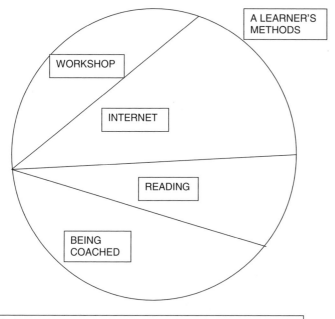

The learner chooses a mix of learning methods to suit their overall learning goals and learning preferences as well as the resources available.

FIGURE 15.1 SML as strategic. The learner chooses a mix of learning methods to suit his/her overall learning goals and learning preferences, as well as the resources available

A simple way of describing this strategic approach is to say that learners initiate their learning programmes with a number of starting points. These are:

- **Problems.** A problem whether in work, or possibly wider, exists when you cannot go from where you are to where you would like to be simply by action. So if a person gets results from a 360 degree feedback exercise which indicate that they are not as good a team player as they would like to be, this usually constitutes a problem. The person typically cannot achieve this simply through action; they are likely to need to learn to operate differently. Hence the person has a learning problem. Note that I am not seeing a problem as a negative; it is merely a starting point for change. And the ability to choose good problems to work on helps a person to be a good learner.
- **Persons.** SML starts with people as they are, with all their values, ideals, skills, knowledge and so on. Obviously the learner starts with themselves as such a person. However they may also need to accommodate other persons, e.g. in their team.
- **Patterns.** People have patterns of behaviour that are commonly labelled habits. These patterns may work well and not need to change, but some do not work so well. To take a common example, people in organisations often feel that they could improve their time management. They may go on courses that provide hints and tips as to how to improve. Sometimes these work but often they don't. If a person has an ingrained habit of procrastinating they may need to address this directly and all the hints and tips in the world may do little to help. So these patterns have to be recognised as one of the starting points for learning.

- **Plans.** The organisation may have plans, e.g. to move into new markets, to bring out new products, to go into e commerce, etc. These organisational plans will also form part of what the learner may need to take on board. For instance new technology may require the learning of new skills.
- **Processes.** The organisation will have its own processes of working; policies, procedures, cultural factors, etc. Again the learner may have to accommodate these. An example would be where the culture is one of continual change; learners are likely to need to learn how to work in such a context e.g. becoming more flexible and adaptable.

Note that there is not one beginning to learning—it is multi-faceted. This 'P' world, of problems, persons, patterns, plans and processes, is the starting point but it is only the start. Learners need to move from this into the 'S' world which can be characterised as follows:

- **Solutions.** The learner will want to move to solving their problems. Therefore searching for or creating appropriate solutions is important. Note that in SML the process goes 'problem to solution'. So much of what has been provided for people in organisations has gone the other way—'solution to problem'—or at least has attempted to. Of course, one difficulty of this latter mode is that it can be highly inefficient. The standardised sheep-dip training course exemplifies the issue.
  Trainers often put people through standard sessions irrespective of the learning needs or learning preferences of the people attending. Hence we find that training at its worst can become a solution looking for a problem to attach itself to. I can remember when I did my training officer training in 1971 being told to look for performance problems or turnover problems (or whatever) and then get in and put on a training course. The notion that there might be other solutions to the problems (selection, work methods, rewards policies, etc) was ignored. Your job as a trainer was to put on training courses. And the idea that other learning modes might be more suitable to meet real development needs was risible. Of course things have become better in the last 30 years but there are still aspects of this thinking around (see later in the research evidence).
- **Subjects.** The traditional academic subjects have their place. People may need to learn more about economics or engineering or marketing. But the learning of these is driven by the needs of the individual and the context in which they work and not by the desires of a professor or a trainer to teach the particular subject. The latter syndrome has been criticised for many years by researchers in the area of management (e.g. see Mintzberg, 1992).
- **Skills/systems/specialisations.** Learners may need to develop new skills; they may need to learn new systems e.g. new software; they may need to acquire new specialist knowledge. All of this learning needs to respond to the 'P' world issues.

In the above I have promulgated the notion of going from 'P to S' as usually the most effective learning route. However, as well as the danger of 'S to P' there is the tendency for some to stay in 'P'. In a reaction against the irrelevance of educational approaches senior managers may suggest that the 'S' world can be rejected totally. They mistakenly believe that just working on existing problems with existing knowledge and skills will work. This can result in an introverted organisational climate where new ideas are not sought. The evidence is that successful businesses do look outside existing processes and modes of operating. They promote learning from their environment by looking for new solutions to their problems (see e.g. de Geus, 1997, on the research conducted by Shell on this).

It's also apparent from studies on effective leaders that they do not stay in the 'P' world. Many commentators have remarked on the voracious learning habits of Bill Gates. He constantly asks questions, invests time in looking for new ways to do things and he uses his travels to learn about other cultures. Note that the learning approach he adopts (along with most CEOs) is not based on attending lots of training courses—it is based mainly on using a whole range of daily experiences. Bennis and Nanus (1985) summarised one aspect of their research on ninety top leaders as follows:

> 'Nearly all leaders are highly proficient in learning from experience. Most were able to identify a small number of mentors and key experiences that powerfully shaped their philosophies, personalities, aspirations and operating styles. And all of them regarded themselves as "stretching", "growing" and "breaking new ground"......leaders have discovered not just how to learn but how to learn in an organizational context' (pp. 188–9).

This last point is crucial – learning in an organisational context is the preferred learning mode of successful people. The researchers that have studied the place of 'communities of practice' confirm this (see Galagan, 1993; Brown and Duguid, 1991).

SML STRUCTURES

The Self Managed Learning approach provides structures within which people can work in the ways indicated above. This is one difference from 'self managed learning'. The latter can be characterised as a more laissez faire approach that essentially hands over total responsibility for development to the employee. In Self Managed Learning we are clear that this is not desirable; the organisation still needs to retain a role in supporting the learner.

A typical SML programme might look like the following:

1. **Ensuring buy-in** from top management. This might take the form of a presentation to the Board and/or one-to-one meetings with key people such as the CEO.
2. **Briefing** the managers of those coming on the programme on their role in supporting learners. Also briefing participants on what SML will mean for them.
3. **Diagnostic activity**. These days, for managers, the favoured mode is to use 360-degree feedback plus optional psychometric tests.
4. **Start-up event** (two/three days). This is where participants start to experience a number of the key structures in SML
   a) They typically join a community of other learners and have the opportunity to continue to access this wider network (perhaps 15 to 25 others).
   b) They join a learning group of five or six participants, that will stay together for the length of the programme (usually nine months to a year).
   c) They are assisted by having a learning group adviser working with the group. This will be someone who has had development in order to fulfil a role that might be characterised as facilitation but actually is somewhat more subtle.
   d) Each participant will start to draft a Strategic Learning Contract which will spell out their learning goals and ways of achieving them. They will discuss this with their learning group.

   e) They will have some assistance in mapping out factors that may influence their
      choice of learning goals (see the P/S discussion above).
5. **Programme in operation**. After the start up event, the learning group usually meets
   about every five weeks to support the learning of each person. Participants will also
   meet with their manager to agree their Strategic Learning Contract and to negotiate
   what support they need from the organisation.
6. **At the end of the programme** participants report back, usually to their Board, on
   what they have learned and what they have done to further the needs of the business.

The above is only one kind of design for an SML programme, but it is one that has
been used in a wide variety of organisations with staff at all levels from secretaries and
technicians to Board members. It exemplifies the SML model of having a clear support
structure which allows the learner significant freedom to learn whatever they want.

It also shows a difference from 'self managed learning' as exemplified in Abbott
and Dahmus's quote (1992) that 'Self managed learning is a less structured alternative
to traditional training.'(p. 50). SML is not less structured but rather it is differently
structured. SML programmes have a consistent structure. It's just that the SML approach
is less directive. SML structures are not driven by curricula or timetables imposed by
teachers or trainers; they enable learners to work with their colleagues to learn what they
choose.

THE E LEARNING EXAMPLE AND SML

This is not the place to make an exhaustive analysis of e learning. Rather what I want
to do is to use this development as an example of where SML deviates from the more
controlled, instructional use of the Internet and company Intranets. I'll start with a few
examples of the problems occurring with e learning.

1. Most web-based training has increased the drop-out rates on 'courses' (see e.g.
   Frankola, 2001).
2. People complain of boredom.
3. Baker (2000) criticises 'electronic page turners' and Staley and MacKenzie (2000)
   found 'many examples' that 'simply automate existing curricula and re-inforce learning processes that have existed for centuries.'(p. 1) In other words, the use of the
   technology may change little in such areas as the empowerment of learners.
4. The 'technolust' syndrome causes many people to fall for the technology without
   evaluating it. This has been going on for decades—witness the failures of teaching
   machines, programmed instruction, interactive video, etc.
5. Print material is often easier to deal with. Throp (2000) quotes research from Russ
   Brown of the University of Toronto that people will only wait 8 seconds for information
   to arrive via the web; 79% of user do not read every word; on-screen reading is 25%
   slower than print; and only 10% of users will scroll.
6. Material is often not easy to find—and most users just want to get what they want and
   don't want to be bothered with what they see as extraneous material (see Rajani and
   Rosenberg, 1999).
7. Motorola (and other companies) have found that it is the young people (18 to 30) who
   are most anti web-based training (see Westerbeck, 2000). It seems that young people

are less tolerant of the mechanistic irrelevances that characterise most web-based training.

8. Most e-learning has a solely individualistic, human capital focus and ignores the value of social interaction (and the development of social capital—see later in this paper).

Some commentators have suggested that the blended approach is the answer i.e. integrating e learning with existing training activity rather than replacing one with the other. This does not solve some of the fundamental problems mentioned above. In the SML approach we have worked differently. I will use the example of the MA in Organisation Design and Effectiveness at the Fielding Institute in California to show how the Internet can be used to support learning.

The kind of learning I am talking about is closest to what David McConnell (2000) describes as 'Computer Supported Cooperative Learning'. In this mode one is using the technology to assist a process of collaboration at a distance. In the Fielding example I used the standard SML structures of learning contract and learning group. The difference from most other programmes was that the groups worked mainly on-line and the course was driven by the learning contracts that participants wrote. (The course description is reproduced as an appendix in Cunningham, 1999).

My written introduction to the course was designed to help learners map out a territory and to make choices about what they wanted to learn. The learners were mostly senior managers or HR professionals working in companies around the world. The learning groups that people belonged to allowed learners to share ideas and support each other's learning, even though they were hundreds or even thousands of miles apart geographically. However, emotionally they became very close. The course I designed had no imposed content upon which people would be assessed. Given the earlier comments on the 'P to S' mode, the participants were helped to undertake a 'P' analysis, i.e. look at themselves, their work situation, their learning needs, etc., so that they could be clear about what 'S' capability they needed.

Participants were advised as to print material that they could acquire and they were directed to web sites if they asked for material that was best accessed via that route. In other words there was no predefined curriculum as per other SML programmes. What we used the technology for was to allow people to interact while being physically separated. There was no web-based training imposed in the way that most e learning is organised.

There are many advantages to working on-line including giving people more time to compose responses to questions and challenges (we never used on-line chat—this was all asynchronous). It also better accommodates people with disabilities. Clearly people with mobility and hearing problems find this mode a lot more convenient. I was also surprised to find that someone with a sight problem could use a speech translation facility and also therefore prefer this mode to face-to-face interaction.

There are many other issues that can be explored in relation to e learning. My sole objective here has been to show how the SML structures can be used in this context and how much they vary from the web-based training most commonly in use. As Staley and MacKenzie (2000) indicate, most trainers are still trapped in the 'S' before 'P' paradigm that I have already criticised. One re-assuring factor is the evidence of young people rejecting this and hence perhaps e learning can develop in a more responsive mode.

THE BASIS FOR SELF MANAGED LEARNING

The structural approach used in SML has not emerged by accident. The approach has been developed in response to significant research that is now available on how best to support learning in organisations. There are also clear theoretical bases for this approach. I will start with a brief review of some research evidence before turning to the theory. I want to make it plain here that when we started SML programmes in the 1970s we did not have all this evidence. We had some ideas and some experience that what we were experimenting with worked. Since those early days we have modified the design of programmes, in part in response to evaluation evidence. However the principles have not changed over time. In this section I will quote from a representative sample of credible research on development issues in organisations.

EVIDENCE FROM RESEARCH IN ORGANISATIONS

Coulson-Thomas (2001) summarises his research on corporate learning strategies as follows:

> 'Many trainers appear to "follow fads". They buy "off the shelf" learning resource packs, rather than assemble or create bespoke responses to specific situations and circumstances. They persuade senior management that all members of staff should receive some standard programme, regardless of individual interests and needs. Enormous sums of money are therefore spent exposing diverse people, working on very different activities, to common experiences that may have little relevance to their particular requirements and priorities.' (p. 28)

He goes on to criticise a range of general courses which he sees as ignoring business needs.

His research seemed to be focused on large companies and to respond to what in our research (Cunningham, 1999) we called the Bureaucratic approach to development. However we found three other types in our research. Firstly there were the *Apathetic/Antagonistic* organisations. These were often small organisations that did not invest in development in any structured way. They would have no development budget and in the worst cases they feared that if people developed they would leave the organisation. Hence they actively avoided providing development opportunities. Note here that I am referring to the management of such organisations and their view of learning. In reality people in these organisations did learn—because it is impossible to stop people learning.

The second kind of organisation we labelled *Reactive*, as they would react to requests for development support and might even have a development budget. But there was no planning involved. People went to conferences or courses or received coaching only if they asked or if their manager took a fancy to something that came in the mail.

The third kind of organisation we called *Strategic*. These were the minority (in our UK sample). They integrated learning and development into the organisation's strategic framework and supported widespread development activity. They only used training and education as one tactical piece in a wider strategic framework.

Our evidence is supported by the unique in-depth studies of Storey et al (Storey et al., 1991; Storey et al., 1997). Their comparative study of UK and Japanese managers showed how little impact training and education had in the development of managers, especially in Japan. However Japanese companies were more systematic in other aspects of development. Peter Wickens (someone with considerable experience of British and Japanese management) reviewed their 1997 book (Wickens, 1997) and pointed out how the most important factor in development was 'challenging assignments' but that in Japan this was managed strategically while in the UK it was more down to luck. However he did also refer to his judgment that there were dangers in the Japanese in-breeding of managers. Allowing for that he opined that a key lesson of the Storey et al research was that 'management development must be long term, not subject to fads and fashions.' (p. 54)

In identifying job-based development as the key, other research that confirms our own comes from Eraut et al (1997 and 1998) and Burgoyne and Reynolds (1997). Indeed what is fascinating in these studies is that they all confirm that training and education contribute around a maximum 10–20% of what makes a person effective at work. The research in the USA also confirms these figures (e.g. see Cohen and Prusak, 2001). Further we see that all the evidence suggests that a more strategic approach is necessary and one that assists people to draw on a wide range of development opportunities.

However, making it more strategic does not mean centralised control. The Storey et al research showed that personal responsibility for development was stronger in Japan than in the UK as was the role of the person's line manager. The importance of these two factors was also identified in the McCall et al. (1988) study in the USA. What is fascinating in looking over the research is how consistent it is and how little notice most managers and HR professionals take of it.

An Economist's Perspective

James Heckman and his colleagues at the University of Chicago have carried out an impressive array of rigorous research studies on education and training. Heckman's conclusions are unequivocal and totally convincing. They are best summarised in Heckman (1999). Here are some of the findings that are relevant to the issues in this chapter.

a) Human capital interventions in most countries over estimate the importance of developing cognitive abilities and underestimate non-cognitive capabilities such as social skills, self discipline etc (all of this is consonant with the evidence from the emotional intelligence research—see Goleman, 1998).
b) Formal education and training should not be at the centre of skill development processes. The education and training establishment have a vested interest in distorting the value of their products as against the influence of the family, the work place, etc. (His evidence for this and other conclusions is firmly rooted in rigorous economic research and not polemic.)
c) The preoccupation with achievement testing and measuring cognitive skills as the sole indicators of success is misguided.
d) It's important to break down 'the artificial separation between the world of work and the world of learning.' (p. 21)
e) Learners can make good judgments about their own learning needs and the key reason why educators and trainers do not believe this is based on prejudiced assumptions not supported by the research evidence.

f) Commenting on the US situation, he shows that increased expenditure by the state on standardised training provision is likely to be of low value. One (rare) example he shows of conspicuous success in adult training is a project which provides development support for so-called 'unskilled' adults. The project responds to each individual's needs and has used technicians from companies, and not trainers, to assist the learners.

Summary so Far

I could go on piling on the research evidence but I'll stop here. One reason for this is that I do not know of any credible research that points in the opposite direction to that indicated by the research studies already quoted. So until there is any it can't be sensible to keep in labouring what seems well founded.

The aspects of the research on learning in organisations that mostly affect thinking about using SML include:

1. Organisations need to take a long term, strategic stance on learning.
2. Strategies have to accommodate both the needs of the learner and the organisation—strategic learning does not mean centralised control but rather balances personal strategies with corporate strategies.
3. Learners are able to make judgments for themselves about what they need to learn—but they may need support to achieve their learning goals.
4. Most learning occurs in the workplace and may be supplemented by courses if the latter meet real defined needs that learners are committed to. However training led approaches, which assume that most learning is in formal settings, are unhelpful and should cease.
5. Good learning must allow for non-cognitive elements—it has to be legitimate for people to learn in these domains and to address issues of ethics, values and feelings.

RESEARCH ON SELF MANAGED LEARNING

Rigorous evaluation studies on Self Managed Learning programmes have been carried out on 1,789 people in the following organisations: Arun District Council, BBC, Birmingham City Council, British Airways, Cable and Wireless, Ericsson, Finland Post, NOP Research Group, PPP healthcare, Reigate and Bansted District Council, SOK (Finland), St Helier NHS Trust, Sainsbury's and Shell, as well as in a consortium programme for managers in Amersham, BP Anoco, Barclays, CT Bowring, EMI, Ladbroke Group, Norwich Union and Nycomed. This is not the sum total of all the evaluation studies but does cover the ones that I know have been independently and rigorously carried out. Nor is this the total of all the organisations that have used SML; most have not undertaken formal evaluation studies.

Chapters on the research in Arun District Council, Ericsson, Sainsbury's, the consortium programme and the work in Finland are in Cunningham et al., 2000. Other research studies are mentioned in Cunningham, 1999, as well as on the website www.selfmanagedlearning.org. It is difficult to summarise the research evidence as individuals learn so much and in so many different ways. Hence any interested reader is advised to consult the texts mentioned.

THEORY

In addition to considering empirical research evidence there are strong theoretical grounds for using SML. The best theories are, of course, underpinned by research but often such research is outside the domain of organisational working. However that need not invalidate it. I will summarise below some key areas of theory that seem important, though the treatment is not encyclopaedic and comprehensive but rather it is indicative of some major themes.

EDUCATION/LEARNING

There is an important strand of educational theory of which perhaps Gardner's (1983) notion of multiple intelligences is an exemplar. By challenging older views of intelligence Gardner most importantly provides the basis for valuing a wider range of capabilities than the educational establishment has traditionally given credit for. He also provides a basis for arguing against the vertical ranking beloved of educationalists. By 'vertical' I mean the placing of learners on a one-dimensional scale (see Figure 15.2), usually driven by marks or grades which do not identify the different qualities being judged. This is especially so when examination methods may emphasise linguistic intelligence, logical-mathematical intelligence and spatial intelligence to the detriment of any evaluation of, for instance, interpersonal intelligence or intrapersonal intelligence.

In Figure 15.2 I have juxtaposed the vertical grading model with a horizontal evaluation of capabilities that a person may offer. While this is an improvement on vertical grading it can still foster an unhelpful reductionism. Also it can still promote a measurement and quantification mode of thinking, with the concomitant danger of ignoring qualitative evidence. In Self Managed Learning programmes people have usually valued the notion that they can balance learning goals across what can be labelled 'hard' and 'soft' factors. So a person might want to improve their score on a 360-degree feedback exercise alongside developing self confidence, which they would assess qualitatively e.g. by asking colleagues how they come over.

This latter point has always been an important dimension of SML programmes. In the early days (the 1970s) we drew on the evidence we had then. Much of this came from experiences in schools and, even then, people such as Rogers (1969) in the USA could quote impressive studies in schools on the efficacy of learner-centred methods. Neill (1968) in the UK was a passionate advocate of what has been called 'free schools' and there is no doubting the success of his Summerhill School over nearly 80 years of its existence. At least I don't doubt it having studied the evidence (see Cunningham, 2000). Interestingly the British Government was forced to accept the case for the continued existence of Summerhill after it failed to close it down in 2000. Indeed the Government agreed to the legitimacy of Neill's educational philosophy in the unique ruling given by the Independent Schools Tribunal at the Summerhill trial.

EPISTEMOLOGY

As in the previous section, here is not the place to go into a detailed philosophical discussion. Rather I want just to allude to the impact of thinking about the status of knowledge

VERTICAL GRADING - MARKING

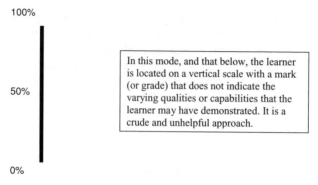

VERTICAL GRADING – GRADES (for example, in UK undergraduate degrees)

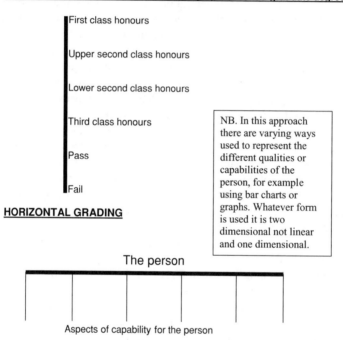

HORIZONTAL GRADING

FIGURE 15.2   Grading approaches

on Self Managed Learning practice. The main issue here is the problem that some trainers and educators argue for a received canon of knowledge that is required, for example in management. Hence business schools have a vested interest in arguing that their choice of subjects to teach constitutes an objectively required curriculum. Similarly the British Government has imposed a national curriculum on state schools on the basis that this is required knowledge for children. Gardner's theory challenges the latter assumption straight away, as does the research evidence quoted earlier, e.g. Heckman (1999).

As regards areas of adult learning, the assertion of an objectively right curriculum is in itself a subjective assertion. The available evidence does not support the business schools in their assumptions. Indeed many business school academics accept this (see Cunningham, 1999, for evidence on this). Also the research studies that I quoted earlier all point away from this objectivist position. Hence in SML programmes we see the value in helping learners to make their own judgments about what to learn since we see this as the only intellectually honest position to take.

Note that I am saying that we provide help. It isn't a question of a pendulum swing to reject all existing knowledge. Rather we find that the metaphor of mapping makes the most sense to people. If a person wants to be more effective at marketing they may want to know what the field of marketing has to offer in order for them to make an informed choice of what to learn. In the part-time SML MBA programme that we designed, experts from various disciplines appeared early in the programme so that participants could interrogate them about what their field offered. However in no sense was there any imposed teaching that was to be assessed. These sessions were purely to help participants make choices of what to pursue later in their programme.

HUMAN AND SOCIAL CAPITAL

There is now substantial evidence that an individualistic focus on human capital development in organisations is too limiting. The case for the development of social capital is becoming more important. As well as scholarly studies at the societal level (e.g. Fukuyama, 1999; Putnam, 1995; Coleman, 1988) there are now emerging equally important texts at the organisational level (Baker, 2000; Cohen and Prusak, 2001). Also, CEOs are starting to identify the need for social capital. Rolf Hüppi the CEO of Zurich Financial Services, has even co-authored a book on the subject (Hüppi and Seemann, 2001). Cohen and Prusak (2001) quote the following two definitions:

> 'The norms and social relationships embedded in social structures that enable people to coordinate action to achieve desired goals' (World Bank).
> 'Social capital refers to features of social organisations such as networks, norms and social trust that facilitate coordination and cooperation for mutual benefit' (Putnam, 1995).

And then they add their own definition:

> 'Social capital consists of the stock of active connections among people: the trust, mutual understanding and shared values and behaviours that bind the members of human networks and communities and make cooperative action possible.' (p. 4).

Most other definitions are similar, except that Hüppi and Seemann deny that trust is an essential part of social capital. The latter also have a neat turn of phrase in saying that 'human capital resides in the people; social capital resides in the relationships among them' (p. 3) and 'human capital represents ability, social capital the means to leverage it' (p. 28). What is interesting is that the authors of the various texts draw on a wide range of research and experience to show how essential the development of social capital is.

As an aside, it could be argued that these ideas are not new. The Organisation Development movement has made a similar case about the importance of social relationships and Burns and Stalker (1968) showed how organismic (or later called 'organic') organisations relied on informal relationships to make them effective. However what seems to be new is the stronger evidence now available for the value of social capital and the new language which links this concept to theories of intellectual capital and human capital.

One danger in social capital becoming a new fad is that we may get the usual pendulum swing—'social capital is the thing so let's ditch the development of human capital'. In SML we want to develop both. The Strategic Learning Contract may have more of a focus on the human capital dimension but even here the negotiation of it with one's peers (in a learning group) and one's manager ensures an organisational dimension to it. The learning group is, par excellence, a major way to develop social capital. Indeed in all the evaluation studies on SML programmes this factor gets high ratings.

When we come to measure business pay-off from SML it is often the social capital dimension that is the most important. People comment time and again on how they have achieved bottom line results through developing trusting relationships on SML programmes. People have, for instance, passed on business to colleagues that they would not have done before. Also Serpis's (2000) research in PPP healthcare indicates that the development of social capital, through almost all their senior managers participating in an SML programme, contributed significantly to the ease with which they managed two major mergers in a matter of months.

One quote from an evaluation report of a local government programme may add to these comments:

> 'The value and power of networking has been a particularly strong feature [of SML] with regard to changing the organisation culture. Many senior managers now choose to meet and discuss situations informally, with a view to resolving problems in a mutually agreed way. This is creating greater flexibility, and speed of response, and reducing unnecessary blocks and misunderstandings—a significant contribution to the devolution of power and accountability which the organisation is trying to encourage'. (Stella Jackson, Head of Management Development, London Borough of Lewisham.)

The two key structures which facilitate the growth of social capital are the learning group and the whole community of learners. This influence spills over into the whole organisation once a critical mass of people have taken part in SML programmes. For instance one company quoted that meetings now end on time (where they didn't before) because enough people have developed the cooperative habits that allow easier team working.

In relation to team working, it's worth noting that some commentators (e.g. Hüppi and Seemann) warn of the dangers of teams that close in on themselves as a result of misguided team building activity. For instance a team can go off together and establish a high degree of camaraderie through an outdoor development experience and as a result exclude others who are not members of their team. And if people take the sporting metaphor too far they start to see the role of their team as needing to compete with other teams in the same organisation. This undermines social capital development, as sharing across the organisation is inhibited. (See also Cunningham, 1994).

In SML we create learning groups with people from different parts of the organisation and we encourage the sharing of ideas and information across the whole learning community. Further the learning group is usually an excellent jumping off point for people to take their own learning out into their own teams. One Managing Director commented that it was so much easier to discuss mistakes and errors now that all his directors had learning contracts. Dialogue around mistakes could now focus on learning needs in a less defensive atmosphere than before.

WHY SML (AND RELATED APPROACHES) ARE NOT USED MORE

It is clear that those in power in the education and training establishment will not change their minds simply by having contradictory evidence quoted at them. Dixon (1976) has shown, from his psychological studies on military incompetence, that authoritarian personalities, for instance, are well shielded from rational argument or evidence that contradicts their prejudices. As he points out:

> 'It is a sad feature of authoritarian organisations that their nature inevitably mili-
> tates against the possibility of learning from experience, through the apportioning
> of blame. The reason is not hard to find. Since authoritarianism is itself the product
> of psychological defences, authoritarian organisations are past masters at deflecting
> blame. They do so by denial, by rationalisation, by making scapegoats, or by some
> mixture of the three.' (p. 43).

Hence the authoritarian HR department deals with the failures of its development strategy by denying that there is a problem; by producing reports which focus on input measures and happy sheets from courses and which avoid looking at outcomes; and by scapegoating trainers through firing one group of consultants and hiring another firm. Vaill (1996) makes a case, in his critique of what he calls 'institutional learning', for why we may be trapped in erroneous assumptions:

> 'The institutional learning model, to retain its power, needs to remain tacit in the
> learner's mind. It makes a lot of assumptions about what is good for the learner that
> a learner might well object to or want to renegotiate if given the opportunity. The
> institutional learning model is built in part on an implicit belief that learners should
> not bother with philosophical considerations about that model.' (p. 84).

He goes on to point out that people do not think through the implications of this model. Indeed they are discouraged from doing this. The institutional model is put forward as the only option for effective learning. Hence people do not realise that this model can be changed or indeed discarded.

Self Managed Learning takes, head on, Vaill's critique. Learners are encouraged to do precisely what the institutional model denies them. They are asked to think consciously about what they want to learn and how and to act on their reflections. They are helped to de-couple their assumptions about learning from the institutional model and are freed up to take charge of their own strategic learning.

CONCLUSION

Despite attempts to force learning on people, adults in organisations will actually choose what they learn. As Postman and Weingartner (1969) point out, learners will interpret any 'teaching' in terms of their own mental frameworks and existing patterns of thinking. Adults especially do not come to a course as tabula rasa; they already have values and ideals. If teaching perfectly transmitted everything from the teacher's brain to the learner's we would not have such wide variations in learning outcomes. As Postman and

Weingartner demonstrate, it is not what the teacher intends that is learned but what the learner chooses to make of it.

In that sense the self managing of learning is inevitable, but it can be highly ineffective and indeed dysfunctional if there is no support given to learners to work though what is useful to learn, and support in carrying it out. The amoral computer virus creators are excellent self managing learners in the techniques that they use, but they are evidence of the failure of the authorities (in schools and organisations) to assist people to learn in the full sense, with all the moral and ethical overtones that are essential for good learning.

Self Managed Learning is an approach that addresses these issues. By locating SML in the social context people have to dialogue with their colleagues in order to plan and implement their own learning activities. In this sense learners decide *for themselves* what and how they want to learn but they do not decide *by themselves.* This distinction is explored more fully in Kegan (1994), and it is an important one. Through the process of dialogue mere solipsistic, self-centred, solitary learning is avoided. Hence individual development in the organisation avoids the trap of being narrowly individualistic. In this sense it contributes to the development of human *and* social capital.

REFERENCES

Abbott, J. and Dahmus, S. (1992) Assessing the appropriateness of self-managed learning. *Journal of Management Development,* 11,1, 50–60.

Baker, W. (2000) *Achieving success through social capital*. San Francisco: Jossey-Bass.

Bennis, W. and Nanus, B. (1985) *Leaders: Strategies for taking charge*. New York: Harper and Row.

Brown, J. S. and Duguid, P. (1991) Organizational learning and communities-of-practice: towards a unified view of working, learning and innovation. *Organization Science*, 2, 1 (February) 40–57.

Burgoyne, J. and Reynolds, M. (Eds) (1997) *Management learning*. London: Sage.

Burns, T and Stalker, G. M. (1968) *The management of innovation* (2nd edn). London: Tavistock.

Cohen, D. and Prusak, L. (2001) *In good company*. Cambridge, Mass.: Harvard Business School Press.

Coleman, J. (1988) Social capital in the creation of human capital. *American Journal of Sociology*, 94, 95–120.

Coulson-Thomas, C. (2001) Entrepreneurship for organisational success. *Journal of Professional Human Resource Management*, January, 25–32.

Cunningham, I. (1994) Against team building. *Organisations and People*, 1, 1 (January) 13–15.

Cunningham, I. (1999) *The wisdom of strategic learning* (2nd edn). Aldershot, Hants: Gower.

Cunningham, I. (2000) (Ed.) *An independent inquiry into Summerhill School*. Brighton: Centre for Self Managed Learning (also available on the Centre's website: www.selfmanagedlearning.org).

Cunningham, I., Bennett, B. and Dawes, G. (2000) (Eds) *Self managed learning in action*. Aldershot, Hants: Gower.

de Geus, A. (1997) *The living company*. Cambridge, Mass.: Harvard Business School Press.

Dixon, N. (1976) *On the psychology of military incompetence*. London: Jonathan Cape.

Eraut, M., Alderton, J., Cole, G. and Senker, P. (1998) *Development of knowledge and skills in employment, Research Report No. 5*. University of Sussex Institute of Education.

Eraut, M. (1998) Learning in the workplace. *Training Officer*, 34, 6, (July/August), 172–4.

Frankola, K. (2000) Why online learners drop out (at www.workforce.com/feature/00/07/29/).

Fukuyama, F. (1999) *The great disruption*. London: Profile.

Galagan, P. A. (1993) The search for the poetry of work. *Training and Development*, (October) 33–7.

Gardner, H. (1983) *Frames of mind: The theory of multiple intelligences*. New York: Basic Books.

Goleman, D. (1998) *Working with Emotional Intelligence*. London: Bantam.

Heckman, J. J. (1999) *Policies to foster human capital*. Aaron Wildavsky Forum, University of California at Berkeley.

Hüppi, R. and Seemann, P. (2001) *Social capital: Securing competitive advantage in the new economy*. London: Financial Times Prentice Hall.

Kegan, R. (1994) *In over our heads: The mental demands of modern life*. Cambridge, Mass.: Harvard Business School Press.

McCall, M. W., Lombardo, M. M. and Morrison, A. M. (1988) *The lessons of experience*. Lexington: Lexington Books.

McConnell, D. (1999) *Implementing computer supported cooperative learning* (2nd edn). London: Kogan Page.

Mintzberg, H. (1992) MBA: Is the traditional model doomed? *Harvard Business Review*, November–December, 129.

Neill, A. S. (1968) *Summerhill*. London: Penguin.

Postman, N. and Weingartner, C. (1969) *Teaching as a subversive activity*. London: Penguin.

Putnam, R. (1995) Bowling alone: America's declining social capital. *Journal of Democracy*, 6, 1, 65–78.

Rajani, R. and Rosenberg, D. (1999) Usable?... or not?... Factors affecting the usability of web sites, (at www.december.com/cmc/mag/1999/jan/rakros.html).

Rogers, C. R. (1969) *Freedom to learn*. Columbus, Ohio: Charles. E. Merrill (NB a second edition appeared in 1983)

Serpis, R., Aspinall, M. and Shorrick, R. (2000) Organisational change through Self Managed Learning—the case of PPP. In Cunningham, I., Bennett, B. and Dawes, G. (Eds) *Self Managed Learning in action*. Aldershot, Hants: Gower.

Staley, A. and MacKenzie, N. (2000) Enabling curriculum re-design through asynchronous learning networks. *Journal of Asynchronous Learning Networks*, 4, 1 (June) 1–14.

Storey, J., Okazaki-Ward, L., Gow, I., Edwards, P. K. and Sissons, K. (1991) Managerial careers and management development: A comparative analysis of Britain and Japan. *Human Resource Management Journal*, 1,3 (Spring) 33–57.

Storey, J., Edwards, P. K. and Sissons, K. (1997) *Managers in the making: careers, development and control in corporate Britain and Japan*. London: Sage.

Throp, N. (2000) Superhighway 61 revisited. *People Management*, 20 July, 49.

Vaill, P. B. (1996) *Learning as a way of being*. San Francisco: Jossey-Bass.

Van der Sluis, E. C. and Hoeksema, L. H. (2001) The palette of management development. *Journal of Management Development*, 20, 2, 1–8.

Westerbeck, T. (2000) Interview with Bill Wiggenhorn, Motorola. (at www.academyonlinee.com/corp_ed/index.htm).

Wickens, P. (1997) Study reveals fickle fate of British management. *People Management*, 28 August, 53–4.

CHAPTER 16

Using Social Networks in Organisations to Facilitate Individual Development

Rob F. Poell and **Ferd J. Van der Krogt**
University of Nijmegen, The Netherlands

SUMMARY

This chapter addresses the question how social networks in various organisational contexts create learning programmes for individual employee development. On the basis of an actor-network approach, four models are proposed for learning programme creation in social networks: a contractual, a regulated, an organic, and a collegiate model. The chapter then relates these different types of learning programme to the prevailing work and learning contexts in which they take place. It is concluded that these contexts have a powerful impact, but that learning networks have their own dynamics as well. Employees as learners, with their specific context interpretations and action strategies, should therefore be considered key to learning-programme creation. The chapter concludes by specifying directions for future research.

INTRODUCTION

This chapter focuses on the way in which individual professional development is organised in the context of work and organisation. Social networks in organisations (e.g., learning groups comprising various actors) play a crucial role in the creation of learning programmes. Key questions for the chapter are how such networks of actors organise learning programmes for employees and how this process is related to the way in which work is organised.

Individual Differences and Development in Organisations. Edited by Michael Pearn.
© 2002 John Wiley & Sons, Ltd.

The chapter firstly presents a conceptual model linking learning-programme creation to social networks and their work contexts. Secondly, the process of learning-programme creation is elaborated upon, comprising such core processes as orientation, learning and optimising, and continuation. Four ideal types of learning programme are distinguished that learning groups can organise: contractual, regulated, organic, and collegiate learning programmes. They provide various mixes of informal and formal learning activities, both on and off the workplace. The way in which the three core processes of the learning programme are conducted differs strongly among these four types, as does the way in which the learning groups organise themselves. Thirdly, the various types of learning programme that learning groups can organise are related to the context in which this process occurs.

The chapter intends to show that social networks can organise learning programmes in a broad variety of ways, depending on how the learning groups organise themselves. Although learning-programme creation is related to the work context, it is certainly not determined by it. Learning also has its own dynamics, which is why learners themselves should be considered core actors in learning-programme creation.

A BRIEF OUTLINE OF THE ACTOR-NETWORK APPROACH

Individual professional development is here viewed as a process of learning-programme creation for employees by social networks in an organisation. The learning-network theory places great emphasis on networks of actors, who form learning groups and create learning programmes with each other (Van der Krogt, 1998; Poell, Chivers, Van der Krogt and Wildemeersch, 2000). Relevant actors are workers, managers, HRD professionals, trade unions, workers' associations, external training providers, and so forth. These actors can organise the process of learning-programme creation in very different ways. It is a process that takes place in the context of the organisation. Over the course of time, various employee training and learning activities have been conducted in the organisation, thus gradually developing into a learning structure. The learning network in every organisation can be characterised by a content and organisational structure, material learning conditions, and a learning climate. This learning structure provides the starting point for actors to undertake new learning activities. They form a learning group together and carry out activities to create a learning programme. Figure 16.1 summarises how a social network of actors create a learning programme in the context of work and learning structure.

As Figure 16.1 indicates, work and existing learning structures both influence the process of learning-programme creation, but actors can individually and collectively exercise their impact on learning programmes as well. This is all the more important since actors give their own (or joint) specific interpretations to their context of work and learning structure. In other words, to a certain extent the existing context leaves room for the actors to act according to their own views and interests.

The complicated nature of the relationship between learning programmes and their context can be expressed in the basic assumption that learning programmes in organisations have a multiple character. Learning programmes are a reflection both of the context (including the work) and of the learning group (the specific set of actors). Furthermore, learning programmes are partly also a reflection of all separate actors making their own

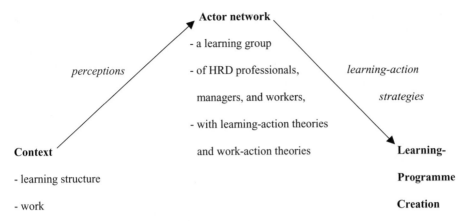

FIGURE 16.1   Learning-programme creation by a social network of actors in its context.

specific contributions to creating the learning programme. To summarise, three factors influence the content and organisation of learning programmes:

1. The context of work and learning structure, and their perception and interpretation by the actors.
2. The views, opinions, action theories, and interests of the separate actors.
3. The creation process by the learning group, producing the specific character of the actor network through the learning-action strategies employed.

We will elaborate on the specific relationships between learning programmes and their contexts in the final part of this chapter. It is firstly intended in the following section to describe the various ways in which social networks can organise different types of learning programmes.

LEARNING-PROGRAMME CREATION: FOUR IDEAL TYPES

Groups within organisations have multiple ways available to create various types of learning programme. Before turning to this diversity, however, we briefly outline three phases that can be distinguished in the creation of every learning programme: the orientation phase, the learning and optimising phase, and the continuation phase (see Poell & Van der Krogt, forthcoming, for a more detailed description).

1. **The orientation phase: from idea to learning contract.** A learning programme begins with an idea that an actor has, to learn about a particular theme with a group. The orientation phase is mainly about getting those involved interested in learning systematically about that theme *(mobilising the actors)* and developing a well-informed plan of action to which they will be willing and able to commit themselves *(analysing the learning theme)*. The team members express what they expect from each other *(drawing up a learning contract)* and make arrangements about the conditions that are necessary to execute the learning programme and to achieve the results they are aiming for *(contextualising the learning programme)*.
2. **The learning and optimising phase: from learning contract to learning results.** During the learning phase, the actors elaborate upon the ideas about the learning

programme that they have developed during the orientation phase. This core phase essentially involves the execution and optimisation of the learning programme. During the execution of the programme, the actors learn about a theme related to their work *(learning in interaction)*. They learn also, however, about the organisation of their learning programme Continual attempts are made to learn from experiences and in doing so to improve the learning programme *(quality control)*.

3. **The continuation phase: from result to permanent effects.** Learning does not come to a halt once the programme has ended; it is a continuous activity. That is why following-up on those activities is of crucial importance. Learning programmes are followed-up in two ways. Firstly, the group members resume their own individual learning paths *(giving them fresh impetus)*. Secondly, on the basis of experience gained during the leaning programme, the organisation can learn to set up and execute new learning programmes *(improving its learning system)*.

It is important to note that in practice not all three phases are necessarily conducted in a highly systematic manner. The core activities of each phase may be less structured in an actual learning programme. They do, however, provide leads as to how learning can be made more systematic.

In the following, we distinguish four ideal models, by which we mean theoretically based, different types of learning programme. We will present the characteristics of: 1) the *liberal, contractual* learning programme; 2) the *vertical, regulated* learning programme; 3) the *horizontal, organic* learning programme; and 4) the *external, collegiate* learning programme. This typology has been derived from Van der Krogt (1998) and Poell (1998). The four learning-programme types provide various mixes of informal and formal learning activities, both on and off the workplace. The way in which the three core processes within the learning programme are conducted differs strongly among these four types, as does the way in which the learning groups organise themselves.

THE LIBERAL CONTRACTUAL LEARNING PROGRAMME

The individual responsibility of the members themselves is central to the liberal, contractual learning programme. They draw up their own programme of learning activities, more explicitly than normally, and utilise the opportunities that the broader framework of the learning group offers them. The individual participants negotiate with each other and with their superior about the programme. A contract is agreed setting out in particular arrangements about the results that are expected, as well as arrangements concerning facilities (such as time, money, and support). Individual participants can call each other to account over whether or not they achieve the expected learning results and with regard to the support that they have agreed to offer each other in their efforts.

This liberal, contractual type of learning programme draws heavily on the self-directed learning ability of the individual group members (Brookfield, 1986). The group context is used to facilitate and enrich the individual learning processes of each member, for which they take their own responsibility (Candy, 1991). Our liberal learning model, however, puts more emphasis on optimisation and continuation than these authors do.

TABLE 16.1 Four ideal types of learning programme

	Liberal, contractual learning programme	Vertical, regulated learning programme	Horizontal, organic learning programme	External, collegiate learning programme
ORIENTATION PHASE				
Mobilising the actors	Learner involves supervisor, superior, and possibly colleagues in own learning plans	Educator and line manager involve expected trainees and experts in planning	Learning group involves all interested parties in provisional problem definition	Professional involves fellow members of profession in learning plans
Analysing the learning theme	Learner familiarises himself with theme with help of supervisor	Educator translates elements of organisation's policy into learning theme	Learning group determines provisional delineation of learning theme	Professional group translates new developments into learning offer
Contextualising the learning programme	Learner ensures involvement/ support of superior and customer	Educator and superior ensure that programme fits within organisation's policy	Learning group ensures all interested parties actively support its mission	Professional ensures that management creates conditions for professionalisa-tion
Drafting a learning contract	Learner lays down arrangements about learning programme, support and output with superior and colleagues	Participants in learning group undertake to attend meetings and action planning	Learning group members assume moral obligations towards each other to work on the problem	Professional agrees with fellow members of profession on participation in learning programme
LEARNING PHASE Executing the learning programme				
Learning in learning situations	Learner solves problems in work independently; private study; individual experiments	Learning group participates in course-based activities off and on the job; manager as workplace trainer	Relatively autonomous learning team works together on defining and solving complex work-related problem	Professional translates new insights from professional domain into own working situation and methods

continues overleaf

TABLE 16.1   (*continued*)

	Liberal, contractual learning programme	Vertical, regulated learning programme	Horizontal, organic learning programme	External, collegiate learning programme
Learning-programme co-ordination	Learner devises programme in consultation with superior	Educator devises learning programme and ensures transfer promoting measures	Learning group develops series of activities while learning	Professional group devises learning programme for professionals
Learning-programme guidance	Supervisor advises learner about approach at his initiative	Educator translates problem and requirements into 'tailor-made' learning programme	Supervisor advises learning group based on progressing insight into work problem	Fellow practitioners help professional to apply new insights in own work

Optimising the learning programme

Tuning to learning views	Learner himself ensures that programme remains tied-in with own learning conceptions	Educator ensures learning programme is attuned to learning style of participants	Learning group reflects continually on own learning conceptions and adjusts them if necessary	Professional group assumes in learning programme that professional is a reflective practitioner
Tuning to work views	Learner himself ensures that programme remains tied-in with own work conceptions	Educator ensures programme is attuned to participants' learning needs; superior monitors this	Learning group reflects continually on own work conceptions and adapts them to progressing insight	Professional group builds in learning programme on work theories deemed to be held by professional
Improving work relevance	Learner himself ensures that programme remains tied-in with developments in work	Educator translates relevant developments in work into learning programme	Learning group continually adapts work problem to new insights	Professional group translates relevant new insights from professional domain into learning programme

TABLE 16.1 *(continued)*

	Liberal, contractual learning programme	Vertical, regulated learning programme	Horizontal, organic learning programme	External, collegiate learning programme
CONTINUATION PHASE				
Resuming one's individual learning path	Learner examines with superior if learning result has been achieved and if learning facilities are used better than previously	Educator takes transfer promoting measures and ensures that participants take part in action planning	Learning group examines extent to which each individual participant has improved ability to solve work problems together in a learning team	Professional reflects with fellow practitioners if introduction of innovative methodology in own work goes better than previously
Improving the learning system of the organisation	Learner examines with superior extent to which liberal learning approach has been refined	Educator assesses whether planning approach and learning group's influence on it worked well	Common reflection on course of process offers insight into learning results via organic approach	Professional examines extent to which organisation enabled innovation to take place

Orientation phase

- *Mobilising the actors.* The initiative for this learning programme comes from the individual employee, who may involve a number of colleagues in his/her learning plans, but who in any case makes arrangements with his/her superior and with a supervisor about the form and substance of the learning programme.
- *Analysing the learning theme.* Once again it is the individual learners who familiarise themselves with the central theme; in doing so they can call in help from the supervisor, who functions as a sort of 'learning broker'. Individual participants in the learning programme try to reach agreement over group activities that each member can use for the improvement of his/her own expertise.
- *Contextualising the learning programme.* The individual learners must ensure the involvement and support of their superior and of their colleagues. In the existing learning and work system, the customer often occupies an important position too; there will be a desire to involve the customer in the learning programme in one way or another (e.g. in trying out particular improvements and in evaluating the results).
- *Drafting a learning contract.* Individual learners lay down the details of the arrangements that they have agreed with each other and with their superior in a contract; it deals with the substance of the learning programme and the support that will be given. The character of the learning contract is that of a contract of exchange: the aim is to seek parity between input and learning results for the various parties involved. The

superior makes time and money available to the employees, in exchange for certain results. The input and results that are expected from each individual are set out in the contract.

Learning and optimising phase

- *Execution: learning in learning situations.* The nature of learning activities is also tied to the actual opportunities that individual learners are able to create for themselves. The learning employee conducts private study and experiments in practice in order to solve problems at work independently. In doing so he/she receives coaching from the superior, the supervisor and/or fellow learners who are wrestling with the same problem.
- *Execution: learning-programme co-ordination.* The co-ordination of the learning programme is in the hands of individual employees themselves. In consultation with their superior and the supervisor, they draw up a programme of learning activities tailored to their own situation, in order to achieve the agreed learning results together.
- *Execution: learning-programme guidance.* A supervisor advises individual learners about the possible approach to and substance of the learning programme; this happens in most cases at the initiative of the participant in the learning programme.
- *Optimising: tuning to learning views.* The individual learning employee ensures that the learning programme continues to correspond with his/her own learning conceptions and opportunities. That is fairly simple, because that individual has the most say over the learning activities that he/she undertakes. Furthermore, arrangements will have been made in this connection with the management and with the supervisor.
- *Optimising: tuning to work views.* The above also applies with respect to taking account of conceptions about work. The learners themselves can ensure that the programme continues to tie in with their own work conceptions and expertise, because they themselves are responsible for the learning programme activities that they undertake. In consultation with their superior and the supervisor, they can alter the content of the learning programme if they develop new knowledge, skills, and views about their work during the course of the programme.
- *Optimising: improving work relevance.* The individual learner is expected to ensure that the programme continues to tie in with relevant developments that occur at work. The learning employees themselves monitor the direction in which their work is developing and take the initiative to undertake the necessary learning activities to keep up with such developments. The promotion of the expertise of individuals is closely tied to reacting to these changes because they are important for the 'employability' and labour market value of those employees.

Continuation phase

- *Resuming the individual learning path.* At the end of the learning programme, individual learners, together with each other and their superior, examine whether the results set out in the learning contract have been achieved, i.e. whether they have obtained new abilities and thereby expanded their range of capabilities. The participants themselves examine the extent to which they are now better able to tackle their work-related problems than they were previously, using the existing learning facilities and working together with others to this end on an exchange basis.

- *Improving the learning system of the organisation.* Together and with the superior, the learners examine what undergoing the learning programme has added to the existing learning system. Has the existing learning approach been refined or optimised? Is there now more emphasis than there was previously upon individual responsibility, self evaluation, and on using the facilities available to learners? Are customers more often involved in the learning of members of the organisation?

THE VERTICAL REGULATED LEARNING PROGRAMME

In the vertical, regulated learning programme, educators and other experts, in consultation with line managers, play a crucial role in the preparation, execution, and evaluation of the activities of the learning group. Much value is attached to careful planning on the basis of policy intentions and requirements analyses. That is carried out by the educator and the experts beforehand, who allow themselves to be influenced in their planning by the possibilities and wishes of the learning employees.

This vertical, regulated type of learning programme fits very well within the training-for-impact approach taken by Robinson and Robinson (1989) and the ideas about structured on-the-job training of Jacobs and Jones (1995). Basically, this means a highly pre-structured way to organise formal off-the-job learning supplemented with transfer enhancing measures (Broad & Newstrom, 1992). Our vertical learning model, however, views learning and transfer activities as part of one coherent learning programme rather than to emphasise the gaps between formal training by the educator and on-the-job application by the employees.

Orientation phase

- *Mobilising the actors.* The educator is often asked by a higher tier of management to organise a learning programme for a group of employees that ties in with particular policy developments or organisational changes. The leader involves a number of those expected to follow the course, their direct superior, and possibly an expert on the particular subject, in devising a plan for the learning programme.
- *Analysing learning themes.* In consultation with experts on particular subjects, the educator translates the relevant elements of the organisation's policy into a learning theme and a design for a learning programme. Express account is taken of capabilities developed previously by the target group that relate to the theme in question and to how they can be built upon.
- *Contextualising the learning programme:* The educator has the job of ensuring that the learning programme fits within the organisation's policy, that it contributes to achieving the changes in work and organisation that it is aiming for. Furthermore, the department where the learning programme is organised must offer the necessary scope for transfer promoting measures, so that the activities of the learning group do not take place in a vacuum. For that reason, the educator must closely involve the direct superior and a representative of the participating group in setting up (and executing) the learning programme.
- *Drafting a learning contract.* Participants in the learning group undertake to attend meetings of the learning programme group and take part in planning its activities. During the sessions, they agree how they will go about applying their new knowledge and skills in the workplace in between meetings of the group proper. To this end, the educator develops such things as handbooks and job-aids beforehand.

Learning and optimising phase

- *Execution: learning in learning situations.* The learning group takes part in courses, designed by the educator, both at the workplace and elsewhere. The educator and superior arrange the working situation in such a way that the participants are able to put into practice what they have learned and agreed in the learning group. The superior acts as an instructor for members of the learning group. Workplace learning forms an important part of this phase.
- *Execution: learning-programme co-ordination.* Programme co-ordination is a task for the educator, who puts together the learning programme and ensures transfer promoting measures are in place before, during, and after the core activities of the learning group.
- *Execution: learning-programme guidance.* Learning path supervision is also a task of the educator, who has translated the central problem and the needs of the participants into a tailor-made learning programme. The superior in the workplace also suggests particular learning activities.
- *Optimising: tuning to learning views.* The educator ensures that the learning programme is attuned to the learning style of the participants in the learning group. That was also focussed on during the orientation phase. During the learning phase, the educator monitors whether the activities correspond sufficiently with the manner in which the participants normally learn. If necessary, the learning programme will be adjusted.
- *Optimising: tuning to work views.* The educator ensures that the learning programme meets the learning requirements of the participants. Those learning requirements will have been examined during the orientation phase. During the learning phase, the educator closely monitors the extent to which the learning programme activities meet those learning requirements, and if necessary will adjust the programme.
- *Optimising: improving work relevance.* This will also have been examined by the educator during the orientation phase. Relevant developments in work and organisation are accommodated into the learning programme, which deals with the necessary capabilities. During the learning phase, the educator should assess the extent to which the learning activities contribute to the acquisition of the required capabilities, in view of those changes. That will also be monitored by the superior.

Continuation phase

- *Resuming the individual learning path.* By taking the applicable transfer promoting measures and motivating participants in the learning group to action planning, the educator and the line manager can ensure that the learners are gradually, but in a structured fashion, able to follow their own learning paths.
- *Improving the learning system of the organisation.* Together with the employees, the educator evaluates whether planning the approach of the learning programme has produced better results than normal. Did the learning group participants have sufficient opportunities to influence the content of the learning programme beforehand and afterwards? Did the educator take proper account of the learning style and learning requirements of the employees in setting up the programme? Was the teaching role of the superior actually realised?

The Horizontal Organic Learning Programme

In the horizontal, organic learning programme, learners work together as a relatively autonomous team, assisted by a process supervisor, in solving complex work-related problems to which there is no standard approach. The members of the learning group often have an extremely diverse range of expertise that must be gathered together in order to devise new creative ideas or solutions. If superiors are involved, they operate in a relationship of equality with the learners or function (in part) as process supervisors. Working as a team in an organic way towards a common product, with a joint mission and aim, is crucial in this respect. This organic method of learning may well be very similar to the participants' everyday work, but in the context of a learning programme those participants are more consciously occupied than they usually would be with making that learning explicit.

This horizontal, organic type of learning programme finds inspiration in the early work on organisational learning by Argyris and Schön (1978). It gained great popularity in the 1990s through the ideas around learning organisations (Senge, 1990). The most recent reference point for this type of learning can be found in literature on communities of practice (Wenger, 1998). While all these authors focus on integrating learning with daily work, our horizontal learning model emphasises also the potential use of collaborative every-day problem solving as a learning opportunity.

Orientation phase

- *Mobilising the actors.* As soon as the realisation arises that there is a complex work-related problem that requires specific learning-attention, the learning group works out which parties have an interest in this and identify those within the organisation who have expertise that can be used. They are involved in formulating a provisional definition of the problem with which the learning group can begin its task.
- *Analysing learning themes.* The members of the learning group determine the provisional delineation of the learning theme. The central problem is examined from the perspective of each individual's expertise, with the specific goal of coming to a common point of view on the most important elements of the problem.
- *Contextualising the learning programme.* The learning group ensures that all of the interested parties are actively involved in the learning programme. Those with an interest in solving the problem and/or who have expertise to contribute must participate in the learning programme, or support its progress in another (more indirect) fashion. The common mission of the team must be able to count on support from the organisation.
- *Drafting a learning contract.* There is no learning contract in a tangible sense, as during the orientation phase the learning group does not usually know how exactly the problem is to be tackled, and it will have at most an idea of what the essential aspects are that require attention. The participants undertake moral obligations to work with each other towards solving the core problem. They may of course put down a number of specific intentions in writing, but as this sort of learning programme is difficult to plan, it is the obligation on everyone to participate that is crucial.

Learning and optimising phase

- *Execution: learning in learning situations.* The programme essentially involves working together as a relatively autonomous team towards the definition and solution of the central problem. During the course of the programme, attempts to grasp the work-related problem will lead to a redefinition of what the group is actually doing until a workable formulation of the problem is reached, which they can tackle together using their combined expertise. The learning group will make progress by continually experimenting with provisional solutions in its work and analysing those experiences together. Education and training may also form part of the programme, if the learning group takes the initiative to call in extra expertise on a particular subject.
- *Execution: learning-programme co-ordination.* Programme co-ordination is a task for the learning group itself; while learning from it own experiences, the group develops a series of connected activities. However, that takes place in an incremental fashion, i.e. on the basis of a progressing insight into what the actual problem is and how it can be tackled.
- *Execution: learning-programme guidance.* In most cases the supervisor is not an expert on a particular subject, but advises the learning group about the possible next steps in their learning process, on the basis of a progressing insight into the work-related problem with which they are occupied. The supervisor assists the group in reflecting upon its experiments and learning experiences and in the selection of its following steps. Individual group members also involve themselves in the learning processes of others, by stimulating them and supporting them in their efforts.
- *Optimising: tuning to learning views.* With the assistance of the process supervisor, the learning group continually reflects upon its own learning conceptions. If it emerges that the chosen learning strategy is not leading to new insights into the problem, the learning group will adjust its common approach. In such learning programmes it is not unusual for this to happen a number of times, because continual adjustment is an integral part of the learning programme.
- *Optimising: tuning to work views.* The above also applies with respect to substantive refinement (to the needs of the programme group members). During the programme, the learning group continually reflects upon its own work conceptions that are related to the problem and applies them on the basis of progressing insight. The learning programme in fact essentially involves the members learning from each others' expertise and creating together new work theories that are suited to tackling the problem at issue.
- *Optimising: improving work relevance.* The learning group ensures work relevance by continuously adjusting the definition of the work-related problem in the light of new insights that they develop together along the way. The programme members' learning and improvements in their work go hand-in-hand and influence each other continuously.

Continuation phase

- *Resuming the individual learning path.* In these learning programmes, everyday learning and working are closely related: the learning in question actually takes the form of solving work-related problems. What the participants do is not all that different to what they would do outside a learning programme, but they do pay more explicit attention to the learning results of the team. To be able to follow their own 'normal' learning paths, it is important that the members of the learning group work out the extent to which they as individuals have improved their abilities to work towards a common team solution, to learn around one particular theme, and to call in the help of the process supervisor in doing so. They must also determine to what extent they have obtained a clearer insight into what one can learn as an individual within a relatively autonomous team.

- *Improving the learning system of the organisation.* Group reflection, with the assistance of a process supervisor, can also generate insights that are useful for optimising the learning system of the organisation. To what extent have the team members improved their abilities to learn from each other in the context of an organic group? And in what respect(s) in particular? How for example did the process of defining and redefining the core problem proceed? Which steps can be distinguished afterwards in approaching and solving the problem? When and why did the most creative experiments and most insightful breakthroughs occur during the programme?

THE EXTERNAL COLLEGIATE LEARNING PROGRAMME

In the external, collegiate learning programme, a learning group of professionals allows itself to be inspired by innovative insights and new methodologies developed within their own professional branch but outside their own individual organisations. The participants often come from several professional organisations and together with fellow professionals they familiarise themselves with professional knowledge, insights, norms, and codes that apply within their own professions. Through the learning programme, they adjust their manner of working in the light of new, scientifically based techniques, that institutions for continuing education pass on to members of their profession.

In this external, collegiate type of learning programme it is assumed that professionals are reflective learners (Schön, 1983), who need to continually develop their expertise within their professional peer group (Daley, 1999). Our external learning model focuses, somewhat more than the continuing professional development literature does, on the appropriation by professionals of new scientific methods to be incorporated in their daily work routine.

Orientation phase

- *Mobilising the actors.* Professionals are stimulated by their profession to keep up-to-date with the professional literature and to take the initiative in maintaining their professional skills. Together with other professionals, often from other institutions, they accept a learning offer from their professional association and prepare their working environment to work in accordance with a new methodology. The professionals inform their superiors of their learning plans.
- *Analysing the learning theme.* The professional group is responsible for translating new professional insights and developing a learning offer. The professionals occupy themselves with adjusting their work to the new insights that they have gained during the learning programme, that programme having been devised elsewhere.
- *Contextualising the learning programme.* The professionals ensure that their management creates opportunities to participate in a professionalisation programme. They also make contact with fellow practitioners outside their own organisations in order to

co-ordinate their own programme activities with the approach that is prevalent in the professional group as a whole.

- *Drafting a learning contract.* The professionals agree to participate in a learning programme with a number of fellow members of their profession. They agree to meet the requirements that the institution offering the learning programme sets for its completion, while they also agree to make themselves proficient in the new methodology and to attune their method of working to it.

Learning and optimising phase

- *Execution: learning in learning situations.* The professionals translate new scientific insights from their professional group into their own working situations and methods, assisted by techniques and materials developed within the professional group.
- *Execution: learning-programme co-ordination.* Programme co-ordination takes place outside the individual organisation, within the professional group. The latter group actually devises the learning programme in which the professionals participate and ensures that they adjust their manner of working to the new insights that they gain.
- *Execution: learning-programme guidance.* The professional group helps the practitioners to apply new insights in their own work. Peer consultation is one tool to enable individual professionals to co-ordinate their new methods of working with what their fellow professionals are doing.
- *Optimising: tuning to learning views.* The professional group assumes that professionals behave as reflective practitioners in the learning programme. It is therefore assumed that their previous professional training enables them to assess (and if necessary, adjust) their learning conceptions. The specific learning culture that prevails within the group plays an important role in such continuing education.
- *Optimising: tuning to work views.* The professional group tailors the programme to its requirements by building upon the working theories deemed to be held by the professionals. Those ideas, which they obtained previously during their extensive professional education, should find expression in their present range of responsibilities and methodologies. The new learning programme should tie in with that.
- *Optimising: improving work relevance.* The work relevance of the programme is also a concern of the professional group. Work relevance is ensured by translating recent scientific research and theories into new working methodologies and the connected offer of continuing education. The professional group also assesses whether its members are succeeding in bringing their own working practices sufficiently into line with the new professional requirements.

Continuation phase

- *Resuming the individual learning path.* Professionals should obtain continuing education in order to continue to be able to comply with the applicable professional norms. That means that they must constantly be adjusting their manner of working in view of innovative insights. The learning programme must enable them to follow their daily learning paths as reflective practitioners. During the continuation phase, it is therefore of great importance to reflect upon the approach taken to the learning programme, particularly with respect to the question of the extent to which the members have improved their abilities, together with professionals from outside their own organi-sations, to translate insights from their professional domain into their own working methodologies.

- *Improving the learning system of the organisation.* The main task of the individual organisation is to offer the professional the essential conditions to participate in pro-moting expertise within the professional group and to adjust his/her own working methodologies on that basis. However, the largest part of the learning system is, from the perspective of the professionals, located outside their own organisations. There-fore, it is very important for them to reflect upon the extent to which their professional group enables them to make the new working methodology their own. Giving feed-back to training and further education institutions, but also to fellow practitioners, about experiences with new working methodologies in practice, can be an important mechanism for optimising the quality of the learning system. Within the individual organisation, it is a question of how far the professionals are enabled to introduce innovations, new impulses from outside, into their own work.

SUMMARY OF THE FOUR MODELS

Table 16.1 provides an overview of the orientation, learning and optimising, and contin-uation phases in each of the four learning-programme types. The sort of activities that participants in the learning programmes carry out in the three phases are the same in all four models, but the specific way in which they are elaborated differs widely from model to model. In the *liberal* model, the individual learners are the dominant actors. They maintain exchange-relationships with their superior and the supervisor; they also involve others in shaping their own learning programme, in as far as it can enrich their own learning paths. In the *vertical* model, the educator and superiors are the dominant actors; they devise the learning programme for the programme group, in the context of strictly regulated relationships with the management and representatives of the employ-ees. In the *horizontal* model, the learning programme group, a relatively autonomous group, is dominant. All of the parties involved work in relationships of equality to-wards solving complex work-related problems. On their way they create the learning programme organically and learn in the group context. Finally, in the *external* model learning programme, the dominant actor is the professional group outside the individual organisation; professional and collegiate relationships prevail. The learning programme largely takes place elsewhere. Following it, professionals from various organisations adjust their working methodologies to their newly gained insights.

LEARNING-PROGRAMME CREATION IN DIFFERENT CONTEXTS

In the above, we have described four different ways in which social networks (i.e., learning groups) can organise themselves to create work-related learning programmes. As alluded to earlier (cf. Figure 16.1), this process of learning-programme creation by an actor network is influenced to a certain extent by the context in which it takes place. In the final part of this chapter, we will elaborate on this idea by relating the various learning-programme types that learning groups can organise to the existing work and learning structure in which they occur.

As the previous section has described in full detail, four ideal types of learning programme can be distinguished, that is, four different ways for actors to form a learning group and create a learning programme. Furthermore, the actor-network approach distinguishes four types of context, namely four types of work (cf. Mintzberg, 1989) and four corresponding learning structures. These will be described in the following two paragraphs.

Four Types of Work in Organisations

1. *Individual work.* Individual work is characterised by individuals performing ill-structured but not too complex jobs. Individual autonomy of employees to prepare, conduct, and evaluate their own work activities is high. Think, for example, of the kind of work performed by a real estate agent in a partnership.
2. *Task work.* Task work is characterised by extensive task division and little complexity. Employees carry out the work programmes that have been laid out for them by staff departments. Line management is in charge of monitoring performance and evaluating outputs. This type of work is conducted, for instance, by counter clerks in a savings bank.
3. *Group work.* Group work features highly complex and ill-structured group tasks for which there are no standardised procedures. This work type represents complex problem solving in an incremental fashion by combining the expertise of participants with different backgrounds. It is carried out, for example, by new product developers working in an IT firm.
4. *Professional work.* Professional work has highly complex but reasonably well defined jobs. Professional associations outside the organisation have developed standardised protocols to deal with a limited number of relatively well defined problems. The professional diagnoses the situation and applies the right procedure to deal with the problem. Think, for instance, of the kind of work that medical doctors conduct in a hospital.

Four Types of Learning Structure in Organisations

1. *A liberal learning structure.* In organisations with a liberal learning structure, individual employees are in charge of their own professional development. They negotiate with their superiors about facilities and expected outputs, with educators about development opportunities and individual guidance, and with colleagues about mutually beneficial learning activities they could conduct together. This is a loosely coupled, relatively unstructured learning structure that expects individuals to deal with their own work problems.
2. *A vertical learning structure.* Organisations with a vertical learning structure have a regulated system to train and develop their employees, in which the learning is very much task oriented. Usually there is a central training department in charge of organising off-the-job training and on-the-job instruction, sometimes delegated to line management. Employees participate in programmes that have been designed for them by training professionals.
3. *A horizontal learning structure.* In organisations with a horizontal learning structure, work and learning are largely integrated in the complex problem solving activities

TABLE 16.2 Similarities and discrepancies between learning programmes and contexts

Contexts (Work and Learning Structure)	Learning Programmes			
	Contractual, Individually oriented	Regulated, Task oriented	Organic, Problem oriented	Collegiate, Methodically oriented
Individual work, Liberal learning structure	X	?	?	?
Task work, Vertical learning structure	?	X	?	?
Group work, Horizontal learning structure	?	?	X	?
Professional work, External learning structure	?	?	?	X

conducted by groups of employees. It is an egalitarian structure with superiors acting as co-learners and educators as process counsellors. Learning is highly problem and organisation oriented.

4. *An external learning structure.* Organisations with an external learning structure draw on continuing development programmes organised by the professional associations of their employees. Learning is externally inspired by new methods and protocols developed within the profession. Professionals, in their respective organisations, have to adapt their work to incorporate the latest professional insights in their repertoire.

SIMILARITIES AND DISCREPANCIES BETWEEN LEARNING PROGRAMMES AND THEIR CONTEXTS

The expected relationships between contexts (work and learning structure) and learning programmes are summarised in the matrix presented in Table 16.2. Contexts are listed from top to bottom, learning programmes from left to right. Contractual, individually oriented learning programmes are expected in a context of individual work and a liberal learning structure. Regulated, task oriented learning programmes are presumed to take place in a context of task work and a vertical learning structure. Organic, problem oriented learning programmes are considered to occur in a context of group work and a horizontal learning structure. Collegiate, methodically oriented learning programmes are expected in a context of professional work with an external learning structure. The x-marks on the diagonal indicate the learning programmes that correspond, theoretically at least, with their context. In these learning programmes actors act according to the context (the existing work and learning structure). The question-marked combinations off the diagonal refer to discrepancies, that is, learning programmes exhibiting characteristics that do not correspond with their context.

Social networks can organise learning programmes for professional development in a variety of ways, more or less corresponding to the existing context of work and learning structure. The context offers, but also limits, the possibilities to create such learning programmes. However, like Figure 16.1 showed, learning groups also produce their own dynamics, since actors develop their own action patterns together. Thus learning groups and programmes come into being that are specific to the particular set of actors and exhibit discrepancies with the context.

Thus, the actor-network approach shows how similarities as well as discrepancies between work and learning programmes can be expected. Work is influential, but actors can individually and collectively leave their mark on the learning programmes that they co-organise. They give their own (joint) specific interpretation to work and learning structures. Moreover, the context is not all-determining and leaves room for the actors to act according to their own views and interests. This is the organisational choice that actors can exert, up to a certain extent.

CONCLUSION

In this chapter, we have presented an actor-network approach to the issue of individual professional development. We have shown how social networks (i.e., learning groups comprised of various actors) can organise learning programmes in many ways, depending on the way in which they organise themselves. Three phases have been introduced for learning groups to organise learning programmes systematically: orientation, learning and optimising, and continuation. Four types of learning programme have been introduced in large detail: the contractual, individually-oriented type; the regulated, task-oriented type; the organic, problem-oriented type; and the collegiate, methodically-oriented type of learning programme. We have indicated how the process of learning-programme creation is related to the context in which it takes place, but that it is not completely determined by it. Work and existing learning structures can have a powerful impact, but social networks such as learning groups can have their own dynamics as well. Learners themselves should, therefore, be considered core actors in any process of learning-programme creation, with their specific context interpretations and action strategies.

The use of the actor-network approach to study the process of learning programme creation has been demonstrated by Van der Krogt (1998) and Poell (1998), including practical cases of the models presented. It has also been applied in the context of workplace training (Harris, Simons & Bone, 2000), project learning (Pluijmen, 2001), and public administration (Mick, 2001). The models can first of all be used to analyse, describe and explain the process of learning programme creation in organisational contexts (Poell, Chivers, Van der Krogt & Wildemeersch, 2000). Moreover, they can provide educators, learners and managers with ideas and alternatives to create learning programmes in their own organisational practice (e.g., Pluijmen, 2001).

We should like to conclude this chapter by presenting two promising directions for future theoretical and empirical research work in this area. Firstly, the relationships between work and learning programmes; secondly, the theme of collaborative learning. We will briefly elaborate on these topics and connect our own ideas to a number of promising other theoretical approaches.

The relation between work and learning programmes is an important theme also in the action learning literature. "Action learning . . . assumes that people learn most effectively when working on real-time problems that occur in their own work setting. Action learning is grounded in the writings of Reg Revans (1971), who theorized that learning results from the interaction between programmed instruction of the type found in coursework (primarily theoretical or explicit knowledge) and the spontaneous questioning that arises from the interpretation of experience (primarily tacit knowledge)." (DeFilippi, 2001, pp. 5–6). In other words, learning can be achieved by reflection but certainly also by action, by doing. These assumptions are very much in line with the approach described in this chapter, as are similar ideas about action learning by Marsick and O'Neil (1999) and by Mumford (1997). Learning programme creation in our view, however, should be based also on the principle that various work contexts offer different learning opportunities. Comparative research into learning programmes in different work contexts could, therefore, focus on the various opportunities of employees to participate in work experiments and gain broad experience.

The topic of social relationships among actors is tackled also in studies of collaborative learning (Sharan & Sharan, 1992; Peterson & Myer, 1995; Gasen & Preece, 1996; Kolmos, 1996). Our approach to learning programme creation pays attention to the positions and roles of the learners themselves, in relationship to the positions and roles of other actors in the learning group. We view the learners as crucial actors, who co-create the contexts in which they learn. Many other approaches, however, put the primary focus on the HRD professional (e.g., McLagan, 1989; Torraco & Swanson, 1995) or on the management (e.g., Nonaka & Takeuchi, 1995; Watkins, Ellinger, & Valentine, 1999) rather than on the learners themselves. Moreover, in our view it is crucial to take into account the diversity in positions and roles of learners. Some other approaches have a tendency to focus solely on organic learning groups, for instance, communities of practice (Wenger, 1998). Organisational practice, however, is still characterised by many more hierarchical, loosely coupled, and professional learning networks, which should also remain an object of investigation. Descriptive and explanatory studies of learning programme creation by social networks in a variety of contexts will greatly enrich our understanding of the possibilities and limitations of such learning networks.

REFERENCES

Argyris, C., & Schön, D. A. (1978). *Organizational learning: A theory of action perspective.* Reading, MA: Addison-Wesley.

Broad, M. L., & Newstrom, J. W. (1992). *Transfer of training: Action-packed strategies to ensure high pay-off from training investments.* San Francisco: Addison-Wesley.

Brookfield, S. D. (1986). *Understanding and facilitating adult learning: A comprehensive analysis of principles and effective practices.* San Francisco: Jossey-Bass.

Candy, P. C. (1991). *Self-direction for lifelong learning: A comprehensive guide to theory and practice.* San Francisco: Jossey-Bass.

Daley, B. J. (1999). Novice to expert: An exploration of how professionals learn. *Adult Education Quarterly, 49*(4), 133–147.

DeFillippi, R. J. (2001). Introduction: Project-based learning, reflective practices and learning outcomes. *Management Learning, 32*(1), 5–10.

Gasen, J. B., & Preece, J. (1996). Collaborative team projects: Key issues for effective learning. *Journal of Educational Technology Systems, 24*(4), 381–394.

Harris, R., Simons, M., & Bone, J. (2000). *More than meets the eye? Rethinking the role of the workplace trainer.* Leabrook: Australian National Training Authority/NCVER.

Kolmos, A. (1996). Reflections on project work and problem-based learning. *European Journal of Engineering Education, 21*(2), 141–148.

Mick, T. D. (2001). *Minority and women entrepreneurs contracting with the federal government.* PhD dissertation, University of Missouri at Kansas City.

Jacobs, R. L., & Jones, M. J. (1995). *Structured on-the-job training: Unleashing employee expertise in the workplace*. San Francisco: Berrett-Koehler.

Marsick, V. J., & O'Neil, J. (1999). The many faces of action learning. *Management Learning, 30*(2), 159–176.

Mintzberg, H. (1989). *Mintzberg on management: Inside our strange world of organizations*. New York: Free Press.

Mumford, A. (Ed.). (1997). *Action learning at work*. Aldershot: Gower.

Peterson, S. E., & Myer, R. A. (1995). The use of collaborative project-based learning in counselor education. *Counselor Education and Supervision, 35*(2), 150–158.

Pluijmen, R. (2001). Learning-action strategies of project managers in a collaborative learning program: An action research project into the learning activities of project managers. In O. A. Aliaga (Ed.), *Exploring the frontiers of Human Resource Development* (pp. 1092–1096). Minneapolis: University of Minnesota.

Poell, R. F. (1998). *Organizing work-related learning projects: A network approach*. PhD dissertation, University of Nijmegen.

Poell, R. F., Chivers, G. E., Van der Krogt, F. J., & Wildemeersch, D. A. (2000). Learning-network theory: Organizing the dynamic relationships between learning and work. *Management Learning, 31*(1), 25–49.

Poell, R. F., & Van der Krogt, F. J. (forthcoming). Project-based learning in organizations: Towards a methodology for learning in groups. *Manuscript submitted for publication.*

Revans, R. W. (1971). *Developing effective managers: A new approach to business education*. New York: Praeger.

Robinson, D. G., & Robinson, J. C. (1989). *Training for impact: How to link training to business needs and measure the results*. San Francisco: Jossey-Bass.

Schön, D. A. (1983). *The reflective practitioner: How professionals think in action*. London: Temple Smith.

Senge, P. M. (1990). *The fifth discipline: The art and practice of the learning organization*. London: Century Business.

Sharan, Y., & Sharan, S. (1992). *Expanding cooperative learning through group investigation*. New York: Teachers College, Columbia University.

Torraco, R. J., & Swanson, R. A. (1995). The strategic roles of human resource development. *Human Resource Planning, 18*(4), 10–21.

Van der Krogt, F. J. (1998). Learning network theory: The tension between learning systems and work systems in organizations. *Human Resource Development Quarterly, 9*(2), 157–177.

Watkins, K. E., Ellinger, A. D., & Valentine, T. (1999). Understanding support for innovation in a large-scale change effort: The manager-as-instructor approach. *Human Resource Development Quarterly, 10*(1), 63–78.

Wenger, E. (1998). *Communities of practice: Learning, meaning, and identity*. Cambridge, MA: University Press.

CHAPTER 17

Online Networking and Individual Development

Gilly Salmon
Open University

SUMMARY

This chapter explores the enormous potential benefits that online networking can add to individual development. It offers four approaches for using networked technologies for development in the future. It reviews and explores what is known to date of the significance of working online. Based on extensive personal experience, gained along with the growth of the Internet for teaching and learning, Gilly Salmon explains how working together online, suitably and carefully supported, offers special benefits and hazards. The chapter offers a well rehearsed and practical 5–step model of development through online networking, together with examples of its application.

INTRODUCTION

Knowledge construction, transmission and learning have been studied throughout the centuries. We now have wonderful opportunities to offer the experience of learning with others through electronic opportunities. The online and e-learning phenomenon is striking at the heart of well-rehearsed and well-loved teaching and learning methods. Four main models are emerging:

Model: 1 T-learning: Information Transmission. Technology can be used mainly as a delivery system. Applications and systems include Content Management Systems,

Individual Differences and Development in Organisations. Edited by Michael Pearn.
© 2002 John Wiley & Sons, Ltd.

multi media, industry standards, DVDs, digital and cable TV. The associated pedagogy is that of the transmission model of teaching, where information is transferred from experts to novices. Content is king. Economies of scale are reached through reduced interaction between teachers and learners. In this model online trainers support the content expert, to develop multimedia programmes and to build online libraries and pathways through resources. T-learning offers the potential for individual development it's learners are focussed, independent and self-motivated.

Model 2: I-learning: Instant and Integrated Learning. A second model, the one most commonly called e-learning is mainly computer based courses, offered from desks at work or in learning centres. Learners work and learn almost simultaneously. Flexibility and 'instantness' are the keywords. Individual learners assess the value of the learning experience asking: is this learning just for me, just in time, just for now and just enough? Employers consider whether learning provision helps to recruit the right people for the organisation. They evaluate the fast delivery of learning by considering the extent to which employee and organisational performance improves. In this model, online trainers support autonomous learning (although many learners exist magically on little human contact to sustain them). Online trainers focus on skills development in employees (to enable them to learn in this way) and on ways of fostering the adoption of a strong in-house knowledge culture. Individual development in this model occurs if learners are able to identify and integrate their individual and organisational needs. They will need to be excellent time managers and comfortable with successfully managing, work, personal and learning time and space.

Model 3: M-learning: Mobile learning. A third model is based on the growth of mobile technologies. Portable learning will reflect mobile working lives. Main technologies in use will be Personal Digital Assistants (PDA) and Palm tops and 3rd generation mobile phones (UMTS together with national and international communications network networks). All students will need laptops, palm tops, text mobiles and access to e-books. Learning devices will be carried or worn. Pedagogy is various so individuals choose based on their cognitive preferences and styles. Development activities and content will be broken down into tiny components that can be transmitted and studied in small chunks. Learners will need to focus on taking ownership the learning process, active learning, independence, the ability to make judgements, self-motivation and a high level of autonomy.

Model 4: N-Learning: networked learning. The fourth model is built around learning communities and interaction, extending access beyond the bounds of time and space, but offering the promise of efficiency and widening access. The key technology is Internet and WWW to allow immediate and satisfying interaction between developers, supporters and learners and between learners and learners. Applications and systems are asynchronous and synchronous group systems to support a wide variety of environments for working and learning together. Both co-located and remotely-located learning communities (clicks *and* mortar) are of key importance. Learners connect through both low and high bandwidth devices and systems. Hence the technologies are seen only as mediating devices, promoting creativity and collaboration. The pedagogy is based on notions of a very strong social context for learning with the model of acquisition, argumentation and application. The roles of reflection (an essential tool of expert learners), personal and professional development, and the sharing of tacit knowledge are of critical importance.

Learning is contextualized and given authenticity by the learning group and the learning community. On and offline resources are important, but electronic and structured information support and stimulate the learning group rather than replace the active, participative learning experience. I consider that this model has the most to offer individual development in organisations. Hence most of this chapter explores its potential and what is already known about how to operate it successfully.

ONLINE NETWORKING FOR DEVELOPMENT

Networking enables people to work across terrestrial boundaries and cultures on a global scale. Concepts of space and time are changing. Working and learning with others who happen to live in a particular locale may become much less important than finding shared professional and personal interests in online environments. Communities of linked collaborators are forming, with many relationships based on common interests rather than place and some are started through informal and chance encounters.

Online networking can be viewed, as a new *context* not just as a tool. This context can be seen as not only mediating the communication but also shaping it. The lack of the traditional hierarchies and online networking's capability to support synthesis of ideas especially supports the constructive approach to knowledge generation (Long, Pence et al., 1995; Phillips, 1995). Networking with others through computer mediation enables the sharing and assimilation of a wide range of experiences. This knowledge is often informal, tacit and continuously developing. Networkers create knowledge for themselves through dynamic online processes. You need a knowledge manager and facilitator (I call them e-moderators) to keep the ideas flowing and to summarise the discussion. Online learners can explore information rather than accepting what the trainer determines should be learnt. They construct knowledge for themselves in this way, through interacting online with peers, usually with guidance.

Networking learning should appeal to all learners and not only the technologically competent and keen. Can you really achieve full-scale collaboration across a distributed corporation? So far, many learners have been just a little disappointed. There are few shining examples. Quality and standards are under debate. Why? The paradox is that whilst interacting through the Internet on a global scale, learners of the 21st Century also want to work more individually, to search and find the information they need and to interact with whom they want from where they happen to be.

Blumer's (1969) view of action learning is of people involved in directing their actions, individually and collectively, around shared understandings of their world. Each carry cultural, philosophical, physical and psychological luggage and shape their learning experiences to meet ends associated with these. It is important that we understand the great value of action learning and how to transfer it into the e-learning world. The aspect of meeting online with colleagues, sharing views and receiving support is a fantastic opportunity for e-learning (Preece, 2000). It is critically important that it does not get submerged and diverted into producing realms of written words, or even highly visual interactive software. The chief benefit of interactive networking for learning is the joy of learning online together.

How Online Networking Works

Online networking through bulletin boards (sometimes called conferencing) works like a series of notice boards each with a title and purpose. Participants can have 24-hour access to the system. Connections for the computers can be part of Local Area Networks, e.g. linking the computers in a department, campus, region or country or they can be connected to the network through the use of a modem and telephone line. The asynchronous nature of online networking is a particular characteristic of the medium. It enables individuals and groups of people to carry on "conversations" and "discussion" over the computer networks based on the written word (Salmon, 2000). Users can log-on from any location and at any time using a computer on campus, at home or in the place of work. The benefits therefore include the convenience of more choice over when to participate. Online networking is non-intrusive compared to face to face conversations or the telephone since the receivers of messages can choose when to access them (Rudy, 1995).

Information sharing through online networking takes various forms and especially encourages the surfacing of tacit, personal and experiential understandings. Caldwell asserts the main advantage of online networking as the reduction of "distance—physically, socially and temporally" (Caldwell and Robertson, 1996, p. 1). Online networking enables large groups of people or selected sub-groups with common interests or purposes to communicate. However, conversely, an individual can receive "attention" that does not occupy group time and users do not need permission to "talk" (McComb, 1993).

A New Context for Development

Online networking involves a hybrid of previously familiar communication. It has some of the elements of writing and its associated thinking and publishing but it also resembles more transient verbal discussion (Mason, 1993). The discursive style lies somewhere between the formality of the written word and the informality of the spoken (Ferrara, Brunner et al., 1991; Rasmussen, Bang et al., 1991). Symbolic emotive messages have been developed to compensate for the lack of non-verbal cues. Some users abbreviate sentences and do not worry about spelling or grammar and all but develop a separate language code for online working (Mason, 1993). The social and contextual cues that regulate and influence group behaviour are largely missing or can be invented during the life of the conference. A major shift can be observed from trainers to learners as the locus of authority and control this change of focus accelerates rapidly as learners become more competent and confident (Salmon, 2000). Face to face identities become less important and the usual discriminators such as race, age and gender are less apparent. Previously existing hierarchies and relationships change and fade (Mason, 1993). It is easier to leave the conference unseen and unembarrassed than is possible with a face to face and synchronous situations (Nixon and Salmon 1996).

Learners' ultimate use and appreciation of online networking does not appear to depend on previous computer literacy and it often appeals to inexperienced computer users (Nipper, 1989). Programmes of study aiming at a spirit of wide access and openness are therefore well served (Mason, 1994).

All relationships and sense of community are based on some degree of commonality-shared space, time, language, and culture or experience (Steele, 1996). The narrower the areas of commonality, the simpler is the task of establishing that particular community (Steele, 1996). Assimilation depends on intensity of exposure, continuity of interaction, competition for attention, and participants' commitment and past experience. The search for relationships and for association with others is a key feature of human behaviour and provides the foundation for an individual's sense of "self" and self-worth (Maslow, 1943). Previously, barriers imposed by space and time limited the available arenas for groups to come together and develop communities. Online networking's interactive capability has a profound implication not only for individuals but the future of working in groups (Steele, 1996). There are endless possibilities for combining and regroupings and hence there is a potential for great diversity. Individuals have great potential for establishment of personal identity within a number of different groupings.

USING ONLINE NETWORKING FOR DEVELOPMENT

Compared to face-to-face group training, for example, networked learning is readily available, and does not require participants to travel to a certain place. If you do not try and emulate synchronous communication (as in the training room) then you'll have the benefit of time as well as place. Many users find that the time lags involved between logging on and taking part, encourages them to consider and think about the experiences they are receiving before replying, rather more than they would in a class situation. Participants can ask questions without waiting in turn. Because of these characteristics, rather different relationships—usually based on shared interests or support—can develop compared to those between learners or trainers who meet face-to-face. Although many people find the lack of visual clues strange, messages are 'neutral' since you cannot see whether the sender is young or old nor need to consider their appearance or race. This characteristic tends to favour minorities of every kind and encourages everyone to 'be himself or herself'. Of course as online courses include more pictures, as they certainly will, this situation may change again. Meanwhile with text based conferencing it is possible to 'rewind' a conversation, to pick out threads and make very direct links. Therefore online discussions have a more permanent feel and are subject to reworking in a way more transient verbal conversation cannot be. This means that the online networked medium is good for giving praise and constructive critiques.

LEARNING AT WORK THROUGH AND WITH OTHERS

Whilst interacting with more global societies, businesses and networks, people are also be able to work more individually, to search and find the information they want and need and to interact with whom they want from where they wish (Dede and Palumbo, 1991). There is a prospect of "unparalleled expression of individual preferences without undue penalty in time or effort" (Steele, 1996, p. 282–3). Online networking offers great opportunities to enable individuals to seek personal relevance whilst learning globally. Thus for the individual, life is becoming richer, more finely structured, more multidimensional, but with greater potential for fragmentation and chaos (Steele, 1996). Changes in the processing and use of information may lead to new personal senses of "reality" and ultimately affect the way humans think (Benjamin, 1994). Steele suggests that a key feature of such changes will be a focus on "smaller events" (Steele, 1996, p. 261) as

Information and Communication Technologies (ICT) will work like a microscope which enable the control of smaller "units of account" but in huge number (Davis, 1997).

Online education is becoming part of the new "info-business" industry (Taylor, 1995). A range of new modes of learning is emerging together with the need for rapid updating of skills and knowledge. Predictions include global learning communication networks and institutions and the ability of students to buy components of their courses from whoever and wherever they wish. Learning resources are becoming more portable, visual and interactive and participative.

Another outcome from widescale networking is proceeding rapidly across the skills for work areas. In the future, the work force must become more adaptive, technical, able to solve problems, able to use intelligent networks and powerful computing capacity. These constitute basic skills, akin to reading and writing (Prahalad, 1996). In addition, the current generation of adults faces a situation, throughout its working life, where it has to train and retrain to respond to constantly changing working environments. Therefore, the distinction between "work" and "learning" is starting to blur.

Some account is being taken by organisations of the need to educate employees for working in more global and networked business environments. Spender emphasises the importance for management education of the "collective aspects of . . . knowledge and practice" which he considers neglected in contrast to the much more individualised scientific-rational management knowledge. He re-conceptualises teamwork as a "community of practice" (Spender, 1994).

Recently, there has been a rise in the number of "corporate universities". The intentions of corporate universities are to provide continuous employee development and enhanced job performance related to problem solving for a specific company's mission or industrial context, often as part of change programmes. Many corporate universities are investing extremely heavily in sophisticated technology and suggest that they can provide learning that is not only relevant but also "online/on-time" (Salmon, 2001)

UNDERLYING CONCEPTUAL MODELS FOR ONLINE DEVELOPMENT

Approaches to teaching based on the scientific objectivist paradigm assume that knowledge about the world can be modelled, mapped and transmitted to the learner, and that the goal of the student is to acquire this reality. Knowledge is seen as externally determined and transmittable from teacher to student, using devices such as books or lectures as a "mirror" of the external world. The role of the learner is to hear or read about a topic and replicate the content and structure of this understanding (Jonassen, 1991). Students' attention may be drawn to issues and their interpretations may be tolerated although the teacher will be the arbitrator (Hendry, 1996). Therefore, the role of the learner is characterised by listening or receiving objective knowledge, with the teacher as the story teller and the learner being persuaded by the use of rewards to acquire it in a replicable form. This concept of teaching is usually appreciated as an efficient and effective way of transmitting information. Understandings of teaching and learning associated with this paradigm have been dominated by cognitive psychology (Jonassen, Davidson et al., 1995).

Another view is of knowledge as *constructed* by individuals in their internal mental worlds (Bruffee, 1993; Oliver and Reeves, 1996). From this, two hypotheses emerge.

One is that knowledge is actively constructed by an individual (Lerman, 1989) through making "sense of material" and through experiences (Kelly, 1955; Rogers, 1993). Personal and unique maps of the world are constructed in an individual's mind and these internal compositions define reality for that person (Jonassen, Davidson et al., 1995). Learning is seen as an active process on the part of the learner, resulting in the changing of these maps of understanding. The second hypothesis is that "coming to know" and the constant adaptation of the constructed maps is achieved through interaction with a community of teachers and peers. These concepts echo Dewey's original view that learning takes place through personal inquiry and that education is a continuing reconstruction of experience (Dworkin, 1959).

The constructivist view, therefore, is of the learner participating in and interacting with the learning environment and with others and learning through a social and dialogical process in which communities of practitioners negotiate their own meanings. This learning paradigm suggests that learning is context-dependent, i.e. "what is learned (the meaning that is constructed by the learner) is indexed by the experience surrounding the learning" (Jonassen, Davidson et al., 1995) p. 9). From this perspective, knowledge is based on the learners' experience and is *not* more or less true, but more or less informed (Guba and Lincoln, 1994). Learning is associated with combining personal experiences with theory especially with the collaboration of teachers and other students (Mezirow, 1996). At its extreme, assessment is based on measuring how effective the learners' knowledge structure is in facilitating thinking or problem solving rather than mastery of "content" (Cunningham, 1992).

Increasingly, thinkers and practitioners in the field of the exploitation of ICTs in teaching are leaning towards constructivism. Eisenstadt challenges the traditional paradigms of teaching, especially when deploying new media:

> "Knowledge is an emergent property which transcends the fixed-size-and-space concepts of media and information, just as it transcends the notion that you can impart it to students by "filling" them up from the teacher's "vessel" . . . knowledge is a dynamic process, a vibrant living thing resting on shared assumptions, beliefs, complex perceptions, sophisticated yet sometimes crazy logic, and the ability to go beyond the information given. "Knowledge" is . . . what people communicate to one another. "Content" is not." (Eisenstadt 1995) p. vi).

Constructivism acknowledges that students *do* learn in taught sessions, that pedagogy can influence the learning environment both positively and negatively but that teaching and learning is accomplished mostly through "talk" (Catt and Eke, 1995). Personal information assimilation has to happen but this is part of the process of "making new and individualised acts of knowing" (Rogers, 1993, p. 200). When teaching environments are constructed on such principles and when a student is confronted with new knowledge, the learner's intentions, previous experiences, preferred learning styles and strategies are *all* elements in determining what becomes of the knowledge.

Although these two views are often presented in the literature as dichotomies, i.e. objective versus constructed knowledge, cognitive learning theories versus eclectic constructivist concepts, their role in underlying instructional design for online learning can be approached in the manner of a continuum, all of which is valuable depending on teaching and learning purposes. This could be seen as especially true when elements of ICTs are involved in providing the construction of an environment that is neither "real world" nor removed from it and that mediate between the learner and some concept of knowledge.

Traditionally, universities offer opportunities for the learning of formalised, scientific knowledge (Grey, Knights et al., 1996). However, where the learning impacts on practice, such as in the education of managers or professionals, a constructivist view may underlie teaching approaches, and learning with peers and practitioners may be important. Lave and Wenger describe how apprenticeships include collaboration as a key way of learning professional practice (Lave and Wenger, 1991). This form of knowledge is often informal, tacit and continuously developing. Knowledge and practice gradually become internalised and ultimately result in the learner supporting and helping his or her own peers (Vygotsky, 1978). Therefore, the role of the learning provider within this model is the "process of exchange of this knowledge, acting as reflective participants in communities of peers" (Lewis, 1996 p. 1). The community and learning environment includes tutors and peers and where ICTs are involved, the software and the design of the programme.

SCAFFOLDING: A MODEL OF ONLINE DEVELOPMENT

Figure 17.1 offers a model of teaching and learning online, researched and developed with business school students over several years, but since applied to corporate training and across many learning disciplines and contexts (Salmon, 2000). The 5-step model provides an example of how an individual can benefit from increasing skill and comfort in working and networking online.

First let me summarise the model, before going into detail. I choose to call all learners, in networked, online and e-learning, "participants" and their trainers, facilitators or teachers, "e-moderators". These words illustrate the different roles that each adopt online compared to face to face teaching and learning situations. Individual access and the ability of participants to use networked learning are essential prerequisites for conference participation (stage one, at the base of the flights of steps). Stage two involves individual participants establishing their online identities and then finding others with whom to interact. At stage three, participants give information relevant to the course to each other. Up to and including stage three, a form of co-operation occurs, i.e. support for each person's goals. At stage four, course-related group discussions occur and the interaction becomes more collaborative. The communication depends on the establishment of common understandings. At stage five, participants look for more benefits from the system to help them achieve personal goals, explore how to integrate networked learning into other forms of learning and reflect on the learning processes.

Each stage requires participants to master certain technical skills (shown in the bottom left of each step). Each stage calls for different e-moderating skills (shown on the right top of each step). The "interactivity bar" running along the right of the flight of steps suggests the intensity of interactivity that you can expect between the participants at each stage. At first, at stage one, they interact only with one or two others. After stage two, the numbers of others with whom they interact, and the frequency, gradually increases, although stage five often results in a return to more individual pursuits.

Given appropriate technical support, e-moderation and a purpose for taking part in online networking nearly all participants will progress through these stages of use in

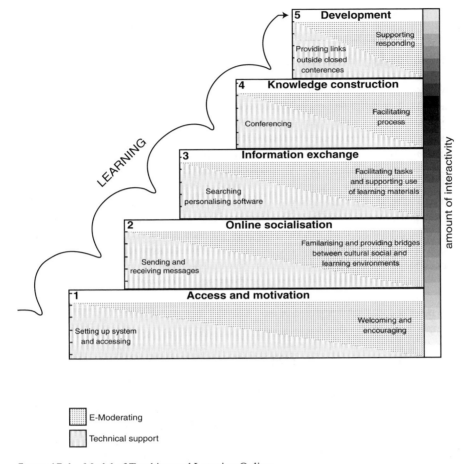

FIGURE 17.1 Model of Teaching and Learning Online

networked learning. There will however be very different responses to how much time they need at each stage before progressing. The model applies to all networked learning software but if experienced participants are introduced to new-to-them networked learning software, they will tend to linger for a while at stages one or two, but then move on quite rapidly up the steps again.

The chief benefit of using the model to design development processes with networked learning is that there is prior knowledge how individuals are likely to exploit the system at each stage and you can avoid common pitfalls. The results should be higher participation rates and increased student satisfaction. E-moderators who understand the model and apply it should enjoy networked learning and find that their work runs smoothly. But let me go into more detail about the stages of the model. If suitable technical and e-moderating help is given to participants at each stage of the model, they are more likely to move up through the stages, to arrive comfortably and happily at stages three-five. These stages are the ones that are more productive and constructive for development purposes.

Scaffolding suggests a way of structuring this interaction and collaboration, starting with "recruitment" of interest, establishing and maintaining an orientation towards task relevant goals, highlighting critical features that might be overlooked, demonstrating how to achieve those goals and helping to control frustration (Wood and Wood, 1996).

CATERING FOR INDIVIDUAL TASTES

Dewar and Whittington explored the relevance of Myers-Briggs Type Indicators to help understand how different personalities interact in online learning situations (Dewar and Whittington, 2000). It may be a comfort to developers to know that similar learning styles manifest themselves in online environments compared to face to face environments. The exception is along the extravert/introvert continiuum, where introverts are *more* at home online (compared to face to face) but extraverts find online appealing for different reasons.

Honey and Mumford suggest that participants use a mixture of active, practical, theoretical and reflective learning (Honey and Mumford, 1986): Activists, as they call their first category, tend to learn best when they are dealing with new problems and experiences. These learners need to have a range of different activities to keep them engaged, and the ability to 'hold the floor' (or in this context, the conference . . .) and to be able to 'bounce ideas' off of others, all of which networked learning caters for extremely well. Pragmatists, on the other hand, need to be able to see an obvious link between what they are learning and problems or opportunities with which they are engaged in their work. They must become fully engaged in the learning process. They tend to want an immediate opportunity to try out what they have learnt in order to evaluate its practical use and value. In designing networked learning, pragmatists can be catered for through activities. Honey and Mumford's theorists need sufficient time to explore the links between ideas and situations. As the asynchronous nature of networked learning builds in a time delay and, with structure and encouragement, the exploration can occur. The high level of peer interaction in networked learning should appeal to theorists, although they are likely to be the first to cry 'it's all rubbish' if topics are not dealt with in depth. Good structure and archiving are important, so they can work in appropriate conferences with serious topics. E-moderators should, as always, encourage questioning, probing and exploring.

Honey and Mumford's reflectors probably benefit most from networked learning opportunities. They engage with the learning task with time to think deeply about the concepts and activities, and to give considered responses that synchronicity and conventional classrooms rarely allow. Activists and pragmatists frequently behave online as if they were extrovert personalities, while the theorists and reflectors have more introverted styles.

Online design of interactive activities (e-tivities) should be planned accordingly. In particular, a clear mixture of engagement in immediately relevant activities, and the opportunity to reflect on online experiences are both important. Activities can either be entirely online, begun face-to-face and extended online, or prepared for online and continued face-to-face. An array of tasks can be provided and groups can be split into smaller learning sets. Such variations are likely to meet a wide variety of learning styles and preferences.

THE ROLES OF THE E-MODERATOR TO SUPPORT DEVELOPMENT

The theme from instructor to facilitator appears in nearly all literature about networking for learning and development (with more or less frustration attached) (Cravener, 1999).

A long string of relevant teaching qualifications or experiences are unlikely to be found at this stage of development of online teachers and trainers. It is most important to look at the potential and at skills. E-moderators will need to learn online communication and e-moderating skills (rather than only learn the software). They will need to understand how to promote appropriate use of own and participants' time online. They will have ability to provide support and counselling through e mail as well as the creativity and flexibility to design and adapt collaborative opportunities for differing purposes, individual and organisational missions and needs. They will be able to work cross culturally and value diversity. They will be flexible in considering approaches to online assessment, evaluation and achievement. They will understand the benefits of online working and hence are able to act as resource guides and monitors. Furthermore they will have personal meta-cognitive and adaptable approaches to learning and the ability to reflect and input into overall course learning processes.

At the moment, there are few people available with these skills so what is most important? The most important are empathy online and flexibility to working, teaching and learning online. Any recruit will have to be willing to be trained and developed into the e-moderating role.

So educators wishing to get the best from e-learning opportunities need to concentrate on engaging their learners (and not just on providing reading materials). I have recently coined the term *"e-tivities"* to bring together the practical aspects of mobilising, engaging and effectively e-moderating in technology mediated teaching and learning environments. My suggestion is that creating e-tivities with attention to both content, process and outcomes will enable students to truly engage—become enchanted even—with the online environment and arrive online frequently in great shape for learning!

Firstly, understanding the importance of the gradual comfort of learning online will increase participation and completion rates. Secondly, understanding that the design of online activities and interaction is as important as sophisticated, but static, design and delivery of "content". Thirdly, that the role of the e-moderator—the human touch—who is much more than just a facilitator or responder to questions, will make or break the experience for the learners. Fourthly, there is considerable evidence that learners become more independent and more responsible for their own development as they "move through" the model, whether in a structured or informal learning settings.

USING THE 5 STAGE MODEL

This five stage framework, diagrammed in Figure 17.1, provides a scaffold for structuring productive networking for learning and development in any community, especially a community of practice in a shared work environment. Here is a summary of advice relevant to each of the five-stages of the model. For each stage, there are ideas on technical support you can provide, on helping participants to learn and develop through online networking opportunities and on e-moderating.

EXAMPLE 1: INDUSTRIAL SUPPLY CHAINS IN THE UK

The Knowledge and Learning in Automotive Supply Systems project (klass.open.ac.uk) was in the automotive component sector, and ran in partnership with four educational institutions and two industry training bodies in the UK. Supporting training and education through work-based networks, especially exploiting the interactive benefits of online working, needs to take account of a much wider variety of factors than learning to use appropriate software. Here, the five-step model frames online training to introduce experienced engineers (used to providing face to face learning and coaching opportunities) to the benefits of online facilitation and the wider use of the Internet, including for e-commerce. We found that an inspiring presentation prior to the commencement of the online training was important to spark of their interest, and, most importantly, to explain the relevance and authenticity of the online training opportunity (Salmon, 2000).

EXAMPLE 2: TELEVISION AND THE INTERNET

In 1999, the opportunity arose for the Open University Business School to create with the BBC a series of magazine-style business television broadcasts linked to an advanced interactive Website. It was called *The Business Café* (www.open.ac.uk/businesscafe). The idea was that television viewers would be drawn to the Web site, and the Web site would add value to their viewing of the broadcasts by offering further knowledge and a chance to collaborate with other viewers.

TV audiences reached 300,000 per programme during the series. Following the first week's broadcast in February 1999, there were around 4,000 visitors to *The Business Café* Web site. This figure rose to around 6,000 for weeks 2–6, reached to 8,000 for week 7 and fell again to 6,000 for weeks 8–9. In total, around 60,000 visits were made to the Café home page during the series. The five step model was used to train the nine e-moderators who interacted with visitors to the Web site over the 10 week period. An open Web-based version of FirstClass was used to provide very large scale open online conferencing (Salmon, 2001).

EXAMPLE 3: PERSONAL AND PROFESSIONAL DEVELOPMENT THROUGH A 6 WEEK ONLINE GLOBAL NETWORK

An online course enables individuals to develop themselves, through structured online networking with others as e-moderators. The course commenced in March 2001, and continues with a monthly start. It is entirely online and global. The course uses the five-step model as a basic framework and the concept of e-tivities (online participative and collaborative activities) as its design. Individuals log in from anywhere in the world and devote up to 5 hours a week, for 5–6 weeks, at times suitable to them to take part.

The course has attracted experienced teachers and trainers from schools, corporate development and universities. Representatives of every continent in the world have appeared and taken part (Salmon, 2001).

CONCLUSION

The ripples flowing over learning and development provision as a result of the large scale introduction of ICTs are increasingly impacting on individual learners. The needs and expectations of individuals and their employers are changing. The future of e-learning is open for shaping. The stakes are extremely high for the impact on learning and development. Each of the four models presented in this chapter will find their own homes and realities. Online networking has a unique and valuable place to take in the debates and the emerging practices. I predict that the *most successful* development experiences will derive from online networking rather than through delivery of static online "content".

Patterns of the use of ICT cannot be easily determined, as the ways individuals use new forms of online learning offerings are unpredictable. Acceptable use and the meaning given to them are a complex mix of "distinctive and perplexing forms of rational and non-rational behaviour" (Silverstone, and Haddon, 1996 p. 45). The examples demonstrated in this chapter show that there is a great richness and diversity of approaches that will work. Using a framework for development increases the likelihood of success. In that way, online networking offers a way forward for effective, individual development which can shape rather than become the victim of the future.

REFERENCES

Benjamin, A. (1994) Affordable, restructured education: A solution through information technology. *RSA Journal*, May, pp. 45–49.

Blumer, H. (1969) *Symbolic interaction*. New Jersey: Prentice Hall.

Bruffee, K. A. (1993) *Collaborative learning; Higher education, interdependence, and the authority of knowledge*. Baltimore: John Hopkins University Press.

Caldwell, B. S. and J. W. Robertson (1996) Community-based information technology services: What some users want. *Interpersonal Computing and Technology* 4 (1) 20–33.

Catt, R. and J. Eke (1995) Classroom talk in higher education: Enabling learning though a reflective analysis of practice. *Innovations in Education & Training International* 32 (4) 362–369.

Cravener, P. A. (1999) Faculty experiences with providing online courses: Thorn among the roles. *Computers in Nursing*, 17 (1) 42–47.

Cunningham, D. (1992) In defense of extremism. In *Constructivism and the technology of instruction*. T. Duffy and D. Jonassen (Eds). Hillsdale New Jersey: Lawrence Erlbaum.

Davis, S. (1997) *Future perfect*. Reading, MA: Addison-Wesley.

Dede, C. and D. Palumbo (1991) Implications of hypermedia for cognition and communication. *Impact Assessment Bulletin*, 9 (1–2) 15–28.

Dewar, T. and D. Whittington (2000) Online learners and their learning strategies. *Journal of Educational Computing Research*, 23 (4) 385–403.

Dworkin, M. (1959) My pedagogic creed. *Dewey on education* (Ed.). New York: Teachers College Press.

Eisenstadt, M. (1995) Overt strategy for global learning. *Time Higher Educational Supplement, Multimedia Section*. London: pp. vi–vii.

Ferrara, K., H. Brunner and G. Whittemore (1991) Interactive written discourse as an emergent register. *Written Communication*, 8 (1) 8–34.

Grey, C., D. Knights and H. Willmott (1996) Is critical pedagogy of management possible? *Rethinking management education*. In R. French and C. Grey (Eds). Sage: London.

Guba, E. G. and Y. S. Lincoln (1994) Competing paradigms in qualitative research. *Handbook of qualitative research*. In N. K. Denzin and Y. S. Lincoln (Eds). Thousand Oaks: Sage.

Hendry, G. (1996) Constructivism and educational practice. *Australian Journal of Education*, 40 (1) 19–45.

Honey, P. and Mumford, A. (1986) *Using your learning styles*. Maidenhead: Honey.

Jonassen, D., M. Davidson, M. Collins, C. Campbell and B. B. Haag (1995) constructivism and computer-mediated communication in distance education. *American Journal of Distance Education*, 9 (2) 7–25.

Jonassen, D. H. (1991) Objectivism versus constructivism: Do we need a new philosophical paradigm? *Educational Technology, Research & Development*, 39 (3) 5–14.

Kelly, G. A. (1955) *The psychology of personal constructs*. New York: Norton.

Lave, J. and E. Wenger (1991) *Situated learning*. Cambridge: Cambridge University Press.

Lerman, S. (1989) Constructivism, mathematics and mathematics education. *Educational Studies in Mathematics*, 20, 211–223.

Lewis, R. (1996) Sharing professional knowledge: Organisational memory. *International Journal of Continuing Engineering Education and Life-long Learning*, 7 (2) 95–107.

Long, G., H. Pence and T. J. Zielinski (1995) New tools vs old: methods: A description of the Chemcomf 93 discussion. *Computers Education*, 24 (4) 259–269.

Maslow, A. H. (1943) A theory of human motivation. *Psychological Review* 50.

Mason, R. (1993) Written interactions. In *Computer Conferencing, The Last Word . . .* R. Mason (Ed.). Victoria, British Colombia: Beach Holme.

Mason, R. (1994). *Using communications media in open and flexible learning*. London: Kogan Page.

McComb, M. (1993) Augmenting a group discussion course with computer mediated communication in a small college setting. *Interpersonal Computing and Technology*, 1 (3) 1–4.

Mezirow, J. (1996) Contemporary Paradigms of Learning. *Adult Education Quarterly*, 46, 3, 158–173.

Nipper, S. (1989) Third generation distance learning and computer conferencing. *Mindweave: Communications, computers & distance education*. R. Mason and A. Kaye (Eds). Oxford: Pergamon.

Nixon, T. T. and G. Salmon (1996) Computer-mediated learning and its potential. In *Supporting open learners*. A. R. Mills and A. W. Tait (Eds). London: Pitman.

Oliver, R. and T. C. Reeves (1996) dimensions of effective interactive learning with telematics for distance education. *ETR&D*, 44 (4) 45–56.

Phillips, G. M. (1995) Creating a real group in a virtual world. *Interpersonal Computing & Technology* 3 (4).

Prahalad, C. K. (1996) A strategy for growth: The role of core competencies in the corporation. In *Training the fire brigade*. B. Conraths (Ed.). Brussels: EFMD.

Preece, J. (2000) *Online communities: Designing usability, supporting sociability*. Chichester: Wiley.

Rasmussen, T., J. Bang and K. Lundby (1991) A social experiment with electronic conferencing. *DEOSNEWS*, 1 (24).

Rogers, A. (1993) Adult learning maps & the teaching process. *Studies in the Education of Adults*, 25 (2) 203–206.

Rudy, I. A. (1995) *A critical review of research on electronic mail*. Cambridge: Judge Institute of Management Studies.

Salmon, G. (2002) *E-tivities: the key to active online learning*. London: Kogan Page.

Salmon, G. (2000) Driving through! Online learning for industrial supply chains. *The Turkish Online Journal of Distance Education*, 1 (July) http://tojde.anadolu.edu.tr/.

Salmon, G. (2000) *E-moderating: the key to teaching and learning online*. London: Kogan Page.

Salmon, G. (2001a) The business cafe project: Viewing to browsing? *British Journal of Educational Technology*, 32 (1) 91–104.

Salmon G. (2001b) 2001 Is this the way it looks like from space? *Proceedings of the Online Educa Conference*, Berlin.

Silverstone, R. and L. Haddon (1996) Design and the implementation of information and communication technologies: Technical change and everyday life. In *Communication by design: The politics of information and communication technologies*. R. Mansell and R. Silverstone (Eds). Oxford: Oxford University Press.

Spender, J. C. (1994) Knowing, managing & learning: A dynamic managerial epistemology. *Management Learning*, 25 (3) 387–412.

Steele, L. W. (1996) And the walls came tumbling down. *Technology in Society*, 18 (3) 261–284.

Taylor, J. (1995) The networked home: Domestication of information. *RSA Journal*, April, 41–53.

Vygotsky, L. S. (1978) *Mind in society*. Cambridge, MA: Harvard University Press.

Wood, D. and Wood, H. (1996) Vygotsky, tutoring & learning. *Oxford Review of Education*, 22 (1)5–15.

PART V

Organisational Context

CHAPTER 18

Developing Individuals for Leadership Roles

Cynthia D. McCauley

Center for Creative leadership, North Carolina, USA

SUMMARY

This chapter examines processes and strategies for developing the capabilities that enable individuals to be effective in leadership roles. It first clarifies the tasks of leaders and the broad human capabilities applicable across many leadership roles. Then, three main avenues for leader development are examined: job experiences, relationships, and formal learning experiences. The chapter summarizes the conclusions of best-practice studies of leadership development and points to factors beyond individual development that affects an organization's leadership capacity. It concludes with a look at the future of leader development.

INTRODUCTION

A priority for any organization is the maintenance of sufficient levels of leadership capacity to keep the organization vital and sustainable. A key factor in maintaining leadership capacity is the ongoing development of individual employees—development that equips employees with the capabilities needed to be effective in leadership roles.

In today's organization there are many different types of leadership roles. Some deal with more complexity than others (Jaques, 1996). Some are synonymous with positions of authority (i.e., supervisor, manager, or executive), while others are more informal

Individual Differences and Development in Organisations. Edited by Michael Pearn.

(Heifetz, 1994). And an organization's strategy for developing individuals for these roles often varies depending on the type of leadership role being targeted. For example, a strategy for developing executives is often long-term, focused on a few individuals, and carefully monitored. Strategies for developing informal leaders among professional staff might emphasize self-selection for and self-management of development. Despite the differences in leadership roles and strategies for development, there are some similarities in the (a) tasks embedded in a leadership role, (b) the kinds of human capabilities needed to be successful at those tasks, and (c) the types of experiences that help develop those capabilities.

LEADERSHIP TASKS AND CAPABILITIES

Any time people come together to work collectively, they need (a) something they are trying to accomplish together (*direction*); (b) to integrate and coordinate their various roles, responsibilities, and tasks so that their efforts are in the same direction (*alignment*); (c) to respond adaptively to unexpected obstacles or changes in the environment (*adaptation*); and (d) to maintain their energy and persistence for the collective work (*commitment*). Leadership is what people working together count on for the group to gain direction, alignment, adaptation, and commitment. I refer to these four key aspects of leadership—setting direction, creating alignment, adapting to new challenges, and maintaining commitment—as *leadership tasks*.

How these leadership tasks are actually carried out varies from group to group and situation to situation. For example, setting direction for an entire company is often carried out by people at the top of the formal management hierarchy (with or without the input of others). Setting direction in a work team might be carried out through a process of mutual influence among team members facilitated by the formal team leader. Setting direction in a community task force might be carried out over time through a series of discussions through which individuals find common ground among diverse views and opinions.

Accomplishing leadership tasks in some situations is more complex or difficult than in others (Drath, 2001). When the group or collective is made up of people with very different perspectives or worldviews, gaining common direction or creating alignment is often more complex than when the people are more homogeneous. Adaptation is likely more difficult for a group that has experienced stable conditions for quite some time as compared to one that has successfully dealt with a rapid succession of new challenges. Alignment is more complex when there are many pieces to align than when there are fewer. Maintaining commitment is more difficult when there is high turnover in organizational membership than when employees tend to stay with the organization over longer periods of time.

Thus, even though there are broad leadership tasks common to all collective work, there is considerable variability in how leadership tasks might be carried out and in how difficult accomplishing these tasks will be. Does all this variability mean that organizations cannot focus on a core set of capabilities to develop in employees who are expected to do leadership work? Yes and no.

Defining a core set of leadership-related capabilities is possible in an organization. First, on many dimensions, there tends to be less variability within organizations than between them (Schneider, Smith, Taylor, & Fleenor, 1998). It doesn't seem unreasonable to assume that organizations have preferred ways of carrying out leadership tasks and that these preferred ways help to define what capabilities are most important. For example, one organization might have a strong hierarchical structure that helps to ensure alignment in the organization. Those in leadership roles in the organization need to be effective at communicating clearly with those directly above and below them in the chain of command. Another organization might have a more fluid structure in which teams form around organizational projects and when the project is completed, the team disbands with members moving on to other project teams. Those in leadership roles in this organization need to be effective at quickly building groups of unrelated people into a high-performing team.

Second, comparisons across many leadership competency models yield similar basic dimensions, suggesting that there are broad human capabilities that are applicable across many leadership roles (Dalton, 1997). For example, a set of broad capabilities used by the Center for Creative Leadership (2000) to assess leadership competencies in managers from many different organizations is presented in Table 18.1.

At the same time, some capabilities are more important in some leadership roles than in others. For example, in studying differences between managers who were effective in

TABLE 18.1 Leadership capabilities

Capabilities	Description
Problem Solving and Decision Making	Ability to identify and analyze problems, make clear decisions, and recognize trade-offs in various decision options.
Innovation and Creativity	Ability to generate new ideas, think "out of the box," seize new opportunities, and introduce and create needed change.
Taking Organizational Action	Ability to translate broad organizational strategy and direction into plans, projects, and actions.
Business Skills and Knowledge	Skills and knowledge in functional areas (e.g., finance, marketing, sales) as well as broad knowledge about how the business operates.
Communication	Ability to communicate clearly and effectively in different media, as well as listen to others.
Building and Maintaining Relationships	Ability to build cooperative relationships; skills relating to many different types of people including superiors, peers, subordinates, and outsides.
Developing People	Ability to coach and encourage others, provide appropriate feedback, and recognize and reward the accomplishments of others.
Valuing Diversity	Respect for varying backgrounds and perspectives.
Drive and Purpose	Personal direction and initiative, perseverance and focus in the face of obstacles, and goal-directed.
Integrity and Values	Honesty, trustworthiness, and credibility.
Self-management	Ability to handle stress and high-pressure situations and to manage time, career, and work-life balance issues.
Self-awareness	Accurate picture of strengths and weaknesses and understanding of own psychological make-up and preferences.
Ability to Learn	Ability to learn from own experiences through action, feedback, and reflection.
Adaptability	Ability to change to meet new challenges and to perform in multiple leadership roles.

domestic roles and those who were effective in global roles (i.e., roles requiring managing across multiple countries and cultures), Dalton, Ernst, Deal, & Leslie (in press) found that both groups of managers needed capabilities in the areas of people management, decision making, communication, business knowledge, and self-management. However, effectiveness in global roles also required international business knowledge (a more specialized type of business knowledge), cultural adaptability, perspective-taking capability (an aspect of ability to learn), and innovation skills.

So how do organizations decide what capabilities to focus on in developing individuals for leadership roles? A common solution is to first articulate a broad competency model for leadership that is applicable across the organization. Since these competency models tend to be similar from organization to organization, the organization can opt to adopt or modify an existing model. Often this includes articulating how the broader competency is operationalized in the organization. For example, "drive and purpose" might mean "doing whatever it takes" in one organization and "being committed to making a difference" in another. If it is important to involve employees in creating the model or if the model needs to reflect language and concepts derived from the organization's history, culture, and experiences, the organization could opt to invest in developing a more tailored model.

Whether adopted or crafted, within the common framework of a competency model, more specific capabilities can be tied to particular types or levels of leadership roles. As in the example cited above, organizations can target particular, more-specific capabilities in developing individuals for global roles. They can also expect to develop more complex aspects of general capabilities as individuals move into higher-level leadership roles. For example, at lower levels in the organization, developing project management capabilities could be the focus of efforts to develop the capability to take organizational action. At higher levels, the developmental emphasis would likely turn to the more complex skills of setting up work systems and processes and of developing alliances throughout the organization.

To summarize, in order to develop individuals for leadership roles, one first has to understand the common tasks embedded in all leadership roles and the capabilities that help individuals carry out these tasks. Developing these capabilities in employees across the organization can increase the organization's leadership capacity. At the same time, organizations will benefit from understanding their own norms and preferences for carrying out leadership tasks because these patterns will suggest capabilities that are particularly important for that organization to develop. In addition, leadership roles within an organization will vary in terms of which tasks are most central and how the tasks are best enacted, thus some specific capabilities will be more important in some roles than in others. Let us now turn to the strategies and methods for developing leadership capabilities.

KEY ELEMENTS OF LEADERSHIP DEVELOPMENT EXPERIENCES

The range of capabilities that contribute to effectiveness in leadership roles is large—from self-awareness to developing people to creativity. To hone such a well-rounded set of capabilities in individuals requires time and a variety of learning experiences. When asked about their developmental experiences, individuals in executive leadership roles point out experiences that occurred at different times throughout their careers and identify different kinds of experiences as developmental (McCall, Lombardo, & Morrison, 1988; Morrison, White, & Van Velsor, 1992; Van Velsor & Douglas, 2001). Some leadership development experiences are formal interventions specifically focused on learning and development, and others are a natural part of a person's career—jobs, relationships, and hardships—that stimulate learning (McCauley, 2001). Whether formal or naturally occurring, experiences are most likely to be developmental when they provide individuals with assessment, challenge, and support (Van Velsor, McCauley, & Moxley, 1998).

ASSESSMENT

An experience provides assessment when it is rich in information about how well a person is doing: what are current leadership strengths, what is the level of current performance or leadership effectiveness, and in what ways could effectiveness be improved. Assessment information can come from many sources: from a person's own observations, from the success or failure of a particular initiative, from other people. It can be formal, as in performance appraisals or 360-degree feedback, or informal, as in conversations with colleagues or personal observation. Assessment data help leaders better understand what works and what does not in various leadership situations and in what ways they need to learn and grow. Assessment information can also motivate developmental effort. A recognized gap between current capabilities and desired or ideal capabilities can stimulate efforts to close the gap by working to learn and improve.

CHALLENGE

An experience provides challenge when it takes people out of their comfort zone, creating disequilibrium and causing them to question the adequacy of their skills, frameworks, or approaches. Challenging experiences require that people develop new capacities if they are going to be successful. Some challenges are due to a lack of experience; they require the person to broaden and acquire new capabilities. Other challenges require changing old habits either because the situation has changed and old responses are no longer adequate, or old responses were never that effective in the first place. New experiences, difficult goals, situations characterized by conflict, and dealing with loss and mistakes are likely sources of challenge in leadership development experiences.

SUPPORT

An experience provides support when people believe they can learn and grow from it and that their effort to learn and grow is valued. Development is not easy. If people do not receive confirming messages and others do not allow and encourage them to change, then the challenge posed by the developmental experience may overwhelm them rather than open them up to learning. Support is also needed to help people handle the strug-gle and pain of developing and to maintain a positive view of themselves as capable of learning. The largest source of support is other people: bosses, co-workers, family, friends, colleagues, coaches, and mentors. But support can also take the form of organi-zational norms and practices that are supportive of development, such as practices that make resources available for learning and reward people for their developmental efforts.

TABLE 18.2   Main sources of leadership development experiences

Job Experience	• New situations with unfamiliar responsibilities • Tasks or projects that call for leadership • High-level or high-latitude responsibilities
Relationships	• Mentoring • Executive coaching • Networks • Manager as coach • A culture of learning and development • Communities of practice
Formal learning experiences	• Feedback-intensive programs • Conceptual/knowledge programs • Skills building programs • Personal growth programs • Action learning programs

In summary, the key elements that make any experience more developmental are assessment, challenge, and support. Whether designing a training program, providing 360-degree feedback, putting someone in a developmental job assignment, or matching the person with a mentor, all three elements need to be part of the experience to maximize its developmental impact.

TYPES OF LEADERSHIP DEVELOPMENT EXPERIENCES

Although individuals experience a wide variety of experiences as developmental, these experiences tend to fall into one of three broad categories: Job experiences, relationships, and formal learning experiences. Organizations generally use all three and weave these types of experiences together in efforts to develop individuals for leadership roles. However, research efforts have often examined these sources of development separately. See Table 18.2 for an overview of the main leadership development experiences.

JOB EXPERIENCES

A number of studies indicate that a great deal of individual development occurs in the course of dealing with the roles, responsibilities, and tasks associated with one's job (McCall et al., 1988; Sternberg, Wagner, Williams, & Horvath, 1995; Wick & Leon, 1993). Focusing primarily on managerial jobs, research has indicated that some types of job assignments foster the development of leadership capabilities more than others do (Davies & Easterby-Smith, 1984; McCauley, Ruderman, Ohlott, & Morrow, 1994). Jobs with high developmental potential tend to have one or more of the following components (McCauley, Ohlott, & Ruderman, 1999):

New situations with unfamiliar responsibilities. This type of experience is most frequently the outcome of a job move (for instance, a promotion or a move to new business, function, organization, or location), but can come from expanded responsibilities with the same job or the redefinition of a job due to reorganizations or changes in the external environment. New situations with unfamiliar responsibilities provide an opportunity to learn because they disrupt routines, call for new skills and behaviors, and yield surprises that cause the individual to reexamine assumptions.

Tasks or projects that require the individual to create change, manage across organizational boundaries, build relationships, or deal with diverse people. These are the types of tasks and projects in which the need for leadership is most apparent—they call for setting direction, creating alignment, adapting to new challenges, and maintaining commitment. Developing the capabilities needed for leadership requires doing the work of leadership. Individuals in these situations are in a rich environment for taking action, observing the consequences of those actions, forming insights and generalizations based on those observations, and testing the new ideas by taking refined actions, thus engaging in an experiential learning cycle (Kolb, 1984).

High-level or high-latitude responsibilities. In these types of jobs, individuals have responsibility for discrete areas of the business, have profit-and-loss responsibility, or make decisions that can have a major impact on the organization. They generally are also given a high degree of latitude in their initiatives and discretion in decision making. Jobs with these characteristics offer developmental opportunities because (a) they often expose the job incumbent to complex systems and the need to make trade-offs between competing demands, (b) the consequences of actions in these jobs often matter a great deal, encouraging individuals to pay more attention to their actions and intended consequences, (c) they allow more freedom to experiment, allowing individuals to test their understanding of a situation by taking actions and seeing the consequences.

Organizations systematically and intentionally use developmental assignments rather than rely solely on their natural occurrence in the workplace. There appear to be three general approaches to using developmental assignments more systematically. First, when choosing people for jobs, the potential development offered by the job is used as one factor in decision making (Clark & Lyness, 1991; Freidman, 1990). For example, if the job contained more new elements for one candidate than for another, the job would be more developmental for this candidate and would thus be a positive in favor of choosing him or her. Second, specific types of assignments are used as part of a development system (Bonoma & Lawler, 1989; Morrison & Hock, 1986). In these situations, the specific kinds of job experiences needed by individuals in particular career paths or people targeted for particular types of leadership roles are identified, and job assignments are given over time to ensure that individuals get these experiences. Finally, employees are encouraged to develop within their current jobs by adding developmental opportunities, such as special projects, task forces, new responsibilities, and boundary-spanning roles (Lombardo & Eichenger, 1989; McCauley et al., 1999). They are also encouraged to use off-the-job experiences, as a volunteer or family member, to develop leadership capabilities (Ruderman & Ohlott, 2000).

Providing developmental assignments is the first step in enhancing on-the-job learning. Organizational practices that enable reflection on recent work experience and that provide support and relieve stress during assignments will likely strengthen the motivation and ability to learn from job experiences (Tesluk & Jacobs, 1998).

RELATIONSHIPS

Relationships play a key role in the development of leadership capabilities. Numerous studies in adult development and career progression have highlighted the impact that a special kind of relationship—a mentoring relationship—can have on personal and professional development (Carden, 1990; Kram, 1985; Levinson, 1978). A mentoring relationship is typically defined as a committed, long-term relationship in which a senior person supports the career and psychosocial development of a junior person. A mentor influences career development through sponsorship, protection, and visibility, and influences psychosocial development by providing acceptance, encouragement, coaching, and counseling (Kram, 1985; Noe, 1988). Receiving support from a mentor is associated with higher performance ratings, more recognition, greater compensation, more career opportunities, and more promotions (Burke & McKeen, 1997; Chao, 1997; Dreher & Ash, 1990; Fagenson, 1989; Orpen, 1995; Scandura, 1992; Turban & Dougherty, 1994; Whitely, Dougherty, & Dreher, 1991).

More recently, scholars and practitioners have looked beyond the traditional mentoring relationship to better understand the network of developmental relationships that provide the assessment, challenge, and support needed for individual development (Higgins & Kram, 2001; McCauley & Douglas, 1998). Supervisors, peers, professional colleagues outside the organization, and role models observed at a distance have all been cited by employees as important sources of learning and development (Kram & Isabella, 1985; McCall et al., 1988; Morrison et al., 1992; Zemke, 1985). These individuals play multiple roles in the learning process. They provide the elements of (a) assessment by giving feedback, helping to interpret feedback from others, and serving as a sounding board; (b) challenge by offering alternative points of view, modeling high competence, helping to access stretch assignments, and holding people accountable for their developmental goals; and (c) support by counseling, encouraging and reinforcing development, and sharing the struggles of learning and development. Higgins & Kram (2001) further propose that the diversity and intensity of relationships in a developmental network varies across individuals, resulting in different types of networks with different developmental outcomes.

Organizations use a number of strategies to enhance learning from relationships. First, they create formal developmental relationships. Formal mentoring programs are likely the most popular form of these intentional relationships. Formal mentors are usually assigned to a particular group of junior employees (e.g., high potentials, new employees, or women and people of color) in the hopes that these relationships will provide some of the same important personal and professional development opportunities as do informal, long-term mentoring relationships. By formalizing the process, the organization is ensuring that all the targeted employees have equal access to a mentor, and it focuses the mentoring effort within a specified time frame (McCauley & Douglas, 1998). Although evaluations of formal mentoring programs have demonstrated positive results (Gaskill, 1993; Noe, 1988; Portwood & Granrose, 1986), there is some evidence that employees participating in formal mentoring programs benefit less than those who have informal mentoring relationships (Chao, Walz, & Gardner, 1992; Raggins & Cotton, 1999). A review of the literature on formal mentoring yielded five common characteristics of more successful mentoring programs: organizational support for the program; clarity of purpose, expectations, and roles; participant choice and involvement; careful selection and matching procedures; and continuous monitoring and evaluation (Douglas, 1997).

Executive coaching is another type of formal developmental relationship. Executive coaching is used to help managers and executives in particular skill areas that have been identified as needing improvement. The process involves a series of one-on-one interactions between an employee and a consultant who specializes in coaching and who is generally external to the organization. Executive coaching takes many shapes and sizes, varying in scope, types of assessment used, participant motivation, organizational involvement, frequency of sessions, and degree of follow-up and support (Peterson, 1996). As a practice, executive coaching is flourishing (HR Focus, 1999; Judge & Cowell, 1997; The Conference Board, 1999). Although there are a number of case studies portraying successful instances of executive coaching (e.g., Diedrich, 1996; Peterson, 1996), little research has been conducted on this practice. A few studies have found that coaching participants find their experiences to be valuable and effective (Edelstein & Armstrong, 1993; Hall, Otazo, & Hollenbeck, 1999).

Other variations of formal relationships include peer mentoring or coaching and mentoring circles. The latter typically involves a group of four to six individuals who meet regularly and are assigned to a senior manager. The senior manager's role is to act as a learning partner by helping the employees analyze and learn from their experiences and to create an environment wherein participants can learn from each other (Kaye & Jacobson, 1995).

A second strategy used by organizations to enhance learning from relationship is to develop managers who can coach all of their employees (Peterson & Hicks, 1996; Waldroop & Butler, 1996). Organizations using this strategy articulate the payback to managers for spending time developing their subordinates, develop coaching skills among managers, and hold managers accountable for the development of their subordinates. Initial research on the impact of manager's coaching on development are encouraging. One study found that preparing managers to act as coaches led subordinates to demonstrate substantially more transfer of training (Olivero, Bane, & Kopelmane, 1997). And supervisor support has been linked to greater employee participation in development activities (Hazucha, Hezlett, & Schneider, 1993; Noe, 1996; Tharenou, 1997). The "manager as coach" approach has several potential advantages over external coaching and formal mentoring: it provides developmental support to more employees, learning may be reinforced more regularly, and it sets the tone that development is important for all employees not just those who find or are assigned a mentor (McCauley & Hezlitt, 2001).

A final organizational strategy to enhance developmental relationships in the workplace is to foster a culture where teaching and learning among employees is the norm. Developing others becomes a shared responsibility across the organization, not just a managerial responsibility. For example, a financial organization launched an initiative to develop more of a "coaching culture" (McCauley & Douglas, 1998). As one part of this effort they identified employees who are particularly good coaches and set out to understand the mind-sets and skills of these people, the tools they use, and the impact they have on those they coach. The organization is using this knowledge to develop a coaching model and a workshop to teach the skills of coaching to others throughout the organization.

Another way that organizations encourage a culture where learning through others is the norm is by supporting the formation of networks and communities of practice. Networks tend to link people with a common perspective or issue in an organization (e.g., women, managers at a particular organizational level, employees in expatriate assignments). They learn from each other by sharing problems and potential solutions associated with their particular role in the organization. Communities of practice are groups of people in an organization with a shared repertoire of tools, concepts, actions, stories, and historical events (Wenger, 1998). As individuals gain membership and participate in community activities they develop particular kinds of knowledge and expertise. Communities of practice that link experts from across an organization are being nurtured in a number of companies as a vehicle for professional development, transfer of best practice, and quick problem solving (Wenger & Snyder, 2000). For example, Daimler-Chrysler supports "tech clubs," groups of engineers who do not work in the same unit but voluntarily meet regularly to talk about problems related to their own area of expertise.

FORMAL LEARNING EXPERIENCES

Conger (1992) identified four basic types of leadership development programs: feedback-intensive programs, conceptual programs, skill-building programs, and personal growth programs. In the last decade, a fifth type of program, action learning programs, have been added to the mix.

Feedback-intensive programs usually last from three to five days and combine 360-degree feedback and assessment center exercises with other forms of assessment—all within a classroom context that provides models and frameworks for thinking about effective leadership. These programs make use of psychological inventories, so participants develop a better understanding of their underlying predispositions toward certain types of behaviors and reactions in the workplace, and they use fellow participants in the program to provide in-the-moment feedback. These programs conclude with the setting of developmental goals and action plans. Follow-up activities (such as a feedback instrument to assess behavioral change or ongoing meetings with a group of fellow participants) may be part of the program design. Feedback-intensive programs have been show to increase self-awareness, broaden and transform managers' perspectives, lead to successful goal attainment, and change leadership behavior (Guthrie & Kelly-Radford, 1998; McCauley & Hughes-James, 1994; Young & Dixon, 1996).

Conceptual programs and skill-building programs fall within what are traditionally thought of as training programs: programs that teach the knowledge and skills that leaders and managers need. Conceptual approaches to leader training focus on a cognitive understanding of what is involved in the task of leadership and what it takes to be an effective leader. These programs tend to be more theory driven and are traditionally offered by universities. Lectures, case studies, and discussion are the predominant pedagogical tools. Conger (1992) reports that conceptual programs are a natural first step for those with little leadership experience; they can help people gain awareness of what leadership is and create enthusiasm for the idea of leading. Conceptual approaches are also a primary way for managers to learn the business knowledge they need in areas such as finance, operations, marketing, and strategic planning.

Skill building is the most commonly employed approach to leader training (Conger, 1992). Programs can range from short workshops focusing on a narrow set of skills to comprehensive programs that cover a wide range of skills and last for as long as a year (Yukl, 1998). Skill-building programs generally consist of modules, each focusing on a specific skill (such as giving feedback, creating a vision statement, or negotiating with external parties). Within a module, participants are given information and strategies for executing the skill, observe the skill in action, and practice the skill themselves. Numerous techniques may be employed: lectures, demonstrations, role modeling, videotapes, role playing, group exercises, and simulations. Training programs are most likely to contribute to lasting change and development when the content of the training is directly relevant to the participant's job, is needed at that time, and can be immediately used in the work setting (McDonald-Mann, 1998). For those in leadership roles, training that focuses on improving interpersonal skills and that helps managers use self-regulation processes to acquire and maintain those skills has received much attention in the last decade (Gist & McDonald-Mann, 2000).

Personal growth programs are "based, generally, on the assumption that leaders are individuals who are deeply in touch with their personal dreams and talents and who will act to fulfill them" (Conger, 1992, p. 45). Therefore, the premise of these programs is that managers need to get in touch with their personal dreams and talents and develop a commitment to making those dreams a reality in order to fulfill their potential as leaders. Programs with this orientation usually take one of two forms: (1) outdoor adventure programs where groups of participants experience increasingly challenging physical activities, many of which require trust and cooperation among group members, and (2) workshops where participants engage in a number of psychological exercises that allow for deep exploration of their personal values and drives. The outdoor programs focus more on developing self-confidence, overcoming fears, and taking risks, while the workshops put more emphasis on self-understanding and tapping into inner resources. Despite the popularity of these programs, there has been few attempts to gather empirical evidence of their impact on leadership capabilities (Gist & McDonald-Mann, 2000).

Action learning was developed by Revans (1982) as an educational approach that encourages people to apply and generate knowledge from real-world situations. Although there are numerous ways that action learning is practiced, the approach has three main components: problems or issues that have no clear solution, people who will take responsibility for action on the issues, and a group of six or so colleagues (often called a 'set') who support and challenge each other to make progress on problems (Pedler, 1997). In a typical action learning program, participants are exposed to theories or knowledge using typical instruction methods. They then apply this knowledge to a project that has potential value to the organization. These projects focus on complex issues that often involve many stakeholders, such as movement into new markets, the introduction of new technology, reorganizations, and decentralization (Marsick, 1990). As they are working on the project, participants meet in groups usually with a facilitator or advisor, to discuss their understanding of the dilemmas they encounter, to question the theories and concepts they are applying in the project, and to discover new ways of thinking or creative alternatives to accomplish their objectives, Through this process of action, debriefing, and feedback with mutual learners, participants gain more in-depth knowledge and effective theories to apply to their work.

As experience with action learning programs has grown, how they are used in organizations has evolved in several directions. Action learning may be (a) a component of an individual development program, (b) part of an organizational change initiative, or (c) part of an ongoing strategy for organizational learning (Dotlich & Noel, 1998; Marsick & O'Neil, 1999). Initial formal evaluations of action learning programs relied heavily on interviews with program participants. Studies reported in Mumford (1997) and Pedler (1997) found that participants experienced learning in the areas of teamwork, communication, effective management, facilitation skills, self-confidence, self-awareness, self-discipline, and networking. More recent research documenting the positive impact of action learning have used multiple sources for assessing learning and change (e.g., coworkers and organizational sponsors) and have begun to address the question of transfer of learning from the program to ongoing work (Dilworth & Willis, 1999; Raelin, 1997; Yorks, Lamm, O'Neil, Kolodny, Marsick, & Nilson, 1998).

LEADERSHIP DEVELOPMENT INITIATIVES IN ORGANIZATIONS

Developing individuals for leadership roles is an ongoing and multi-faceted activity in most organizations, and one into which organizations continue to invest increasing amounts of money and energy. In recent years, studies of best practice in leadership development (Fulmer & Wagner, 1999; Fulmer, Gibbs, & Goldsmith, 2000; Vicere & Fulmer, 1997) and reviews of how the practice of leadership development is evolving (Conger & Benjamin, 1999; Day, 2000; Moxley & Wilson, 1998) are consistent in highlighting several key themes in successful leadership development initiatives:

Leadership development initiatives should be closely linked to the organization—its goals and strategies, business issues, and challenges. This is most frequently reflected in an organization's efforts to closely align leadership development with corporate strategy and use it to support the company's goals (Fulmer & Wagner, 1999). For example, Conger & Benjamin (1999) attribute a large part of the success of Ernst & Young's Leadership 2000 program to the clear strategic framework that drove its program design. Ernst & Young had articulated a growth strategy for remaining competitive, and Leadership 2000 provided a learning experience that would foster the leadership capabilities and organizational strategies that would advance this objective. The imperative to link leadership development and the organization's needs is also reflected in additional advice to practitioners, e.g., make leadership development a joint responsibility of human resource professionals and line managers, use action learning projects that address real business needs, assess the organization's learning needs before designing development interventions, involve senior managers in teaching roles, and anticipate future business needs and their leadership development implications.

Leadership development initiatives should utilize multiple learning and development methods. People learn in numerous ways, and development happens over time through a series of experiences. Thus, organizations do not rely on a particular type of developmental experience (i.e., jobs, relationships, or formal learning experiences), but rather work to provide a variety of experiences to create the assessment, challenge, and support needed for individual development. For example, a national nonprofit organization's initiative to develop bench strength for top-level leadership positions included a feedback-intensive formal program, several knowledge and skill-building programs, formal and informal mentoring, and the support of peer networks (McCauley, 2001).

Leadership development initiatives should be linked across organizational levels in an effort to develop consistent leadership at all levels. Best practice organizations believe that a talent pool of leaders is needed at all levels of the organization (Vicere & Fulmer, 1997). Creating linkages in leadership development efforts targeted to different levels of the organization ensures more of a shared understanding of the tasks of leadership, the company's strategic direction, and the leadership demands embedded in that direction.

There are numerous ways to create linkages: use a consistent leadership model, link each program or activity to an overall leader competency model, cascade initiatives from top-levels downward in the organization, and design curricula to elicit collective dialogue across levels.

Leadership development initiatives should be constantly evaluated and adapted to meet changing needs. Best practice organizations always assess the impact of their leadership development initiatives (Fulmer & Wagner, 1999). They monitor the views of program participants, the perceived value of the initiative to those sponsoring and supporting it, and progress toward meeting the objectives of the initiative. Some organizations also consider impact on business results. For example, to the staff of an action-learning-based leadership development program at Shell International, a program adds value only if the projects generate revenues at least 25 times greater than the project's cost (Fulmer et al., 2000). Demonstrating the success of leadership development allows for continued high-level support of the initiative. Monitoring also allows for adaptation to changing needs.

Other organizational systems and practices need to support the outcomes and objectives of leadership development initiatives. These initiatives are part of a larger human resource management system that includes recruitment, selection, development, appraisal, and reward. These components need to align with and support the leader capabilities being developed in individuals. For example, one organization's leadership development program focused on helping people develop the skills needed to effectively operate in a flatter, more team-based environment. Yet the performance appraisal and compensation system put more emphasis on individual performance (Moxley & Wilson, 1998). Succession planning systems in particular need to be aligned with leadership development initiatives. These systems identify individuals who have the potential to take on higher levels of responsibility in the organization (which will expose them to broader and more complex leadership challenges) and articulate what kind of preparation each individual needs before taking on these higher-level jobs. Although they have overlapping goals, succession planning and leadership development have often been separate activities in organizations. However, best practice company's link these two functions either formally (through organizational structure) or informally (Fulmer & Wagner, 1999).

Friedman (2001) provides a case study of leadership development at Ford Motor Company that illustrates how one organization worked to put these principles in place. Ford's senior executives have articulated a new direction—one that is designed to take the company from a traditional manufacturer to a 21st-century consumer company that delivers excellent products and services and strives to make the world a better place. It required a new mindset at Ford: adopting a consumer mindset as well as one of environmental and social responsibility. Ford's Leadership Development Center saw as its mission to support and accelerate this organizational change. Their initiatives were directed at challenging and supporting participants to be transformational leaders—to think "outside the box" and to learn how to capitalize on the talents of their people for maximum business impact. They used action learning, online learning tools, and managers as teachers in programs directed at four different levels in the organization. They also supported the leadership development needs of five strategic change initiatives that cut across the organization. They pioneered a new frame for understanding leadership at Ford—total leadership—that sought to integrate all aspects of a person's life and which was consistent with the multiple stakeholder view behind the organization's new direction. Finally, demonstrating the impact of their programs on the organization and its finances is an ongoing part of the Leadership Development Center's responsibility.

BEYOND INDIVIDUAL DEVELOPMENT: OTHERS ASPECTS OF LEADERSHIP DEVELOPMENT

As noted at the beginning of this chapter, developing the leadership capabilities of individual employees is a key factor in maintaining leadership capacity in organizations. But it is not the only factor. The principles used in successful leadership development initiatives (described above) begin to point to factors outside of individual development that affects an organization's leadership capacity.

DEVELOPING PRODUCTIVE RELATIONSHIPS AMONG EMPLOYEES

Day (2000) makes the distinction between leader development and leadership development. By leader development, he means the development of human capital—knowledge, skills, and abilities associated with leadership roles. In Day's framework, the current chapter focuses on leader development. By leadership development, he means the development of social capital—"building networked relationships among individuals that enhance cooperation and resource exchange in creating organizational value" (p. 585). Although many of the activities and experiences associated with leader development can also enhance leadership development (e.g., shared leader development experiences can create strong relationships, networks for learning can create bonds for cooperation and resource exchange), they do not specifically address the development of social capital. The tasks of leadership—direction, alignment, adaptation, and commitment—require relationships and interpersonal exchange. Enhancing mutual obligations and reciprocated trust and respect among organizational members is another route to increasing leadership capacity in organizations.

DEVELOPING A SHARED LEADERSHIP PHILOSOPHY

The tasks of leadership are carried out more effectively in organizations when organizational members hold shared principles of leadership or implicit theories about how leadership is carried out. Cognitive leadership research has been building evidence that collective leadership schemas—socially constructed ways of understanding leadership derived from exchanges and interactions among multiple individuals in an organization—are used by organizational members to generate leadership behavior and perceptions (Lord & Emrich, 2000). Thus in addition to developing individual capabilities and social relations, leadership development also involves developing shared implicit theories of leadership which will guide the actions and behaviors of organizational members.

EVOLVING ORGANIZATIONAL SYSTEMS AND PRACTICES

Many organizations find themselves facing more complexity in their leadership challenges. The Ford Motor Company case provides a good example. The organization's new direction is more complex than its old one, i.e., producing excellent products for consumers *and* making the world a better place is more complex than simply returning profits to shareholders. Gaining the commitment of multiple stakeholder (shareholders, employees, customers, and the larger community) is more complex than gaining the commitment of one or two of these groups. Focusing on the individual capabilities needed to lead in this more complex organization and on the leadership philosophy that will guide leadership actions (e.g., "total leadership") is necessary but not sufficient. Embedded in the company's existing organizational systems are practices—everything from performance appraisals to accounting practices to communication patterns—that reflect and support the existing leadership culture. Thus, particularly in times of change, leadership development also involves the intentional evolution of organizational systems and practices to create better alignment with new ways of enacting leadership.

THE FUTURE OF INDIVIDUAL DEVELOPMENT FOR LEADERSHIP ROLES

Future directions can be examined in terms of emerging capabilities needed in leadership roles, new methods or processes for developing the capabilities of leaders, and evolving frameworks for understanding leadership development in organizations. As organizations and the challenges they face become more complex, one would expect an increasing need for capabilities that help those in leadership roles make sense of and act in the face of chaos, ambiguity, and rapid change. Technology also enables groups and teams to work at a distance, raising questions about capabilities needed to carry out leadership tasks across space and time. Technology is also having an impact on methods of learning and development. In what ways might we effectively use online or "e-learning" to better develop individuals for leadership roles? Another trend—connected to changing employer-employee relationships and to the attitudes and values of a new generation of employees—is for individuals to be more proactive in shaping and directing their own development. What new development strategies might emerge from this trend? And finally, our frameworks for thinking about leadership development are becoming more systemic. Best practice companies are already seeing leadership development as an evolving process embedded in the organization. A systemic perspective does not ignore the role of individual development in leadership development, but recognizes the role of relationships, culture, and systems in sustaining leadership capacity in organizations.

REFERENCES

Bonoma, T.V., & Lawler, J.C. (1989). Chutes and ladders: Growing the general manager. *Sloan Management Review, 30(3)*, 27–37.

Burke, R.J., & McKeen, C.A. (1997). Benefits of mentoring relationships among managerial and professional women: A cautionary tale. *Journal of Vocational Behavior, 51*, 43–57.

Carden, A.D. (1990). Mentoring and adult career development: The evolution of a theory. *Counseling Psychologist, 18*, 275–299.

Center for Creative Leadership. (2000). *The CCL library of scales available on 360 By Design*. Greensboro, NC: Author.

Chao, G.T. (1997). Mentoring phases and outcomes. *Journal of Vocational Behavior, 51*, 15–28.

Chao, G.T., Walz, P.M., & Gardner, P.D. (1992). Formal and informal mentorships: A comparison of mentoring functions and contrast with non-mentored counterparts. *Personnel Psychology, 45*, 619–636.

Clark, L.A., & Lyness, K.S. (1991). Succession planning as a strategic activity at Citicorp. In L.W. Foster (Ed.), *Advances in applied business strategy, Vol. 2* (pp. 205–224). Greenwich, CT: JAI Press.

Conference Board. (1999). Developing leaders. *HR Executive Review, 7(1)*, 1–18.

Conger, J.A. (1992). *Learning to lead: The art of transforming managers into leaders.* San Francisco: Jossey-Bass.

Conger, J.A., & Benjamin, B. (1999). *Building leaders: How successful companies develop the next generation.* San Francisco: Jossey-Bass.

Dalton, M. (1997). Are competency models a waste? *Training & Development, 51(10)*, 46–49.

Dalton, M., Ernst, C., Deal, J., & Leslie, J. (in press). *Success for the new global manager: What you need to know about managing others across distance, countries, and cultures.* San Francisco: Jossey-Bass.

Davies, J., & Easterby-Smith, M. (1984). Learning and development from managerial work experiences. *Journal of Management Studies, 21*, 169–183.

Day, D.V. (2000). Leadership development: A review in context. *Leadership Quarterly, 11*, 581–613.

Diedrich, R.C. (1996). An iterative approach to executive coaching. *Consulting Psychology Journal: Practice and Research, 48(2)*, 61–66.

Dilworth, R.L., & Willis, V.J. (1999). Action learning for personal development and transformative learning. In L. Yorks, J. O'Neil, & V.J. Marsick (Eds.), *Action learning: Successful strategies for individual, team, and organizational development* (pp. 75–82). San Francisco: Berrett-Koehler.

Dotlich, D.L., & Noel, J.L. (1998). *Action learning: How the world's top companies are re-creating their leaders and themselves.* San Francisco: Jossey-Bass.

Douglas, C.A. (1997). *Formal mentoring programs in organizations: An annotated bibliography.* Greensboro, NC: Center for Creative Leadership.

Drath, W.H. (2001). *The deep blue sea: Rethinking the source of leadership.* San Francisco: Jossey-Bass.

Dreher, G.F., & Ash, R.A. (1990). A comparative study of mentoring among men and women in managerial, professional, and technical position. *Journal of Applied Psychology, 75*, 539–546.

Edelstein, B.C., & Armstrong, D.J. (1993). A model for executive development. *Human Resource Planning, 16(4)*, 51–64.

Fagenson, E.A. (1989). The mentor advantage: Perceived career/job experiences of protégés versus non-protégés. *Journal of Organizational Behavior, 10*, 309–320.

Friedman, S.D. (1990). Succession systems in the public sector: Lessons from the Oklahoma Department of Corrections. *Public Personnel Management, 19*, 291–303.

Friedman, S.D. (2001). Leadership DNA: The Ford Motor story. *Training & Development, 55(3)*, 22–29.

Fulmer, R.M., & Wagner, S. (1999). Leadership: Lessons from the best. *Training & Development, 53(3)*, 29–32.

Fulmer, R.M., Gibbs, P.A., & Goldsmith, M. (2000). Developing leaders: How winning companies keep on winning. *Sloan Management Review, 42(1)*, 49–59.

Gaskel, L.R. (1993). A conceptual framework for the development, implementation, and evaluation of formal mentoring programs. *Journal of Career Development, 20*, 147–160.

Gist, M.E., & McDonald-Mann, D. (2000). Advances in leadership training and development. In C.L. Cooper, & E.A. Locke (Eds.), *Industrial and organizational psychology: Linking theory with practice.* Oxford: Blackwell.

Guthrie, V., & Kelly-Radford, L. (1998). Feedback intensive programs. In C.D. McCauley, R.S. Moxley, & E. Van Velsor (Eds.), *The Center for Creative Leadership handbook of leadership development* (pp. 66–105). San Francisco: Jossey-Bass.

Hall, D.T., Otazo, K.L., & Hollenbeck, G.P. (1999). Behind closed doors: What really happens in executive coaching. *Organizational Dynamics, 27(3)*, 39–53.

Hazucha, J.F., Hezlett, S.A., & Schneider, R.J. (1993). The impact of 360-degree feedback on management skills development. *Human Resource Management, 32*, 325–351.

Heifetz, R.A. (1994). *Leadership without easy answers*. Cambridge, MA: Harvard University Press.

Higgins, M.C., & Kram, K.E. (2001). Reconceptualizing mentoring at work: A developmental network perspective. *Academy of Management Review, 26*, 265–288.

HR Focus. (1999). Corporate coaching growing as retention tool, *HR Focus, 76(10)*, 4.

Jaques, E. (1996). *Requisite organization*. Gloucester, MA: Cason Hall & Co.

Judge, W.Q., & Cowell, J. (1997). The brave new world of executive coaching. *Business Horizons, 40(4)*, 71–77.

Kaye, B., & Jacobson, B. (1995). Mentoring: A group guide. *Training & Development, 49(4)*, 22–27.

Kolb, D. (1984). *Experiential learning: Experience as the source of learning and development*. Englewood Cliffs, NJ: Prentice Hall.

Kram, K.E. (1985). *Mentoring at work*. Glenview, IL: Scott, Foresman.

Kram, K.E., & Isabella, L.A. (1985). Mentoring alternatives: The role of peer relationships in career development. *Academy of Management Journal, 28*, 119–132.

Levinson (1978). *Seasons of a man's life*. New York: Knopf.

Lombardo, M.M., & Eichenger, R.W. (1989). *Eight-eight assignments for development in place: Enhancing the developmental challenge of existing jobs*. Greensboro, NC: Center for Creative Leadership.

Lord, R.G., & Emrich, C.G. (2000). Thinking outside the box by looking inside the box: Extending the cognitive revolution in leadership research. *Leadership Quarterly, 11*, 551–579.

Marsick, V.J. (1990). Experience-based learning: Executive learning outside the classroom. *Journal of Management Development, 9(4)*, 50–60.

Marsick, V.J., & O'Neil, J. (1999). The many faces of action learning. *Management Learning, 30*, 159–176.

McCall, M.W., Jr., Lombardo, M.M., & Morrison, A.M. (1988). *The lessons of experience: How successful executives develop on the job*. San Francisco: New Lexington Press.

McCauley, C.D. (2001). Leader training and development. In S.J. Zaccaro, & R.J. Klimoski (Eds.), *The nature of organizational leadership* (pp. 347–383). San Francisco: Jossey-Bass.

McCauley, C.D., & Douglas, C.A. (1998). Developmental relationships. In C.D. McCauley, R.S. Moxley, & E. Van Velsor (Eds.), *The Center for Creative Leadership handbook of leadership development* (pp. 160–193). San Francisco: Jossey-Bass.

McCauley, C.D., & Hezlett, S.A. (2001). Individual development in the workplace. In N. Anderson, D.S. Ones, H.K. Sinangil, & C. Viswesvaran (Eds.), *Handbook of industrial, work, and organizational psychology*. London: Sage.

McCauley, C.D., & Hughes-James, M.W. (1994). *An evaluation of the outcomes of a leadership development program*. Greensboro, NC: Center for Creative Leadership.

McCauley, C.D., Ohlott, P.J., & Ruderman, M.N. (1999). *Job Challenge Profile: Facilitator's guide*. San Francisco: Jossey-Bass/Pfeiffer.

McCauley, C.D., Ruderman, M.N., Ohlott, P.J., & Morrow, J.E. (1994). Assessing the developmental components of managerial jobs. *Journal of Applied Psychology, 79*, 544–560.

McCauley, C.D., & Young, D.P. (1993). Creating developmental relationships: Roles and strategies. *Human Resource Management Review, 3*, 219–230.

McDonald-Mann, D. (1998). Skill-based training. In C.D. McCauley, R.S. Moxley, & E. Van Velsor (Eds.), *The Center for Creative Leadership handbook of leadership development* (pp. 106–126). San Francisco: Jossey-Bass.

Morrison, A.M., White, R.P., & Van Velsor, E. (1992). *Breaking the glass ceiling: Can women reach the top of America's largest corporations?* (Updated ed.). Reading, MA: Addison-Wesley.

Morrison, R.F., & Hock, R.R. (1986). Career building: Learning from cumulative work experience. In D.T. Hall (Ed.), *Career development in organizations* (pp. 236–273). San Francisco: Jossey-Bass.

Moxley, R.S., & Wilson, P.O. (1998). A systems approach to leadership development. In C.D. McCauley, R.S. Moxley, & E. Van Velsor (Eds.), *The Center for Creative Leadership handbook of leadership development* (pp. 194–214). San Francisco: Jossey-Bass.

Mumford, A. (1997). *Action learning at work*. Aldershot: Gower.

Noe, R.A. (1996). Is career management related to employee development and performance? *Journal of Organizational Behavior, 17*, 119–133.

Noe, R.A. (1988). An investigation of the determinants of successful assigned mentoring relationships. *Personnel Psychology, 41*, 457–479.

Olivero, G., Bane, K.D., & Kopelman, R.E. (1997). Executive coaching as a transfer of training tool: Effects on productivity in a public agency. *Public Personnel Management, 26*, 461–469.

Orpen, C. (1995). The effects of mentoring on employees' career success. *Journal of Social Psychology, 135*, 667–668.

Pedler, M. (1997). *Action learning in practice* (3rd edn). Brookfield, VT: Gower.

Peterson, D.B. (1996). Executive coaching at work: The art of one-on-one change. *Consulting Psychology Journal: Practice and Research, 48(2)*, 78–86.

Peterson, D.B., & Hicks, M.D. (1996). *Leader as coach: Strategies for coaching and developing others*. Minneapolis, MN: Personnel Decisions International.

Portwood, J.D., & Granrose, C.S. (1986). Organizational career management programs: What's available? What's effective? *Human Resource Planning, 9*, 107–119.

Raelin, J.A. (1997). Individual and situational precursors of successful action learning. *Journal of Management Education, 21*, 368–394.

Ragins, B.R., & Cotton, J.L. (1999). Mentor functions and outcomes: A comparison of men and women in formal and informal mentoring relationships. *Journal of Applied Psychology, 84*, 529–550.

Revans, R.W. (1982). *The origin and growth of action learning*. Bromley: Chartwell Bratt.

Ruderman, M.N., & Ohlott, P.J. (2000). Putting some life into your leadership. *Leadership in Action, 20(5)*, 6–10.

Scandura, T.A. (1992). Mentorship and career mobility: An empirical investigation. *Journal of Organizational Behavior, 13*, 169–174.

Schneider, B., Smith, D.B., Taylor, S., & Fleenor, J. (1998). Personality and organizations: A test of the homogeneity of personality hypothesis. *Journal of Applied Psychology, 83*, 462–470.

Sternberg, R.J., Wagner, R.K., Williams, W.M., & Horvath, J.A. (1995). Testing common sense. *American Psychologist, 50*, 912–927.

Tesluk, P.E., & Jacobs, R.R. (1998). Toward an integrated model of work experience. *Personnel Psychology, 51*, 321–350.

Tharenou, P. (1997). Organisational, job, and personal predictors of employee participation in training and development. *Applied Psychology: An International Review, 46*, 112–113.

Turban, D.B., & Dougherty, T.W. (1994). Role of protégé personality in receipt of mentoring and career success. *Academy of Management Journal, 37*, 688–702.

Van Velsor, E., & Douglas, C.A. (2001). Lessons of a diverse workforce: Comparing the lessons of experience of African-American and white managers. Paper presented at the annual meeting of the Society for Industrial and Organizational Psychology, San Diego, CA.

Van Velsor, E., McCauley, C.D., & Moxley, R.S. (1998). Our view of leadership development. In C.D. McCauley, R.S. Moxley, & E. Van Velsor (Eds.), *The Center for Creative Leadership handbook of leadership development* (pp. 1–26). San Francisco: Jossey-Bass.

Vicere, A.A., & Fulmer, R.M. (1997). *Leadership by design*. Boston: Harvard Business School Press.

Waldroop, J., & Butler, T. (1996). The executive as coach. *Harvard Business Review, 74 (6)*, 111–117.

Wenger, E.C. (1998). *Communities of practice: Learning, meaning and identity*. Cambridge: Cambridge University Press.

Wenger, E.C., & Snyder, W.M. (2000). Communities of practice: The organizational frontier. *Harvard Business Review, 78(1)*, 139–145.

Whitely, W., Dougherty, T.W., & Dreher, G.F. (1991). Relationship of career mentoring and socioeconomic origin to managers' and professionals' early career progress. *Academy of Management Journal, 34*, 331–351.

Wick, C.W., & Leon, L.S. (1993). *The learning edge: How smart managers and smart companies stay ahead*. New York: McGraw-Hill.

Yorks, L., Lamm, S., O'Neil, J., Kolodny, R., Marsick, V.J., & Nilson, G. (1998). Transfer of learning from an action reflection learning program. *Performance Improvement Quarterly, 11(1)*, 59–73.

Young, D., & Dixon, N. (1996). *Helping leaders take effective action: A program evaluation.* Greensboro, NC: Center for Creative Leadership.

Yukl, G. (1998). *Leadership in organizations* (4th edn). Upper Saddle River, NJ: Prentice Hall.

Zemke, R. (1985). The Honeywell studies: How managers learn to manage. *Training, 22(8)*, 46–51.

CHAPTER 19

Developing Innovation in Organizations

Nigel King
University of Huddersfield, UK

SUMMARY

This chapter provides an overview of the literature in work and organizational psychology on innovation in organizations. It starts by considering the definition of the concept, and the ways in which the relationship between creativity and innovation may be understood. It then examines individual, group and organizational-level research, distinguishing between that which conceives of innovation as a product, as a process, and as a characteristic of organizations. The need for research and practice to recognise the importance of context (at differing levels) is emphasised, as is the crucial role of relationships and communication. It is also argued that greater attention should be paid to the ways in which innovativeness relates to organizational, group and personal identities. In conclusion, the chapter stresses the limited value of general prescriptions for enhancing innovation, and suggests qualities required of those facing the task of managing a process which by its very nature is uncertain and hard to control.

INTRODUCTION

For more than twenty years, organizational innovation has remained a key topic in work and organizational psychology and related disciplines. Though classic contributions can be traced back at least as far as the 1950s and 1960s (e.g. Lewin, 1951, Burns and Stalker, 1961), it was the early 1980s that saw an explosion of interest in the area, both academic and popular. Political and economic changes in the USA and Europe (especially Britain) focused attention on competitiveness, the empowerment of managers, and the dominance

Individual Differences and Development in Organisations. Edited by Michael Pearn.
© 2002 John Wiley & Sons, Ltd.

of "the market" in private and public sectors. In this context, books by management writers such as Peters and Waterman (1982) and Kanter (1983) reached a huge audience with their prescriptions for stimulating innovation by structural and cultural change. Delayering, teamwork and participative leadership were widely promoted as essential to organizational innovativeness. The economic downturn of the late 1980s and early 1990s saw growing criticism of these, sometimes simplistic, universal recipes for success (e.g. Dunphy and Stace, 1988; Wilson, 1992), but the importance of innovation continued to be recognized. Current literature justifies this emphasis in terms of the impact of globalization, new technology, and consumerism; however, many of the research topics focused on by contemporary innovation scholars are the same as those that dominated the earlier literature: leadership styles, the role of teams, the nature of innovative climates, and so on. Although there have been some important new theoretical contributions in recent years, for example from a social constructionist perspective (e.g. Bouwen and Fry, 1996), and new substantive areas that have risen to prominence (e.g. temporal issues, diversity), overall I would argue that the more recent development of the area has been somewhat disappointing.

DEFINING INNOVATION

A difficulty for those new to the innovation literature is the wide variety of definitions employed by writers. To some extent this reflects the differing concerns of the disciplines involved in the area, but even within work and organizational (w/o) psychology, there is limited agreement over how the term should be used. The only consensus is that it relates to newness (note that the word is derived from the latin for new—"nova"), but even here, researchers disagree as to how novel a new "something" has to be to count as an innovation. Thus many writers argue that an innovation need only be new to the organization (or organizational sub-unit) into which it is introduced (e.g. Zaltman, Duncan and Holbek, 1973; King and West, 1987), but Kimberly (1981) insists that it should be a "truly" novel phenomenon. Similarly, some researchers include within the concept relatively small-scale changes (e.g. West and Wallace, 1991; King, 1992) while others restrict it to those changes which have a substantial impact on the organization adopting them (Kimberly, 1981). Furthermore, a distinction can be drawn between definitions of innovation as product, process or characteristic. In the first of these, the term is used to describe specific new products or procedures which meet the criteria of novelty and scale. In contrast, process approaches define innovation in terms of the activities involved in introducing the new product or procedure, while the final type of definition stipulates the characteristics by which individuals, groups (or teams) and organizations may be identified as "innovative".

A final definitional issue to consider is how innovation should be distinguished from other related concepts, particularly creativity and organizational change. Again, there are numerous views on this in the literature. Taking creativity first, the concept tends to be understood in a more individualistic way than innovation, often focusing on cognitive processes or personality characteristics. In the context of organizations, it is commonly applied more to the initiation of new ideas than to their implementation. (I will explore the relationship between creativity and organizational innovation in more depth in the next section of this chapter, and will highlight some of the criticisms that have been made of this conventional view of creativity.) With regard to the distinction between innovation and organizational change, writers have mostly seen the former as a sub-set of the latter, and have attempted to draw boundaries by specifying the types of organizational change which are excluded from the concept of innovation. West and Farr (1990) are quite typical here in excluding routine, maturational and predictable seasonal changes. They also exclude "unintended or undesired change" which is perhaps more problematic, given clear research evidence that the innovation process rarely unfolds as intended, and often produces undesired effects (e.g. Van de Ven, Polley, Garud and Venkataraman, 1999; Lewis and Seibold, 1993).

While it is important that researchers make it clear how they are using the term "innovation", it seems to me unlikely that there will ever be a single definition that meets the requirements of all scholars in the field, with their different aims and interests. For the purposes of this chapter, I will take an inclusive approach, not insisting on "absolute novelty" and covering research into intentional change of any scale within organizations. Nicholson (1990) argues that definitional variation is not an impediment to progress in the area, but a reflection of the indeterminate nature of the phenomenon itself. Innovations are inevitably understood differently, according to the perspectives of those involved:

> "My thesis is that, rather than viewing this indeterminacy as a problem to be circum- vented, it is fruitful to let the social construction of innovation occupy the centre of our attention." (pp. 197–198).

I have considerable sympathy with this view, which resonates with my arguments con- cerning innovation and organizational identity presented towards the end of this chapter.

AIMS OF THIS CHAPTER

The present chapter seeks to provide a critical overview of the literature on innovation in organizations. I will draw principally on psychological theory and evidence but will bring in relevant material from allied disciplines where this is required to inform the psychological argument. Given the enormous scope of the field, I will concentrate par- ticularly on areas where there are important implications for individual development in organizations. The first section below will focus on the relationship between creativity and innovation, followed by a review of research into innovation as an organizational product (where the majority of the literature is located). Subsequent sections will con- sider innovation as an organizational process and characteristic, and I will conclude by outlining implications for practice.

CREATIVITY AND INNOVATION

The relationship between creativity and innovation has been conceptualized in many ways, but the most common formulation is to depict creativity as strongly involved in the initiation of innovations, but not necessarily required in their adoption and imple- mentation. This is summed up nicely by Rosenfeld and Servo (1990):

> "Creativity is the starting point for any innovation: in many cases, a solitary process, conjuring up the image of an eccentric scientist buried under mounds of papers, or of an artist surrounded by half-finished canvases and multicoloured palettes. Innovation is the hard work that follows idea conceptions and usually involves the labour of many people with varied, yet complementary, skills" (page 252).

Such a depiction of the role of creativity in organizational innovation provides the rationale for many of the strategies advocated for enhancing organizational innovativeness, including idea generation techniques, some forms of creativity training, and selection procedures based on identifying creative individuals. The rationale is that if more creative people can be recruited, or existing staff trained to perform more creatively, more and/or better innovative ideas will be produced. However, although this view is widely held, by no means all writers accept the notion that the major role of creativity in innovation is the generation of new ideas which serve as the start of the process. Some see creative thinking skills as being involved throughout the innovation process, not just at the stage of idea initiation. Min Basadur and colleagues, for example, characterize creativity as involving both divergent (ideation) and convergent (evaluation) thinking at all stages of an innovation attempt, from problem-finding, through problem solving to solution implementation (Basadur, Graen, and Green, 1982; Basadur, Graen and Scandura, 1986).

Other writers have argued that even if we accept the traditional distinction between the two concepts (creativity as an individual process and innovation as social), it is wrong to assume that the relationship between the two is necessarily a positive one. As I have highlighted elsewhere (King, 1995), some typical characteristics of "creative" people are not necessarily congruent with the requirements of successful innovation implementation—independence and non-conformity, for example. Equally, there may be conflict between the external drivers for organizational innovation, such as the need to compete in a particular market, and the personal needs of highly creative people to pursue ideas which capture their interest and imagination. A further limitation to the view that creativity is antecedent to innovation stems from the fact that most definitions of innovation—as noted earlier—only require the product, process or procedure to be new to the organizational unit of adoption, and not necessarily to the person introducing the idea. Thus an individual manager importing into an organization an innovation with which they are already familiar (perhaps from a previous job in another organization) does not need to be particularly creative in terms of cognitive abilities or personality traits. In fact, other types of skill or personality characteristic may be more important—persistence and persuasiveness, for instance.

Rather than trying to reformulate the creativity-innovation link to encompass the issues raised above, some scholars have rejected the notion that creativity and innovation are separate phenomena—at least when considered in the context of organizations (e.g. Unsworth, 2001). The distinction between the two can be seen as one of research focus and level of analysis, with work on "creativity in organizations" tending to concentrate on individual-level factors at the initiation stage of the innovation process, while "organizational innovation" research is more concerned with social factors (e.g. structure, team function, culture) and the adoption and implementation of new ideas. This reflects divisions in the literature quite accurately, and therefore may be a convenient way of categorising it, but care must be taken to avoid giving the misleading impression that the initial stages of the innovation process can be understood in purely individualistic terms. Such a position is not supported by research which has looked in detail at the development of particular innovations (e.g. King, 1992; Van de Ven et al., 1999), as we will see in the later section on the innovation process.

It is a common argument that precise definitions which clearly delineate between concepts are a requirement for progress in any field (see Parkhurst, 1999, in relation to creativity). Contrary to this, I would contend that in the area of innovation research, there are real benefits to be gained by accepting that the boundaries between the concepts of innovation and creativity are inevitably blurred, as this encourages cross-fertilization of ideas from the two research traditions rather than futile attempts to carve up the territory of each. This is especially true in relation to developments in social psychological understandings of creativity since the late 1980s, which have effectively challenged the "lone genius" myth of creativity, even in areas where it as deeply entrenched in public and academic consciousness, such as fine art (Montuori and Purser, 1995; Freeman, 1993). Csikszentmihalyi's highly influential systems model of creativity (1988) recognizes that "the person" introduces variation in an area, but can do so only because of his or her access to a body of relevant knowledge ("domain") and can only succeed if the variation is validated by those gatekeepers who have power to accept or reject changes to the domain (known as the "field"). The relevance of this kind of understanding of creativity to organizational innovation seems self-evident (see Ford, 1995).

INNOVATION AS ORGANIZATIONAL PRODUCT

Research which conceptualizes innovation as an organizational product[1] has been predominant in the literature. It has had as its central concern the identification of factors which enhance or impede an organization's ability to produce more and/or better innovations. Reviews of the literature commonly divide it into individual, group and organizational levels of analysis (e.g. Staw, 1984; Anderson and King, 1993); though not without its limitations, this provides a comprehensible framework for organizing a huge and diverse body of published material.

INDIVIDUAL LEVEL RESEARCH

Theory and evidence relating to the role of individuals in innovation mostly centers on three types of person; leaders, change agents and idea champions. The part played by individuals outside of these influential and generally senior positions is most often restricted to a discussion of "resistance to change".

Regarding leaders, work in the innovation area has largely followed developments in wider leadership research, though often with rather a lag. Thus early research attempted to identify personal characteristics of innovative leaders, with limited success (e.g. Mohr, 1969). The emphasis then changed from characteristics to leader behaviours that facilitated innovation, generally referred to in terms of leadership style. Influenced by hugely successful popular texts on organizational change and excellence (Peters and Waterman, 1982; Kanter, 1983), from the early 1980s onwards there was considerable agreement amongst writers in the area that a democratic and participative (though not laissez faire) leadership style is most appropriate to nurture innovation, as it encourages subordinates to become involved in innovation decisions, to feel safe to take the risks often associated with innovation, and to develop a sense of commitment to the changes they participate in. By the late 1980s, some scholars were arguing against the notion of a universal "best style" for innovation and the adoption of a contingency approach (Dunphy and Stace,

---

[1] N.B. This usage of the term "innovation as organizational product" must not be confused with the much narrower concept of "product innovation" which refers to a specific body of literature concerned with innovation in manufactured products.

1988; Manz, Barstein, Hostager and Shapiro, 1989), though the unqualified recommendation of participative leadership is still seen in some contemporary writing. From the
late 1980s onwards, researchers have begun to examine the potential contribution of
transformational leadership to innovation production (Howell and Higgins, 1990), and
have emphasized the importance of a leaders' ability to utilize different styles over the
course of the innovation process (Quinn, 1988; Van de Ven et al., 1999).

"Ideas champions" are those who voluntarily take on the role of promoting the introduction and implementation of an innovation. In some cases an idea may be championed
by its originator, but often championing is taken up by another person, perhaps because
the originator lacks the power, influence or skills of persuasion to succeed on their own.
It therefore follows that ideas champions do not necessarily need to possess the characteristics of a "creator" (in the narrow, idea-generating sense of the word). Instead, it
is commonly argued that the success of a champion depends upon the person holding a
position of influence within an organization and the skills to develop and effectively use
wide networks. Howell and Higgins (1990) found that ideas champions displayed transformational leadership qualities, enabling them to inspire others. A study by Dougherty
and Hardy (1996) showed that senior, long-serving members of staff in large, mature
organizations were more able to successfully champion ideas than newer, more junior
members, because of the former's ability to "work" personal networks.

While some innovations are facilitated by informal champions who choose to take on
such a role, often a formal change agent is assigned responsibility for overseeing the
innovation process. The nature of the task such a person faces is strongly shaped by
whether he or she is an internal change agent (i.e. a member of the organization into
which the change is being introduced) or an external agent, working on a consultancy
basis. An internal change agent has some similarities to an idea champion, in that he
or she is likely to benefit from positional power and networking abilities. However,
change agents (unlike ideas champions) are usually in a situation where the decision
to adopt an innovation has already been taken; the challenge is to foster support and
gather resources to facilitate implementation. They can draw on "insider" knowledge
of the organization to do this, but may also be constrained by their own involvement
in the politics and personal relationships that constitute the organization's history, and
by their own (and others') awareness that they will have to live with the consequences
of the innovation. In contrast, external change agents have the advantages of distance
and independence from internal politics, but the disadvantage of a necessarily limited
understanding of the organization. Furthermore, they always face the potential danger of
suspicion and even hostility from members who may see them as unwelcome outsiders
threatening a comfortable status quo. The knowledge, skills and abilities required for an
effective external change agent have been widely discussed in the literature, especially
from the perspective of Organizational Development (OD). The list of eight actions and
characteristics suggested by Rogers (1983; see Table 19.1) is reflected in more recent
accounts. It should be noted, though, that the importance of particular aspects of change
agent practice is itself likely to vary between organizations and over time, as the nature
of organizational life changes (Van Eynde and Bledsoe, 1990).

While a great deal of attention has been paid to the role of key individuals in the
innovation process—leaders, idea champions and change agents—the involvement of
other organizational members has mostly been considered in the form of "resistance"
and how it should be overcome. Managers commonly see resistance to change as in some

TABLE 19.1 Change agent actions and characteristics likely to facilitate successful innovation

---

The amount of effort the change agent makes to contact clients.
An orientation towards clients rather than towards the change agency.
The degree to which the innovation program is compatible with clients' needs.
The empathy of the change agent with clients.
The degree to which the change agent and his or her clients share the same outlook and
    background.
The change agent's credibility to clients.
The extent to which the change agent is able and willing to work through opinion leaders in
    the organization.
The extent to which he or she is able to increase the clients' own ability to evaluate innovations.

Adapted from Rogers (1983).

sense "natural", and some of the research literature encourages the view that certain types of people are simply resistant to change—perhaps because of their age, tenure, educational level and so on. The classic innovation diffusion literature, for example, focuses on characteristics of adopters and resistors, often with a pro-innovation and individual-blame bias, memorably characterised by Rogers (1983) as implying that "if the shoe doesn't fit, there's something wrong with your foot". Another substantial body of literature focuses on situational antecedents of resistance, emphasizing that it often occurs not through hostility to a new idea *per se*, but because of the actual or feared negative impact of change on interpersonal relationships and the climate of the organization (e.g. Lawrence, 1969; DuBrin, 1974). This approach, stemming from the "human relations" tradition, has stimulated a considerable volume of work dedicated to advising managers on how to overcome resistance, through attention to the social aspects of innovation (e.g. Kotter and Schlesinger, 1979).

Even where resistance is construed in terms of situational factors, the concept tends to be used in a way which oversimplifies the way that organizational members are involved in the innovation process, and overstates the extent to which it is controlled by management. Detailed case-studies of innovations by Meston and King (1996) and Shue (1998) showed a complex range of responses amongst different groups within an organization, and demonstrated the relationship between the way innovation impacts on power relations, values and cultures and the various forms of resistance. In these cases, and in those studied in the Minnesota program (Van de Ven et al., 1999), it was clear that the ability of managers to control the unfolding of the innovation process was very limited, and that the involvement of many people outside of managerial positions had a major shaping influence on the course of what Van de Ven et al call "the innovation journey".

A final point to make concerning resistance to innovation is that academics and managers alike need to avoid assuming that it is necessarily a bad thing for organizations. Resistance at any level beyond the intransigence of isolated individuals is rarely (if ever) simply a manifestation of an unthinking refusal to accept the new. Instead, it reflects perceived threats to valued aspects of people's working lives—be it power, status, quality of relationships, pride in work achievements or a cherished set of cultural values. Shue's (1998) study of a medical education innovation, mentioned above, showed that the group who were most resistant—mid-ranking administrative and support staff—were those who saw themselves as losing most in terms of power and culture, and gaining least.

Rather than seeing resistance as an obstacle to "overcome", managers may benefit from viewing it diagnostically; as a pointer to areas where they have perhaps failed to properly consider the impact of the innovation, and where further attention is required. Managers are often at some remove from the day-to-day consequences of innovation, and formal feedback mechanisms about innovation progress may be distorted by subordinates' desire not to appear to be attacking a "pet project". Resistance—and other forms of member response—can be a valuable source of information for those leading an innovation attempt.

GROUP LEVEL RESEARCH

Although historically there has been less research at the group level than either the individual or the organizational, over the last decade or so it has attracted a considerable amount of attention, and has been the subject of several review articles (King and Anderson, 1990; Anderson, 1992; Agrell and Gustafson, 1996). In this overview I will concentrate on two broad areas that encompass a substantial proportion of the group-level innovation research—group composition and group climate. For the sake of coherence, I will consider work on temporal aspects of group innovation in the later section on "innovation as an organizational process", although I recognize that some of this material takes more of a "product" approach.

Within the literature on group composition and innovation, there has been considerable discussion of the effects of group heterogeneity—or more recently diversity—on innovativeness. Earlier work (e.g. Geschka, 1983; Kanter, 1983) tended to propose that heterogeneity was likely to facilitate innovation, because of the opportunity it provided to bring a wider range of perspectives to bear on a problem and thus to avoid some of the pitfalls of group decision-making identified by social psychologists (see below). More recent research has tended to paint a more complex picture. Diversity in membership may potentially enhance innovation through the wider expertise and experience it can bring to a group, but equally it may have the opposite effect, because of conflict and communication difficulties that can arise amongst people with very different backgrounds and perspectives. Conversely, homogenous groups may lack breadth in the intellectual resources available to them, but benefit from greater cohesiveness, which has often been associated with innovation success. (It should be noted, however, that cohesiveness may be at least as much a product of successful performance as it is a cause of it—see Mullen and Cooper, 1994).

Given the apparently contradictory arguments about the likely effect of diversity on innovative performance, it make sense to attempt a more sophisticated analysis, recognizing that we should not expect a general relationship between heterogeneous membership and innovation, regardless of context. Agrell and Gustafson (1996) break down work group diversity into four different types: professional, tenure, demographic and functional. They contend that these different types of diversity have different implications for work group innovation. The limited evidence to date provides support for the general notion that the type of diversity present in a group matters for innovative performance. O'Reilly III, Williams and Barsade (1998) found that ethnic diversity in a large clothing manufacturer was positively related to innovation (though only for certain ethnic mixes), tenure diversity negatively related and gender diversity unrelated. The value of this kind of work, taking a more fine-grained approach to studying the impact of diversity, is that instead of encouraging bland generalizations about how diversity influences innovation, it draws attention to the social psychological processes involved in the actual working through of innovation attempts in groups. In so doing it can help rectify the neglect of context in much of the literature (as urged by Triandis, 1996 and Nkomo, 1996, for example).

Along with composition, group climate has been a popular topic for writers on innovation, though the concept is frequently not clearly defined. In general, researchers have simply imported organizational-level definitions of climate to the group level, and taken it to refer to the characteristic "feelings, attitudes and behavioural tendencies" (Nystrom, 1990) of the group. Research has often focused on particular dimensions of climate, rather than attempting to consider it holistically, with group cohesiveness being one of the most popular group climate variables to be examined in relation to innovation. Cohesiveness refers to the extent to which group members feel a sense of identity with and attachment to the group as a whole and to their fellow members. Quite commonly, it is viewed as a facilitator of innovation, because members of a highly cohesive work group are likely to derive more satisfaction from the success of group action (Nystrom, 1979) and to have better internal communication than less cohesive groups (Danowski, 1980). However, cohesiveness can lead to an excessive focus on protecting the group from anything which might disrupt its pleasurable inter-personal relations, with the consequence that poor decisions about innovation (and other matters) are made—a situation very similar to the phenomenon of "group think" described by Janis (1982).

The limitations of single-dimensional conceptualizations of group climate led to attempts to produce a more sophisticated understanding of the way climate is related to innovation. The "four factor" model of group climate proposed by West (1990), from which the Team Climate Inventory (TCI) was derived (Anderson and West, 1994) has been an influential attempt to achieve such an understanding. This predicts that group innovation will be facilitated by four climate factors; shared vision, participative safety, task orientation and support for innovation. Support for the importance of these (or very similar) variables has come from West and colleagues' own work in a variety of health care organization settings (e.g. West and Anderson, 1996; West and Wallace, 1992) and from a study of 17 teams in Swedish organizations by Agrell and Gustafson (1994). There remains a need to examine whether other climate factors identified as facilitators or inhibitors at the organizational level are also important at the group level—for example, playfulness, challenge and dynamism (Ekvall, 1996).

Although group composition and climate are typically treated as separate variables, in reality they are of course interdependent. The "feelings, attitudes and behavioural tendencies" of a group can hardly be independent of the particular mix of people that make up the group. Many of the arguments about how diversity influences group innovation can be recast in climate terms, for example, through their effects on cohesiveness. It would be wrong, though, to conclude that climate is no more than a product of the interaction between specific individuals with specific characteristics. Group climate, I would argue, is always shaped by the wider organizational climate in which it is embedded, though not in a simple, deterministic way. Thus a general climate of risk-aversion is likely to infect that of organizational sub-units, damaging their innovative potential, but the extent to which this happens is likely to vary between groups—more autonomous groups may be able to resist the dominant climate better than those under more centralised control. There is a need for w/o psychologists to devote much more attention to the question of how groups relate to the wider organization, and what implications this has for innovation, with reference to climate and a range of other concepts such as leadership and culture.

ORGANIZATIONAL LEVEL RESEARCH

The organizational level encompasses the largest proportion of the literature, and also covers the widest span of disciplines, including psychology, sociology, management studies, communication studies and Organization Development (OD). Numerous factors have been studied as probable antecedents to, or influences on, organizational innovativeness, of which the most prominent are structure, strategy, climate, culture and the nature of the organization's relationship with its environment (see King and Anderson, 2002, for a recent review of this area). There is insufficient space here to evaluate the evidence relating to each of these main factors in any depth, and in any case the interconnections between factors are so strong and important that considering them in isolation from each other is of limited value. After all, the practical aim of this literature is to determine whether there are some forms of organizing which foster innovation more successfully than others. This emphasis is reflected in the long tradition of providing leaders and decision-makers with prescriptions for how to design their organizations to maximize innovative performance. In this section I will therefore describe some of the most influential of such accounts, before discussing critiques of this kind of approach to understanding innovation.

Organic versus mechanistic organizations

Burns and Stalker's (1961) work relating the organization's structure to the nature of its environment played a truly seminal role in this field, and remains widely cited to this day. Based on studies of a cross-section of British firms in the 1950s, they defined a continuum from mechanistic to organic. Mechanistic organizations are hierarchical, sub-divided by functions with rigid job definitions, and are dominated by vertical patterns of communication. Organic organizations, in contrast, have a flatter structure with many temporary project-based work groups, flexible job definitions, more devolved decision-making based on the needs of particular projects, and a high degree of lateral communication. Burns and Stalker found that mechanistic organizations operated well in stable environments with little need for innovation, but were very poor at coping with rapidly changing or turbulent environments—for which organic forms were best suited.

The "excellence" model

The early 1980s saw an upsurge of interest in organizational innovation and change, closely linked to the political and economic changes of the time in America and Western Europe (as I noted in the introduction to this chapter). These circumstances ensured a receptive audience for best-selling texts which drew lessons from successful innovative companies (e.g. Peters and Waterman's "In Search of Excellence" (1982) and Kanter's "The Change Masters" (1983)) and stimulated a boom in academic research into organizational innovation and change. The recommendations from this work had much in common with Burns and Stalker's description of the organic organization: flat structures, project team organization, lateral communications. However, there was more emphasis than before on the less tangible aspects of organization—the need for a playful and risk-tolerant climate, the need to embed innovative values in the organization culture, and so on.

New forms of organizing for a new millennium

From the 1990s and into the new millennium, many writers have argued that major technological and social changes are producing new forms of organizing, in which inno-vation-potential is a key attribute. They point in particular to globalization, consumerism (in the public as well as the private sector), and developments in IT—above all, the in-ternet. Characteristics of the "new" organization include some which are familiar from the early 1980s if not from Burns and Stalker: delayering, project-based structures and participative leadership. However, structure in itself is seen as much less important than it traditionally has been, and it is stressed that organizing should be around processes and strategies. Internal and external networking is seen as crucially important, as is the building of strategic alliances between organizations. The most radical predictions are for an increasing number of organizations which largely exist on a virtual basis, with interactions amongst members and with clients/customers predominantly via the inter-net. Pettigrew and Fulton (2000) have recently presented findings from a major survey of large and medium-sized organizations in Europe, which showed substantial evidence of changes in structure, processes and the nature and management of organizational boundaries. However, the survey only found a small minority who showed wholesale transformation to new organizational forms, with changes in all three of the key areas of structure, processes and boundaries. Interestingly, these organizations showed signif-icantly better performance than the rest, though of course we must be cautious about assuming a causal relationship from such a correlation.

Research into organizational characteristics has made a substantial contribution to our understanding of innovation at work. Contrary to earlier claims (Downs and Mohr, 1976), there appears to be a fair degree of consistency in the relationship between innovation adoption and such features as centralization, specialization, the availability of slack resources, managerial attitudes to change, and external and internal communication (see Damanpour's meta-analysis, 1991). Also, for at least some of the common prescriptions there is a sound psychological rationale; for instance, the importance of networking can be understood in terms of access to diverse sources of information and opportunities for building support for change (Dougherty and Hardy, 1996; Weenig, 1999).

Despite these strengths, the literature has some important weaknesses. There is a ten-dency to over-generalize from successful innovators, and to underestimate the extent to which such success may be related to business circumstances at a particular historical moment. Wilson (1992) points out that many of the organizations held up as role models by Peters and Waterman (1982) subsequently suffered serious problems as markets, tech-nology and the global politico-economic system changed. (Of course, there are examples of organizations that have maintained successful innovative performance for many years, adapting to changing circumstances along the way—3M being perhaps the best known; Gundling, 2000.) Even if we can establish that certain forms present an overall advantage in innovation, it does not mean that organizations can ensure innovativeness by changing to such a form. Any major transformation needs to take into account the organization's unique context, including its history. King and Anderson (2002) give the example of the introduction of autonomous work groups; while these may generally facilitate innovation, if in a specific case there is a history of members feeling that management has been remote and uninvolved, the sudden granting of greater autonomy may be construed as yet further evidence of neglect.

LIMITATIONS OF RESEARCH INTO "INNOVATION AS ORGANIZATIONAL PRODUCT"

The problem of over-generalized prescriptions noted in the previous section with regard to organizational level research also apply at individual and group levels, but it is only one of the limitations of the whole "organizational product" approach. These include methodological weaknesses in research design and the measurement of innovation as a dependent variable, and theoretical weaknesses in conceptualizing the dynamic nature of innovation.

Much of the research in this tradition has used a cross-sectional design, raising difficulties of judging directions of causality. This is compounded by the tendency to take for granted that innovation is an outcome of organizational processes—for instance, that if groups with more participative leaders are more innovative, it is reasonably safe to assume that leadership style influenced innovation production. In fact, it may be the case that failure to innovative encourages a more coercive style (and the opposite in successful groups), or—as is most likely—that over time innovation and leadership shape each other. (Note Mullen and Cooper's conclusions, cited earlier, that group climate can be both an antecedent and a product of group performance.) Although there has been a growing awareness of the advantages of longitudinal studies, many of these rely on a simple two-stage design, where a set of factors at time 'A' is used to predict innovation performance at time 'B'. Preferable though this is to a cross-sectional design, it still presents a rather static picture of innovation—showing that the possession of certain attributes tends to lead to a certain level of innovation, but revealing little about *how* this happens.

For a research approach that is centrally interested in innovation as an outcome variable, the quality of the innovation measures used is naturally of great importance. Unfortunately, innovation is an extraordinarily difficult construct to measure, and the two main methods used both have serious flaws. The first and most direct method is to produce some sort of tally of innovations over a set period (e.g. Daft, 1978). An obvious issue here is scale. Does *any* change which meets the criteria used, count as an innovation, or does it have to have a certain level of impact on the organization (or sub-unit)? We have already seen that scholars differ considerably in the scale they require of a change for it to be considered an innovation. Even more problematic is how one deals with a selection of innovations of varying scale—is a group which produces ten minor innovations more or less innovative than one which produces two major ones? Researchers may define some kind of weighting system, but arguably this would always have an arbitrary quality to it, regarding the boundaries between different degrees of innovativeness. In any case, at what stage in its development is the scale of an innovation determined? An innovation may initially seem quite minor and local in impact, but over time become far more pervasive and radical in its impact; alternately, a change announced and initially appearing as a "big bang" may turn out to be little more than a damp squib! A final complication is that it is often quite difficult to determine whether one is dealing with a single innovation or a group of innovations. A new computer system may be counted as one innovation according to some criteria, but a number of separate though linked innovations (in software, hardware, role definitions, working practices, etc.) by other criteria.

Despite these difficulties, tallying systems may have some utility where they are being used to compare the performance of groups in the same of very similar contexts—especially in the same organization—so long as the criteria are defined with great care and are properly validated (e.g. West and Anderson, 1996). As soon as they are used to compare across contexts they become, in my opinion, irredeemably compromised. Can anything meaningful be learnt by comparing the number of innovations produced by, say, a cancer research team to those of a team of advertising executives or aero-engine designers for an equivalent time period?

The main alternative to the tallying approach is the use of expert ratings of individual, group or organizational innovativeness (e.g. West and Wallace, 1991). This parallels Amabile's (1983) "consensual assessment" technique, which is widely employed in the measurement of creativity, and has demonstrated that if judges with appropriate expertise are chosen and are provided with clear enough criteria, high levels of inter-rater agreement can be obtained. As well as being easier to carry out than a properly-constructed tallying system, this means of measurement has the advantage that experts can draw on intimate contextual knowledge to give validity to their ratings. Against this, it is highly likely that expert raters will draw on other characteristics than just the propensity to produce effective innovations in their judgments—self-promotional abilities of the targets, broad performance reputation, high-profile "past glories" and so on. Expert ratings are of little more use than tallies for comparing innovativeness in different contexts; it is unlikely that a single team of raters would be expert enough to make reliable and valid judgments in two or more different contexts, and if different teams are used for each context, one cannot assume that they are applying the same standards.

The difficulties in measuring innovation production are matched by theoretical difficulties with the "organizational product" approach as a whole. Most importantly, this kind of innovation research pays minimal attention to what goes on in the process of bringing an innovation from the initiation of an idea to implementation and routinization into organizational life. Rogers (1983) says: "Essentially, this approach amounts to making the innovation process 'timeless'. It is convenient for the researcher but intellectually deceitful with respect to the process he is investigating" (page 177).

Failure to attend to the process is closely linked to a second major theoretical weakness; the decontextualizing of innovation. Most of the research has a strongly positivistic orientation, seeking to produce generalizable theories which—it is hoped—will allow innovative performance to be predicted and ultimately controlled. It requires the reduction of the phenomena of innovation to a set of variables, to be measured quantitatively, and the data aggregated across cases for analysis. This may provide information on the factors which normally facilitate or inhibit innovation, but it ignores they way that any specific innovation is shaped by its unique social and historical context within an organization. If this is the only kind of innovation research which is reaching a wide academic and professional audience, we are in danger of producing an understanding of the "typical" innovation which bears little resemblance to any one individual case. To avoid such an eventuality, we need to turn to process-based approaches to innovation research.

INNOVATION AS ORGANIZATIONAL PROCESS

Process-oriented research into innovation addresses a different set of research questions from product-oriented research; instead of asking what makes some organizations (or organizational sub-units) more innovative than others, it asks how innovations develop within organizations, what factors shape the unfolding process, and what the role of managers—and other organizational members—can and should be in directing it towards desired outcomes. Some writers seek to move towards generalizable models of the process through the accumulation of case evidence, but they tend to do so in a more cautious manner than much of the work from a product approach, showing reluctance to make simple prescriptions for success. Because this kind of research is by its nature attentive to context, it tends to make more use of qualitative techniques such as unstructured observation, depth interviews, and documentary analysis, sometimes on their own and sometimes in combination with survey instruments.

STAGE MODELS OF THE PROCESS

In most of the literature, where the innovation process is described it is in terms of a series of relatively discrete steps or stages. Zaltman, Duncan and Holbek (1973) describe two main stages of *initiation* and *implementation*, with the point of innovation adoption marking the boundary between the two. These in turn are further sub-divided; initiation includes knowledge/awareness, formation of attitudes, and decision, while implementation includes initial and continued/sustained implementation sub-stages. Rogers (1983) also identifies main stages of initiation and implementation but defines the substages somewhat differently; agenda-setting and matching within the former, and redefining/restructuring, clarifying and routinizing within the latter. Note the more detailed account of post-adoption activities in Rogers' model, reflecting the concerns of the innovation diffusion literature with which he is strongly associated. These models and others like them (e.g. Hage and Aiken, 1970; Kimberly, 1981; Staw, 1990) are not derived directly from innovation case data, but from their authors' general knowledge of the literature, and doubtless in most cases from personal experience too. Although usually presented as descriptive, they are sometimes interpreted in more prescriptive tones, as depictions of how the process *ought* to occur.

Although stage models of innovation like these will be highly familiar to anyone who has read even a modest amount of the organizational innovation literature, they have rarely been subject to any kind of empirical test of their accuracy. The handful of studies over more than two decades which have sought to do so present a rather mixed picture, perhaps not surprisingly given the wide variety of types of organization and innovation they embrace. Ettlie (1980) found that a six-stage model was seen as at least adequately describing the innovation process in 21 out of 34 transportation innovations, based on the reports of managers from the companies involved. Pelz (1983) found support for discrete stages in relatively simple urban innovations but not in more complex ones, while Witte (1972) found no consistent evidence for a stage model in a study of the adoption of a technological innovation across 233 organizations. My own participant observation study of small-scale innovation on a hospital psycho-geriatric ward (King, 1992) found little support for Zaltman et al's (1973) stage model. Axtell, Holman,

Unsworth, Wall, Waterson and Harrington (2000) did find that a sample of engineering designers perceived different factors as influences on innovation at the initiation stage from the implementation stage, suggesting that this is a meaningful division of the process. It is worth noting, however, that the innovation process may appear more ordered and rational in hindsight than it does when it is ongoing (Anderson and King, 1993); a point potentially relevant to Ettlie's (1980) study too.

An Alternative Approach: The Minnesota Innovation Research Program

I would contend that this limited and diverse evidence suggests that traditional stage-based models may fail to adequately describe the innovation process in many—though perhaps not all—circumstances. They are therefore of questionable utility as a basis for making sense of the innovation process in specific cases. An alternative approach has been developed in the highly influential Minnesota Innovation Research Program (MIRP). Here a large team of researchers closely tracked the development of fourteen varied innovations over a period of up to ten years, using a mixture of quantitative and qualitative methods (Van de Ven, Polley, Garud and Venkataraman, 1999). On the basis of this they identified a set of observations of common features of the innovation process which occurred in most cases, but not in a rigid sequence of developmental stages. These observations are summarised in table 19.2.

In my psycho-geriatric ward study, mentioned above, I found better support for the kind of approach to the innovation process developed in MIRP—as described by Schroeder,

TABLE 19.2   Process observations from the Minnesota Innovation Research Program

Initiation Period
1. Most innovations have a long gestation period prior to initiation
2. Internal or external "shocks" trigger initiation
3. Plans are developed, more to "sell" the idea than as realistic scenarios for development

Developmental Period
4. The initial idea proliferates
5. Setbacks and mistakes are frequently encountered
6. Criteria of success and failure often change during the process
7. Organizational members participate in the innovation in highly fluid ways
8. Senior managers and/or investors intervene in the process throughout development
9. Relationships with other organizations develop during the process and shape its course
10. Innovation participants often work with external organizations and agencies to build infrastructures for their innovations

Implementation/Termination Period
11. During the innovation, the "new" and "old" are linked and integrated
12. The innovation process stop at implementation or is terminated through lack of resources. Attributions of success or failure are made, though are often misdirected.

Van de Ven, Scudder and Polley (1989)—than for a conventional stage-based approach. The Minnesota studies clearly illustrate the richness of understanding that can be achieved from process-based research, although they also show the resource-intensive and time-consuming nature of such work, which has doubtless inhibited the wider employment of such an approach. A key message of this work is that the "innovation journey" (as Ven de Ven et al. call it) cannot be controlled by management, as it almost always takes unexpected twists and turns and is influenced by a wide range of social forces within and outside the organization. I will consider the implications of this for managerial practice in the concluding section of this chapter.

TEMPORAL PROCESSES AND WORK GROUP INNOVATION

There has been even less research into the process of innovation in work groups than into organizational-level processes. I therefore very much welcome the fact that research into temporal processes in groups has begun to be applied to the topic of innovation. Gersick's work on pacing in experimental and real world groups (Gersick, 1989, 1994) has been influential here. She showed experimentally that when given a simulated project task, groups of fixed longevity displayed without any prompting a marked change in their activity at around the midpoint of their life-span. Kelly, Futoran and McGrath (1990) found that the kind of timing problems groups experienced in earlier tasks shaped the way they responded to new problems. King and Anderson (2002) point out that such findings are potentially relevant for groups involved in innovation attempts, suggesting that changes in pacing are probably inevitable over the course of an innovation process in a group especially where a fixed deadline is imposed—and that efforts to "force the pace" early in the process are likely to be fruitless, and may even be harmful.

As well as attending to the internal pacing of innovations, groups and those managing them need to consider the synchronizing of work to external temporal patterns—a concept known as "entrainment". Relevant external patterns can include such things as seasonal variations in supply and demand, fixed administrative schedules such as the financial year, or the unfolding of change processes elsewhere in the organization. Careful entrainment may enable an innovating group to benefit from exploiting "windows of opportunity" (Ancona and Chong, 1999) that maximize their chances of success, while poor entrainment can be a major inhibitor of effective innovation, as Ancona (1990) showed in a study of programme innovation in an American education department (education is, of course, a sector where there are particularly strong and important temporal patterns within the overall structure of the "academic year").

INNOVATION AS ORGANIZATIONAL CHARACTERISTIC

It is commonplace for organizations to describe themselves as "innovative"—in recruitment advertising, in formal reports, in newsletters, and a whole range of other documentation. However, the notion of innovation as an organizational characteristic has not received much attention from researchers in w/o psychology and related disciplines. I suspect that this is largely because it has not been seen as an issue of interest in its own right, being "merely" self-promotional rhetoric, or else reducible to the level of product (an organization's "true" innovativeness being measurable in terms of innovation production). I would argue that this misses an important point. Innovativeness is not an objectively quantifiable property of an organization, but rather an aspect of the way the organization sees and presents itself—in other words its identity. (One may also look and individual and group innovative identities in the same way.) The relationship between this identity and the actual production of innovation is not a straightforward one; it is likely to be shaped by a whole range of historical, cultural and (in the broadest sense) commercial factors. Thus a company such as Jack Daniels presents an identity of tradition and continuity in its advertising, downplaying the many technological, managerial and organizational changes that have occurred in the distilling industry since its foundation in the 1880s. In contrast, 3M takes every opportunity to present innovativeness as central to the company's identity, and the words of Senior Vice President William Coyne make it clear that innovativeness relates to culture, philosophy and values as much as to the actual production of new ideas:

> "3M's culture of innovation has formed the bedrock of our success for nearly 100 years. It is an amalgam of superb scientific discipline and stubborn individualism fuelled by a passion for solving customer problems. If you haven't grown up in it, it's difficult to understand and even more difficult to explain." (Quoted on back cover of Gundling, 2000).

The study of how innovative (or anti-innovative) organizational identities are constructed, maintained and promoted requires different methodologies from the positivist approaches which have dominated the field, with their reliance on surveys and quasi-experimental designs. We are dealing here with questions of meaning and of the use of language in specific contexts with specific purposes, for which non-positivist approaches utilising qualitative methods are suited. Social constructionist researchers have already begun to address questions of organizational innovation (e.g. Bouwen and Fry, 1996; Symon, 2000), while others have approached the area from the perspective of grounded theory (Carrero, Pieró & Salanova, 2000) and phenomenological psychology (Ross and King, 2001). It must be noted that there are considerable differences amongst these qualitative approaches in the kinds of assumptions they make about the nature of social reality and of the research process (see, for example, Symon and Cassell, 1998, and Symon, Cassell and Dickson, 2000). What they have in common is a recognition that the study of organizational innovation must be closely concerned with specific contexts, and that language is essentially the medium through which organizational life is constructed. This is an area which is likely to be of growing importance in future research.

CONCLUSION

Innovation is an area where there is no shortage of recommendations for managers. Indeed, a key message of this chapter has been the need to be wary of general prescriptions for how to innovate effectively that abound in popular texts (and can be found in some of the academic literature too). This does not mean that managers cannot learn anything useful from "best practice" in other organizations, but that they should not uncritically follow the lead of those trumpeted as heroic exemplars of innovation success. Organizational innovation is a social process, heavily dependent on context, and as the pioneering work of MIRP shows (Van de Ven et al, 1999; see above), the course of the "innovation journey" cannot be known in detail in advance.

If we understand the innovation process in this way, the implications for practice are less about specific structures to set up or procedures to follow, and more about the way managers interact with other people and the relationships they develop and use in the process of steering an innovation attempt. Good communications at all levels are likely to be important to enable managers to be aware of how an innovation is developing and to spot unexpected problems earlier enough to do something about them. To extend the "journey" metaphor, managers need to be able to provide a clear vision of the destination of an innovation, without being rigid about the means of getting there or the precise route to follow. In terms of the personal qualities required to achieve this, flexibility, responsiveness to change and interpersonal networking skills are highly desirable.

Despite my scepticism about prescriptive advice, I am happy to acknowledge that the literature offers much that is useful for anticipating likely pitfalls in the innovation process, and identifying means of avoiding them. Many of these have been addressed in this chapter: the role of creativity throughout the innovation process; the innovative potential of diversity in teams, and the kind of climate factors that facilitate innovation; the importance of temporal factors such as pacing and entrainment; the key role of networking and alliance-building; the inhibiting effects of hierarchy and authoritarian leadership. I would emphasize, though, that managers must always consider these points in the specific context of their organization, including such intangible things as its values, traditions, internal politics and so on. Take as an example the near universal preference in the literature for participative over authoritarian leadership. In the vast majority of cases, that managers would be safe to assume that the former style would be more conducive to innovation than the latter. However, there are countless ways in which participation can be enacted in practice, and in any one case some ways are likely to be much more successful than others. It is in the detailed application of general recommendations that the manager's contextual knowledge is crucial.

REFERENCES

Agrell, A. & Gustafson, R. (1994) The team climate inventory (TCI) and group innovation: A psychometric test on a Swedish sample of work groups. *Journal of Occupational and Organizational Psychology*, 67, 143–52.

Agrell, A. & Gustafson, R. (1996) Innovation and creativity in work groups. In M.A. West (Ed.), *Handbook of work group psychology*. Chichester: Wiley.

Amabile, T.M. (1983) *The social psychology of creativity*. New York: Springer-Verlag.

Ancona, D.G. (1990) Outward bound: Strategies for team survival in the organization. *Academy of Management Journal*, 33, 334–365.

Ancona, D.G. & Chong, C. (1999) Cycles and synchrony: The temporal role of context in team behavior. In R. Wageman (Ed.), *Research on Managing Groups and Teams: Volume 2, Groups in Context*, JAI Press, Stamford, Connecticut.

Anderson, N.R. (1992) Work-group innovation: A state-of-the-art review. In D.M. Hosking and N.R. Anderson (Eds), *Organizational change and innovation: Psychological perspectives and practices in Europe*. London: Routledge.

Anderson, N.R. & King, N. (1993) Innovation in organizations. In C.L. Cooper and I.T. Robertson (Eds), *International Review of Industrial and Organizational Psychology, Volume 8*. Chichester: Wiley.

Anderson, N.R. & West, M.A. (1994) *The team climate inventory*. Windsor, Berks: ASE.

Axtell, C.M., Holman, D.J., Unsworth, K.L., Wall, T.D., Waterson, P.E. and Harrington, E. (2000) Shopfloor innovation: Facilitating the suggestion and implementation of ideas. *Journal of Occupational and Organizational Psychology*, 73, 265–285.

Basadur, M., Graen, G.B. & Green, G. (1982) Training in creative problem-solving: Effects on ideation and problem finding and solving in an industrial research organization. *Organizational Behavior and Human Performance*, 30, 41–70.

Basadur, M., Graen, G.B. & Scandura, T.A. (1986) Training effects on attitudes towards divergent thinking among manufacturing engineers. *Journal of Applied Psychology*, 71, 612–17.

Bouwen, René & Fry, Ron (1996) Facilitating group development: Interventions for a relational and contextual construction. In M.A.West (Ed.), *Handbook of Work Group Psychology*. Chichester: Wiley.

Burns, T. & Stalker, G.M. (1961) *The management of innovation*. London: Tavistock.

Carrero, Virginia, Peiró, José, & Salanova, Marisa (2000) Studying radical organizational innovation through grounded Theory. *European Journal of Work and Organizational Psychology*, 9(4), 489–514.

Csikszentmihalyi, M. (1988) Society, culture and person: A systems view of creativity. In R.J. Sternberg (Ed.), *The Nature of Creativity*. Cambridge: Cambridge University Press.

Daft, R.L. (1978) A dual-core model of organizational innovation. *Academy of Management Journal*, 21, 193–210.

Damanpour, F. (1991) Organizational innovation: A meta-analysis of effects of determinants and moderators. *Academy of Management Journal*, 34, 555–590.

Danowski, J.A. (1980) Group attitude uniformity and connectivity of organizational communication netwroks for production, innovation, and maintenance control. *Human Communication Research*, 6, 299–308.

Dougherty, D. & Hardy, C. (1996) Sustained product innovation in large, mature organizations: Overcoming innovation-to-organization problems. *Academy of Management Journal*, 39, 1120–53.

Downs, G.W. Jr, & Mohr, L.B. (1976) Conceptual issues in the study of innovation. *Administrative Science Quarterly*, 21, 700–14.

DuBrin, A.J. (1974) *Fundamentals of organizational behavior: An applied perspective*. New York: Pergamon Press.

Dunphy, D.C. & Stace, D.A. (1988) Transformational and coercive strategies for planned organizational change: Beyond the OD model. *Journal of Personality and Social Psychology*, 53, 497–509.

Ekvall, G. (1996) Organizational climate for creativity and innovation. *European Journal of Work and Organizational Psychology*, 5, 105–23.

Ettlie, J.E. (1980) Adequacy of stage models for decisions on adoption of innovation. *Psychological Reports*, 46, 991–995.

Ford, C.M. (1995) Striking inspirational sparks and fanning creative flames: A multi-domain model of creative action taking. In C.M. Ford and D.A. Gioia (Eds), *Creative Action in Organizations: Ivory Tower Visions and Real World Voices*. Thousand Oaks, CA: Sage.

Freeman, M. (1993) *Finding the Muse: A Sociopsychological Inquiry into the Conditions of Artistic Creativity*. Cambridge: Cambridge University Press.

Geschka, H. (1983) Creativity techniques in product planning and development: A view from West Germany. *R&D Management*, 13, 9–41.

Gersick, C.J.G. (1989) 'Marking time: Predictable transitions in work groups' *Academy of Management Journal*, 32, 274–309.

Gersick, Connie J.C. (1994) Pacing strategic change: The case of a new venture. *Academy of Management Journal*, 37, 9–45.

Gundling, E. (2000) *The 3M way to innovation: Balancing people and profit*. Tokyo: Kodansha.

Hage, J. & Aiken, M. (1970) *Social change in complex organizations*. New York: Random House.

Howell, J.M. & Higgins, C.A. (1990) Champions of technological innovation. *Administrative Science Quarterly*, 35, 317–41.

Janis, I.L. (1982) *Groupthink*, 2nd edition. Boston: Houghton Mifflin.

Johnson, D.M., Parrott, G.L. & Statton, R.P. (1968). Production and judgement of solutions to five problems. *Journal of Educational Psychology Monograph Supplement*, 59, 6 (2).

Kanter, R.M. (1983) *The change masters*. New York: Simon & Schuster.

Kelly, J.R., Futoran, G.C. & McGrath, J.E. (1990) Capacity and capability: Seven studies of entrainment of task performance rates. *Small Group Research*, 21 (3), 283–314.

Kimberly, J.R. (1981) Managerial innovation. In P.C. Nystrom and W.H. Starbuck (Eds), *Handbook of Organizational Design*. Oxford: Oxford University Press.

King, N. (1992) Modelling the innovation process: An empirical comparison of approaches. *Journal of Occupational and Organizational Psychology*, 65, 89–100.

King, N. (1995) Creativity and innovation: An uncertain link. In C.M. Ford and D.A. Gioia (Eds), *Creative Action in Organizations: Ivory Tower Visions and Real World Voices*. Thousand Oaks, CA: Sage.

King, N. & Anderson N.R. (1990) Innovation and creativity in working groups. In West, M.A. and Farr, J.L. (Eds), *Innovation and Creativity at Work: Psychological and Organizational Strategies*. Chichester: Wiley.

King, N. & Anderson N.R. (2002) *Managing innovation and change: A critical guide for organizations*. Thomson Learning: London.

King, N. & West, M.A. (1987) Experiences of innovation at work. *Journal of Managerial Psychology*, 2, 6–10.

Kotter, J.P. & Schlesinger, L.A. (1979) Choosing strategies for change. *Harvard Business Review*, March-April, 106–14.

Lawrence, P.R. (1969) How to deal with resistance to change. *Harvard Business Review*, January–February, 115–22.

Lewin, K. (1951) *Field theory in social science*. New York: Harper & Row.

Lewis, Laurie K. & Seibold, David R. (1993) Innovation modification during intraorganizational adoption. *Academy of Management Review*, 18 (2), 322–354.

Manz, C.C., Barstein, D.T., Hostager, T.J. & Shapiro, G.L. (1989) Leadership and innovation: A longitudinal process view. In A. Van de Ven, H.L. Angle and Poole, M.S. (Eds), *Research on the Management of Innovation: The Minnesota Studies*. New York: Harper and Row.

Meston, C.M. & King, N. (1996) Making sense of "resistance": Responses to organizational change in a private nursing home for the elderly. *European Journal of Work and Organizational Psychology*, 5, 91–102.

Mohr, L.B. (1969) Determinants of innovation in organizations. *American Political Science Review*, 63, 111–26.

Montuori, A. & Purser, R.E. (1995) Deconstructing the lone genius myth: Toward a contextual view of creativity. *Journal of Humanistic Psychology*, 35, 69–112.

Mullen, B. & Cooper, C. (1994) The relation between group cohesiveness and performance: An integration. *Psychological Bulletin*, 115, 210–227.

Nicholson, N. (1990) Organizational innovation in context: culture, interpretation and application. In West, M.A. and Farr, J.L. (Eds), *Innovation and Creativity at Work: Psychological and Organizational Strategies*. Chichester: Wiley.

Nkomo, S. (1996) Identities and the complexities of diversity. In S.E. Jackson and M.N. Ruderman (Eds), *Diversity in work teams: Research paradigms for a changing workplace*. Washington, DC: American Psychological Association.

Nystrom, H. (1979) *Creativity and innovation*. Chichester: Wiley.

Nystrom, H. (1990) Organizational Innovation. In West, M.A. and Farr, J.L. (Eds), *Innovation and creativity at work: Psychological and organizational strategies*. Chichester: Wiley.

O'Reilly III, C.A., Williams, K.Y. & Barsade, S. (1998). Group demography and innovation: Does diversity help? In D.H. Gruenfeld (Ed.), *Research on Managing Groups and Teams: Volume 1, Composition*. Stamford, Connecticut: JAI Press.

Pelz, D.C. (1983) Quantitative case histories of urban innovations: Are there innovation stages? *IEEE Transactions on Engineering Management*, 30, 60–67.

Peters, T. & Waterman, R.H. (1982) *In search of excellence: Lessons from America's best-run companies*. New York: Harper & Row.

Pettigrew, A.M. & Fulton, E.M. (2000) *The innovating organization*. London: Sage.

Quinn, R.E. (1988) *Beyond rational management: Mastering the paradoxes and competing demands of high performance*. San Francisco: Jossey-Bass.

Rogers, E.M. *Diffusion of innovations*, 3rd edition. New York: Free Press.

Rosenfeld, R. & Servo, J.C. (1990) Facilitating innovation in large organizations. In West, M.A. and Farr, J.L. (Eds), *Innovation and creativity at work: Psychological and organizational strategies*. Chichester: Wiley.

Ross, A. & King, N. (2001) Professional diversities and interprofessional relations. Paper presented at 3rd *International Conference on Social Work in Health and Mental Health*. Tampere, Finland, July 1–5.

Schroeder, R.G., Van de Ven, A., Scudder, G.D. & Polley, D. (1989) The development of innovation ideas. In Van de Ven, A., Angle, H.L. and Poole, M.S. (Eds), *Research on the Management of Innovation: The Minnesota Studies*, New York: Harper & Row.

Shue, L.L. (1998) Teaching an old system new tricks. Unpublished Ph.D. thesis, Ohio State University.

Staw, B.M. (1984) Organizational behavior: A review and reformulation of the field's outcome variables. *Annual Review of Psychology*, 35, 627–66.

Staw, B.M. (1990) An evolutionary approach to creativity and innovation. In West, M.A. and Farr, J.L. (Eds), *Innovation and creativity at work: Psychological and organizational strategies*. Chichester: Wiley.

Symon, G. (2000) Everyday rhetoric: Argument and persuasion in everyday life. *European Journal of Work and Organizational Psychology*, 9 (4), 477–488.

Symon, G. & Cassell, C. (1998) *Qualitative methods and analysis in organizational research: A practical guide*. London: Sage.

Symon, G., Cassell, C. & Dickson, R. (2000) (Eds), *Qualitative methods in organizational research and practice*. Hove, East Sussex: Psychology Press.

Triandis, H.C. (1996) The importance of contexts in studies of diversity. In S.E. Jackson and M.N. Ruderman (Eds), *Diversity in work teams: Research paradigms for a changing workplace*. Washington, DC: American Psychological Association.

Unsworth, K.L. (2001) Unpacking innovation. Unpublished Ph.D. thesis, Institute of Work Psychology, University of Sheffield, U.K.

Van de Ven, Andrew H., Polley, Douglas E., Garud, Raghu, & Venkataraman, Sankaran (1999) *The innovation journey*. New York: Oxford University Press.

Van Eynde, D.F. & Bledsoe, J.A. (1990) The changing practice of Organization Development. *Leadership and Organization Development Journal*, 11 (2), 25–30.

West, M.A. (1990) The social psychology of innovation in groups. In M.A. West and J.L. Farr (Eds), *Innovation and creativity at work: Psychological and organizational strategies*. Chichester: Wiley.

West, M.A. & Anderson, N.R. (1996) Innovation in top management teams. *Journal of Applied Psychology*, 81, 680–693.

West, M.A. & Farr, J.L. (1990) *Innovation and creativity at work: Psychological and organizational strategies*. Chichester: Wiley.

West, M.A. & Wallace, M. (1991) Innovation in healthcare teams. *European Journal of Social Psychology*, 21, 303–15.

Wilson, D.C. (1992) *A strategy of change: Concepts and controversies in the management of change*. London: Routledge.

Witte, E. (1972) Field research on complex decision-making processes—the phase theorem. *International Studies of Management and Organization*, 156–182.

Zaltman, G., Duncan, R. & Holbek, J. (1973) *Innovations and organizations*. New York: Wiley.

CHAPTER 20

Diversity and Individual Development

Rajvinder Kandola and Satya Kartara

Pearn Kandola, Oxford, UK

SUMMARY

In this chapter we review models and strategies for managing diversity and present a vision of a diversity-orientated organisation. We examine the practice of managing diversity and how it applies to key fields of activity, such as recruitment, selection, promotion, individual development and appraisal. We then describe several diversity competencies for the diversity-orientated organisations. Finally we present a model for the effective implementation of an integrated diversity strategy.

The key argument is that culturally sensitive, and diversity-aware development of all individuals comprising an organisation can only be effective within the context of an integrated diversity strategy of the kind described in this chapter.

INTRODUCTION

This chapter looks at the nature of diversity, and in particular the drivers of diversity in organisations today.

In Britain, the USA and many industrially advanced economies there exists hugely diverse and culturally rich societies. To a greater or lesser extent, organisations are microcosms of society and to varying degrees that diversity is reflected in the organisations and companies in which we all work. However, in many organisations traditional systems, procedures and processes have remained intact for a long, long time. This means

Individual Differences and Development in Organisations. Edited by Michael Pearn.
© 2002 John Wiley & Sons, Ltd.

that it can be difficult for organisations to embrace wholly the diversity that exists in society. This has a number of consequences. Firstly, it will make it difficult for many organisations to attract a diverse workforce. Secondly, if they are able to attract this diversity then they may be unable to harness fully the different skills that these employees bring to the organisation. Thirdly, it will mean they are unable to retain them.

The definition of diversity used in this chapter is as follows:

> 'The basic concept of managing diversity accepts that the workforce consists of a diverse population of people. The diversity consists of visible and non-visible differences which will include sex, age, background, race, disability, personality and workstyle. It is founded on the premise that harnessing these differences will create a productive environment in which everybody feels valued, where their talents are being fully utilised, and in which organisational goals are met.' (Kandola and Fullerton, 1998)

MODELS AND STRATEGIES FOR MANAGING DIVERSITY

This section describes a number of different approaches to managing diversity, viz. models for managing diversity: the evolution of diversity-related initiatives; and the concept of global diversity.

Table 20.1 shows a number of models of managing diversity some of which focus on the processes that should be followed in successfully managing diversity, while others include a mix of both process and content, i.e. the initiatives that should be put in place.

Gardenswartz & Rowe (1998) state that the diversity arena is rapidly changing and evolving. Whilst areas of focus continue to shift, what does not change is the need to address the issues. A culture of inclusion, demographic trends, globalisation, competitive marketplaces and the need for top talent all point to the fact that diversity does matter in a highly complex and competitive world. They go on to outline 'Seven Strategic Steps' of questioning to help an organisation see where it stands in its diversity strategy:

1. Executive Level Commitment: What concrete indicators from executives illustrate their support and commitment?
2. Assessment and Diagnosis: What data have you used to identify obstacles and steer your initiative? How current is it? Does it reflect all levels of the organisation?
3. Diversity Task Force: What group is acting as shepherd and advocate of the initiative? What kind of team building and education has enabled them to develop common goals and language?
4. Systems Changes: What systems changes are needed? How are people being held accountable for making these changes the norm?
5. Training: What objectives is training designed to accomplish? How has the content been tailored to suit all levels and skills throughout the organisation? How is diversity integrated into training?
6. Measurement and evaluation: What are your stated outcomes and how will you know if you are successful? What data can you collect to use in measurement?
7. Integration: How will you make your efforts stick?

TABLE 20.1 Models of managing diversity

Process models of managing diversity
Thomas (1990)
- Clarify your motivation
- Clarify your vision
- Expand your focus
- Audit your corporate culture
- Modify your assumptions
- Modify your systems
- Modify your models
- Help your people pioneer
- Apply the special considerations test
- Continue affirmative action

McEnrue (1993)
- The role of top management
- Identifying needs
- Methods of managing diversity: use of customised methods
- Scope and timeframe of efforts: realistic expectation of scope and timeframes
- Required skills: skills development
- Measuring progress: establish controls tied to business results

Cox and Blake (1991)
- Leadership: enlist top management support and commitment
- Training: managing and valuing diversity training
- Research: collecting information pertaining to diversity-related issues
- Analysis and change of culture and human resource management systems
- Follow-up: conduct analyses of change of culture and HRM system

Process and content models of managing diversity
Jamieson and O'Mara (1991)
- Matching people and jobs
    individualise job profiles, assessment methods, orientation, careers
    assess individual strengths and weaknesses
    review and change key HRC processes
- Matching and rewarding performance
    examine different ways of work planning, motivating and rewarding mentoring,
    coaching, feedback
    flexibility of approach in dealing with appraisal, development
- Informing and involving people
    keep people informed
    use flexible systems, e.g. ongoing and temporary groups
    suggestion schemes; attitude surveys; focus groups
- Supporting lifestyle and life needs
    identify people's needs and interests and create supportive options, e.g. childcare, work
        hours, leave options
    new benefits policies
    special interest networks
    supportive and creative managers

Bartz et al. (1990)
- Organisational acceptance and commitment
- Understanding the concept of diversity and attributes of major sub-populations
- Identify work styles and motivation
- Developmental needs and career aspirations
- Personal needs, including flexible working

continues overleaf

TABLE 20.1   (*continued*)

Motwani et al. (1993)
- Assessment
- Planning
- Programming
- Implementation
- Evaluation

Rossett and Bickman (1994)
- Link diversity with business priorities
- Top management support
- Specify acceptable/unacceptable behaviours
- Role models
- Communication
- Measure results

Ross and Schneider (1992)
- Diagnosis
- Setting aims
- Spreading ownership
- Policy development
- Training

Hammond and Kleiner (1992)
- Acknowledge differences of the workplace
- Examine policies and procedures—eliminate areas of bias or discrimination
- Conduct a needs assessment
- Develop training programmes
- Communication, ensure management proves its commitment and openness by follow-up
- Be constantly aware of cultural differences and biases

Thiederman (1994)
- Organisational soul searching
- Accountability
- Senior management involvement
- Communication
- Create hospitable workplace
- Adjust strategies and processes
- Set up special interest groups
- Measure results

Harrington (1993)
- Top management support and commitment
- Open aptitude to new ways of working
- Distinguish between three approaches to managing diversity
- Audit your workforce and customers
- Create a vision
- Training in managing diversity awareness
- Be flexible
- Skills training
- Help reduce work/family conflicts

Kandola & Fullerton (1996): Strategic Implementation Model
- Organisational vision
- Senior management commitment
- Auditing and assessment of needs
- Clarity of objectives
- Clear accountability
- Effective communication
- Co-ordination of activities

MOSAIC: A Vision of a Diversity-Oriented Organisation

Kandola and Fullerton (1994) propose a vision of the diversity-oriented organisation. This model incorporates ideas from a number of other writers on diversity. The chief characteristics of a diversity-oriented organisation are encompassed within the MOSAIC framework: Mission and values; Objective and Fair; Skilled workers—aware and fair; Active flexibility; Individual focus; and a Culture that empowers.

- **Mission and values.** Strong, positive mission and core values which make managing diversity a necessary long-term business objective for the organisation and responsibility for all employees. They should be clearly outlined to all employees and the practical implication of values needs to be communicated to everyone. Everyone is held accountable for adherence to the values.
- **Objective and Fair.** Auditing and re-auditing of all processes and systems (recruitment, selection, induction, performance appraisal) to ensure no one group predominates at any one level. Hindrances to diversity have been removed and the tools and techniques for assessment are regularly examined.
- **Skilled workforce—aware and fair.** Workforce aware of, and guided by, principles of managing diversity and know of its importance to the business objectives. Are also trained to recognise prejudices and can prevent them affecting decisions. Having managers who manage—both to develop themselves and their employees. They keep up to date with developments in the field; solicit feedback and act upon it; harness potential; understand individual motivation; appraise employees considering individual differences; do not leave development to chance; ultimate aim is to maximise the potential of all employees to meet organisational goals; are accountable for own and employees development.
- **Active flexibility.** There is an increase in flexibility in a diversity-oriented organisation in: Working arrangements; Policies; Practices; and Procedures. The emphasis is on output. Individuals are not expected to conform to a set of patterns and regulations laid down by the predominant culture.
- **Individual Focus.** This is the overarching principle of all actions in a diversity-oriented organisation. Focuses on developing all employees based on their needs and not on group membership.
- **Culture that empowers.** Culture must be consistent with and complementary to managing diversity. Awareness of organisational culture and how it impacts on individuals. All employees understand how the organisation operates, its values and behaviour expectations. Key aspects are an open, trusting environment free from harassment and discrimination; devolved decision-making; participation and consultation encourages experimentation is valued and encourages objective and fair allocation of duties and projects.

THE EVOLUTION OF DIVERSITY-RELATED INITIATIVES

Gardenswartz & Rowe (1998) state that there are four major trends that signal the evolutionary direction of diversity-related initiatives. These are

- **Systems changes.** This relates to organisational change, which is essential in bringing accountability and longevity to diversity initiatives. Without a long-term culture change, initiatives such as awareness raising and training may not succeed. If done correctly, the organisation becomes more humane and productive, clear in its objectives and flexible enough to respond to multiple employee needs. The key to systems change is to think long-term, have patience and to hold people accountable for the agreed changes.

- **Skills set training.** To date awareness raising diversity training has been the most commonly set objective. Future training is most likely to emphasise managerial and team skills, with a focus on two audiences: *Internal* (i.e. employee to employee) and *External* (i.e. employee to customer). Internally, staff at all levels often need conflict resolution, cross-cultural communication and productive problem-solving skills in a pluralistic environment. At managerial level, understanding interviewing biases and assumptions is key to broadening the hiring profile. Giving performance reviews to employees from different cultural backgrounds or running meetings with employees who may be used to deferential relationship requires an additional set of skills and competencies. Externally-focused, selling and marketing skills which understand and appeal to diverse customers or focusing on improving customer service can be improved. Defining what constitutes excellent service and particular contexts and teaching people how to demonstrate these behaviours, is a central part of skill set training.

- **Integration.** This refers to diversity being woven into all aspects of the organisation. A broader array of skills needs to be brought into all curricula. Whether participants are learning about conflict, time management or stress, culture helps shape realities and should shape content. Its influence needs to be fully a part of all classes, all policies and all procedures because in reality, it effects the work environment daily.

- **Global focus.** This is now unavoidable whether you are a multinational doing business abroad or a company dealing with a diverse population. Thought needs to be given on how policies relating to sexual harassment or gender equality will transfer to other countries, or how people of other cultures look at issues around say, sexual orientation. Consideration needs to be given to whether or not the concept of individualism, or equality and justice have any ring of truth or relevance in other parts of the world or in all parts of the workforce. Any successful business today needs global eyes that pay close attention to all strategic and operational issues.

THE CONCEPT OF GLOBAL DELIVERY

Wilson (2000) has argued:

> "We need a concept of diversity that is transferable. The exact words may not be transferable, but an inclusive definition is about equity, the fair treatment of people. We share the humanness, we react the same. The template (diversity) doesn't change. Success is linking it into the business. Globalisation pushes the quest for measurement."

With the globalisation of the work environment and organisations, the term 'global diversity' has emerged. Consideration needs to be given to this topic when considering strategies for MD. Diversity as a global concept is problematic for a number of reasons. First, diversity is seen as a US-born initiative and is therefore associated with black/white integration and social marginalisation. Many countries in Europe, for example, do not deal with the issue of race. There are implications for this when looking at diversity in a global context, in that if say, a US based company wants to transfer a North American diversity programme to Italy or Greece it probably will not work.

An additional problem is that often communication and standards are not in place within an organisation, so diversity initiatives pursued by a company in the U.S. may be unknown to a subsidiary of that company in, say, Italy. Thus, the issue of global diversity presents a complex challenge for organisations and individuals.

Global diversity, Wilson (1999) says, needs to consider government, culture, social institutions, economy and resources as well as race and gender. When considering diversity programme results and realities, it is difficult to make comparisons between countries because the 'global villages' from which they come are so different. Whilst diversity is a popular word, it means different things in different organisations.

According to Graham Shaw, diversity project manager with European Business Network for Social Cohesion (EBNSC), European corporations are starting to see the practical business applications for diversity:

> "Europe is experiencing many of the same trends that are going on in North America. We have significant populations of visible minorities, and large immigrant populations that vary in size and type among different countries. Other changes regarding women in the workplace and people with disabilities are also similar".

Discrimination cannot be dealt with as a global concept because different issues affect different countries, e.g. class is the main issue affecting Belgium and England—if you are not born into a certain class, you are not going to make it. Canada has issues of language and education. In Africa the issues are tribe and language. A transferable concept of diversity is needed.

Wilson recognises that when he started doing diversity work in the early 80s, like many practitioners he was excluding white men. He now focuses on moving the diversity discussion forward and thinking about what is going to really make a difference, while at the same time recognising that sexism, racism and homophobia are alive and well. It is no longer justifiable to deal with fairness issues for certain people only. If it is fairer for a black man than it is for a white woman, then it is no longer fair. Due to these dynamics, the differences in and diversity in people have to be managed.

The EBNSC have put together a Global Diversity Standard. This standard brings together eight business processes, including commitment, accountability, measurement, policy; and ten business practices, such as promotion, retention, and marketing and sales into an overall structure. Using a series of questions an organisation can work through a software tool to undertake an objective analysis of the current position across the business or in specific business units. The answers determine where they fall on a rating scale of one to five. (A 'one' is a company that creates a program as a knee jerk reaction to external pressure; a 'three' sees the business case for diversity, for example, new markets by reaching certain target groups; and 'five' is close to the ideal.)

Diversity experts agree that understanding diversity from a global perspective may also make it easier to understand local diversity issues. Wilson sees standardisation of processes, measurement and proof of the business case as the way forward.

BP, the international oil and energy company, uses the concept of 'inclusion' as a global strategy for managing diversity within the different regions of a country, so that specific and relevant issues can be focused upon. The regions are used to drive the strategy forward for the country. Influence from any one country or region is avoided as each region has autonomy for dealing with its own diversity issues.

MANAGING DIVERSITY PRACTICES

The importance of diversity and equality initiatives being fully integrated into key management processes has already been mentioned in the previous section. This section considers key fields of activity, i.e. how to integrate diversity into recruitment, selection, induction, appraisal, development and promotion. The implications for organisations and individual development will be considered at the end of the chapter.

Recruitment

In order to recruit a diverse workforce, Carr-Ruffino (1996) suggests that organisations should focus on two key principles: (1) to actively seek diverse applicants for all types and levels of jobs; and (2) To make sure that word-of-mouth recruitment reaches all types of potential applicants.

Carr-Ruffino emphasises the importance of actively recruiting from universities that have large numbers of ethnic minority students; contacting all types of minority student organisations, giving them job postings, going to their job fairs, and speaking at their meetings. In addition, she suggests getting lists of various types of minority organisations—community, social, professional, business etc. and making regular and systematic contact with the formal and informal leaders of these organisations; and encouraging minority employees to spread the word among their friends, family and other contacts.

Selection

A recent IPD Recruitment Survey in the UK shows that 23% of UK firms recruit internationally. Of these, 71% look for "awareness of international issues"; 81% look for the ability to "manage in culturally diverse teams"; 85% look for a "positive attitude to cultural diversity" (Sparrow, 1999).

It is important to be sure that all job criteria, such as experience, degrees and certificates are really good predictors of job success and do not unreasonably exclude certain groups whose members could succeed. All tests and exams must be valid. The selection process should reflect as closely as possible the skills required for the job.

One challenge in terms of selection is that of finding the correct balance between shared values and diversity of viewpoints. Many businesses invest time and effort in selecting employees who fit their organisation's style. However, by focusing too keenly on cultural fit in the selection process, they may be inadvertently discriminating against certain groups and may develop a workforce that lacks complementary skills and personalities. Identifying the competencies that predict success in a position can be difficult and time consuming, but it is critical to ensure that selection is based on objective criteria and to quantify the softer, cultural issues (Grensing-Pophal, 1999).

Induction

Induction itself is a relatively under-researched area, although more attention is now being focused on it. Research has revealed that the socialisation processes that take place early on in a person's career within an organisation can have an extremely long-lasting impact. Bauer & Green (1994) found that early involvement in work-related activities led to better integration into the organisation and greater productivity. Minorities may take longer to be inducted and socialised into organisations.

If managers have made assumptions about the capabilities of newcomers based on stereotypes, or if they feel uncomfortable dealing with people from different groups, then this could have an adverse effect on minorities. If an organisation's induction processes are not effective significant numbers of staff could leave relatively quickly and this could reflect on the validity of the selection processes. Kandola & Fullerton (1998) suggest that in order to improve induction processes, organisations should make it clear to all individuals the organisation's values and what people need to do in order to make progress within it. They should also have a mentoring process; ensure there is some flexibility in the induction process so that individual concerns about the organisation, development etc. can be handled; and ensure that managers responsible for inducting new staff are properly trained and aware of the issues minority groups may face on entering the organisation.

APPRAISAL

In terms of the appraisal process used for evaluating performance, Kandola & Fullerton (1998) stress that the criteria on which people are being evaluated must be relevant to the job and the organisation as a whole and that they should be behaviourally focused. The process for setting performance objectives needs to be clear and measurable. An examination of the extent to which different ways of achieving those objectives are to be acceptable, i.e. in terms of how people conform to the organisation's values. In addition, employees need to know what they should expect from the appraisal process and what to do if these expectations are not being met. Appraisal training needs to be given, including how managers identify and develop potential. Finally, regular auditing and quality checks need to be carried out to ensure standards are being maintained.

DEVELOPING THE INDIVIDUAL

Monitoring and tracking *all* employees' career paths and progress towards achieving their career goals is an initiative that demonstrates a commitment to the development of all employees, especially with a focus on developmental opportunities that help prepare people for promotion.

Ruderman, Ohlott and Kram (1995) found that promotion decision processes can undermine women's advancement, even in organisations that are known for their progressive work on a number of diversity-related concerns. Without careful examination of the subtle yet powerful dynamics that shape assignments and promotion decisions, it is all too likely that decision makers will continue to choose candidates with whom they feel most comfortable and will use different criteria for promoting men and women. Strategies for making these complex dynamics visible, and discussible, include undertaking an assessment of current practices, putting in place an infrastructure of accountability for proactive development of women and minorities, and providing opportunities for personal inquiry about promotion possibilities. These actions help enable decision-makers to make personal development an effective diversity practice.

Carr-Ruffino (1996) emphasises the importance of having a diverse panel of employees making promotion decisions, as they are less likely to make biased promotion decisions than a homogenous panel or an individual decision-maker. Further she suggests publicising the criteria for promotion. Having a policy of 'development for promotability' is another possibility. The organisation must first discover and then create the conditions under which minority groups can thrive at all levels of the organisation.

Support, in the form of encouragement, training targeted at specific groups, access to developmental opportunities should be available for *all* employees. Other developmental activities such as mentoring, coaching, secondments, projects, and formal programmes should be communicated equally to all members of the organisation.

DIVERSITY COMPETENCY FRAMEWORKS

A diversity competency framework can be used as a basis for selecting and developing employees. Kim Cromwell, director of workforce effectiveness at BankBoston Corp (Digh, 1998) defines diversity competence, as " the ability to demonstrate a thorough understanding of how diversity [affects] the organisation's success". The goal is to develop employees who deal effectively with colleagues and customers from many different backgrounds; seek to learn about and optimise the unique contribution inherent in the culture of each individual; anticipate the impact of cultural biases on business relationships and processes; and seek to remove obstacles to equity and inclusion wherever possible.

Diversity competence is rated 'not effective', 'moderately effective', or 'role model'. Each rating has a detailed definition which gives individuals ample opportunity to improve performance. For example, 'not effective' is defined in the following way:

- has difficulty dealing with people of different cultures and styles
- exhibits disdain toward workplace diversity
- excludes people of different cultural backgrounds from personal networks
- lacks understanding of the impact of diversity on business relationships
- discourages people of different styles and cultures from participating in the work environment

The definition of 'role model' includes reference to:

- is familiar with and able to address diverse market opportunities and the needs of diverse internal and external customers
- actively participates in creating an environment where various styles are welcome
- initiates personal development related to diversity

Hofstede (1999) outlines the following broad framework for building the competencies required for operating on a cross-cultural basis: Building of awareness both of individuals' own cultures and the differences between national cultures; Development of knowledge of the effect of cultural difference, and the relative strengths and weaknesses of different cultures in a managerial context; Building of skills in the areas of managerial cultural sensitivity.

McEnrue (1993) describes the qualities needed for effective cross-cultural communication as the capacity to accept the relativity of one's own knowledge and perceptions;

the capacity to be non-judgemental; a tolerance for ambiguity; the capacity to appreciate and communicate respect for other people's ways, backgrounds, values and beliefs. In addition it includes the capacity to demonstrate empathy; to be flexible; a willingness to acquire new patterns of behaviour and belief; and finally the humility to acknowledge what one does not know.

Other skills that have been identified are managing change under circumstances where people are likely to have a variety of opinions about what should be done, or where too few resources exist to do what everyone wants; being open-minded enough to learn to recognise and appreciate the differences (Dreyfuss, 1990); being prepared and able to understand the values and attitudes of others and of sensitivity to the stress of being in a minority (Kanter, 1977); being able to 'understand our own cultural filters and to accept differences in people so that each person is treated and valued as a unique individual' (Kennedy and Everest, 1991).

The skills required fall mainly into the interpersonal and communication skills arena and have been described in other fields of research without any reference to managing diversity. For example, Argyris (1962) constructed a model that defined five conditions necessary for authentic relationships or interpersonal competence in organisations. These are giving and receiving non-evaluative, descriptive feedback; owning, and helping others to own, values, attitudes, ideas and feelings; openness to new values, attitudes and feelings as well as helping others to develop their own degree of openness; experimenting and helping others to do the same with new values, attitudes, ideas and feelings; taking risks with new values, attitudes, ideas and feelings.

Kandola and Fullerton (1998) cite research by Stodgill (1974) and Vaught & Abraham (1992) which emphasises the link between effective communication and interpersonal skills with satisfaction, employee performance, lower work stress and leadership style. They conclude that the competencies managers require to manage a diverse workforce appear very similar to the skills of communication competence that have been described for the last 30 years at least.

The major British bank, Lloyds TSB, have developed a diversity competency framework with behavioural indicators. These have been used as a competency framework for a diversity development centre. The competencies are:

- Practising objectivity
- Flexible thinking
- Understanding and knowledge of diversity
- Communication
- Developing/managing teams
- Championing diversity
- Strategic diversity focus

This serves to highlight the central importance of communication and other core managerial skills to diversity management. Thus communication skills need to be emphasised in training managers in the diversity-oriented organisation. Good managers of diversity are good managers, and good managers are those who deal with employees as individuals rather than expect everyone to be equally motivated and to work in similar ways.

Diversity competency frameworks are an appropriate means of focusing on behaviours for assessment and development purposes. Linking pay and bonuses to achievement of diversity objectives appears to be an effective way of encouraging behaviour change at work issues more routinely. Diversity issues need to be incorporated into competency frameworks and associated training. Competency frameworks should reflect diversity as a goal of the organisation.

POLICIES INTO PRACTICE

A challenge facing many organisations is making diversity goals survive in the organisation long after the initial diversity training is over. Increasingly, employers are looking for ways to make diversity an integral part of the organisation's culture, it's custom and practice. Digh (1998) suggests that the answer for both these issues lies in holding managers accountable for diversity efforts at all levels. According to her, employers are starting to realise that you get what you pay for and that if you pay for performance and hold people accountable for behavioural and business changes in the diversity arena, you will begin to build an organisational culture supportive of diversity. Wheeler (1998) agrees that initially it may be necessary to sponsor specific diversity-specific courses, but eventually, diversity management should be incorporated into normal leadership training or mentoring programmes.

Another dilemma facing many organisations is whether to instigate or continue with special training and development programmes targeted solely at identifiable underrepresented or underperforming groups identified by race, gender or other group characteristics. The view of the authors of this chapter is that such initiatives should not be necessary, except in special circumstances, e.g. following periods of sustained following sustained unlawful discriminatory practices. In organisations that are genuinely committed to harnessing diversity as a strategic goal and which also put in place the sorts of measures described earlier in this chapter, including incorporating diversity into leadership and management development, and the use of diversity competency frameworks, individuals identified by reference to group membership should not be disadvantaged. The truth, of course lies in systematic collection of data, so monitoring and evaluation of diversity goals is still crucial.

There is a risk that special treatment and developmental provisions for targeted groups, as distinct from individuals, result in marginalising rather than mainstreaming, the people whom the initiatives are designed to assist.

Diversity is about change, but the power of inertia for maintaining the organisational status quo, is immense. In order to help overcome organisational resistance we have developed a simple strategic framework for taking action, which is summed up in the acronym FAME which stands for Future and Vision; Auditing; Mainstreaming; and Evaluation.

FUTURE/VISION

It is important for an organisation embarking on the diversity journey to have some idea about the intended destination, in other words a clear vision of what it is trying to achieve. An example comes from the Ford Motor Company in the UK. The senior management team at one of the main manufacturing sites worked with the diversity manager to create a vision for diversity for the site:

'To recruit, retain and develop a committed and diverse workforce at all levels within the Dagenham estate. To understand, value and effectively manage a skilled and diverse workforce. Business transformation and customer satisfaction are the ultimate measures of our success.'

This vision focuses the attention of key people in the organisation on where they wanted to get to. It has local ownership and buy-in, it has not been imposed from above.

Another example can be taken from Oxford City Council. The council had what could be described as a traditional equal opportunities approach in that it focused on the areas of race, gender, and disability discrimination. This approach only helped to 'ghettoise' particular groups and marginalised the issues they faced. A 'new way' was required that saw equality of opportunity as important to everyone and not just to some. The new diversity strategy encompassed the needs and aspirations of all groups represented in the council's employment as well as the local communities they served. For this vision to become a reality it would not only need to get buy-in from local politicians and community groups. It was also necessary to change the council committee structure. The Council set about developing and implementing a new structure which meant disbanding log-established committees such as the Women's Committee, and the Race Committee. Whilst this was difficult to do it was necessary to remove the old structure if the organisation was to embrace a new philosophy.

The organisation's diversity vision indicates where the organisation wants to get to. The next step on the journey is to take stock of the current situation, and that is where Auditing becomes important.

AUDITING

There are three distinct aspects of auditing, viz. examining policies; examining processes; and examining employee perceptions.

The first part involves looking at the policies that exist, in areas such as recruitment, selection, development, promotion and finding out how they have been communicated and implemented. Processes goes beyond the policies and looks at the extent to which they are being followed. Often we have found that an organisation will have excellent policies on paper but they are not being implemented properly by managers because of a lack of defined process.

Employee perceptions are a key part of auditing. Employee perceptions have invariably provided a valuable perspective on how policies, practices and good intentions are felt and perceived by the people who work in the organisation.

A lot of interesting issues come to light through carrying out an audit for example, some organisations have very antiquated policies which are retained merely because they have been in existence a long time. In one organisation employees' length of services (seniority) was used as the basis for promotion decisions. Originally the practice had been adopted to prevent discriminatory practices whereby managers were promoting people they happened to like. The policy was well-intentioned but as more women and people from minority groups joined the company it became apparent that the practice of seniority was actually discriminatory to many of the more recently arrived employees. Abolishing this practice and moving towards a promotion on merit policy was initially resisted but later given full support.

To sum, up auditing enables organisations to identify what needs to done and to develop a strategy which focuses on the needs and aspirations of the organisation and *all* its people.

MAINSTREAMING

Diversity touches all parts of an organisation's life and operations. Diverity should therefore be made the responsibility of all managers, indeed all employees and not just those working in the Diversity Department. Mainstreaming is about ensuring that managing diversity becomes an integral part of the organisation's daily operation and that it becomes 'the way we do things around here' and not just an added extra, in effect a natural feature of the organisation's culture.

Sometimes it is necessary to challenge peoples' views about these issues especially those in positions of influence and power. They have to recognise that diversity is something that cannot be separated from good management. Being a good manager therefore means managing diversity well.

Communication is a key issue. Many large organisations have excellent policies which are either directly or indirectly related to diversity. The problem often is though is that many managers may not even believe that the organisation is serious about its diversity strategy. If managers do not know, understand, or believe in the policies, they cannot implement them. Ensuring that all managers take responsibility for implementing the diversity strategy is a key part of mainstreaming, and it is only in this context that culturally sensitive individual development that harnesses the talents of all employees can take place.

EVALUATION

The vision, followed by audits, leads to co-ordinated action followed by evaluation. Without this we will not know what has worked and what has not. Unfortunately, however very little evaluation of diversity initiatives seems to take place. Activities, policies and initiatives must be evaluated to ensure that we are achieving the results that we set out to achieve, and that we are not doing things that may be done with good intentions but which actually make little difference.

CONCLUSION

Diversity is essentially a values driven approach. Many major organisations, in the private, public and voluntary sectors have recognised that it is important to create an inclusive environment where everyone feels valued, their potential is fulfilled and through which organisational goals are met.

This means having systems, processes and ways of working which enable people to perform at their best and to develop to their full potential. This is much easier said than done. To achieve it successfully requires us to take an honest look at the way we do things and decide if there are not better ways. This requires a different form of leadership where variation and differences in people are not only permitted but genuinely welcomed. Managers and leaders in organisations can be resistant to change. Sometimes they do not realise that they are becoming an obstacle themselves. In some instances it is a question of education, demonstrating that other ways of working can bring results.

We need to ensure that people get the personal development that is best suited to them. If we are to create organisations which value diversity then development needs to be given to those in key positions. Work we have carried out with Lloyds TSB shows clearly that given the right form of development, senior managers in an organisation can become more convinced of the need to change. In this case we have run diversity development centres for the bank. These events are designed to simulate work settings and to give the senior managers an opportunity to demonstrate how they handle a range of diversity issues. Each person leaves with a personal development plan.

Without this opportunity to learn and develop there can be little doubt that the rate of change would be much slower. Part of the workshop focuses on how much flexibility they allow their teams. What this demonstrates is that saying 'we are going to change' is not enough. People need guidance on how to change, and to know what is expected of them.

There is much that organisations can do to improve practices and processes. There are obviously implications for people working in each of those areas. People working in or responsible for key activity areas need to ensure that they are considering the diversity issues in everything that they do.

This requires education, knowledge and a willingness to be open to new ideas and a preparedness to experiment. The competencies required to manage diversity effectively are also becoming better defined. These need to be incorporated into competency frameworks and assessed appropriately. It is by these means that diversity becomes woven into the fabric of an organisation, or mainstreamed. Diversity can seem like a constantly moving target. Just when we seem to have it cracked something happens that makes us question our assumptions and approaches. It might be a grievance, or a tribunal, or new legislation. That has been the trend and there seems little evidence that will change. This means that to develop diversity in organisations and develop diverse people requires continuous feedback and learning in order to move forward. Without this cycle there will be little chance of genuine change.

REFERENCES

Browne, A. (2000) UK whites will be minority by 2100. *The Observer Newspaper*, London, 3/8/00.
Conway, C. (1996) Mentoring to Diversity. *The Ashridge Journal*, March 1996.
Digh, P. (1998) The next challenge: holding people accountable. *HRMagazine*, October, 63–69.
Equal Opportunities Commission (1999) Glass ceiling still solid in Wales. *Equal Opportunities Review, No 88*.
European Union Commission, Telework 1998: Status Report on European Telework, Brussels, August 1998.
Fernandez, J.P. (1993) *The diversity advantage*. Lexington Books.
Gardenswartz & Rowe (1998) Why diversity matters. *HRFocus (USA)* 98 (75/7).
Grensing-Pophal, L. (1999) Hiring to fit your corporate culture. *HRMagazine*, August, 51–54.
Hardy, (1998) Mentoring: a long-term approach to diversity. *HRFocus* (USA).
Hayles, R. (1997) *The diversity directive: why some initiatives fail and what to do about it*. McGraw-Hill.
Higgs, M. (1999) Developing international management teams through diversity. In Joynt, P. and Morton, B. (1999) *The Global HR Manager*.
Hofstede, G. (1999) in Higgs, M. Developing international management teams through diversity. In Joynt, P. & Morton, B. (1999) *The Global HR Manager*.

Javaid, M. (2000) Liberte, egalite, legality. *People Management,* 20 July.

Kandola, R. & Fullerton, J. (1998) *Diversity in action.* London: IPD.

Kramar, R. (1997) Developing and implementing work and family policies: The implications for HR policies. *Asia Pacific Journal of Human Resources,* 35, 3, 1–18.

Lewis, D. (2000) *The soul of the new consumer.* London: NB Publishing.

McEnrue (1993) in Kandola & Fullerton (1998) Diversity in action. London: IPD.

Morrison, A. et al. (1994) *Breaking the glass ceiling.* Addison Wesley Publishing Company.

Rice, M. (2000) Age of the flex exec. *Management Today* 2.8.00.

Rosenzweig, P. (1998) Managing the new global workforce: fostering diversity, forging consistency. *European Management Journal,* 16, 6, 644–652.

Ruderman, M.N., Ohlott, P.J. & Kram, K.E. (1995) Promotion decisions as a diversity practice. *Journal of Management Development,* 14, 2.

Simons, T., Pelled, L.H. & Smith, K.A. (1999) Making use of difference: Diversity, debate, and decision-making comprehensiveness in top management teams. *Academy of Management Journal,* 42, 6, 662–673.

Sparrow, P. (1999) International Recruitment, Selection and Assessment. In the *Global HR Manager Creating the Seamless Organisation.*

Wheeler (1998) in Digh, P. The next challenge: holding people accountable. *HRMagazine,* 63–69.

Wilson, R. (1998) Workplace diversity—new challenges, new opportunities. *Equal Opportunities Review,* no 78.

Vernon, (1999) It takes all sorts. *HR Resources (UK),* 43, 40–44.

Wilson, T. (1999) in Norm Bond 'A Global Diversity Standard' @ *http://www.diversityatwork.com.*

Author Index

Subject Index

Added to a page number 't' denotes a table, 'f' denotes a figure.